UNIVERSITY OF EDINBURGH INTRODUCTION
TO POLITICS AND INTERNATIONAL RELATIONS

UNIVERSITY OF EDINBURGH INTRODUCTION TO POLITICS AND INTERNATIONAL RELATIONS

Compiled for
UGUR OZDEMIR

 macmillan education   palgrave

First published 2017 by
PALGRAVE

Palgrave in the UK is an imprint of Macmillan Publishers Limited,
registered in England, company number 785998, of 4 Crinan Street,
London, N1 9XW.

Palgrave® and Macmillan® are registered trademarks in the United States,
the United Kingdom, Europe and other countries.

ISBN: 978-1-352-00147-1 paperback

This book is printed on paper suitable for recycling and made from fully
managed and sustained forest sources. Logging, pulping and manufacturing
processes are expected to conform to the environmental regulations of the
country of origin.

A catalogue record for this book is available from the British Library.

A catalog record for this book is available from the Library of Congress.

CONTENTS

LIST OF FIGURES

LIST OF TABLES

LIST OF MAPS

LIST OF SOURCES

This custom publication has been compiled for us in the
University of Edinburgh. The chapters included are reproduced
from the following works:

Chapter 1 from **Gerry Stoker**: *Why Politics Matter (2nd edition)* © Gerry Stoker 2017

Chapter 2 from **Heather Savigny & Lee Marsden**: *Doing Political Science
and International Relations* © **Heather Savigny & Lee Marsden** 2011

Chapter 3 from **Heather Savigny & Lee Marsden**: *Doing Political Science
and International Relations* © **Heather Savigny & Lee Marsden** 2011

Chapter 4 from **Andrew Heywood**: *Politics (4th edition)* © **Andrew Heywood** 2013

Chapter 5 from **Andrew Heywood**: *Politics (4th edition)* © **Andrew Heywood** 2013

Chapter 6 from **Heather Savigny & Lee Marsden**: *Doing Political Science
and International Relations* © **Heather Savigny & Lee Marsden** 2011

Chapter 7 from **Andrew Heywood**: *Politics (4th edition)* © **Andrew Heywood** 2013

Chapter 8 from **Andrew Heywood**: *Politics (4th edition)* © **Andrew Heywood** 2013

Chapter 9 from **Andrew Heywood**: *Politics (4th edition)* © **Andrew Heywood** 2013

Chapter 10 from **Andrew Heywood**: *Global Politics (2nd edition)*
© **Andrew Heywood** 2014

Chapter 11 from **Andrew Heywood**: *Politics (4th edition)* © **Andrew Heywood** 2013

Chapter 12 from **Andrew Heywood**: *Politics (4th edition)* © **Andrew Heywood** 2013

Chapter 13 from **Andrew Heywood**: *Politics (4th edition)* © **Andrew Heywood** 2013

Chapter 14 from **Andrew Heywood**: *Politics (4th edition)* © **Andrew Heywood** 2013

Chapter 15 from **Andrew Heywood**: *Politics (4th edition)* © **Andrew Heywood** 2013

Chapter 16 from **Andrew Heywood**: *Politics (4th edition)* © **Andrew Heywood** 2013

Chapter 17 from **Andrew Heywood:** *Global Politics (2nd edition)*
© **Andrew Heywood** 2014

Chapter 18 from **Andrew Heywood:** *Global Politics (2nd edition)*
© **Andrew Heywood** 2014

Chapter 19 from **Mike Bourne:** *Understanding Security* © **Mike Bourne** 2014

Chapter 20 from **Mike Bourne:** *Understanding Security* © **Mike Bourne** 2014

Chapter 21 from **Andrew Heywood:** *Global Politics (2nd edition)*
© **Andrew Heywood** 2014

Chapter 22 from **Joseph Grieco, G. John Ikenberry & Michael Mastand-uno:** *Introduction to International Relations* © **Joseph Grieco, G. John Ikenberry & Michael Mastanduno** 2015

Chapter 23 from **Joseph Grieco, G. John Ikenberry & Michael Mastand-uno:** *Introduction to International Relations* © **Joseph Grieco, G. John Ikenberry & Michael Mastanduno** 2015

Chapter 24 from **Andrew Heywood:** *Global Politics (2nd edition)*
© **Andrew Heywood** 2014

Note: any cross-references within this book refer to the original sources from which these chapters have been extracted and should therefore be ignored.

1. Introduction

The Dynamics of Politics

Negativity about the practice of politics is not news to many politicians anymore. Indeed, some politicians seem to be intent on taking advantage of it by offering populist stances on issues and by distancing themselves very clearly from something called the 'political establishment'. The top nominations for 2016 might well have been Donald Trump in the United States and Boris Johnson in Britain, leading the Leave campaign in the EU membership referendum, but as we shall see later in the book there are plenty of competitors. Many politicians have developed something of a gallows humour about it. Gavin Shuker, a UK Member of Parliament (MP), writes:

> Every MP has their own favourite moment on 'The Tour'. It's a routine that each Member must develop – a witty and insightful commentary to accompany the leading of visitors around the Palace of Westminster. Mine is the revelation that, as fire destroyed the old building in 1834, crowds gathered on the south bank of the Thames to celebrate and applaud its destruction. Anti-politics sentiment has always run deep in Britain.[1]

Other politicians offer convoluted apologies to public audiences for being a politician. Isobel Harding, a journalist at a meeting I was chairing in 2016, argued that she would throw up if she heard another politician explain how they only took up the job 'by accident'. They were an engineer or doctor – or some other occupation deemed socially acceptable – turned up at some political event and then, seemingly through forces outside their control, found themselves as a candidate for election and then eventually an elected representative.

If politicians are aware they are close to being social pariahs as a group, then most citizens would not try to persuade them that the situation is otherwise. In 2011–12, we asked people to indicate what words they associated with politics.[2] We grouped the words they overwhelmingly chose under eight headings: deception, corruption, feather-nesting, self-serving, politicking, privileged, boring and incomprehensible (see Table 2.2 on p. 41 for more detail). Not a terribly positive list, I think you would agree. Would citizens want the job themselves? An excellent study of young Americans asked exactly that question and came up with a very clear 'no chance' response. Aliza, an 18-year-old student from Ohio, spoke for many when she told the researchers: 'I'm pretty sure that whatever I do, I won't run for office. I'd hate to live my life like that, the way that people act in politics.'[3]

We know that millions around the world like the idea of democratic governance in the abstract but struggle to be convinced by the politics essential to its delivery. This book tries to understand this contradiction and, because politics matters, it asks what, if anything, we could do to make it work better.

The book takes a broad view of the main issues confronting all democracies in the twenty-first century, but given the limitations of space and the experiences and capacities of the author it gives more attention to the politics of longer-established industrial democracies. While the problems and solutions to the current malaise of democratic politics will vary from country to country, I believe that my focus on common features and key comparisons provides a good starting point for discussion of where we are, and what needs to be done.

The negative response to politics that many of us share is, I think, a very human reaction to the way politics works. As an intricate mechanism in our multifaceted and complex societies, politics exists because we do not agree with one another. Politics is about choosing between competing interests and views often demanding incompatible allocations of limited resources. Crucially, because it is a collective form of decision making, once a choice has been made then that choice has to be imposed on us all. There is no point having a rule that vehicles on a road must stop at a red traffic light unless it is universally observed and enforced. Politics at the level of today's large-scale, interconnected and diverse societies is on a tough beat. Our collective will – which is what politics is supposed to express – is not easy to fathom, or always comfortable to accept once it is decided upon. The central argument of this book is that politics matters and getting it right matters.

The external environment for politics has arguably got harder. Globalization appears to be taking decisions out of the hands of politicians and citizens rooted in nation states. Institutions such as the EU have become a focus of debate, with some claiming they allow us to extend some sort of democratic influence in a globalized world and others arguing that its powers and reach undermine national democracy. The rapid scale of our technological development and issues such as the global warming of our planet create challenges that some fear may be beyond the capacity of sovereignty politics to tackle effectively. Do we need government by authoritative experts to save our planet? Finally, a wide range of social and cultural changes seems to be making many of our societies more individualistic and less cohesive. Added together, these factors may well have made politics harder, and may explain in part our sense of disenchantment with it. But politics is not just failing because the challenges are tougher.

There are a number of internal pathologies to the dynamics of politics that need to be examined. The way that politics is done today rubs up people the wrong way. People have a number of common fears or preconceptions when it comes to living in society and politics tends to bring those fears and preconceptions to the fore. People don't like to be taken for a sucker or treated like an idiot. Politics as experienced on a daily basis often seems calculated to feed that fear. When politicians debate issues in simplistic terms, when they imply that we can have it all at no cost and appear to manufacture arguments they think will play well to different groups, it is hardly surprising that we think they are taking us for a ride. Nor is it odd that cynicism becomes a common coping response. People often find it difficult to think beyond their own experiences and therefore tend to judge political decisions according to their own interests and circumstances. Naïve aspirations and assumptions about politics often flow from these preconceptions. People tend to assume that most other people agree with them (or would do if only the issue was explained to them properly) and that the ideal outcome is one that suits them in every detail. People generally do not like making a lot of effort for little reward. Accordingly, offloading responsibility onto others is a very common coping mechanism in political exchanges.

I argue in this book that politics matters more than most people in democracies give it credit for, and it is more demanding of them than they fully realize. Equally I am clear that we need to change some of the practices of politics. You can have politics without democracy – that is, you can have authoritarian government with people making collective decisions on your behalf without accountability to you – but you *can't have democracy without politics*. For democracy to work, citizens need opportunities to engage and they need to understand the messiness and demands of politics. Social media may be changing the technological expression of politics but it does not mean the fundamental nature of politics has changed.

Why Politics?

This book is premised on a belief that politics matters, and that it matters so much we can't afford to be stupid, naïve or cynical about it, and moreover we cannot afford to entirely offload our responsibilities to engage in it. To explore this statement a little further, it is first worth dwelling on the issues of what politics is, and whether it has to exist. There have been many disputes over these two questions stretching over centuries.[4] I have already suggested that politics reflects the existence of conflicts of interests and opinions. But is it inevitable that politics must exist? You might argue that politics persists only because humans make the wrong choices: if they followed the right path, set down by religion or some other moral guide, they would all choose the same thing and as a result politics would not be necessary. You might alternatively argue that politics operates only in societies that are structured so that people's interests are fundamentally opposed, but that it might be possible to structure a society where people's interests were always aligned and as a result politics would not be required. The former argument has at various times been made by some religious and other moralizing opinion leaders. The latter is one used by some radicals and utopians of various hues. Neither is particular convincing to me, and neither can take much succour from the historical record to date. There is little to suggest that human beings or human societies are perfectible, as implied by these contrasting understandings.

It is difficult to be certain about human nature. But I think it is reasonable to take as a starting point the idea that people are capable of terrible deeds, but also capable of great acts. It is equally difficult to always be sure what is in someone's best interests, so it seems impossible to establish a society where some interests do not clash. Given human society as it has been, and as it might reasonably be expected to be in the future, people will make their own judgements about what is right for themselves and for others and there is no basis to assume that those judgements will be shared. Equally, it is clear that as humans we need to find ways to act together, to engage in collective action and to resolve the problems and challenges of living together. So politics, as John Dunn defines it, can be seen as:

> [T]he struggles which result from the collisions between human purposes: most clearly when these collisions involve large numbers of human beings ... It takes in, too, the immense array of expedients and practices which human beings have invented to cooperate, as much as to compete, with one another.[5]

Politics is constructed in order to express conflicts and allow different interests to shape our collective endeavours. So politics is about trying to get what you want for yourself, or alongside others, for a common cause. Politics is also ultimately something to do with rule, with the ordering of our societies. Politics is about reaching a compromise, and finding ways for those who disagree to rub along with one another.

Some people argue that there is a strong distinction between a 'big P' politics of government conducted at a national (or perhaps an international) level and a 'small p' politics of civil society that takes place in communities and associations of citizens.[6] There are, indeed, different sites or locations for politics, and part of a better approach to politics in democracies might be to extend the scope of a politics of civil society alongside allowing citizens greater access to the more mainstream 'big P' politics. We shall cover these issues in Part III of the book. For now, it is important to emphasize that there is no escape from politics. Whether at a 'big P' level or 'small p' level, politics involves expressing and resolving differences and findings ways of cooperating to achieve collective actions. In civil society, differences exist as much as they do in the 'big P' politics of nation states and international relations. Romantic thinking about community and civil society should not blind us to the reality that because we are human we disagree and seek different things. We need politics not only to express but also to manage those disagreements and, if possible, find ways to cooperate.

Why Politics Matters

Politics matters because collective decisions matter. Perhaps the very richest in society are in a position where they could opt out and live on a desert island free from the rest of us, but even there they can't escape the impact of global warming and our collective effect on our environment as sea levels rise. For almost everyone else, what happens in the wider society makes a huge difference to their ability to get a job, access education or receive health care. What happens in the wider society matters to us all – and that means that politics matters too, because it is through politics that we can influence what happens in that wider world. And that does not only apply to politics on the grand stage of national and international politics, but also to the politics of civil society, the communities in which you live and the associations that structure your life.

Politics matters because there are conflicts and differences of perspective in society about what to do, what resources to collect for public use and how those resources should be spent. The idea that people disagree may at first seem uncontroversial; but one constant suspicion that people have about politics is that many disagreements are trumped up and that the great show of difference that politicians and the media sometimes try to emphasize is somehow false.[7] Sometimes it is true that disagreements are a result of misunderstanding and that discussion and debate can mitigate it, but on many occasions conflict has a very solid base. To understand politics, one must above all understand the inevitable *partiality* of judgement. Judgement is particular to an individual because it reflects their unique set of experiences.

Throughout the ages, people have hoped that wise and incorruptible individuals could be found to make judgements on all our parts, avoiding the unpleasant necessity of politics by allowing others, more expert and gifted, to decide. But judgement is always partial because it comes from the whole breadth of human experience. As John Dunn puts it: 'what partiality rests on is the lives which each of us live'.[8] No one else can live our life and therefore no one else can make all judgements for us.

People can value some things more than others. At the very grand level, a lot of politics is about different views of 'the good life'. A central divide for much of the last two centuries has been between those who prefer liberty over equality and those who privilege equality over liberty. At a more prosaic level, a lot of politics is about hanging on to what you have got, and politics often involves crude power struggles over who gets what. Politics does not always involve grand visions of right and wrong, but rather its focus is on fighting to get or keep a share of resources. More challenging still can be political arguments about identity and entitlements. Issues of ethnicity and the rights of different social groups can often lead to great problems in finding sustainable political solutions if those basic rights are disputed or challenged by another group. The concern to define who and what you are is a constant source of political conflict in our diverse societies, and it is a form of disagreement that is very hard to manage within democracies. Violent conflict, civil wars and even genocide can result from these types of conflict.

Some matters are just more important to some people than others. And at different stages of your life you may be concerned about different things, from student loans to pensions. So a lot of politics involves the 'don't cares' on a particular issue versus the 'care-a-lots', because they are directly affected. Indeed, one of the main things that people disagree about is what should be on the political agenda of society and therefore be something that politics should do something about. A lot of politics is about getting something on the 'to-do list' of governments at all levels.

If everyone agreed we should value the environment and the future of the earth (and it is difficult to argue we should not) there would be plenty of scope for disagreement about what to do, what course of action to take and at what level of urgency. So if people agree about the goal there remain a lot of arguments to be had about the means to achieve the goal. A lot of collective decision making involves *redistribution*, and so politics can involve intense arguments about who gets what. Politics often involves regulation or intervention that passes costs on to some rather than others. And in the details of implementation – the way that a policy is put into effect – there is plenty of scope for further differences of opinion and interest.

Politics matters because it reflects the tensions created when human beings rub against each other and at times it does more than just express those conflicts: it finds a way of settling them. Politics is one way to address and potentially patch up the disagreements that characterize our societies without recourse to illegitimate coercion or violence. Politics, especially in democratic societies, enables people to compromise and reach an agreement. It is a means to orderly and legitimate self-rule. As Bernard Crick puts it in his classic book *In Defence of Politics*:

> Politics is simply the activity by which government is made possible when differing interests in an area to be governed grow powerful enough to need to be conciliated … Other paths are always open. Politics is simply … that solution to the problem of order which chooses conciliation rather than violence and coercion, and chooses it as an effective way by which varying interests can discover that level of compromise best suited to their common survival.[9]

In other words, politics can provide a means of getting on with your fellow human beings that aims to find a way forward through reconciliation and compromise without recourse to straightforward coercion or outright violence. It provides a way to live in an ordered manner with your neighbours, but one that unavoidably often calls on you to sign up to deals and compromises that might not be your first or even tenth choice, but which nevertheless have something in them that enables you to put up with them. It might not be very inspiring, but when it works, politics delivers one great benefit: it enables you to choose, within constraints, the life you want without fear of physical coercion and violence being used against you. Politics creates space for human choices and diverse lifestyles. Politics, if done well, creates the positive context and stable environment for you to live your life. That's why politics matters.

Democratic Politics in Trouble: An Overview of the Argument

Democracy as a particular way of practising politics has gained considerable ground in the last few decades. Around two-thirds of all the countries in the world have a basic set of democratic institutions built around competitive elections that enable all adult citizens to choose and remove their government leaders. As we shall see, some countries have struggled to maintain even these basic democratic requirements and in most democracies there appears to be a considerable amount of discontent and disenchantment about the operation of politics. Mass democracy, practised with a universal suffrage, has less than a century's worth of experience. Democracy is a demanding way of doing the politics of compromise and reconciliation because it rests on the fundamental idea that all adult citizens have a right to a say in matters that affect them. So perhaps we should not be surprised that democratic politics is proving to have difficulties in practice that we still need to learn to overcome. According to the social theorist Max Weber:

> Politics is a strong and slow boring of hard boards. It takes both passion and perspective ... And even those who are neither leaders nor heroes must arm themselves with that steadfastness of heart which can brave even the crumbling of all hopes.[10]

Max Weber, writing at the beginning of the twentieth century, thought that modern democratic politics would be the preserve of professional politicians and activists for whom politics was a vocation. These activists and leaders would require imagination and commitment but also willingness to compromise and make hard choices. Yet even the mostly unengaged citizenry would require a certain steadfastness of heart to stay with the political process. But today many citizens appear to be alienated by the professionalization of politics and dissatisfied with their allocated position as passive and patient observers of the decision making of others.

The book is not a dispassionate analysis, although it aims to offer clear analytical frameworks for thinking through the issues and to provide an accurate account of some of the most important ways that we currently conduct politics in democracies. Alongside the analysis there is a concern with how things ought to be, as well as a focus on how they are. This book looks at the rights and wrongs of our current democratic politics and eventually, in Part III, how we might go about improving our practice of politics. Part I of the book provides an analytical and empirical account of our discontents with democracy and how they might be explained, alongside normative judgements about what democratic politics is about and, by implication, how it should be conducted. Part II of the book is the most heavily empirical. It analyses the ways that citizens are engaged, or not engaged, in politics in democracies, but it too does not shy away from normative judgements about whether certain types of engagement are good or bad for democracy. Part III of the book is the most straightforwardly normative, in that it turns its attention to how politics in democracies might be made to work better. However, there are strong analytical and empirical strands even in this section as the aim of the book is not just to explore ideas about what might be done but also point towards new practices.

Mass Democracy: Triumph and Disappointment

Chapter 1 begins our exploration by arguing that getting politics in democracies to work is a worthwhile challenge. Democracy is rightly a celebrated guide to how we should take collective decisions in our societies. The starting idea of democracy is that all adult citizens should have a voice in respect of decisions made in the societies in which they live. The practice of democratic governance requires free and fair elections to choose government leaders and a range of other freedoms (such as freedom of speech and assembly) and basic respect for human rights. Beyond these basic starting points there are, of course, differences of view about how democracy can best be expressed and achieved. Above all, democracy needs to be seen as a universal value. It is not simply a Western ideology. People everywhere have reason to see its basic premises as valuable. It is an integral part of human nature to value the opportunity to be involved in decisions about issues that affect you. Democracy, in turn, protects a wider commitment to freedom and respect for human rights. Your right to engage is only validated by the rights of others to engage also being respected. Democracy also delivers at a basic level. It cannot guarantee you a happy life, but it makes government and power-holders in society inclined to look after your basic necessities. Finally, democracy helps by using the knowledge embedded in different parts of society to find solutions to intractable problems. The ideas behind democratic governance appear to have wide support in many countries of the world, across a range of cultures and contexts. Most people think that democracy may have some problems, but they are clear that it is better than other forms of government. Yet establishing and maintaining effective democratic practices are no easy tasks, especially in divided societies. Democracy has spread as a practice to many countries but some countries have stepped back from its use and all countries have struggled to deliver its full ambitions.

Within both established and newer democracies, there appears to be a considerable disenchantment with politics. Detailed evidence from many parts of the globe is provided to illustrate this point in Chapter 2. What emerges is a complex picture of overall decline and a set of discontents that range from a lack of confidence in the way that politics works to extreme cynicism about the process. Some degree of scepticism about politics might well be considered healthy and there may be a cycle to public engagement in politics, depending on the nature of the issues at stake. But it is difficult to escape the idea that the scale and breadth of discontent about politics raises some questions about the long-term health of democracy. People perhaps naturally do not trust politicians but, more than that, many of the key institutions of democracies – parties, parliaments and polls – do not command sufficient respect and engagement. Democracy cannot survive if its lifeblood of politics is seen as a sort of necessary evil – or, worse still, a pointless waste of time.

Chapter 3 explores various explanations of why disenchantment might have grown. We examine whether social changes might be driving anti-politics or whether changing norms and attitudes among citizens might be behind the phenomenon. These first two categories of explanations imply that something has changed about citizens that have made politics a more alienating or challenging experience for them. However, two other categories of explanation rest on the idea that the practice or performance of politics may have changed the relationship of politics with citizens for the worse. The political system or politicians may have changed in a way that makes citizens find the inherently difficult processes of politics even harder to accept. Moreover, positive outcomes from politics may have become more complicated to deliver, leaving more citizens pondering what its point is. In different countries, it is likely that various mixes of the dozen factors identified under our four headings have played their part in creating political negativity.

Chapter 4 suggests that there may be one overarching factor that also helps to explain political disenchantment: that a number of misunderstandings of the political process have taken hold in the discourse of democracies. The pressure from the increased prominence given to market-based consumerism in the culture of many democracies has led key aspects of politics to be overlooked. As a result, many citizens fail to fully appreciate that politics in the end involves the collective imposition of decisions, demands a complex communication process and generally produces messy compromise. Yes, the big 'sell' of politics is the imposition of collective decisions, the dull dynamics, the mendacity, the compromises and the reconciliation of opponents. In that sense politics is designed to disappoint. Its outcomes are often messy, ambiguous and never final. Part of the trick is to recognize that it is possible to return to an issue later. Politics involves that hardest of human skills: listening carefully to the opinions of others and their expressions of their interests. Doing politics in a small group is hard enough and the greater prospects of misinformation, muddle and malaise in our large complex societies are bound to create some frustration. Democracy cannot wish away that reality.

The Pathologies of Political Practice

Part II of the book explores the argument that it is not just that we characterize and understand politics in a mistaken way, but that there are problems and difficulties with the way we practise it as well. Most citizens' engagement has a sporadic and mundane character and an uneven and very limited quality. As Chapter 5 shows, for all the opportunities that in theory might be afforded them, most people engage very little beyond occasionally casting a vote; and in some countries the number willing to do even that appears to be declining. Research indicates that when citizens do engage, they tend to undertake relatively simple acts such as signing a petition or boycotting a product as a way of sending a political message. Even in terms of these types of political activity there are significant differences between the civic capacity of different countries and within countries between more and less educated people. The emergence of digital forms of political engagement has been taken up across the generations – of course especially among younger citizens – but what is clear activism even in these new digital forms is still a sport for a minority of citizens. The broad empirical message of this chapter stands that citizens do engage in politics in a variety (and shifting) ways but they tend to do so occasionally rather than regularly. In terms of the quality of the engagement, there is a sense in which what counts as 'politics' for most people is not much more than an extension of their activities as consumers. There is nothing wrong with such expressions of citizenship; they are just rather limited. Much engagement is directed towards something that brings personal benefit or perhaps provides an expressive statement about a person's sense of themselves and their identity. These atomized forms of citizenship mean that people often have only a surface engagement with political issues and complexities. There is hope in the range and diversity of engagement in democracies, but there are also concerns because of its uneven spread and shallow quality.

Most of the real politics is done in a space where we are spectators. It is the sphere of professionals not amateurs. Chapter 6 examines the roles of high-intensity activists in party politics, citizen lobby groups and protest movements. The cohesion brought by parties, the advocacy of special interests by the lobby and the challenge and dissent offered through various forms of protest offer vital links in the democratic chain between governors and governed. But all are failing to engage citizens-at-large in politics. The committed activists for democracy constitute maybe fewer than 1 in 600 in any population. Activists are odd people, very much in a minority in our society. They do a lot of the work of politics for us, and we should be grateful to them but the way their organizations work is in part responsible for people's sense of alienation from politics.

As parties have lost membership, they have become reliant on professional campaigners and organizers and operate in a way that treats citizens as passive political observers that just need to be mobilized at elections to back the party. Citizen lobby organizations – such as Friends of the Earth – have large-scale memberships, but their involvement is generally restricted to providing the necessary funding. They, too, rely on professional organizers and experts. Members provide the cash but the professional politicos in the lobby organizations decide what to campaign on. Citizens are a passive audience to be exhorted about particular campaigns through the media and occasionally galvanized to send in letters or cards of support or join a public demonstration based on often rather simplistic messages. Citizens are offered little in terms of depth of analysis or understanding of the issues at stake by these organizations. Even more radical protest organizations tend to be professionalized in their style of behaviour and their use of the media in both old and new versions. The occasional engagement by a wider group of citizens in a protest 'event', online campaign or rally is in danger of being more a lifestyle statement than a serious engagement with a political debate.

Chapter 7 argues against the corrosive influence of cynicism in the way that so many of us view politics and politicians. It challenges the academic literature that lends support to a very cynical take on politics. A central part of the chapter addresses the issue that might make the most direct case for cynicism – namely, that politicians lie all the time. There is no point in denying that politicians do lie some of the time, but the case for the defence rests on two main points. First, we all lie some of the time. Second, between lying at one end of the spectrum and the full, unvarnished truth at the other, there are many halfway houses that our expectations and the circumstances under which they may operate often force politicians uncomfortably to occupy.

The final section of Chapter 7 examines the role of the mainstream media in promoting a culture of cynicism. There are several aspects of this argument to consider. First, there has been a 'dumbing down' in news coverage, which means that people are less likely to understand underlying issues or complexities with respect to politics and politics can often be seen to fail when what it is delivering is judged in a simplistic framework. Second, the fusing of news reporting and comment, which is a characteristic of modern media coverage of politics, probably feeds a culture where fact, opinion and speculation merge into one another and which lends itself to a cynical take on political life. A third argument is that the media in some countries has actively spread a culture of contempt; a fourth argument is that we have seen the emergence of a style of journalism that presents itself as the champion of the people and takes a strongly adversarial position to politicians, asking all the time why is this politician lying to me and you, the viewers and listeners. The first two arguments perhaps hold true across more countries than the last two. However, we should stop glorifying journalists and journalism that makes its reputation by being constantly cynical about politics and politicians. The problem with cynicism is that it is ultimately a fatalistic creed: it feeds disengagement, because it tells us that in the end selfishness and mendacity will triumph, so why bother?

I am not arguing that you should trust politicians without qualification. I am happy to agree that politicians sometimes make politics worse by their behaviour. Some politicians are dishonest, some are time-serving compromisers and some are dangerous ideologues. In some senses, in all of these ways they are representative of us, the citizens. But beyond that, many politicians are not as venal, incompetent or divisive as we sometimes think. Democracy needs us to strike a pose of healthy scepticism towards politicians, rather than corrosive cynicism.

Chapter 8 looks at another problematic approach to democratic politics that is commonly to be observed in today's world: *populism*. Populists are not really troubled by the mood of anti-politics, rather they are trying to exploit it. Populists see themselves as true democrats, defending the neglected interests of the people. Modern populism finds an accommodation with democratic practice and thought and is reflected in the rapid rise of 'anti-politicians' of various hues and persuasions: right-wing, left-wing and centrists. It is often reflected in the spectacular rejection of political elite-supported referendum propositions that are put to the people. Modern populism draws in people from all walks of life, not just the uneducated or the underclass. It feeds on the discontent with politics and produces short bursts of engagement, but offers little that could sustain a tolerant and viable approach to politics.

My main criticism of populism is that it fails to see the complexities of politics. Ironically for a creed that holds that the common sense of the people should be lauded, populism tends towards a very high-octane faith in redemptive politics. Changing the world in the direction you want is a matter of capturing the will of the people. Democracy should deliver what the people want, and if it does not it's down to corrupt politicians or the malign influence of do-gooders, big business or some other unrepresentative lobby. It tends to a view that a powerful personality and strong leadership could overcome all the problems and institutional complexities that appear to bedevil the practices of democratic governments. The irony is that common sense might tell you to be more pragmatic and view politics as the art of the possible, a matter of compromise, its tone as driven by respect for toleration and diversity, its rewards as stability and peace rather than any utopia. Populism should not be viewed as simply anti-democratic or undesirable. Populism can express a belief central to democracy – that the people can change their world for the better. It fails when it collapses into aggressive intolerance of other people's legitimate viewpoints and generally the rather simplistic understanding of political processes and prospects that it conveys.

Searching for Solutions

The understanding of politics in democracies offered here provides a framework for interpreting the sense of disenchantment and divorce from politics that pervades those democracies and simultaneously points towards ways to improve the practice of politics in democracies. We now need to consider what changes are needed, and how positive change could be delivered. This book takes a long, hard look at how people participate in politics. It finds that people are often cynical about politics, that many have naïve aspirations about what it can offer and achieve, that people tend to offload responsibilities for engagement and that most prefer to join in themselves only in a way that minimizes effort and maximizes potential gain.

The troubling issue is that these dominant forms of citizen engagement are not sustainable as a way of conducting democratic politics. They feed a cycle of disaffection that ultimately runs the risk of undermining public support for democracy. Rampant cynicism, populism and a stark gap between high-intensity activists and the political practice of the rest of us makes politics more difficult and less likely to succeed. We need to rethink the way that we do politics. It matters for the future of democracy that we do.

In Chapter 9 I argue, however, that we should start from where people are and then seek to mould political institutions and a wider civic infrastructure to enable people to engage in politics more effectively without transforming them into new model citizens. When it comes to politics, most people are amateurs: they have no intention of making it their vocation or career. There is nothing wrong with being an amateur, but there is a difference between a vaguely competent amateur and a completely inadequate layperson – as any golfer, sailor or birdwatcher will tell you. Moreover, being an incompetent amateur when it comes to these leisure activities can be very irritating to others, and occasionally even dangerous. The same argument can be applied when considering democratic politics. So the first plea of this book is that people should be more self-critical and reflective about their approach to politics. They should seek to become more competent amateurs.

Politics is a place for amateurs, but we need to design institutions, structure processes and develop support systems to make it easier for people to engage. My solution to the problem of disenchantment with politics is thus deceptively simple. It is to expand the opportunities for citizens to have a say about the issues they care about. There are two insights hidden away in this formula that run as threads throughout this book. First, it is vital to recognize the *range of issues* that people think are important. One person's 'big issue' can mean nothing to another. This is so because politics rests on a fundamental truth about human beings: because we, and only we, can live our different lives, we all see the world through the lens of that experience. Most of us probably carry around in our heads a set of (usually unarticulated) understandings of what range and type of issues matter to us; they will be different to those held by others. We need a politics that allows citizens to have a say over what is important to them, not what professional politicians, lobbyists, journalists or scientists tell them is important. The second is that having a say does not mean, for most people, having a veto or being the final judge. As amateurs, citizens are cautious about claiming decision-taking responsibility. Having a say means wanting to *influence*, but not having to *decide*.

The implications of these challenges are taken up in Chapters 10 and 11. Chapter 10 explores how to make representative politics more legitimate and open. Representative politics needs to be understood as a more active exchange between citizen and representative and restructured to give more scope for local and global decision making. We need to learn to love local politics and argue for a world where local political actors – mayors – have both more power and are held to account by a more dynamic community politics. We need to find ways to embrace global politics and get the voices of citizens heard. The EU may be a way of dealing on the global stage for much of Europe but there can be little doubt that it suffers from a democratic deficit.

Chapter 11 looks at the broader civic arena that surrounds politics. It argues for some big changes. The first set of initiatives goes under the broad heading of democratic innovations and is about new ways of offering public engagement in politics. The second set of options rests on a critical use of new social media and other new technologies to do politics differently. The third option explores how citizens can use a range of monitoring and challenging devices to build on their distrust of politics in order to hold politicians and other decision-makers to account. The fourth option is to consider how to improve understanding of politics and goes on to examine the roles of civic education, key civic institutions and in particular the mainstream media in creating a positive environment for democratic politics.

2. Introduction

What is it that we 'do' when we engage in Political Science or International Relations? Clearly, we study the world of politics, but what does this activity entail? The aim of this book is to provide an understanding of what it means to be a political scientist/analyst; that is, to demonstrate what it is that we as students or analysts of politics do, and how we do it. In this book we reflect upon the different ways in which we might go about: tackling a particular question or political problem; analyzing an issue or event; discussing the potential for political and/or social transformation; or challenging dominant interpretations of the political world. Our central argument is that the 'doing' of political analysis is an active, and interactive, process of critical evaluation and application of theory, and it is this skill which we hope to shed some light on in the pages that follow.

This book is designed as a new kind of introduction to Political Science and International Relations (which we will refer to by its abbreviation – IR). We focus in particular upon the different ways in which we might analyze a similar issue or problem in both disciplines. Of interest to Political Science and IR are questions such as: why do states go to war? Is world peace politically possible? Why are some societies more unequal than others? In whose interests does the political system work? Is a solution to climate change possible? These questions are all concerned with issues, problems or events which affect and transcend both the domestic and international levels of politics. The disciplines of Political Science and IR provide differing theoretical explanations as a means to analyze or seek to provide answers to these questions. With this in mind our book has a particular focus on the existence of a wide range of theoretical perspectives and shows how they might be applied. We also suggest that just as political questions and issues cross-cut domestic and international boundaries, so our analysis needs to do the same.

Our book has three starting assumptions: first, that the 'doing' of political analysis is theoretically informed; second, that there are several different ways that we can approach our studies, all of which are legitimate; and, third, that the disciplines of Political Science and International Relations are not discrete but overlap, asking similar questions, albeit with a slightly different vocabulary and a slightly different focus of enquiry. In part these differences stem from differences in subject matter – a disciplinary divide. In part these differences stem from approaches, or ways that we carry out our analysis; there is also a methodological divide. Political Science and IR both ask important questions about our contemporary environment. They might explore the way history or economics shapes our understandings of today. Both disciplines also enable us to reflect upon and analyze the complexity of the 'real world' of politics and the possibilities of changing it. Nevertheless, this reflection is shaped not only by what we see in the 'real world' of politics, but also by the way in which our disciplines have developed and have taught us what are regarded as legitimate areas of enquiry. That is, the important point here is that debates centre around not only what we study, but *how* we study it.

The debate over how we study is an important one, but one which can be incredibly complex and confusing. Our aim here is to simplify this debate through illustrating that there are different ways to address similar political questions and issues. We might have intuitive thoughts about what the answer to a particular political problem is. What we are trying to do in this book is show how these intuitions can be systematically and logically developed, to enable us to do coherent and rigorous analysis. We are seeking to demystify some of the vocabulary that is used within our disciplines, and give labels to those intuitions which lie behind the analysis that we do.

We might have particular views about what the political world is like, or what it should be like. These views translate into differing ways in which we undertake our study. Our first example of how these differences manifest themselves can be found in the title of this book. While this book is entitled 'Doing Political Science and International Relations' there are two key contentious issues here that are worth briefly reflecting on. First, to term the study of politics 'Political Science' reflects a set of assumptions about the way in which the discipline can and should be studied – as a science. For us this definition provides only a partial account of what the analysis of politics entails (the debate over whether Politics may be considered a 'science' will be explicitly addressed in the following chapter and is a theme which runs throughout the book). Second, the title acknowledges the existence of a disciplinary split between Politics and IR, but another aim of the book is to suggest that this is somewhat limiting. What we are seeking to do here is to reflect upon these divisions which we do through a series of substantive topics.

We proceed in the introduction by giving a short discussion of the terminology which will be used to describe the two disciplines, and a brief overview of what is conventionally regarded as their legitimate areas of enquiry. As the need for theory to show us how we 'do' what it is we do is a key theme of this book, the main part of the introduction provides an overview of why theory is crucial in our analytical 'toolkit'.

A brief note on terminology: Politics and International Relations

It is easy to get confused about the terms IR, Political Studies and Political Science, and whether they refer to the world 'out there' or the study that we do. Conventionally, when referring to the discipline, the words begin with uppercase – Political Science/ Political Studies and International Relations. However, given our assumption that these divisions are arbitrary and limiting, we use the word Politics as an overarching umbrella term to include the whole field of Politics/Political Science/International Relations. We also assume an overlap of methodologies in both disciplines and so we use the term 'political analysis' to refer to the activity engaged in by both disciplines.

What is Politics (Political Science and International Relations)?

So what is it that we study when we analyze politics? For some people, politics is about war. For others, war is the consequence of a breakdown or failure of politics. For some politics is about government and the institutions of the state, whereas for others, notably, but not exclusively, politics is not only what happens in public life but is played out in private lives too through the politics of family relationships. For some politics is what happens on the news, while for others politics characterizes what happens in popular culture, where we are taught values of citizenship and political identities outside of a formal news setting (see, for example, Street, 1997).

Arguably, politics is also about the allocation of scarce resources, asking Laswell's (1936) famous question: who gets what, when and how? Related to this is the idea of collective bargaining, the interests of which might then be represented in public policy. Political study can also be about political behaviour, for example of politicians or the electorate. For some politics is about class conflict and the way in which this forms the basis of systems of exploitation. Politics can also be about the possibility of social transformation and as such provides an opportunity through which this is possible. Politics can be about challenging the status quo and envisioning alternative ways in which society can exist and operate.

Underlying this diversity of content, Leftwich (2004) suggests, are two broad approaches to defining the study of politics. First is the 'arena' approach, which suggests politics is something which takes place in a certain site, or set of institutions within certain kinds of societies, and is linked to the idea of states. Second, Leftwich suggests, is a 'procedural' approach, which is concerned with the processes of politics. That is, politics is not confined to geographic location or formal institutions, but takes place between people and is a process. Feminists, for example, argue that the 'personal is the political'. In their definition politics does not only occur in public life, but also in the private lives of citizens. Feminism is interesting as it blurs the boundaries of Leftwich's definitions and shows us how politics becomes a process of interaction, yet can also be embodied in institutions (so can combine a processural and arena account). However, arguably what underpins these definitional debates, and both disciplines, is a concern with power. Who has it or where is it located? How is it used and with what effects? Whose interests does it operate in? While these questions may not always be explicitly addressed in the work that we read, they do inform and shape the kind of questions that we ask about what we study. Given the centrality of the notion of power for understanding both how politics in the 'real world' works and in understanding how we, as analysts, formulate our research, power is discussed in more depth in Chapter 2. However, the study of politics isn't simply about the topic, it is also about the approach that we adopt, that is *how* we study our area of enquiry. We make a series of assumptions before we even begin our analysis, and so it is useful, and provides for much better analysis, if we are aware of our theoretical predispositions before we begin.

What are we trying to do as analysts of politics?

When considering what it is we do when we analyze politics, we need to think first about what it is that we are seeking to do. Are we seeking to provide causal explanation of phenomena? Are we aiming to uncover statistically measurable regularities and generate general unifying laws in order to provide both explanation and the possibility of predictions? Or are we trying to understand a set of phenomena through reference to its historical and cultural context? Do we need an awareness of the actions and intentions of the participants and the meaning they attach to them? These questions are related to one of the most fundamental questions that underpins Politics: can it be conceived of as 'scientific'? There is an enormous debate around this issue within the disciplines and given its importance in shaping the way in which we approach the study of politics, this will be addressed in more detail in the following chapter.

How do we 'do' Politics (Political Science and International Relations)?

In short, in this book we argue that the way in which we 'do' Politics is through the application of a theoretical framework to a particular political phenomenon, question, issue, process or event. Our argument is that theory provides a mechanism through which we can make sense of the world, but also we need to reflect on this. We also need to be aware of the limitations and strengths of our theories. That is, the way we use theory enables us to *critically evaluate* the world, but we should also *critically evaluate* our theories. This is a skill which we learn and refine and the aim of this book is to introduce the differing ways in which we might do this.

When we do our political analysis we might begin by looking at a particular problem or issue and think about how we might resolve it, such as: why are some tax regimes more progressive than others? How might participation in universities be widened? Why are ideas about neo-liberalism dominant and largely unchallenged? How can wealth be redistributed to address problems of inequality? Or we might have a particular question that we want to answer, such as what caused World War II? Why was a decision taken by the UK and US to invade Iraq? We may want to ask how we can address problems of social inequality, or how we can bring about political change. However, before we can apply theoretical frameworks to address these kinds of questions, we need to think about the assumptions that we are making about what is real, what we can know about reality and how we can find out about it.

Before we do any kind of analysis we have already made a set of assumptions about what the political world looks like and how we can know about it. This discussion about our ability to know about political reality reflects a complicated debate which we engage in throughout our lives as political analysts. We give an overview of this debate in the next chapter as it is crucial in helping us think about the way in which we analyze Politics. One reason we need to think about this issue is that it informs the theories that we adopt and a key argument in this book is that critical use of theory is central for us in doing our political analysis. We now turn to discuss why.

The importance of theory

The way in which we analyze politics and international relations is through the use of theoretical frameworks. Much like a mechanic needs a toolkit to do his/her job, so in order to do our job – to analyze political phenomena – we need a toolkit. However, the toolkit of the political analyst is not made up of spanners and screwdrivers; rather it comprises theoretical frameworks which provide us with a means through which we can analyze, explain, understand and potentially change the world.

Theory is crucial for a number of reasons. First, what makes political analysis different from journalism, or the kind of conversations we might have in the pub, is that theory is employed not only to describe events or issues but also to look for causation. It allows us to ask how and why particular events have happened, and to enable us to think about the likely implications of particular outcomes and observations. Theory helps us establish what we are looking for and why what we are looking for is relevant. When we analyze politics, we can collect stylized 'facts', but how do we put them together to make a coherent story or argument? It is not enough to establish what is (and so provide a descriptive analysis); we need to establish *why* something might be the case. Why do a certain set of 'facts' appear as they are? To ask these 'how' and 'why' questions, we need to use theory. Theory provides the framework through which we can understand or at least analyze why a certain set of 'facts' or a certain set of behaviours link together in the way that they do.

Second, theory provides us with a way to simplify the world so that we can analyze it. Political phenomena are inherently messy and so theory enables us to identify the key features, which are significant in analysis and so providing for understanding or explanation, and this would seem intuitively appealing as, *ceteris paribus*, we tend to be attracted to parsimony. However, this already raises complications. The more simplified a theory is the more abstract it is from what is happening, or what is being observed or analyzed, so it may miss important factors. But, at the same time, the more complex theory becomes the more difficult it is to identify the cause or conditions which produce that observation. So, getting the balance between simplification and reflecting the complexity of political life is crucial. Third, relatedly, through a critical evaluation of the theory we are using, we are able to see what is missing from our analysis – are there other factors which we should pay attention to? This then enables us to engage in theory building, to provide for more sophisticated analysis in later work. As we set out below, one of the key differences in the development of International Relations as a discipline was its atheoretical approach, its lack of theory. This led to a series of failings and weaknesses within the discipline (such as its inability to predict the outbreak of World War II or the collapse of communism). Although, this is discussed, and widely accepted as a 'failure' of the discipline, it raises the question: is it possible for any theory to make such a prediction? Whether the function of theory is to produce predictions or to help us to make sense of the world is something which we need to reflect upon when we do our analysis. Today the leading IR journals focus on publishing theoretical work, which aim to build and develop theory, not just for its own sake, but to provide us with more comprehensive 'tools' with which to do our job.

Fourth, for those who adhere to a scientific approach to politics, theory is also used to ask 'what if' questions. That is, theory is used to generate hypotheses to be tested. This can be used to explore counterfactuals (e.g., if A happens, then B *might* happen). Counterfactuals explore what might have happened or what may have been the case given certain conditions (for example, whether there would still have been a Democrat president if Hillary Clinton had won the nomination, or whether the UK would not have gone to war on Iraq if Blair had not been prime minister). Theory can also be used to establish causal relationships (e.g., if A happens, then B *will* happen) and can be also be used to make predictions about what happens if certain conditions are fulfilled. For example, there has been a great deal of research which has argued that the reason we voted for whom we did was related to our socio-economic background. A causal theory of voting behaviour was premised upon the following: in the UK, if you were middle class you were likely to vote Conservative; working class, you would vote Labour. Therefore, we would not need to observe someone in the ballot box, it is enough to know their social class and we would be able to predict their likely voting behaviour from that. Theories of voting behaviour, such as this, provide a simplification of reality. Using this theory, it is possible that we could have explained why the Conservatives might have won seats at election time if there were a high number of middle-class voters in the constituency. While this argument has been subject to much debate (as summarized in Denver, 1994/2003) the point to be made here is that the theory has been used to simplify reality so that predictions can be made, and an explanation and account of political reality can be offered. In this way, theory shows us where to look, and what is important for our analysis. For those who adhere to a 'scientific' approach it also provides the opportunity to offer a causal explanation.

Fifth, theory can also provide us with a way in which we can generate social and political transformation. For critical theorists, the use of theory enables us to reflect upon how we can challenge the existing order, through analysis of how it operates. This in turn provides us with the basis from which we can explore alternative conceptions of our social and political world.

Sixth, and linked to the previous point, theory provides us with a way to problematize the world. That is, it may not necessarily produce a definitive solution to a political problem or issue, but it provides us with a means through which we can understand the complexity of a political issue. Crucially, it helps us to understand the questions that we need to

---

Box 2.1   Summary: the role of theory in political analysis

- Distinguishes the discipline from journalism in providing the opportunity for rigorous analysis

- Helps us to know what to look for and why this is relevant

- Simplifies the world to help us try and make sense of it

- Enables us to ask 'how' and 'why' questions

- Makes it possible for us to recognize the existence of different 'worldviews'

- Allows for a critical consideration of implications and possible outcomes

- For scientific approaches it provides for the possibility of predictions

- For critical accounts it provides a way to think about possibilities for social and political change

- Helps us to formulate the questions that we need to ask

- Theory also provides a language for communities of scholars, giving us terminologies to engage in dialogue

---

ask. Seventh, theory also gives us a language, a community with which to share that language, and a set of terminologies and 'labels' which we can use to define our intuitive and logical responses or thoughts about topics. It also gives us a vocabulary through which to discuss issues with other scholars in the community.

To be aware of differing theoretical perspectives enables us to understand that not everyone sees the world in the way that we do and so theory draws our attention to differing perspectives and ways in which people understand the political world.

Using theory enables us to think about what we should look for and why that particular aspect is relevant to our analysis. One of the ways in which theory does this is through the 'framing' of underlying issues or concerns. That is, what is it that we look at through a theoretical framework, what do we use theory to tell us? There are a number of issues which underpin all our theoretical frameworks both prior to and during our analysis. Some of these are discussed in Chapter 12, and below we draw out three of the key concerns that we need to be aware of: what is the level of analysis; what is the relationship between structures and agents; and are we accounting for/describing or explaining continuity or change? Our answers to these questions inform the way in which we approach our topic and influence the kind of outcomes we may produce. A brief account of these issues is outlined below.

Spatial levels of analysis

Something which theory has done much to highlight is the issue of 'levels of analysis'. That is, what is it that we look at when we analyze politics? Do we look at the actions of politicians, such as prime ministers and presidents? Do we look at the actions of nation-states? So, do we analyze the individual or an individual unit? Or, do we look at the systems or structures that are in place? Should we focus attention on the anarchic structure of the international system, the structure of capitalism, or the regulatory structure within states? To some the study of the international arena is macro level, where the domestic state is seen as a micro-level actor. Yet at the domestic level, the state can also be viewed as a macro-level actor, with political actors/individuals regarded as micro-level units of analysis. As this suggests we not only use theory to help us identify what we are looking for; it also helps us to think about the positioning of what we are looking at. An awareness of this enables us to reflect upon both what we are explaining or accounting for, and what we are missing.

Structure and agency

This levels of analysis debate focuses our attention on the geographical location that we may look at the international arena, the workings of the domestic state apparatus, or, as is being recently discussed in IR, the role of cities. However, is it enough only to think about the physical location of politics? Our argument is that it is not. We need also to think about the individuals who take part in the political process and the historical and institutional structures which shape and influence their behaviour. The interaction between the two has been widely debated across the social sciences, and has been labelled the 'structure/agency' debate. For some this debate is framed as a problem, which implies the need for a solution. However, philosophers have debated this issue throughout history and a solution has yet to be found. We prefer to go with the notion of the interaction with structure and agency not as a problem requiring a solution, but as a means to problematize the world. That is, through reference to the interaction between structure and agency, we can see what issues need to be addressed.

The tensions between structure and agency are inherent in both disciplines and there is a wealth of literature surrounding this theoretical issue (see, for example, Giddens, 1984; Hay, 2002, McAnulla, 2002; Wendt, 1987). This is also important because it influences what we might study and what we might miss in our theoretical frameworks. For example,

Marxist accounts will draw our attention to the way in which the world is shaped by capitalism (so providing an account which privileges the role of structures in explaining events); whereas elitist accounts would look at the role of leaders (so thereby privileging the role of agents, or individuals). We would endorse the argument that we need to reflect upon the role of both structures and agents to understand politics. That is, we cannot understand how structures operate, without understanding the role of individuals within them, at the same time, we cannot look at individuals divorced from their context. While this may seem a fairly obvious statement, many of the theoretical frameworks we explore through this book will (often implicitly) privilege one over the other.

An understanding of the underlying interaction and tensions between structures and agents in whatever theoretical framework we adopt is useful in that it reminds us of the complexity of the social and political world. It also enables us to reflect upon what is missing from our analysis. For example, if we explain the political world in terms of capitalist structures, are we missing the role that individuals (such as politicians, businessmen/women and bureaucrats) play in shaping those structures? If we explain the world in terms of individuals within it, are we missing the wider structures which constrain or facilitate our behaviour? In economic recession it may seem wise for the individual to be careful with their hard-earned cash – in this case the level of analysis would be upon the individual and the benefits to them of this frugal behaviour. However, if every individual chooses to behave in this way, then the sum total of this behaviour is a lack of money in circulation and so recession deepens. Analysis here might then instead focus upon the economy as a whole in recession, which misses the role of individuals (collectively) acting within it. Combining an analysis of structures and agents in this example would suggest that what is needed within a recession is government intervention to facilitate greater spending within the economy, by providing individuals with the means (i.e., jobs and wages) to make this interaction possible. The aim of this example is thus to illustrate that it is useful to consider the role of both structures and agents in our analysis. It is worth noting, however, that the choice to introduce this level of complexity contains a trade-off: if we study both structures and agents we may increase the complexity of our analysis at the expense of parsimony.

Change or continuity?

The other way in which we use theory is not just to look at static phenomena, but also to understand why things are the way they are, how they have come to be a particular way. The point being that we are not simply concerned to describe what is the case, but our aim is to seek to understand *why* something has come to be the case. What particular set of circumstances has facilitated this particular event, issue or outcome? We are not only looking to understand or explain what is, but more importantly we are seeking to understand why things are the way they are. To do this we need to be able to understand why things change and why they don't. So, when we are seeking to understand or account for events, or resolve particular problems, what is it that we are looking for? Are we looking to explain or understand why things have changed, why change happens? (For example, why are voters in contemporary society less likely to vote according to their socio-economic class compared to 50 years ago?) Or are we seeking to understand why things stay the same? (For example, why is capitalism so enduring?)

Each of the theories that we look at throughout this text includes assumptions about what the level of analysis should be when explaining or analysing political phenomena. The theories we use are also underpinned by assumptions about the relationship between structure and agency. These may not always be explicitly spelled out within the theoretical frameworks, but an awareness of this is important for understanding what it is the theory is doing and what it is missing. Likewise, it is important to reflect upon the issue of continuity and change, as this enables us to think about the role that theory is playing in our analysis. Is our theory providing for a description of what is? Or does it enable us to understand why particular issues or events or problems are framed the way they are? Does this theory provide us with an opportunity to reflect upon the political world differently? This is important for two reasons. First, if we want to understand why things are the way they are and, second, because a more critical analyst of politics, again to paraphrase Marx, is not simply seeking to observe the world but seeking to change it too. In this way, theoretical frameworks provide us with an opportunity to reflect upon how things may be different. Second, the theory we adopt influences the outcomes available to us, be those outcomes ones which reinforce the status quo or those that bring about change. However, given the way in which theory shapes what it is possible to establish, we need to have this critical awareness of the assumptions that we make before we begin.

In summary, we argue that the way in which we 'do' political analysis is that we apply a particular theoretical framework and evaluate political phenomena against it. This enables us to simplify political phenomena, look for key aspects which we may use to explain events, or answer particular questions, to understand why and how something has happened, consider an alternative and possibilities of change and, depending upon our standpoint, address 'what if' questions. These issues are of concern to all students of Politics and given our suggestion that the disciplines are closely linked, we now turn to provide a brief overview of how the disciplines have been separated and what unites them.

What is the difference between IR and Politics and how are they connected?

Disciplinary contexts

Politics and IR have developed as separate disciplines. For some this is strange, as the subject area of enquiry for both disciplines is often similar (e.g., political institutions, ideas and behaviour, differentiated only by spatial levels of analysis). Moreover, if we look closely we can see a lot of similarities, not only in what is studied, but also in the way in which political phenomena are studied. The next section gives a general overview of how the two disciplines have developed historically and then draws out some of their similarities. It is important to draw attention to what may be one of the dangers of providing such a brief disciplinary history, in that this neglects the influence of broader disciplines, such as communications and media studies, gender studies, as well as psychology and, more recently, neuro-science. The aim here, however, is to illustrate how the two disciplines have emerged independently of each other, and yet to also highlight their shared approaches and concerns. In addition, we argue against the demarcation of the two disciplines, which a) may prevent insights into the other and b) while these boundaries may facilitate parsimony in analysis we believe that political life is inherently more complex than the superficial boundaries suggest.

This brief overview is not intended to suggest cohesion within the disciplines (and, indeed, there are debates about the historical development of the disciplines; see, for example, Schmidt, 2008; Adcock and Bevir, 2005; Savigny, 2010). Rather, the aim is to suggest that while Politics and IR may have had differing starting points, there are two main areas of agreement. First, as suggested earlier in this introduction and as reflected in the substantive chapters of this book, there are overlaps in terms of subject matter. Second, both disciplines are united in containing a number of divergent views upon how we actually proceed in analyzing the content matter.

Politics

Politics as a discipline was established in the late nineteenth/early twentieth century across Europe and in the US (although its roots in Europe – for example, in Sweden – date back to the mid-nineteenth century).

Historically, in the US and UK, the emphasis was upon political philosophy and normative political theory, although more recent variants have to varying degrees been informed by the natural sciences and economics. Politics as a broader discipline, concerning the study of ideas, institutions and interests, in the UK was formally established in the 1950s. Theoretical development more recently moved beyond philosophy and, in the US, Political Science has tended to focus upon quantitative approaches and formal modelling, strongly influenced by work from economics, and institutions. The 'scientific' quantitative approach still dominates the pages of the leading US journals. British Political Science (also referred to in the UK as Political Studies) has tended to be more qualitative, with a focus upon political philosophy (also known as normative theory), history and institutions, while European Political Science tended towards humanities, particularly history and sociology (for discussion of its contemporary character see special issue of *European Political Science*, e.g. Savigny (and other papers) 2010). Historically, the study of politics was concerned with normative issues such as the nature of (good) government. The behavioural 'revolution' meant an increasing focus upon the behaviour and workings of political systems, and analysis focused on voters and electoral outcomes. More recently the challenges came from a group of political analysts who are referred to as the *perestroika* movement. They sought to challenge the mainstream status quo and their emphasis is upon the need for a wider remit of methods and approaches. Nonetheless, Political Science has also tended to be dominated by white males, and written as a reflection of their interests. In recent years greater prominence has been achieved by feminists and female writers and we have sought to mainstream their approaches within this text.

In recent years, as noted above, challenges have also come from outside, although still within academia, from, among others, economics, media and communications and psychology. However, Politics as a discipline has also had to respond to 'real world' events which challenge the primacy of the nation-state (Politics' original focus of analysis). Political processes, issues and structures, such as globalization, climate change and the European Union, have meant that the discipline has had to rethink, or at least re-evaluate, what is studied and how it proceeds. One way this can be seen is through the increasing number of academic articles and papers. In recent years we have seen a proliferation of specialist journals, and sub-fields within the discipline (Taggart and Lees, 2006), which reflects not only a widening of remit of subject matter, but also increasing influence from other disciplines and a recognition of changes in the real world of politics.

International Relations

Historically, the main concern of IR was *policy relevance*. The primary motivation for the emergence of IR was to analyze the events that had led to war, with a view to preventing its reoccurrence. The main focus of scholars in this tradition was to ensure their work had *policy relevance*, and to advise decision-makers how to avoid war. Scholars in this school of thinking were referred to as Idealists and in the early twentieth century they were concerned explicitly with the *policy relevance* and application of their work. There was also an important normative aspect, in that scholars sought to prescribe to policy-makers. In this way, IR developed as a distinctly empirical, practical atheoretical and historically focused prescriptive discipline. Idealism largely collapsed with the outbreak of World War II and realism came to take its place as the dominant organizing paradigm (and this is discussed in more detail in Chapter 3).

IR's subsequent historical development was also shaped by theoretical innovations, again, which can be characterized by cultural differences. In Germany, IR was a sub-discipline of Political Science, and although theoretical developments occurred within the field between the 1960s and 80s, this was largely in the area of peace research and was aimed at international audiences (Waever, 1998: 705). In France IR did not develop as a separate discipline, and where it is studied it is largely practical rather than theoretical, with a key focus on Area Studies. In the UK, the 'English school' developed (usually associated with the work of Martin Wight and Hedley Bull). In the UK, IR was not originally considered part of Political Science but a field which drew on many disciplines (sociology, history, law, political philosophy) (Waever, 1998). As with American IR, in the UK the development was a response to foreign policy, an aim to influence policy-makers in the postwar period.

As with Political Studies/Political Science, IR's analysis traditionally began with the state, although, in contrast, it assumed the state was a unitary actor. However, IR has also been faced with the same challenges as Politics (e.g., globalization, climate change and interconnectivity of markets, to name but a few), plus a recognition that issues transcend the domestic and international divide. For example, security (one of the key concerns of IR) is no longer only concerned with military issues and the balance of power in the international arena, but also with the security of individual citizens within states. In this way, the boundaries between IR and Political Science/Studies, in terms of their 'real world' subject matter, have become increasingly blurred. At the same time, the influences of economics and natural science have been as significant in IR as Politics. Like Politics, IR has also been dominated by Western white men. Feminist IR theory has achieved increasing prominence in

Box 2.2   Disciplinary boundaries

These serve to demarcate what counts as a legitimate area of concern within a particular discipline. For some, though, these boundaries are socially constructed and serve to obscure debates, prevent insights being realized (Wilson, 1998). It could also be suggested that the boundaries are constructed through institutional developments and the separation of learning into departments within universities. These boundaries are also reinforced through the existence of specialist journals within disciplines. This is less pronounced in the natural sciences, where there are a number of leading journals which transcend disciplinary boundaries. The top journals are *Science* (in the US) and *Nature* (in the UK). In the social sciences, however, the equivalent does not exist.

the discipline, and done much to challenge the dominant orthodoxy, providing for both fresh insights into the discipline and possibilities of emancipation for women across the globe.

The broader context

It is also important to remember that while the shaping of disciplines is identified within particular schools of thought (which are discussed in more detail in the following chapter), these did not emerge in a vacuum. Rather they are reflective and constitutive of a wider environment of ideas, not only in terms of what is happening in the 'real' world of politics, but also in terms of how knowledge is gathered and studied, and how this is institutionalized within universities and research communities, through the construction of disciplinary boundaries.

One of the main problems in thinking about IR and Politics as separate disciplines is that it leads us to downplay the importance of factors usually regarded as the preserve of the other discipline. It may also lead us to neglect particular theoretical insights which may be of use in our analysis.

Similarities and differences

The earlier atheoretical development of IR has in some ways been one of the dividing features between the disciplines. However, as noted above, 'real world' events, such as the inability of IR to explain or predict the collapse of communism has led to an increased emphasis upon the role of theory. Indeed, now both disciplines have strong theoretical components to them and both are characterized by disagreement over what constitute legitimate fields of enquiry. For example, should the study of globalization or the European Union occur within Political Science or IR? Should the environment be studied in terms of its domestic impact, or in terms of the effect it has internationally and, if studied internationally, does this absolve people within states from any kind of responsibility to act? Should war be discussed only in military terms, or should the effects upon civil society within states also be the concern of political science? Do domestic women bear the adverse costs of internationally pursued war?

The separation of the domestic from the international characterizes much of what is taking place in the two disciplines at present. However, should we not consider both international and domestic elements in our analysis? Might we not benefit from discussing the interrelationship between individual human action, the action of individual states and the impact this has on the global climate, necessitating global solutions as well as individual ones? Should we not think about both the effects of war upon the international community and its impacts upon citizens and civilians who live in those war zones? Our argument in this book is that these questions, while separated by disciplinary boundaries, are inherently interlinked. We argue that the disciplines overlap in subject matter and, in turn, need to be considered together.

Despite debates over the legitimate areas of study within the disciplines, and differences in historical development, what we have seen more recently has been a move to broader debates around methodology. That is, both disciplines have become increasingly concerned with how they proceed and how analysis should be done. The big methodological debate is centred around whether Politics may be conceived of as 'scientific' and given the significance of this not only for how we understand the development of the disciplines we are in, but also the implications this has for how we study; this issue is addressed in the following chapter.

Cultural factors have also played an important role in the development of the disciplines and both are characterized by a strong US dominance in their respective fields. Many of the 'top' journals are located in America; for example, *American Political Science Review* and *International Organization*. While this may provide some cohesion to the disciplines, what this can also mean is that significant variables in analysis may be missed.

Recognizing the significance of culture can enable us to reflect upon questions such as: is liberal capitalist democracy something which is possible in all states across the globe? Or are other forms of democracy possible and more 'workable' given a particular cultural context? Happily, in our disciplines, physical violence is less likely to be a response to the issues; however, crucially, failure to discuss these cultural differences in the 'real world' may well lead to conflict and war.

The aim here has been to provide an overview of the differing ways in which both disciplines have developed and to suggest that the disciplinary boundaries between them may serve to obscure rather than enhance

---

Box 2.3 Journals

Journals are an important source of up-to-date scholarship in the field. There are generalist journals such as *American Political Science Review* and *International Studies Quarterly*, which give an overview of the shape of the discipline, and also more specialist journals such as *British Politics* and *Journal of Middle East Studies*. While journals are often available electronically, these are not to be confused with other internet sites. Articles published in academic journals go through a peer-review process; this means the information contained within these journals may be considered authentic and authoritative in a way in which information published elsewhere on the web may not (for example, on sites such as Wikipedia).

---

opportunities for political analysis. Awareness of the historical development of the disciplines can enable us to understand why politics is studied in the way that it is today and can also provide us with a basis from which to move both the disciplines and our analysis forward.

Layout of book

In this book our aim is to encourage reflection upon how we 'do' Politics. We argue that the way in which we undertake political analysis is principally through the application of theoretical frameworks to a particular area of enquiry. The following chapters are by no means an exhaustive account of the topics of interest for students of politics. What they are intended to do, however, is to address some of the central areas of study within our disciplines and show how we use the theory within each area. One of our main aims is to highlight the contingent nature of political analysis; that is, there is not one, but competing ways in which to 'do' the study of politics and this issue is discussed explicitly in the next chapter, and reflected throughout the book.

Chapter 2 provides a discussion of a central concept in the study of Politics: power. While the study of power could be said to define and underpin the disciplines, its own definition is considerably more difficult. A contested concept, power can mean differing things depending upon our definition of power and our starting point. Clearly, where we look for power influences where we might find it. If we think power is something which belongs to politicians, then the likelihood is, we will analyze the behaviour of politicians to establish the nature of the power relationship. Suppose, though, that politicians are not the only sources or sites of power. Consider the notion that the actions of politicians are limited by their positioning in a liberal democratic capitalist system. This suggests we would need to have an awareness of this system: we may not necessarily be able to see the system, but it may be powerful in influencing how politicians, states and others behave. Alternatively, suppose we think that power is located in the ideas which shape our society – analysis then might begin by exploring the role of a particular set of ideas (such as neo-liberalism) and how they inform behaviour within a political context.

The background of the Introduction and Chapters 1 and 2 then sets the context for the substantive chapters which deal with topics of interest to both Political Science and IR: the state; public policy; institutions; representation and participation; the media; security; globalization; political economy; and the environment. While it is not possible to cover all areas which fall under the remit of Politics, the intention is to highlight that while debates occur within the disciplines over what the legitimate area of study is, simultaneously within those areas of study there are also debates about how and what should be studied. The intention is also to show that Politics is broadly defined and fluid, characterized by 'grey' areas, and that reflexivity is a key component in analysis. Each of the substantive chapters is structured in the same way to reflect the differing ways in which political analysts may approach the same issue or problem. Consistent with our view that there is an overlap in Political Science and IR, we introduce the dominant theories, not by their disciplinary split, but with reference to the things which we think really divide them, their ontological and epistemological positions.

Much of Political Science, and to a lesser degree IR, is dominated by positivist approaches (cf. Marsh and Savigny, 2004). We are not seeking to deny the contribution of positivism to the discipline; however, we are aiming to challenge its dominance. By dividing the frameworks according to their underlying claims to knowledge, we are seeking to reinforce the idea that, to paraphrase Marsh and Smith (2002), there is more than one way to "do" Political Science (and IR). Each chapter is divided into three sections which broadly reflect the assumptions that are made within the discipline about what the real world is like and how we find out about it. (These are labelled: foundationalist/positivist; foundational critical realist; and anti-foundational interpretivist – and as they reflect quite complex debates, we discuss their definitions in the following chapter). Within each section we then apply approaches and theories from within these positions to an example where Political Science or IR is likely to analyze or ask questions. Our point is that, when faced with the same problem, differing explanations and outcomes are possible depending upon the assumptions which we make prior to our analysis.

Each chapter illustrates these differing analytical processes and outcomes through reference to a case study. It then summarizes the key features and compares differing theories and approaches, drawing out not only their differences but also their similarities. A set of reflective questions and seminar activities is also provided at the end of each chapter.

Clearly, these chapters do not exhaust the potential topics which we might analyze, so the final chapter (12) provides a discussion of the wider considerations that we need to make when we do our own political analysis. One of the driving assumptions of this book is that theory plays a crucial role in helping us analyze political reality. The wider aim of the book is thus to encourage a critical reflection upon the way in which we use a theory or approach, its purpose, assumptions and the implications that flow from it.

Conclusion

Our aim and arguments in this book are threefold. First, we argue that to 'do' political analysis we must be theoretically informed, meaning that that we use theory to structure and guide our analysis. However, we need also be aware of the underlying assumptions that those theories or approaches make (more widely discussed in Chapters 1 and 12). Second, we have sought to challenge the dominant forms of theorizing about politics by 'mainstreaming' alternate approaches in each chapter. This means we have given equal weighting to different positions in each topic. Third, we have sought to highlight the parallels between Political Science and IR. The socially constructed division between the disciplines, we argue, means that operating solely within one discipline means that we miss an awareness of the insights of the others. In short, we argue that political analysis is an active process. We need to be critically evaluating our assumptions both prior to and throughout our analysis so that we can produce coherent, rigorous and potentially emancipatory political analysis.

Reflection

Do you think the following should be studied by Political Science or IR?

Water scarcity

GM foods

Social mobility

'Honour' killings

War and peace

Do you think we should we look at the individuals who are affected by these issues? Or the individuals who cause them? Or the systems they take place in?

Can you think of a topic or issue that can only be studied by Politics or IR?

Do you find the division useful or unhelpful?

Seminar activities

Identify five journals in the disciplines of Politics and IR (perhaps one from the UK, one from the US, one from Europe and from the fields of both Politics and IR).

What issues do they discuss?

What is the difference between the articles in the Politics journals and those in the IR journals?

What are the differences between the European, UK-specific and US journals?

Why do you think these differences exist?

Can you identify theory in these articles?

What purpose has it been used for, what is the theory 'doing'?

What difference has the theory made to what is being studied?

Why do you think there are these differences?

Evaluation of electronic sources

A lot of the information we gain these days is via electronic means, but there is a wide variety of quality and problems of authenticity in some of these sources.

Having identified the journal articles above:

What is the difference between an article in an e-journal and that on Wikipedia?

How can we identify reliable and credible online sources?

Why is this important to producing coherent political research?

Why should we not rely upon sources such as Wikipedia?

Chapter 3

Themes and Issues in Political Science and International Relations

Introduction

As we identified in the introduction, one of the biggest debates within Politics is about how we actually go about doing our analysis: how do we actually 'do' Politics? How do we decide what it is we are looking at? How do we find out what the real world of politics looks like and how can we find out information about it? How do we decide what questions to ask? How do we decide what theoretical position to adopt and which theory to apply? Once we start to think about these questions, we realize that there are bigger issues at stake; we don't simply randomly pick what it is that we analyze. Rather we make a series of assumptions and judgements about what it is that is important, what it is we are seeking to do. These assumptions may often be implicit in the work of some of the scholars that we read, but it is important to be aware of them. Why? Because it enables us to recognize the strengths and limitations of the work we are analyzing and to enable us to be more rigorous in our own work. Awareness of these assumptions also enables us to be able to reflect upon differing positions and contributions of other approaches and enables us to make a decision about why that particular perspective provides the most useful account. It also provides a vocabulary through which we are able to articulate to others why we see the world in the way that we do.

The aim of this chapter is to introduce some of the debates around how we decide what it is we are looking at when we look at the world of politics, and how we can access that information: these are centred around ontology and epistemology. We begin by reflecting upon the nature of reality, and the assumptions that inform our analysis; that is we start with a discussion of ontology. The next issue we need to consider when beginning analysis is how we can gain access to that reality. How can we have knowledge of it? This leads us to introduce a brief discussion about epistemology. As such, we introduce one of the key debates in our disciplines; that is, can we know about the political world through the assumptions and methods of the natural sciences? Can we have a 'science' of Politics? What can this tell us about the way in which we can know about the 'real world' of politics? This debate is crucial to our studies.

We should point out that we see the 'doing' of political analysis as very much a learned skill. It is a skill which we continually refine and think about throughout our academic lives and the aim of this book is to reflect upon how we acquire this ability. As one of the reviewers helpfully observed, when we began our studies we had no idea what an ontological and epistemological position was, and it was something that we learned about (and we very much agree with this point). What we are seeking to do here is to demystify the vocabulary and processes that we engage in when we do Politics. That is not to say, however, that once we grasp the basics we stop learning or thinking about what we do. Rather like learning a musical instrument, once we master the basics we continue throughout our lives to practise, reflect, improve and refine.

Having introduced the philosophical issues that inform our work, the second part of the chapter is concerned to give an overview of the different approaches we may adopt when studying Politics. There is a number of different perspectives, but we will focus our attention on some of the main ones within the discipline: behaviouralism; rational choice theory; Marxism; feminism; poststructuralism; and constructivism. When discussing these approaches we also show how their differing ontological and epistemological assumptions are important in shaping what they focus on. Throughout the rest of the book each of the theoretical frameworks that we introduce makes assumptions about ontology and epistemology and is also informed by one of the approaches detailed below.

A note of caution!

The debates outlined in the first half of this chapter are incredibly complex and have generated vast discussion throughout the history of philosophy. We are not seeking to reconcile those debates here! Nor are we seeking to suggest that they can be reconciled. Rather we argue that they are a means for understanding why people do Politics in different ways. What we are seeking to do here is give a brief, simple and accessible introduction to these issues, the positions outlined below represent a starting point. Rather than a definitive attempt to demarcate rigid boundaries, we argue that the borders around these positions and approaches are fluid and open to contestation (as we have hoped to illustrate in Figure 3.1 and Table 3.1). Much like the way in which theory is used to simplify the world, our aim here is to simplify these debates so that we can understand the starting points. Thereafter, further reading (beyond this book) is useful to understand some of the greater complexities of these debates.

The first section of this chapter draws substantially on the work of David Marsh and Paul Furlong (2002). We should note that their arguments have been subject to criticism (for their presentation of these positions as having tightly defined boundaries [see, for example, Bates and Jenkins, 2007]) and more critical accounts reflecting the 'fuzziness' of these boundaries are offered by Hay (2002) and in later work (Marsh 2010). However, we believe that in order to engage in these debates we need to understand the basics. Much like building a house, we begin with a few basic building blocks and it is only once we start to lay these foundations that we can see the different forms that may be available to us. We are simply aiming to provide those basic building blocks.

Underlying philosophical issues

Ontology and epistemology

As we have suggested, before we begin our analysis we have already made a series of assumptions about what we think political reality looks like, what it is possible to know and how we can find out about that reality. At first glance this might seem a quite straightforward idea, but consideration of this is crucial for our analysis. The assumptions that we make about what the real political world looks like and how we can know about it inform all the analysis that we will go on to do. More specifically for us as political analysts it enables us to ask: what does the real world of politics look like? How can we know what is really happening in the world of politics? These, then, are questions of ontology (the former) and epistemology (the latter). Because there are a variety of ways in which we can answer these questions, it is useful to have the language to do so and we use the terms ontology and epistemology to discuss these ideas and issues. Ontology and epistemology are philosophical positions, but they also provide us with a vocabulary with which to talk about the assumptions that we make about what is real, what is out there to discover and how we can discover it.

Ontological and epistemological positions

Articulating responses to questions of ontology is often done through reference to two main positions: foundationalism and anti-foundationalism. Once we have established our ontological position this then informs our epistemological position (although this ordering has been challenged; see, for example, Hay, 2002), and we continue with an overview of some of their key features. Our view that ontology underpins epistemology is illustrated in Figure 3.1.

Ontology: foundationalism and anti-foundationalism

When we think about what is out there in the world, we make assumptions about what it is we think exists. For some people (foundationalists) the world exists as a reality out there and is largely independent of us. It is possible to establish a truth about this world. For others (anti-foundationalists), it is the way that we interpret and interact with the world that is important, so in this way we are intimately involved in the creation of reality. As people interact differently with the world out there, so different realities are created. For anti-foundationalists there is not one truth about the real world, but competing truths and interpretations.

Think of the age-old question that confounds philosophers and scientists alike. If a tree falls in the woods, and there is no one there to see it, does it make a sound? Foundationalists would argue with some certainty that the answer is yes. Every other tree that has been observed falling has made a sound, and therefore it can be said with conviction, that yes, that tree made a sound. This is because the world is thought to exist independently of us, and crucially our understanding of how the world works is not dependent on us being there to interpret it. In contrast, anti-foundationalists would say we cannot be sure. Rather, trees may have fallen noisily elsewhere at other points in time, but this particular tree, which no one observes, may well have fallen silently. Indeed, it is the act of hearing the noise that brings noise into existence, rather than the physical event itself.

This debate may seem abstract; however, what it does do is highlight that we need to be sure of the assumptions that we make when we do political analysis, as the differing ways in which we think about what the real world looks like can lead us to make different assumptions about how it is possible to know about the 'real' world. It is important to be aware of the assumptions that we make prior to our analysis because this not only informs the positions that we adopt when we do our analysis, but also shapes what is possible for us to find. These positions are summarized in Figure 3.1 and are discussed below.

Epistemology: positivism, interpretivism, scientific/critical realism

So how can we know about the real world? This question can be discussed through reference to epistemology, and one way in which epistemological issues present themselves to us as students of Politics is through the debate around science. Is it possible to have a science of Politics? By this we mean is it possible to adopt the methods of science? Is it possible to generate predictions about political behaviour? Is it possible to establish universal covering laws, in the way that we are able to do in the natural sciences? (For a much more detailed discussion of this, see Moses and Knutsen, 2007.)

The issue, in part, is informed by the assumptions that we make about the kind of knowledge we think it is possible to have about the political world. If we believe a science of politics is possible, then we are likely to adopt a scientific methodology. From this vantage point the way in which we can know about the political world is through empirical investigation. This would suggest that we can gain knowledge of the political world through that which is available to our senses: sight, sound, taste, smell and touch. Observations which flow from these are assumed to be measurable and can subsequently be quantified. Adherence to a scientific methodology and the assumptions that inform it also enable us to make scientific claims to knowledge about the political world.

Juxtaposed to this scientific perspective is the view that the subject matters of natural and social science are fundamentally different and therefore the methods of natural science are deemed simply inappropriate. In this view, the study of Politics is about the study of human beings, who simply do not behave in predictable ways, like numbers and atoms. Moreover, unlike the subject matter in natural science human beings also have subjective values, which raises the question: can we ever be value-neutral in the analysis of our subject matter? For example, it is possible to say that Hitler and Nelson Mandela were powerful leaders given that they were able to mobilize vast numbers of people in support of their aims. But, normatively, would we want to equate the two? Would we not want to differentiate between the 'rightness' or legitimacy of their actions? Some would argue that a science of Politics is just not possible, in part because of the normative aspects, which are an inherent part of our analyses which simply do not feature in the natural world.

The issue of whether we can have a science of Politics is reflected through debates around how we can know what we do about our political world. These debates are enormously complex and we have sought here to simplify and introduce them. (For much greater depth, see Hay, 2002; Stoker and Marsh, 2002; Marsh and Furlong, 2002; Agger, 1991.) These debates are often presented as polarized around two mutually exclusive positions, positivism and interpretivism, of which we give a brief overview below. We then move to outline a position which draws from both and provides for a kind of middle ground between the two, scientific or critical realism. We also illustrate and summarize the key points of each position in Figure 3.1.

Positivism

Positivism is the dominant perspective in contemporary political analysis. Many of the articles and books we read are underpinned by the assumptions of positivism. It is beyond the scope of this book to discuss why positivism is dominant (and this has been done elsewhere; see, for example, Marsh and Savigny, 2004), but what we do here is give a brief overview of what its main assumptions are.

Positivism is underpinned by a foundational ontology. It assumes that there is a singular real world out there, which is available to be discovered though recourse to the senses. This is informed by empiricism as derived from the work of Comte, which assumes that all that we can know can be counted and empirically measured and states that we can discover and establish regular relationships between phenomena. This school of thought seeks to apply the methods and thinking behind the natural sciences to the subject matter of the social 'sciences'. Through observation and measurement of the 'real world' we are able to establish laws and certainties like those established in the natural sciences. For example Michels' (1911/1959) Iron Law of Oligarchy states that society will always be dominated by elites. This relationship was established by observing regular patterns in elite and societal behaviour. A generalization and covering law was then proposed, which could be empirically tested, akin to the testing of hypotheses in the experiments of the natural sciences. Underlying this notion of covering laws is the wider aim of providing causal explanation.

Informed by the methods and assumed certainties provided by science, positivists are concerned to establish the cause of an event or phenomena, to explain why something happens. Cause and explanation are two words strongly associated with positivism. For example, consider the statement – 'female voters are more likely to vote Democrat'. This statement would form the function of a hypothesis which would be tested against empirical evidence. If the outcome confirmed the hypothesis then gender may be used as an explanator of electoral success for a candidate like Obama. This may then provide an explanation of why people have voted for Obama (because they are women) and also establishes a causal link between gender and political preferences.

Finally, positivism also claims to be able to separate facts and values. Positivists argue they analyze facts and that their goal is not to address normative questions. They view this separation as legitimate and possible. The argument is that because scientific method is assumed to have no content it therefore has no politics (Villmoore, 1990: 150).

Objective knowledge can be generated through this value-free approach. Positivists, in their academic research, are only concerned with empirical questions about what the case is, rather than the legitimacy, or rightness or wrongness of an issue. For example positivists may measure the rate of inequalities of income between rich and poor (as has been evidenced in both the UK and US). However, they would not seek to make normative judgements about the legitimate or illegitimate nature of that inequality.

Interpretivism

Interpretivism can be usefully contrasted with positivism. Interpretivism is generally viewed as anti-foundational as it assumes that there is more than one way in which reality can be understood. Rather than seeking universal laws and to establish regularities in relationships, interpretivists seek to provide understanding of a particular issue or event. They argue that facts and values cannot be separated as the nature of the enquiry (human beings) is inherently value-laden. That is, as human beings we all make judgements, from the seemingly simply judgement about what is fashionable to wear (although once considering the ethics of the producers of clothing, debates become more complex) to establishing responsibility for societal inequalities. Interpretivists reject the notion of causation; rather they seek to provide understanding of, or the meaning of, a given context of political issue. Interpretivists would seek to explore the context which gave rise to a set of political conditions, so they may not argue that a change in the tax regime *caused* an increase in social inequality. However, what they would seek to explore would be the conditions that made this possible; in so doing they may also seek to transform these conditions. In this way interpretivists might look at the ideas and social structures that are dominant in society. They might look at the discourses which informed and shaped the creation of tax reduction legislation. They may draw attention to a political discourse which emphasized entrepreneurship and, more importantly, the role of individuals, over the existence of society (think about Thatcher's infamous (mis)quote – there is no such thing as society!). In this way then we can start to understand the role that ideas and discourse may play in enabling us to understand present political conditions.

The important point to note is that interpretivists draw attention to the contingent nature of social reality and, rather than providing explanation, they seek to provide understanding. This is informed by the assumption that there is no one overarching truth about the 'real world' out there. Rather, they suggest, there are a series of competing truths which are dependent upon our interpretation of the world and if we are to understand this we need to move analysis beyond only what is available to the senses. All action is meaningful, and our role as analysts is to uncover that meaning. Moreover, rather than assume that analysis is value-free, they highlight the value-laden nature of social and political analysis (so their work may be explicitly informed, for example, by particular ideas of what a just society should look like).

Scientific/critical realism

Scientific realism or, as it is also referred to, critical realism offers something of a middle ground between positivism and interpretivism. While it accepts the possibility of causality in explanation and can aim to make predictions (a feature of the scientific approach), it also admits interpretivist features into its analysis with its assumption of unobservable layers of reality.

Scientific/critical realists argue that there are differing layers of reality which comprise the real world out there. They claim that we cannot see all these layers, but we know that they exist because we can see causal consequences. For example, capitalism is a layer of reality, and we know that capitalism exists. We cannot see it but we know that it exists as it has causal consequences which we can observe. For example, we might take some money into a shop and exchange it for a product. This is an outcome and a causal consequence of the underlying mechanism of capitalism. Capitalism determines the value of both the product and the money that we hand over in exchange for the good. Here we see influence from the positivist approach, that it is possible to establish causal explanation. However, as noted, this position, also admits from the interpretivists that there are influencing features which we cannot see; there is a reality which exists beyond that which our physical senses can access. Indeed, there is also argued to be a difference between reality and appearance (see, for example, Hollis and Smith, 1990). So, in the example of capitalism, we know there is this reality called capitalism, but what we see is not capitalism itself; rather we see evidence of the existence of capitalism, in the transaction which takes place in the act of consumption.

The idea of unobservable, underlying causal mechanisms, means that critical realism tends to be associated with Marxism. Similarly, it is also a position within feminist analysis. For example, patriarchy can be argued to be an underlying causal mechanism; we cannot see 'patriarchy' but we can see its effects (as we will see through some of the frameworks we use within the book). (It should be noted that this discussion about the layers of reality in scientific/critical realism has led to debate as to whether it represents an ontological or epistemological position. We recognize this debate; however, for the purposes of providing a starting point into these debates we begin by accepting the more widely held view that it is more epistemological in its positioning than ontological.)

Figure 3.1   *Summary of epistemological positions and their underlying ontologies*

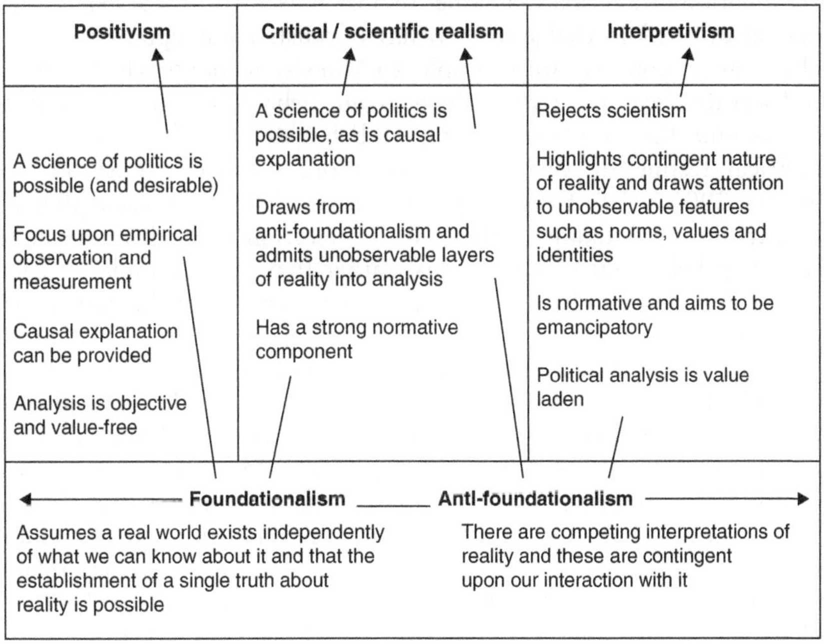

Positivism	Critical / scientific realism	Interpretivism
A science of politics is possible (and desirable) Focus upon empirical observation and measurement Causal explanation can be provided Analysis is objective and value-free	A science of politics is possible, as is causal explanation Draws from anti-foundationalism and admits unobservable layers of reality into analysis Has a strong normative component	Rejects scientism Highlights contingent nature of reality and draws attention to unobservable features such as norms, values and identities Is normative and aims to be emancipatory Political analysis is value laden

◄————— **Foundationalism** ———— **Anti-foundationalism** —————►

Assumes a real world exists independently of what we can know about it and that the establishment of a single truth about reality is possible

There are competing interpretations of reality and these are contingent upon our interaction with it

Approaches

The ontological and epistemological assumptions that we make subsequently inform the approach that we adopt when we come to do our political analysis. These assumptions, positions and approaches underpin many of the theoretical frameworks that we may use (as we will see in the substantive chapters that follow). This in turn can lead us towards some outcomes and close off other possibilities. This is one reason why we need to be clear about our prior assumptions. Another is so that we can maintain logic, rigour and consistency in our analysis whichever approach we adopt. We now turn to give an overview of some of the main approaches within the disciplines.

Behaviouralism

Behaviouralism has been one of the dominant schools of thought in Politics during the twentieth century. It emphasizes the explanation of behaviour (in reaction to the normative philosophical approaches which had gone before). Behaviouralism emerged in the 1920s/1930s and was consolidated by the 1950s/60s. Its development was influenced by psychology, is committed to the methods of the natural sciences and as such it is highly empiricist and positivist in its approach. Behaviouralism is foundationalist in that it assumes that there is a world that exists independent of our knowledge of it. Behaviouralists focus upon observable behaviour (in contrast, for example, to Marxist accounts which suggest unobservable features may influence our behaviour). Behaviouralists also assume that any explanation of behaviour can be subjected to empirical testing or verification (for more detailed exposition, see Sanders, 2002/2010). For example, behaviouralists might argue that we can explain the outcome of the 2008 US election through reference to the voting behaviour of US citizens (rather than, for example, because of the campaigns run by the politicians, the economy or the personality of the politicians themselves). A behavioural approach to voting behaviour would observe who voted for Obama and who voted for McCain (through the use of methods such as opinion polls). They would then categorize these people into groups (which have traditionally been around race and class). While the techniques for categorizing voters become more sophisticated, they rely on the assumption that we can observe certain characteristics. Once data has been gathered behaviouralists would argue they can then generate knowledge as they are able to offer analysis which enables them to make predictions about the likely behaviour of voters and, in turn, this would lead to predictions about outcomes of future elections. We not only see this kind of analysis in the academic literature, but also more publicly in opinion polls.

In this view, to understand political phenomena behaviour needs to be observed. From this data can be gathered and hypotheses generated and tested. For example, using these observations we could hypothesize that if your income is below x then you are more likely to vote for Obama (H1). From here, then, we could hypothesize that if your income exceeds x then you are more likely to vote for McCain (H2). Testing these assumptions against the data gathered means that in future elections we could make predictions about the likelihood of a particular class of the electorate and their likelihood to vote Democrat or Republican.

With this adherence to 'science' also goes the assumption that it is possible to separate facts from values, and the possibility of objective, value-free political analysis arises. So, for example, we may be able to observe what different classes of voters do, and how they behave, but we would not be able to make any normative statements about how they should behave, or about what is desirable for them. This may seem intuitively appealing; however, we highlight within this book that many scholars conflate normative and observational statements. For example, Dahl's work on pluralism (that we discuss in Chapter 3) is a classic piece of behaviouralism in that he focused upon decisions made in government, and used this as a means to describe how government worked. However, his work was not entirely objective, as this was underpinned by a normative proposition: not only was this how government worked, he argued, but this was how government should work. This brief illustration suggests that the separation of facts and values, while in principle may seem a laudable objective, becomes problematic, in large part because of the subject matter of the discipline (as noted above; this issue is also discussed in more depth in Chapter 12).

Rational choice theory (RCT)

The next approach we consider is rational choice theory (RCT, sometimes known as public choice theory). This came to prominence during the 1980s partly as a response to, and partly because of its influence upon, the wider political conditions at the time (Thatcherism and Reaganism). Rational choice accounts, like behaviouralism, are foundational and positivist. They assume a truth exists about the political world and this can be discovered and measured. For RCT adherence to the 'scientific' method is derived from the influence of economics.

The rational choice approach (which is also sometimes referred to as a method) argues that individual choice is the basis of action (and inaction). Directly informed by theorizing and models drawn from economics, rational choice accepts a series of starting assumptions. First, that individuals are the unit of analysis, and that they are assumed to be rational; that is, individuals will pursue rational strategies to maximize their utility. We are able to chart these courses of actions and choices that are made, through reference to other information and assumptions we make about behaviour. Rational choice also assumes that an individual has a fixed set of preferences which they have identified, can express and rank order. Behaviour is assumed to be means–ends without specification of what the ends are or should be and rational behaviour is pursued to achieve a specific end (see, for example, Elster, 1986). As such, to be able to establish the choices that individuals will make, we simply need to identify their preferences. Once we know these preferences, we are then able to make predictions about the behaviour of that individual, as we assume that they will seek to maximize their utility. (Rational choice is sometimes referred to as formal political theory, or as a form of political economy, and will be discussed in more depth in Chapter 9.) For the purposes of this section, however, suffice to note the basic assumptions. Analysis focuses attention upon the criteria for rational action, so assumptions are made and the method suggests that if we accept those assumptions then particular outcomes, or courses of action will follow. These assumptions of rationality are then used to construct models, again so we can make predictions about how individuals will behave. For example, a rational choice model of voting will assume that rational individuals will look at both/all candidates in an election and chose the one which best satisfies their preferences (which are identifiable and expressed). Therefore, in order to predict election outcomes, we can simply establish voters' preferences and then match that to candidates' policies.

Again, we can see there are problems here not only in the separation of facts and values (as above), but also in the way in which we separate the individual from their wider context. In the voting example, can we really say that individuals approach the voting booth as a 'blank sheet', without reference to their personal history and experiences, and to the society within which they live, which may also influence how they decide to vote? In this sense, we need to reflect upon what we gain by adopting these parsimonious assumptions (i.e., simplicity of explanation) and what we miss (the complexity of motivations for individual behaviour and the social context in which it takes place).

On a methodological note, we may also see that just as behaviouralists have conflated normative and observational claims, so rational choice theorists have implied normative statements. (For a fascinating critique of rational choice theory as individualism, see Taylor, 2006.) The purpose of models and modelling is to simplify behaviour, so we can isolate key features which in turn facilitate the possibility of predictions. However, when we do this, we abstract from reality; models are used to simplify reality so we can try to understand it. Models do not provide a template for how reality should be (a normative claim). What became evident during the 1980s was that the works of rational choice theorists (such as Niskanen, 1971; Buchanen and Tullock, 1962) were used not only to describe the nature of politics, but also to make prescriptive (and normative) claims about how it should operate.

Marxism

Marxism as an approach is unusual in that it combines aspects of positivism and interpretivism, which tend to be viewed as mutually exclusive. Marxism does have a foundational view of the world, seeks to establish truth through scientific methods and enables us to make causal statements, which links into positivism. However, it also acknowledges the role of intangible and unobservable features (for example, ideology) in shaping the real world around us, and so Marxism can be located in the epistemological 'middle ground' and tends to be associated with scientific or critical realism (as noted above) (for an extension of this, see Marsh, 2002).

Marxism draws attention to the class basis of social and political relationships and the way in which this basis results in exploitative relationships of power. For some Marxism is a political doctrine – communism, and it has been expressed through the political actions of Stalin, Lenin and others. For those who view Marxism through its manifestation as a regime, the collapse of these political systems may suggest Marxism has little left to offer. However, it is not simply the political systems that Marxism informed that matter to us as political analysts, but the tools that Marxism provides. Here, Marxism is able to expose and offer an opportunity for us to question existing power structures within society. Through doing so we can make sense of inequalities within our society. This enables us not to simply consider them as immutable and therefore unchangeable, but also to understand them as a consequence of the way in which society has developed, allowing us to play a role in changing them. Marx, in *Theses on Feuerbach* (1845/1969:15), draws attention to those who have sought to gain knowledge and offers a critique: 'The philosophers have only interpreted the world, in various ways; the point is to change it.' In this sense, Marx also introduces an explicit normative aspect to his work; that we are not only, or merely, to interpret what happens in the world, but we can, or indeed should, use this to attempt to effect change.

Marxism is often criticized for its structuralism: its over-emphasis upon the role of structures as guiding behaviour, and downplaying the role of individuals who are, critiques suggest, powerless, like automatons, with very limited room for manoeuvre within these structures. Despite this criticism, Marxism does draw our attention to the role of ideas, in particular, the importance of ideology which functions to ensure that the proletariat accept their role in the system. Marxism highlights the structural basis of inequality in our society, which for Marx is located in the economic divisions that exist in the class divisions which form the basis of our society (between the bourgeoisies and the proletariat). These find expression through the mechanisms of capitalism, which in turn is reliant upon and reinforces inequalities (while primarily economic, these are also intimately linked with political and social inequalities). Rising levels of economic and social inequality in contemporary capitalist Western societies (see Barry, 2005; Sandel, 1982/1998) suggest that Marxist analysis still has much to offer.

Feminism

Feminism is perhaps the most methodologically unusual of approaches as it straddles the epistemological spectrum. There are a number of differing strands of feminism. The central feature within feminism is to draw attention to the role of women and gender within society, and feminism(s) is/are overt about its/their normative positioning. It seeks

to achieve equality and emancipation for women, but differing epistemological assumptions and positions within feminism lead to this being
manifested in very different guises.

For example, positivist feminists may argue that in order to understand
equality for women, we need to look at the role of women in public
life. To establish if women have achieved equality in the workforce, for
example, we can know this through reference to observable features we
can measure, such as pay scales, or counting the number of women in
public life (for example, those who hold senior positions such as judges,
or are in office in such bodies as Congress or Parliament, see, e.g., Childs,
2008; Lovenduski, 2005). Feminism may also draw attention to the
masculine nature of political systems and the way in which women's
rights are subsumed and seconded to ideas of how political systems should
operate. For example, the 2009 elections in Afghanistan were largely
supported by the West, irrespective of the retrograde legislation which had
been recently introduced which downplayed women's' rights in the home
and relegalized rape within marriage. This focus upon the observable
position of women in formal political systems means that some feminism
can be located within the positivist position.

Alongside this positivist account, critical feminists argue that understanding the role of women in society is about understanding relationships
of power, which are gendered, and we need to consider why it is that we
observe that which we do. Here the concept of patriarchy is crucial and,
in this discussion of deep-rooted underlying unobservable structures with
causal effects, means that some critical feminism can be located within
the scientific/critical realist position. For example, in this perspective
feminists highlight the way in which patriarchal societies have constructed
a gendered division of labour, where women's work was traditionally
thought of as being tied to the home, male work the public sphere of the
workplace. The slogan 'the personal is the political' encapsulates the idea
that to understand women's role within contemporary society we need to
explore the way in which society constructs personal relationships as well
as those located in formal employment.

Constructivist and/or poststructuralist feminists tend to be located in
the interpretivist position and, in contrast, draw attention to the way
in which the role of women in society needs to be understood through
reference to the way in which their roles are articulated. For example,
the common reference to an abstract person as 'he', suggests that the
'norm' is male and in turn society privileges the expectations of the
'norm'. Natasha Walter's (2010) recent book refers to the way in which
social practices (supported through legislation) have constructed a very
narrow public perception of what it means to be a woman (see also
Mulvey, 1975). In this way, Walter suggests, far from achieving the

equality and empowerment that 'first-wave' feminist fought for, while women may have suffrage, the way in which society teaches women to behave is through a dominant male view of what women should be like, rather than one which reflects parity between men and women. This suggests then that the position of women in society is something which we need to understand through recognition of underlying unobservable structures, or with reference to language and social practices.

Feminism takes a variety of forms and is largely subject to internal critique; so while liberal feminists might argue we need to look at numbers of women in the workplace, feminist critical theorists might argue we need to look at the structural conditions which defined their opportunities (or lack of) to engage in the workplace. Constructivist feminists might draw attention to the way in which women are socially constructed and their roles defined through dominant discourses, prevalent at work, in the media, in government and in everyday life.

Constructivism

Constructivism is widely debated and contested, and as with feminism and poststructuralism, it is not an overarching approach, rather it takes a variety of forms. A uniting feature is that it highlights the importance of norms and values in analysis. However, this manifests itself in different ways, and here we are concerned with how constructivism draws our attention to the contingent nature of the world around us. The way in which we present constructivism here is anti-foundational and linked to interpretivism. This suggests that to understand the world around us we need to understand the way in which it has been constructed according to particular norms and values. In this perspective, our interpretation and articulation of the world around us plays a role in the way in which it is constructed. For example, we can say that education exists. But what is this thing called 'education'? We can see features which serve to support the idea of education, such as schools, colleges and universities, but the notion of education itself is something that we cannot see, we cannot touch; but it is something which we, as a society, consider to be important (albeit to varying degrees). But that we discuss education, its purpose and how we might engage with it, in short, that we articulate the notion of education, from this perspective, plays a role in its construction and so its existence. In this view, education exists through our experience of and our interaction with it.

Constructivism has had varying degrees of influence within the disciplines, and has been much more successful in becoming part of the orthodoxy in IR than in Politics. Therefore, throughout this book we highlight that we are much more likely to see fully formed constructivist theories in IR.

Constructivism has been criticized for its focus upon the specific and its lack of ability to make generalizations. However, constructivism provides a significant challenge to the positivist view of scientific ways through which to understand the world. Moreover, crucially it draws our attention to the role of ideas and norms in structuring processes and social and political relationships. In this way constructivism as an approach is concerned to explore and evaluate social patterns and relationships rather than making a set of specific claims or hypotheses about interactions or relations in world or domestic politics. In order to discern these processes and values constructivists have drawn from critical theory and provided compelling critiques of existing power relationships.

Poststructuralism

As with constructivism, poststructuralism is also linked to anti-foundational interpretivism and is subject to similar criticisms. Finlayson and Martin (2006: 155) suggest there is no single version of poststructuralism, but what it does is provide a challenge to the dominant Enlightenment view and draw attention to some of the problems associated with the Westernized scientific (and liberal) worldview. Here, then, poststructuralism proceeds not quite as an alternative to the positivistic accounts detailed above, but as a discipline which draws attention to the existence of competing truths about the social and political world. In contrast to approaches which assume that the subject matter of social science (human beings) can be understood in the same way as the subject matter of social sciences, poststructuralism does not assume a uniform behaviour of individuals. Rather it highlights that individuals are reflexive, reassessing their activities and behaviour, not only in the context of that behaviour but also within the context or system of meaning that they are situated in. This system of meaning is characterized by cultural and ideological norms. Thus, the way to understand individual behaviour is not simply through reference to that behaviour, but through an understanding of the system of meaning within which that action takes place. For example, we may witness an individual place an X on a sheet of paper, but we cannot establish the meaning of that action without recourse to the context within which it takes place. If that action takes place in a polling booth then we understand the action through reference to our understanding of the function of elections in society. As such, we cannot understand what is going on without reference to concealed meanings and contextualization (for detailed discussion of the philosophers whose thinking informs this approach, see Agger, 1991).

But how is this system of meaning constructed? Here poststructuralists draw attention to the ways in which many actors and institutions negotiate and organize these systems of meaning so that political claims are legitimated, making particular actions seem normal or inevitable. In order to understand the 'rules of the game' one must be conversant in the particular language game which is being played or used. For example, we cannot understand why someone would kick a ball in a net, unless we understood the language game associated with football, which suggests that the side who kicks the most balls in the net is the winner. These language games and systems of meaning also function as a mechanism to include and exclude certain options, ideas and possibilities. In this way, in order to understand power relations, we need to understand how systems of meaning are constructed. To do this, poststructuralists explore the role of discourse in institutionalizing norms and behaviours. A discourse is an 'historically, socially, and institutionally specific structure of statements, terms, categories and beliefs' (Scott, 1988: 35). That is, it moves beyond language and text, and explores the processes, interactions and social relationships which embed meaning. Crucially, poststructuralists alert attention to the notion that there is not one system of meaning, rather there are competing interpretations, which may clash. As such, at the heart of this is contestation and political struggle; through recognition of which comes the opportunity to challenge the dominant order and effect transformation.

The differing approaches we are using within this book, and outlined above, are summarized in Table 3.1. We have sought to highlight that the boundary between each approach is not fixed. Each approach may be predominantly associated with a particular ontology and epistemology, but that is not to suggest that their boundaries are fixed. As theoretical work progresses the boundaries between approaches can become blurred. This is most evident within feminisms, which can adopt differing ontological and epistemological positions while having shared and overlapping concerns.

A word on method: quantitative and qualitative approaches

The approaches detailed above also inform the method, or methods that we may adopt. A discussion of the reflection of the method that we use is called methodology, and so when we reflect methodologically we think about not only the methods that we actually use, but also the assumptions that inform those methods. We argue that the boundaries around these positions and approaches are not discrete, but fluid and open to contestation (as we noted earlier). One of the ways this fluidity

Table 3.1 *Overview of differing approaches informed by their underlying positions (note: all boundaries assumed to be fluid rather than fixed)*

Foundational positivism	Foundational scientific/ critical realism	Anti-foundational interpretivism
Behaviouralism	**Marxism and critical theory**	**Constructivism**
Empirically testable theory	Accepts scientism in that it provides for universal laws (such as capitalism)	Analysis focuses around the way in which norms are constructed and guide behaviour
Assumes a real world exists and that knowledge of this is empirically accessible	Seeks to make predictions and causal explanations	
	Makes foundational assumption of a real world out there, but draws from anti-foundationalism in admitting unobservable features into analysis	Highlights the contingent nature of reality and the social construction of meaning
Aims to generate causal explanation, predictions and general laws		
Political analysis is and should be objective and value-free	Political analysis is normative and can be emancipatory	Political analysis is inherently value-laden
Rational choice theory		**Poststructuralism**
A method which adheres to scientific principles		Reflexive behaviour of subject of analysis
Seeks to generate predictions and general laws		Competing truths about the political world available
Assumption of individual rationality		Aims to challenge dominant power relations
Political analysis is (and should be) objective and value-free		Political analysis value-laden but has emancipatory potential

◄————————Feminism————————►

Liberal feminism	Critical feminism	Poststructural feminism
Institutional and reformist	Systemic inequalities reflected in patriarchy	Challenges dominant gendered power relations
Focus on public role of women		
Observation of behaviour	Overtly normative and aims for emancipation	

between ontology and epistemology is reflected is in the division over method. Quantitative and qualitative methods are often juxtaposed and have tended to be treated as mutually exclusive. Over recent years, however, there has been an increase in methodological triangulation – or combining methods (see, for example, Tashakkori and Teddlie, 1998). What is briefly summarized here is how the differing methods (categorized as quantitative or qualitative) are linked to the ontological and epistemological positions outlined above.

Foundational and positivist assumptions tend to lead to quantitative methods. These are often (but not always) statistical methods. But as suggested by the scientific approach, they are concerned with counting and observing what is available to our senses. The key here is empirical observation and the way in which it can be quantified. This is often through the use of statistics: for example, 66 per cent of new voters voted for Obama in the 2008 election (www.bbc.co.uk), which suggests targeting new voters was crucial to securing Obama's electoral success. Here, then, positivists would focus upon observable and quantifiable behaviour and make a claim to knowledge on the basis of their empirical evidence.

In contrast, anti-foundational interpretivist approaches tend to adopt qualitative methods such as discourse analysis that would draw attention to the importance of language, such as the symbolism invoked by Obama's continued campaign rhetoric of 'change' and 'hope' which suggests electoral victory was about the mobilization of ideas. This approach would thus emphasize the contingent nature of political reality and that, while slogans such as these depicted above may have mobilized support, we might also look at the way in which the campaigns were symbolic and reflective of a clash or conflict of wider political interests.

The methods that we adopt are informed by the meta-theoretical decisions we make, the approaches that we adopt and the theories that we use. Our aim here is not to discuss these methods (as this has been comprehensively done elsewhere, see, for example, Burnham *et al.*, 2004; Bryman, 2008); rather our aim is to discuss what assumptions we make and how this might influence the way in which we do our analysis.

Adjudicating between competing perspectives

As becomes clear, the choice of which theory to adopt in order to do political analysis is not straightforward. So how do we decide which approach to use? This simple question belies a complex set of thought processes and assumptions that we make, and while we are not concerned with the psychology of how we choose, we think it is important that we understand and are able to reflect upon the consequences of what we choose.

It might be that we choose a particular position because of the audience we want to influence; for example, if we were trying to influence policy-makers we may choose a more 'scientific' approach. If we were seeking to get an article published in the *American Journal of Political Science*, then we may be well advised to choose a method that enables us to use sophisticated econometric techniques. If we were trying to engage a lay audience a narrative approach might be more useful. Considerations of our audience may form one part of our decision as to which approach or position best serves our purpose. However, we argue that, less instrumentally perhaps, what we consider to be important is to acknowledge that it is the assumptions that we make about the world prior to our study that will influence the theoretical framework which we adopt. As we have discussed in this chapter, if we believe that all that we can know about the world is based upon what is available to our empirical senses, then we are likely to adopt a positivist approach to our study. If we believe that there are structures which, although we may not be able to directly observe, still may shape or inform our behaviour, then we are more likely to adopt a scientific/critical realist approach. If we believe that ideas play an important role in shaping our approach to understanding the world, then we are more likely to adopt an interpretivist approach. We argue that our response to these issues then tends to inform how we choose the theoretical framework that we adopt.

This may raise the following questions. Can we not have a theory which does everything? Why do we have separate theories? While some have attempted to discover a general theory of politics, the main reason that this doesn't happen is twofold. First, because political reality is so inherently complex that it would be impossible to find a theory which was able to explain every detail of behaviour at all times. Second, because of the competing ways in which people think that it is possible to do Politics and, while there are blurrings of these boundaries, at the same time their aims and fundamental assumptions are incommensurate.

Some argue we need to adopt an epistemological position and stick to it (Marsh and Furlong, 2002). Others suggest that different theories capture different aspects of the world and thereby we choose theory accordingly; we need to acknowledge that differing epistemologies can capture differing aspects of reality. Our objective here is not to resolve these debates (indeed, these debates reflect hundreds of years of philosophical discussion). Rather our aim is to suggest that these are not issues which need a solution. Instead we see these debates like a prism which we call 'Politics'. Depending upon the perspective that we adopt, we shine light on a particular angle of a puzzle, issue or problem. In this way, we are using these debates to problematize issues, and to reflect upon their causes and the likely consequences, rather than to provide solutions to them.

Conclusion

The aim of this chapter has been to introduce the different philosophical assumptions and the dominant approaches that we use to inform our analysis of the real world of politics. It is important to stress that these are not the only approaches; indeed, as we are very aware, our narrative expresses a particular view of what political analysis is that reflects the roots of these approaches – that is, these are very Western-centric. Our aim here is not to give an exhaustive account, but to introduce some of the dominant assumptions and approaches, so that when we engage with other readings and research within Politics we can understand how other scholars and students may come to the conclusions that they do. In short, we have aimed to give a brief summary of the some of the ways in which we 'do' political analysis. The following chapters now apply these assumptions and approaches more explicitly by introducing a range of theoretical perspectives and illustrating how they tell us about the world of politics.

Reflection

Do you think the political world is characterized by a 'clash of civilizations'?

Do you think we have seen the 'end of ideology'?

Do you think that women are more likely to vote for left-wing candidates?

Do you think war is inevitable?

How do you know these things?

Is it possible to establish them scientifically?

What do you think are the key components of the political world?

What do you think exists? Can you draw or map the political world?

How do you know what is in there?

Do you think you are a positivist, critical/scientific realist or interpretivist?

Can you give reasons for your answer?

Do you think your position may change?

Can you see what the position you adopted enables you to do?

Can you see what it misses or its limitations?

Seminar activities

Identify one journal article from the field of Politics and another from an IR journal.

What is the article about?

Do the authors assume explicitly or implicitly (this is more likely) that a science of politics is possible?

What assumptions are they making about what the world of politics 'looks like'? (Again, this assumption is likely to be implicit.)

Can you identify the authors' epistemological position?

How did you do this?

What are the differences or similarities between the approaches in the articles?

Which do you find the most credible and why?

What are kinds of questions are they asking?

Can the questions they ask be categorized as either Politics or IR or do you think the boundaries around the subject matter are blurred?

CHAPTER 4

Politics and the State

> 'The purpose of the State is always the same: to limit the individual, to tame him, to subordinate him, to subjugate him.'
>
> MAX STIRNER, *The Ego and His Own* (1845)

PREVIEW

The shadow of the state falls on almost every human activity. From education to economic management, from social welfare to sanitation, and from domestic order to external defence, the state shapes and controls; where it does not shape or control it regulates, supervises, authorizes or proscribes. Even those aspects of life usually thought of as personal or private (marriage, divorce, abortion, religious worship and so on) are ultimately subject to the authority of the state. It is not surprising, therefore, that politics is often understood as the study of the state, the analysis of its institutional organizations, the evaluation of its impact on society and so on. Ideological debate and party politics, certainly, tend to revolve around the issue of the proper function or role of the state: what should be done by the state and what should be left to private individuals and associations? The nature of state power has thus become one of the central concerns of political analysis. This chapter examines the feature that are usually associated with the state, from both a domestic and an international perspective. It considers the issue of the nature of state power, and, in the process, touches on some of the deepest and most abiding divisions in political theory. This leads to a discussion of the contrasting roles and responsibilities of the state and the different forms that states have assumed. Finally, it looks whether, in the light of globalization and other developments, the state is losing its central importance in politics.

KEY ISSUES

- What is the state, and why does it play such a crucial role in politics?
- How has state power been analysed and explained?
- Is the state a force for good or a force for evil?
- What roles have been assigned to the state? How have responsibilities been apportioned between the state and civil society?
- To what extent does politics now operate outside or beyond the state?

The state

The state is a political association that establishes sovereign jurisdiction within defined territorial borders, and exercises authority through a set of permanent institutions. These institutions are those that are recognizably 'public', in that they are responsible for the collective organization of communal life, and are funded at the public's expense. The state thus embraces the various institutions of government, but it also extends to the courts, nationalized industries, social security system, and so forth; it can be identified with the entire 'body politic'.

DEFINING THE STATE

The term 'state' has been used to refer to a bewildering range of things: a collection of institutions, a territorial unit, a philosophical idea, an instrument of coercion or oppression, and so on. This confusion stems, in part, from the fact that the state has been understood in four quite different ways; from an idealist perspective, a functionalist perspective, an organizational perspective and an international perspective. The *idealist* approach to the state is most clearly reflected in the writings of G. W. F. Hegel (see p. 59). Hegel identified three 'moments' of social existence: the family, civil society and the state. Within the family, he argued, a 'particular altruism' operates that encourages people to set aside their own interests for the good of their children or elderly relatives. In contrast, civil society was seen as a sphere of 'universal egoism' in which individuals place their own interests before those of others. Hegel conceived of the state as an ethical community underpinned by mutual sympathy – 'universal altruism'. The drawback of idealism, however, is that it fosters an uncritical reverence for the state and, by defining the state in ethical terms, fails to distinguish clearly between institutions that are part of the state and those that are outside the state.

Functionalist approaches to the state focus on the role or purpose of state institutions. The central function of the state is invariably seen as the maintenance of social order (see p. 400), the state being defined as that set of institutions that uphold order and deliver social stability. Such an approach has, for example, been adopted by neo-Marxists (see p. 64), who have been inclined to see the state as a mechanism through which class conflict is ameliorated to ensure the long-term survival of the capitalist system. The weakness of the functionalist view of the state, however, is that it tends to associate *any* institution that maintains order (such as the family, mass media, trade unions and the church) with the state itself. This is why, unless there is a statement to the contrary, an organizational approach to the definition of the state is adopted throughout this book

The *organizational* view defines the state as the apparatus of government in its broadest sense; that is, as that set of institutions that are recognizably 'public', in that they are responsible for the collective organization of social existence and are funded at the public's expense. The virtue of this definition is that it distinguishes clearly between the state and civil society (see p. 6). The state comprises the various institutions of government: the bureaucracy (see p. 361), the military, the police, the courts, the social security system and so on; it can be identified with the entire 'body politic'. The organizational approach allows us to talk about 'rolling forward' or 'rolling back' the state, in the sense of expanding or contracting the responsibilities of the state, and enlarging or diminishing its institutional machinery.

In this light, it is possible to identify five key features of the state:

- The state is *sovereign*. It exercises absolute and unrestricted power, in that it stands above all other associations and groups in society. Thomas Hobbes (see p. 61) conveyed the idea of sovereignty (see p. 58) by portraying the state as a 'leviathan', a gigantic monster, usually represented as a sea creature.
- State institutions are recognizably '*public*', in contrast to the 'private' institutions of civil society. Public bodies are responsible for making and

● **Idealism**: A view of politics that emphasizes the importance of morality and ideals; philosophical idealism implies that ideas are more 'real' than the material world.

● **Civil society**: A private sphere of autonomous groups and associations, independent from state or public authority.

CONCEPT

Sovereignty

Sovereignty, in its simplest sense, is the principle of absolute and unlimited power. However, sovereignty can be understood in different ways. *Legal* sovereignty refers to supreme legal authority, defined in terms of the 'right' to command compliance, while *political* sovereignty refers to absolute political power, defined in terms of the 'ability' to command compliance. *Internal* sovereignty is the notion of supreme power/authority within the state (e.g. parliamentary sovereignty: see p. 336). *External* sovereignty relates to a state's place in the international order and its capacity to act as an independent and autonomous entity.

enforcing collective decisions, while private bodies, such as families, private businesses and trade unions, exist to satisfy individual interests.

- The state is an exercise in *legitimation*. The decisions of the state are usually (although not necessarily) accepted as binding on the members of society because, it is claimed, they are made in the public interest, or for common good; the state supposedly reflects the permanent interests of society.
- The state is an instrument of *domination*. State authority is backed up by coercion; the state must have the capacity to ensure that its laws are obeyed and that transgressors are punished. For Max Weber (see p. 82), the state was defined by its monopoly of the means of 'legitimate violence'.
- The state is a *territorial* association. The jurisdiction of the state is geographically defined, and it encompasses all those who live within the state's borders, whether they are citizens or non-citizens. On the international stage, the state is therefore regarded (at least, in theory) as an autonomous entity.

The *international* approach to the state views it primarily as an actor on the world stage; indeed, as the basic 'unit' of international politics. This highlights the dualistic structure of the state; the fact that it has two faces, one looking outwards and the other looking inwards. Whereas the previous definitions are concerned with the state's inward-looking face, its relations with the individuals and groups that live within its borders, and its ability to maintain domestic order, the international view deals with the state's outward-looking face, its relations with other states and, therefore, its ability to provide protection against external attack. The classic definition of the state in international law is found in the Montevideo Convention on the Rights and Duties of the State (1933). According to Article 1 of the Montevideo Convention, the state has four features:

- a defined territory
- a permanent population
- an effective government
- the capacity to enter into relations with other states.

This approach to the state brings it very close to the notion of a 'country'. The main difference between how the state is understood by political philosophers and sociologists, and how it is understood by IR scholars is that while the former treat civil society as *separate from* the state, the latter treat civil society as *part of* the state, in that it encompasses not only an effective government, but also a permanent population. For some, the international approach views the state essentially as a legal person, in which case statehood depends on formal recognition by other states or international bodies. In this view, the United Nations (UN) is widely accepted as the body that, by granting full membership, determines when a new state has come into existence. Nevertheless, while, from this perspective, states may be legally equal, they are in political terms very different. Although their rights and responsibilities as laid out in international law may be identical, their political weight in world affairs varies dramatically. Some states are classified as '**great powers**', or even 'superpowers' (see p. 422), whereas others are 'middle' or 'small' powers and, in cases such as the small highland countries of the Caribbean and the Pacific, they may be regarded as 'micro-states'.

● **Great power**: A state deemed to rank amongst the most powerful in a hierarchical state system, reflecting its influence over minor states.

Georg Wilhelm Friedrich Hegel (1770–1831)

German philosopher. Hegel was the founder of modern idealism and developed the notion that consciousness and material objects are, in fact, unified. In *Phenomenology of Spirit* (1807), he sought to develop a rational system that would substitute for traditional Christianity by interpreting the entire process of human history, and indeed the universe itself, in terms of the progress of absolute Mind towards self-realization. In his view, history is, in essence, a march of the human spirit towards a determinate endpoint. His major political work, *Philosophy of Right* (1821), portrays the state as an ethical ideal and the highest expression of human freedom. Hegel's work had a considerable impact on Marx and other so-called 'young Hegelians'. It also shaped the ideas of liberals such as T. H. Green (1836–82), and influenced fascist thought.

Regardless of the different ways in which the state has been understood, there is general agreement about when and where it emerged. The state is a historical institution: it emerged in sixteenth- and seventeenth-century Europe as a system of centralized rule that succeeded in subordinating all other institutions and groups, including (and especially) the Church, bringing an end to the competing and overlapping authority systems that had characterized Medieval Europe. By establishing the principle of territorial sovereignty, the Peace of Westphalia (1648), concluded at the end of the Thirty Years' War, is often taken to have formalized the modern notion of statehood, by establishing the state as the principal actor in domestic and international affairs. There is less agreement, however, about why the state came into existence. According to Charles Tilly (1990), for instance, the central factor that explains the development of the modern state was its ability to fight wars. In this view, the transformation in the scale and nature of military encounters that was brought about from the sixteenth century onwards (through, for instance, the introduction of gun powder, the use of organized infantry and artillery, and the advent of standing armies) not only greatly increased the coercive power that rulers could wield, but also forced states to extend their control over their populations by developing more extensive systems of taxation and administration. As Tilly (1975) thus put it, 'War made the state, and the state made war'. Marxists, in contrast, have explained the emergence of the state largely in economic terms, the state's origins being traced back to the transition from feudalism to capitalism, with the state essentially being a tool used by the emerging bourgeois class (Engels, [1884] 1972). Michael Mann (1993), for his part, offered an account of the emergence of the state that stresses the state's capacity to combine ideological, economic, military and political forms of power (sometimes called the 'IEMP model').

The state nevertheless continued to evolve in the light of changing circumstances. Having developed into the **nation-state** during the nineteenth century, and then going through a process of gradual democratization, the state acquired wider economic and social responsibilities during the twentieth century, and especially in the post-1945 period, only for these, in many cases, to be 'rolled back' from the 1980s and 1990s. The European state model, furthermore, spread

● **Nation-state**: A sovereign political association within which citizenship and nationality overlap; one nation within a single state (see p. 124).

to other lands and other continents. This occurred as the process of decolonization accelerated in the decades following World War II, independence implying the achievement of sovereign statehood. One result of this process was a rapid growth in UN membership. From its original 51 member states in 1945, the UN grew to 127 members by 1970, and reached 193 members by 2011 (with the recognition of South Sudan). The state has therefore become the universal form of political organization around the world. However, in order to assess the significance of the state, and explore its vital relationship to politics, two key issues have to be addressed. These deal with the nature of state power and with the roles and responsibilities the state has assumed and should assume.

DEBATING THE STATE

Rival theories of the state

What is the nature of state power, and whose interests does the state represent? From this perspective, the state is an 'essentially contested' concept. There are various rival theories of the state, each of which offers a different account of its origins, development and impact on society. Indeed, controversy about the nature of state power has increasingly dominated modern political analysis and goes to the heart of ideological and theoretical disagreements in the discipline. These relate to questions about whether, for example, the state is autonomous and independent of society, or whether it is essentially a product of society, a reflection of the broader distribution of power or resources. Moreover, does the state serve the common or collective good, or is it biased in favour of privileged groups or a dominant class? Similarly, is the state a positive or constructive force, with responsibilities that should be enlarged, or is it a negative or destructive entity that must be constrained or, perhaps, smashed altogether? Four contrasting theories of the state can be identified as follows:

- the pluralist state
- the capitalist state
- the leviathan state
- the patriarchal state.

The pluralist state

The **pluralist** theory of the state has a very clear liberal lineage. It stems from the belief that the state acts as an 'umpire' or 'referee' in society. This view has also dominated mainstream political analysis, accounting for a tendency, at least within Anglo-American thought, to discount the state and state organizations and focus instead on 'government'. Indeed, it is not uncommon in this tradition for 'the state' to be dismissed as an abstraction, with institutions such as the courts, the civil service and the military being seen as independent actors in their own right, rather than as elements of a broader state machine. Nevertheless, this approach is possible only because it is based on underlying, and often unacknowledged, assumptions about state neutrality. The state can be ignored only because it is seen as an impartial arbiter or referee that can be bent to the will of the government of the day.

● **Pluralism**: A belief in, or commitment to diversity or multiplicity; or the belief that power in modern societies is widely and evenly distributed (see p. 100).

Thomas Hobbes (1588–1679)

English political philosopher. Hobbes was the son of a minor clergyman who subsequently abandoned his family. He became tutor to the exiled Prince of Wales Charles Stewart, and lived under the patronage of the Cavendish family. Writing at a time of uncertainty and civil strife, precipitated by the English Revolution, Hobbes developed the first comprehensive theory of nature and human behaviour since Aristotle.

His classic work, *Leviathan* (1651), discussed the grounds of political obligation and undoubtedly reflected the impact of the Civil War. It provided a defence for absolutist government but, by appealing to reasoned argument in the form of the social contract, also disappointed advocates of divine right.

• **Divine right**: The doctrine that earthly rulers are chosen by God and thus wield unchallengeable authority; a defence for monarchical absolutism.

• **Political obligation**: The duty of the citizen towards the state; the basis of the state's right to rule.

• **State of nature**: A society devoid of political authority and of formal (legal) checks on the individual; usually employed as a theoretical device.

• **Anarchy**: Literally, 'without rule'; anarchy is often used pejoratively to suggest instability, or even chaos.

The origins of this view of the state can be traced back to the social-contract theories (see p. 62) of thinkers such as Thomas Hobbes and John Locke (see p. 31). The principal concern of such thinkers was to examine the grounds of **political obligation**, the grounds on which the individual is obliged to obey and respect the state. They argued that the state had arisen out of a voluntary agreement, or social contract, made by individuals who recognized that only the establishment of a sovereign power could safeguard them from the insecurity, disorder and brutality of the **state of nature**. Without a state, individuals abuse, exploit and enslave one another; with a state, order and civilized existence are guaranteed and liberty is protected. As Locke put it, 'where there is no law there is no freedom'.

In liberal theory, the state is thus seen as a neutral arbiter amongst the competing groups and individuals in society; it is an 'umpire' or 'referee' that is capable of protecting each citizen from the encroachments of fellow citizens. The neutrality of the state reflects the fact that the state acts in the interests of *all* citizens, and therefore represents the common good or public interest. In Hobbes' view, stability and order could be secured only through the establishment of an absolute and unlimited state, with power that could be neither challenged, nor questioned. In other words, he held that citizens are confronted by a stark choice between absolutism (see p. 268) and **anarchy**. Locke, on the other hand, developed a more typically liberal defence of the limited state. In his view, the purpose of the state is very specific: it is restricted to the defence of a set of 'natural' or God-given individual rights; namely, 'life, liberty and property'. This establishes a clear distinction between the responsibilities of the state (essentially, the maintenance of domestic order and the protection of property) and the responsibilities of individual citizens (usually seen as the realm of civil society). Moreover, since the state may threaten natural rights as easily as it may uphold them, citizens must enjoy some form of protection against the state, which Locke believed could be delivered only through the mechanisms of constitutional and representative government.

These ideas were developed in the twentieth century into the pluralist theory of the state. As a theory of society, pluralism asserts that, within liberal democracies, power is widely and evenly dispersed. As a theory of the state, pluralism holds that the state is neutral, insofar as it is susceptible to the influence of

Focus on . . .

Social-contract theory

A social contract is a voluntary agreement made amongst individuals through which an organized society, or state, is brought into existence. Used as a theoretical device by thinkers such as Hobbes, Locke and Rousseau (see p. 97), the social contract has been revived by modern theorists such as John Rawls (see p. 45). The social contract is seldom regarded as a historical act. Rather, it is used as a means of demonstrating the value of government and the grounds of political obligation; social-contract theorists wish individuals to act as if they had concluded the contract themselves. In its classic form, social-contract theory has three elements:

- The image of a hypothetical stateless society (a 'state of nature') is established. Unconstrained freedom means that life is 'solitary, poor, nasty, brutish and short' (Hobbes).
- Individuals therefore seek to escape from the state of nature by entering into a social contract, recognizing that only a sovereign power can secure order and stability.
- The social contract obliges citizens to respect and obey the state, ultimately in gratitude for the stability and security that only a system of political rule can deliver.

various groups and interests, and all social classes. The state is not biased in favour of any particular interest or group, and it does not have an interest of its own that is separate from those of society. As Schwarzmantel (1994) put it, the state is 'the servant of society and not its master'. The state can thus be portrayed as a 'pincushion' that passively absorbs pressures and forces exerted upon it. Two key assumptions underlie this view. The first is that the state is effectively subordinate to government. Non-elected state bodies (the civil service, the judiciary, the police, the military and so on) are strictly impartial and are subject to the authority of their political masters. The state apparatus is therefore thought to conform to the principles of public service and political accountability. The second assumption is that the democratic process is meaningful and effective. In other words, party competition and interest-group activity ensure that the government of the day remains sensitive and responsive to public opinion. Ultimately, therefore, the state is only a weather vane that is blown in whichever direction the public-at-large dictates.

Modern pluralists, however, have often adopted a more critical view of the state, termed the neopluralist (see p 63) theory of the state. Theorists such as Robert Dahl (see p. 250), Charles Lindblom and J. K. Galbraith (see p. 155) have come to accept that modern industrialized states are both more complex and less responsive to popular pressures than classical pluralism suggested. Neopluralists, for instance, have acknowledged that business enjoys a 'privileged position' in relation to government that other groups clearly cannot rival. In *Politics and Markets* (1980), Lindblom pointed out that, as the major investor and largest employer in society, business is bound to exercise considerable sway over any government, whatever its ideological leanings or manifesto commitments. Moreover, neopluralists have accepted that the state can, and does, forge its own sectional interests. In this way, a state elite, composed of senior civil servants,

CONCEPT

Neopluralism

Neopluralism is a style of social theorizing that remains faithful to pluralist values while recognizing the need to revise or update classical pluralism in the light of, for example, elite, Marxist and New Right theories. Although neopluralism embraces a broad range of perspectives and positions, certain central themes can be identified. First, it takes account of modernizing trends, such as the emergence of postindustrial society. Second, while capitalism is preferred to socialism, free-market economic doctrines are usually regarded as obsolete. Third, western democracies are seen as 'deformed polyarchies', in which major corporations exert disproportionate influence.

● **Bourgeoisie**: A Marxist term, denoting the ruling class of a capitalist society, the owners of productive wealth.

judges, police chiefs, military leaders and so on, may be seen to pursue either the bureaucratic interests of their sector of the state, or the interests of client groups. Indeed, if the state is regarded as a political actor in its own right, it can be viewed as a powerful (perhaps the most powerful) interest group in society. This line of argument encouraged Eric Nordlinger (1981) to develop a state-centred model of liberal democracy, based on 'the autonomy of the democratic state'.

The capitalist state

The Marxist notion of a capitalist state offers a clear alternative to the pluralist image of the state as a neutral arbiter or umpire. Marxists have typically argued that the state cannot be understood separately from the economic structure of society. This view has usually been understood in terms of the classic formulation that the state is nothing but an instrument of class oppression: the state emerges out of, and in a sense reflects, the class system. Nevertheless, a rich debate has taken place within Marxist theory in recent years that has moved the Marxist theory of the state a long way from this classic formulation. In many ways, the scope to revise Marxist attitudes towards the state stems from ambiguities that can be found in Marx's (see p. 41) own writings.

Marx did not develop a systematic or coherent theory of the state. In a general sense, he believed that the state is part of a 'superstructure' that is determined or conditioned by the economic 'base', which can be seen as the real foundation of social life. However, the precise relationship between the base and the superstructure, and in this case that between the state and the capitalist mode of production, is unclear. Two theories of the state can be identified in Marx's writings. The first is expressed in his often-quoted dictum from *The Communist Manifesto* ([1848] 1967): 'The executive of the modern state is but a committee for managing the common affairs of the whole bourgeoisie'. From this perspective, the state is clearly dependent on society and entirely dependent on its economically dominant class, which in capitalism is the **bourgeoisie**. Lenin (see p 99) thus described the state starkly as 'an instrument for the oppression of the exploited class'.

A second, more complex and subtle, theory of the state can nevertheless be found in Marx's analysis of the revolutionary events in France between 1848 and 1851, *The Eighteenth Brumaire of Louis Bonaparte* ([1852] 1963). Marx suggested that the state could enjoy what has come to be seen as 'relative autonomy' from the class system, the Napoleonic state being capable of imposing its will upon society, acting as an 'appalling parasitic body'. If the state did articulate the interests of any class, it was not those of the bourgeoisie, but those of the most populous class in French society, the smallholding peasantry. Although Marx did not develop this view in detail, it is clear that, from this perspective, the autonomy of the state is only *relative*, in that the state appears to mediate between conflicting classes, and so maintains the class system itself in existence.

Both these theories differ markedly from the liberal and, later, pluralist models of state power. In particular, they emphasize that the state cannot be understood except in a context of unequal class power, and that the state arises out of, and reflects, capitalist society, by acting either as an instrument of oppression wielded by the dominant class, or, more subtly, as a mechanism through which class antagonisms are ameliorated. Nevertheless, Marx's attitude towards

Neo-Marxism

Neo-Marxism (sometimes termed 'modern' or 'western' Marxism) refers to attempts to revise or recast the classical ideas of Marx while remaining faithful to certain Marxist principles or aspects of Marxist methodology. Neo-Marxists typically refuse to accept that Marxism enjoys a monopoly of the truth, and have thus looked to Hegelian philosophy, anarchism, liberalism, feminism, and even rational-choice theory. Although still concerned about social injustice, neo-Marxists reject the primacy of economics over other factors and, with it, the notion that history has a predictable character.

the state was not entirely negative. He argued that the state could be used constructively during the transition from capitalism to communism in the form of the 'revolutionary dictatorship of the proletariat'. The overthrow of capitalism would see the destruction of the bourgeois state and the creation of an alternative, proletarian one.

In describing the state as a proletarian 'dictatorship', Marx utilized the first theory of the state, seeing the state as an instrument through which the economically dominant class (by then, the proletariat) could repress and subdue other classes. All states, from this perspective, are class dictatorships. The 'dictatorship of the proletariat' was seen as a means of safeguarding the gains of the revolution by preventing counter-revolution mounted by the dispossessed bourgeoisie. Nevertheless, Marx did not see the state as a necessary or enduring social formation. He predicted that, as class antagonisms faded, the state would 'wither away', meaning that a fully communist society would also be stateless. Since the state emerged out of the class system, once the class system had been abolished, the state, quite simply, loses its reason for existence.

Marx's ambivalent heritage has provided modern Marxists, or neo-Marxists, with considerable scope to further the analysis of state power. This was also encouraged by the writings of Antonio Gramsci (see p. 175), who emphasized the degree to which the domination of the ruling class is achieved by ideological manipulation, rather than just open coercion. In this view, bourgeois domination is maintained largely through 'hegemony' (see p. 174) : that is, intellectual leadership or cultural control, with the state playing an important role in the process.

Since the 1960s, Marxist theorizing about the state has been dominated by rival instrumentalist and structuralist views of the state. In *The State in Capitalist Society* ([1969] 2009), Miliband portrayed the state as an agent or *instrument* of the ruling class, stressing the extent to which the state elite is disproportionately drawn from the ranks of the privileged and propertied. The bias of the state in favour of capitalism is therefore derived from the overlap of social backgrounds between, on the one hand, civil servants and other public officials, and, on the other, bankers, business leaders and captains of industry. Nicos Poulantzas, in *Political Power and Social Classes* (1968), dismissed this sociological approach, and emphasized instead the degree to which the *structure* of economic and social power exerts a constraint on state autonomy. This view suggests that the state cannot but act to perpetuate the social system in which it operates. In the case of the capitalist state, its role is to serve the long-term interests of capitalism, even though these actions may be resisted by sections of the capitalist class itself. Neo-Marxists have increasingly seen the state as the terrain on which the struggle amongst interests, groups and classes is conducted. Rather than being an 'instrument' wielded by a dominant group or ruling class, the state is thus a dynamic entity that reflects the balance of power within society at any given time, and the ongoing struggle for hegemony.

The leviathan state

The image of the state as a 'leviathan' (in effect, a self-serving monster intent on expansion and aggrandizement) is one associated in modern politics with the New Right. Such a view is rooted in early or classical liberalism and, in particular,

● **Proletariat**: A Marxist term, denoting a class that subsists through the sale of its labour power; strictly speaking, the proletariat is not equivalent to the working class.

CONCEPT

Patriarchy

Patriarchy literally means 'rule by the father', the domination of the husband–father within the family, and the subordination of his wife and his children. However, the term is usually used in the more general sense of 'rule by men', drawing attention to the totality of oppression and exploitation to which women are subject. Patriarchy thus implies that the system of male power in society at large both reflects and stems from the dominance of the father in the family. Patriarchy is a key concept in radical feminist analysis, in that it emphasizes that gender inequality is systematic, institutionalized and pervasive.

a commitment to a radical form of individualism (see p. 158). The New Right, or at least its neoliberal wing, is distinguished by a strong antipathy towards state intervention in economic and social life, born out of the belief that the state is a parasitic growth that threatens both individual liberty and economic security. In this view, the state, instead of being, as pluralists suggest, an impartial umpire or arbiter, is an overbearing 'nanny', desperate to interfere or meddle in every aspect of human existence. The central feature of this view is that the state pursues interests that are separate from those of society (setting it apart from Marxism), and that those interests demand an unrelenting growth in the role or responsibilities of the state itself. New Right thinkers therefore argue that the twentieth-century tendency towards state intervention reflected not popular pressure for economic and social security, or the need to stabilize capitalism by ameliorating class tensions but, rather, the internal dynamics of the state.

New Right theorists explain the expansionist dynamics of state power by reference to both demand-side and supply-side pressures. Demand-side pressures are those that emanate from society itself, usually through the mechanism of electoral democracy. As discussed   Chapter 4   in connection with democracy, the New Right argue that electoral competition encourages politicians to 'outbid' one another by making promises of increased spending and more generous government programmes, regardless of the long-term damage that such policies inflict on the economy in the form of increased taxes, higher inflation and the 'crowding out' of investment. Supply-side pressures, on the other hand, are those that are internal to the state. These can therefore be explained in terms of the institutions and personnel of the state apparatus. In its most influential form, this argument is known as the 'government oversupply thesis'.

The oversupply thesis has usually been associated with public-choice theorists (see p. 252), who examine how public decisions are made on the assumption that the individuals involved act in a rationally self-interested fashion. Niskanen (1971), for example, argued that, as budgetary control in legislatures such as the US Congress is typically weak, the task of budget-making is shaped largely by the interests of government agencies and senior bureaucrats. Insofar as this implies that government is dominated by the state (the state elite being able to shape the thinking of elected politicians), there are parallels between the public-choice model and the Marxist view discussed above. Where these two views diverge, however, is in relation to the interests that the state apparatus serves. While Marxists argue that the state reflects broader class and other social interests, the New Right portrays the state as an independent or autonomous entity that pursues its own interests. In this view, bureaucratic self-interest invariably supports 'big' government and state intervention, because this leads to an enlargement of the bureaucracy itself, which helps to ensure job security, improve pay, open up promotion prospects and enhance the status of public officials. This image of self-seeking bureaucrats is plainly at odds with the pluralist notion of a state machine imbued with an ethic of public service and firmly subject to political control.

The patriarchal state

Modern thinking about the state must, finally, take account of the implications of feminist theory. However, this is not to say that there is a systematic feminist theory of the state. As emphasized in Chapter 2, feminist theory encompasses a range of traditions and perspectives, and has thus generated a range of very different attitudes towards state power. Moreover, feminists have usually not regarded the nature of state power as a central political issue, preferring instead to concentrate on the deeper structure of male power centred on institutions such as the family and the economic system. Some feminists, indeed, may question conventional definitions of the state, arguing, for instance, that the idea that the state exercises a monopoly of legitimate violence is compromised by the routine use of violence and intimidation in family and domestic life. Nevertheless, sometimes implicitly and sometimes explicitly, feminists have helped to enrich the state debate by developing novel and challenging perspectives on state power.

Liberal feminists, who believe that sexual or gender (see p 163) equality can be brought about through incremental reform, have tended to accept an essentially pluralist view of the state. They recognize that, if women are denied legal and political equality, and especially the right to vote, the state is biased in favour of men. However, their faith in the state's basic neutrality is reflected in the belief that any such bias can, and will, be overcome by a process of reform. In this sense, liberal feminists believe that all groups (including women) have potentially equal access to state power, and that this can be used impartially to promote justice and the common good. Liberal feminists have therefore usually viewed the state in positive terms, seeing state intervention as a means of redressing gender inequality and enhancing the role of women. This can be seen in campaigns for equal-pay legislation, the legalization of abortion, the provision of child-care facilities, the extension of welfare benefits, and so on.

Nevertheless, a more critical and negative view of the state has been developed by radical feminists, who argue that state power reflects a deeper structure of oppression in the form of patriarchy. There are a number of similarities between Marxist and radical feminist views of state power. Both groups, for example, deny that the state is an autonomous entity bent on the pursuit of its own interests. Instead, the state is understood, and its biases are explained, by reference to a 'deep structure' of power in society at large. Whereas Marxists place the state in an economic context, radical feminists place it in a context of gender inequality, and insist that it is essentially an institution of male power. In common with Marxism, distinctive instrumentalist and structuralistversions of this feminist position have been developed. The *instrumentalist* argument views the state as little more than an agent or 'tool' used by men to defend their own interests and uphold the structures of patriarchy. This line of argument draws on the core feminist belief that patriarchy is rooted in the division of society into distinct 'public' and 'private' spheres of life, men dominating the former while women are confined to the later. Quite simply, in this view, the state is run *by* men, and *for* men.

Whereas instrumentalist arguments focus on the personnel of the state, and particularly the state elite, *structuralist* arguments tend to emphasize the degree to which state institutions are embedded in a wider patriarchal system. Modern radical feminists have paid particular attention to the emergence of the welfare state, seeing it as the expression of a new kind of patriarchal power. Welfare may uphold patriarchy by bringing about a transition from private dependence (in which women as 'home makers' are dependent on men as 'breadwinners') to a system of public dependence in which women are increasingly controlled by the institutions of the extended state. For instance, women have become increasingly dependent on the state as clients or customers of state services (such as child-care institutions, nursery education and social work) and as employees, particularly in the so-called 'caring' professions (such as nursing, social work and education).

The role of the state

Contrasting interpretations of state power have clear implications for the desirable role or responsibilities of the state. What should states do? What functions or responsibilities should the state fulfil, and which ones should be left in the hands of private individuals? In many respects, these are the questions around which electoral politics and party competition revolve. With the exception of anarchists, who dismiss the state as fundamentally evil and unnecessary, all political thinkers have regarded the state as, in some sense, worthwhile. Even revolutionary socialists, inspired by the Leninist slogan 'smash the state', have accepted the need for a temporary proletarian state to preside over the transition from capitalism to communism, in the form of the 'dictatorship of the proletariat'. Nevertheless, there is profound disagreement about the exact role the state should play, and therefore about the proper balance between the state and civil society. Among the different state forms that have developed are the following:

- minimal states
- developmental states
- social-democratic states
- collectivized states
- totalitarian states
- religious states

Minimal states

The minimal state is the ideal of classical liberals, whose aim is to ensure that individuals enjoy the widest possible realm of freedom. This view is rooted in social-contract theory, but it nevertheless advances an essentially 'negative' view of the state. From this perspective, the value of the state is that it has the capacity to constrain human behaviour and thus to prevent individuals encroaching on the **rights** and liberties of others. The state is merely a protective body, its core function being to provide a framework of peace and social order within which citizens can conduct their lives as they think best. In Locke's famous simile, the state acts as a nightwatchman, whose services are called upon only when orderly existence is threatened. This nevertheless leaves the 'minimal' or 'nightwatchman' state with three core functions. First and foremost, the state exists to maintain domestic order. Second, it ensures that contracts or voluntary agreements made between private citizens are enforced, and third it provides protection against external attack. The institutional apparatus of a minimal state is thus limited to a police force, a court system and a military of some kind. Economic, social, cultural, moral and other responsibilities belong to the individual, and are therefore firmly part of civil society.

● **Rights**: Legal or moral entitlements to act or be treated in a particular way; civil rights differ from human rights.

Robert Nozick (1938–2002)

US academic and political philosopher. Nozick's major work, *Anarchy, State and Utopia* (1974), had a profound influence on New Right theories and beliefs. He developed a form of libertarianism that was close to Locke's and clearly influenced by nineteenth-century US individualists such as Spooner (1808–87) and Tucker (1854–1939). He argued that property rights should be strictly upheld, provided that wealth has been justly acquired in the first place, or has been justly transferred from one person to another. This position means support for minimal government and minimal taxation, and undermines the case for welfare and redistribution. Nozick's rights-based theory of justice was developed in response to the ideas of John Rawls (see p. 45). In later life, Nozick modified his extreme libertarianism.

The cause of the minimal state has been taken up in modern political debate by the New Right. Drawing on early liberal ideas, and particularly on free-market or classical economic theories, the New Right has proclaimed the need to 'roll back the frontiers of the state'. In the writings of Robert Nozick, this amounts to a restatement of Lockean liberalism based on a defence of individual rights, especially property rights. In the case of free-market economists such as Friedrich von Hayek (see p. 37) and Milton Friedman (see p 138), state intervention is seen as a 'dead hand' that reduces competition, efficiency and productivity. From the New Right perspective, the state's economic role should be confined to two functions: the maintenance of a stable means of exchange or 'sound money' (low or zero inflation), and the promotion of competition through controls on monopoly power, price fixing and so on.

Developmental states

The best historical examples of minimal states were those in countries such as the UK and the USA during the period of early industrialization in the nineteenth century. As a general rule, however, the later a country industrializes, the more extensive will be its state's economic role. In Japan and Germany, for instance, the state assumed a more active 'developmental' role from the outset. A developmental state is one that intervenes in economic life with the specific purpose of promoting industrial growth and economic development. This does not amount to an attempt to replace the market with a 'socialist' system of planning and control but, rather, to an attempt to construct a partnership between the state and major economic interests, often underpinned by conservative and nationalist priorities.

The classic example of a developmental state is Japan. During the Meiji Period (1868–1912), the Japanese state forged a close relationship with the *zaibutsu*, the great family-run business empires that dominated the Japanese economy up until World War II. Since 1945, the developmental role of the Japanese state has been assumed by the Japanese Ministry of International Trade and Industry (MITI), which, together with the Bank of Japan, helps to shape private investment decisions and steer the Japanese economy towards international competitiveness (see

p. 372). A similar model of developmental intervention has existed in France, where governments of both left and right have tended to recognize the need for economic planning, and the state bureaucracy has seen itself as the custodian of the national interest. In countries such as Austria and, to some extent, Germany, economic development has been achieved through the construction of a 'partnership state', in which an emphasis is placed on the maintenance of a close relationship between the state and major economic interests, notably big business and organized labour. More recently, economic globalization (see p 142) has fostered the emergence of 'competition states', examples of which are found amongst the tiger economies of East Asia. Competition states are distinguished by their recognition of the need to strengthen education and training as the principal guaranteeing economic success in a context of intensifying transnational competition.

Social-democratic states

Whereas developmental states practise interventionism in order to stimulate economic progress, social-democratic states intervene with a view to bringing about broader social restructuring, usually in accordance with principles such as fairness, equality (see p. 454) and social justice. In countries such as Austria and Sweden, state intervention has been guided by both developmental and social-democratic priorities. Nevertheless, developmentalism and social democracy do not always go hand-in-hand. As Marquand (1988) pointed out, although the UK state was significantly extended in the period immediately after World War II along social-democratic lines, it failed to evolve into a developmental state. The key to understanding the social-democratic state is that there is a shift from a 'negative' view of the state, which sees it as little more than a necessary evil, to a 'positive' view of the state, in which it is seen as a means of enlarging liberty and promoting justice. The social-democratic state is thus the ideal of both modern liberals and democratic socialists.

Rather than merely laying down the conditions of orderly existence, the social-democratic state is an active participant; in particular, helping to rectify the imbalances and injustices of a market economy. It therefore tends to focus less upon the generation of wealth and more upon what is seen as the equitable or just distribution of wealth. In practice, this boils down to an attempt to eradicate poverty and reduce social inequality. The twin features of a social-democratic state are therefore Keynesianism and social welfare. The aim of Keynesian economic policies is to 'manage' or 'regulate' capitalism with a view to promoting growth and maintaining full employment. Although this may entail an element of planning, the classic Keynesian strategy involves 'demand management' through adjustments in fiscal policy; that is, in the levels of public spending and taxation. The adoption of welfare policies has led to the emergence of so-called 'welfare states', whose responsibilities have extended to the promotion of social well-being amongst their citizens. In this sense, the social-democratic state is an 'enabling state', dedicated to the principle of individual empowerment.

Collectivized states

While developmental and social-democratic states intervene in economic life with a view to guiding or supporting a largely private economy, collectivized

● **Competition state**: A state which pursues strategies to ensure long-term competitiveness in a globalized economy.

● **Tiger economies**: Fast-growing and export-orientated economies modelled on Japan: for example, South Korea, Taiwan and Singapore.

● **Social justice**: A morally justifiable distribution of material rewards; social justice is often seen to imply a bias in favour of equality.

● **Welfare state**: A state that takes primary responsibility for the social welfare of its citizens, discharged through a range of social security, health, education and other services (albeit different in different societies).

Debating...
Is the state a force for good?

Political and ideological debate so often revolves around the issue of the state and, in particular, the proper balance between the state and civil society. At one extreme, anarchists claim that states and, for that matter, all systems of rule are illegitimate. Other views range from a grudging acceptance of the state as a necessary evil to a positive endorsement of the state as a force for good. Does the state have a positive or negative impact on our lives? Should it be celebrated or feared?

YES

Key to civilized existence. The most basic argument in favour of the state is that it is a vital guarantee of order and social stability. A state is absolutely necessary because only a sovereign body that enjoys a monopoly of the means of coercion is able to prevent (regrettable, but inevitable) conflict and competition from spilling over into barbarism and chaos. Life in the absence of a state would be, as Hobbes famously put it, 'solitary, poor, nasty, brutish and short'. This is a lesson that is underlined by the sad misfortunes suffered by so-called 'failed' states (see p 76), where civil war and warlordism take hold in the absence of a credible system of law and order.

Foundation of public life. The state differs from other bodies and institutions in that it is the only one that represents the common or collective interests, rather than the selfish or particular ones. The state speaks for the whole of society, not just its parts. As such, the state makes possible a 'public' realm of existence, which allows people to be involved in something larger than themselves, discharging responsibilities towards fellow citizens and, where appropriate, participating in making collective decisions. In a tradition that dates back to Aristotle and Hegel, the state can therefore be seen to be morally superior to civil society.

Agent of social justice. The state is a key agent of modernization and delivers a range of economic and social benefits. Even supporters of free-market economics acknowledge this in accepting that the economy can only function in a context of civic order that can only be established by the state. Beyond this, the state can counter the inherent instability of a market economy by intervening to ensure sustainable growth and full employment, and it can protect people from poverty and other forms of social disadvantage by delivering publicly-funded welfare services that no amount of private philanthropy can rival in terms of reach and quality.

NO

Cause of disorder. As anarchists argue, the state is the cause of the problem of order, not its solution. The state breeds conflict and unrest because, by robbing people of their moral autonomy and forcing them to obey rules they have not made themselves, it 'infantalizes' them and blocks their moral development. This leaves them under the sway of base instincts and allows selfishness, greed and aggression to spread. As moral development flourishes in conditions of freedom and equality, reducing the authority of the state or, preferably, removing it altogether, will allow order to arise 'from below', naturally and spontaneously.

Enemy of freedom. The state is, at best, a necessary evil. Even when its benefits in terms of upholding order are accepted, the state should be confined to a strictly minimal role. This is because, as state authority is sovereign, compulsory and coercive, the 'public' sphere is, by its nature, a realm of oppression. While anarchists therefore argue that all states are illegitimate, others suggest that this only applies when the state goes beyond its essential role of laying down the conditions for orderly existence. Freedom is enlarged to the extent that the 'public' sphere contracts, civil society being morally superior to the state.

Recipe for poverty. The economy works best when it is left alone by the state. Market economies are self-regulating mechanisms; they tend towards long-term equilibrium, as the forces of demand and supply come into line with one another. The state, in contrast, is a brute machine: however well-meaning state intervention in economic and social life may be, it inevitably upsets the natural balance of the market and so imperils growth and prosperity. This was a lesson most graphically illustrated by the fate of orthodox communist systems, but it has also been underlined by the poor economic performance of over-regulated capitalist systems.

CONCEPT

Statism

Statism (or, in French, *étatisme*) is the belief that state intervention is the most appropriate means of resolving political problems, or bringing about economic and social development. This view is underpinned by a deep, and perhaps unquestioning, faith in the state as a mechanism through which collective action can be organized and common goals can be achieved. The state is thus seen as an ethical ideal (Hegel), or as serving the 'general will' or public interest. Statism is most clearly reflected in government policies that regulate and control economic life, possibly extending to Soviet-style state collectivization.

● **Collectivization:** The abolition of private property in favour of a system of common or public ownership.

● **Totalitarianism:** An all-encompassing system of political rule, involving pervasive ideological manipulation and open brutality (see p. 269).

states bring the entirety of economic life under state control. The best examples of such states were in orthodox communist countries such as the USSR and throughout Eastern Europe. These sought to abolish private enterprise altogether, and set up centrally planned economies administered by a network of economic ministries and planning committees. So-called 'command economies' were therefore established that were organized through a system of 'directive' planning that was ultimately controlled by the highest organs of the communist party. The justification for state **collectivization** stems from a fundamental socialist preference for common ownership over private property. However, the use of the state to attain this goal suggests a more positive attitude to state power than that outlined in the classical writings of Marx and Engels (1820–95).

Marx and Engels by no means ruled out nationalization; Engels, in particular, recognized that, during the 'dictatorship of the proletariat', state control would be extended to include factories, the banks, transportation and so on. Nevertheless, they envisaged that the proletarian state would be strictly temporary, and that it would 'wither away' as class antagonisms abated. In contrast, the collectivized state in the USSR became permanent, and increasingly powerful and bureaucratic. Under Stalin, socialism was effectively equated with statism, the advance of socialism being reflected in the widening responsibilities and powers of the state apparatus. Indeed, after Khrushchev announced in 1962 that the dictatorship of the proletariat had ended, the state was formally identified with the interests of 'the whole Soviet peoples'.

Totalitarian states

The most extreme and extensive form of interventionism is found in totalitarian states. The essence of **totalitarianism** is the construction of an all-embracing state, the influence of which penetrates every aspect of human existence. The state brings not only the economy, but also education, culture, religion, family life and so on under direct state control. The best examples of totalitarian states are Hitler's Germany and Stalin's USSR, although modern regimes such as Saddam Hussein's Iraq arguably have similar characteristics. The central pillars of such regimes are a comprehensive process of surveillance and terroristic policing, and a pervasive system of ideological manipulation and control. In this sense, totalitarian states effectively extinguish civil society and abolish the 'private' sphere of life altogether. This is a goal that only fascists, who wish to dissolve individual identity within the social whole, are prepared openly to endorse. It is sometimes argued that Mussolini's notion of a totalitarian state was derived from Hegel's belief in the state as an 'ethical community' reflecting the altruism and mutual sympathy of its members. From this perspective, the advance of human civilization can clearly be linked to the aggrandisement of the state and the widening of its responsibilities.

Religious states

On the face of it, a religious state is a contradiction in terms. The modern state emerged largely through the triumph of civil authority over religious authority, religion increasingly being confined to the private sphere, through a separation between church and state. The advance of state sovereignty thus usually went hand in hand with the forward march of secularization. In the USA, the secular nature of the state was enshrined in the First Amendment of the constitution, which guarantees that freedom of worship shall not be abridged, while in France the separation of church and state has been maintained through a strict emphasis on the principle of *laïcité*. In countries such as Norway, Denmark and the UK, 'established' or **state religions** have developed, although the privileges these religions enjoy stop well short of theocratic rule, and their political influence has generally been restricted by a high level of social secularization.

Nevertheless, the period since the 1980s has witnessed the rise of the religious state, driven by the tendency within religious fundamentalism (see p. 53) to reject the public/private divide and to view religion as the basis of politics. Far from regarding political realm as inherently corrupt, fundamentalist movements have typically looked to seize control of the state and to use it as an instrument of moral and spiritual regeneration. This was evident, for instance, in the process of 'Islamization' introduced in Pakistan under General Zia-ul-Haq after 1978, the establishment of an 'Islamic state' in Iran as a result of the 1979 revolution, and, despite its formal commitment to secularism, the close links between the Sri Lankan state and Sinhala Buddhism, particularly during the years of violent struggle against Tamil separatism. Although, strictly speaking, religious states are founded on the basis of religious principles, and, in the Iranian model, contain explicitly theocratic features, in other cases religiously-orientated governments operate in a context of constitutional secularism. This applies in the case of the AKP in Turkey (see p. 280) and, since 2012, the Muslim Brotherhood in Egypt.

ECLIPSE OF THE STATE?

Since the late 1980s, debate about the state has been overshadowed by assertions about it 'retreat' or 'decline'. The once-mighty leviathan – widely seen to be co-extensive with politics itself – had seemingly been humbled, state authority having been undermined by the growing importance of, amongst other things, the global economy, the market, major corporations, non-state actors and international organisations. The clamour for 'state-centric' approaches to domestic and international politics to be rethought, or abandoned altogether, therefore grew. However, a simple choice between 'state-centrism' and 'retreat-ism' is, at best, misleading. For instance, although states and markets are commonly portrayed as rival forces, they also interlock and complement one another. Apart from anything else, markets cannot function without a system of property rights that only the state can establish and protect. Moreover, although states may have lost authority in certain respects; in others, they may have become stronger.

Decline and fall of the state

Globalization and state transformation

The rise of globalization has stimulated a major debate about the power and significance of the state in a globalized world. Three contrasting positions can be identified. In the first place, some theorists have boldly proclaimed the emergence of 'post-sovereign governance' (Scholte, 2005), suggesting that the rise of

● *Laïcité*: (French) The principle of the absence of religious involvement in government affairs, and of government involvement in religious affairs.

● **State religion**: A religious body that is officially endorsed by the state, giving it special privileges, but (usually) not formal political authority.

globalization is inevitably marked by the decline of the state as a meaningful actor. Power shifts away from the state and towards global marketplaces and transnational corporations (TNCs) (see p. 149) in particular. In the most extreme version of this argument, advanced by so-called 'hyperglobalists', the state is seen to be so 'hollowed out' as to have become, in effect, redundant. Others, nevertheless, deny that globalization has altered the core feature of world politics, which is that, as in earlier eras, sovereign states are the primary determinants of what happens within their borders, and remain the principal actors on the world stage. In this view, globalization and the state are not separate or, still less, opposing forces; rather, and to a surprising degree, globalization has been created by states and thus exists to serve their interests. Between these two views, however, there is a third position, which acknowledges that globalization has brought about qualitative changes in the role and significance of the state, and in the nature of sovereignty, but emphasizes that these have transformed the state, rather than simply reduced or increased its power.

Developments such as the rise of international migration and the spread of cultural globalization have tended to make state borders increasingly 'permeable'. However, most of the discussion about the changing nature and power of the state has concerned the impact of economic globalization.(discussed in more detail in Chapter 6). The central feature of economic globalization is the rise of 'supraterritoriality', the process through which economic activity increasingly takes place within a 'borderless world' (Ohmae, 1989). This is particularly clear in relation to financial markets that have become genuinely globalized, in that capital flows around the world seemingly instantaneously; meaning, for example, that no state can be insulated from the impact of financial crises in other parts of the world. If borders have become permeable and old geographical certainties have been shaken, state sovereignty, at least in its traditional sense, cannot survive. This is the sense in which governance (see p 74) in the twenty-first century has assumed a genuinely postsovereign character. It is difficult, in particular, to see how economic sovereignty can be reconciled with a globalized economy. Sovereign control over economic life was only possible in a world of discrete national economies; to the extent that these have been, or are being, incorporated into a single globalized economy, economic sovereignty becomes meaningless. However, the rhetoric of a 'borderless' global economy can be taken too far. For example, there has been, if anything, a growing recognition that market-based economies can only operate successfully within a context of legal and social order that only the state can guarantee (Fukuyama, 2005).

Increased global competition has also generated pressure to develop more efficient and responsive means of developing public policy and delivering public services. For many, this reflected a shift from government to 'governance'. As societies became more complex and fluid, new methods of governing have had to be devised that relied less on hierarchical state institutions and more on networks and the market, thus blurring the distinction between the state and society. The 'governance turn' in politics has been characterized by what has been called the 'reinvention' of government, reflected, in particular, in a move away from direct service provision by the state to the adoption of an 'enabling' or 'regulating' role. Such developments have led, some argue, to the transformation of the state itself, reflecting the rise of what has variously been called the 'competition' state, the 'market' state or the 'postmodern' state. Philip Bobbitt (2002)

● **Supraterritoriality**: The reconfiguration of geography that has occurred through the declining importance of state borders, geographical distance and territorial location.

● **Economic sovereignty**: The absolute authority of the state over national economic life, involving independent control of fiscal and monetary policies, and control over trade and capital flows.

● **Market state**: A state that aims to enlarge citizens' rights and opportunities, rather than assume control over economic and social life.

● **Political globalization**: The growing importance of international bodies and organizations, and of transnation political forces generally.

went as far as to argue that the transition from the nation-state to what he termed the 'market state' heralded a profound shift in world politics, in that it marked the end of the 'long war' between liberalism, fascism and communism to define the constitutional form of the nation-state. The core feature of the market state is a shift away from 'top-down' economic management, based on the existence of discrete national economies, to an acceptance of the market as the only reliable principle of economic organization. Instead of trying to 'tame' capitalism, market states 'go with the flow'. Whereas states were previously judged on their effectiveness in promoting growth and prosperity, alleviating poverty and narrowing social inequality, market states base their legitimacy on their capacity to maximize the opportunities available to citizens, and their ability to ensure effective and unimpeded market competition. The speed with which this has happened varies in different parts of the world, as states embrace the market-state model with greater or less enthusiasm, and try to adapt it to their political cultures and economic needs.

Non-state actors and international bodies

A further manifestation of the decline of the state is evident in the rise of non-state or transnational actors and the growing importance of international organizations. This reflects the fact that, increasingly, major aspects of politics no longer take place merely in or through the state but, rather, outside or beyond the state. Amongst non-state actors, TNCs are often regarded as the most significant, their number having risen from 7,000 in 1970 to 38,000 in 2009. TNCs often dwarf states in terms of their economic size. Based on the (rather crude) comparison between corporate sales and countries' GDP, 51 of the world's 100 largest economies are corporations; only 49 of them are countries. General Motors is broadly equivalent, in this sense, to Denmark; Wal-Mart is roughly the same size as Poland; and Exxon Mobil has the same economic weight as South Africa. However, economic size does not necessarily translate into political power or influence. States, after all, can do things that TNCs can only dream about, such as make laws and raise armies. Non-governmental organizations (NGOs) (see p. 248) have also steadily grown in number and influence, particularly since the 1990s. Estimates of the total number of international NGOs usually exceed 30,000, with over 1,000 groups enjoying formal consultative status by the UN. Their expertise, moral authority and high public profiles enable NGOs such as Greenpeace, Amnesty International and Care International to exert a level of influence within international organizations that may at times rival, or even surpass, that of national governments. NGOs are therefore the key agents of what is increasingly called 'global civil society' (see p. 106). Other non-state actors range from the women's movement and the anti-capitalist movement to terrorist networks, such as al-Qaeda, guerrilla armies and transnational criminal organizations. As such groups have a 'trans-border' character, they are often able to operate in ways that elude the jurisdiction of any state.

The growth of politics beyond the state has also been apparent in the trend towards **political globalization**. However, its impact has been complex and, in some ways, contradictory. On the one hand, international bodies such as the UN, the European Union (EU) and the World Trade Organization (WTO) have undermined the capacity of states to operate as self-governing political units. As the range and importance of decisions that are made at intergovernmental or supranational level has increased, states have been forced to exert influence in and through regional or global bodies, or to operate within frameworks established by them. In the case of the EU, a growing range of decisions (for example, on monetary policy, agriculture and fisheries policy, defence and foreign affairs) are made by EU institutions, rather than member states. This has led to the phenomenon of multilevel governance, as discussed in Chapter 17. The WTO, for its part, acts as the judge and jury of global trade disputes and serves as a forum for negotiating trade deals between and amongst its members. On the other hand, political globalization opens up opportunities for the state as well as diminishes them. This occurs through the 'pooling' of sovereignty. For example, the EU Council of Ministers, the most powerful policy-making body in the EU, is very much a creature of its member states and provides a forum that allows national politicians to make decisions on a supranational level. By 'pooling' sovereignty, member states of the EU arguably gain access to a larger and more meaningful form of sovereignty. The 'pooled' sovereignty of the EU may be greater than the combined national sovereignties of its various member states.

Failed states and state-building

In the developing world, debate about the decline of the state has sometimes been displaced by concern about weak, failing or collapsed states. Cooper (2004) portrayed what he called the 'pre-modern' world as a world of postcolonial chaos, in which such state structures as exist are unable to establish (in Weber's words) a legitimate monopoly of the use of force, thus leading to endemic **warlordism**, widespread criminality and social dislocation. Such conditions do not apply consistently across the developing world, however. In cases such as India, South Korea and Taiwan, developing world states have been highly successful in pursuing strategies of economic modernization and social development. Others, nevertheless, have been distinguished by their weakness, sometimes being portrayed as 'quasi-states' or 'failed states'(see p. 76) . Most of the weakest states in the world are concentrated in sub-Saharan Africa, classic examples being Somalia, Sierra Leone, Liberia and the Democratic Republic of the Congo. These states fail the most basic test of state power: they are unable to maintain domestic order and personal security, meaning that civil strife and even civil war become almost routine.

The failure of such states stems primarily from the experience of colonialism (see p 122), which, when it ended (mainly in the post-1945 period), bequeathed formal political independence to societies that lacked an appropriate level of political, economic, social and educational development to function effectively as separate entities. As the borders of such states typically represented the extent of colonial ambition, rather than the existence of a culturally cohesive population, postcolonial states also often encompass deep ethnic, religious and tribal divisions. Although some explain the increase in state failure since the 1990s primarily in terms of domestic factors (such as a disposition towards authoritarian rule, backward institutions and parochial value systems which block the transition from pre-industrial, agrarian societies to modern industrial ones), external factors have also played a major role. This has applied not least through the tendency of globalization to re-orientate developing world economies

● **Warlordism**: A condition in which locally-based militarized bands vie for power in the absence of a sovereign state.

CONCEPT

Failed state

A failed state is a state that is unable to perform its key role of ensuring domestic order by monopolizing the use of force within its territory. Examples of failed states in recent years include Cambodia, Haiti, Rwanda, Liberia and Somalia. Failed states are no longer able to operate as viable political units, in that they lack a credible system of law and order. They are no longer able to operate as viable economic units, in that they are incapable of providing for their citizens and have no functioning infrastructure. Although relatively few states collapse altogether, a much larger number barely function and are dangerously close to collapse.

● **State-building:** The construction of a functioning state through the establishment of legitimate institutions for the formulation and implementation of policy across key areas of government.

---

around the dictates of global markets, rather than domestic needs, and to widen inequality.

State failure is not just a domestic problem, however. Failed states often have a wider impact through, for example, precipitating refugee crises, providing a refuge for drug dealers, arms smugglers and terrorist organizations, generating regional instability, and, sometimes, provoking external intervention to provide humanitarian relief and/or to keep the peace. In this light, there has been a growing emphasis on **state-building**, typically associated with the larger process of peace-building and attempts to address deep-rooted, structural causes of violence in post-conflict situations. The provision of humanitarian relief and the task of conflict resolution become almost insuperably difficult in the absence of a functioning system of law and order. The wider acceptance of humanitarian intervention (see p. 424) since the early 1990s has meant that ordered rule is often provided, initially at least, by external powers. However this does not constitute a long-term solution. As examples such as Somalia, Iraq and Afghanistan demonstrate, externally-imposed order is only sustainable for a limited period of time, both because the economic and human cost to the intervening powers may be unsustainable in the long run, and because, sooner or later, the presence of foreign troops and police provokes resentment and hostility. Foreign intervention has therefore come, over time, to focus increasingly on the construction of effective indigenous leadership and building legitimate national institutions, such as an army, a police force, a judiciary, a central bank, a tax collection agency and functioning education, transport, energy and healthcare systems. As examples such as Liberia demonstrate, state-building is often a profoundly difficult task

Return of the state?

Discussion about the state in the early twenty-first century has been dominated by talk of retreat, decline, or even collapse. The reality is more complex, however. For instance, although globalization may make state borders more 'porous', globalization has not been imposed on unwilling states; rather, it is a process that has been devised by states in pursuit of what they identify as their national interests. Similarly, international organizations typically act as forums through which states can act in concert over matters of mutual interest, rather than as bodies intent on usurping state power. Moreover, a number of developments in recent years have helped to strengthen the state and underline its essential importance. What explains the return of the state? In the first place, the state's unique capacity to maintain domestic order and protect its citizens from external attack has been strongly underlined by new security challenges that have emerged in the twenty-first century; notably, those linked to transnational terrorism (as discussed in Chapter 18). This underlines what Bobbitt (2002) viewed as a basic truth: 'The State exists to master violence'; it is therefore essentially a 'warmaking institution'. The decline in military expenditure that occurred at the end of the Cold War, the so-called 'peace dividend', started to be reversed in the late 1990s, with global military expenditure rising steeply after the September 11 terrorist attacks and the launch of the 'war on terror'. Furthermore, counter-terrorism strategies have often meant that states have imposed tighter border controls and assumed wider powers of surveillance, control and sometimes detention, even becoming 'national security states'.

POLITICS IN ACTION . . .

Liberia: a failed state rebuilt?

Events: During the 1990s, Liberia was often cited as a classic example of a failed state. Its ethnic and religious mixes, widespread poverty, endemic corruption, collapse of institutions and infrastructure, and tendency towards warlordism and violence imperilled the security and welfare of its citizens and affected other states, notably neighbouring Sierra Leone. Liberia, Africa's oldest republic, had collapsed into civil war in the late 1980s when Charles Taylor's National Patriotic Front of Liberia (NPFL) rebels overran much of the countryside, seizing the capital, Monrovia, in 1990. Around 250,000 people were killed and many thousands more fled the country as fighting intensified between rebel splinter groups, the Liberian army and West African peacekeepers. The 14-year civil war ended in 2003 when, under mounting international pressure and hemmed in by rebels, Taylor stepped down and went into exile in Nigeria (he was later found guilty of war crimes by an international tribunal in The Hague, linked to atrocities carried out in Sierra Leone). A transitional government steered the country towards elections in 2005, which brought the Harvard-educated economist Elaine Johnson-Sirleaf to power, becoming Africa's first female head of state. Sirleaf was re-elected in an uncontested run-off presidential election in November 2011.

Significance: Successful state-building has to overcome at least three challenges. First, new institutions and structures have to be constructed in a context of often deep political and ethnic tension, economic and social dislocation, and endemic poverty. In Liberia, the process of reconstructing the economic and social infrastructure was accelerated once Sirleaf and her Unity Party (UP) assumed power in 2005. Central Monrovia was transformed with improved roads and shining new buildings; investment in education and health saw the building of hundreds of new schools and health facilities, some of them free and affordable; and, alongside the elected presidency and legislature, progress was made in establishing an independent judiciary, and a disciplined police and military. Other important institutions have included Liberia's Truth and Reconciliation Commission, modelled on the experience of South Africa, and the National Election Commission (NEC), which presided over its first elections in 2011. Nevertheless, many development goals have yet to be achieved, despite considerable sums of money having been provided by international donors. For example, most people in Monrovia still do not have elec-

tricity or running water, and unemployment remains extremely high, with young people being most affected.

Second, the indigenous leadership and new institutions need to enjoy a significant measure of legitimacy. This is why state-building is invariably linked to the promotion of 'good governance', with the eradication of corruption being a key goal. Before contesting the presidency, Sirleaf had resigned her post as head of the Governance Reform Commission, criticizing the transitional government's inability to fight corruption. However, her opponents claim that her administration is guilty of some of the crimes it associates with previous governments. In 2009, the Truth and Reconciliation Commission implicated Sirleaf in the civil war and recommended that she be banned from public office for 30 years. The 2011 elections were also highly divisive. Sirleaf's main opponent, Winston Tubman, boycotted the run-off election, claiming that the NEC was biased in favour of the president and had manipulated vote-counting in her favour.

Third, successful state-building often requires external support, although this may become more of a hindrance than a help. State-building 'from above', associated with military intervention, as in Afghanistan and Iraq, clearly has its drawbacks, not least because indigenous leaders and new institutions are in danger of being seen to serve external interests rather than domestic ones. In the case of Liberia, the support of the Economic Community of West African States (ECOWAS) and the presence of a 15,000-strong UN peacekeeping force certainly aided economic development and helped to keep civil strife under control. Nevertheless, Liberia's peace may be fragile, and this may be tested either when the UN peacekeeping forces withdraw, or when President Sirleaf leaves office.

Second, although the days of command-and-control economic management may be over, the state has sometimes reasserted itself as an agent of modernization. Competition states have done this by improving education and training in order to boost productivity and provide support for key export industries. States such as China and Russia each modernized their economies by making significant concessions to the market, but an important element of state control has been retained or re-imposed (these developments are examined in more detail in Chapter 6 in relation to 'state capitalism'). On a wider level, the state's vital role in economic affairs was underlined by the 2007–09 global financial crisis. Although the G20 may have provided states with a forum to develop a coordinated global response, the massive packages of fiscal and other interventions that were agreed were, and could only have been, implemented by states. Indeed, one of the lessons of the 2007–09 crash, and of subsequent financial and fiscal crises, may be that the idea that the global economy works best when left alone by the state (acting alone, or through international organizations) has been exposed as a myth.

SUMMARY

- The state is a political association that exercises sovereign jurisdiction within defined territorial borders. As a system of centralized rule that emerged in Europe between the seventeenth and nineteenth centuries, and succeeded in subordinating all other institutions and groups, the state came to dominate political life in all its forms. The spread of the European model of the state to other lands and continents has seen the state become the universal form of political organization around the world

- There are a number of rival theories of the state. Pluralists hold that the state is a neutral body that arbitrates between the competing interests of society. Marxists argue that the state maintains the class system by either oppressing subordinate classes or ameliorating class conflict. The New Right portrays the state as a self-serving monster that is intent on expansion and aggrandizement. Radical feminists point to patriarchal biases within the state that support a system of male power.

- Those who support the state see it either as a means of defending the individual from the encroachments of fellow citizens, or as a mechanism through which collective action can be organized. Critics, however, tend to suggest that the state reflects either the interests of dominant social groups, or interests that are separate from, and antithetical to, society.

- States have fulfilled very different roles. Minimal states merely lay down the conditions for orderly existence. Developmental states attempt to promote growth and economic development. Social-democratic states aim to rectify the imbalances and injustices of a market economy. Collectivized states exert control over the entirety of economic life. Totalitarian states bring about all-encompassing politicization and, in effect, extinguish civil society. Religious states are used as instruments of moral and spiritual renewal.

- Modern debate about the state is dominated by talk of retreat, decline and even collapse. The decline of the state is often explained in terms of the impact of globalization, the rise of non-state actors and the growing importance of international organizations. Most dramatically, some postcolonial states have collapsed, or barely function as states, having a negligible capacity to maintain order. However, the retreat of the state may have been exaggerated and, in relation to security and economic development in particular, the state may be reviving in importance.

Questions for discussion

- How should the state be defined?
- Would life in a stateless society really be 'nasty, brutish and short'?
- Why has politics traditionally been associated with the affairs of the state?
- Can the state be viewed as a neutral body in relation to competing social interests?
- Does the nature and background of the state elite inevitably breed bias?
- What is the proper relationship between the state and civil society?
- Does globalization mean that the state has become irrelevant?
- Have nation-states been transformed into market states?
- To what extent can state capacity be 're-built'?

Further reading

Hay, C., M. Lister and D. Marsh, *The State: Theories and Issues* (2006). An accessible, comprehensive and contemporary introduction to the theoretical perspectives on the state and to key issues and controversies.

Jessop, B., *State Theory: Putting Capitalist States in Their Place* (1990). A demanding but worthwhile collection of essays through which Jessop develops his own approach to state theory.

Pierre, J. and B. Guy Peters, *Governance, Politics and the State* (2000). A useful discussion of the phenomenon of governance, and of its implications for the role and nature of the state.

Sørensen, G., *The Transformation of the State: Beyond the Myth of Retreat* (2004). A systematic analysis of the contemporary state that assesses the nature and extent of its transformation in a global era.

CHAPTER 5

Governments, Systems and Regimes

'That government is best which governs not at all.'

HENRY DAVID THOREAU, *Civil Disobedience* (1849)

PREVIEW Classifying the various forms of government has been one of the principal concerns of political analysis through the ages. This process can be traced back to the fourth century BCE, when Aristotle made the first recorded attempt to describe the political regimes then in existence, using terms such as 'democracy', 'oligarchy' and 'tyranny' that are still commonly employed today. From the eighteenth century onwards, governments were increasingly classified as monarchies or republics, or as auto-cratic or constitutional regimes. During the twentieth century, these distinctions were further sharpened. The 'three worlds' classification of political systems, which was particularly fashionable during the Cold War period, created an image of world politics dominated by a struggle between democracy and totalitarianism. However, in the light of modern developments, such as the collapse of communism, the rise of East Asia, and the emergence of political Islam, all such classifications appear outdated. Nevertheless, it is not entirely clear what these shifts mean. Some inter-pret them as an indication that democratization, modelled around the principle and structures of western liberal democracy, is a natural and inevitable process. In this view, liberal democracy constitutes the final form of human government. Others, nevertheless, argue that the modern world is becoming politically more diffuse and fragmented. From this perspective, not only is liberal democracy culturally-bound rather than universally applicable, but alternative regimes including authoritarian systems and forms of illiberal democracy, may prove to be more successful and enduring than expected.

KEY ISSUES
- What is the difference between governments, political systems and regimes?
- What is the purpose of classifying systems of government?
- On what basis have, and should, regimes be classified?
- What are the major regimes of the modern world?
- Has western liberal democracy triumphed worldwide?

Government

Government in its broadest sense, refers to any mechanism through which ordered rule is maintained, its central features being the ability to make collective decisions and the capacity to enforce them. However, the term is more commonly understood to describe the formal and institutional processes that operate at the national level to maintain public order and facilitate collective action. The core functions of government are, thus, to make law (legislation), implement law (execution) and interpret law (adjudication). In some cases, the political executive alone is referred to as 'the government'.

● **Political system**: A network of relationships through which government generates 'outputs' (policies) in response to 'inputs' (demands or support) from the general public.

● *Coup d'état*: (French) A sudden and forcible seizure of government power through illegal and unconstitutional action.

● **Government gridlock**: Paralysis resulting from institutional rivalry within government, or the attempt to respond to conflicting public demands.

TRADITIONAL SYSTEMS OF CLASSIFICATION

Before we examine how different systems of rule have been classified, it is necessary for us to reflect on both what is being classified, and why such classifications have been undertaken. First, what is 'government', and how do governments differ from 'political systems' or 'regimes'? 'Government' refers to the institutional processes through which collective and usually binding decisions are made; its various institutions constitute the subject matter of Chapters 12–16 of this book. A **political system** or regime, on the other hand, is a broader term that encompasses not only the mechanisms of government and the institutions of the state, but also the structures and processes through which these interact with the larger society.

A political system is, in effect, a subsystem of the larger social system. It is a 'system', in that there are interrelationships within a complex whole; and 'political', in that these interrelationships relate to the distribution of power, wealth and resources in society. Political regimes can thus be characterized as effectively by the organization of economic life as they are by the governmental processes through which they operate. A regime is therefore a 'system of rule' that endures despite the fact that governments come and go. Whereas governments can be changed by elections, through dynastic succession, as a result of *coups d'état*, and so on, regimes can be changed only by military intervention from without, or by some kind of revolutionary upheaval from within.

Why classify political systems?

The interest in classifying political systems stems from two sources. First, classification is an essential aid to the *understanding* of politics and government. As in most social sciences, understanding in politics is acquired largely through a process of comparison, particularly as experimental methods are generally inapplicable. It is not possible, for instance, to devise experiments to test whether, say, US government would be less susceptible to institutional **government gridlock** if it abandoned the separation of powers (see p. 313), or whether communism (see p. 275) could have survived in the USSR had reforms been instigated a generation earlier. In consequence, we look to comparison to throw into relief what we are studying. Through the highlighting of similarities and differences between what might otherwise be bewildering collections of facts, comparison helps us to distinguish between what is significant and meaningful, and what is not. In this process, we are able both to develop theories, hypotheses and concepts, and, to some extent, to test them. As Alexis de Tocqueville (see p. 245) put it, 'without comparisons to make, the mind does not know how to proceed'. The attempt to classify systems of rule is, therefore, merely a device for making the process of comparison more methodical and systematic.

The second purpose of classification is to facilitate *evaluation*, rather than analysis. Since Aristotle (see p. 6), those who have sought to understand political regimes have often been as keen to 'improve' government as to understand it. In other words, descriptive understanding is closely tied up with normative judgements: questions about what *is* are linked to questions about what *should* be. In

CONCEPT

Utopia, utopianism

A utopia (from the Greek *outopia*, meaning 'nowhere', or *eutopia*, meaning 'good place') is literally an ideal or perfect society. Although utopias of various kinds can be envisaged, most are characterized by the abolition of want, the absence of conflict, and the avoidance of violence and oppression. Utopianism is a style of political theorizing that develops a critique of the existing order by constructing a model of an ideal or perfect alternative. However, the term is often used in a pejorative sense to imply deluded or fanciful thinking, a belief in an impossible goal.

its extreme form, this process may involve a search for an 'ideal' system of rule, or even a utopia, and this can be seen in works such as Plato's (see p. 13) *Republic*, Thomas More's *Utopia* ([1516] 1965), and Peter Kropotkin's *Fields, Factories and Workshops* (1912). In a more modest form, this type of classification allows for qualitative judgements to be made in relation to political structures and governmental forms. Only a comparative approach, for instance, enables us to consider questions such as 'Should the transition to liberal democracy in Russia and other former communist states be welcomed and encouraged?', 'Should India abandon federalism in favour of either a unitary system or regional independence?' and 'Should the UK adopt a "written" constitution?'

All systems of classification have their drawbacks, however. In the first place, as with all analytical devices, there is a danger of simplification. The classification of regimes under the same heading draws attention to the similarities that they share, but there is a risk that the differences that divide them will be ignored or disguised. A related problem is a possible failure to see that a phenomenon may have different meanings in different contexts. For instance, in Japan and throughout East Asia, 'the state' may be different in kind and significance from 'the state' as generally understood in the context of the West. Comparative analysis is therefore hampered by the constant danger of **ethnocentrism**. Second, value biases tend to intrude into the classification process. This can be seen in the tendency to classify communist and fascist regimes as 'totalitarian', implying that western liberal democracies were fighting the *same* enemy in the Cold War as they had done in World War II. Finally, all systems of classification have the drawback that they are necessarily state-bound: they treat individual countries as coherent or independent entities in their own right. Although this approach is by no means invalid, it is now widely viewed as incomplete in the light of the phenomenon of globalization (see p. 142).

Classical typologies

Without doubt, the most influential system of classification was that devised by Aristotle in the fourth century BCE, which was based on his analysis of the 158 Greek city-states then in existence. This system dominated thinking on the subject for roughly the next 2,500 years. Aristotle held that governments could be categorized on the basis of two questions: 'Who rules?', and 'Who benefits from rule?' Government, he believed, could be placed in the hands of a single individual, a small group, or the many. In each case, however, government could be conducted either in the selfish interests of the rulers, or for the benefit of the entire community. He thus identified the six forms of government shown in Figure 5.1.

Aristotle's purpose was to evaluate forms of government on normative grounds in the hope of identifying the 'ideal' constitution. In his view, tyranny, oligarchy and democracy were all debased or perverted forms of rule in which a single person, a small group and the masses, respectively, governed in their own interests and, therefore, at the expense of others. In contrast, monarchy, aristocracy and polity were to be preferred, because in these forms of government the individual, small group and the masses, respectively, governed in the interests of all. Aristotle declared tyranny to be the worst of all possible constitutions, as it reduced citizens to the status of slaves. Monarchy and aristocracy were, on the

● **Ethnocentrism:** The application of values and theories drawn from one's own culture to other groups and peoples; ethnocentrism implies bias or distortion.

CONCEPT

Absolutism

Absolutism is the theory or practice of absolute government, most commonly associated with an absolute monarchy.
Government is 'absolute', in the sense that it possesses unfettered power: government cannot be constrained by a body external to itself. The absolutist principle, nevertheless, resides in the claim to an unlimited right to rule (as in divine right), rather than the exercise of unchallengeable power. As it is based on a principled claim, whether religious or rational, absolutism does not invest government with arbitrary power, unlikely dictatorship.

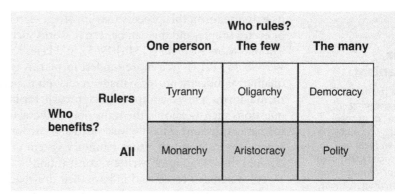

Figure 5.1   Aristotle's six forms of government

other hand, impractical, because they were based on a God-like willingness to place the good of the community before the rulers' own interests. Polity (rule by the many in the interests of all) was accepted as the most practicable of constitutions. Nevertheless, in a tradition that endured through to the twentieth century, Aristotle criticized popular rule on the grounds that the masses would resent the wealth of the few, and too easily fall under the sway of a **demagogue**. He therefore advocated a 'mixed' constitution that combined elements of both democracy and aristocracy, and left the government in the hands of the 'middle classes', those who were neither rich nor poor.

The Aristotelian system was later developed by thinkers such as Thomas Hobbes (see p. 61) and Jean Bodin (1530–96). Their particular concern was with the principle of sovereignty (see p. 58), viewed as the basis for all stable political regimes. Sovereignty was taken to mean the 'most high and perpetual' power, a power that alone could guarantee orderly rule. Bodin's *The Six Bookes of a Commonweale* ([1576] 1962) offered a wider-ranging account of the locus of sovereignty in political regimes, both contemporary and classical. He concluded that absolutism was the most defensible of regimes, as it established a sovereign who makes law but is not bound by those laws. The overriding merit of vesting sovereignty in a single individual was that it would then be indivisible: sovereignty would be expressed in a single voice that could claim final authority. Bodin nevertheless argued that absolute monarchs were constrained by the existence of higher law in the form of the will of God or natural law. On the other hand, in *Leviathan* ([1651] 1968), Hobbes portrayed sovereignty as a monopoly of coercive power, implying that the sovereign was entirely unconstrained.

These ideas were later revised by early liberals such as John Locke (see p. 31) and Montesquieu (see p. 312), who championed the cause of constitutional government. Locke, in *Two Treatises of Government* ([1690] 1965), argued that sovereignty resided with the people, not the monarch, and he advocated a system of limited government to provide protection for natural rights; notably, the rights to life, liberty and property. In his epic *The Spirit of the Laws* ([1748] 1949), Montesquieu attempted to develop a 'scientific' study of human society, designed to uncover the constitutional circumstances that would best protect individual liberty. A severe critic of absolutism and an admirer of the English parliamentary tradition, he proposed a system of checks and balances in the form of a 'separation of powers' between the executive, legislative and judicial

● **Demagogue:** A political leader whose control over the masses is based on the ability to whip up hysterical enthusiasm.

CONCEPT

Totalitarianism

Totalitarianism is an all-encompassing system of political rule, typically established by pervasive ideological manipulation and open terror. Totalitarianism differs from autocracy and authoritarianism (see p. 277), in that it seeks to politicize every aspect of social and personal existence, rather than just suppress political opposition. Totalitarian regimes are sometimes identified through a 'six-point syndrome' (Friedrich and Brzezinski, 1963): (1) an official ideology; (2) a one-party state, usually led by an all-powerful leader; (3) a system of terroristic policing; (4) a monopoly of the means of mass communication; (5) a monopoly of the means of armed combat; and (6) state control of all aspects of economic life.

● **Republicanism**: The principle that political authority stems ultimately from the consent of the people; the rejection of monarchical and dynastic principles.

● **Gross domestic product**: The total financial value of final goods and services produced in an economy over one year.

institutions. This principle was incorporated into the US constitution (1787), and it later came to be seen as one of the defining features of liberal democratic government.

The 'classical' classification of regimes, stemming from the writings of Aristotle, was rendered increasingly redundant by the development of modern constitutional systems from the late eighteenth century onwards. In their different ways, the constitutional republicanism established in the USA following the American War of Independence of 1775–83, the democratic radicalism unleashed in France by the 1789 French Revolution, and the form of parliamentary government that gradually emerged in the UK created political realities that were substantially more complex than early thinkers had envisaged. Traditional systems of classification were therefore displaced by a growing emphasis on the constitutional and institutional features of political rule. In many ways, this built on Montesquieu's work, in that particular attention was paid to the relationships between the various branches of government. Thus, monarchies were distinguished from republics, parliamentary government (see p. 310) was distinguished from presidential government (see p. 289), and unitary systems were distinguished from federal systems.

The 'three worlds' typology

During the twentieth century, historical developments once again altered the basis of political classification. The appearance in the interwar period of new forms of authoritarianism (see p. 277), particularly in Stalinist Russia, Fascist Italy and Nazi Germany, encouraged the view that the world was divided into two kinds of regime: democratic states and totalitarian states. The stark contrast between democracy and totalitarianism dominated attempts at regime classification through much of the 1950s and 1960s, despite the fact that the fascist and Nazi regimes had collapsed at the end of World War II. Nevertheless, there was a growing awareness that this approach was shaped by the antagonisms of the Cold War, and that it could perhaps be seen as a species of Cold War ideology, and this stimulated the search for a more value-neutral and ideologically impartial system of classification. This led to the growing popularity of the so-called 'three worlds' approach – the belief that the political world could be divided into three distinct blocs:

- a capitalist 'first world'
- a communist 'second world'
- a developing 'third world'.

The three-worlds classification had economic, ideological, political and strategic dimensions. Industrialized western regimes were 'first' in economic terms, in that their populations enjoyed the highest levels of mass affluence. In 1983, these countries generated 63 per cent of the world's gross domestic product (GDP) while having only 15 per cent of the world's population (World Bank, 1985). Communist regimes were 'second', insofar as they were largely industrialized and capable of satisfying the population's basic material needs. These countries produced 19 per cent of the world's GDP with 33 per cent of the world's population. The less-developed countries of Africa, Asia and Latin America were

CONCEPT

Liberal democracy

A liberal democracy is a political regime in which a 'liberal' commitment to limited government is blended with a 'democratic' belief in popular rule. Its key features are: (1) the right to rule is gained through success in regular and competitive elections, based on universal adult suffrage; (2) constraints on government imposed by a constitution, institutional checks and balances, and protections for individual and minority rights; and (3) a vigorous civil society including a private enterprise economy, independent trade unions and a free press. The terms liberal democracy and and pluralist democracy are often used interchangeably.

'third', in the sense that they were economically dependent and often suffered from widespread poverty. They produced 18 per cent of the world's GDP with 52 per cent of the world's population.

The first and second worlds were further divided by fierce ideological rivalry. The first world was wedded to 'capitalist' principles, such as the desirability of private enterprise, material incentives and the free market; the second world was committed to 'communist' values such as social equality, collective endeavour, and the need for centralized planning. Such ideological differences had clear political manifestations. First-world regimes practised liberal-democratic politics based on a competitive struggle for power at election time. Second-world regimes were one-party states, dominated by 'ruling' communist parties. Third-world regimes were typically authoritarian, and governed by traditional monarchs, dictators or, simply, the army. The three-worlds classification was underpinned by a bipolar world order, in which a USA-dominated West confronted a USSR-dominated East. This order was sustained by the emergence of two rival military camps in the form of NATO and the Warsaw Pact. Not infrequently, the 'non-aligned' third world was the battleground on which this geopolitical struggle was conducted, a fact that did much to ensure its continued political and economic subordination.

Since the 1970s, however, this system of classification has been increasingly difficult to sustain. New patterns of economic development have brought material affluence to parts of the third world; notably, the oil-rich states of the Middle East and the newly industrialized states of East Asia, Southeast Asia, and, to some extent, Latin America. In contrast, poverty became, if anything, more deeply entrenched in parts of sub-Saharan Africa which, in the 1990s, in particular, constituted a kind of 'fourth world'. Moreover, the advance of democratization (see p. 272) in Asia, Latin America and Africa, especially during the 1980s and 1990s, has meant that third-world regimes are no longer uniformly authoritarian. Indeed, the phrase 'third world' is widely resented as being demeaning, because it implies entrenched disadvantage. The term 'developing world' is usually seen as preferable.

Without doubt, however, the most catastrophic single blow to the three-worlds model resulted from the eastern European revolutions of 1989–91. These led to the collapse of orthodox communist regimes in the USSR and elsewhere, and unleashed a process of political liberalization and market reform. Indeed, Francis Fukuyama (see p. 271) went so far as to proclaim that this development amounted to the 'end of history' (see p. 44). He meant by this that ideological debate had effectively ended with the worldwide triumph of western liberal democracy. Quite simply, second-world and third-world regimes were collapsing as a result of the recognition that only the capitalist first world offered the prospect of economic prosperity and political stability.

REGIMES OF THE MODERN WORLD

Since the late 1980s, the regime-classification industry has been in a limbo. Older categories, particularly the 'three worlds' division, were certainly redundant, but the political contours of the new world were far from clear. Moreover, the 'end of history' scenario was only fleetingly attractive, having been sustained by the wave

Francis Fukuyama (born 1952)

US social analyst and political commentator. Fukuyama was born in Chicago, USA, the son of a Protestant preacher. He was a member of the Policy Planning Staff of the US State Department before becoming an academic; he is currently at Johns Hopkins University. A staunch Republican, he came to international prominence as a result of his article 'The End of History?' (1989), which he later developed into *The End of History and the Last Man* (1992). These works claimed that the history of ideas had ended with the recognition of liberal democracy as 'the final form of human government'. In *Trust* (1996) and *The Great Disruption* (1999), Fukuyama discussed the relationship between economic development and social cohesion. In *The Origins of Political Order* (2011), he laid down the basis for a theory of political development.

of democratization in the late 1980s and early 2000s, and drawing impetus in particular from the collapse of communism. In some senses, this liberal-democratic triumphalism reflected the persistence of a western-centric viewpoint, and it may, anyway, have been a hangover from the days of the Cold War. The image of a 'world of liberal democracies' suggested the superiority of a specifically western model of development, based perhaps especially on the USA, and it implied that values such as individualism (see p. 158), rights and choice are universally applicable. One result of this was a failure to recognize the significance, for instance, of Islamic and Confucian political forms, which tended to be dismissed as mere aberrations, or simply as evidence of resistance to the otherwise unchallenged advance of liberal democracy.

However, one of the difficulties of establishing a new system of classification is that there is no consensus about the criteria on which such a system should be based. No system of classification relies on a single all-important factor. Nevertheless, particular systems have tended to prioritize different sets of criteria. Among the parameters most commonly used are the following:

- Who rules? Is political participation confined to an elite body or privileged group, or does it encompass the entire population?
- How is compliance achieved? Is government obeyed as a result of the exercise or threat of force, or through bargaining and compromise?
- Is government power centralized or fragmented? What kinds of check and balance operate in the political system?
- How is government power acquired and transferred? Is a regime open and competitive, or is it monolithic?
- What is the balance between the state and the individual? What is the distribution of rights and responsibilities between government and citizens?
- What is the level of material development? How materially affluent is the society, and how equally is wealth distributed?
- How is economic life organized? Is the economy geared to the market or to planning, and what economic role does government play?
- How stable is a regime? Has the regime survived over time, and does it have the capacity to respond to new demands and challenges?

CONCEPT

Democratization

Democratization refers to the process of transition from authoritarianism to liberal democracy. Democratization encompasses three, sometimes overlapping, processes. (1) The breakdown of the old regime; this usually involves a loss of legitimacy (see p. 81) and the faltering loyalty of the police and military. (2) 'Democratic transition' witnesses the construction of new liberal-democratic structures and processes. (3) 'Democratic consolidation' sees these new structures and processes becoming so embedded in the minds of elites and the masses that democracy becomes 'the only game in town' (Przeworski, 1991).

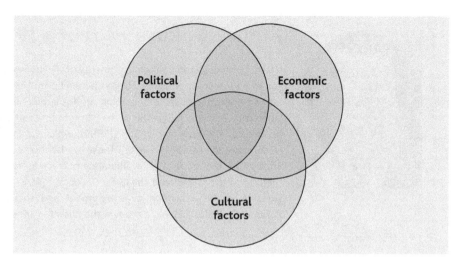

Figure 5.2 Key regime features

A *constitutional–institutional* approach to classification that was influenced by 'classical' typologies was adopted in the nineteenth and early twentieth centuries. This approach highlighted, for instance, differences between codified and uncodified constitutions, parliamentary and presidential systems, and federal and unitary systems. A *structural–functional* approach, however, was developed out of systems theory, which became increasingly prominent in the 1950s and 1960s. This approach was concerned less with institutional arrangements than with how political systems work in practice, and especially with how they translate 'inputs' into 'outputs'. The 'three worlds' approach was *economic–ideological* in orientation, as it paid special attention to a systems level of material development and its broader ideological orientation. The approach adopted here, however, is in some ways different from each of these three. It attempts to take account of three key features of a regime: its political, economic and cultural aspects. The assumption in this approach is that regimes are characterized not so much by particular political, economic or cultural factors as by the way in which these interlock in practice (see Figure 5.2).

The significance of this approach is that it emphasizes the degree to which formal political and economic arrangements may operate differently depending on their cultural context. For instance, multiparty elections and a market economy may have very different implications in western liberal societies than they do in non-western ones. Nevertheless, in view of the profound political upheavals since the late twentieth century, it would be foolish to suggest that any system of classification can be anything but provisional. Indeed, regimes are themselves fluid, and the regime-classification industry is constantly struggling to keep up to date with an ever-changing political reality. Nevertheless, five regime types can be identified in the modern world:

- western polyarchies
- new democracies
- East Asian regimes

CONCEPT

Polyarchy

Polyarchy (literally, 'rule by many') refers, generally, to the institutions and political processes of modern representative democracy. Polyarchy can be understood as a rough or crude approximation of democracy, in that it operates through institutions that force rulers to take account of the public's wishes. Its central features are (Dahl, 1989): (1) government is based on election; (2) elections are free and fair; (3) practically all adults have the right to vote; (4) the right to run for office is unrestricted; (5) there is free expression and a right to criticize and protest; (6) citizens have access to alternative sources of information; and (7) groups and associations enjoy at least relative independence from government.

● Liberalization: The introduction of internal and external checks on government power and/or shifts towards private enterprise and the market.

- Islamic regimes
- military regimes.

Western polyarchies

Western polyarchies are broadly equivalent to regimes categorized as 'liberal democracies', or even simply 'democracies'. Their heartlands are therefore North America, western Europe and Australasia. Huntington (see p. 425) argued that such regimes are a product of the first two 'waves' of democratization: the first occurred between 1828 and 1926, and involved countries such as the USA, France and the UK; the second occurred between 1943 and 1962, and involved countries such as West Germany, Italy, Japan and India. Although polyarchies have, in large part, evolved through moves towards democratization and liberalization, the term 'polyarchy' is preferable to 'liberal democracy' for two reasons. First, liberal democracy is sometimes treated as a political ideal, and is thus invested with broader normative implications. Second, the use of 'polyarchy' acknowledges that these regimes fall short, in important ways, of the goal of democracy.

The term 'polyarchy' was first used to describe a system of rule by Dahl and Lindblom in *Politics, Economics, and Welfare* (1953), and it was later elaborated in Dahl's *Polyarchy: Participation and Opposition* (1971). In the view of these authors, polyarchical regimes are distinguished by the combination of two general features. In the first place, there is a relatively high tolerance of opposition that is sufficient at least to check the arbitrary inclinations of government. This is guaranteed in practice by a competitive party system, by institutionally guaranteed and protected civil liberties, and by a vigorous and healthy civil society. The second feature of polyarchy is that the opportunities for participating in politics should be sufficiently widespread to guarantee a reliable level of popular responsiveness. The crucial factor here is the existence of regular and competitive elections operating as a device through which the people can control and, if necessary, displace their rulers. In this sense, there is a close resemblance between polyarchy and the form of democratic elitism described by Joseph Schumpeter (see p. 202) in *Capitalism, Socialism and Democracy* (1942). Nevertheless, Lindblom (1977) and Dahl (1985) both acknowledged the impact on polyarchies of the disproportional power of major corporations. For this reason, the notion of 'deformed polyarchy' has sometimes been preferred.

Thus defined, the term 'polyarchy' may be used to describe a large and growing number of regimes throughout the world. All states that hold multi-party elections have polyarchical features. Nevertheless, western polyarchies have a more distinctive and particular character. They are marked not only by representative democracy and a capitalist economic organization, but also by a cultural and ideological orientation that is largely derived from western liberalism. The most crucial aspect of this inheritance is the widespread acceptance of liberal individualism. Individualism, often seen as the most distinctive of western values, stresses the uniqueness of each human individual, and suggests that society should be organized so as to best meet the needs and interests of the individuals who compose it. The political culture of western polyarchies is influenced by liberal individualism in a variety of ways. It generates, for example, a heightened sensitivity to individual rights (perhaps placed above duties), the

The West

The term the West has two overlapping meanings. In a general sense, it refers to the cultural and philosophical inheritance of Europe, as exported through migration or colonialism. The roots of this inheritance lie in Judeo-Christian religion and the learning of 'classical' Greece and Rome, shaped in the modern period by the ideas and values of liberalism. In a narrower sense, fashionable during the Cold War, the West meant the USA-dominated capitalist bloc, as opposed to the USSR-dominated East. Although Eastern Europe no longer belongs to the East in this sense, it has always been unclear whether Russia belongs to the West in the broader sense.

● **Westminster model**: A system of government in which the executive is drawn from, and (in theory) accountable to, the assembly or parliament.

● **Consociational democracy**: A form of democracy that operates through power-sharing and a close association amongst a number of parties or political formations.

● **Exceptionalism**: The features of a political system that are unique or particular to it, and thus restrict the application of broader categories.

general perception that choice and competition (in both political and economic life) are healthy, and a tendency to fear government and regard the state as, at least, a potential threat to liberty.

Western polyarchies are not all alike, however. Some of them are biased in favour of centralization and majority rule, and others tend towards fragmentation and pluralism. Lijphart (1990, 1999) highlighted this fact in distinguishing between 'majority' democracies and 'consensus' democracies. Majority democracies are organized along parliamentary lines according to the so-called 'Westminster model'. The clearest example of this is the UK system, but the model has also, in certain respects, been adopted by New Zealand, Australia, Canada, Israel and India. Majoritarian tendencies are associated with any, or all, of the following features:

- single-party government
- a fusion of powers between the executive and the assembly
- an assembly that is either unicameral or weakly bicameral
- a two-party system
- a single-member plurality, or first-past-the-post, electoral system (see p. 208)
- unitary and centralized government
- an uncodified constitution and a sovereign assembly.

In contrast, other western polyarchies are characterized by a diffusion of power throughout the governmental and party systems. The US model of pluralist democracy (see p. 101) is based very largely on institutional fragmentation enshrined in the provisions of the constitution itself. Elsewhere, particularly in continental Europe, consensus is underpinned by the party system, and a tendency towards bargaining and power sharing. In states such as Belgium, Austria and Switzerland, a system of consociational democracy has developed that is particularly appropriate to societies that are divided by deep religious, ideological, regional, cultural or other differences. Consensual or pluralistic tendencies are often associated with the following features:

- coalition government (see p. 239)
- a separation of powers between the executive and the assembly
- an effective bicameral system
- a multiparty system
- proportional representation (see p. 207)
- federalism (see p. 382) or devolution
- a codified constitution and a bill of rights.

On another level, of course, each polyarchical regime – and, indeed, every regime – is unique, and therefore exceptional. US exceptionalism, for instance, is often linked to the absence of a feudal past, and the experience of settlement and frontier expansion. This may explain the USA's deeply individualist political culture, which, uniquely amongst western polyarchies, does not accommodate a socialist party or movement of any note. The USA is also the most overtly religious of western regimes, and it is the only one, for instance, in which Christian fundamentalism has developed into a major political force.

CONCEPT

Communism

Communism, in its simplest sense, is the communal organization of social existence on the basis of the collective ownership of property. For Marxists, communism is a theoretical ideal, characterized by classlessness, rational economic organization and statelessness. 'Orthodox' communism refers to the societies founded in the twentieth century, supposedly on the basis of Marxist principles. In such societies: (1) Marxism-Leninism was used as an 'official' ideology; (2) the communist party had a monopoly of power, based on its 'leading and guiding' role in society; and (3) economic life was collectivized and organized through a system of central planning.

● Transition countries: Former Soviet Bloc countries that are in the process of transition from central planning to market capitalism.

● New democracies: Regimes in which the process of democratic consolidation is incomplete; democracy is not yet the 'only game in town' (Przeworski, 1991).

India is a still more difficult case. It is certainly not part of the West in cultural, philosophical or religious terms. In contrast to the 'developed' polyarchies of Europe and North America, it also has a largely rural population and a literacy rate of barely 50 per cent. Nevertheless, India has functioned as an effective polyarchy since it became independent in 1947, even surviving Indira Gandhi's 'state of emergency' during 1975–7. Political stability in India was undoubtedly promoted by the cross-caste appeal of the Congress Party and the mystique of the Nehru–Gandhi dynasty. However, the decline of the former and the end of the latter has perhaps transformed modern India into something approaching a consociational democracy. Turkey is another example of a political system that, in some respects, hovers between the East and the West (see p. 280).

New democracies

A third wave of democratization began, according to Huntington (1991), in 1974. It witnessed the overthrow of right-wing dictatorships (see p. 281) in Greece, Portugal and Spain; the retreat of the generals in Latin America; and, most significantly, the fall of communism. Of the 151 countries comprising the world at that time, in 1973 only 45 were electoral democracies. However, by 2003, 63 per cent of states, accounting for about 70 per cent of the world's population, exhibited some of the key features of liberal-democratic governance. Most prominently, this process has been characterized by the adoption of multi-party elections and market-based economic reforms. Nevertheless, many of these states are 'transition countries', often classified as new democracies. The process of democratic transition has been both complex and difficult, highlighting the fact that liberal democracy may not be the 'default position' for human societies (see p. 276). New democracies not only lack developed democratic political cultures, they also have to handle the strains produced by the external forces of globalization, as well as rapid internal change. The most dramatic evidence of their vulnerability is the re-emergence of the armed forces into politics, as occurred, for example, in military *coups* in Pakistan in 1979 and in Thailand in 2006. However, particular problems are faced by postcommunist states in bringing about democratization.

One feature of postcommunist regimes is the need to deal with the politico-cultural consequences of communist rule, especially the ramifications of Stalinist totalitarianism. The ruthless censorship and suppression of opposition that underpinned the communist parties' monopoly of power guaranteed that a civic culture emphasizing participation, bargaining and consensus failed to develop. In Russia, this has produced a weak and fragmented party system that is apparently incapable of articulating or aggregating the major interests of Russian society. As a result, communist parties, or former communist parties, have often continued to provide a point of stability. In Romania and Bulgaria, for example, the institutions of the communist past have survived into the postcommunist era while, in states such as Hungary, Poland and Russia, communist parties – now embracing, if with differing degrees of conviction, the principles of social democracy – have retained a measure of electoral credibility.

A second set of problems stems from the process of economic transition. The 'shock therapy' transition from central planning to *laissez-faire* capitalism, initially advocated by the International Monetary Fund, unleashed deep insecu-

Debating . . .
Is liberal democracy the 'default position' for human societies?

The seemingly relentless advance of democratization since the early nineteenth century has encouraged some to believe that it is a natural and inevitable process. From this perspective, all systems of rule are destined, sooner or later, to collapse and be remodelled on liberal-democratic lines. Is liberal democracy the only 'normal' political regime?

YES

Mandate of history. Modernization clearly wears a liberal-democratic face. Although the liberal-democratic mix of limited government and popular rule has only been around for about 200 years, it has become the dominant form of government worldwide. Although initially confined to Western Europe and North America, its western 'homeland', liberal democracy demonstrated its universal appeal through its spread to India and Japan after World War II, into Latin America and across Eastern Europe from the 1980s onwards and, more recently, into the Muslim world through the Arab Spring. This, and further waves of democratization, seems set to culminate in the establishment of a world of liberal democracies.

The 'transition paradigm'. Democratization is driven forward through a strong internal dynamic, helping to explain why dictatorship eventually crumbles in the face of advancing liberal democracy. Following an opening phase in which cracks appear in a dictatorial regime that has lost legitimacy, the regime itself collapses and a new, democratic system emerges in its place. Over time, democratic structures gain greater substance, as the new democratic 'rules of the game' come to be accepted by both political elites and the mass of the population. In this view, once competitive elections have been held, even if democratic imperfections persist for some time, a return to dictatorship is unlikely, and may be impossible.

Unrivalled performance. Liberal democracy brings a unique collection of humanitarian, economic and political benefits in its wake. Liberal democracy's humanitarian benefits derive from its capacity to uphold human rights and afford citizens the widest possible sphere of freedom unchecked by the state. Its economic benefits stem from its intrinsic relationship with capitalist economic structures, helping to explain why liberal-democratic regimes are also prosperous and developed. Its political benefits are evident in its tendency towards stability and consensus, open and pluralist politic, ensuring that no significant section of the population is permanently left ignored.

NO

Global context. In the aftermath of World War II, the advance of liberal democracy was underpinned in significant ways by the global hegemony of the USA. This both gave US-style liberal democracy a powerful appeal worldwide and was reflected in the adoption by the USA of a strategy of 'democracy promotion', using diplomatic, economic and, sometimes, military means. However, the shift in global power, from the US-led West to Asia in particular, has not only diminished the USA's willingness and ability to promote democracy elsewhere, but also tarnished the US political and economic model. It is also notable that rising powers such as China and Russia represent very different political models.

Rise of illiberal democracy. Since the late 1990s, the democratization process has slowed down, leading to a 'democratic recession' in the first decade of the twenty-first century (Fukuyama, 2011). Instead of the overthrow of dictatorship and holding of elections leading irresistibly to democratic consolidation, many transition countries have been left, perhaps permanently, in a 'grey area'. These states have become 'managed' or 'illiberal' democracies, in which a form of electoral democracy operates alongside weak checks and balances, and the routine intimidation of oppositional forces. Such arrangements reflect the capacity of political elites to bend democratic politics to their own ends.

Discontents of liberal democracy. It is by no means clear that liberal democracy has performance advantages over other systems of rule. Liberal democracy's difficulties and discontents include: a tendency towards plutocracy, reflecting the fact that capitalism is ultimately incompatible with popular rule; a trend towards atomism and declining civic engagement; and trade-offs between personal freedom and majority opinion that flow from the inherent tension between liberalism and democracy. The rise of state capitalism also challenges the idea that liberal-democratic regimes will always be more prosperous than other regimes, and liberal democracy may be culturally unsuitable for the non-western world.

CONCEPT

Authoritarianism

Authoritarianism is a belief in, or practice of, government 'from above', in which authority is exercised regardless of popular consent. Authoritarianism thus differs from authority, as the latter rests on legitimacy, and so arises 'from below'. Authoritarian regimes emphasize the claims of authority over those of individual liberty. However, authoritarianism is usually distinguished from totalitarianism. Authoritarianism, associated with monarchical absolutism, traditional dictatorships, and most forms of military rule, seeks to exclude the masses from politics rather than abolish civil society.

rity because of the growth of unemployment and inflation, and it significantly increased social inequality. Since the heady days of the early 1990s, the pace of economic liberalization has sometimes been greatly reduced as a consequence of a backlash against market reforms, often expressed in growing support for communist or nationalist parties. A final set of problems result from the weakness of state power, particularly when the state is confronted by centrifugal forces effectively suppressed during the communist era. This has been most clearly demonstrated by the re-emergence of ethnic and nationalist tensions. The collapse of communism in the USSR was accompanied by the break-up of the old Soviet empire and the construction of 15 new independent states, several of which (including Russia) continue to be afflicted by ethnic conflict. Czechoslovakia ceased to exist in 1992 with the creation of the Czech Republic and Slovakia. Ethnic conflict was most dramatic in Yugoslavia, where it precipitated full-scale war between Serbia and Croatia in 1991, and led to civil war in Bosnia in 1992–96.

Important differences between postcommunist states can also be identified. The most crucial of these is that between the more industrially advanced and westernized countries of 'central' Europe, such as the Czech Republic, Hungary and Poland, and the more backward, 'eastern' states such as Romania, Bulgaria and, in certain respects, Russia. In the former group, market reform has proceeded swiftly and relatively smoothly; in the latter, it has either been grudging and incomplete, or it has given rise to deeper political tensions. This was reflected in early membership of the EU for the Czech Republic, Hungary, Poland, Slovakia, Slovenia and the Baltic states (Estonia, Latvia and Lithuania), achieved in 2004. However, Bulgaria and Romania joined the EU in 2007, with other Balkan postcommunist states, including Croatia, Albania, Bosnia-Herzegovina and Serbia, still waiting to join. Another distinction is between the states on which communism was 'imposed' by the Soviet Red Army at the end of World War II and those that were once part of the USSR. Since the late 1990s, the process of democratization in many successor states to the USSR has slowed down and, in some cases, been reversed, leaving them in what Carothers (2004) called a 'grey zone' between dictatorship and liberal democracy. In countries such as Moldova, Kazakhstan, Uzbekistan and Belarus, sometimes dubbed 'Europe's last dictatorship', an official acceptance of democratic legitimacy has been accompanied, albeit in different ways, by the systematic removal of checks on executive power and the erosion of the rule of law. In the case of Russia, the emergence of Putin as the government's leading force has led to a strengthening of executive control over television, the judiciary and the provinces, as well as a more ruthless approach to dealing with potential opponents. However, cracks in what has been portrayed variously as Russia's 'managed democracy' or 'electoral authoritarianism' became apparent after the parliamentary elections of December 2011, both because Putin's United Russia party saw its share of the vote drop to 49 per cent from 64 per cent four years earlier, and because of popular protests against vote rigging that were unprecedented for the Putin era.

East Asian regimes

The rise of East Asia from the final decades of the twentieth century onwards may ultimately prove to be a more important world-historical event than the

CONCEPT

Confucianism

Confucianism is a system of ethics formulated by Confucius (551–479 BCE) and his disciples that was primarily outlined in *The Analects*. Confucian thought has concerned itself with the twin themes of human relations and the cultivation of the self. The emphasis on *ren* (humanity or love) has usually been interpreted as implying support for traditional ideas and values; notably, filial piety, respect, loyalty and benevolence. The stress on *junzi* (the virtuous person) suggests a capacity for human development and potential for perfection realized, in particular, through education.

● **Asian values**: Values that supposedly reflect the history, culture and religious backgrounds of Asian societies; examples include social harmony, respect for authority and a belief in the family.

collapse of communism. Certainly, the balance of the world's economy shifted markedly from the West to the East in this period. Since the 1980s, economic growth rates on the western rim of the Pacific Basin have been between two and four times higher than those in the 'developed' economies of Europe and North America. However, the notion that there is a distinctively East Asian political form is a less familiar one. The widespread assumption has been that 'modernization' means 'westernization'. Translated into political terms, this implies that industrial capitalism is always accompanied by liberal democracy. Those who advance this position cite, for example, the success of Japan's 1946 constitution, bequeathed by the departing USA, and the introduction of multiparty elections in countries such as Thailand, South Korea and Taiwan in the 1980s and 1990s. However, this interpretation fails to take account of the degree to which polyarchical institutions operate differently in an Asian context from the way they do in a western one. Most importantly, it ignores the difference between cultures influenced by Confucian ideas and values, and those shaped by liberal individualism. This has led to the idea that there are a specific set of **Asian values** that are distinct from western ones, although this notion has attracted less attention since the Asian financial crisis of 1997/8.

East Asian regimes tend to have similar characteristics. First, they are orientated more around economic goals than around political ones. Their overriding priority is to boost growth and deliver prosperity, rather than to enlarge individual freedom in the western sense of civil liberty. This essentially practical concern is evident in the 'tiger' economies of East and South East Asia (those of South Korea, Taiwan, Hong Kong, Singapore and Malaysia), but it has also been demonstrated in the construction of a thriving market economy in China since the late 1970s, despite the survival there of monopolistic communist rule. Second, there is broad support for 'strong' government. Powerful 'ruling' parties tend to be tolerated, and there is general respect for the state. Although, with low taxes and relatively low public spending (usually below 30 per cent of GDP), there is little room for the western model of the welfare state, there is nevertheless general acceptance that the state as a 'father figure' should guide the decisions of private as well as public bodies, and draw up strategies for national development. This characteristic is accompanied, third, by a general disposition to respect leaders because of the Confucian stress on loyalty, discipline and duty. From a western viewpoint, this invests East Asian regimes with an implicit, and sometimes explicit, authoritarianism. Finally, great emphasis is placed on community and social cohesion, embodied in the central role accorded to the family. The resulting emphasis on what the Japanese call 'group think' tends to restrict the scope for the assimilation of ideas such as individualism and human rights, at least as these are understood in the West.

There is also differentiation between East Asian regimes. The most significant difference is that, although China's acceptance of capitalism has blurred the distinction between it and other East Asian regimes, profound political contrasts survive. China, in political terms at least, and North Korea, in both political and economic terms, are unreconstituted communist regimes, in which a monopolistic communist party still dominates the state machine. China's 'market Stalinism' contrasts sharply with the entrenched and successful electoral democracy of, for instance, Japan. Moreover, East Asian regimes are becoming industrialized and increasingly urbanized, China, despite its dramatic economic growth,

Theocracy

Theocracy (literally 'rule by God') is the principle that religious authority should prevail over political authority. A theocracy is therefore a regime in which government posts are filled on the basis of the person's position in the religious hierarchy. Theocratic rule is illiberal in two senses. First, it violates the public/private divide, in that it takes religious rules and precepts to be the guiding principles of both personal life and political conduct. Second, it invests political authority with potentially unlimited power, because, as temporal power is derived from spiritual wisdom, it cannot be based on popular consent, or be properly constrained within a constitutional framework.

● **Shari'a**: Islamic law, believed to be based on divine revelation, and derived from the Koran, the Hadith (the teachings of Muhammad), and other sources.

sill has a significant agricultural sector. To some extent, this also explains different modes of economic development. In Japan and 'tiger' economies such as Taiwan and Singapore, growth is now based largely on technological innovation, and an emphasis on education and training, whereas China continues, in certain respects, to rely on her massive rural population to provide cheap and plentiful labour. A final range of differences stems from cultural contrasts between overwhelmingly Chinese states such as Taiwan and China, and Japan and ethnically mixed states such as Singapore and Malaysia. For example, plans to introduce Confucian principles in Singapore schools were dropped for fear of offending the Malay and Indian populations. Similarly, Malaysian development has been based on a deliberate attempt to reduce Chinese influence and emphasize the distinctively Islamic character of Malay culture.

Islamic regimes

The rise of Islam as a political force has had a profound effect on politics in North Africa, the Middle East, and parts of Asia. In some cases, militant Islamic groups have challenged existing regimes, often articulating the interests of an urban poor since the disillusionment in the 1970s with Marxism–Leninism. In other cases, however, regimes have been constructed or reconstructed on Islamic lines. Since its inception in 1932, Saudi Arabia has been an Islamic state. The Iranian revolution of 1979 led to the establishment of an Islamic republic under Ayatollah Khomeini (see p. 164), an example later followed in Pakistan, the Sudan and Afghanistan.

Islam is not, however, and never has been, simply a religion. Rather, it is a complete way of life, defining correct moral, political and economic behaviour for individuals and nations alike. The 'way of Islam' is based on the teachings of the Prophet Muhammad (570–632) as revealed in the Koran, regarded by all Muslims as the revealed word of God, and the Sunna, or 'beaten path', the traditional customs observed by a devout Moslem that are said to be based on the Prophet's own life. Political Islam thus aims at the construction of a theocracy in which political and other affairs are structured according to 'higher' religious principles. Nevertheless, political Islam has assumed clearly contrasting forms, ranging from fundamentalist to pluralist extremes.

The fundamentalist version of Islam is most commonly associated with Iran. The Iranian system of government is a complex mix of theocracy and democracy. The Supreme Leader (currently Ali Khamenei) presides over a system of institutionalized clerical rule that operates through the Islamic Revolutionary Council, a body of 15 senior clerics. Although a popularly elected president and parliament have been established, all legislation is ratified by the Council for the Protection of the Constitution, which ensures conformity to Islamic principles. Shari'a law continues to be strictly enforced throughout Iran as both a legal and a moral code. The forces of revolutionary fundamentalism also asserted themselves through the Taliban regime in Afghanistan, 1997–2001, which was characterized by the imposition of strict theocratic rule and the exclusion of women from education, the economy and public life in general. Fundamentalism (see p. 53) is no less significant in Saudi Arabia, where it has similarly absolutist implications, although the temper of the essentially conservative Sunni regime in Saudi Arabia differs markedly from the revolutionary populism (see p. 307) of Shi'a Iran.

Turkey: between East and West?

Events: Although the republic of Turkey, founded in 1923 by Mustafa Kemal Atatürk (1881–1938), was firmly rooted in secularism, Islamist political parties have been gaining strength since the 1990s. The Welfare Party briefly led a coalition government in 1996, before being broken up by the army and, in the 2002 parliamentary elections, the Justice and Development Party (AKP) won two-thirds of the seats on the basis of 34 per cent of the vote (thanks to the 10 per cent electoral threshold, which excluded all but two parties from representation). In the 2007 election, AKP increased its share of the vote to 47 per cent, which rose again in 2011, this time reaching 50 per cent. Since 2003, AKP's leader Recep Tayyip Erdoğan has been prime minister and, when Abdullah Gül was appointed president in 2007, he became the first openly devout Muslim president in the history of modern Turkey.

Significance: Turkey, a country of 79 million people, lies at the crossroads of Europe and Asia. Its geographical position is, nevertheless, also reflected in its political character, which has been shaped by a shifting combination of polyarchic, military and Islamic features. In line with 'Kemalism' (after Kemal Atatürk), modern Turkey is a constitutional republic committed to the rule of law, popular sovereignty, and a strict separation of politics and religion. In this context, the rise of political Islam during the 1990s and, especially, the rule of the AKP since 2002 have raised major questions about the country's future political direction. Its critics warn that the AKP plans to overturn the secular nature of the Turkish state, possibly establishing an Iranian-style Islamic republic. The ban on the wearing of the Islamic headscarf in Turkish universities (only enforced since the 1980s) was lifted in 2010, and restrictions on the sale of alcohol have been imposed in some parts of Turkey. Turkey has also increasingly looked to build ties with the Arab world and has become increasingly critical of Israel (particularly after Israeli soldiers raided a Turkish-led aid flotilla heading for Gaza in May 2010, causing the deaths of nine Turkish civilians). However, supporters of the AKP argue that it practises a constitutional form of Islamism very different from that found in

Iran, in which moderate conservative politics based on Islamic values are balanced against an acceptance of Turkey's secular democratic framework. Rather than choosing between East and West, the AKP thus tries to establish a Turkish identity that is confident in being part of both. A key aspect of this compromise has been the quest, under the AKP, for membership of the EU, and, related to this, a willingness to introduce reforms in areas such as women's rights, and Kurdish language and cultural rights.

These developments have, nevertheless, had major implications for military-civilian relations in Turkey. The army played a crucial role in the establishment of the Turkish republic, coming to be the custodian of 'Kemalism' and establishing strong links to the bureaucracy, the judiciary and the media. Four times between 1960 and 1997, Turkey's generals have staged military *coups*, the last of which forced from office the country's first Islamist prime minister. While some see the 1 million strong army as the greatest obstacle to Turkey's onward march towards democracy and EU membership, others view it as the vital guarantee of secular and open politics, an obstacle preventing the AKP's moderate Islamism from becoming revolutionary Islamism. Although relations between the AKP government and Turkey's generals remain frayed, a gradual shift in power from the military to civilians, with, for instance, the military becoming more accountable to civilian courts, creates the possibility that the Turkish army may, in future, remain in barracks and out of politics.

CONCEPT

Dictatorship

A dictatorship is, strictly, a form of rule in which absolute power is vested in one individual; in this sense, dictatorship is synonymous with autocracy. Dictators are thus seen as being above the law and as acting beyond constitutional constraints. Early examples of dictators were Sulla, Julius Caesar and Augustus Caesar in Rome, more recent ones are Hitler, Mussolini and Saddam Hussein. More generally, dictatorship is characterized by the arbitrary and unchecked exercise of power, as in 'class dictatorship', 'party dictatorship', 'military dictatorship' and 'personal dictatorship'.

Muslims themselves, however, have often objected to the classification of any Islamic regime as 'fundamentalist', on the grounds that this perpetuates long-established western prejudices against an 'exotic' or 'repressive' East, serving as examples of 'orientalism' (Said, 1978). Evidence that Islam is compatible with a form of political pluralism can be found in Malaysia. Although Islam is the official state religion of Malaysia, with the Paramount Ruler serving as both religious leader and head of state, a form of 'guided' democracy operates as the dominance of the United Malays National Organization (UMNO), operating as a broad coalition, the Barisan Nasional, and within a multiparty framework. The UMNO has, since 1981, pursued a narrowly Islamic and pro-Malay strategy fused with an explicitly Japanese model of economic development. Authoritarian tendencies have, nevertheless, re-emerged since 1988, when the independence of the judiciary effectively collapsed following a wave of political arrests and the imposition of press censorship. Turkey also offers an interesting example of the relationship between Islam and democracy (see p. 280), as does the Arab Spring and developments in countries such as Egypt, Tunisia and Libya.

Military regimes

Whereas most regimes are shaped by a combination of political, economic, cultural and ideological factors, some survive through the exercise, above all, of military power and systematic repression. In this sense, military regimes belong to a broader category of dictatorship. Military dictatorship has been most common in Latin America, the Middle East, Africa and Southeast Asia, but it also emerged in the post-1945 period in Spain, Portugal and Greece. The key feature of a military regime is that the leading posts in the government are filled on the basis of the person's position within the military chain of command. Normal political and constitutional arrangements are usually suspended, and institutions through which opposition can be expressed, such as elected assemblies and a free press, are either weakened or abolished.

Although all forms of military rule are deeply repressive, this classification encompasses a number of regime types. In some military regimes, the armed forces assume direct control of government. The classical form of this is the military junta, most commonly found in Latin America. This operates as a form of collective military government centred on a command council of officers who usually represent the three armed services: the army, navy and air force. *Junta* regimes are often characterized by rivalry between the services and between leading figures, the consequence being that formal positions of power tend to change hands relatively frequently.

The second form of military regime is a military-backed personalized dictatorship. In these cases, a single individual gains pre-eminence within the *junta* or regime, often being bolstered by a cult of personality (see p. 302) designed to manufacture charismatic authority. Examples are Colonel Papadopoulos in Greece in 1974–80, General Pinochet in Chile after the 1973 military *coup*, and General Abacha in Nigeria, 1993–98. In the final form of military regime, the loyalty of the armed forces is the decisive factor that upholds the regime, but the military leaders content themselves with 'pulling the strings' behind the scenes. This, for example, occurred in post-1945 Brazil, as the armed forces generally recognized that the legitimacy of the regime would be strengthened by the

● *Junta*: (Spanish) Literally, 'a council'; a (usually military) clique that seizes power through a revolution or *coup d'état*.

maintenance of a distinction between political and military offices and personnel. Such a distinction, however, may fuel an appetite for constitutional and representative politics, and reduce the scope for direct military intervention, thereby, over time, encouraging polyarchical tendencies. However, in what circumstances does the military seize power? Military *coups* appear to be associated with four key sets of circumstances. In the first place, there is a clear link between the incidence of military *coups* and economic underdevelopment. The vast majority of countries that have experienced military government are in the developing world. By the same token, growing prosperity appears to be an antidote to military intervention, as demonstrated by the tendency in Latin America, since the 1970s, for the military to return to the barracks. Second, the military is likely to intervene in politics only when it senses that the legitimacy of the existing institutions and the ruling elite is challenged, and when it calculates that its intervention is going to be successful. The armed forces thus rarely interfere directly in politics when a stable democratic culture has been successfully established. Third, military intervention is associated with the degree to which the values, goals and interests of the armed forces differ from those of the broader regime. In many newly-independent developing states, the military thus took over to 'save the nation', seeing itself as a 'westernizing' or 'modernizing' force confronting a traditionalist, rural, hierarchical and frequently divided political elite. This, for instance, occurred in Nigeria, Indonesia and Pakistan. Finally, the military's decision to seize power may also be affected by international considerations. In some cases, international pressures undoubtedly encourage military action. This was clearly the case with the Pinochet *coup* in Chile. Not only did Pinochet receive covert advice and encouragement from the US Central Intelligence Agency (CIA), but he was also guaranteed US diplomatic support once his new military regime was established.

SUMMARY

- Government is any mechanism through which ordered rule is maintained, its central feature being its ability to make collective decisions and enforce them. A political system, or regime, however, encompasses not only the mechanisms of government and institutions of the state, but also the structures and processes through which these interact with the larger society.

- The classification of political systems serves two purposes. First, it aids understanding by making comparison possible, and helping to highlight similarities and differences between otherwise shapeless collections of facts. Second, it helps us to evaluate the effectiveness or success of different political systems.

- Regimes have been classified on a variety of bases. 'Classical' typologies, stemming from Aristotle, concentrated on constitutional arrangements and institutional structures, while the 'three worlds' approach highlighted material and ideological differences between the systems found in 'first world' capitalist, 'second world' communist and 'third world' developing states.

- The collapse of communism and advance of democratization have made it much more difficult to identify the political contours of the modern world, making conventional systems of classification redundant. It is, nevertheless, still possible to distinguish between regimes on the basis of how their political, economic and cultural characteristics interlock in practice, even though all systems of classification are provisional.

- 'End of history' theorists have proclaimed that history has ended, or is destined to end, with the worldwide triumph of western liberal democracy. Indeed, the most common form of regime in the modern world is now some form of democracy. However, there is evidence that regime types have become both more complex and more diverse. Significant differences can be identified among western polyarchies, new democracies, East Asian regimes, Islamic regimes and military regimes.

- Those who view democratization as an irresistable process usually argue that, once instigated, democratic reform gains an internal momentum, deriving from the ways in which the holding of competitive elections alter public expectations about the political process. Others, however, point out that many transition countries have been left, perhaps permanently in a 'grey area' between democracy and authoritarianism.

Questions for discussion

- Does Aristotle's system of political classification have any relevance to the modern world?
- Is there any longer such a thing as the 'third world'?
- To what extent have postcommunist regimes discarded their communist past?
- Why have liberal-democratic structures proved to be so effective and successful?
- Have some new democracies got stuck in a 'grey zone' between dictatorship and liberal democracy?
- How democratic are western polyarchies?
- Do Confucianism and Islamism constitute viable alternatives to western liberalism as a basis for a modern regime?
- Are military regimes doomed to be short-lived?

Further reading

Brooker, P., *Non-Democratic Regimes; Theory, Government and Politics* (2009). A useful and wide-ranging survey of the different forms of non-democratic regime.

Carothers, T., *Critical Mission: Essays on Democracy Promotion* (2004). A stimulating collection of essays that reflect on strategies for aiding democracy and the nature of the democratic process.

Hague, R. and M. Harrop, *Comparative Government and Politics: An Introduction* (2013). A succinct and stimulating introduction to comparative politics that adopts a genuinely international approach.

Lijphart, A., *Patterns of Democracy: Government Forms and Performance in Thirty-Six Countries* (1999). An updated version of a classic and highly influential attempt to distinguish between forms of democratic rule.

Chapter 6

Power

Introduction

Open any book on Politics and we do not have to turn too many pages before seeing the concept of power discussed. Indeed, the pursuit and exercise of power is traditionally presented as the very cut and thrust of both domestic and international politics, and theorists go to great lengths to conceptualize and contextualize this power. Politicians go into politics to be able to exercise 'power' in order to achieve their personal and party political objectives; electorates may be said to exercise power when they choose who governs them. Power can also be exercised in the suppression or expression of a particular political debate or issue. Power might be the property of individuals, or might be located within systems. Power may be a 'thing' or it may be a process. So what do we really understand by the concept of power? In seeking to do political analysis for ourselves how should we approach the subject of power? There will certainly be questions that need addressing such as: what is power? Who has it? Where is it located? How is it exercised? In whose interest does it operate? The ontological and epistemological approaches we adopt will also largely determine how we explore 'power'. Because of the assumptions that we make prior to our analysis about what is possible to establish, our theoretical perspectives emphasize different facets of power. Indeed, so important is the concept of power to Politics that in each of the subsequent chapters we address the implications for, and the impact of, power on each of the topics covered. In locating the sources, exercise and consequences of power we are able to analyze and interpret how individuals, states and systems operate in domestic and international spheres.

In this chapter, we seek to provide an overview of the different ways in which power is conceptualized. Using Steven Lukes' seminal text *Power: A Radical View* (1974) as a starting point, we examine his three dimensions of power to discover how such understandings of power can serve as an analytical tool. In doing so, we explore pluralist, elitist and Marxist approaches to power and how these fit into theories of power that have grown up within Political Science and IR. We consider: realism, in its classical and neo-realist variants; liberal institutionalism; neo-Marxism; world systems theory, with its global stratification of class; feminism; constructivism; and poststructuralism. Through outlining these different approaches, we highlight the contested nature of power. Indeed, a number of these theories reject the very idea that they are concerned with power, arguing that they are about cooperation or identity, providing an antidote or a different way of looking at the world other than through the prism of power relationships. We argue, however, that the way in which power is studied is crucial in all aspects of Politics. In short, what this chapter seeks to do is to discover what power is and how we can study it.

Three dimensions of power

In 1974, Steven Lukes produced a small book entitled *Power: A Radical View* which neatly encapsulates three different approaches to power: the one-dimensional behaviouralist view pioneered by Robert Dahl (1957, 1958, 1961), a slightly more critical two-dimensional view championed by Peter Bachrach and Morton S. Baratz (1970) and Lukes' own three-dimensional view, which criticizes the behavioural focus of the first two dimensions. Robert Dahl's work has been heavily influential in a school of thought known as pluralism. Dahl studied the behaviour of political elites by examining all the decisions taken in the policy-making process in New Haven, Connecticut. During the period of his study he observed who initiated, vetoed or proposed alternatives and who had their initiatives turned down and by whom. A positive and negative ratio recording defeats and successes was tabulated, which, according to Dahl, was sufficient to determine who had most power or influence (Dahl, 1961). (The terms 'power' and 'influence' are often used interchangeably by pluralists.) The underlying normative assumption held by Dahl (as with other pluralists) is that government's role is to mediate between differing interests. Power or influence is assumed to be located in political actors (we can establish this assumption, as this is who Dahl observed, and, following observation of their behaviour, went on to make claims about their power). For pluralists, then, the amount of power that political actors have can be determined simply by observing who gets what, when and how, in the decision-making process.

In Dahl's formulation power can be defined as A having power over B to the extent that A can get B to do something they would not otherwise do (Dahl, 1957; Lukes, 1974: 11–12). This view of power has been the most influential approach to understanding power because of its simplicity. This one-dimensional view of power focuses on the behaviour of political actors who are involved in decision-making; it prioritizes the key issues and looks for observable conflict. Participation in the political process reveals interests as policy preferences (Lukes, 1974: 25). Dahl's formulation relies on overt observation, which is readily available in the public domain. But what about those decisions that are not observable, which take place outside formal decision-making structures?

Bachrach and Baratz argue that power has two aspects – Dahl's one-dimensional view *and* Schattschneider's (1960) 'mobilization of bias'. They posit that political scientists should not just be concerned with observable behaviour but also with that which takes place beyond public scrutiny. In particular, who, what, why and how is it determined what is to be included or excluded from decision-making? For Bachrach and Baratz personal or group power is manifest to the extent 'that a person or group – consciously or unconsciously – creates or reinforces barriers to the public airing of policy conflicts' (Bachrach and Baratz, 1970: 8). In distinguishing between overt and covert faces of power, where those exercising power are able to determine what is included or excluded from discussion, Bachrach and Baratz challenge Dahl's assumptions of an open and democratic process. They argue that the mobilization of bias determines what is included and excluded from the decision-making process. In this way the vested interests of individuals or groups are able to control policy agendas. In short, power is still assumed to be identifiable through the observation of the behaviour of individuals (as with Dahl's formulation). However, power in this view lies in the capacity to determine which decisions get made and, crucially, which don't (non-decisions). Power is the ability to 'set the agenda'. For example, there is no longer discussion in the UK about unilateral nuclear disarmament, which, within this perspective, would represent power being exercised by political elites (and the nuclear industry?) in their ability to keep this issue from the public agenda.

Those who determine such decisions or non-decisions are policy elites who can mobilize through:

> A set of predominant values, beliefs, rituals, and institutional proce-dures ('rules of the game') that operate systematically and consistently to the benefit of certain persons and groups at the expense of others. Those who benefit are placed in a preferred position to defend and promote their vested interests. (Bachrach and Baratz, 1970: 43–4)

Whereas Dahl and other pluralists predetermine what are, or are not, political issues through insisting on observerability, Bachrach and Baratz also try to discover those political issues that non-decision-making prevents from taking place, thereby wholly or partly excluding people from the political system (Lukes, 1974: 19–20). Lukes describes this position as a two-dimensional view of power, which includes a qualified critique of behaviouralism and focuses on decision-making and non-decision-making, issues and potential issues, overt and covert observable conflict, and policy preferences or grievances defined as interests (Lukes, 1974: 25). Here, then, we can see that power is still assumed to be observable and the property of individuals.

Lukes challenges the two-dimensional view outlined above, arguing there is a third dimension to power. Power has structural features, he suggests, and, while the two previous approaches highlight the exercise of power as located at a site of conflict, in the structural view, power in the third dimension is the prevention of conflict emerging in the first place. Power is thus more than just conflict; it is also about manipulation and authority (Lukes, 1974: 23):

> Decisions are choices consciously and intentionally made by individuals between alternatives, whereas the bias of the system can be mobilised, recreated and reinforced in ways that are neither consciously chosen nor the intended result of particular individual's choices. (Lukes, 1974: 21)

Lukes argues that it is not enough to simply examine open conflict or consider what is and is not discussed (as suggested by the first two dimensions); we also need to recognize that 'the most effective and insidious use of power' actually prevents conflict even happening (Lukes, 1974: 23). Herein lie the seeds of latent conflict where the real interests of the people represented are diametrically opposed to the interests of their representatives. Lukes warns that just because there might appear to be an absence of grievance it is not necessarily the case. Indeed, a grievance consensus can be reached by a 'false or manipulated consensus' (Lukes, 1974: 24). By this Lukes does not imply a Marxist false consciousness of privileged access to truths but rather the 'power to mislead' people (Lukes, 1974: 149). Lukes critiques behaviouralist approaches to power and instead focuses on decision-making and considerations of who controls the political agenda, which is not always through decisions being taken. For Lukes, both the issues and potential issues are important. He is concerned about observable conflict but also latent conflict, and not simply subjective interests but also real interests (Lukes, 1974: 25). Lukes widens Dahl's formulation that *A has power over B to the extent to which A can get B to do something B would not otherwise do* to *A exercises power over B when A affects B in a manner contrary to B's interests* (Lukes, 1974: 34).

Approaches to power

Pluralism, elitism and Marxism

The discussion above has focused on Lukes' three dimensions of power. In this next section, we briefly reprise the key aspects of pluralism and elitism before introducing Marxist approaches to power. Pluralism takes both a positivist and subjectivist approach to power in which the subject discovers power relationships and seeks to identify who prevails in decision-making. The decisions, which are taken, involve real and observable conflict, the outcomes of which determine whether or not there is a ruling elite. Power is about consciously made and articulated decisions (or preferences) resulting in conflict. For the pluralist, preferences are always articulated, observable and actors are always aware of their own interests without being mistaken (Dahl, 1958: 463–9; Lukes, 1974: 13–14).

Bachrach and Baratz's neo-elitism is somewhat softer than the approach of C. Wright Mills or Lasswell, for example, who saw a powerful elite existing in the United States, where the holders of power use it to advance their own interests and prevent others achieving their objectives (Wright Mills, 1956; Lasswell, 1936). For elitists, power is a permanent feature of political life and even human existence (Dunleavy and O'Leary, 1987: 148). Classical elitists and ruling-class theorists including Pareto, Mosca and Michels would subscribe to this position. A key criticism of both elitist and pluralist theories, with their common subjectivist core, is that they only consider one form of power and are unable to account for social change (Therborn, 1982: 229–30). Dahl, Bachrach, Baratz and Lukes, despite different emphases, are all subjectivists and concentrate on interrelationships to the exclusion of other aspects of power. The key question for them is the study of power 'in' society rather than power 'over' society. They want to know who governs in society, whether it is an elite or competing leadership groups, and how stable such groupings are:

> What they have been debating is whether there is an *interpersonal* relation between the different moments of power in society; Is there a cohesive elite which unites the different exercises of power by making the decisions in different areas? (Therborn, 1982: 230)

This rather narrow perspective on power, about who governs in any given polity, is expanded considerably by Marxist approaches that question the focus of pluralists and elitists. Why should the study of society be so restricted when it could, and they would argue should, also include the process of reproduction. Therborn argues that in adopting this approach, the key question now becomes: 'What kinds of society, what fundamental relations of production, are being produced?' (Therborn, 1982: 232).

Marxist approaches emphasize that the relationship to the means of production determines class relationships based on exploitation and domination. The two key classes within capitalism are the bourgeoisie and the proletariat: those who control the means of production and those who are exploited. While pluralism and elitism focus on the subject holding or exercising power, Marxist approaches are more concerned with relationships to the means of production and the way in which the ruling class is organized to maintain and develop capitalism (Therborn, 1982).

The perpetuation of domination and exploitation sets the basis for class rule in which the given social structure and the individuals who occupy positions within it are reproduced, thereby enabling capitalism to develop (Therborn, 1982: 233; Poulantzas, 1973a: 49). Some neo-Marxists, such as Althusser (1967, 1969) and Poulantzas (1967), analyze the structures which support the exercise of power in society, arguing that the way society is organized is itself a power relationship. Domination and exploitation, in this understanding, are built into societies' 'social structures and practices' (Joseph, 1988: 49). Pluralist, elitist and Marxist approaches, which we have discussed from a Political Science perspective, also resonate within the field of IR and in the next section we will seek to develop these themes.

Realism

Realism purports to describe the world as it really is, to get to the basics of how the world actually operates, how countries interact with one another and what their role and purpose is. In brief, classical and neo-realists (also known as structural realists) are united in their identification of statism, survival and self-help as the way the world operates. Statism highlights states as the key international actors, even in a globalized world with international organizations and transnational actors. States in this view operate as rational and autonomous actors in pursuit of their own national interest. In an international system, unlike domestic systems, there is no overarching authority and sovereign states must compete for power and ensure their survival in an anarchical world. In the last resort, states have to rely on themselves to ensure their survival.

Realists are the power theorists in IR. Drawing on a classical literature that dates back at least as far as Thucydides' history of the Peloponnesian wars (431–404 BCE), and includes Sun Tzu's *The Art of War*, Niccolò Machiavelli's *The Prince* (1532) and Thomas Hobbes' *Leviathan* (1651), realists form a particular worldview through the prism of power. Classical realists emphasize human nature as a main driver for international relations. They adopt a pessimistic view of human nature that suggests that if there is no overarching authority then humans will pursue their own interests, selfishly and to the detriment of others. In other words, they will seek to maximize their own power. In a world in which every state is compelled to act in the same way, the most successful will be those with most power. The greater the power the state has, the greater its prospects of survival.

When realists talk of power, what they really mean is military power, the ability of the state to achieve its objectives and ensure its survival because it has the military capability to do so. Clearly, power is not evenly distributed and states will be involved in an ongoing competition for greater power. Pecking orders are established and either accepted or contested based on power distribution. States are 'powerful to the extent that they affect others more than others affect them' (Goldstein and Pevehouse, 2010: 45). Realists expect states to behave in certain ways based on their interpretation of human nature, which Hans Morgenthau, describes as 'the desire to live, to propagate, and to dominate' (Morgenthau, 1955: 30). Powerful states in such thinking are obliged to act in such a way that maximizes their power and prevents challenges emerging. Thucydides depicts the Peloponnesian wars as a conflict in which Sparta and Athens are both obliged to go to war, the former to avoid domination by Athens and the latter to preserve its empire. Further down the pecking order, the islanders of Melos are given a salutary lesson in the realist worldview when caught up in the war between Sparta and Athens and given an ultimatum to surrender by the Athenians:

> you know as well as we do that, when these matters are discussed by practical people, the standard of justice depends on the equality of power to compel and that in fact the strong do what they have the power to do and the weak accept what they have to accept. (Thucydides, 1954: 360)

For realists, power and justice are a matter of a capacity, which do not just depend on the size, quality and preparedness of the military and its weaponry, although this is crucial, but also on a state's ability to attract allies, its diplomacy, the size of its economic strength and territory, its geographical terrain and location, and natural resources. Weaker states will need to appease or satisfy the interests of stronger states in order to survive or form alliances with rival strong states, thus balancing the power of opposing stronger states. Alternatively, weak states could choose to ally with the strongest state, or hegemon, to promote national interests as far as possible within prescribed limits. States constantly have to adapt to the changing configurations of power that occur within international politics. Realists tend to divide the world up into great, middle and small powers and focus on military polarity to describe world order. In this view, we can see how the multipolarity of the nineteenth- and early twentieth-century great powers gave way to the bipolarity of the Cold War era and subsequent unipolarity, with the United States as global hegemon (following the fall of the Berlin Wall).

Structural realists, inspired by Kenneth Waltz during the Cold War, agree with classical realists that international politics is all about the struggle for power but rather than emphasize that this is due to human nature, argue that it owes more to the anarchic structure of the international system and the relative distribution of power within it. Waltz argues that anarchy creates an international environment in which each state has to protect its own interests and seek to maximize its own security. While all states have different capabilities we can only understand international outcomes through recognizing those differences, the number of great powers that exist and the rank order of each of them. For Waltz, power is simply a means to the greater end of achieving security for the state. Indeed, power maximization might be counterproductive by persuading other states to join forces to counterbalance against the power-maximizing state (Waltz, 1979, 1989).

> The opportunity and at times the necessity of using force distinguishes ... the balances of power that form inside a state ... The balance of power among states becomes a balance of all the capabilities, including physical force, that states choose to use in pursuing their goals. (Waltz, 1959: 205)

For Waltz, the most stable form of world order is one based on bipolarity where nuclear weapons and the threat of mutually assured destruction equalize military power and therefore maximize security. John Mearsheimer, however, rejects this defensive premise and adopts a structural realism that emphasizes offensive capability. He argues that, in an uncertain world, it is impossible to second guess rivals' intentions and therefore states need to maximize their military might. There can be no satisfied or status quo states but each must seek to increase their relative power against other states. Rather than seeing bipolarity as ideal, Mearsheimer looks to a global hegemon as the most stable world order, albeit one that is continually tested by great power rivalry (Mearsheimer, 2003).

If we return for a moment to Lukes' three dimensions of power, then a realist understanding of power in its various classical, defensive and offensive structural guises lies within the approach adopted by Robert Dahl: power and security maximization both involve state A persuading state B to do what it would not otherwise do. The extent to which it is successful in doing so indicates the power that the state has within the international system. We can know this takes place based upon our observation of behaviour of political actors (for realism these are states).

Realists argue that there are fundamental differences between hierarchical domestic politics, where the state imposes order on its citizens, and anarchical international politics, where there is survival of the fittest or most powerful. As a result, realists argue that domestic and international politics need to be considered independently. Realists are largely unconcerned with politics at the domestic level, considering that they have little bearing on decisions taken at the international level. Given the dominance of realism in IR in the post-war era, we can perhaps also understand why within IR it sees itself as distinct from the remit of Political Science.

Epistemologically, the realist claim is to objectivity: through empirical observation they argue that the social scientist standing outside events is able to record the world as it actually is. In this perspective 'the evidence' reveals an international system where states are forced to maximize power and/or security. States behave the way they do because, as rational actors who make an ontological assumption of the existence of an anarchical world order, they cannot do anything else.

Realists deny that their approach is overtly normative. Faced with accusations that their worldview is amoral, or even immoral, realists argue that international morality consists in the survival of the state to enable it to continue to pursue domestic politics. Such a position, however, does have significant normative implications, laying realists open to the charge that in seeking to maximize security and/or power and reifying the state, they promote a world order in which such thinking becomes the norm and a conflictual world order a self-fulfilling prophecy.

Liberal institutionalism

Liberal views of world politics tend to be rather more optimistic about human nature and seek to emphasize cooperation and interdependence rather than antagonism and power maximization. Whereas realism separates domestic and international politics, liberalism considers that international politics develop from the domestic realm. John Locke's three *Letters Concerning Toleration* (1689–92), *Two Treatises on Government* (1690) and *An Essay Concerning Human Understanding* (1690) underpin subsequent liberal thinking. Locke advances a theory of government within states and good governance between states and their peoples. Good governance consisting of order, liberty, justice and tolerance at the domestic level is the blueprint for an international order based on those same values. As Tim Dunne would have it: 'In a sense, the historical project of liberalism is the domestication of the international' (Dunne, 2008: 110).

Immanuel Kant develops this theme in his *Perpetual Peace: A Philosophical Essay*, arguing that a peaceful world order could exist among like-minded states, which were republican and liberal. For a 'perpetual peace' to exist Kant (1795) insists that nine points must be established, which he summarizes in six preliminary articles:

1. 'No Treaty of Peace Shall Be Held Valid in Which There Is Tacitly Reserved Matter for a Future War
2. No Independent States, Large or Small, Shall Come under the Dominion of Another State by Inheritance, Exchange, Purchase, or Donation
3. Standing Armies (miles perpetuus) Shall in Time Be Totally Abolished
4. National Debts Shall Not Be Contracted with a View to the External Friction of States
5. No State Shall by Force Interfere with the Constitution or Government of Another State
6. No State Shall, *during* War, Permit Such Acts of Hostility Which Would Make Mutual Confidence in the Subsequent Peace Impossible: Such Are the Employment of Assassins (percussores), Poisoners (venefici), Breach of Capitulation, and Incitement to Treason (perduellio) in the Opposing State.'

Three Definitive Articles provide a foundation on which a lasting peace could be established and perpetuated:

1. 'The Civil Constitution of Every State Should Be Republican
2. The Law of Nations Shall be *Founded on* a Federation of Free States
3. The Law of World Citizenship Shall Be Limited to Conditions of Universal Hospitality.'

Whatever the merits of Kant's claims, what is apparent here is that such thinking represents a radical departure from realist thought. Kant's premise that domestic governance has international implications and application is anathema to realists. The rejection of unjust treaties and contracts, domination, the ending of standing armies, non-interference in the internal affairs of other countries fly in the face of all that realists hold dear. Here, Kant presents a world that is interconnected and interdependent, where power is of secondary consideration to cooperation and mutual benefit. Woodrow Wilson took up and developed these themes during and after World War I. Wilson's *Fourteen Points* found expression in a League of Nations that substituted balance of power politics for collective security and, in principle, the right of self-determination. Power, in its military context, when it is used is to be exercised collectively in defence of maintaining peace. The failure of this liberal experiment, resulting in a second world war, ushered in the dominant realist paradigm in international relations. This paradigm is inspired by E. H. Carr's forensic analysis of the failings of liberalism to prevent war and the necessity to see the world as it really is, rather than how it ought to be in an ideal world (see Carr, 1946).

Liberalism refuses to be restricted to realism's prioritization of military and strategic power. Trade and commerce are also of importance and states develop organizations and rules of conduct to facilitate this. Greater interaction will encourage best practice between states in terms of governance and promote peace through the reciprocal benefit of trade. Liberal institutionalists argue that rational actors are able and willing to forgo short-term gains for longer-term benefits and that what matters are not relative gains but absolute gains benefiting all states involved in transactions. The risk of cheating or resort to violence can be overcome through institutionalizing processes of trade and other international relations in international institutions. International institutions and international law enable states to develop confidence in the good faith of other states while acknowledging that it is in each national interest to cooperate. The rules and expectations, which facilitate cooperation, become embedded and normalized.

Although the international system is still anarchic the worst and most violent excesses can be ameliorated by working together in permanent institutions such as the World Bank, International Monetary Fund, or the World Trade Organization. For liberal institutionalists the realist problem of state survival has largely been overcome through participation in security regimes such as the United Nations, NATO or the European Union. In this new world, it is transnational actors, transnational corporations and international non-governmental organizations rather than states as such that are increasingly important (Keohane and Nye, 1972, 1977). When states act, they should use more tools than are available in the realist box, including soft power, the power to attract rather than naked aggression (Nye, 2004). For liberal institutionalists, institutions are actually an antidote to power and the way forward for a more pacific world (see Keohane, 1984).

Liberalism overtly rejects the military associations of power, rather than power per se. Liberalism focuses its attention on the actions and behaviour of key political actors, NGOs and organizations. Power, in this perspective, is exercised through the facilitation of cooperation at elite level. Power is observable and in the hands of elite-level actors, with shades of both pluralism and elitism characterizing this perspective, as outlined in Lukes' first two dimensions of power.

Although liberal institutionalists seek to distance themselves from realist or military power, with their emphasis on interdependence, they nonetheless perpetuate power relationships through 'the control actors exercise indirectly over others through diffuse relations of interaction' and the 'behavioural constraints and governing biases of institutions' (Barrett and Durrell, 2005: 43, 52). E. H. Carr castigates the claims of those who present international institutions as an antidote to power as mere hubris. He contends that the idea that these institutions represent a gain for all parties is deceitful and that they introduce a new set of power relations of dependency and exploitation that leads to domination as surely as military power. This is achieved through those dominated submitting to their own domination through a false consciousness that the international system operates for mutual benefit (Barrett and Durrell, 2005: 68; Carr, 1946).

Neo-Marxism

Marxist approaches to power in international relations have their origins in Lenin's *Imperialism, the Highest Stage of Capitalism* (1917). Lenin argues that as capitalism reached its highest state of development in the industrialized countries of Europe, monopoly capitalism developed, which in order to generate sufficient profit necessitated exporting excess capital abroad. In order to control this, the major powers acquire and seek to maintain colonies with the super-profits generated returned to them. European capitalists and skilled labourers are financially rewarded, reducing the latter's revolutionary potential. Lenin concludes that the new proletariat in this developing world, such as Russia, possessed greater revolutionary potential at capitalism's weakest point. The revolutionary fervour of the new proletariat, he argues, would then spread to the developed world. Power resided with the monopoly capitalists of the colonial powers, but this would be taken from them by proletarian revolution.

Lenin, along with all Marxist theorists, sees society, and indeed the world, as divided by class. In an international system where there is an uneven distribution of capital and resources, not only do class relationships of exploiter and exploited prevail, but also the proletariat is divided between developed and developing states and the idea of harmony of interests among all workers is lost. The nature of capitalism necessitates that the world system is considered in its entirety to determine who has power and how these power relationships work out. What can be observed is that class relations now exist around the world and the total accumulation of the surplus value produced by labour moves from poor developing countries to the rich developed ones. If the developing countries of the global South retain their surplus they would be considerably better off and yet neo-Marxists would argue they are constrained from doing so by false consciousness and the constraints of an international system based on the needs of global capitalism. This suppression of interests is also articulated in Lukes' third dimension of power, to which Marxist approaches are often linked.

The basic unfairness of the capitalist system and its attendant power structures are evident in all modern societies and yet Marx's prediction of workers rising up and casting off the chains that bind them has largely failed to materialize. Antonio Gramsci (1971) rejects traditional Marxist teaching that emphasizes state violence, politically and economically coercive practices, as an inadequate or incomplete explanation of why the masses fail to rise up. Instead, he presents a conceptualization of power that introduces the concept of hegemony. Here, it is not so much coercion as consent that determines working-class passivity. Consent is produced and reproduced by societal institutions such as the media, the education system, third-sector organizations and religious institutions, which are at least partly autonomous from the state (Hobden and Wyn Jones, 2008: 150).

Whereas traditionally Marxists consider that the base of socio-economic relations is the dominant aspect in explaining power relations, Gramsci insists that the superstructure of political and cultural practices is more significant. The interaction of the base and superstructure is the key to understanding hegemony. The 'mutually reinforcing and reciprocal relationships' between socio-economic relations, culture and ideology serves to strengthen the existing capitalist order (Hobden and Wyn Jones, 2008: 150). Rather than coercion, the working class cooperates in their own subjugation by absorbing and reproducing bourgeois values and aspirations. Ruling-class values become normalized and, if unchallenged, maintain the existing status quo. The only antidote to this ruling-class hegemony, Gramsci suggests, is to build a counter-hegemonic struggle leading to the creation of an alternative power bloc. Given the international character of global capitalism, IR and international political economy, theorists in the Gramscian tradition, argue that the counter-hegemonic struggle needs to take place at the level of national and international civil society. The anti-globalization, solidarity, global justice movements and international labour organizations with emancipatory agendas fit within this Gramscian tradition.

Robert Cox has emerged as one of the leading thinkers in linking Gramsci's hegemony within individual capitalist states to the international sphere (see Cox, 1981, 1983, 1987). Cox argues that dominant powers in the international system have shaped the world for their own benefit using both coercion and consent. The most successful, like the United States, are able to reproduce systems and values that advance their hegemony. The universal norms of world hegemony are established in part by international organizations. Cox describes the features that express this hegemonic role:

> (1) the institutions embody the rules which facilitate the expansion of hegemonic world orders; (2) they are themselves the product of the world order; (3) they ideologically legitimate the norms of world order; (4) they co-opt the elites from peripheral countries; and (5) they absorb counter-hegemonic ideas. (Cox, 2010: 222)

International organizations and institutions are established and exist to perpetuate and advance dominant social and economic forces throughout the world. The rules are set by the hegemonic state with the cooperation of a hierarchy of other states – for example, the United States in the Bretton Woods Agreements. The international institutions perform an ideological role shaping a discourse and universal norms that reinforce a dominant consensus, which reflects the interest of the core countries. Talented members of elites in the developing world are co-opted into the organizations, reducing the prospects for a counter-hegemonic movement (Cox, 2010: 223).

Where Gramsci identifies workers absorbing ruling-class values Cox identifies developing nations' acceptance of free trade, which operates in the interest of developed countries. For Cox, traditional theories of IR perpetuate and seek to legitimate the existing world order. Realism and structural realism in particular present a worldview that is not subject to change because either human nature or the international system will always serve to maintain inequalities of power. Realists reinforce the status quo which favours ruling elites in the industrialized world and perpetuates the subordinate status of the global south.

Cox rejects the notion of a scientific, value-free, positivist approach to international relations, insisting that '[t]heory is always for someone, and for some purpose' (Cox, 1981: 128). The theoretical impulse to solve problems actually masks an agenda that maintains the existing order. Instead, critical theory (which is derived from Marxist thought) has emancipatory potential to understand the existing system and its unequal power relationships and how those dynamics can be transformed to create a fairer world. Cox is clear though that the existing structure of the world order cannot be changed by international movements or wresting control of international institutions. A new historic bloc can only emerge through building up a national socio-political base for change (Cox, 2010: 224).

Another way of understanding power relationships in a global capitalist system, which has its origins in Marxist thought, is world system theory. World system theorists expand the class struggle within states and use a global analysis to project regional class divisions. For IR scholars such as Immanuel Wallerstein (1974; 1980; 1989), the most important class divisions are those between regions of the world. Wallerstein identifies developed manufacturing states as constituting the core region. This core uses its power, derived from its wealth, to concentrate surplus from the poorer countries in what he terms the periphery. While Lenin foresaw developed capitalist nations exporting capital to their colonies, world system theorists believe the failure to do so perpetuates regional inequality. The manufacturing regions in the core have greater capital, higher wages and a more highly skilled workforce than the peripheral nations situated in the global south. The periphery is an extraction region defined by agricultural economies with raw materials, low-paid and low-skilled workers.

When conflict occurs among the great powers, as it did during the two world wars and the Cold War, such conflict is the result of competition among the core states for the right to exploit the periphery. Between the core and the periphery a buffer zone of semi-peripheral regions exist, which have some manufacturing and capital accumulation. States in the periphery cooperate in this system through not only the coercion of core states but also the assimilation of norms and a system, which is flexible enough for peripheral states to become semi-peripheral or core. The prospect of progression to the core keeps disaffected states in the periphery from rebellion against the overall system. Understandings of core, semi- and periphery are not confined to nations but are also found within them. The power relationship is based on relationship to (and access to) the means of production.

Feminism

So far, our discussion has been concerned with power relationships that consider states, institutions or classes. We now turn our attention to those based on gender relations. Feminist theorists have tended to be marginalized in disciplines that have been largely dominated by privileged middle- and upper-class white men. In Martin Griffiths' book *Fifty Key Thinkers in International Relations* (1999) it is not without significance that only four of those selected were women (three of whom specialized in gender). However, gender is beginning to play a far more significant role in providing an alternative lens to mainstream IR approaches and a critique to norms of unequal gendered power relations. Although there are a number of different feminist approaches, all are united in using gender to highlight inequalities in the power relationships between men and women and seek to increase women's visibility as actors within international relations.

A critique of realism, the dominant paradigm in IR for much of the second half of the twentieth century, tends to be the starting point of feminist understanding in IR theory. Realism's separation of domestic and international politics reflects the division between the public and private sphere that traditionally consigned women to the role of supporting actors in a man's world. The social and cultural construction of gendered identities with masculinity associated with power, authority, aggression, rationality, calculation and an assumption of leadership in public roles fits into a realist perception of how states should and do behave (Viotti and Kauppi, 2010: 378). Femininity, on the other hand, stereotypically defines women as passive, submissive, nurturing, sensitive, caring and more focused on the private realm. Therefore, according to the implied assumptions in realism, for women to play a part in international politics they are required to assume a masculine role, which incorporates power, balance of power politics, coercive diplomacy and a willingness to act unilaterally.

This assumption is embodied in the following examples. Margaret Thatcher, UK prime minister during the Falklands conflict, and Secretaries of State Madeleine Albright and Condoleezza Rice personified this masculine approach to international relations. Albright infamously declared that the death of half a million Iraqi children, through the imposition of sanctions in Iraq during the 1990s, was a 'price worth paying' to contain Saddam Hussein, and Rice was George W. Bush's national security advisor and as such a leading proponent of the decision to invade Iraq in 2003. Difference feminists have adopted an essentialist approach and argued that men and women are equal but different and that promoting women to leading positions within the military and foreign policy-making hierarchy would substantively change the course of international relations. Others, citing the actions of women when placed in positions of power, suggest that the international system is masculine and this is what needs to be radically overhauled to end the imbalance in gendered power relationships. This is equally true of neo-liberal theorists who adopt masculinist assumptions about the interactions of autonomous actors (Goldstein and Pevehouse, 2010: 136–48).

Radical feminists are far more concerned about the referent object in international relations and security. While realist and liberal scholars emphasize states or the system as the referent object, radical feminists such as Cynthia Enloe (1989) and Sandra Whitworth (1994) highlight the individual. In order to understand power relationships we need to consider who and what are omitted as much as are included. Enloe's study of what goes on in and around military bases demonstrates previously ignored issues of gendered domination and exploitation. The patriarchal role of the military is portrayed in traditional theory as selflessly protecting 'good' women – that is, wives, mothers, sisters and daughters – while simultaneously overlooking or exploiting the contribution of other women and ethnic minorities that sustain the system by providing cooking, cleaning and sexual services.

Radical feminists, including constructivists, critical theorists, post-modernists and post-colonialists reject positivist assumptions and argue instead that the underlying assumptions of traditional IR need challenging. While there are clearly differences in perspective between these different theoretical positions, they each challenge the claims to truth adopted by traditional approaches. Post-colonialists reject the notion that females can be categorized as a homogeneous entity and highlight the imbalance in power relationships resulting from race, class, sexuality and history. Postmodernists and constructivists challenge the notion of femininity and masculinity as socially constructed and seek to deconstruct those taken-for-granted assumptions. They see such a revised discourse as emancipatory in seeking to challenge prevailing norms in IR by providing visibility to the role of women as both referent objects (the focus of academic attention) and actors in IR.

Constructivism

Constructivist thinking also emerged as a result of a critique of structural realist thinking. Alexander Wendt's seminal article 'Anarchy is What States Make of It' (1992) and subsequent book *The Social Theory on International Politics* (1999) attempted to present a different reality ignored by neo-realism. For Wendt, the ontological depiction of power-maximizing autonomous actors seeking to survive in an anarchic world order becomes a self-fulfilling prophecy. Instead, what is needed, according to Wendt and fellow constructivists, is an appreciation of how and why states act in the way they do: how do identity and ideas actually shape the foreign policy options that are pursued? For constructivists, norms and new ideas drive state action rather than naked power interests. Constructivists are therefore concerned to examine how debates are framed and ideas and identities constructed to determine which issues are securitized and the discourse used to shape those identities.

> To analyze the social construction of international politics is to analyze how processes of interaction produce and reproduce the social structures – cooperative or conflictual – that shape actors' identities and interests and the significance of their material contexts. (Wendt, 1995: 79)

Constructivist accounts of domestic and international politics demonstrate how social movements, non-governmental organizations and international organizations each play their part in helping shape identity and norms of appropriate behaviour. While rejecting the inevitability and permanence of existing power relations, constructivists are not necessarily part of an emancipatory project in that examining how ideas and identities form and how they shape behaviour at individual, state and system level does not mean that relationships can or should change. Power is not the raison d'être of constructivist theory, but in examining identity and norm formation power can be seen to reside with those who construct those norms and identities.

Poststructuralism

Poststructuralists, inspired by philosophers such as Michel Foucault, Jean-François Lyotard, Jacques Derrida and Jean Baudrillard, seek to go beyond the structuralist claims of neo-Marxists such as Althusser and Wallerstein and positivist approaches to politics. They reject the idea that structure takes precedence over agency and express a commitment to analytical principles that deconstruct texts, explore subtexts and seek out omissions in discourse on issues as diverse as race, class, gender and individuals to reveal the meanings underneath what we say and mean. Poststructuralism is both normative and critical in that it deconstructs traditional interpretations of reality, especially those that would posit a grand theory of the world or a linear approach to human progress. They reject notions of a single objective truth or value-free science and turn their attention, following Foucault (1979, 2002), to the three key areas of identity, power/knowledge and representations/interpretation (Jørgensen, 2010: 165).

For Foucault power is located everywhere, in all relationships, in institutions and is 'rooted in the whole network of the social' (Foucault, 2002: 346–7). We all operate according to rules and power relationships that we have no control over. We all live out roles that are constructed rather than innate, and determined by power relationships that may change from one role into another. Power and the subject are indivisible and, once a role is constructed, that construction defines how we act and what we say (Smith, 2009: 44). Foucault is particularly interested in 'projects of docility', about how society is disciplined and controlled by processes of surveillance through a combination of 'supervision, control and correction' (Foucault, 1979, 2002: 345). Rather than coercion Foucault, like Gramsci (1971), believes that socialization – the acceptance of values and norms by society – comes about through discourse rather than material structures. While the state increases its power and control over daily life, Foucault contends that all power relationships are resisted and, along with identity, contested (Foucault, 2002: 345).

Conclusion

Power is one of the defining characteristics of the study of Politics. Some theories such as pluralism and elitism seek to locate power in individuals or agents, through examining the behaviour of different actors. Others, such as Marxism and some feminists, suggest that power is located in the political, economic and social system that we operate within. In this chapter we have discussed some of the different facets of power and sought to highlight how the way in which we view power is shaped by our perception of the world. The study of politicians' behaviour favours an agency over a structural approach to power. Individual or group political actors identified by pluralist and elitist approaches are assumed to have power because of the decisions they take or do not take and what is and is not discussed or placed on policy agendas.

In contrast to the above emphasis upon individual elite level behaviour, Marxist and neo-Marxist writers have taken a more structural approach and argued that agency, when it is exerted, is exerted by the bourgeoisie or ruling class. In this way, power has systemic features. The individuals are interchangeable but capitalism operates exclusively in the interest of the ruling class nationally and internationally. Globalization extends class domination and exploitation to the developing world in the periphery and semi-periphery of world regions. Gramsci and Cox suggest that no longer does this exploitation involve coercion, but through rewarding working-class elites, and rulers in developing countries cooperate in their own exploitation by consenting to prevailing ruling-class norms. We have seen how realists have reduced the power relationship in IR to power maximization in a system based on statism, survival and self-help in which the powerful states maintain their privileged status and dominate the weaker. Liberal institutionalists consider that the world is far more interconnected and has the potential through increased cooperation to be more pacific. In emphasizing the democratic peace and international institutions as overcoming anarchy, liberal institutionalists actually situate power within the status quo of the developed nations.

Feminists insist that traditional approaches to Political Science and IR theory ignore the role of women and perpetuate gender inequality throughout the world. They draw attention to patriarchal systems that promote a masculinist worldview, reinforcing exploitative social systems and relationships. We also considered constructivist approaches that highlight the importance of identity and ideas in establishing norms of behaviour, which serve to highlight that power resides with those framing and talking the debate. Poststructuralists who deconstruct texts, subtexts and omissions from dominant narratives in order to expose dominant power relationships and challenge that which is taken for granted also develop this approach.

When it comes to doing Politics, we need to consider which approach is best suited to explain whatever issue we are seeking to explore. Many theorists will make use of one approach to explain every area they research, while others will use a combination governed by the issue concerned. If a theorist argues that that class or gender is the most important issue and that this discourse underpins everything else, they will necessarily see every aspect of the private and public realms as being governed by power relationships reflecting this. In examining power relationships, it is necessary to inject a final note of caution. By their very nature power and influence are very difficult concepts to prove. As we have seen, power consists in assumptions and is as much about what is unseen as what is seen, about consent as much as coercion, about structures and agency; but the key question is: how do we prove power and influence? The counterfactual argument must always occupy our attention: would anything different have occurred if this hypothesized power relationship did not exist? Over the remainder of the book we consider power as one aspect among many as we examine substantive issues at the heart of Politics.

Reflection

Why do you think power is so important in the study of Politics?

What are the weaknesses of Robert Dahl's pluralist approach to power?

Lukes identifies three dimensions of power; which do you think is the most convincing and why?

Can you think of other dimensions of power?

What are the similarities and differences between Political Science and IR theorizations on power?

How effective are pluralists and elitists at accounting for political change?

Which do you consider more important – military or economic power?

Why do you think this?

Do you agree with Robert Cox that 'theory is always for someone, and for some purpose'?

How important are class relationships today and what, if anything, can they teach us about power?

Is Foucault right to suggest that all power is resisted and identity contested?

Seminar activities

Examine the lead political story in today's newspaper. Consider and discuss the importance of power in the story.

What evidence is there of power at work?

How can we tell?

Who is exercising power and for what purpose?

Does the story provide us with enough information to make a judgement?

If not, what other information would we need?

Which theory best explains the use of power within the story?

Are there other explanations that would explain power as well?

CHAPTER **7** **Politics, Society and Identity**

'Society is inside man and man is inside society.'

ARTHUR MILLER, *The Shadow of the Gods* (1958)

PREVIEW   To suggest, as textbooks tend to do, that politics takes place in a social context fails to convey just how intimately politics and social life are related. Politics, by its very nature, is a social activity, and it is viewed by some as nothing more than the process through which the conflicts of society are articulated and, perhaps, resolved. In this sense, society is no mere 'context', but the very stuff and substance of politics itself. Although later chapters examine the interaction between society and politics in relation to particular channels of communication, such as the media, elections, political parties, interest groups and so on, this chapter focuses on the broader political implications of how society is structured and how it has changed and continues to change. For example, the transition from agrarian societies to industrial societies and then to so-called post-industrial society has profoundly altered levels of social connectedness and given rise to new political battle lines. Not only has post-industrialism been associated with the declining significance of social class, but technological change, particularly in the fields of information and communication, has altered the breadth and depth of connections between people, as well as the nature of these connections. These and related factors have been linked to the strengthening of individualism, with major political consequences. Modern thinking about the relationship between politics and society is, nevertheless, increasingly focused on the question of identity, many claim, giving rise to a new politics of group self-assertion, or identity politics. This trend has helped, amongst other things, to highlight the political significance of race and ethnicity, gender, religion and culture.

KEY ISSUES
- What have been the political implications of the emergence of post-industrial societies?
- Is the 'information society' a myth or a reality?
- How has the growth of individualism affected community and social cohesion?
- Why has the politics of identity become so prominent in recent years?
- How have race and ethnicity, gender, religion and culture provided the basis for identity politics?
- Is identity politics a liberating force or a political dead-end?

POLITICS AND SOCIETY

CONCEPT

Status

Status is a person's position within a hierarchical order. It is characterized by the person's role, rights and duties in relation to the other members of that order. As status is a compound of factors such as honour, prestige, standing and power, it is more difficult to determine than an essentially economic category such as class. Also, because it is a measure of whether someone is 'higher' or 'lower' on a social scale, it is more subjective. Although status hierarchies have faded in significance in modern societies, they continue to operate in relation to factors such as family background, gender, and race and ethnicity.

What do we mean by 'society'? In its most general sense, a society is a collection of people who occupy the same territorial area. However, not every group of people constitutes a society. Societies are characterized by regular patterns of social interaction. This suggests the existence of some kind of social *structure*; that is, a usually stable set of interrelationships amongst a number of elements. Moreover, 'social' relationships involve a sense of connectedness, in the form of mutual awareness and, at least, a measure of cooperation. For instance, strictly speaking, warring tribes do not constitute a 'society', even though they may live in close proximity to one another and interact regularly. Societies are also usually characterized by social *divisions*, in which groups and individuals occupy very different positions, reflecting an unequal distribution of status, wealth and/or power within the society. The nature of these divisions or cleavages, and the political significance of particular divisions (class, race, gender, age, religion and so on), of course, differ from society to society.

In all cases, though, society can be seen to shape politics in a number of important ways:

- The distribution of wealth and other resources in society conditions the nature of state power.
- Social divisions and conflicts help to bring about political change in the form of legitimation crises.
- Society influences public opinion and the political culture.

- The social structure shapes political behaviour; that is, who votes, how they vote, who joins parties and so on.

The nature of society, however, is one of the most contentious areas of political and ideological debate, being no less controversial, in fact, than the attempt to define the content of human nature. For example, whereas Marxists and others hold that society is characterized by irreconcilable conflict, liberals tend to emphasize that harmony exists amongst competing interests and groups. Similarly, while liberals are inclined to view society as an artefact fashioned by individuals to satisfy their various needs, conservatives have traditionally portrayed it as organic, ultimately shaped by the forces of natural necessity. Nevertheless, the nature of society, and therefore of social connectedness, have changed significantly over time. Modern society appears to be characterized by a 'hollowing out' of social connectedness, a transition from the 'thick' connectedness of close social bonds and fixed allegiances to the 'thin' connectedness of more fluid, individualized social arrangements. These changes have been linked to developments such as the advent of 'post-industrialism' and the fading significance of social class (see p. 153), the emergence of so-called 'information societies', and the growth of individualism.

From industrialism to post-industrialism

Industrialization has been the most powerful factor shaping the structure and character of modern societies. It has, for instance, contributed to a dramatic

CONCEPT

Social class

A class is, broadly, a group of people who share a similar social and economic position. For Marxists, class is linked to economic power, which is defined by the individual's relationship to the means of production. From this perspective, the key class division is between the owners of productive wealth (the bourgeoisie) and those who live off the sale of their labour power (the proletariat). Non-Marxist definitions of class are usually based on income and status differences between occupational groups. Distinctions are thus made between 'middle' class (or non-manual) workers and 'working' class (or manual) workers.

● *Gemeinschaft*: (German) Community; social ties typically found in traditional societies and characterized by natural affection and mutual respect.

● *Gesellschaft*: (German) Association; the loose, artificial and contractual bonds typically found in urban and industrial societies.

● Class consciousness: A Marxist term denoting a subjective awareness of a class's objective situation and interests; the opposite of 'false consciousness'.

● Post-industrial society: A society based on service industries, rather than on manufacturing industries, and accompanied by a significant growth in the white-collar workforce.

increase in geographical mobility through the process of urbanization (by the early 2000s, most of the world's then 6.3 billion people had come to live in towns and cities, rather than in rural areas). In the process, the nature of social connectedness underwent significant changes. One of the most influential attempts to convey this transition was undertaken by the German sociologist Ferdinand Tönnies (1855–1936). Tönnies distinguished between *Gemeinschaft* and *Gesellschaft*. The advance of industrialization also changed the structure of society, with economically-based class divisions displacing the fixed social hierarchies of more traditional societies, which were usually based on status and linked to land ownership. Social class thus emerged as the central organizing principle of society.

However, any analysis of the relationship between class and politics is bedevilled by problems, not least about how social class should be defined and the role that social classes play. The leading protagonists of class politics have come from the Marxist tradition. Marxists regard class as the most fundamental, and politically the most significant, social division. As Marx (see p. 41) put it at the beginning of the *Communist Manifesto* ([1848] 1967), 'the history of all hitherto existing societies is the history of class struggle'. From the Marxist perspective, capitalist societies are dominated by a 'ruling class' of property owners (the bourgeoisie) who oppress and exploit a class of wage slaves (the proletariat). This gives rise to a two-class model of industrial capitalism that emphasizes irreconcilable conflict and progressive polarization, with social classes being the key actors on the political stage. Marx predicted that, as capitalist development would be characterized by deepening crises, the proletariat would eventually achieve **class consciousness** and fulfil its destiny as the 'gravedigger' of capitalism. The proletariat would thus be transformed from a 'class in-itself' (an economically defined category) and become a 'class for-itself' (a revolutionary force).

Decline of class politics

The Marxist two-class model has, however, been discredited by the failure of Marx's predictions to materialize, and by declining evidence of class struggle, at least in advanced capitalist societies. Even by the end of the nineteenth century, it was clear that the class structure of industrial societies was becoming increasingly complex, and that it varies from system to system, as well as over time. Max Weber (see p. 82) was one of the first to take stock of this shift, developing a theory of stratification that acknowledged economic or class differences, but also took account of the importance of political parties and social status. In drawing attention to status as a 'social estimation of honour' expressed in the lifestyle of a group, Weber helped to prepare the ground for the modern notion of occupational class, widely used by social and political scientists. For some, however, the late twentieth century was characterized by the final eclipse of class politics. By the 1960s, neo-Marxists such as Herbert Marcuse (see p. 42) were lamenting the deradicalization of the urban proletariat, and looked instead to the revolutionary potential of students, women, ethnic minorities and the developing world. The traditional link between socialism and the working class was formally abandoned in works such as André Gorz's *Farewell to the Working Class* (1982).

Most commentators agree that, behind the declining political significance of class, lies the emergence of so-called '**post-industrial societies**'. One of the

Fordism, post-Fordism

Fordism refers to the large-scale mass-production methods pioneered by Henry Ford in Detroit in the USA. These used mechanization and highly-regimented production-line labour processes to produce standardized, relatively cheap products. Fordist societies were structured largely by solidaristic class loyalties. Post-Fordism emerged as the result of the introduction of more flexible microelectronics-based machinery that gave individual workers greater autonomy and made possible innovations such as subcontracting and batch production. Post-Fordism has been linked to decentralization in the workplace and a greater emphasis on choice and individuality.

● **Atomism**: The tendency for society to be made up of a collection of self-interested and largely self-sufficient individuals, operating as separate atoms.

● **Underclass**: A poorly defined and politically controversial term that refers, broadly, to people who suffer from multiple deprivation (unemployment or low pay, poor housing, inadequate education and so on)

● **Internet**: A global 'network of networks' that connects computers around the world; 'virtual' space in which users can access and disseminate online information.

key features of such societies has been the process of de-industrialization, reflected in the decline of labour-intensive 'heavy' industries such as coal, steel and shipbuilding. These tended to be characterized by a solidaristic culture rooted in clear political loyalties and, usually, strong union organization. In contrast, the expanding service sectors of economies foster more individualistic and instrumentalist attitudes. Post-industrial societies are therefore distinguished by growing atomism and the weakening of social connectedness. The term 'post-industrialism' was popularized by Daniel Bell in *The Coming of Post-industrial Society* (1973). For Bell, post-industrial societies were characterized, amongst other things, by the transition from a labour theory of value to a knowledge theory of value, as implied by the idea of an 'information society' (see p. 156), discussed below. Piore and Sabel (1984) interpreted the transition as part of a shift from a Fordist to a post-Fordist era. In this light, the eclipse of the system of mass production and mass consumption, the chief features of Fordism, has produced more pluralized and fluid class formations.

The shrinkage of the traditional working class has led to the development of so-called 'two-thirds, one-third' societies, in which the two-thirds are relatively prosperous, a product of a marked tendency towards social levelling associated with mass education, rising affluence and consumerism (Hutton, 1995). One of the most influential attempts to discuss the political implications of this development is found in J. K. Galbraith's *The Culture of Contentment* (1992). Galbraith (see p. 155) pointed to the emergence in modern societies, at least amongst the politically active, of a 'contented majority' whose material affluence and economic security encourages them to be politically conservative. This contented majority, for instance, has provided an electoral base for the anti-welfarist and tax-cutting policies that have become fashionable since the 1970s. Debate about the plight of the one-third and about the nature of social inequality in modern societies has increasingly focused not so much on social class, but more on what has been called the 'underclass'. The underclass suffers less from poverty as it has been traditionally understood (deprivation of material necessities) and more from social exclusion, reflected in cultural, educational and social impediments to meaningful participation in the economy and society. However, attitudes towards social differentiation and debates about the appropriate response to the growth of an underclass are rooted in deeper disagreements about the causes and political implications of social inequality.

New technology and the 'information society'

One of the features most commonly associated with post-industrialism is the increased importance that is placed on knowledge and information generally, on intellectual capital (ideas), rather than material capital (things). This is often seen as a consequence of what has been called the 'third' modern information revolution, which has witnessed the advent of so-called 'new' media; notably, mobile phones, cable and satellite television, cheaper and more powerful computers, and, most importantly, the internet. (The first revolution involved the development of the telegraph, telephone and radio, while the second centred on television, early-generation computers and satellites). The third information

John Kenneth Galbraith (1908–2006)

Canadian economist and social theorist. Following wartime service as the Director of the US Strategic Bombing Survey, Galbraith became a professor of economics at Harvard University and served as the US Ambassador to India, 1961–63. Galbraith was closely identified with the Democratic Party, and was perhaps the leading modern exponent of Keynesian economics (and certainly its most innovative advocate). He became one of the USA's most eminent social commentators. In *The Affluent Society* (1958), Galbraith highlighted the contrast between private affluence and public squalor, arguing that economic resources are often used in the wasteful gratification of trivial wants. *The New Industrial State* (1967) advanced a critique of corporate power in the USA. His other major works include *The Culture of Contentment* (1992).

revolution has concerned the technologies of **connectivity**, and have been particularly significant. The extraordinary explosion that has occurred in the quantity of information and communication exchanges, made possible by digital technologies, has marked, some argue, the birth of the 'information age' (in place of the industrial age). Society has been transformed into an 'information society' and the economy has become a **'knowledge economy'**, even a 'weightless' economy.

The emergence of new media has helped to alter both the scope and the nature of social connectedness. As far as the scope of social connectedness is concerned, new media have given huge impetus to the process of globalization. Indeed, so-called 'hyperglobalist' theorists subscribe to a kind of technological determinism in arguing that accelerated globalization became inevitable once new information and communication technologies (ICT) became widely available (Ohmae, 1989). While the industrial age (and the first two communications revolutions) created new mechanisms for communicating at a national, rather than a local level (via national newspapers, telephone systems, radio and television services, and so on), the technologies of the information age are, by their nature, transnational: mobile phones, satellite television and the internet (usually) operate regardless of borders. This, in turn, has facilitated the growth of transborder groups, bodies and institutions, ranging from non-governmental organizations (NGOs) (see p. 248), protest movements and transnational corporations (TNCs) (see p. 149) to international criminal organizations and global terrorist groups such as al-Qaeda. Not only do states struggle to control and constrain groups and organizations that have transborder structures, but they also have a greatly reduced capacity to control what their citizens see, hear and know. For instance, although states such as China, Burma and Iran have, at various times, tried to restrict transborder communications via mobile phones and the internet, the pace of technological change is very likely to weaken such controls in the longer term. The former US Presient Bill Clinton likened China's attempts to control the internet to trying to nail Jell-O to the wall.

Not only do information societies connect more people to more other people – and, increasingly, to people who live in other societies – but the nature

● **Connectivity**: A computer buzzword that refers to the links between one device (usually a computer) and others, affecting the speed, ease and extent of information exchanges.

● **Knowledge economy**: An economy in which knowledge is the key source of competitiveness and productivity, especially through the application of information and communications technology.

Debating . . .
Does social equality matter?

The issue of social equality lies at the heart of ideological debate and argument. While left-wingers tend to support equality, seeing it as the key to social justice, right-wingers typically accepted inequality as inevitable if not desirable. How does material inequality, particularly income inequality, affect politics and society? Do governments have a moral obligation to promote social equality, and, if so, on what grounds?

YES	NO
Inequality and social dysfunction. Socialists have long argued that social inequality breeds resentment, hostility and strife, even, in the case of Marxists, associating class inequality with inevitable social revolution. Such concerns have also been borne out by empirical studies that link inequality to a range of negative personal and social outcomes. Comparative studies of 'high' inequality countries, such as the USA, the UK and Portugal, and 'low' inequality countries, such as Japan and the Scandinavian states, suggests that inequality leads to shorter, unhealthier and unhappier lives, reflected in increased rates of, for instance, teenage pregnancies, violence, obesity, imprisonment and addiction (Wilkinson and Pickett, 2010).	***Inequality and economic growth.*** Liberal political economists link social equality to economic stagnation. This occurs because social 'levelling' serves to cap aspirations and remove the incentive for enterprise and hard work. The sterility and inertia of communist states was thus in large part a consequence of high levels of job security and low income differentials. In contrast, the USA, the world's leading economy, demonstrates how inequality promotes economic vigour, as the rich can always get richer and the poor can always become more poor. Indeed, by strengthening incentives, inequality may actually benefit the poor, whose living standards may be higher in relatively unequal societies than they are in relatively equal societies.
Justice as equality. The moral case in favour of equality includes that poverty and social disadvantage impair people's opportunities and life chances. As social differentiation more often results from unequal treatment by society than from unequal natural endowment, justice dictates that social rewards should generally be distributed more equally, and that this should be done through policies of welfare and redistribution. According to John Rawls (see p. 45), if people were unaware of their personal attributes and qualities, most would favour equality over inequality, as their fear of being destitute would outweigh their desire for great wealth.	***Justice as inequality.*** Inequality is justifiable quite simply because people are different: they have different aspirations, talents, dispositions and so forth. To treat them as equals must therefore result in injustice. As Aristotle (see p. 6) put it, injustice arises not only when equals are treated unequally, but also when unequals are treated equally. Justice may require equality of opportunity, giving each person the same starting point in life, but certainly not equality of outcome. In line with the principle of meritocracy, the talented and hardworking should rise, while the lazy and feckless should fall. Pursuing equality thus involves penalizing talent.
Social citizenship. Social equality (or, more accurately, reduced social inequality) is a necessary condition for healthy democracy and meaningful citizenship. Citizens have to enjoy freedom from poverty, ignorance and despair if they are to participate fully in the affairs of their community, an idea embodied in the concept of social citizenship. Groups such as women, ethnic minorities, the poor and the unemployed, commonly regard themselves as 'second class citizens' if social disadvantage prevents their full civic and political participation (see p. 444). Social inequality thus correlates with low voter turnout and fuels dissent and civil unrest.	***Politics of envy.*** The socialist principle of equality is based on social envy, the desire to have what others possess. Instead of encouraging the less well-off to focus on improving their own living standards, it encourages them to resent the wealthy, seeing them, somehow, as the architects of their misfortune. As the politics of envy grows, individual freedom is diminished, both through the emergence of an extensive system of manipulation and 'social engineering', and by the fact that redistribution, in effect, legalizes theft (as government transfers wealth from one group of people to another without their consent).

CONCEPT

Information society

An information society is a society in which the creation, distribution and manipulation of information are core economic and cultural activities, underpinned, in particular, by the wider use of computerized processes and the internet. Information and knowledge are thus seen to have replaced physical capital as the principal source of wealth. In an 'information age', or 'cyber age', the principal responsibility of government is to improve education and training, both to strengthen international competitiveness and to widen opportunities for the individual.

● Network: A means of co-ordinating social life through loose and informal relationships between people or organizations, usually for the purpose of knowledge dissemination or exchange.

of those connections has also changed. One of the most influential attempts to explain this was advanced in Manuel Castells' (1996) notion of the 'network society'. Whereas the dominant mode of social organization in industrial societies had been hierarchies, more complex and pluralized information societies operate either on the basis of markets (reflecting the wider role of market economics, as well as the impact of economic globalization, as discussed in Chapter 6), or on the basis of looser and more diffuse networks. According to Castells, businesses increasingly function as 'network corporations'. Many TNCs, for instance, are organized as networks of franchises and subsidiaries. Similar trends can be witnessed in social and political life. For example, hierarchical bodies such as trade unions and pressure groups have increasingly lost influence through the emergence of network-based social movements (see p. 260), such as the anti-globalization movement and the environmental movement.

Nevertheless, opinions are divided over the implications of the wider use of new communications technologies for politics and society. Dating back to Ivan Illich's pioneering *Tools for Conviviality* (1973), the potential for computer-based technologies to give individual citizens independent access to specialized knowledge, allowing them to escape from dependency on technocratic elites, has been lauded. In this light, new media are a source of citizen empowerment and (potentially) a significant constraint on government power. Critics, in contrast, point out that the internet does not discriminate between good ideas and bad ones. It provides a platform for the dissemination not only of socially-worthwhile and politically-neutral views, but also of political extremism, racial and religious bigotry, and pornography of various kinds. A further danger has been the growth of a 'cult of information', whereby the accumulation of data and information becomes an end in itself, impairing the ability of people to distinguish between information, on the one hand, and knowledge, experience and wisdom, on the other (Roszak, 1994). Such a criticism is linked to allegations that 'surfing' the internet actually impairs people's ability to think and learn by encouraging them to skim and jump from one piece of information to the next, ruining their ability to concentrate. New media may therefore be making people stupid, rather than better-informed (Carr, 2008, 2010). The impact of new media on democracy and governance is examined in greater detail in Chapter 8.

No such thing as society?

Although the advent of post-industrialism and the spread of IT-based, network relationships have encouraged the 'thinning' of social connectedness, at the heart of this trend lies a deeper process: the rise of individualism. In many parts of the world, the notion of 'the individual' is now so familiar that its political and social significance, as well as its relatively recent origins, are often overlooked. In traditional societies, there was typically little idea of individuals having their own interests, or possessing personal and unique identities. Rather, people were seen as members of the social groups to which they belonged: their family, village, tribe, local community and so on. Their lives and identities were largely determined by the character of these groups in a process that had changed little from one generation to the next. The rise of individualism is widely seen as a conse-

CONCEPT

Individualism

Individualism is the belief in the supreme importance of the individual over any social group or collective body. As such, individualism has two key implications. First, each individual has a separate, indeed unique, identity, reflecting his or her 'inner' or personal qualities. This is evident in the idea of individuality, and is linked to the notion of people as self-interested, and largely self-reliant, creatures. Second, all individuals share the same moral status as 'persons', irrespective of factors such as race, religion, nationality, sex and social position. This is reflected in the idea of rights, and especially in the doctrine of human rights.

● **Economic individualism:** The belief that individuals are entitled to autonomy in matters of economic decision-making; economic individualism is lo0sely linked to property rights.

● **Community:** A principle or sentiment based on the collective identity of a social group; bonds of comradeship, loyalty and duty.

● **Anomie:** A weakening of values and normative rules, associated with feelings of isolation, loneliness and meaninglessness.

quence of the establishment of industrial capitalism as the dominant mode of social organization, first in western societies and, thanks to globalization, beyond. Industrial capitalism meant that people were confronted by a broader range of choices and social possibilities. They were encouraged, perhaps for the first time, to think for themselves, and to think of themselves in personal terms. A peasant, for example, whose family may always have lived and worked on the same piece of land, became a 'free man' and acquired some ability to choose who to work for, or maybe the opportunity to leave the land altogether and look for work in the growing towns or cities. As individuals, people were more likely to be self-seeking, acting in accordance with their own (usually material) interests, and they were encouraged to be self-sufficient, in the sense of taking responsibility for their economic and social circumstances. This gave rise to the doctrine of **economic individualism**.

A child of industrial capitalism, individualism has been further strengthened by the growth, especially since the 1960s, of the consumer society and, later, by the general shift in favour of neoliberal economics, as examined in Chapter 6, Whereas earlier versions of industrial capitalism had linked people's status in society to their productive roles (most clearly demonstrated by the importance traditionally placed on social class, a consumer society, or consumer capitalism), encouraged people to define themselves increasingly in terms of what they own and how much they own. While an emphasis on production tends to foster social solidarity, in that it highlights what people have in common with other people, consumerism encourages people to think and act more in individual terms, focusing on personal gratification, even seeing consumption as a form of self-expression. Daniel Bell (1976) interpreted this as evidence of a cultural contradiction that lies at the heart of the capitalist system, arguing that the ethic of acquisitiveness and immediate gratification (which encourages consumers to consume) was winning out over the ethic of asceticism and delayed gratification (which encourages workers to work). The growing prominence of neoliberalism (see p. 144) from the 1980s onwards, especially in countries that had embraced free-market thinking with the greatest enthusiasm, such as the USA and the UK, further strengthened individualism. This occurred both through the tendency to extol the virtues of entrepreneurialism and individual self-striving, creating, critics argued, a philosophy of 'greed is good', and through the rolling back of welfare, based on the desire for people to 'stand on their own two feet'. Margaret Thatcher's famous assertion, that 'There is no such thing as society . . . only individual men and women and their families', is often seen to encapsulate the thrust of neoliberal individualism.

However, there is deep disagreement over the implications of the spread of individualism. For many, the spread of individualism has profoundly weakened **community** and our sense of social belonging. For instance, academic sociology largely arose in the nineteenth century as an attempt to explore the (usually negative) social implications of the spread of industrialization and urbanization, both of which had encouraged increasing individualism and competition. The French sociologist Émile Durkheim (1858–1917) thus emphasized the degree to which the weakening of social codes and norms had resulted in the spread of '**anomie**'. For Durkheim (1897), this had led to an increase in the number of suicides in industrial societies. Similar misgivings about the rise of individualism have been expressed by modern communitarian thinkers, who have linked the

CONCEPT

Consumerism

Consumerism is a psychic and social phenomenon whereby personal happiness is equated with the acquisition and consumption of material possessions. Its growth has been shaped by the development of new advertising and marketing techniques that took advantage of the emergence of the mass media and the spread of mass affluence. Rising consumerism has important socio-economic and cultural implications. Whereas 'productionist' societies emphasize the values of discipline, duty and hard work (the Protestant work ethic, for example), consumer societies emphasize materialism, hedonism and immediate, rather than delayed, gratification.

● Social reflexivity: The tendency of individuals and other social actors to reflect, more or less continuously, on the conditions of their own actions, implying higher levels of self-awareness, self-knowledge and contemplation.

growth of egoism and atomism to a weakening of social duty and moral responsibility. Communitarian theorists, such as Michael Sandel (1982) and Alisdair MacIntyre (1981), have thus argued that, in conceiving the individual as logically prior to and 'outside' the community, liberal individualism has legitimized selfishness and greed, and downgraded the importance of the public good. Robert Putnam (2000) and others have associated such trends with a decline of social capital (see p. 175) across many modern societies, as discussed at greater length in Chapter 8.

On the other hand, liberal theorists, in particular, have viewed rising individualism as a mark of social progress. In this view, the forward march of individualism has been associated with the spread of progressive, even 'enlightened', social values; notably, toleration and equality of opportunity. If human beings are thought of, first and foremost, as individuals, they must be entitled to the same rights and the same respect, meaning that all forms of disadvantage or discrimination, based on factors such as gender (see p. 163), race (see p. 112), colour, creed, religion or social background, are viewed as morally questionable, if not indefensible. All modern societies have, to a greater or lesser extent, been affected by the spread of such ideas, not least through the changing gender roles and family structures that have resulted from the spread of feminism. The link between individualism and the expansion of choice and opportunity has also been highlighted by the spread in modern societies of social reflexivity (Giddens, 1994). This has occurred for a variety of reasons, including the development of mass education; much wider access to information through radio, television, the internet and so on; and intensified cultural flows within and between societies. However, social reflexivity brings both benefits and dangers. On the one hand, it has greatly widened the sphere of personal freedom, the ability of people to define who they are and how they wish to live, a tendency reflected in the increasing domination of politics by so-called 'lifestyle' issues. On the other hand, its growth has coincided with a strengthening of consumerism and materialist ethics.

Nevertheless, it is important not to overstate the advance of individualism or, for that matter, the erosion of community. Individualism has been embraced most eagerly in the English-speaking world, where it has been most culturally palatable, given the impact of Protestant religious ideas about personal salvation and the moral benefits of individual self-striving. In contrast, Catholic societies in Europe and elsewhere have been more successful in resisting individualism and in maintaining the ethics of social responsibility, reflected in a stronger desire to uphold welfare provision as both an expression of social responsibility and a means of upholding social cohesion. However, the best examples of successful anti-individualist societies can be found in Asia, especially in Japan, China and Asian 'tiger' states such as Taiwan, South Korea and Singapore. This has led to a debate about the viability of a set of so-called 'Asian values', and especially those associated with Confucianism (see p. 278), as an alternative to the individualism of western, liberal societies. In addition, the image of modern societies being increasingly dominated by 'thin' forms of social connectedness is undermined by evidence of the resurgence of 'thick' social connectedness in many societies; notably, through the rise of identity politics and the growing importance of ethnicity, gender (see p. 160), culture and religion in many parts of the world.

Ethnicity

Ethnicity is the sentiment of loyalty towards a distinctive population, cultural group or territorial area. The term is complex because it has both racial and cultural overtones. The members of ethnic groups are often seen, correctly or incorrectly, to have descended from common ancestors, and the groups are thus thought of as extended kinship groups, united by blood. More commonly, ethnicity is understood as a form of cultural identity, albeit one that operates at a deep and emotional level. An 'ethnic' culture encompasses values, traditions and practices but, crucially, it also gives a people a common identity and sense of distinctiveness, usually by focusing on their origins.

● **Identity politics**: A style of politics that seeks to counter group marginalization by embracing a positive and assertive sense of collective identity.

● **Eurocentrism**: A culturally biased approach to understanding that treats European, and generally western, ideas, values and assumptions as 'natural'.

● **Race**: A group of people who share a common ancestry and 'one blood': 'racial' differences linked to skin and hair colour and facial features have no scientific basis (see p. 112).

IDENTITY POLITICS

Rise of identity politics

One of the prominent features of modern politics has been a growing recognition of the significance of cultural differences within society, often portrayed as 'identity politics', or the 'politics of difference'. Identity politics is an orientation towards social or political theorizing, rather than a coherent body of ideas with a settled political character. It seeks to challenge and overthrow oppression by reshaping a group's identity through what amounts to a process of politico-cultural self-assertion. This reflects two core beliefs. The first is that group marginalization operates through stereotypes and values developed by dominant groups that structure how marginalized groups see themselves and are seen by others. These typically inculcate a sense of inferiority, even shame. The second belief is that subordination can be challenged by reshaping identity to give the group concerned a sense of pride and self-respect (for instance, 'black is beautiful' or 'gay pride'). In seeking to reclaim a 'pure' or 'authentic' sense of identity, identity politics expresses defiance against marginalization and disadvantage, and serves as a source of liberation. This is what gives identity politics its typically combative character and imbues it with psycho-emotional force.

The foundations for identity politics were laid by the postcolonial theories that emerged from the collapse of the European empires in the early post-1945 period. The significance of postcolonialism (see p. 52) was that it sought to challenge and overturn the cultural dimension of imperial rule by establishing the legitimacy of non-western – and sometimes anti-western – political ideas and traditions. For example, Franz Fanon (1926–61) developed a theory of imperialism (see p. 427) that gave particular emphasis to the psychological dimension of colonial subjugation. For Fanon (1968), decolonization was not merely a political process, but one through which a new 'species' of man is created. He argued that only the cathartic experience of violence is powerful enough to bring about this psycho-political regeneration. Edward Said (see p. 161) developed a critique of Eurocentrism through his notion of 'orientalism' (Said, 1978). Orientalism highlights the extent to which western cultural and political hegemony over the rest of the world, but over the Orient in particular, had been maintained through elaborate stereotypical fictions that belittled and demeaned non-western people and culture. Examples of this would include notions such as the 'mysterious East', 'inscrutable Chinese' and 'lustful Turks'. However, manifestations of identity politics are varied and diverse. This is because identity can be shaped around many principles. The most important of these are:

- race and ethnicity
- gender
- religion
- culture.

Race and ethnicity

Racial and ethnic divisions are a significant feature of many modern societies. There is nothing new, however, in the link between race and politics. The first

Edward Said (1935–2003)

A Jerusalem-born US academic and literary critic, Said was a leading literary critic, a prominent advocate of the Palestinian cause and a founding figure of postcolonial theory. From the 1970s onwards, he developed a humanist critique of the western Enlightenment that uncovered its links to colonialism and highlighted 'narratives of oppression', cultural and ideological biases that disempowered colonized peoples by representing them as the non-western 'other'. He is best known for the notion of 'orientalism', which operated through a 'subtle and persistent Eurocentric prejudice against Arabo-Islamic peoples and culture'. His key texts include *Orientalism* (1978) and *Culture and Imperialism* (1993).

explicitly racialist (see p. 120) political theories were developed in the nineteenth century against the background of European imperialism. Works such as Gobineau's *Essay on the Inequality of Human Races* (Gobineau, [1855] 1970) and H. S. Chamberlain's *The Foundations of the Nineteenth Century* ([1899] 1913) attempted to provide a pseudoscientific justification for the dominance of the 'white' races of Europe and North America over the 'black', 'brown' and 'yellow' peoples of Africa and Asia. Anti-Semitic (see p. 121) political parties and movements emerged in countries such as Germany, Austria and Russia in the late nineteenth century. The most grotesque twentieth-century manifestation of such racialism was found in German Nazism, which, through the so-called 'Final Solution', attempted to carry out the extermination of European Jewry. Apartheid (Afrikaans for 'apartness') in South Africa consisted of the strict segregation of whites and non-whites between the election of the Nationalist Party in 1948 and the establishment of a non-racial democracy under the leadership of the African National Congress (ANC) in 1994. Elsewhere, racialism has been kept alive through campaigns against immigration, organized, for example, by the British National Party (BNP) and Le Pen's *Front National* (FN) in France.

Very different forms of racial or ethnic politics have, nevertheless, developed out of the struggle against colonialism (see p. 122) in particular, and as a result of racial discrimination and disadvantage in general. Indeed, in seeking to challenge economic and social marginalization, black nationalism in the USA and elsewhere constituted the prototype for identity politics, especially through its emphasis on '**consciousness raising**'. The origins of the black consciousness movement date back to the early twentieth century and the emergence of a 'back to Africa' movement, inspired by activists such as Marcus Garvey (see p. 162). Black politics, however, gained greater prominence in the 1960s with an upsurge in both the reformist and revolutionary wings of the movement. In its reformist guise, the movement took the form of a struggle for civil rights that reached national prominence in the USA under the leadership of Martin Luther King (1929–68) and the National Association for the Advancement of Coloured People (NAACP). The strategy of protest and non-violent civil disobedience was, nevertheless, rejected by the emerging Black Power movement, which supported black separatism and, under the leadership of the Black Panther Party, founded

● Consciousness raising: Strategies to remodel social identity and challenge cultural inferiority by an emphasis on pride, self-worth and self-assertion.

Marcus Garvey (1887–1940)

Jamaican political thinker and activist, and an early advocate of black nationalism. Garvey was the founder in 1914 of the Universal Negro Improvement Association (UNIA). He left Jamaica for New York in 1916, where his message of black pride and economic self-sufficiency gained him a growing following, particularly in ghettos such as Harlem. Although his black business enterprises failed, and his call for a return to Africa was largely ignored, Garvey's emphasis on establishing black pride and his vision of Africa as a 'homeland' provided the basis for the later Black Power movement. Rastafarianism is also based largely on his ideas. Garvey was imprisoned for mail fraud in 1923, and was later deported, eventually dying in obscurity in London.

in 1966, promoted the use of physical force and armed confrontation. Of more enduring significance in US politics, however, have been the Black Muslims, who advocate a separate creed based on the idea that black Americans are descended from an ancient Muslim tribe. Founded in 1930, the Black Muslims were led for over 40 years by Elijah Muhammad (1897–1975), and they counted amongst their most prominent activists in the 1960s the militant black leader Malcolm X (1925–65). Renamed the Nation of Islam, the movement continues to exert influence in the USA under the leadership of Louis Farrakhan. Other manifestations of ethnic consciousness include the secessionist nationalist movements that sprang up in many parts of western Europe and North America in the 1960s and early 1970s. This was most evident in Quebec in Canada, Scotland and Wales in the UK, Catalonia and the Basque area in Spain, Corsica in France, and Flanders in Belgium.

The rise of ethnic consciousness has by no means occurred only in the West. Although ethnic rivalry (often portrayed as 'tribalism') is sometimes seen as an endemic feature of African and Asian politics, it is better understood as a phenomenon linked to colonialism (see p. 122). However, the divide-and-rule policies of the colonial period often bequeathed to many newly-independent 'nations' a legacy of bitterness and resentment. In many cases, this was subsequently exacerbated by the attempt of majority ethnic groups to consolidate their dominance under the guise of 'nation-building'. Such tensions, for instance, resulted in the Biafran war in Nigeria in the 1960s, a long-running civil war in Southern Sudan, and a resort to terrorism by the predominantly Christian Tamils in Sri Lanka. The worst recent example of ethnic bloodshed, however, occurred in Rwanda in 1994, where an estimated 800,000 Tutsis and moderate Hutus were slaughtered in an uprising by militant Hutus. The spectre of ethnic rivalry and regional conflict has also been created by the collapse of communism in Eastern Europe. In the former USSR, Czechoslovakia and Yugoslavia, for example, this led to state collapse and the creation of a series of new states. Nevertheless, these newly-created states have themselves been subject to deep ethnic rivalries and tensions. This has been demonstrated by the rebellion of the Chechens in Russia, and the fragmentation of the former Yugoslav republic of Bosnia into 'ethnically pure' Muslim, Serb and Croat areas.

Gender

Gender refers to social and cultural distinctions between males and females, (as opposed to 'sex' which highlights biological, and therefore ineradicable, differences between men and women). Gender is therefore a social construct, usually based on stereotypes of 'feminine' and 'masculine' behaviour. Feminists typically emphasize the distinction in order to demonstrate that physical or biological differences (sexual differences) need not mean that women and men must have different social roles and positions (gender differences). In short, gender equality is based on the belief that sexual differences have no social or political significance.

● **First-wave feminism:** The early form of feminism, dating from the mid-nineteenth century to the 1960s, which sought to achieve gender equality in the areas of legal and political rights, particularly suffrage rights.

● **Second-wave feminism:** The form of feminism that emerged in the 1960s and 1970s, and was characterized by a more radical concern with 'women's liberation', including, and perhaps especially, in the private sphere.

Gender politics

An awareness of the political significance of gender dates back to the emergence of so-called 'first-wave feminism', which emerged in the nineteenth century and was shaped, above all, by the campaign for female suffrage: the right to vote. Its core belief was that women should enjoy the same legal and political rights as men, with a particular emphasis being placed on female suffrage on the grounds that if women could vote, all other forms of other sexual discrimination or prejudice would quickly disappear. This essentially liberal form of feminism was nevertheless 'difference-blind', in that its goal was the achievement of genderless 'personhood', allowing women and men to transcend 'difference'. However, the emergence of second-wave feminism in the 1960s and 1970s served to recast feminism as a form of identity politics. Radical feminists, such as Kate Millett (1970) and Mary Daly (1978), argued that gender divisions are the deepest and most politically significant of all social cleavages. All contemporary and historical societies are therefore seen to be characterized by patriarchy (see p. 65); that is, the dominance of men and the subordination of women, usually rooted in the rule of the husband-father within the family. From this perspective, nothing short of a 'sexual revolution' that would fundamentally transform cultural and personal relationships, as well as economic and political structures, could bring an end to gender inequality.

The emphasis within feminism on identity and difference increased with the emergence of strains within radical feminism that emphasized the fundamental and unalterable differences between women and men. An example of this was the 'pro-woman' position, which has been particularly strong in France and the USA. This position extols the positive virtues of fertility and motherhood, and rejects the idea that women should try to be 'more like men'. Instead, they should recognize and embrace their sisterhood, the bonds that link them to all other women. The pro-woman position therefore accepts that women's attitudes and values are different from men's, but implies that, in certain respects, women are superior, possessing qualities of creativity, sensitivity and caring which men can never fully appreciate or develop. The acknowledgement of deep, and possibly ineradicable, differences between women and men also led some feminists to argue that the roots of patriarchy lie within the male sex itself. In this view, 'all men' are physically and psychologically disposed to oppress 'all women'; in other words, 'men are the enemy'. In *Against Our Will* (1975), Susan Brownmiller therefore argued that men dominate women through a process of physical and sexual abuse. Men have created an 'ideology of rape', which amounts to a 'conscious process of intimidation by which all men keep all women in a state of fear'. Such a line of argument leads in the direction of feminist separatism, whereby women retreat from corrupt and corrupting male society. For some radical feminists, this had important implications for women's personal and sexual conduct. Only women who remain celibate or choose lesbianism can regard themselves as 'woman-identified women'. In the slogan attributed to Ti-Grace Atkinson: 'feminism is the theory; lesbianism is the practice' (Charvet, 1982).

Since the 1990s, a younger generation of feminist theorists have sought to articulate a feminist 'third wave', distinct from the campaigns and demands of the women's movement of the 1960s and 1970s. This has usually involved a more radical engagement with the politics of difference, especially going beyond those

Ayatollah Khomeini (1900–89)

Iranian cleric and political leader. Khomeini was one of the foremost scholars in the major theological centre of Qom until he was expelled from Iran in 1964. His return from exile in 1979 sparked the 'Islamic Revolution', leaving the Ayatollah (literally, 'gift of Allah') as the supreme leader of the world's first Islamic state until his death. Breaking decisively with the Shi'a tradition that the clergy remain outside politics, Khomeini's world-view was rooted in a clear division between the oppressed (under-stood largely as the poor and excluded of the developing world) and the oppressors (seen as the twin Satans: the USA and the USSR, capitalism and communism). Islam thus became a theo-political project aimed at regenerating the Islamic world by ridding it of occupation and corruption from outside.

strands within radical feminism that had emphasized that women are different from men, to a concern with differences between women. In so doing, third-wave feminists have tried to rectify an over-emphasis within earlier forms of feminism on the aspirations and experiences of middle-class, white women in developed societies, meaning that the contemporary women's movement is characterized by diversity, hybridity, and even contradiction. This has allowed the voices of, amongst others, low-income women, women in the developing world and 'women of colour' to be heard more effectively. Black feminism has been particularly effective in this respect, challenging the tendency within conventional forms of feminism to ignore racial differences and suggesting that women endure a common oppression by virtue of their sex. Especially strong in the USA, black feminism portrays sexism and racism as linked systems of oppression, and highlights the particular and complex range of gender, racial and economic disadvantages that confront women of colour.

Religion and politics

● **Hybridity:** A condition of social and cultural mixing; the term derives from cross-breeding between genetically dissimilar plants or animals.

● **Secularism:** The belief that religion should not intrude into secular (worldly) affairs, usually reflected in the desire to separate church from state.

● **Secularization thesis:** The theory that modernization is invariably accompanied by the victory of reason over religion and the displacement of spiritual values by secular ones.

The impact of religion on political life had been progressively restricted by the spread of liberal culture and ideas, a process that has been particularly prominent in the industrialized West. Nevertheless, liberal secularism is by no means an anti-religious tendency. Rather, it is concerned to establish a 'proper' sphere and role for religion. Emphasizing the importance of the public/private divide, it has sought to confine religion to a private arena, leaving public life to be organized on a strictly secular basis. However, the emergence of new, and often more assertive, forms of religiosity, the increasing impact of religious movements and, most importantly, a closer relationship between religion and politics, especially since the 1970s, has confounded the so-called 'secularization thesis'. This was dramatically demonstrated by the 1979 'Islamic Revolution' in Iran, which brought the Ayatollah Khomeini to power as the leader of the world's first Islamic state. Nevertheless, it soon became clear that this was not an exclusively Islamic development, as 'fundamentalist' movements emerged within Christianity, particularly in the form of the so-called 'new Christian Right' in the USA, and within Hinduism and Sikhism in India. Other manifestations of this

CONCEPT

Islamism

Islamism (also called 'political Islam' or 'radical Islam') is a politico-religious ideology, as opposed to a simple belief in Islam. Although Islamist ideology has no single creed or political manifestation, certain common beliefs can be identified, as follows. (1) Society should be reconstructed in line with the ideals of Islam. (2) The modern secular state should be replaced by an 'Islamic state'. (3) The West and western values are viewed as corrupt and corrupting, justifying, for some, the notion of a *jihad* against them. However, distinct Sunni and Shi'a versions of Islamism have been developed, the former linked to Wahhabism, the latter to Iran's 'Islamic Revolution'.

● **Moral relativism:** A condition in which there is deep and widespread disagreement over moral issues. (see p. 453).

● **Theocracy:** Literally, rule by God; the principle that religious authority should prevail over political authority, usually through the domination of church over state.

● **Shari'a** (Arabic): Literally, the 'way' or 'path'; divine Islamic law, based on principles expressed in the Koran.

● **Clash of civilizations thesis:** The idea that twenty-first century conflict will be primarily cultural in character, rather than ideological, political or economic (Huntington, 1996).

include the spread of US-style Pentecostalism in Latin America, Africa and East Asia; the growth in China of Falun Gong, a spiritual movement that has been taken by the authorities to express anti-communism and is reportedly supported by 70 million people; the regeneration of Orthodox Christianity in post-communist Russia; the emergence of the Aum Shinrikyo Doomsday cult in Japan; and growing interest across western societies in myriad forms of Eastern mysticism, and spiritual and therapeutic systems (yoga, meditation, Pilates, Shiatsu and so forth).

Although religious revivalism can be seen as a consequence of the larger upsurge in identity politics, religion has proved to be a particularly potent means of regenerating personal and social identity in modern circumstances. As modern societies are increasingly atomistic, diffuse and pluralized, there is, arguably, a greater thirst for the sense of meaning, purpose and certainty that religious consciousness appears to offer. This applies because religion provides believers with a world-view and moral vision that has higher, or indeed supreme, authority, as it stems from a supposedly divine source. Religion thus defines the very grounds of people's being; it gives them an ultimate frame of reference, as well as a moral orientation in a world increasingly marked by moral relativism. In addition, religion generates a powerful sense of social solidarity, connecting people to one another at a 'thick' or deep level, as opposed to the 'thin' connectedness that is conventional in modern societies.

The link between religion and politics has been clearest in relation to Islam, where it has been reflected in an upsurge in Islamic fundamentalism, often termed 'Islamism'. Fundamentalism in Islam does not imply a belief in the literal truth of the Koran, for this is accepted by all Muslims and, in that sense, all Muslims are fundamentalists. Instead, it means an intense and militant faith in Islamic beliefs as the overriding principles of social life and politics, as well as of personal morality. Islamic fundamentalists wish to establish the primacy of religion over politics. In practice, this means the founding of an 'Islamic state', a theocracy, ruled by spiritual rather than temporal authority, and applying the Shari'a. The Shari'a lays down a code for legal and religious behaviour, including a system of punishment for most crimes, as well as rules of personal conduct for both men and women. However, Islam should be distinguished from Islamism. Islamism refers either to a political creed based on Islamic ideas and principles, or to the political movement that has been inspired by that creed. It has had three core aims. First, it promotes pan-Islamic unity, distinguishing Islamism from traditional political nationalism. Second, it seeks the purification of the Islamic world through the overthrow of 'apostate' leaders of Muslim states (secularized or pro-western leaders). Third, it calls for the removal of western, and especially US, influence from the Muslim world, and possibly a wider politico-cultural struggle against the West itself. The rise of Islamism has sometimes been interpreted as evidence of an emerging 'clash of civilizations' between Islam and the West, a notion that has profound implications for both global politics and for western societies which have significant Muslim communities (see p. 168).

Cultural diversity

One of the most powerful factors underpinning the global significance of identity politics has been the growth of international migration, particularly since

Transnational community

A transnational community is a community whose cultural identity, political allegiances and psychological orientations cut across or transcend national borders. Transnational communities can therefore be thought of as 'deterritorialized nations' or 'global tribes'. The strength of transnational allegiances depends on factors such as the circumstances of migration and the length of stay in the new country. Nevertheless, transnational communities typically have multiple attachments, as allegiances to a country of origin do not preclude the formation of attachments to a country of settlement.

● **Diaspora**: Literally, dispersion (from the Hebrew); implies displacement or dispersal by force, but is also used to refer to the communities that have arisen as a result of such dispersal.

● **Affirmative action**: Reverse or 'positive' discrimination which accords preferential treatment to groups on the basis of their past disadvantage.

● **Assimilation**: The process through which immigrant communities lose their cultural distinctiveness by adjusting to the values, allegiances and lifestyles of the 'host' society.

the 1950s. This has given an increasing number of societies a distinctively multi-cultural character, with examples of still highly homogenous countries, such as Japan, becoming rarer. Ethnic minority communities developed in many European countries as a result of the end of empire and of deliberate attempts by governments to recruit workers from abroad to help in the process of postwar reconstruction. Since the 1980s, however, there has been a significant intensification of cross-border migration across the globe, creating what some have seen as a 'hyper-mobile planet'. This has happened for two main reasons. First, there have been a growing number of refugees (reaching a peak of about 18 million in 1993), which resulted from war, ethnic conflict and political upheaval in areas ranging from Algeria, Rwanda and Uganda to Iraq and Afghanistan. Second, economic globalization (see p. 142) has intensified pressures for international migration, both because people have been 'pushed' to migrate through the disruption that has been caused to many developing economies by the pressures generated by global markets and because they have been 'pulled' to migrate by the growth of a stratum of low-paid, low-skilled and low-state jobs in developed societies that indigenous populations are increasingly unwilling to fill. This has led to a position in which, for instance, roughly one-third of the total population of the Gulf states, and two-thirds of their working populations, are (predominantly female) non-nationals, largely from South and Southeast Asia. Such trends have significantly strained national identity in many countries and contributed to the development of so-called 'transnational communities', sometimes call **diasporic** communities.

As a growing number of countries have come to accept as an irreversible fact that their populations have a multi-ethnic, multireligious or multicultural character, various attempts have been made to reconcile cultural diversity and identity-related difference with civic and political cohesion. However, how is political stability to be maintained in societies in which the monocultural bonds of political nationalism have been fatally undermined? Some, indeed, view this as the central political challenge of the twenty-first century. Attempts to balance diversity against cohesion are usually dubbed 'multiculturalism'.

Multiculturalism is a broad and often ill-defined term, which may simply stress cultural differentiation that is based on race, ethnicity or language. However, multiculturalism not only recognizes the fact of cultural diversity; it also holds that such differences should be respected and publicly affirmed.

Although the USA, as an immigrant society, has long been a multicultural society, the cause of multiculturalism in this sense was not taken up until the rise of the black consciousness movement and the advent of '**affirmative action**'. Australia has been officially committed to multiculturalism since the early 1970s, in recognition of its increasing 'Asianization' through an acceptance of the rights of its aboriginal peoples. In New Zealand, multiculturalism is linked to a recognition of the role of Maori culture in forging a distinctive national identity. In Canada, the country that has demonstrated the greatest official commitment to multiculturalism, it is associated with attempts to achieve reconciliation between French-speaking Quebec and the English-speaking majority population (see p. 114), and an acknowledgement of the rights of the indigenous Inuit peoples. In the UK, multiculturalism recognizes the existence of significant black and Asian communities, and abandons the demand that they **assimilate** into white society. In Germany, this applies to Turkish groups.

Multiculturalism

Multiculturalism is used as both a descriptive and a normative term. As a descriptive term, it refers to cultural diversity arising from the existence within a society of two or more groups whose beliefs and practices generate a distinctive sense of collective identity. As a normative term, multiculturalism implies a positive endorsement of communal diversity, based on either the right of cultural groups to respect and recognition, or the alleged benefits to the larger society of moral and cultural diversity. Multiculturalism, in this sense, acknowledges the importance of beliefs, values and ways of life in establishing a sense of self-worth for individuals and groups alike.

The central theme within all forms of multiculturalism is that individual identity is culturally embedded, in the sense that people largely derive their understanding of the world and their framework of moral beliefs from the culture in which they live and develop. Distinctive cultures therefore deserve to be protected or strengthened, particularly when they belong to minority or vulnerable groups. This leads to the idea of minority or multicultural rights, sometimes seen as 'special' rights. Will Kymlicka (1995) identified three kinds of minority rights: self-government rights, polyethnic rights and representation rights. Self-government rights belong, Kymlicka argued, to what he called 'national minorities', peoples who are territorially concentrated, possess a shared language and are characterized by a 'meaningful way of life across the full range of human activities'. Examples would include the Native Americans, the Inuits in Canada, the Maoris in New Zealand and the Aborigines in Australia. In these cases, he argued, the right to self-government should involve the devolution of political power, usually through federalism (see p. 382), although it may extend to the right of secession and, therefore, to sovereign independence. Polyethnic rights are rights that help ethnic groups and religious minorities, that have developed through immigration to express and maintain their cultural distinctiveness. They would, for instance, provide the basis for legal exemptions, such as the exemption of Jews and Muslims from animal slaughtering laws, the exemption of Sikh men from wearing motorcycle helmets, and the exemption of Muslim girls from school dress codes. Special representation rights attempt to redress the under-representation of minority or disadvantaged groups in education, and in senior positions in political and public life. Such rights, which in the USA take the form of affirmative action, imply the practice of reverse or 'positive' discrimination, which attempts to compensate for past discrimination or continuing cultural subordination. Their justification is not only that they ensure full and equal participation, but also that they are the only means of guaranteeing that public policy reflects the interests of all groups and peoples, and not merely those of traditionally dominant groups.

However, there is neither a settled view of how multicultural societies should operate, nor of how far multiculturalism should go in positively endorsing communal diversity. There are three main models of multiculturalism:

- Liberal multiculturalism
- Pluralist multiculturalism
- Cosmopolitan multiculturalism.

Liberal multiculturalism is rooted in a commitment to freedom and toleration: the ability to choose one's own moral beliefs, cultural practices and way of life, regardless of whether these are disapproved of by others. However, the liberal model of multiculturalism only provides a qualified endorsement of communal diversity, highlighting the dangers that may also be implicit in identity politics. In particular, liberals are only prepared to tolerate views, values and social practices that are themselves tolerant; that is, to those that are compatible with personal freedom and autonomy. Liberal multiculturalists may therefore be unwilling to endorse practices such as female circumcision, forced (and possibly arranged) marriages and female dress codes, however much the groups concerned may believe that these are crucial to the maintenance of their cultural identity.

POLITICS IN ACTION ...

Muslims in the West: an internal clash of civilizations?

Events: In 2011, estimates of the number of Muslims living in the European Union ranged from 15 to 20 million. In the early post-1945 period, immigration mainly came from former colonies. The majority of France's Muslim population (about 6 million – the largest in Europe) thus have a heritage in Algeria, Morocco and Tunisia, while most of the UK's Muslims (almost 2 million) came originally from Pakistan. Later Muslim immigration has often been linked to war and civil strife in countries such as Bosnia, Iraq, Afghanistan and Somalia. Nevertheless, in recent years several incidents have raised issues about the relationship between western European states in particular and, at least, elements in their Muslim populations, including the following:

- the 1989 'Rushdie affair', in which Muslim protesters in several countries denounced Salman Rushdie's *The Satanic Verses* as blasphemous and Ayatollah Khomeini issued a *fatwa* condemning the author to death
- the 2004 murder of Theo van Gogh, a Dutch film director who had collaborated on a film criticizing the treatment of women in Muslim countries
- the 2004 Madrid train bombings, carried out by an 'al-Qaeda-inspired' group
- the 2005 'Danish cartoons affair', in which the publication of 12 cartoons of the Prophet Mohammad by the newspaper *Jyllands-Posten* provoked protests across the Muslim world
- the 2005 London bombings, carried out by so-called 'home-grown' Islamist terrorists.

Significance: The existence of significant Muslim populations in the West has been seen by some as a threat to social cohesion and possibly national security (Caldwell, 2009). Such a view is in line with Huntington's (1996) 'clash of civilizations' thesis, which suggests that Islamic values and beliefs are fundamentally incompatible with those of the liberal-democratic West. Clashes over issues such as whether protecting 'sacred' beliefs justifies the curtailment of free speech and press freedom thus highlight a more profound divide over whether the public realm should be strictly secular, or shaped by Islamic ideas and values. As, in this view, Islam is anti-liberal and anti-pluralist, the politics of cultural recognition threatens to entrench Muslim separatism and sow the seeds of civic conflict. The most appropriate response to Muslim communities in the West is therefore to reject multi-culturalism and insist on a strategy of integration. Such a stance has been adopted most clearly in France, where, in 2004, a law was passed forbidding the wearing of any 'ostentatious' religious articles, including Islamic head-scarves, in state-funded schools, with a ban on the wearing of face-covering headgear, including *niqads* and other veils, in public places coming into force in 2011.

Others, however, view multiculturalism as the most appropriate response to what has been called the 'Muslim question' (Modood, 2007; Parekh, 2008). From this perspective, the image of Muslims in the West as an 'enemy within' is based on a serious misrepresentation of Islam and of the views of Muslim populations. Surveys, for instance, consistently show that Muslims in the Europe are predominantly satisfied with the secular nature of western society and hold political views little different from other cultural groups. Moreover, when Muslim identity politics has become entangled with extremism, even violence, this is better explained by social or political factors than by cultural incompatibility. Muslim communities in Europe, for example, tend to be socially marginalized, facing higher unemployment and poverty rates, and having lower educational achievement than the general population. Moreover, international developments since 9/11 have seen a range of western states participating in wars against and occupations of Muslim countries. In this light, the politics of cultural recognition is likely to weaken the trend towards extremism and violence, by giving Muslim populations a clearer stake in society, while a strategy of 'enforced' integration threatens to be counter-productive, being perceived as evidence of 'Islamophobia' and helping to deepen alienation and resentment.

Isaiah Berlin (1909–97)

UK historian of ideas and philosopher. Berlin was born in Riga, Latvia, and came to Britain in 1921. He developed a form of liberal pluralism that was grounded in a life-long commitment to empiricism and influenced by the ideas of counter-Enlightenment thinkers, including Vico (1668–1744), Herder (see p. 110) and Alexander Herzen (1812–70). Basic to Berlin's philosophical stance was a belief in moral pluralism, the idea that conflicts of values are intrinsic to human life. His best-known political writing is *Four Essays on Liberty* (1958), in which he extolled the virtues of 'negative' freedom over 'positive' freedom. Berlin's writings constitute a defence of western liberalism against totalitarianism.

Pluralist multiculturalism provides firmer foundations for a theory of cultural diversity because it is based on the idea of **value pluralism**. Developed in particular in the writings of Isaiah Berlin, this holds that people are bound to disagree about the ultimate ends of life. As values conflict, the human predicament is inevitably characterized by moral conflict. In this view, liberal or western beliefs, such as support for personal freedom, democracy and secularization, have no greater moral authority than rival beliefs. This form of multiculturalism also focuses more explicitly on unequal power relations in society, particularly the extent to which the dominant culture in western societies reflects the values and interests of the majority group and so subordinates minority communities. Cultural recognition therefore counters oppression and serves to expose the corrupt and corrupting nature of western culture, values and lifestyles, believed to be tainted by the inheritance of colonialism and racialism, or by materialism and 'godless' permissiveness. Such thinking has been especially controversial in relation to Muslim minorities in western societies (see p. 168).

Cosmopolitan multiculturalism endorses cultural diversity and identity politics, but, in contrast to both liberal and pluralist views, sees them more as transitional states in a larger reconstruction of political sensibilities and priorities. This form of multiculturalism celebrates diversity on the grounds of what each culture can learn from other cultures, and because of the prospects for personal self-development offered by a world of wider cultural opportunities and lifestyle choices. Its acceptance of multiple identities and hybridity lead to a kind of pick-and-mix multiculturalism, which portrays society as a 'melting pot', as opposed to a 'cultural mosaic' of separate ethnic or religious groups.

● **Value pluralism:** The theory that there is no single, overriding conception of the 'good life' but, rather, a number of competing and equally legitimate conceptions.

SUMMARY

● Societies are characterized by regular patterns of social interaction. However, the 'thick' social connectedness of close bonds and fixed allegiances is giving way to the 'thin' connectedness of more fluid, individualized social arrangements. This reflects, in large part, the transition from industrial to so-called post-industrial society, and, particularly, the declining importance of social class.

● Post-industrialism is characterized, amongst other things, by an increasing emphasis on knowledge and information generally, with the advent of the internet and the wider use of computer-based technologies having given rise to the 'information society'. Not only do information societies connect more people to more other people, but the nature of those connections has also changed, especially through the development of looser and more diffuse networks.

● At the heart of the trend towards the 'thinning' of social connectedness is the rise of individualism. Individualism was a child of industrial capitalism, but it has been boosted by a growing ethic of materialism and consumerism, given greater prominence, from the 1980s onwards, by the wider influence of neoliberal or free-market thinking. However, the spread of individualism may weaken community and people's sense of social belonging, a trend that may be particularly evident in the English-speaking world.

● The rise of identity politics has been evident in the growing recognition of cultural and other forms of difference, especially providing a vehicle through which groups can challenge marginalization by adopting a more positive and assertive sense of identity. Nevertheless, identity politics does not have a settled political character and it has been shaped around many principles, the most important of which are race and ethnicity, gender, religion and culture.

● Attempts to regenerate personal and social identity have given rise to new, and sometimes more radical, forms of politics. These include forms of ethnic assertiveness, often associated with black nationalism; second-wave feminism and a stronger emphasis on issues of gender equality and gender difference; religious revivalism, commonly expressed through fundamentalist movements, especially in Islam; and multiculturalism and the 'celebration' of cultural diversity.

Questions for discussion

● Why has social connectedness become 'thinner'?

● Has class conflict in modern society been resolved or merely suppressed?

● Has the network society substituted 'virtual' communities for real communities, and with what consequences?

● Is individualism the enemy of social solidarity and cohesion?

● Does consumerism liberate people or enslave them?

● What are the main factors explaining the growth of identity politics?

● Is identity politics a liberating or oppressive force?

● To what extent has the recognition of ethnic and gender divisions produced meaningful political change?

● Do modern societies need to be protected from cultural diversity?

Further reading

Bauman, Z. *Liquid Modernity* (2000). An examination of the changing nature of human connectedness in the light of the emergence of 'liquid' or 'light' modernity.

Beck, U. and E. Beck-Gernsheim, *Individualization: Institutionalized Individualism and its Social and Political Consequences* (2001). A critical examination of the process of individualization that examines both its causes and its wide-ranging consequences.

Kumar, K. *From Post-Industrial to Post-Modern Society: New Theories of the Contemporary World* (2004). A lucid and insightful study of the idea of the information society and theories of post-Fordism and post-modernity.

Parekh, B. *A New Politics of Identity: Political Principles of an Interdependent World* (2008). A wide-ranging analysis of the impact of global interconnectedness on ethnic, religious, national and other identities.

CHAPTER 8

Political Culture and the Media

*'Mankind, in general, judge more by their eyes than their hands;
for all can see the appearance, but few can touch the reality.'*

NICCOLÒ MACHIAVELLI, *The Prince* (1532)

PREVIEW Much of politics takes place in our heads; that is, it is shaped by our ideas, values and assumptions about how society should be organized, and our expectations, hopes and fears about government. Ultimately, what we believe about the society in which we live may be more important than the reality of its power structure, and the actual distribution of resources and opportunities within it. Perception may not only be more important than reality; in practical terms, perception may *be* reality. This highlights the vital role played by what is called 'political culture'. People's beliefs, symbols and values structure both their attitude to the political process and, crucially, their view of the regime in which they live. However, there is significant disagreement about the nature and role of the political culture, not least over whether it sustains democracy or is aligned with the interests of dominant groups. Others have highlighted concerns about the political culture's (apparently) declining capacity to foster civic engagement and a sense of social belonging. The issue of the political culture also draws attention to the extent to which the politics of modern societies is conducted through the media – newspapers, television, the internet, mobile phones and so on. The media constitute much more than a channel of communications; they are part of the political process itself, affecting, and not merely reflecting, the distribution of power in society at large. Long-standing debate about the media's relationship with democracy and styles of governance have been given a fresh twist by the advent of electronic-based 'new' media, while media influence generally has been associated with a growing emphasis in politics on 'news managment' and so-called 'spin'.

KEY ISSUES
- How do individuals and groups acquire their political attitudes and values?
- Do democratic regimes depend on the existence of a distinctive 'civic culture'?
- Are modern societies characterized by free competition between values and ideas, or by a 'dominant' culture?
- To what extent do the media shape political attitudes?
- How do the media affect the distribution of political power?
- Is the politics of 'spin' inevitable in the media age?

CONCEPT

Political culture

Culture, in its broadest sense, is the way of life of a people. Sociologists and anthropologists tend to distinguish between 'culture' and 'nature', the former encompassing that which is passed on from one generation to the next by learning, rather than through biological inheritance. Political scientists, however, use the term in a narrower sense to refer to a people's psychological orientation, political culture being the 'pattern of orientations' to political objects such as parties, government, the constitution, expressed in beliefs, symbols and values. Political culture differs from public opinion in that it is fashioned out of long-term values rather than simply people's reactions to specific policies and problems.

POLITICAL CULTURE

Political thinkers through the ages have acknowledged the importance of attitudes, values and beliefs. However, these past thinkers did not see them as part of a 'political culture'. Burke (see p. 36), for instance, wrote about custom and tradition, Marx (see p. 41) about ideology, and Herder (see p. 110) about national spirit. All of them, nevertheless, agreed about the vital role that values and beliefs play in promoting the stability and survival of a regime. Interest amongst political scientists in the idea of political culture emerged in the 1950s and 1960s as new techniques of behavioural analysis displaced more traditional, institutional approaches to the subject. The classic work in this respect was Almond and Verba's *The Civic Culture* (1963), which used opinion surveys to analyse political attitudes and democracy in five countries: the USA, the UK, West Germany, Italy and Mexico. This work was stimulated, in part, by a desire to explain the collapse of representative government in interwar Italy, Germany and elsewhere, and the failure of democracy in many newly-independent developing states after 1945. Although interest in political culture faded in the 1970s and 1980s, the debate has been revitalized since the 1990s as a result of efforts in Eastern Europe to construct democracy out of the ashes of communism, and growing anxiety in mature democracies, such as the USA, about the apparent decline of social capital (see p. 175) and civic engagement. However, there is also debate about whether or not political culture is shaped by the ideas and interests of elite groups. This, in turn, is linked to rival views of the mass media (see p. 179) and the extent to which government can now manipulate political communication, considered later in the chapter.

Civic culture or ideological hegemony?

Debate about the nature of political culture has often focused on the idea of civic culture, usually associated with the writings of Almond and Verba (1963, 1980). Almond and Verba set out to identify the political culture that most effectively upheld democratic politics. They identified three general types of political culture:

- A *participant* political culture. This is one in which citizens pay close attention to politics, and regard popular participation as both desirable and effective.
- A *subject* political culture. This is characterized by more passivity amongst citizens, and the recognition that they have only a very limited capacity to influence government.
- A *parochial* political culture. This is marked by the absence of a sense of citizenship, with people identifying with their locality, rather than the nation, and having neither the desire nor the ability to participate in politics.

● Civic culture: A set of specific attitudes which are crucial to the success of modern democracies.

Although Almond and Verba accepted that a participant culture came closest to the democratic ideal, they argued that the 'civic culture' is a blend of all three, in that it reconciles the participation of citizens in the political process with the vital necessity for government to govern. Democratic stability, in their view, is underpinned by a political culture that is characterized by a blend of activity and passivity on the part of citizens, and a balance between obligation and performance on the part of government.

In their initial study (1963), Almond and Verba concluded that the UK came closest to the civic culture, exhibiting both participant and subject features. In other words, while the British thought that they could influence government, they were also willing to obey authority. The USA also scored highly, its relative weakness being that, as participant attitudes predominated over subject ones, Americans were not particularly law-abiding. The difficulty of building or rebuilding a civic culture was underlined by the examples of both West Germany and Italy. By the early 1960s, neither country appeared to have a strong participant culture; while the subject culture was dominant in Germany, parochial attitudes remained firmly entrenched in Italy. Almond and Verba's later study (1980) highlighted a number of shifts, notably declining national pride and confidence in the UK and the USA, which contrasted with a rise in civic propensities in Germany.

The civic-culture approach to the study of political attitudes and values has, however, been widely criticized. In the first place, its model of the psychological dispositions that make for a stable democracy is highly questionable. In particular, the emphasis on passivity and the recognition that deference to authority is healthy has been criticized by those who argue that political participation

is the very stuff of democratic government. Almond and Verba suggested a 'sleeping dogs' theory of democratic culture that implies that low participation indicates broad satisfaction with government, which politicians, in turn, will be anxious to maintain. On the other hand, when less than half the adult population bothers to vote, as regularly occurs in the USA, this could simply reflect widespread alienation and ingrained disadvantage. (The link between declining participation rates and the health of the political system is discussed in greater detail in Chpater 20.)

Second, the civic-culture thesis rests on the unproven assumption that political attitudes and values shape behaviour, and not the other way round. In short, a civic culture may be more a consequence of democracy than its cause. If this is the case, political culture may provide an index of the health of democracy, but it cannot be seen as a means of promoting stable democratic rule. Finally, Almond and Verba's approach tends to treat political culture as homogeneous; that is, as little more than a cipher for national culture or national character. In so doing, it pays little attention to political subcultures and tends to disguise fragmentation and social conflict. In contrast, radical approaches to political culture tend to highlight the significance of social divisions, such as those based on class, race and gender. (see Chapter 7).

A very different view of the role and nature of political culture has been developed within the Marxist tradition. Although Marx portrayed capitalism as a system of class exploitation and oppression operating through the ownership of the means of production, he also acknowledged the power of ideas, values and beliefs. As Marx and Engels put it in *The German Ideology* ([1846]1970), 'the ideas of the ruling class are in every epoch the ruling ideas, i.e. the class which is the ruling *material* force of society, is at the same time the ruling *intellectual* force'. In Marx's view, ideas and culture are part of a 'superstructure' that is conditioned or determined by the economic 'base', the mode of production.

CONCEPT

Hegemony

Hegemony (from the Greek *hegemonia*, meaning 'leader') is, in its simplest sense, the ascendancy or domination of one element of a system over others. In Marxist theory, the term is used in a more specific sense. In the writings of Gramsci, (see p. 175), hegemony refers to the ability of a dominant class to exercise power by winning the consent of those it subjugates, as an alternative to the use of coercion. As a non-coercive form of class rule, hegemony typically operates through the dissemination of bourgeois values and beliefs throughout society.

● **Bourgeois ideology:** A Marxist term, denoting ideas and theories that serve the interests of the bourgeoisie by disguising the contradictions of capitalist society.

These ideas have provided Marxism with two theories of culture. The first suggests that culture is essentially class-specific: as members of a class share the same experiences and have a common economic position and interests, they are likely to have broadly similar ideas, values and beliefs. In Marx's words, 'it is not the consciousness of men that determines their existence, but their social existence that determines their consciousness'. Proletarian culture and ideas can therefore be expected to differ markedly from bourgeois ones. The second theory of culture emphasizes the degree to which the ideas of the ruling class (what Marx referred to as 'ideology') pervade society and become the 'ruling ideas' of the age. In this view, political culture, or even civic culture, is thus nothing more than **bourgeois ideology**. What is important about this view is that it sees culture, values and beliefs as a form of power. From the Marxist perspective, the function of ideology is to reconcile subordinate classes to their exploitation and oppression by propagating myths, delusions and falsehoods (in Engels' words, 'false consciousness'). Later Marxists have understood this process in terms of bourgeois 'hegemony'.

Modern Marxists have been quick to acknowledge that, in no sense, do the 'ruling ideas' of the bourgeoisie monopolize intellectual and cultural life in a capitalist society, excluding all rival views. Rather, they accept that cultural, ideological and political competition does exist, but stress that this competition is unequal. Quite simply, ideas and values that uphold the capitalist order have an overwhelming advantage over ideas and values that question or challenge it. Such ideological hegemony may, in fact, be successful precisely because it operates behind the illusion of free speech, open competition and political pluralism – what Herbert Marcuse (see p. 42) termed 'repressive tolerance'.

The most influential twentieth-century exponent of this view was Antonio Gramsci (see p. 175). Gramsci drew attention to the degree to which the class system is upheld not simply by unequal economic and political power, but also by bourgeois hegemony. This consists of the spiritual and cultural supremacy of the ruling class, brought about through the spread of bourgeois values and beliefs via 'civil society'; the mass media, the churches, youth movements, trade unions and so forth. What makes this process so insidious is that it extends beyond formal learning and education into the very common sense of the age. The significance of Gramsci's analysis is that, in order for socialism to be achieved, a 'battle of ideas' has to be waged through which proletarian principles, values and theories displace, or at least challenge, bourgeois ideas.

The Marxist view of culture as ideological power rests on the distinction between subjective or *felt* interests (what people think they want) and objective or *real* interests (what people would want if they could make independent and informed choices). This draws attention to what Stephen Lukes (2004) called a 'radical view of power' (see p. 9): '*A* exercises power over *B* when *A* affects *B* in a manner contrary to *B*'s interests'. Such a view of political culture has, however, attracted considerable criticism. Some have argued that it is unwarrantedly patronizing to suggest that the values and beliefs of ordinary people have been foisted upon them by manipulation and indoctrination. The acceptance of capitalist values and beliefs by the working classes may, for instance, merely reflect their perception that capitalism works.

The dominant-ideology model of political culture may also overstate the degree of homogeneity in the values and beliefs of modern societies. While a

Antonio Gramsci (1891–1937)

Italian Marxist and social theorist. The son of a minor public official. Gramsci joined the Socialist Party in 1913, and in 1921 became the General Secretary of the newly-formed Italian Communist Party. Although an elected member of parliament, he was imprisoned by Mussolini in 1926. He remained in prison until his death. His *Prison Notebooks* (Gramsci, 1971), written in 1929–35, tried to counterbalance the emphasis within orthodox Marxism on 'scientific' determinism by stressing the importance of the political and intellectual struggle. Although proponents of Eurocommunism have claimed him as an influence, he remained throughout his life a Leninist and a revolutionary.

CONCEPT

Social capital

The concept of social capital was developed in the 1970s to highlight the social and cultural factors that underpin wealth creation. The term has since been used to refer to social connectiveness, as represented by networks, norms and trust that promote civic engagement. In common with economic assets, social capital can decline or rise, usually through education and a stress on active citizenship. The alleged decline in social capital in modern society has been linked, variously, to the 'parenting deficit', the rise of individualism and the increase in social and geographical mobility.

'ruling' ideology may provide a dominant class with self-belief and a sense of purpose, it is less clear, as Abercrombie *et al.*, (1980) argued, that subordinate classes have been successfully integrated into this value system. Finally, the Marxist view, which purports to establish a link between unequal class power and cultural and ideological bias, may do nothing more than describe a tendency found in all societies for powerful groups to propagate self-serving ideas. Whether this constitutes a dominant value *system*, in which a coherent and consistent message is disseminated through the media, schools, the churches and so on, is rather more questionable.

Decline of social capital?

The process of political and economic reconstruction in former communist states has stimulated renewed interest in the issue of political culture since the 1990s. This is because pervasive state control over a number of generations had evidently destroyed or suppressed the social connections and sense of civic responsibility that usually sustain democratic politics. In other words, there was a perceived need to rebuild civil society (see p. 6), in the sense of a realm of autonomous groups and associations, including businesses, interest groups, clubs and so on. Indeed, such ideas can be traced back to Alexis de Tocqueville (see p. 245), who, in the nineteenth century, had explained the USA's egalitarian institutions and democratic practices by reference to the American's propensity for participation and civic association. No sooner had this revived concern with political culture arisen in relation to postcommunist states than it was being applied to perceived problems in mature democracies.

Robert Putnam (see p. 176), for example, argued that variations in the quality of local government in different regions of Italy were determined by the presence, or absence, of traditions of civic engagement, reflected in differing levels of voter turnout, newspaper readership, and membership of choral societies and football clubs. In *Bowling Alone* (2000), Putnam drew attention to the USA's declining 'social capital', and argued that other industrialized countries are likely to follow US trends. He highlighted the emergence of a 'post-civic' generation. This was demonstrated by a 25–50 per cent drop in the number of voluntary

Robert D. Putnam (born 1941)

US political scientist and social commentator. Putnam's work has revived interest in civil society and focused attention on the importance of 'social capital': the social networks in a society that build trust and cooperation and develop 'the "I" into the "we"'. His most influential work, *Bowling Alone: The Collapse and Revival of American Community* (2000), used the image of a man bowling alone, rather than in a team, to illustrate the decline of community activity and political engagement in the USA. Amongst the causes of this decline, Putnam identifies the growing influence of television, two-career families and longer commutes. His other works include *Making Democracy Work: Civic Traditions in Italy* (1993).

CONCEPT

Communitarianism

Communitarianism is the belief that the self or person is constituted through the community, in the sense that individuals are shaped by the communities to which they belong and thus owe them a debt of respect and consideration. *Left-wing* communitarians hold that community demands unrestricted freedom and social equality. *Centrist* communitarians hold that community is grounded in reciprocal rights and responsibilities. *Right-wing* communitarians hold that community requires respect for authority and established values.

clubs and associations since 1965, and by sharp declines in attendance at public, town and school meetings, as well as in the membership of, and work done for, political parties. Putnam's view, which is influenced by communitarianism, explains declining social capital in a variety of ways. These include the spread of suburbanization and, therefore, of longer journeys to work; the rise of two-career families and their impact on the quantity and quality of parenting; and the tendency of television to privatize leisure time, misshape social perceptions and reduce achievement levels in children. From an alternative social-democratic perspective, however, the decline of civic engagement is explained by the triumph of consumer capitalism and the spread of materialist and individualist values.

Conservative thinkers have long supported their own view of social capital in the form of tradition (see p. 82) and, in particular, 'traditional values'. These are values and beliefs that have supposedly been passed down from earlier generations and so constitute a kind of cultural bedrock. Conservative politicians regularly call for such values to be 'strengthened' or 'defended', believing that they are the key to social cohesion and political stability. In the UK in the 1980s, for example, Margaret Thatcher called for the resurrection of what she called 'Victorian values', while John Major's ill-starred 'Back to Basics' initiative attempted much the same in the 1990s. In the USA, Ronald Reagan embraced the notion of the 'frontier ideology', harking back to the conquest of the American West and the virtues of self-reliance, hard work and adventurousness that he believed it exemplified. Not uncommonly, such values are linked to the family, the church and the nation; that is, to long-established institutions that supposedly embody the virtues of continuity and endurance.

In his essay 'Rationalism in Politics', Michael Oakeshott (1962) developed a further defence of continuity and tradition. Oakeshott (see p. 177) argued that traditional values and established customs should be upheld and respected on account of their familiarity, which engenders a sense of reassurance, stability and security. This suggests that there is a general human disposition to favour tradition over innovation, the established over the new. To be a conservative, Oakeshott suggested, is 'to prefer the familiar to the unknown, to prefer the tried to the untried, fact to mystery, the actual to the possible, the

Michael Oakeshott (1901–90)

UK political philosopher. Oakeshott was a professor of political science at the London School of Economics from 1951 until his retirement in 1968. His collection of essays *Rationalism in Politics and Other Essays* (1962) and his more systematic work of political philosophy *On Human Conduct* (1975) are often seen as major contributions to conservative traditionalism. By highlighting the importance of civil association and insisting on the limited province of politics, he also developed themes closely associated with liberal thought. Though often seen as an advocate of a non-ideological style of politics, in line with the ideas of Edmund Burke (see p. 36), Oakeshott influenced many of the thinkers of the New Right.

CONCEPT

Postmaterialism

Postmaterialism is a theory that explains the nature of political concerns and values in terms of levels of economic development. It is loosely based on Abraham Maslow's (1908–70) 'hierarchy of needs', which places esteem and self-actualization above material or economic needs. Postmaterialism assumes that conditions of material scarcity breed egoistical and acquisitive values, meaning that politics is dominated by economic issues. However, in conditions of widespread prosperity, individuals express more interest in 'postmaterial' or 'quality of life' issues, typically concerned with morality, political justice and personal fulfilment.

limited to the unbound, the near to the distant, the sufficient to the super abundant, the convenient to the perfect, present laughter to utopian bliss' (Oakeshott, 1962).

The defence of traditional values and established beliefs has been one of the central themes of neoconservatism, advanced in the USA by social theorists such as Daniel Bell (1976) and Irving Kristol (1983), who have warned against the destruction of spiritual values brought about both by market pressures and by the spread of permissiveness. The problem with this position, however, is that it assumes there is an authoritative moral system upon which order and stability can be based. The simple fact is that, in modern multicultural and multireligious societies, it is doubtful whether any set of values can be regarded as authoritative. To define certain values as 'traditional', 'established' or 'majority' values may simply be an attempt to impose a particular moral system on the rest of society. Indeed, empirical evidence appears to support the view that political culture is becoming increasingly fragmented, and that modern societies are characterized by growing moral and cultural diversity.

An alternative view of the social capital debate suggests not that there has been a decline of civic engagement or social connectedness, but that the forms these have taken have changed. According to Inglehart (1977, 1990), such shifts are linked to the spread of affluence and to the growth, particularly amongst young people, of 'postmaterial' values. As new generations have grown up since the 1960s accustomed, in advanced industrial countries at least, to economic security and material well-being, 'traditional' ideas about subjects such as sex, marriage and personal conduct have been displaced by more 'liberal' or 'permissive' attitudes. At the same time, traditional political attitudes and allegiances have been weakened and sometimes replaced by growing interest in issues such as feminism, nuclear disarmament, animal rights and environmental protection. Thus party membership and electoral turnout may have declined but there has been a growth of interest in single-issue protest politics and campaigning groups. Post-Fordist (see p. 154) theorists argue that such cultural changes are irresistible, because they are linked to a wholesale shift in economic and political organization that is bringing about a decline in deference and a rise of individualism (see p. 158).

CONCEPT

Political socialization

Political socialization is the process through which individuals acquire political beliefs and values, and by which these are transmitted from one generation to the next. Families and schools are usually viewed as 'primary' agents of political socialization, while the workplace, peer groups and the media are viewed as 'secondary' agents of political socialization. Interest in political socialization peaked during the so-called 'behavioural revolution', as external stimuli were seen to explain (and possibly determine) political attitudes or behaviour.

THE MEDIA AND POLITICAL COMMUNICATION

Any examination of the factors that influence people's psychological orientation to politics, whether their long-term beliefs and values (political culture) or their short-term reaction to particular policies or problems (public opinion), must, in modern circumstances, take account of the crucial role played by the media. The mass media have been recognized as politically significant since the advent of mass literacy and the popular press in the late nineteenth century. However, it is widely accepted that, through a combination of social and technological changes, the media have become increasingly powerful political actors and, in some respects, more deeply enmeshed in the political process. Three developments are particularly noteworthy. First, the impact of the so-called 'primary' agents of political socialization, such as the family and social class, has declined. Whereas once people acquired, in late childhood and adolescence in particular, a framework of political sympathies and leanings that adult experience tended to modify or deepen, but seldom radically transformed, this has been weakened in modern society by greater social and geographical mobility, and by the spread of individualist and consumerist values. This, in turn, widens the scope for the media's political influence, as they are the principal mechanism through which information about issues and policies, and therefore political choices, is presented to the public.

Second, the development of a mass television audience from the 1950s onwards, and more recently the proliferation of channels and media output associated with the 'new' media, has massively increased the media's penetration of people's everyday lives. This means that the public now relies on the media more heavily than ever before. For instance, television is a much more important source of news and current-affairs information than political meetings; many more people watch televised sport than participate in it; and even shopping is increasingly being carried out through shopping channels and the internet. Particular interest has focused on the burgeoning political significance of the internet, with, by 2011, two billion people worldwide having access to it. Although the highest internet penetration is in North America (78 per cent), Oceania/Australia (60 per cent) and Europe (58 per cent), the highest usage growth is in Africa, the Middle East and Latin America.

Third, the media have become more powerful economic actors. Not only are major media corporations major global players, but also a series of mergers has tended to incorporate the formerly discrete domains of publishing, television, film, music, computers and telecommunications into a single massive 'infotainment' industry (Scammel, 2000). Media businesses such as Microsoft, Time Warner Inc, Disney and News Corporation have accumulated so much economic and market power that no government can afford to ignore them.

● 'New' media: A generic term for the many different forms of electronic communication made possible through digital or computer technology.

Theories of the mass media

Few commentators doubt the media's ability to shape political attitudes and values or, at least, to structure political and electoral choice by influencing public perceptions about the nature and importance of issues and problems, thereby.

CONCEPT

Mass media

The media comprise those societal institutions that are concerned with the production and distribution of all forms of knowledge, information and entertainment. The 'mass' media channel communication towards a large and undifferentiated audience using relatively advanced technology. The clearest examples are the 'broadcast' media (television and radio) and the 'print' media (newspapers and magazines). The 'new' media (cable and satellite telecommunications, the Internet and so on) has, subverted the notion of mass media by dramatically increasing audience fragmentation.

However, there is considerable debate about the political significance of this influence. A series of rival theories offer contrasting views of the media's political impact. The most important of these are the following:

- the pluralist model
- the dominant-ideology model
- the elite-values model
- the market model.

Pluralist model

Pluralism (see p. 100) highlights diversity and multiplicity generally. The pluralist model of the mass media portrays the media as an ideological marketplace in which a wide range of political views are debated and discussed. While not rejecting the idea that the media can affect political views and sympathies, this nevertheless suggests that their impact is essentially neutral, in that they tend to reflect the balance of forces within society at large.

The pluralist view, nevertheless, portrays the media in strongly positive terms. In ensuring an 'informed citizenry', the mass media both enhance the quality of democracy and guarantee that government power is checked. This 'watchdog' role was classically demonstrated in the 1974 *Washington Post* investigation into the Watergate scandal, which led to the resignation of Richard Nixon as US president. Some, moreover, argue that the advent of the new media, and particularly the internet, has strengthened pluralism and political competition by giving protest groups, including 'anti-capitalist' activists, a relatively cheap and highly effective means of disseminating information and organizing campaigns, as discussed later in the chapter. However, the pluralist model suffers from significant deficiencies. For example, weak and unorganized groups are excluded from access to mainstream publishing and broadcasting, meaning that the media's ideological marketplace tends to be relatively narrow and generally pro-establishment in character. In addition, private ownership and formal independence from government may not be sufficient to guarantee the media's oppositional character in the light of the increasingly symbiotic relationship between government and journalists and broadcasters.

Dominant-ideology model

The dominant-ideology model portrays the mass media as a politically conservative force that is aligned to the interests of economic and social elites, and serves to promote compliance or political passivity amongst the masses. In its Marxist version, rooted in the larger Marxist critique of political culture (discussed earlier in the chapter) and particularly the ideas of Gramsci, it suggests that the media propagate bourgeois ideas and maintain capitalist hegemony, acting in the interests of major corporations and media moguls. Ownership, in other words, ultimately determines the political and other views that the mass media disseminate, and ownership is increasingly concentrated in the hands of a small number of global media conglomerates. The six largest are Time Warner Inc, News Corporation, Viacom, Disney, CBS and Bertelsmann.

From this perspective, the media play an important role in promoting globalization (see p. 142), in that their tendency to spread ideas, images and values that are compatible with western consumerism (see p. 159) helps to open up new markets and extend business penetration worldwide.

One of the most influential and sophisticated versions of the dominant-ideology model was developed by Noam Chomsky (see p. 181) and Ed Herman in *Manufacturing Consent* (2006), in the form of the 'propaganda model'. They identified five 'filters' through which news and political coverage are distorted by the structures of the media itself. These filters are as follows:

- the business interests of owner companies
- a sensitivity to the views and concerns of advertisers and sponsors
- the sourcing of news and information from 'agents of power', such as governments and business-backed think-tanks
- 'flak' or pressure applied to journalists, including threats of legal action
- an unquestioning belief in the benefits of market competition and consumer capitalism.

Chomsky's analysis emphasizes the degree to which the mass media can subvert democracy, helping, for example, to mobilize popular support in the USA for imperialist foreign policy goals. The dominant-ideology model is, nevertheless, also subject to criticism. Objections to it include that it underestimates the extent to which the press and broadcasters, particularly public service broadcasters, pay attention to progressive social, racial and development issues. Moreover, the assumption that media output shapes political attitudes is determinist and neglects the role played by people's own values in filtering, and possibly resisting, media messages.

Elite-values model

The elite-values model shifts attention away from the ownership of media corporations to the mechanism through which media output is controlled. This view suggests that editors, journalists and broadcasters enjoy significant professional independence, and that even the most interventionist of media moguls are able only to set a broad political agenda, but not to control day-to-day editorial decision-making. The media's political bias (see p. 183) therefore reflects the values of groups that are disproportionally represented amongst its senior professionals. However, there are a number of versions of this model, depending on the characteristics that are considered to be politically significant.

One version of the elite-valuies model holds that the anti-socialist and politically conservative views of most mainstream newspapers, magazines and television stations derive from the fact that their senior professionals are well-paid and generally from middle-class backgrounds. A quite different version is sometimes advanced by conservatives, who believe that the media reflect the views of university-educated, liberal intellectuals, whose values and concerns are quite different from those of the mass of the population. In its feminist version, this model highlights the predominance of males amongst senior journalists and broadcasters, implying that this both explains the inadequate attention given to

Noam Chomsky (born 1928)

US linguistic theorist and radical intellectual. Chomsky first achieved distinction as a scholar in the field of linguistic studies. His *Syntactic Structures* (1957) revolutionized the discipline with the theory of 'transformational grammar', which proposed that humans have an innate capacity to acquire language. Radicalized during the Vietnam War, Chomsky subsequently became the leading radical critic of US foreign policy, developing his views in an extensive range of works including *American Power and the New Mandarins* (1969), *New Military Humanism* (1999) and *Hegemony and Survival* (2004). In works such as (with Edward Herman) *Manufacturing Consent* ([1988] 2006), he developed a radical critique of the mass media and examined how popular support for imperialist aggression is mobilized.

women's views and issues by the mass media, and accounts for the confrontational style of interviewing and political discussion sometimes adopted by broadcasters and journalists. Although the elite-values model helps to explain why the range of political views expressed by the mass media is often more restricted than pluralists suggest, it also has its limitations. Chief amongst these is that it fails to take full enough account of the pressures that bear upon senior media professionals; these, for example, include the views and interests of owners and commercial considerations; notably, 'ratings' figures.

Market model

The market model of the mass media differs from the other models, in that it dispenses with the idea of media bias: it holds that newspapers and television *reflect*, rather than shape, the views of the general public. This occurs because, regardless of the personal views of media owners and senior professionals, private media outlets are, first and foremost, businesses concerned with profit maximization and thus with extending market share. The media therefore give people 'what they want', and cannot afford to alienate existing or potential viewers or readers by presenting political viewpoints with which they may disagree. Such considerations may be less pressing in relation to public service broadcasters, such as the BBC, which are more insulated from commercial and advertiser pressures but, even here, the tyranny of 'ratings' is increasingly evident.

Nevertheless, although this model dispenses with the idea that at least the privately-owned mass media should be seen as part of the political process, it helps to explain some significant trends in political life. One of these may be growing popular disenchantment with politics resulting from the trivialization of political coverage. Fearful of losing 'market share', television companies in particular have reduced their coverage of serious political debate, and thus abandoned their responsibility for educating and informing citizens, in favour of 'infotainment'.

Media, democracy and governance

Custodians of democracy?

The impact that the media have on democracy is one of the most widely-debated aspects of the relationship between the media and politics. For many, the existence of a free press is one of the key features of democratic governance. However, how do the media act as custodians of democracy? And why have some questioned the media's democratic credentials, even arguing that they may undermine it? The media has traditionally been said to promote democracy in two key ways: by fostering public debate and political engagement, and by acting as a 'public watchdog' to check abuses of power. (The specific impact of the new media on democracy and politics more generally is considered later in the chapter.)

The capacity to provide a civic forum in which meaningful and serious political debate can take place is often viewed as the key democratic role of the media. The virtue of this is that better-informed citizens with more independent and considered views will be more politically engaged. The media are therefore agents of political education. Indeed, the media may have largely replaced formal representative institutions, such as assemblies, parliaments and local councils, as arenas for the dialogue, debate and deliberation that are the very stuff of democratic politics. This has happened because the media are, arguably, better-suited to this role than are traditional representative bodies. In addition to offering the public perhaps its only meaningful opportunity to watch politicians in action (through, for example, interviews with politicians and televised assembly debates), the media provide a forum for the expression of a much wider range of viewpoints and opinions than is possible within representative institutions composed only of elected politicians. Thus, academics and scientists, business leaders and trade union bosses, and representatives of interest groups and lobbyists of all kinds are able to express views and engage in public debate through the mechanism of media. Not only do the media substantially widen the range of views and opinions expressed in political debate, but they also present debate and discussion in a way that is lively and engaging for the general public, devoid of the formality, even stuffiness, that characterizes the exchanges that take place in assemblies and council chambers around the world.

The 'watchdog' role of the media is, in a sense, a subset of the political debate argument. The role of the media, from this perspective, is to ensure that public accountability takes place, by scrutinizing the activities of government and exposing abuses of power. Once again, in carrying out this role the media is supplementing and, to some extent, replacing the work of formal representative institutions. Media professionals such as researchers, journalists and television presenters are particularly suited to this role because they are 'outside' politics and have no interest other than to expose incompetence, corruption or simply muddled thinking whenever and wherever it can be found. By contrast, if public accountability is left solely in the hands of professional politicians, it may be constrained by the fact that those who attempt to expose ineptitude or wrongdoing wish themselves, at some stage, to hold government power. This may not only taint their motives, but it may also discourage them from criticizing processes and practices that they may wish to take advantage of in the future.

● **Free press**: Newspapers (and, by extension, other media outlets) that are free from censorship and political interference by government and, usually, are privately owned.

CONCEPT

Political bias

Political bias refers to political views that systematically favour the values or interests of one group over another as opposed to 'balanced' or 'objective' beliefs. Bias, however, may take various forms (McQuail, 1992). *Partisan* bias is explicit and deliberately promoted (newspaper editorials). *Propaganda* bias is deliberate but unacknowledged ('lazy' students or 'militant' Muslims). *Unwitting* bias occurs through the use of seemingly professional considerations (the 'newsworthiness' of a story). *Ideological* bias operates on the basis of assumptions and value judgements that are embedded in a particular belief system (wealth is gained through talent and hard work).

However, the media can only perform this role effectively if they are properly independent, and not dominated by government. Democratic governance therefore requires either that the publicly financed media are accountable to an independent commission, or that there is an appropriate level of competition from 'free' or privately financed media. The example of WikiLeaks nevertheless highlight how controversial the media's 'watchdog' role can be in practice.

However, reservations have also been expressed about the capacity of the media to promote effective democratic governance. The first of these, as advanced by dominant-ideology and elite-values theorists, is that, far from providing citizens with a wide and balanced range of political views, the content of the media is tainted by clear political biases. Whether political bias stems from the opinions and values of editors, journalists and broadcasters, or from a more general alignment between the interests of the media and those of economic and social elites, it is difficult to see how the media's duty to provide objective information and remain faithful to public-service principles can be discharged reliably and consistently in practice. Particular emphasis has, in this respect, been placed on the implications of media ownership, and the fact that the views and interests of major corporations or powerful media moguls cannot but, at some level, influence media output. Insofar as the mass media affects the political agenda, this agenda is likely to be politically conservative and, at least, compatible with the interests of dominant groups in society.

Second, as the mass media is not subject to public accountability, it is the classic example of 'power without responsibility' (Curran and Seaton, 2009). However well-informed, knowledgeable and stimulating the views of journalists and broadcasters may be, and however eager they may be to portray themselves as the 'voice of the people', media professionals – unlike elected politicians – 'represent' no one other than themselves, and have no meaningful basis for claiming to articulate public opinion. Third, there are reasons for doubting the independence of the media from government. As discussed in the final section of this chapter, all too often a symbiotic relationship develops between media professionals and the political elite which constrains both the mass media's political views and its capacity to act as an effective 'watchdog'.

The media and governance

Apart from its impact (for good or ill) on democracy, the prominence of the mass media in an 'information age' has affected the processes of governance in a variety of ways. The most significant of these include the transformation of political leadership and, with it, a reapportionment of government power; changes to the political culture that, some have warned, are leading to a growing disenchantment with politics and making societies more difficult to govern; and alterations to the behaviour of governments and the nature of policy-making.

The chief way in which the media has transformed political leadership is through growing interest in the personal lives and private conduct of senior political figures, at the expense of serious and 'sober' policy and ideological debate. This, in part, stems from the media's, and particularly television's, obsession with image rather than issues, and with personality rather than policies. In the UK and other parliamentary systems, it is evident in a tendency towards the

POLITICS IN ACTION . . .

WikiLeaks: speaking truth to power?

Events: WikiLeaks was launched in 2006 as a project of the Sunshine Press. Since January 2007, its key spokesperson has been Julian Assange, an Australian internet activist, often described as the 'founder of WikiLeaks'. The main purpose of Wikileaks is to publish and comment on leaked documents alleging government and corporate misconduct, with documents and other materials being submitted anonymously through an electronic 'drop box'. Either directly, or through collaboration with other media (including, at times, *The Guardian*, the *New York Times* and *Der Spiegel*), WikiLeaks has published a massive quantity of documents on issues ranging from war, killing, torture and detention to the suppression of free speech and free press, and ecology and climate change. Many of the most high profile leaks have shed light on US military, security and intelligence activities. These have included almost 400,00 previously secret US military field reports about the Iraq War; secret US files on the war in Afghanistan which reveal civilian killings, 'friendly fire' deaths and the activities of special forces; more than 250,000 US state department cables, sent from, or to, US embassies around the world (so-called 'CableGate'); and US military files containing secret assessments of the 779 detainees held at the Guantánamo Bay detention centre.

Significance: Making use of the new internet culture and modern technology, WikiLeaks has been responsible for the biggest leak of secret information in history. However, assessments of the implications and value of its work have varied starkly. Supporters have used two key arguments to uphold media freedom. The first is that transparency is the only effective means of preventing, or at least reducing, conspiracy, corruption, exploitation and oppression. Quite simply, those in power, whether in government, the military, the security forces or in the world of business and finance will be less likely to abuse their positions and engage in unethical activities if they know that their actions are likely to be publicly exposed. Open governance thus promotes good governance. Second, media freedom underpins democracy, in that it allows citizens to make up their own minds, having access to information from all sources and not merely 'official' sources. There is therefore a clear public interest defence for 'whistleblowing', or 'principled leaking'. This was accepted by the 1971 'Pentagon Papers' case, in which the US Supreme Court upheld the right of the *New York Times*

to publish classified documents about the conduct of the Vietnam War, leaked by Daniel Ellsberg, on the grounds that 'only a free and unconstrained press can effectively expose deception in government'.

WikiLeak's activities have also attracted criticism, however. These have included that WikiLeaks has been over-concerned with generating publicity for itself and with promoting funding (especially in the light of restrictions imposed by the financial industry on online payments to WikiLeaks). However, the most serious criticisms have alleged that WikiLeaks has allowed information to get into the public domain that could both threaten national security and leave intelligence operatives working in foreign countries, together with those who assist them, vulnerable to identification and reprisals. This has been claimed, in particular, in relation to CableGate, where the alleged source of the leaked embassy cables, Private Bradley Manning, a US army intelligence analyst, was accused in a pre-trial military court hearing in December 2011 of 'aiding the enemy'. The release of the CableGate documents stimulated a wave of criticism not only from governments around the world, but also from human rights groups and former sympathizers and partners, including *The Guardian*. Some have accused Wikileaks of going beyond a traditional liberal defence of openness and transparent government in supporting 'free information fundamentalism', a stance that has deeply libertarian, if not anarchist, implications. For example, the private rituals of the Masons, Mormons and other groups were published even though this did not serve a clear political purpose.

'presidentialization', or 'Americanization', of politics.

Such trends reflect not so much conscious bias on the part of the media, as an attempt to 'sell' politics to a mass audience that is deemed to be little interested in issues and policies. This also accounts for the tendency to treat elections as 'horse races', the public's attention being focused less on policy significance of the outcome and more on who is going to win. These two tendencies invariably coincide, turning elections into 'beauty contests' between leading politicians, each of whom serves as the 'brand image' of their party. Leaders are therefore judged largely on the basis of their 'televisual' skills (relaxed manner, sense of humour, ability to demonstrate the 'popular touch' and so on), rather than their mastery of political issues and capacity for serious political debate. However, has exposing leading politicians to the unrelenting glare of media attention merely given them celebrity status, or has media attention affected the location of power within the governmental system?

There can be little doubt that the advent of the 'media age' has changed the behaviour of political leaders, as well as affected the career prospects of individual politicians. For example, presentational factors, such as personal appearance, hairstyle, dress sense and so on, have become more important in determining political preferment or advancement. However, such developments have not merely changed the 'face' of modern politics; they have reordered power relationships both within the political executive and between the executive and the assembly. The growth of 'celebrity politics' gives presidents, prime ministers and other party leaders the ability to make personalized appeals to the voters, creating the phenomenon of spatial leadership. This allows leaders to appeal 'over the heads' of their senior colleagues, parties and government institutions, directly to the public. Furthermore, the messages they give, and the policy and ideological stances they adopt, are increasingly determined by leading politicians personally, supported, it appears, by an ever-expanding band of public relations consultants, 'spin doctors', media managers, pollsters and publicity directors. One of the consequences of this is that junior politicians may have an additional reason for deferring to their leaders: their fear of damaging their leader's image and reputation. If the leader is damaged, especially by splits and internal criticism, all members of his or her party or government suffer. Political power thus comes to be structured on the basis of the publicity and media attention received by individual politicians. The greater the media attention, the greater the political leverage. However, media attention is far from an unqualified benefit for political leaders. Although their triumphs and successes can be publicly trumpeted, their flaws, failings and transgressions can also be ruthlessly exposed. Indeed, the ultimate vulnerability of contemporary political leaders may well be that negative media coverage may turn them into 'electoral liabilities', encouraging their parties and colleagues to remove them in order to 'save the party', or their own political careers.

The second way in which the media has affected governance is through its impact on the political culture. The media is sometimes charged with having created a climate of corrosive cynicism amongst the public, leading to growing popular disenchantment with politics generally, and a lack of trust in governments and politicians of all complexions (Lloyd, 2004). This may, in turn, be linked to trends that have afflicted mature democracies in particular, such as declining voter turnout and falling party membership. The UK is often seen as

● **Presidentialization**: A growing emphasis on personal leadership, in line with the role and powers of an executive president.

● **Celebrity politics**: Either or both the cultivation of 'celebrityhood' by elected politicians, or interventions by stars of popular culture into the political domain.

● **Spatial leadership**: The tendency of political leaders to distance themselves from their parties and governments by presenting themselves as 'outsiders', or developing their own political stance or ideological position.

CONCEPT

E-democracy

E-democracy (sometimes called 'digital democracy' or 'cyberdemocracy') refers to the use of computer-based technologies to enhance citizens' engagement in democratic processes. This nevertheless, may happen in different ways. (1) In the *representative* model, e-democracy seeks to strengthen the operation of established democratic mechanisms (e-voting and e-petitions,). (2) In the *deliberative* model, e-democracy aims to open up new opportunities for direct popular participation (electronic direct democracy). (3) In the *activist* model, e-democracy attempts to strengthen political and social movements and bolster citizen power generally ('virtual' communities and ICT-based protests).

the most advanced example of such a media-driven 'culture of contempt', but similar tendencies are evident elsewhere; notably, in the USA, Australia and Canada. Why has this happened? A critical stance towards politicians in general and governments in particular is, of course, vital to the maintenance of democratic governance. However, the distinction between legitimate criticism and systematic and relentless negativity may, in practice, be difficult to uphold. This occurs, in part, because increasingly intense commercial pressures have forced the media to make their coverage of politics 'sexy' and attention-grabbing. The media, after all, is a business, and this places inevitable pressure on the coverage of news and current affairs. Facts are absorbed progressively more quickly into a swirl of comment and interpretation, blurring, seemingly altogether, the distinction between what happens and what it means. Similarly, routine political debate and policy analysis receive less and less attention, as the media focus instead on – or 'hype' – scandals of various kinds and allegations of incompetence, policy failure or simple inertia. Leading politicians have, as a result, come to live in a kind of ongoing reality-television programme, the sole purpose of which appears to be to embarrass and denigrate them at every possible turn. The public, for their part, tend to view politicians as untrustworthy and deceitful, according them the same level of respect they would accord any other reality-television programme participant (The implications of such developments are examined further.)

The final way in which the media has influenced governance is through its impact on the policy-making process. This has happened in at least two ways. The first is that, just like everyone else in society, government is bombarded by a much greater quantity of information arriving almost immediately. Knowing too much can sometimes be as dangerous as knowing too little. An example of this can be found in the USA's inability to predict and prevent the September 11 terrorist attacks in 2001. The problem the USA faced was not that it lacked information about al-Qaeda, its plans and movements, but that the sheer quantity of national-security intelligence available made effective analysis almost impossible. Moreover, as news and information spreads around the globe at a faster pace, governments are forced to react to events more quickly, and often before they have been fully discussed and digested. An age of '24/7 news' inevitably becomes one of '24/7 government'. Politicians are encouraged, even forced, to take a stance on issues simply to avoid being criticized for inertia or inactivity, leaving little time for the analysis of policy options and their implications. Second, greater reliance on the media means that it is often the media, and not government, that sets the political agenda and dictates the direction of policy-making. For example, the fact that television pictures of the Asian tsunami in December 2004 were broadcast almost immediately across the globe, creating an outpouring of public sympathy for its victims and leading to unprecedented levels of private charitable donations, forced governments around the world, within days, to make substantial increases in the scale of their of aid and support.

New media and the rise of e-politics

The revolution in communication technologies, brought about since the 1990s especially by the spread of satellite and cable television, mobile phones, the internet and digital technology generally, has transformed the media and society, helping to create what has been called an 'information society' or a 'network society' (as discussed in Chapter 7). This is also a process that has occurred with remarkably rapidity. For instance, internet penetration worldwide went from about 1 in 17 of the world's population in 2000, to almost 1 in 3 by 2012, and Twitter, Facebook, YouTube, Wikipedia and Google, unknown only a few years ago, have become part of many people's everyday lives. But how, and to what extent, has new media affected politics? The most common claim is that new media are a progressive force, helping to improve the quality of political life, in particular by contributing to a general transfer power from governments and political elites to the public at large. This is often summed up in the idea of 'e-democracy'. However, e-democracy is a vague and contested term which covers a diverse range of activities, some of which may be 'top-down' (initiated by government or other public bodies) while others are 'bottom-up' (initiated by citizens and activists), with a further distinction being made between those that involve a one-way flow of information from government to citizens and those involving a two-way process of interaction. Examples of e-democracy include the following:

- online voting (e-voting) in elections or referendums
- online petitions (e-petitions) organized by governments or other bodies
- the use of ICT to publicize, organize, lobby or fundraise (e-campaigning)
- accessing political information, news and comments via websites, blogs (web-logs) and so on
- the use of interactive television or social networking sites, or **social media**, to allow citizens to engage in political debate and, possibly, policy-making
- the use of mobile phones and social media to organize popular protests and demonstrations.

New media can be seen to have changed, or be changing, politics in at least three key ways. In the first place, electronic mechanisms have altered the conduct of elections. This is particularly apparent in the case of election campaigns, which increasingly revolve around internet-based activities. Websites, emails and podcasts provide political candidates and parties with a fast and cheap means of getting their message across to a (potentially) large audience, in the process allowing them also to recruit campaign volunteers and raise campaign funds. E-campaigning has the advantage that it is particularly effective in reaching younger people, who are often the most difficult section of the population to engage through conventional strategies. Although the internet has been used in campaigning since the mid-1990s, particularly in the USA, it became particularly prominent during Barack Obama's 2008 presidential campaign. Obama's team used forums and social media such as Facebook and MySpace to build relationships particularly with supporters and would-be supporters aged 18–29, also encouraging the spread of wider networks of support via the website MyBarackObama.com. Sympathizers were also sent regular updates on events and policy positions via emails and text messages. Nevertheless, new technologies were certainly not the be-all and end-all of the Obama campaign, which also relied heavily, and spent most of its money, on more traditional strategies such as television advertising and poster campaigns.

A further way in which digital innovations have affected elections is through growing experiments in electronic voting, sometimes portrayed as 'push-button

● **Social media**: Forms of elecronic communication that facilitate social interaction and the formation of online communities through the exchange of user-generated content.

democracy'. E-voting has been particularly important in countries such as India, where it has proved to be the only practicable solution to the problem of tallying some 400 million votes without substantial delays occurring in announcing election results. The first experiments in India in the use of electronic voting machines located at polling stations started in 1982, with e-voting subsequently being adopted, first, for state elections and, later, for national elections. Similar electronic mechanisms have been used in countries ranging from France, Germany and Finland to Romania and the Philippines. However, although trials have taken place in the use of 'remote' e-voting, through use of the internet (sometimes called 'i-voting'), its wider adoption has been hampered because fears about the greater likelihood of electoral fraud have yet to be allayed.

Second, new media offer citizens wider and easier access to political information and political comment. This has occurred in a number of ways. For example, governments in all parts of the world have, albeit at different speeds, recognized the advantage of making government information available online, and, in a growing number of cases, of allowing citizens to access government services through websites, so-called 'e-government'. The most significant new sources of information are, nevertheless, non-governmental in character. The proliferation of websites developed, variously, by professional groups, businesses, lobbying bodies and think-tanks means that, for the first time, citizens and citizen groups are privy to a quantity and quality of information that may rival that of government. This has generally empowered non-state actors at the expense of national governments and traditional political elites. Non-governmental organizations (see p. 248) and interest groups (see p. 247) have thus become more effective in challenging the positions and actions of government and, sometimes, even displaced government as an authoritative source of views and information about specialist subjects ranging from the environment and global poverty to public health and civil liberties. A further development has been the impact of new media on journalism. This has occurred in two ways. In the first, the rise of the blog has greatly expanded the contours of political commentary, as the growing 'blogosphere' allows writers, academics, politicians and others to share their observations and opinions about political matter with whoever may be interested in accessing them. In the second, there has been a growth of 'user-generated content', stemming from the increased willingness of private citizens, often in newsworthy or politically-charged situations, to share their thoughts, experiences and, frequently, pictures with other via social media.

Third, new media have supported the development of political and social movements, and increased their effectiveness, thus giving rise to a new style of activist politics, sometimes called the 'new politics', and contributing, some argue, to a general shift of power from governments to citizens. The key advantage of new media, from this perspective, is not just that they open up new opportunities for political participation, but also that these forms of participation are, by their nature, decentralized and non-hierarchic. Armed with mobile phones and through the use of the internet, anti-globalization or 'anti-capitalist' protesters have been able to mount demonstrations, and engage in agitation and direct action, a trend that first became apparent during the so-called 'Battle of Seattle' in 1999, when some 50,000 activists forced the cancellation of the opening ceremony of a World Trade Organization meeting. Social media such as Twitter and Facebook were, similarly, instrumental in facilitating the spread of pro-democracy protests during the 2011 Tunisian revolution, at the beginning of the Arab Spring (see p. 88). Their capacity to promote self-management and grass-roots organization has made new media particularly attractive for modern anarchist and libertarian groups, sometimes dubbed 'new' anarchists. Old-style anarchist collectives have therefore given way to online anarchist (or anarchist-style) networks such as Anonymous, which, since 2008, has engaged in campaigns and protests, usually associated with internet freedom or exposing corporate malpractice, and sometimes associated with what has been called 'hacktivism'.

New media have, nevertheless, also attracted criticism. These have, for instance, linked the trend towards e-democracy with the growth of a privatized and consumerist form of citizenship. How meaningful is democratic participation if it lacks a genuinely public dimension and fails to engender meaningful debate and discussion. Perhaps an underlying problem with the debate over the impact of new media is the tendency to believe that political problems (such as low voter turnout rates or declining party membership), can be solved by 'technical fixes'. Similarly, it is perhaps a mistake to suggest that technology, in itself, has a particular political character, whether positive or negative; rather, technology may be either liberating or oppressive, depending on who is using it and the uses to which it is put. It is worth remembering, for instance, that the same technologies that helped in the spread and coordination of pro-democracy demonstrations during the Tunisian revolution were the same technologies that, only six months later, were also used to organize looting during riots in London and other English cities.

Media globalization

An aspect of the media's influence that has attracted growing political attention is its role in strengthening globalization. Radio and television started this process, as it became increasingly difficult to insulate the populations of one country from news, information and images broadcast from other countries. An example of this was the extent to which the communist regimes of Eastern Europe were destabilized by the growing penetration of pro-western, and therefore pro-capitalist, radio and television broadcasts from Western Europe and the USA, contributing to the revolutions of 1989–91. New media, and especially satellite television, mobile phones and the internet, have dramatically intensified this process, both because of their dramatic spread and because of their inherently transnational characters. China and Singapore are amongst the few countries still trying to censor the internet, with such attempts likely to become less and less successful over time. Insofar as the media facilitates, or even fuels, globalization, it has contributed to a far-reaching range of political developments, including the growth of a globalized capitalist economy, the declining (or, at least, changing) role of the state, and the emergence of what some see as a homogenized global culture.

The role of the media in promoting cultural globalization has been an area of particular controversy. The power of the media, allied to the growth of transnational corporations (see p. 149) and trends such as mass tourism, is often held to be responsible for the development of a single global system that imprints itself on all parts of the world; this results, in effect, in a global mono-

● Hacktivism: The use of computers and computer networks to achieve political ends by methods including 'denial-of-service' attacks on targeted websites.

● Cultural globalization: The process whereby information, commodities and images produced in one part of the world enter into a global flow that tends to 'flatten out' cultural differences between nations and regions.

Debating...
Does the wider use of new media enrich politics?

It is generally accepted that new digital or computer technologies are having a profound impact on society and politics, but it is less clear what that impact is. Is ICT a motor for decentralization and democracy, or may new technologies debase politics and threaten freedom?

YES

Modernizing politics. Technological development reflects an ongoing desire to use science and innovation to make human existence more convenient and comfortable, and this applies in politics as well as other spheres of life. E-voting and 'virtual' referendums thus enable citizens to express their views easily and conveniently, possibly without having to leave home. Falling electoral turnouts may therefore simply be a consequence of the failure of the democratic process to keep up-to-date with how citizens in an 'information society' wish to participate in politics.

Knowledge is power. New technologies massively enlarge citizens' access to information, making possible, for the first time, a truly free exchange of ideas and views. The internet already makes available to private citizens specialist information that was once only available to governments. Accessing information through Wikipedia and the myriad other online sources is not only almost instantaneous, but it also exposes the public to a rich diversity of views, including radical and dissident ones.

Citizen empowerment. The great advantage of new technologies is that they make possible a two-way transmission of views, thereby promoting active and engaged citizenship. Instead of participating in politics simply through the act of voting every few years, citizens can express views and opinions on an almost continuous basis, through, for instance, online consultations on draft legislation and online petitions. More radically, new media may foster direct popular participation, making a reality of Athenian-style democracy, for so long dismissed as impracticable, or relevant only to township meetings.

Decentralized activism. The broadest claim made for new media is that, in contributing to a wholesale shift in power from political elites to the public at large, it is bringing about a process of radical democratization. This occurs because new technologies are implicitly egalitarian (being relatively cheap, easily accessible and simple to use), and also facilitate decentralized and spontaneous social action. As modern protest movements clearly demonstrate, the use of mobile phones and social media in particular helps to make leadership and formal organization unnecessary, even irrelevant.

NO

Technological 'Big Brother'. Technology has always been developed to serve the interests of elite or powerful groups, and ICT is no exception. Contrary to the popular image that they are tools of liberation, mobile phones and the internet actually provide the police, security forces, tax officials and so on with access to a massive amount of information about the movements, views and activities of private citizens. As such, new media provide a highly effective means of controlling dissident behaviour and containing political opposition.

Dangers of information anarchy. Many of the new political spaces opened up by new media have been polluted by both the nature of the views they feature and the style of expression they tend to encourage. The internet provides a platform for religious fundamentalists, racists, ethnic nationalists and other extremists, who would otherwise struggle to attract public attention. Similarly, the blogosphere tends to be dominated by shrill, uncivil and opinionated views, fashioned, seemingly, by the desire to create notoriety.

New inequalities. The claim that new technologies are implicitly egalitarian is bogus. Most obviously, a 'digital divide' has opened up based on the fact that access to new communication technologies is not universal. The 'information rich' have come to dominate the 'information poor'. In the feminist version of this argument, computers and technology generally have been seen to benefit men, since they reflect essentially male interests and patterns of thought. New media also provide private business with new opportunities to advertise, generate profits and improve their public image.

Impoverished, debased democracy. E-democracy, or 'virtual' democracy, threatens to turn the democratic process into a series of push-button referendums while citizens sit alone in their own living rooms. This further erodes the 'public' dimension of political participation, reducing democratic citizenship to a set of consumer choices, somewhat akin to voting in the television show *Big Brother*. By weakening face-to-face human interaction, the danger is that people will be consumed by their own opinions, and become indifferent to those of others.

Propaganda

Propaganda is information (or disinformation) disseminated in a deliberate attempt to shape opinions and, possibly, stimulate political action. Propaganda is a pejorative term, implying both untruth or distortion, and a (usually crude) desire to manipulate and control public opinion. Propaganda differs from political bias, in that it is systematic and deliberate, whereas the latter may be partial and unintentional. A distinction is sometimes drawn between 'black' propaganda (blatant lies), 'grey' propaganda (distortions and half truths) and 'white' propaganda (the truth).

culture. The most prominent feature of this process has been the worldwide advance of consumerism and of the materialistic values and appetites that underpin burgeoning global capitalism. Benjamin Barber (1995) dubbed this emerging world 'McWorld', to capture the idea that mass communications and modern commerce, tied together by technology, has created a world in which people everywhere are mesmerized by 'fast music, fast computers, fast food – with MTV, McIntosh and McDonald's pressing nations into one commercially homogeneous theme park'. In this view of cultural globalization, the rich diversity of global cultures, religions, traditions and lifestyles is being subverted by a process of 'westernization' or 'Americanization', made possible by what has been called 'media imperialism'. The western – or, more specifically, American – character of cultural globalization stems not only from the fact that the West is the home of consumer capitalism, but also from the tendency of global media content to derive disproportionately from the West, and particularly from the USA. This is reflected in the rise of English as the global language, and in the global dominance of Hollywood films and US-produced television programmes.

However, this image of cultural homogenization fuelled by the global mass media fails to capture what is, in practice, a complex and often contradictory process. Alongside the media's tendency to 'flatten out' cultural differences, there are also strong tendencies towards diversity and pluralization. This has occurred in a number of ways and for a variety of reasons. In the first place, as Barber (1995) argued, the rise of McWorld has been symbiotically linked to the emergence of countervailing forces, the most notable of which is militant Islam, or what Barber called '*Jihad*'. The second development is that new media have substantially reduced the cost of mass communication, as well as widened access to it. An example of this is the success of the Qatar-based television station Al Jazeera, launched in 1996, in providing a forum for the expression of non-western views and opinions across the Arab world and beyond, offering a rival to, for instance, CNN, Voice of America and the BBC. Third, cultural exchange facilitated through the media is by no means a 'top-down' or one-way process; instead, all societies, including the economically and politically powerful, have become more varied and diverse as a result of the emergence of a globalized cultural marketplace. In return for Coca-Cola, McDonald's and MTV, developed states have increasingly been 'penetrated' by Bollywood films, Chinese martial arts epics, 'world music', and non-western religions and therapeutic practices.

Political communication

Propaganda machines

The notion that government and the media are always opposing forces, the latter exposing the failings and flaws of the former (either for the public's benefit or for commercial advantage), is highly misleading. Instead, the media have often been controlled, directly or indirectly, by government and used as a form of propaganda machine. The classic example of a propaganda machine was that constructed under Joseph Goebbels in Nazi Germany. The Nazis set out to 'coordinate' German society through an elaborate process of ideological indoctrination. For example, youth organizations were set up in the form of the Hitler Youth and the League of German Maidens; the school curriculum was entirely revised and all teachers coerced to join the Nazi Teachers' League; and the German Labour Front replaced free trade unions, providing workers with recreational facilities through the 'Strength through Joy' organization. As chief propagandist of the Nazi Party, in 1933 Goebbels created a new department, the Reich Ministry of Information and Propaganda, which inundated Germany with an unending flood of propaganda. Little in the field of mass communication and entertainment escaped the **censorship** of Goebbels' ministry. It supervised all the writing, music, theatre, dance, painting, sculpture, film and radio. Goebbels placed particular stress on radio broadcasting and encouraged the manufacture of a cheap 'people's' radio set, which resulted in huge and ever-growing audiences for his propaganda through the radio. He began the world's first regular television service in 1935, which, although restricted to closed-circuit showing in Berlin, kept going until near the end of World War II.

Media propaganda was also a significant feature of communist regimes. The Soviet Union, for example, not only operated a system of strict censorship over the mass media, but also fostered a journalistic culture (the 'internal censor') that demanded total support of the ideology and policies of the Communist Party, or CPSU. Both the print and broadcast media were used as propaganda tools by the Soviet authorities, with media content unwaveringly mirroring the policies of the state at each stage in the history of the Soviet Union (Oates, 2005). However, the introduction of '*glasnost*' by Mikhail Gorbachev when he became CPSU General Secretary in 1985 initiated changes in the Soviet media that were to have far-reaching, and ultimately unstoppable, political implications. The high point of the media's influence came in August 1991, when journalists and broadcasters defied the *coup* that had toppled Gorbachev and was intended to reinstate authoritarian rule. In so doing, they contributed both to the collapse of the *coup* and, later in the year, to the downfall of the Soviet regime itself. Russia's record of media freedom in the postcommunist era has nevertheless been patchy. Despite the formal abolition of censorship in 1990 and the inclusion of freedom from censorship in the 1993 Russian Constitution (Article 29), the Russian media, and television in particular, continue to be dominated by state interests. Television channels such as Channel 1, NTV and RTR have been criticized during election campaigns of systematic bias towards Vladimir Putin and the government-backed United Russia party, and Russia remains one of the most dangerous places in the world to be a journalist (Shiraev, 2010).

Criticisms of the use of the media as a propaganda machine are not restricted to totalitarian regimes and new democracies, however. For instance, controversy was sparked in Italy by Silvio Berlusconi's periods as prime minister in 1994–05, 2001–06 and 2008–11. Berlusconi, who is Italy's richest person, owns Mediaset, which controls three of Italy's six privately-owned television channels. In 1993 he founded the Forza Italia political movement, in part to further his own political ambitions. The success of Forza Italia was certainly linked to widespread disenchantment with Italy's sclerotic party system, but the movement undoubtedly also benefited from the consistently positive coverage it received in the Berlusconi-owned media. During his period in power, however, Berlusconi was frequently criticized for trying to extend his media control beyond the Mediaset channels, bringing pressure to bear also on the publicly-owned RAI television channels. This, his critics alleged, gave Berlusconi control of almost all television sources of information in Italy, ensuring favourable coverage for Berlusconi

● **Censorship**: A policy or act of control over what can be said, written, published or performed in order to suppress what is considered morally or politically unacceptable.

● *Glasnost*: (Russian) Literally, 'openness' or 'transparency'; the liberalization of controls over political expression and the media.

personally and for the centre-right views of Forza Italia. Although the Italian example is unusual because of Berlusconi's joint role as media mogul and political leader, attempts by democratic politicians to exert influence over the media are by no means uncommon. Indeed, they have become routine in an emerging age of 'spin' and news management.

Politics of spin

In addition to political biases that operate in and through the mass media, growing concern has been expressed about the closer relationship in modern politics between government and the media, and about how each uses the other for its own purposes. This has led to a transformation in the style and substance of political communication in democratic regimes, affecting both public opinion and, more widely, the political culture. Governments of whatever complexion have always had an unreliable relationship with truth. Politicians are concerned primarily with winning and retaining power, and are thus ever sensitive to the need to maintain public support. The desire to accentuate the positive and conceal the negative is therefore irresistible. In a liberal-democratic context, in which the existence of free media rules out 'official' propaganda and crude ideological manipulation, governments have come to shape the news agenda by new techniques for the control and dissemination of information, often described as 'news management' or 'political marketing'. The favourable presentation of information and policies, or what has come to be called 'spin', has thus become a major preoccupation of modern governments.

The art of 'spin', practised by so-called 'spin-doctors', has many facets. These include the following:

- the careful 'vetting' of information and arguments before release to the media
- the control of sources of information to ensure that only an official 'line' is presented
- the use of unattributable briefings or 'leaks'
- the feeding of stories only to sympathetic media sources
- the release of information close to media deadlines to prevent checking or the identification of counter-arguments
- the release of 'bad' news at times when other, more important events dominate the news agenda.

News management of this kind is most advanced in the USA, where it has become common for election strategists and campaign managers to take up senior White House posts, if their candidate wins the presidency. The Clinton administration was widely seen to have taken 'spin' and the skills of policy presentation to new and more sophisticated levels. The Blair government in the UK also devoted particular attention to the 'packaging' of politics, leading some to criticize it for being concerned more with style than with substance. Amongst the developments that occurred under Blair were the centralizing of government communications under the control of the prime minister's press office; a 'carrot and stick' approach to journalists, who were rewarded with information for sympathetic coverage but penalized for criticism; and the politicization of

● **Spin**: The presentation of information so as to elicit a desired response, or being 'economical with the truth'.

departmental information offices through the imposition of control from Downing Street. Blair also employed a former senior editor of a tabloid newspaper (Alistair Campbell) as his director of communications, 1997–2003, as did David Cameron, 2007–10, (Andy Coulson).

It would be a mistake, however, to assume that the media have been reluctant or passive players in the development of news management. The media need government as much as government needs the media. Government has always been an important source of news and information, but its role has become even more vital as the expansion in media outlets – television channels, websites, magazines and newspapers – has created greater pressure for the acquisition of 'newsworthy' stories. In some cases, publishers, editors and journalists conspire with 'spin-doctors' to manage the news for mutual benefit. This was alleged in the UK in relation to the Blair government and the Murdoch press, as, for instance, the government's unwillingness to press ahead with privacy legislation coincided with the (temporary) conversion of, first, the *Sun*, the UK's largest selling tabloid, and then *The Times* into Labour-supporting newspapers.

In addition to undermining the rigour and independence of political reporting, the advent of media-orientated government has a range of other implications. Some, for example, argue that it strengthens democracy by allowing government to deal with the public more directly and to respond more effectively to popular views and concerns. Others, however, see it as a threat to the democratic process, in that it widens the scope for manipulation and dishonesty, and weakens the role of representative institutions such as assemblies or parliaments. Moreover, it may engender apathy and undermine interest in conventional forms of political activity; in particular, voting and party membership. This occurs because 'spin', style and presentation themselves become the focus of media attention, strengthening the image of government as a vast publicity machine that is disengaged from the lives and concerns of ordinary people.

SUMMARY

- There are rival theories of the media's political impact. Pluralists portray the media as an ideological market-place that enhances debate and electoral choice. However, others highlight systematic media bias, stemming either from links between the media and economic and social elites, or from the personal views of the editor, broadcasters and journalists. The market model suggests that the media output simply reflects the views of the general public.

- The media play a key democratic role in four senses. They promote political education by providing a public forum for meaningful and serious debate; act as a public watchdog, exposing abuses of power; tend, through the 'new' media in particular, to widen access to information and facilitate political activism; and serve as a mechanism through which democracy takes place. Concerns have, nevertheless, been raised about the political views of the media, their lack of democratic accountability and their over-close links to government.

- The mass media has affected governance in various ways. These include that they have transformed political leadership and, in the process, reapportioned government power. They have also changed the political culture and, some have warned, contributed to declining respect for politicians and politics in general. Finally, the growing influence of the media is evident in a policy-making process that has to react more rapidly and make sense of a vast amount of information.

- The use of new media has been defended on the grounds that it facilitates political participation, widens citizen's access to information, and stimulates new forms of decentralized political activism. Critics, nevertheless, warn against the growth of a consumerist form of citizenship and doubt the value of 'technological fixes'.

- The role of the media in promoting globalization has provoked particular controversy. Some have warned against 'media imperialism', drawing attention to the media's role in spreading a global culture of consumerism and in strengthening 'westernization or 'Americanization'. However, cultural exchange facilitated by the mass media is by no means always a 'top-down' or one-way process.

- Governments have sometimes used the media as a propaganda machine. This involves direct control over all kinds of media output to ensure that only 'official' views and ideas are distributed. Classic examples of this can be found in Nazi Germany and in communist regimes, but there has been a growing tendency for democratic regimes to engage in news management and the politics of 'spin', providing evidence of a symbiotic relationship that tends to develop between government and the media.

Questions for discussion

- Is civic culture a cause or a consequence of effective democratic rule?
- Do the mass media reflect public opinion or shape it?
- Is a free media vital for democratic rule?
- How has the media changed the nature of political leadership? Are leaders stronger or weaker as a result?
- What is new about the 'new' media?
- Is the media an agent of cultural homogenization?
- Do all governments use propaganda, or only some?
- Are modern governments more concerned with political marketing than with political performance?

Further reading

Almond, G. A. and S. Verba (eds), *The Civic Culture Revisited* (1989). An updated version of the authors' classic 1963 analysis of the conditions required for democratic stability.

Jenkins, H. and D. Thorburn (eds), *Democracy and New Media* (2004). A wide-ranging collection of essays that discuss, from a variety of perspectives, the relationship between democracy and cyberspace.

Putnam, R. *Bowling Alone: The Collapse and Revival of American Community* (2000). A highly influential anaysis of the decline of civic engagement and social participation in the USA.

Street, J., *Mass Media, Politics and Democracy*, 2nd edn (2011). A readable and wide-ranging overview of all aspects of the relationship between the media and politics.

CHAPTER 9

Nations and Nationalism

'*Nationalism is an infantile disease. It is the measles of mankind.*'

ALBERT EINSTEIN, *Letter* (1921)

PREVIEW

For the last 200 years, the nation has been regarded as the most appropriate (and perhaps the only proper) unit of political rule. Indeed, international law is largely based on the assumption that nations, like individuals, have inviolable rights; notably, the right to political independence and self-determination. Nowhere, however, is the importance of the nation more dramatically demonstrated than in the potency of nationalism as a political creed. In many ways, nationalism has dwarfed the more precise and systematic political ideologies examined.

It has contributed to the outbreak of wars and revolutions. It has caused the birth of new states, the disintegration of empires and the redrawing of borders; and it has been used to reshape existing regimes, as well as to bolster them. However, nationalism is a complex and highly diverse political phenomenon. Not only are there distinctive political and cultural forms of nationalism, but the political implications of nationalism have been wide-ranging and sometimes contradictory. This has occurred because nationalism has been linked to very different ideological traditions, ranging from liberalism to fascism. It has therefore been associated, for instance, with both the quest for national independence and projects of imperial expansion. Nevertheless, there are reasons to believe that the age of the nation may be drawing to a close. The nation-state, the goal that generations of nationalists have strived to achieve, is increasingly beset by pressures, both internal and external.

KEY ISSUES

- What is a nation?
- How do cultural nationalism and political nationalism differ?
- How can the emergence and growth of nationalism be explained?
- What political forms has nationalism assumed? What causes has it articulated?
- What are the attractions or strengths of the nation-state?
- Does the nation-state have a future?

WHAT IS A NATION?

Many of the controversies surrounding the phenomenon of nationalism can be traced back to rival views about what constitutes a nation. So widely accepted is the idea of the nation that its distinctive features are seldom examined or questioned; the nation is simply taken for granted. Nevertheless, confusion abounds. The term 'nation' tends to be used with little precision, and is often used interchangeably with terms such as 'state', 'country', 'ethnic group' and 'race'. The United Nations, for instance, is clearly misnamed, as it is an organization of states, not one of national populations. What, then, are the characteristic features of the nation? What distinguishes a nation from any other social group, or other sources of collective identity?

The difficulty of defining the term 'nation' springs from the fact that all nations comprise a mixture of objective and subjective features, a blend of cultural and political characteristics. In objective terms, nations are cultural entities: groups of people who speak the same language, have the same religion, are bound by a shared past and so on. Such factors undoubtedly shape the politics of nationalism. The nationalism of the Québecois in Canada, for instance, is based largely on language differences between French-speaking Quebec and the predominantly English-speaking rest of Canada (see p. 114). Nationalist tensions in India invariably arise from religious divisions, examples being the struggle of Sikhs in Punjab for a separate homeland (Khalistan), and the campaign by Muslims in Kashmir for the incorporation of Kashmir into Pakistan. Nevertheless, it is impossible to define a nation using objective factors alone. All nations encompass a measure of cultural, ethnic and racial diversity. The Swiss nation has proved to be enduring and viable despite the use of three major languages (French, German and Italian), as well as a variety of local dialects. Divisions between Catholics and Protestants that have given rise to rival nationalisms in Northern Ireland have been largely irrelevant in mainland UK, and of only marginal significance in countries such as Germany.

This emphasizes the fact that, ultimately, nations can only be defined *subjectively* by their members. In the final analysis, the nation is a psycho-political construct. What sets a nation apart from any other group or collectivity is that its members regard themselves as a nation. What does this mean? A nation, in this sense, perceives itself to be a distinctive political community. This is what distinguishes a nation from an ethnic group. An **ethnic group** undoubtedly possesses a communal identity and a sense of cultural pride, but, unlike a nation, it lacks collective political aspirations. These aspirations have traditionally taken the form of the quest for, or the desire to maintain, political independence or statehood. On a more modest level, however, they may consist of a desire to achieve a measure of autonomy, perhaps as part of a federation or confederation of states.

The complexity does not end there, however. Nationalism is a difficult political phenomenon, partly because various nationalist traditions view the concept of a nation in different ways. Two contrasting concepts have been particularly influential. One portrays the nation as primarily a cultural community, and emphasizes the importance of ethnic ties and loyalties. The other sees it essentially as a political community, and highlights the significance of civil bonds and allegiances. These rival views not only offer alternative accounts of the origins of nations, but have also been linked to very different forms of nationalism.

CONCEPT

Nation

Nations (from the Latin *nasci*, meaning 'to be born') are complex phenomena that are shaped by a collection of factors. *Culturally*, a nation is a group of people bound together by a common language, religion, history and traditions, although nations exhibit various levels of cultural heterogeneity. *Politically*, a nation is a group of people who regard themselves as a natural political community, classically expressed through the quest for sovereign statehood. *Psychologically*, a nation is a group of people distinguished by a shared loyalty or affection in the form of patriotism (see p. 118).

● **Ethnic group**: A group of people who share a common cultural and historical identity, typically linked to a belief in common descent.

Johann Gottfried Herder (1744–1803)

German poet, critic and philosopher, often portrayed as the 'father' of cultural nationalism. A teacher and Lutheran clergyman, Herder travelled throughout Europe before settling in Weimar in 1776, as the clerical head of the Grand Duchy. Although influenced in his early life by thinkers such as Kant, (see p. 410), Rousseau (see p. 97) and Montesquieu (see p. 312), he became a leading intellectual opponent of the Enlightenment and a crucial influence on the growth in Germany of the romantic movement. Herder's emphasis on the nation as an organic group characterized by a distinctive language, culture and 'spirit' helped both to found cultural history, and to give rise to a particular form of nationalism that emphasized the intrinsic value of national culture.

Nations as cultural communities

The idea that a nation is essentially an ethnic or cultural entity has been described as the 'primary' concept of the nation (Lafont, 1968). Its roots can be traced back to late eighteenth-century Germany and the writings of figures such as Herder and Fichte (1762–1814). For Herder, the innate character of each national group was ultimately determined by its natural environment, climate and physical geography, which shaped the lifestyle, working habits, attitudes and creative propensities of a people. Above all, he emphasized the importance of language, which he believed was the embodiment of a people's distinctive traditions and historical memories. In his view, each nation thus possesses a *Volksgeist*, which reveals itself in songs, myths and legends, and provides a nation with its source of creativity. Herder's nationalism therefore amounts to a form of culturalism that emphasizes an awareness and appreciation of national traditions and collective memories instead of an overtly political quest for statehood. Such ideas had a profound impact on the awakening of national consciousness in nineteenth-century Germany, reflected in the rediscovery of ancient myths and legends in, for example, the folk tales of the brothers Grimm and the operas of Richard Wagner (1813–83).

The implication of Herder's **culturalism** is that nations are 'natural' or organic entities that can be traced back to ancient times and will, by the same token, continue to exist as long as human society survives. A similar view has been advanced by modern social psychologists, who point to the tendency of people to form groups in order to gain a sense of security, identity and belonging. From this perspective, the division of humankind into nations reflects nothing more than the natural human propensity to draw close to people who share a culture, background and lifestyle that is similar to their own. Such psychological insights, however, do not explain nationalism as a historical phenomenon; that is, as one that arose at a particular time and place, specifically in early nineteenth-century Europe.

In *Nations and Nationalism* (1983), Ernest Gellner emphasized the degree to which nationalism is linked to modernization and, in particular, to the process of industrialization. Gellner stressed that, while premodern or 'agroliterate' soci-

● *Volksgeist*: (German) Literally, the spirit of the people; the organic identity of a people reflected in their culture and, particularly, their language.

● Culturalism: The belief that human beings are culturally-defined creatures, culture being the universal basis for personal and social identity.

CONCEPT

Cultural nationalism

Cultural nationalism is a form of nationalism that places primary emphasis on the regeneration of the nation as a distinctive civilization, rather than as a discrete political community. Whereas political nationalism is 'rational', and usually principled, cultural nationalism is 'mystical', in that it is based on a romantic belief in the nation as a unique, historical and organic whole, animated by its own 'spirit'. Typically, it is a 'bottom-up' form of nationalism that draws more on 'popular' rituals, traditions and legends than on elite, or 'higher', culture.

eties were structured by a network of feudal bonds and loyalties, emerging industrial societies promoted social mobility, self-striving and competition, and so required a new source of cultural cohesion. This was provided by nationalism. Nationalism therefore developed to meet the needs of particular social conditions and circumstances. On the other hand, Gellner's theory suggests that nationalism is now ineradicable, as a return to premodern loyalties and identities is unthinkable. However, in *The Ethnic Origins of Nations* (1986) Anthony Smith challenged the idea of a link between nationalism and modernization by highlighting the continuity between modern nations and premodern ethnic communities, which he called 'ethnies'. In this view, nations are historically embedded: they are rooted in a common cultural heritage and language that may long predate the achievement of statehood, or even the quest for national independence. Smith nevertheless acknowledged that, although ethnicity is the precursor of nationalism, modern nations came into existence only when established ethnies were linked to the emerging doctrine of political sovereignty. This conjunction occurred in Europe in the late eighteenth century and early nineteenth century, and in Asia and Africa in the twentieth century.

Regardless of the origins of nations, certain forms of nationalism have a distinctively cultural, rather than political, character. Cultural nationalism commonly takes the form of national self-affirmation; it is a means through which a people can acquire a clearer sense of its own identity through the heightening of national pride and self-respect. This is demonstrated by Welsh nationalism, which focuses much more on attempts to preserve the Welsh language and Welsh culture in general than on the search for political independence. Black nationalism in the USA, the West Indies and many parts of Europe also has a strong cultural character. Its emphasis is on the development of a distinctively black consciousness and sense of national pride, which, in the work of Marcus Garvey (see p. 162) and Malcolm X (1925–65), was linked to the rediscovery of Africa as a spiritual and cultural 'homeland'. A similar process can be seen at work in modern Australia and, to some extent, New Zealand. The republican movement in Australia, for example, reflects the desire to redefine the nation as a political and cultural unit separate from the UK. This is a process of self-affirmation that draws heavily on the Anzac myth, the relationship with indigenous peoples, and the rediscovery of a settler folk culture.

The German historian Friedrich Meinecke (1907) went one step further and distinguished between 'cultural nations' and 'political nations'. 'Cultural' nations are characterized by a high level of ethnic homogeneity; in effect, national and ethnic identities overlap. Meinecke identified the Greeks, the Germans, the Russians, the English and the Irish as examples of cultural nations, but the description could equally apply to ethnic groups such as the Kurds, the Tamils and the Chechens. Such nations can be regarded as 'organic', in that they have been fashioned by natural or historical forces, rather than by political ones. The strength of cultural nations is that, bound together by a powerful and historical sense of national unity, they tend to be stable and cohesive. On the other hand, cultural nations tend to view themselves as exclusive groups. Membership of the nation is seen to derive not from a political allegiance, voluntarily undertaken, but from an ethnic identity that has somehow been inherited. Cultural nations thus tend to view themselves as extended kinship groups distinguished by common descent. In this sense, it is not possible to 'become' a German, a Russian

Race

Race refers to physical or genetic differences amongst humankind that supposedly distinguish one group of people from another on biological grounds such as skin and hair colour, physique, and facial features. A race is thus a group of people who share a common ancestry and 'one blood'. The term is, however, controversial, both scientifically and politically. Scientific evidence suggests that there is no such thing as 'race' in the sense of a species-type difference between peoples. Politically, racial categorization is commonly based on cultural stereotypes, and is simplistic at best and pernicious at worst.

or a Kurd simply by adopting the language and beliefs of the people. Such exclusivity has tended to breed insular and regressive forms of nationalism, and to weaken the distinction between nations and races.

Nations as political communities

The view that nations are essentially political entities emphasizes civic loyalties and political allegiances, rather than cultural identity. The nation is thus a group of people who are bound together primarily by shared citizenship, regardless of their cultural, ethnic and other loyalties. This view of the nation is often traced back to the writings of Jean-Jacques Rousseau (see p. 97), sometimes seen as the 'father' of modern nationalism. Although Rousseau did not specifically address the nation question, or discuss the phenomenon of nationalism, his stress on popular sovereignty, expressed in the idea of the 'general will' (in effect, the common good of society), was the seed from which nationalist doctrines sprang during the French Revolution of 1789. In proclaiming that government should be based on the general will, Rousseau developed a powerful critique of monarchical power and aristocratic privilege. During the French Revolution, this principle of radical democracy was reflected in the assertion that the French people were 'citizens' possessed of inalienable rights and liberties, no longer merely 'subjects' of the crown. Sovereign power thus resided with the 'French nation'. The form of nationalism that emerged from the French Revolution therefore embodied a vision of a people or nation governing itself, and was inextricably linked to the principles of liberty, equality and fraternity.

The idea that nations are political, not ethnic, communities has been supported by a number of theories of nationalism. Eric Hobsbawm (1983), for instance, highlighted the degree to which nations are 'invented traditions'. Rather than accepting that modern nations have developed out of long-established ethnic communities, Hobsbawm argued that a belief in historical continuity and cultural purity was invariably a myth, and, what is more, a myth created by nationalism itself. In this view, nationalism creates nations, not the other way round. A widespread consciousness of nationhood (sometimes called 'popular nationalism') did not, for example, develop until the late nineteenth century, perhaps fashioned by the invention of national anthems and national flags, and the extension of primary education. Certainly, the idea of a 'mother tongue' passed down from generation to generation and embodying a national culture is highly questionable. In reality, languages live and grow as each generation adapts the language to its own distinctive needs and circumstances. Moreover, it can be argued that the notion of a 'national' language is an absurdity, given the fact that, until the nineteenth century, the majority of people had no knowledge of the written form of their language and usually spoke a regional dialect that had little in common with the language of the educated elite.

Benedict Anderson (1983) also portrayed the modern nation as an artefact, in his case as an 'imagined community'. Anderson pointed out that nations exist more as mental images than as genuine communities that require a level of face-to-face interaction to sustain the notion of a common identity. Within nations, individuals only ever meet a tiny proportion of those with whom they supposedly share a national identity. If nations exist, they exist as imagined artifices, constructed for us through education, the mass media and a process of political socialization (see p. 178). Whereas in Rousseau's view a nation is animated by ideas of democracy and political freedom, the notion that nations are 'invented' or 'imagined' communities has more in common with the Marxist belief that nationalism is a species of bourgeois ideology. From the perspective of orthodox Marxism, nationalism is a device through which the ruling class counters the threat of social revolution by ensuring that national loyalty is stronger than class solidarity, thus binding the working class to the existing power structure.

Whether nations spring out of a desire for liberty and democracy, or are merely cunning inventions of political elites or a ruling class, certain nations have an unmistakably political character. Following Meinecke, these nations can be classified as 'political nations'. A 'political' nation is one in which citizenship has greater political significance than ethnic identity; not uncommonly, political nations contain a number of ethnic groups, and so are marked by cultural heterogeneity. The UK, the USA and France have often been seen as classic examples of political nations. The UK is a union of what, in effect, are four 'cultural' nations: the English, the Scottish, the Welsh and the Northern Irish (although the latter may comprise two nations, the Protestant Unionists and the Catholic Republicans). Insofar as there is a distinctively British national identity, this is based on political factors such as a common allegiance to the Crown, respect for the Westminster Parliament, and a belief in the historic rights and liberties of the British people. As a 'land of immigrants', the USA has a distinctively multi-ethnic and multicultural character, which makes it impossible for it to construct a national identity on the basis of shared cultural and historical ties. Instead, a sense of American nationhood has been consciously developed through the educational system, and through the cultivation of respect for a set of common values, notably those outlined in the Declaration of Independence and the US Constitution. Similarly, French national identity is closely linked to the traditions and principles of the 1789 French Revolution.

What such nations have in common is that, in theory, they were founded on a voluntary acceptance of a common set of principles or goals, as opposed to an existing cultural identity. It is sometimes argued that the style of nationalism that develops in such societies is typically tolerant and democratic. If a nation is primarily a political entity, it is an inclusive group, in that membership is not restricted to those who fulfil particular language, religious, ethnic or suchlike criteria. Classic examples are the USA, with its image as a 'melting pot' nation, and the 'new' South Africa, seen as a 'rainbow society'. On the other hand, political nations may at times fail to experience the organic unity and sense of historical rootedness that is found in cultural nations. This may, for instance, account for the relative weakness of specifically British nationalism in the UK, by comparison with Scottish and Welsh nationalism and the insular form of English nationalism that is sometimes called 'little Englander' nationalism.

Developing-world states have encountered particular problems in their struggle to achieve a national identity. Such nations can be described as 'political' in two senses. First, in many cases, they have achieved statehood only after a struggle against colonial rule (see p. 122). In this case, the nation's national identity is deeply influenced by the unifying quest for national liberation and freedom. Developing-world nationalism therefore tends to have a strong anti-

POLITICS IN ACTION ...

Canada: one nation or two?

Events: Canada is a federation comprising ten provinces and three territories, the former enjoying wider political autonomy than the latter. Almost 24 per cent of Canadians are francophones, who speak French as their first language and largely live (85 per cent) in the Atlantic province of Quebec. Since the 1970s, Canadian domestic politics has been dominated by the issue of Quebec's relationship to predominantly anglophone Canada. The paramilitary Quebec Liberation Front, was active during 1963–70; the separatist political party, *Parti Québécois* (PQ), won power in Quebec in 1976; since 1990, PQ has operated on a federal level through the *Bloc Québécois* (BQ). Referendums on independence for Quebec were held in 1980 and 1995, but both failed, the latter by a margin of 1 per cent. Attempts to address the challenge of Quebec nationalism through constitutional reform, notably through the Meech Lake Accord of 1987, also failed. However, the principles of multiculturalism and biculturalism have been enshrined in law through section 27 of the 1982 Canadian Charter of Rights and Freedoms and the 1988 Canadian Multiculturalism Act. In 2006, the Canadian House of Commons passed a motion recognizing that the 'Québécois form a nation within a united Canada'.

Significance: The nationalism of the Québécois in Canada raises important questions about both the nature of nationalism and the circumstances in which it rises or falls. From the mid-nineteenth to the mid-twentieth century, Quebec nationalism was distinctively cultural in orientation, being shaped by conservative clerical allegiances, centred on the Catholic Church, and reflecting the rural and familial values of a historically agricultural territory. However, by the 1960s, this elite version of society was being unsettled by trends such as urbanization, secularization, Americanization, and the spread of liberal and progressive values. In this context, Québécois identity started to be re-articulated, becoming more self-confident and assertive, and expressing itself increasingly through political demands, especially for independence. Political factors also facilitated this process. The introduction, in the early 1960s, of the so-called 'Quiet Revolution' by the province's Liberal government promoted social and cultural modernization and, by increasing the power of the provincial government, sparked the growth of popular demands for secession. Similarly, under the premierships of Pierre Trudeau (1968–79, 1980–84), the Canadian

government attempted to satisfy Quebec nationalism by making concessions in terms of language rights and by adjusting both Canada's and Quebec's constitutional status, which strengthened the tide of nationalism, rather than containing it.

However, despite the transition from cultural concerns to political demands, language remained central to Quebec nationalism, and, in some respects, became more important. This occurred both because of the perception that French was being threatened by the spread of English (and other languages) due to growing immigration (Canada has one of the highest per capita immigration rates in the world), and because language was increasingly equated with identity, and thus became part of a politics of politico-cultural self-assertion. Nevertheless, following the failure of the 1995 referendum, the tide started to turn against secessionist nationalism. In the 2007 provincial election, PQ was defeated by both the Liberals and the conservative *Action démocratique du Québec* (ADQ), marking the first time since 1973 that the party did not form either the government or the official opposition. The reasons for this include a growing recognition of the economic benefit of remaining within the Canadian federation, and the fact that progress in securing Quebec's cultural and language rights has, over time, weakened the sense of threat and injustice that had once helped to fuel secessionist politics. In many respects, multiculturalism (see p. 167), rather than nationalism, has proved to be the solution to the 'Quebec problem', especially as, since the 1990s, Canada has acknowledged the territorial and self-government rights of its so-called 'First Nations'.

colonial character. Second, these nations have often been shaped by territorial boundaries inherited from their former colonial rulers. This has particularly been the case in Africa. African 'nations' often encompass a wide range of ethnic, religious and regional groups that are bound together by little more than a shared colonial past. In contrast to the creation of classic European cultural nations, which sought statehood on the basis of a pre-existing national identity, an attempt has been made in Africa to 'build' nations on the foundations of existing states. However, the resulting mismatch of political and ethnic identities has bred recurrent tensions, as has been seen in Nigeria, Sudan, Rwanda and Burundi, for example. However, such conflicts are by no means simply manifestations of ancient 'tribalism'. To a large extent, they are a consequence of the divide-and-rule policies used in the colonial past.

VARIETIES OF NATIONALISM

Immense controversy surrounds the political character of nationalism. On the one hand, nationalism can appear to be a progressive and liberating force, offering the prospect of national unity or independence. On the other, it can be an irrational and reactionary creed that allows political leaders to conduct policies of military expansion and war in the name of the nation. Indeed, nationalism shows every sign of suffering from the political equivalent of multiple-personality syndrome. At various times, nationalism has been progressive and reactionary, democratic and authoritarian, liberating and oppressive, and left-wing and right-wing. For this reason, it is perhaps better to view nationalism not as a single or coherent political phenomenon, but as a series of 'nationalisms'; that is, as a complex of traditions that share but one characteristic – each, in its own particular way, acknowledges the central political importance of the nation.

This confusion derives, in part, from the controversies examined above as to how the concept of a nation should be understood, and about whether cultural or political criteria are decisive in defining the nation. However, the character of nationalism is also moulded by the circumstances in which nationalist aspirations arise, and by the political causes to which it is attached. Thus, when nationalism is a reaction against the experience of foreign domination or colonial rule, it tends to be a liberating force linked to the goals of liberty, justice and democracy. When nationalism is a product of social dislocation and demographic change, it often has an insular and exclusive character, and can become a vehicle for racism (see p. 120) and xenophobia. Finally, nationalism is shaped by the political ideals of those who espouse it. In their different ways, liberals, conservatives, socialists, fascists and even communists have been attracted to nationalism (of the major ideologies, perhaps only anarchism is entirely at odds with nationalism). In this sense, nationalism is a cross-cutting ideology. The principal political manifestations of nationalism are:

- liberal nationalism
- conservative nationalism
- expansionist nationalism
- anticolonial nationalism.

● **Tribalism**: Group behaviour characterized by insularity and exclusivity, typically fuelled by hostility towards rival groups.

● **Xenophobia**: A fear or hatred of foreigners; pathological ethnocentrism.

Giuseppe Mazzini (1805–72)

Italian nationalist and apostle of liberal republicanism. Mazzini was born in Genoa, Italy, and was the son of a doctor. He came into contact with revolutionary politics as a member of the patriotic secret society, the Carbonari. This led to his arrest and exile to France and, after his expulsion from France, to Britain. He returned briefly to Italy during the 1848 Revolutions, helping to liberate Milan and becoming head of the short-lived Roman Republic. A committed republican, Mazzini's influence thereafter faded as other nationalist leaders, including Garibaldi (1807–82), looked to the House of Savoy to bring about Italian unification. Although he never officially returned to Italy, Mazzini's liberal nationalism had a profound influence throughout Europe, and on immigrant groups in the USA.

Liberal nationalism

Liberal nationalism can be seen as the classic form of European liberalism; it dates back to the French Revolution, and embodies many of its values. Indeed, in continental Europe in the mid-nineteenth century, to be a nationalist meant to be a liberal, and vice versa. The 1848 Revolutions, for example, fused the struggle for national independence and unification with the demand for limited and constitutional government. Nowhere was this more evident than in the '*Risorgimento*' (rebirth) nationalism of the Italian nationalist movement, especially as expressed by the 'prophet' of Italian unification, Guiseppe Mazzini. Similar principles were espoused by Simon Bolívar (1783–1830), who led the Latin-American independence movement in the early nineteenth century, and helped to expel the Spanish from Hispanic America. Perhaps the clearest expression of liberal nationalism is found in US President Woodrow Wilson's 'Fourteen Points'. Drawn up in 1918, these were proposed as the basis for the reconstruction of Europe after World War I, and provided a blueprint for the sweeping territorial changes that were implemented by the Treaty of Versailles (1919).

In common with all forms of nationalism, liberal nationalism is based on the fundamental assumption that humankind is naturally divided into a collection of nations, each possessed of a separate identity. Nations are therefore genuine or organic communities, not the artificial creation of political leaders or ruling classes. The characteristic theme of liberal nationalism, however, is that it links the idea of the nation with a belief in popular sovereignty, ultimately derived from Rousseau. This fusion was brought about because the multinational empires against which nineteenth-century European nationalists fought were also autocratic and oppressive. Mazzini, for example, wished not only to unite the Italian states, but also to throw off the influence of autocratic Austria. The central theme of this form of nationalism is therefore a commitment to the principle of **national self-determination**. Its goal is the construction of a nation-state (see p. 124); that is, a state within which the boundaries of government coincide as far as possible with those of nationality. In J. S. Mill's ([1861] 1951) words:

● **National self-determination**: The principle that the nation is a sovereign entity; self-determination implies both national independence and democratic rule.

CONCEPT

Internationalism

Internationalism is the theory or practice of politics based on transnational or global cooperation. It is rooted in universalist assumptions about human nature that put it at odds with political nationalism. The major internationalist traditions are drawn from liberalism and socialism. *Liberal* internationalism is based on individualism reflected in the assumption that human rights have a 'higher' status than claims based on national sovereignty. *Socialist* internationalism is grounded in a belief in international class solidarity (proletarian internationalism), underpinned by assumptions about a common humanity. Feminism and green politics have also advanced distinctively internationalist positions.

● **Universalism**: The theory that there is a common core to human identity shared by people everywhere.

● **Human rights**: Rights to which people are entitled by virtue of being human; universal and fundamental rights.

When the sentiment of nationality exists in any force, there is a prima facie case for uniting all members of the nationality under one government, and a government to themselves apart. This is merely saying that the question of government should be decided by the governed.

Liberal nationalism is, above all, a principled form of nationalism. It does not uphold the interests of one nation against other nations. Instead, it proclaims that each and every nation has a right to freedom and self-determination. In this sense, all nations are equal. The ultimate goal of liberal nationalism, then, is the construction of a world of sovereign nation-states. Mazzini thus formed the clandestine organization Young Italy to promote the idea of a united Italy, but he also founded Young Europe in the hope of spreading nationalist ideas throughout the continent. Similarly, at the Paris Peace Conference that drew up the Treaty of Versailles, Woodrow Wilson advanced the principle of self-determination not simply because the break-up of European empires served US national interests, but because he believed that the Poles, the Czechs, the Yugoslavs and the Hungarians all had the same right to political independence that the Americans already enjoyed.

From this perspective, nationalism is not only a means of enlarging political freedom, but also a mechanism for securing a peaceful and stable world order. Wilson, for instance, believed that World War I had been a consequence of an 'old order' that was dominated by autocratic and militaristic empires bent on expansionism and war. In his view, democratic nation-states, however, would be essentially peaceful, because, possessing both cultural and political unity, they lacked the incentive to wage war or subjugate other nations. In this light, nationalism is not seen as a source of distrust, suspicion and rivalry. Rather, it is a force capable of promoting unity within each nation and brotherhood amongst nations on the basis of mutual respect for national rights and characteristics.

There is a sense, nevertheless, in which liberalism looks beyond the nation. This occurs for two reasons. The first is that a commitment to individualism (see p. 158) implies that liberals believe that all human beings (regardless of factors such as race, creed, social background and nationality) are of equal moral worth. Liberalism therefore subscribes to universalism, in that it accepts that individuals everywhere have the same status and entitlements. This is commonly expressed nowadays in the notion of human rights. In setting the individual above the nation, liberals establish a basis for violating national sovereignty, most clearly through 'humanitarian intervention' (see p. 424) designed to protect the citizens of another country from their own government. The second reason is that liberals fear that a world of sovereign nation-states may degenerate into an international 'state of nature'. Just as unlimited freedom allows individuals to abuse and enslave one another, national sovereignty may be used as a cloak for expansionism and conquest. Freedom must always be subject to the law, and this applies equally to individuals and to nations. Liberals have, as a result, been in the forefront of campaigns to establish a system of international law supervised by supranational bodies such as the League of Nations, the United Nations and the European Union. In this view, nationalism and internationalism are not rival or mutually exclusive principles; rather, from a liberal perspective, the latter compliments the former.

Patriotism

Patriotism (from the Latin *patria*, meaning 'fatherland') is a sentiment, a psychological attachment to one's nation (a 'love of one's country'). The terms 'nationalism' and 'patriotism' are often confused. Nationalism has a doctrinal character and embodies the belief that the nation is in some way the central principle of political organization. Patriotism provides the affective basis for that belief. Patriotism thus underpins all forms of nationalism; it is difficult to conceive of a national group demanding, say, political independence without possessing at least a measure of patriotic loyalty.

● Ethnic cleansing: The forcible expulsion or extermination of 'alien' peoples; often used as a euphemism for genocide.

● Euroscepticism: Opposition to further European integration, usually not extending to the drive to withdraw from the EU (anti-Europeanism).

Criticisms of liberal nationalism tend to fall into two categories. In the first category, liberal nationalists are accused of being naive and romantic. They see the progressive and liberating face of nationalism; theirs is a tolerant and rational nationalism. However, they perhaps ignore the darker face of nationalism; that is, the irrational bonds of tribalism that distinguish 'us' from a foreign and threatening 'them'. Liberals see nationalism as a universal principle, but they have less understanding of the emotional power of nationalism, which, in time of war, can persuade people to fight, kill and die for 'their' country, almost regardless of the justice of their nation's cause. Such a stance is expressed in the assertion: 'my country, right or wrong'.

Second, the goal of liberal nationalism (the construction of a world of nation-states) may be fundamentally misguided. The mistake of Wilsonian nationalism, on the basis of which large parts of the map of Europe were redrawn, was that it assumed that nations live in convenient and discrete geographical areas, and that states can be constructed to coincide with these areas. In practice, all so-called 'nation-states' comprise a number of linguistic, religious, ethnic and regional groups, some of which may consider themselves to be 'nations'. This has nowhere been more clearly demonstrated than in the former Yugoslavia, a country viewed by the peacemakers at Versailles as 'the land of the Slavs'. However, in fact, it consisted of a patchwork of ethnic communities, religions, languages and differing histories. Moreover, as the disintegration of Yugoslavia in the early 1990s demonstrated, each of its constituent republics was itself an ethnic patchwork. Indeed, as the Nazis (and, later, the Bosnian Serbs) recognized, the only certain way of achieving a politically unified and culturally homogeneous nation-state is through a programme of **ethnic cleansing**.

Conservative nationalism

Historically, conservative nationalism developed rather later than liberal nationalism. Until the latter half of the nineteenth century, conservative politicians treated nationalism as a subversive, if not revolutionary, creed. As the century progressed, however, the link between conservatism and nationalism became increasingly apparent; for instance, in Disraeli's 'One Nation' ideal, in Bismarck's willingness to recruit German nationalism to the cause of Prussian aggrandisement, and in Tsar Alexander III's endorsement of pan-Slavic nationalism. In modern politics, nationalism has become an article of faith for most, if not all, conservatives. In the UK, this was demonstrated most graphically by Margaret Thatcher's triumphalist reaction to victory in the Falklands War of 1982, and it is evident in the engrained '**Euroscepticism**' of the Conservative right, particularly in relation to its recurrent bogey: a 'federal Europe'. A similar form of nationalism was rekindled in the USA through the adoption of a more assertive foreign policy; by Ronald Reagan in the invasion of Grenada (1983) and the bombing of Libya (1986), and by George W. Bush in the invasion of Afghanistan (2001) and Iraq (2003).

Conservative nationalism is concerned less with the principled nationalism of universal self-determination, and more with the promise of social cohesion and public order embodied in the sentiment of national patriotism. Above all, conservatives see the nation as an organic entity emerging out of a basic desire of humans to gravitate towards those who have the same views, habits, lifestyles and appearance as themselves. In short, human beings seek security and identity through membership of a national community. From this perspective, patriotic loyalty and a consciousness of nationhood is rooted largely in the idea of a shared past, turning nationalism into a defence of values and institutions that have been endorsed by history. Nationalism thus becomes a form of traditionalism. This gives conservative nationalism a distinctively nostalgic and backward-looking character. In the USA, this is accomplished through an emphasis on the Pilgrim Fathers, the War of Independence, the Philadelphia Convention and so on. In the case of British nationalism (or, more accurately, English nationalism), national patriotism draws on symbols closely associated with the institution of monarchy. The UK national anthem is God Save the Queen, and the Royal Family play a prominent role in national celebrations, such as Armistice Day, and on state occasions, such as the opening of Parliament.

Conservative nationalism tends to develop in established nation-states rather than in those that are in the process of nation-building. It is typically inspired by the perception that the nation is somehow under threat, either from within or from without. The traditional 'enemy within' has been class antagonism and the ultimate danger of social revolution. In this respect, conservatives have seen nationalism as the antidote to socialism: when patriotic loyalties are stronger than class solidarity, the working class is, effectively, integrated into the nation. Calls for national unity and the belief that unabashed patriotism is a civic virtue are therefore recurrent themes in conservative thought.

The 'enemies without' that threaten national identity, from a conservative perspective, include immigration and supranationalism. In this view, immigration poses a threat because it tends to weaken an established national culture and ethnic identity, thereby provoking hostility and conflict. This fear was expressed in the UK in the 1960s by Enoch Powell, who warned that further Commonwealth immigration would lead to racial conflict and violence. A similar theme was taken up in 1979 by Margaret Thatcher in her reference to the danger of the UK being 'swamped' by immigrants. Anti-immigration campaigns waged by the British National Party, Le Pen's National Front in France, and far-right groups such as the Freedom Party in Austria and the Danish People's Party also draw their inspiration from conservative nationalism. National identity and, with it, our source of security and belonging, is threatened in the same way by the growth of supranational bodies and by the globalization of culture. Resistance in the UK and in other EU member states to a single European currency reflects not merely concern about the loss of economic sovereignty, but also a belief that a national currency is vital to the maintenance of a distinctive national identity.

Although conservative nationalism has been linked to military adventurism and expansion, its distinctive character is that it is inward-looking and insular. If conservative governments have used foreign policy as a device to stoke up public fervour, this is an act of political opportunism, rather than because conservative nationalism is relentlessly aggressive or inherently militaristic. This leads to the criticism that conservative nationalism is essentially a form of elite manipulation or ruling-class ideology. From this perspective, the 'nation' is invented, and certainly defined, by political leaders and ruling elites with a view to manufacturing consent or engineering political passivity. In crude terms, when in

CONCEPT

Racialism, racism

The terms racialism and racism tend to be used interchangeably. Racialism refers to any belief or doctrine that draws political or social conclusions from the idea that humankind is divided into biologically distinct races (a notion that has no, or little, scientific basis). Racialist theories are thus based on that assumption the cultural, intellectual and moral differences amongst humankind derive from supposedly more fundamental genetic differences. In political terms, racialism is manifest in calls for racial segregation (apartheid), and in doctrines of 'blood' superiority and inferiority (Aryanism and anti-Semitism).

• Jingoism: A mood of public enthusiasm and celebration provoked by military expansion or imperial conquest.

trouble, all governments play the 'nationalism card'. A more serious criticism of conservative nationalism, however, is that it promotes intolerance and bigotry. Insular nationalism draws on a narrowly cultural concept of the nation; that is, the belief that a nation is an exclusive ethnic community, broadly similar to an extended family. A very clear line is therefore drawn between those who are members of the nation and those who are alien to it. By insisting on the maintenance of cultural purity and established traditions, conservatives may portray immigrants, or foreigners in general, as a threat, and so promote, or at least legitimize, racialism and xenophobia.

Expansionist nationalism

The third form of nationalism has an aggressive, militaristic and expansionist character. In many ways, this form of nationalism is the antithesis of the principled belief in equal rights and self-determination that is the core of liberal nationalism. The aggressive face of nationalism first appeared in the late nineteenth century as European powers indulged in 'the scramble for Africa' in the name of national glory and their 'place in the sun'. Nineteenth-century European imperialism (see p. 427) differed from the colonial expansion of earlier periods in that it was fuelled by a climate of popular nationalism in which national prestige was linked to the possession of an empire, and each colonial victory was greeted by demonstrations of popular enthusiasm, or jingoism. To a large extent, both world wars of the twentieth century resulted from this expansionist form of nationalism. When World War I broke out in August 1914, following a prolonged arms race and a succession of international crises, the prospect of conquest and military glory provoked spontaneous public rejoicing in all the major capitals of Europe. World War II was largely a result of the nationalist-inspired programmes of imperial expansion pursued by Japan, Italy and Germany. The most destructive modern example of this form of nationalism in Europe was the quest by the Bosnian Serbs to construct a 'Greater Serbia' in the aftermath of the break-up of Yugoslavia in the early 1990s.

In its extreme form, such nationalism arises from a sentiment of intense, even hysterical, nationalist enthusiasm, sometimes referred to as 'integral nationalism', a term coined by the French nationalist Charles Maurras (1868–1952), leader of the right-wing Action Française. The centrepiece of Maurras' politics was an assertion of the overriding importance of the nation: the nation is everything and the individual is nothing. The nation thus has an existence and meaning beyond the life of any single individual, and individual existence has meaning only when it is dedicated to the unity and survival of the nation. Such fanatical patriotism has a particularly strong appeal for the alienated, isolated and powerless, for whom nationalism becomes a vehicle through which pride and self-respect can be regained. However, integral nationalism breaks the link previously established between nationalism and democracy. An 'integral' nation is an exclusive ethnic community, bound together by primordial loyalties, rather than voluntary political allegiances. National unity does not demand free debate, and an open and competitive struggle for power; it requires discipline and obedience to a single, supreme leader. This led Maurras to portray democracy as a source of weakness and corruption, and to call instead for the re-establishment of monarchical absolutism.

Anti-Semitism

'Semites' are by tradition the descendants of Shem, son of Noah. They include most of the peoples of the Middle East. Anti-Semitism is prejudice or hatred specifically towards Jews. In its earliest form, *religious* anti-Semitism reflected the hostility of the Christians towards the Jews, based on their alleged complicity in the murder of Jesus and their refusal to acknowledge him as the son of God. *Economic* anti-Semitism developed from the Middle Ages onwards, and expressed distaste for Jews in their capacity as moneylenders and traders. *Racial* anti-Semitism developed from the late nineteeth century onwards, and condemned the Jewish peoples as fundamentally evil and destructive.

● **Pan-nationalism**: A style of nationalism dedicated to unifying a disparate people through either expansionism or political solidarity ('pan' means all or every).

This militant and intense form of nationalism is invariably associated with chauvinistic beliefs and doctrines. Derived from the name of Nicolas Chauvin, a French soldier noted for his fanatical devotion to Napoleon and the cause of France, chauvinism is an irrational belief in the superiority or dominance of one's own group or people. National chauvinism therefore rejects the idea that all nations are equal in favour of the belief that nations have particular characteristics and qualities, and so have very different destinies. Some nations are suited to rule; others are suited to be ruled. Typically, this form of nationalism is articulated through doctrines of ethnic or racial superiority, thereby fusing nationalism and racialism. The chauvinist's own nation is seen to be unique and special, in some way a 'chosen people'. For early German nationalists such as Fichte and Jahn (1783–1830), only the Germans were a true *Volk* (an organic people). They alone had maintained blood purity and avoided the contamination of their language. For Maurras, France was an unequalled marvel, a repository of all Christian and classical virtues.

No less important in this type of nationalism, however, is the image of another nation or race as a threat or enemy. In the face of the enemy, the nation draws together and gains an intensified sense of its own identity and importance, achieving a kind of 'negative integration'. Chauvinistic nationalism therefore establishes a clear distinction between 'them' and 'us'. There has to be a 'them' to deride or hate in order for a sense of 'us' to be forged. The world is thus divided, usually by means of racial categories, into an 'in group' and an 'out group'. The 'out group' acts as a scapegoat for all the misfortunes and frustrations suffered by the 'in group'. This was most graphically demonstrated by the virulent anti-Semitism that was the basis of German Nazism. Hitler's *Mein Kampf* ([1925] 1969) portrayed history as a Manichean struggle between the Aryans and the Jews, respectively representing the forces of light and darkness, or good and evil.

A recurrent theme of expansionist nationalism is the idea of national rebirth or regeneration. This form of nationalism commonly draws on myths of past greatness or national glory. Mussolini and the Italian Fascists looked back to the days of Imperial Rome. In portraying their regime as the 'Third Reich', the German Nazis harked back both to Bismarck's 'Second Reich' and Charlemagne's Holy Roman Empire, the 'First Reich'. Such myths plainly give expansionist nationalism a backward-looking character, but they also look to the future, in that they mark out the nation's destiny. If nationalism is a vehicle for re-establishing greatness and regaining national glory, it invariably has a militaristic and expansionist character. In short, war is the testing ground of the nation. At the heart of integral nationalism there often lies an imperial project: a quest for expansion or a search for colonies. This can be seen in forms of **pan-nationalism**. However, Nazi Germany is, again, the best-known example. Hitler's writings mapped out a three-stage programme of expansion. First, the Nazis sought to establish a 'Greater Germany' by bringing ethnic Germans in Austria, Czechoslovakia and Poland within an expanded Reich. Second, they intended to achieve *Lebensraum* (living space) by establishing a German-dominated empire stretching into Russia. Third, Hitler dreamed of ultimate Aryan world domination.

Colonialism

Colonialism is the theory or practice of establishing control over a foreign territory and turning it into a 'colony'. Colonialism is thus a particular form of imperialism. Colonialism is usually distinguished by settlement and by economic domination. As typically practised in Africa and Southeast Asia, colonial government was exercised by a settler community from a 'mother country'. In contrast, *neocolonialism* is essentially an economic phenomenon based on the export of capital from an advanced country to a less developed one (for example, so-called US 'dollar imperialism' in Latin America).

Anticolonial and postcolonial nationalism

The developing world has spawned various forms of nationalism, all of which have in some way drawn inspiration from the struggle against colonial rule. The irony of this form of nationalism is that it has turned doctrines and principles first developed through the process of 'nation-building' in Europe against the European powers themselves. Colonialism, in other words, succeeded in turning nationalism into a political creed of global significance. In Africa and Asia, it helped to forge a sense of nationhood shaped by the desire for 'national liberation'. Indeed, during the twentieth century, the political geography of much of the world was transformed by anticolonialism. Independence movements that sprang up in the interwar period gained new impetus after the conclusion of World War II. The overstretched empires of Britain, France, the Netherlands and Portugal crumbled in the face of rising nationalism.

India had been promised independence during World War II, which was eventually granted in 1947. China achieved genuine unity and independence only after the 1949 communist revolution, having fought an eight-year war against the occupying Japanese. A republic of Indonesia was proclaimed in 1949 after a three-year war against the Netherlands. A military uprising forced the French to withdraw from Vietnam in 1954, even though final liberation, with the unification of North and South Vietnam, was not achieved until 1975, after 14 further years of war against the USA. Nationalist struggles in Southeast Asia inspired similar movements in Africa, with liberation movements emerging under leaders such as Nkrumah in Ghana, Dr Azikiwe in Nigeria, Julius Nyerere in Tanganyika (later Tanzania), and Hastings Banda in Nyasaland (later Malawi). The pace of decolonization in Africa accelerated from the late 1950s onwards. Nigeria gained independence from the UK in 1960 and, after a prolonged war fought against the French, Algeria gained independence in 1962. Kenya became independent in 1963, as did Tanzania and Malawi the next year. Africa's last remaining colony, South-West Africa, finally became independent Namibia in 1990.

Early forms of anticolonialism drew heavily on 'classical' European nationalism and were inspired by the idea of national self-determination. However, emergent African and Asian nations were in a very different position from the newly-created European states of the nineteenth century. For African and Asian nations, the quest for political independence was inextricably linked to a desire for social development and for an end to their subordination to the industrialized states of Europe and the USA. The goal of 'national liberation' therefore had an economic as well as a political dimension. This helps to explain why anticolonial movements typically looked not to liberalism but to socialism, and particularly to Marxism–Leninism, as a vehicle for expressing their nationalist ambitions. On the surface, nationalism and socialism appear to be incompatible political creeds. Socialists have traditionally preached internationalism, since they regard humanity as a single entity, and argue that the division of humankind into separate nations breeds only suspicion and hostility. Marxists, in particular, have stressed that the bonds of class solidarity are stronger and more genuine than the ties of nationality, or, as Marx put it in the *Communist Manifesto* ([1848] 1967): 'Working men have no country'.

The appeal of socialism to the developing world was based on the fact that the values of community and cooperation that socialism embodies are deeply established in the cultures of traditional, pre-industrial societies. In this sense, nationalism and socialism are linked, insofar as both emphasize social solidarity and collective action. By this standard, nationalism may simply be a weaker form of socialism, the former applying the 'social' principle to the nation, the latter extending it to cover the whole of humanity. More specifically, socialism, and especially Marxism, provide an analysis of inequality and exploitation through which the colonial experience could be understood and colonial rule challenged. In the same way as the oppressed and exploited proletariat saw that they could achieve liberation through the revolutionary overthrow of capitalism, developing-world nationalists saw 'armed struggle' as a means of achieving both political and economic emancipation, thus fusing the goals of political independence and social revolution. In countries such as China, North Korea, Vietnam and Cambodia, anticolonial movements openly embraced Marxism–Leninism. On achieving power, they moved to seize foreign assets and nationalize economic resources, creating Soviet-style planned economies. African and Middle Eastern states developed a less ideological form of nationalistic socialism, which was practised, for example, in Algeria, Libya, Zambia, Iraq and South Yemen. The 'socialism' proclaimed in these countries usually took the form of an appeal to a unifying national cause or interest, typically championed by a powerful 'charismatic' leader.

However, nationalists in the developing world have not always been content to express their nationalism in a language of socialism or Marxism borrowed from the West. Especially since the 1970s, Marxism–Leninism has often been displaced by forms of religious fundamentalism (see p. 53) and, particularly, Islamic fundamentalism. This has given the developing world a specifically non-western – indeed an anti-western, voice. In theory at least, Islam attempts to foster a transnational political identity that unites all those who acknowledge the 'way of Islam' and the teachings of the Prophet Muhammad within an 'Islamic nation'. However, the Iranian revolution of 1979, which brought Ayatollah Khomeini (1900–89) to power, demonstrated the potency of Islamic fundamentalism as a creed of national and spiritual renewal. The establishment of an 'Islamic republic' was designed to purge Iran of the corrupting influence of western materialism in general, and of the 'Great Satan' (the USA) in particular, through a return to the traditional values and principles embodied in the Shari'a, or divine Islamic law. By no means, however, does Islamic nationalism have a unified character. In Sudan and Pakistan, for example, Islamification has essentially been used as a tool of statecraft to consolidate the power of ruling elites.

A FUTURE FOR THE NATION-STATE?

Since the final decades of the twentieth century, it has become fashionable to declare that the age of nationalism is over. This has not been because nationalism had been superseded by 'higher' cosmopolitan allegiances, but because its task had been completed: the world had become a world of nation-states. In effect, the nation had been accepted as the sole legitimate unit of political rule. Certainly, since 1789, the world had been fundamentally remodelled on nationalist lines. In 1910, only 15 of the 193 states recognized in 2011 as full members

CONCEPT

Nation-state

The nation-state is a form of political organization and a political ideal. In the first case, it is an autonomous political community bound together by the overlapping bonds of citizenship and nationality. In the latter, it is a principle, or ideal type (see p. 20), reflected in Mazzini's goal: 'every nation a state, only one state for the entire nation'. As such, the nation-state principle embodies the belief that nations are 'natural' political communities. For liberals and most socialists, the nation-state is largely fashioned out of civic loyalties and allegiances. For conservatives and integral nationalists, it is based on ethnic or organic unity.

of the United Nations existed. Well into the twentieth century, most of the peoples of the world were still colonial subjects of one of the European empires. Only 3 of the current 72 states in the Middle East and Africa existed before 1910, and no fewer than 108 states have come into being since 1959. These changes have been fuelled largely by the quest for national independence, with these new states invariably assuming the mantle of the nation-state.

History undoubtedly seems to be on the side of the nation-state. The three major geopolitical upheavals of the twentieth century (World War I, World War II and the collapse of communism in Eastern Europe) each gave considerable impetus to the concept of the nation as a principle of political organization. Since 1991, at least 22 new states have come into existence in Europe alone (15 of them as a result of the disintegration of the USSR), and all of them have claimed to be nation-states. The great strength of the nation-state is that it offers the prospect of both cultural cohesion and political unity. When a people who share a common cultural or ethnic identity gain the right to self-government, community and citizenship coincide. This is why nationalists believe that the forces that have created a world of independent nation-states are natural and irresistible, and that no other social group could constitute a meaningful political community. They believe that the nation-state is ultimately the only viable political unit. This view implies, for instance, that supranational bodies such as the European Union will never be able to rival the capacity of national governments to establish legitimacy and command popular allegiance. Clear limits should therefore be placed on the process of European integration because people with different languages, cultures and histories will never come to think of themselves as members of a united political community.

Nevertheless, just as the principle of the nation-state has achieved its widest support, other, very powerful forces have emerged that threaten to make the nation-state redundant. A combination of internal pressures and external threats has produced what is commonly referred to as a 'crisis of the nation-state'. Internally, nation-states have been subject to centrifugal pressures, generated by an upsurge in ethnic, regional and multicultural politics. This heightened concern with ethnicity and culture may, indeed, reflect the fact that, in a context of economic and cultural globalization (see p. 142), nations are no longer able to provide a meaningful collective identity or sense of social belonging. Given that all nation-states embody a measure of cultural diversity, the politics of ethnic assertiveness cannot but present a challenge to the principle of the nation, leading some to suggest that nationalism is in the process of being replaced by multiculturalism (see p. 167). Unlike nations, ethnic, regional or cultural groups are not viable political entities in their own right, and have thus sometimes looked to forms of federalism (see p. 382) and confederalism to provide an alternative to political nationalism. For example, within the framework provided by the European Union, the Belgian regions of Flanders and Wallonia have achieved such a degree of self-government that Belgium remains a nation-state only in a strictly formal sense. The nature of such centrifugal forces is discussed more fully in Chapter 17.

External threats to the nation-state have a variety of forms. First, advances in the technology of warfare, and especially the advent of the nuclear age, have brought about demands that world peace be policed by intergovernmental or supranational bodies. This led to the creation of the League of Nations and, later,

Debating...
Are nations 'natural' political communities?

Nationalism is based on two core assumptions: first, that humankind is naturally divided into distinct nations and, second, that the nation is the most appropriate, and perhaps only legitimate, unit of political rule. This is why nationalists have strived, wherever possible, to bring the borders of the state into line with the boundaries of the nation. But is humankind 'naturally' divided into distinct nations? And why should the national communities be accorded this special, indeed unique, political status?

YES

'Natural' communities: For primordialist scholars, national identity is historically embedded: nations are rooted in a common cultural heritage and language that may long predate statehood or the quest for independence (Smith, 1986). In this view, nations evolve organically out of more simple ethnic communities, reflecting the fact that people are inherently group-orientated, drawn naturally towards others who are similar to themselves because they share the same cultural characteristics. Above all, national identity is forged by a combination of a sense of territorial belonging and a shared way of life (usually facilitated by a common language), creating deep emotional attachments that resemble kinship ties.

Vehicle for democracy: The nation acquired a political character only when, thanks to the doctrine of nationalism, it was seen as the ideal unit of self-rule, a notion embodied in the principle of national self-determination. Nationalism and democracy therefore go hand-in-hand. Bound together by ties of national solidarity, people are encouraged to adopt shared civic allegiances and to participate fully in the life of their society. Moreover, democratic nations are inclusive and tolerant, capable of respecting the separate identities of minority groups. Nationality, thus, does not suppress other sources of personal identity, such as ethnicity and religion.

Benefits of national partiality: Nationalism inevitably implies partiality, the inclination to favour the needs and interests of one's 'own' people over those of other peoples. This, as communitarian theorists argue, reflects the fact that morality begins at home. From this perspective, morality only makes sense when it is locally-based, grounded in the communities to which we belong, and which have shaped our lives and values. National partiality is thus an extension of the near universal inclination to accord moral priority to those we know best, especially our families and close friends. There is no reason, moreover, why national partiality should preclude a moral concern for 'strangers'.

NO

'Invented' communities: Rather than being natural or organic entities, nations are, to a greater or lesser extent, political constructs. Nations are certainly 'imagined communities', in the sense that people only ever meet a tiny proportion of those with whom they supposedly share a national identity (Anderson, 1983). Marxists and others go further and argued that ruling or elite groups have 'invented' nationalism in order to bind the working class, and the disadvantaged generally, to the existing power structure (Hobsbawm, 1983). National anthems, national flags and national myths and legends are thus little more than a form of ideological manipulation.

'Hollowed-out' nations: The nation has had its day as a meaningful political unit and as a basis for democracy and citizenship. Nations were appropriate political communities during an industrial age that was shaped though the development of relatively discrete national economies. However, the growth of an interdependent world, and the transfer of decision-making authority from national governments to intergovernmental or supranational bodies, has seriously weakened the political significance of the nation. Not only have nations been 'hollowed-out' in terms of their political role, but the seemingly remorseless trends towards international migration and cultural diversity has fatally compromised the nation's organic unity (if it ever existed).

Miniaturizing humanity: National identity encourages people to identify with part of humanity, rather than with humanity as a whole. As such, it narrows our moral sensibilities and destroys our sense of a common humanity. Worse, nationalism breeds inevitable division and conflict. If one's own nation is unique or 'special', other nations are inevitably seen as inferior and possibly threatening. Nationalism therefore gives rise to, not a world of independent nation-states, but a world that is scared by militarism, aggression and conquest. For humankind to progress beyond struggle and war, nationalism must be abandoned and treated like the infantile disease it has always been.

the United Nations. Second, economic life has been progressively globalized. Markets are now world markets, businesses have increasingly become transnational corporations (see p. 149), and capital is moved around the globe in the blink of an eye. Is there a future for the nation-state in a world in which no national government can control its economic destiny? Third, the nation-state may be the enemy of the natural environment and a threat to the global ecological balance. Nations are concerned primarily with their own strategic and economic interests, and most pay little attention to the ecological consequences of their actions. The folly of this was demonstrated in the Ukraine in 1986 by the Chernobyl nuclear accident, which released a wave of nuclear radiation across Northern Europe that will cause an estimated 2000 cancer-related deaths over 50 years in Europe.

Finally, distinctive national cultures and traditions, the source of cohesion that distinguishes nation-states from other forms of political organization, have been weakened by the emergence of a transnational, and even global, culture. This has been facilitated by international tourism and the dramatic growth in communications technologies, from satellite television to the 'information superhighway'. When US films and television programmes are watched throughout the world, Indian and Chinese cuisine is as popular in Europe as native dishes, and people can communicate as easily with the other side of the world as with their neighbouring town, is the nation-state any longer a meaningful entity? These and related issues are discussed in greater depth.

SUMMARY

- Nations are defined by a combination of cultural and political factors. Culturally, they are groups of people who are bound together by a common language, religion, history and traditions. Ultimately, however, nations define themselves through the existence of a shared civic consciousness, classically expressed as the desire to achieve or maintain statehood.

- Distinctive cultural and political forms of nationalism can be identified. Cultural nationalism emphasizes the regeneration of the nation as a distinctive civilization on the basis of a belief in the nation as a unique, historical and organic whole. Political nationalism, on the other hand, recognizes the nation as a discrete political community, and is thus linked with ideas such as sovereignty and self-determination.

- Some political thinkers portray nationalism as a modern phenomenon associated with industrialization and the rise of democracy, while others trace it back to premodern ethnic loyalties and identities. The character of nationalism has varied considerably, and has been influenced by both the historical circumstances in which it has arisen and the political causes to which it has been attached.

- There have been a number of contrasting manifestations of political nationalism. Liberal nationalism is based on a belief in a universal right to self-determination. Conservative nationalism values the capacity of national patriotism to deliver social cohesion and political unity. Expansionist nationalism is a vehicle for aggression and imperial conquest. Anticolonial nationalism is associated with the struggle for national liberation, often fused with the quest for social development.

- The most widely recognized form of political organization worldwide is the nation-state, which is often seen as the sole legitimate unit of political rule. Its strength is that it offers the prospect of both cultural cohesion and political unity, thus allowing those who share a common cultural or ethnic identity to exercise the right to independence and self-government.

- The nation-state now confronts a number of challenges. Nation-states have been subject to centrifugal pressures generated by the growth in ethnic politics. Externally, they have confronted challenges from the growing power of supranational bodies, the advance of economic and cultural globalization, and the need to find international solutions to the environmental crisis.

Questions for discussion

- Where do nations come from? Are they natural or artificial formations?
- Why have national pride and patriotic loyalty been valued?
- Does cultural nationalism merely imprison a nation in its past?
- Why has nationalism proved to be such a potent political force?
- Does nationalism inevitably breed insularity and conflict?
- Can nationalism be viewed as a form of elite manipulation?
- Are nationalism and internationalism compatible?
- Is the nation-state the sole legitimate unit of political rule?
- Is a postnationalist world possible?

Further reading

Brown, D., *Contemporary Nationalism: Civic, Ethnocultural and Multicultural Politics* (2000). A clear and illuminating framework for understanding nationalist politics.

Hearn, J., *Rethinking Nationalism: A Critical Introduction* (2006). A comprehensive account of approaches to understanding nationalism that draws on sociology, politics, anthropology and history, and develops its own critique.

Hobsbawm, E., *Nations and Nationalism Since 1780* (2nd edn) (1993). An analysis of the phenomenon of nationalism from a modern Marxist perspective.

Spencer, P. and H. Wollman (eds), *Nations and Nationalism: A Reader* (2005). A wide-ranging and stimulating collection of mainstream and less mainstream writings on nationalism.

CHAPTER **10** # The Nation in a Global Age

'Nations are the irreplaceable cells of the human community.'

FRANJO TUDJMAN, *Nationalism in Contemporary Europe* (1981)

PREVIEW   Nationalism has, arguably, been the most powerful force in world politics for over 200 years. It has contributed to the outbreak of wars and revolutions. It has been closely linked to the birth of new states, the disintegration of empires and the redrawing of borders; and it has been used to reshape existing regimes as well as to bolster them. The greatest achievement of nationalism has been the establishment of the nation as the key unit for political rule, meaning that the so-called 'nation-state' has come to be accepted as the most basic – and, nationalists argue, the only legitimate – form of political organization. However, the character of nationalism and its implications for world politics are deeply contested. Has nationalism advanced the cause of political freedom, or has it simply legitimized aggression and expansion? Nevertheless, modern nations are under pressure perhaps as never before. Globalization is widely seen to have weakened nationalism as territorial nation-states have been enmeshed in global political, economic and cultural networks, and significantly increased international migration has led to the development of transnational communities, giving a growing number of societies a multicultural character and creating other strains. Is nationalism a political force in retreat? Can nationalism survive in a world on the move? Finally, despite frequent predictions to the contrary, there is evidence of the resurgence of nationalism. Since the end of the Cold War, new and often highly potent forms of nationalism have emerged, often linked to cultural, ethnic or religious self-assertion. Nationalism has also re-emerged as a reaction against the homogenizing impact of globalization and as a means of resisting immigration and multiculturalism. How can the revival of nationalism best be explained, and what forms has it taken?

KEY ISSUES

- What is a nation? How is nationalism best understood?
- How, and to what extent, has nationalism shaped world politics?
- Why has international migration increased in recent decades?
- How has population movement affected world politics?
- Why has nationalism resurfaced since the end of the Cold War?
- Does contemporary nationalism differ from earlier forms of nationalism?

The Nation

Nations (from the Latin *nasci*, meaning 'to be born') are complex phenomena that are shaped by a collection of cultural, political and psychological factors. *Culturally*, a nation is a group of people bound together by a common language, religion, history and traditions, although all nations exhibit some degree of cultural heterogeneity. *Politically*, a nation is a group of people who regard themselves as a 'natural' political community, usually expressed through the desire to establish or maintain sovereignty. *Psychologically*, a nation is a group of people who are distinguished by a shared loyalty or affection, in the form of patriotism, although people who lack national pride may still, nevertheless, recognize that they 'belong' to the nation.

● **Patriotism**: Literally, love of one's fatherland; a psychological attachment of loyalty to one's nation or country.

● **Race**: A group of people who (supposedly) share the same physical or biological characteristics, based on common descent.

NATIONALISM AND WORLD POLITICS

Modern nations and the idea of nationalism were born in the late eighteenth century; some commentators see them as a product of the 1789 French Revolution (Kedourie 1966). Previously, countries had been thought of as 'realms', 'principalities' or 'kingdoms'. The inhabitants of a country were 'subjects', their political identity being formed by allegiance to a ruler or ruling dynasty, rather than any sense of national identity or patriotism. However, the revolutionaries in France who rose up against Louis XVI did so in the name of the people, and understood the people to be the 'French nation'. Nationalism was therefore a revolutionary and democratic creed, reflecting the idea that 'subjects of the crown' should become 'citizens of France'. Such ideas, nevertheless, were not the exclusive property of the French. In the early nineteenth century, a rising tide of nationalism spread throughout Europe, exploding in 1848 in a series of revolutions that affected the mainland of Europe from the Iberian peninsula to the borders of Russia. During the twentieth century, the doctrine of nationalism, which had been born in Europe, spread throughout the globe as the peoples of Asia and Africa rose in opposition to colonial rule.

Making sense of nationalism

However, nationalism is a complex and deeply contested political phenomenon. In the most simple sense, nationalism is the belief that the nation is, or should be, the most basic principle of political organization. But what is a nation? In everyday language, words such as 'nation', 'state', 'country' and even 'race' are often confused or used as if they are interchangeable. The United Nations, for instance, is clearly misnamed, as it is an organization of states, not one of national populations. It is common in international politics to hear references to 'the Americans', 'the Chinese', 'the Russians' and so on, when in fact it is the actions of these people's governments that are being discussed. In the case of the UK, there is confusion about whether it should be regarded as a nation or as a state that comprises four separate nations: the English, the Scots, the Welsh and the Northern Irish (who may, indeed, constitute two nations, Unionists viewing themselves as British, while Republicans define themselves as Irish). The Arab peoples of North Africa and the Middle East pose very similar problems. For instance, should Egypt, Libya, Iraq and Syria be treated as nations in their own right, or as part of a single and united Arab nation, based on a common language (Arabic), a common religion (Islam), and descent from a common Bedouin tribal past?

Such difficulties spring from the fact that all nations comprise a mixture of objective and subjective factors, a blend of cultural and political characteristics. On the most basic level, nations are cultural entities, collections of people bound together by shared values and traditions, in particular a common language, religion and history, and usually occupying the same geographical area. From this point of view, the nation can be defined by objective factors: people who satisfy a requisite set of cultural criteria can be said to belong to a nation; those who do not can be classified as non-nationals or members of foreign nations. Such factors certainly shape the politics of nationalism. The nationalism of the Québécois in Canada, for instance, is based largely on language differences between French-speaking Quebec and the predominantly English-speaking rest of Canada. Nationalist tensions in India invariably arise from religious divisions, examples being the struggle of Sikhs in the Punjab for a separate homeland (Khalistan), and the campaign by Muslims in Kashmir for the incorporation of Kashmir into Pakistan. Nevertheless, it is impossible to define the nation using objective factors alone. All nations, to a greater or lesser extent, are characterized by cultural heterogeneity, and some to a high degree. The Swiss nation has proved to be enduring and viable despite the use of three major languages (French, German and Italian), as well as a variety of local dialects. Divisions between Catholics and Protestants that has given rise to rival nationalisms in Northern Ireland have been largely irrelevant in mainland UK, and have only marginal significance in countries such as Germany.

The cultural unity that supposedly expresses itself in nationhood is therefore difficult to pin down. It reflects, at best, a varying combination of cultural factors, rather than any precise formula. This emphasizes the fact that, ultimately, nations can only be defined subjectively, by their members. In the final analysis, the nation is a psycho-political entity, a group of people who regard themselves as a natural political community and are distinguished by shared loyalty and affection in the form of patriotism. The political dimension of nationhood is evident in the difference between a nation and an **ethnic group**. An ethnic group undoubtedly possesses a communal identity and a sense of cultural pride, but, unlike a nation, it lacks collective political aspirations: it does not seek to establish or maintain sovereign independence or political autonomy. The psychological dimension of nationhood is evident in the survival of nationalist aspirations despite the existence of profound objective difficulties, such as the absence of land, a small population or lack of economic resources. Latvia, for example, became an independent nation in 1991 despite having a population of only 2.6 million (barely half of whom are Lats), no source of fuel and very few natural resources. Likewise, the Kurdish peoples of the Middle East retain nationalist aspirations, even though the Kurds have never enjoyed formal political unity and are presently spread over parts of Turkey, Iraq, Iran and Syria.

Confusions over the factors that define the nation are nevertheless compounded by controversy over the phenomenon of nationalism. Is nationalism a feeling, an identity, a political doctrine, an ideology or a social movement? Or is it all these things at once? Moreover, how can the emergence of nationalism best be explained: is it a natural phenomenon, or has it somehow been invented? Since the 1970s, students of nationalism have increasingly fallen into two great camps: primordialists versus modernists (Hearn 2006). **Primordialism** portrays national identity as historically embedded: nations are rooted in a common cultural heritage and language that may long predate statehood or the quest for independence. All nationalists, in this sense, are primordialists. The dominant themes of primordialism are:

- People are inherently group-orientated and nations are a manifestation of this.
- National identity is forged by three key factors: common descent, a sense of territorial belonging, and a shared language.

● **Ethnic group**: A group of people who share a common cultural and historical identity, typically linked to a belief in common descent.

● **Primordialism**: The theory that nations are ancient and deep-rooted, fashioned variously out of psychology, culture and biology.

● To describe a collection of people as a nation is to imply that they share a common cultural heritage. In that sense, all nations are myths or illusions, as no nation is culturally homogeneous (the Japanese being perhaps the closest thing to an exception in this respect). Nations, in that sense, are 'invented' or 'imagined'.

Deconstructing . . .

'NATION'

● Nations appear to be cohesive entities, which act as organically unified wholes. This gives rise to what is called 'methodological nationalism', an approach to understanding in which discrete nations are taken to be the primary global actors. In practice, this apparent cohesiveness is achieved only by the fact that the leading actors on the world stage are states or governments, which legitimize their actions by claiming to act on behalf of 'the nation'. To refer to, say, 'the Chinese', 'the Russian' or 'the Americans' as global actors is therefore deeply misleading.

● The assumption that people are members of a nation suggests that national identity is the principal form of collective identity. Other sources of collective identity – based, for instance, on social class, gender, ethnicity or religion – are thus of secondary importance, especially as each of these has transnational or subnational implications.

● Nations are historical entities: they evolve organically out of more simple ethnic communities.
● Nationalism is characterized by deep emotional attachments that resemble kinship ties.

Such views can be traced back to the writings of the German philosopher Johann Herder (1744–1803), who argued that each nation possesses a *Volksgeist*, which reveals itself in songs, myths and legends, and provides a nation with its source of creativity. The implications of Herder's culturalism is that nations are natural or organic identities that can be traced back to ancient times and will, by the same token, continue to exist as long as human society survives. Modern commentators have advanced similar ideas. Anthony Smith, (see p. 169), for instance, highlighted the continuity between modern nations and pre-modern ethnic communities, which he called 'ethnies'. This implies that nationalism is a variant of ethnicity (see p. 193), modern nations essentially being updated versions of immemorial ethnic communities.

● *Volksgeist*: (German) Literally, the spirit of the people; the organic identity of a people revealed in their culture and particularly their language.

By contrast, modernist approaches to nationalism suggest that national identity is forged in response to changing social and historical circumstances. In many cases, modernism links the origins of nationalism to the process of modernization and, in particular to the emergence of industrialization. Although different modernist theorists place an emphasis on different factors, modernism can be associated with three broad themes:

- The emergence of industrial and capitalist economies weakened traditional social bonds and generated new social tensions, so creating a need for a unifying national identity.
- States often play a key role in forging a sense of national identity, implying that the state predates and, in a sense, 'constructs' the nation.
- The spread of mass literacy and mass education contributed significantly to the construction of national identity.

Ernest Gellner (see p. 169) thus stressed that while premodern or 'agro-literate' societies were structured by a network of feudal bonds and loyalties, emerging industrial societies promoted social mobility, self-striving and competition, and so required a new source of cultural cohesion (as discussed in Chapter 6). This new source of cultural cohesion was provided by nationalism, which, in effect, means that nationalism invented the nation, not the other way round. Although Gellner's theory suggests that nations coalesced in response to particular social conditions and circumstances, it also implies that the national community is deep-rooted and will be enduring, as a return to premodern loyalties and identities is unthinkable. Benedict Anderson (see p. 169) also portrayed modern nations as a product of socio-economic change, in his case stressing the combined impact of the emergence of capitalism and the advent of modern mass communications, which he dubbed 'print-capitalism'. In his view, the nation is an 'imagined community', in that, within nations, individuals only ever meet a tiny proportion of those with whom they supposedly share a national identity (Anderson 1983). If nations exist, they exist as imagined artifices, constructed for us through education, the mass media, and the process of political socialization. Marxists, such as Eric Hobsbawm (1992), tend to view nationalism as a device through which the ruling class counters the threat of social revolution by ensuring that national loyalty is stronger than class solidarity, thereby binding the working class to the existing power structure.

A world of nation-states

Nationalism has helped to shape and reshape world politics for over 200 years. However, the nature of its impact has been the subject of considerable debate. Nationalism is a chameleon-like ideology, capable of assuming a bewildering variety of political forms. At different times, it has been progressive and reactionary, democratic and authoritarian, liberating and oppressive, aggressive and peaceful, and so on. Some, as a result, distinguish between good and bad nationalism, dispensing altogether with the idea of nationalism as a single, coherent political force. The liberating or progressive face of nationalism is evident in what is often seen as classical political nationalism. Classical nationalism dates back to the French Revolution, and embodies many of its values. Its ideas spread

NATIONALISM

Realist view

Realists do not generally place an emphasis on nation-alism as such. In their view, the crucial stage in the development of the modern international system was the emergence of sovereign states in the 1500–1750 period (particularly through the 1648 Peace of Westphalia), rather than the transformation of these states, from the early nineteenth century onwards, into nation-states through the advent of nationalism. The international system is thus, more accurately, viewed as an inter-state system. Despite this, realists have tended to view nationalism in broadly positive terms. From the realist perspective, nationalism is a key auxiliary component of state power, a source of internal cohe-sion that consolidates the external effectiveness of a nation-state. By interpreting state interests (generally) as 'national interests', realists recognize nationalism as a force that sustains international anarchy, limits the scope for cooperation between and among states, and implies that universal values, such as human rights (see p. 311), are defective.

Liberal view

Liberals have long endorsed nationalism. Indeed, in nineteenth-century Europe in particular, to be a liberal meant to be a nationalist. Liberal nationalism is a prin-cipled form of nationalism, based above all on the notion of national self-determination, which portrays the nation as a sovereign entity and implies both national independence and democratic rule. Although liberal nationalists, like all nationalists, view the nation as a 'natural' community, they regard nations as essen-tially civic entities, based on the existence of common values and political loyalties. This makes their form of nationalism tolerant and inclusive. From the liberal perspective, the nation-state (see p. 168) is a political ideal, representing the goal of freedom and the right of each nation to fashion its own destiny. Self-determination, moreover, is a universal right, reflecting the equality of nations (at least in a moral sense) and implying that liberals aim not merely to achieve sover-eign statehood for their particular nation but to construct a world of independent nation-states. Liberals argue that such a world would be character-ized by peace and harmony, both because nation-states are likely to respect each other's rights and freedoms, and because no nation-state would wish to endanger its own civic and cultural unity. Liberals nevertheless view

nationalism and internationalism (see p. 67) as complementary, not conflicting, principles. The most prominent forms of liberal internationalism are support for free trade to promote economic interde-pendence, making war so costly it becomes almost unthinkable, and the construction of intergovernmen-tal or supranational bodies to ensure an international rule of law.

Critical views

Critical views of nationalism have been developed within the Marxist, social constructivist, poststruc-turalist and feminist traditions. For Marxists, national-ity is an example of 'false consciousness', an illusion that serves to mystify and confuse the working classes, preventing them from recognizing their genuine inter-ests. In particular, in emphasizing the bonds of nation-hood over those of social class, nationalism serves to distort, and conceal, the realities of unequal class power and prevent social revolution. Social constructivists have been particularly critical of the primordialist image of 'fixed' ethnic and national identities, empha-sizing instead that the sense of national belonging is 'constructed' though social, political and other processes. They therefore tend to argue that nations are fashioned by nationalism itself, sympathizing with Eric Hobsbawm's (1983) image of nations as 'invented traditions'.

Poststructuralist and postmodernist approaches to nationalism tend to suggest that at the heart of the nationalist project is a narrative, or collection of narra-tives. The story of the nation is told by history books, works of fiction, symbols, myths and so on, with partic-ular importance being given to a foundational myth that locates the origins of the nation in a time long ago and imbues the nation with special qualities. Feminist theories of nationalism build to these ideas by empha-sizing the gender dimension of national identity. The nation is often depicted as female – as the 'motherland' rather than the 'fatherland' – a tendency that draws from an emphasis on women as the (biological) reproducers of the nation and as symbols of the nation's values and culture (usually emphasizing the home, purity and selflessness). On the other hand, when the nation is constructed as masculine, this often links national identity to heroism, self-assertion and aggression, tending to conflate nationalism with militarism.

Focus on . . .
The two nationalisms: good and bad?

Does nationalism embrace two, quite distinct traditions? Does nationalism have a 'good' face and a 'bad' face? The idea that there are, in effect, 'two nationalisms' is usually based on the belief that nationalism has contrasting civic and ethnic forms. What is often called civic nationalism is fashioned primarily out of shared political allegiances and political values. The nation is thus an 'association of citizens'. Civic nationalism has been defended on the grounds that it is open and voluntaristic: membership of the nation is based on choice and self-definition, not on any pre-determined ethnic or historical identity. It is a form of nationalism that is consistent with toleration and liberal values generally, being forward-looking and compatible with a substantial degree of cultural and ethnic diversity. Critics, however, have questioned whether civic nationalism is meaningful (Kymlicka 1999). Most citizens, even in a 'civic' or 'political' nation, derive their nationality from birth, not choice. Moreover, divorced from the bonds of ethnicity, language and history, political allegiances and civic values may simply be incapable of generating the sense of belonging and rootedness that gives nationalism its power.

By contrast, ethnic nationalism is squarely rooted in ethnic unity and a deep sense of cultural belonging. This form of nationalism is often criticized for having a closed or fixed character: it is difficult, and perhaps impossible, for non-citizens to become members of the nation. Nationalism therefore acquires a homogenizing character, breeding a fear or suspicion of foreigners and strengthening the idea of cultural distinctiveness, often interwoven with a belief in national greatness. Ethnic nationalism is thus irrational and tends to be tribalistic, even bloodthirsty. On the other hand, its capacity to generate a closed and fixed sense of political belonging may also be a virtue of ethnic nationalism. 'Ethnic' or 'cultural' nations tend to be characterized by high levels of social solidarity and a strong sense of collective purpose.

● **Civic nationalism:** A form of nationalism that emphasizes political allegiance based on a vision of a community of equal citizens, allowing respect for ethnic and cultural diversity that does not challenge core civic values.

● **Ethnic nationalism:** A form of nationalism that emphasizes the organic and usually ethnic unity of the nation and aims to protect or strengthen its national 'spirit' and cultural sameness.

quickly through much of Europe and were expressed, for example, in the emergence of unification movements in the Italian states and the Germanic states in particular, and through the growth of independence movements in the Austro-Hungarian empire and later in the Russian empire and the Ottoman empire. The ideas and aspirations of classical European nationalism were most clearly expressed by the prophet of Italian unification, Giuseppe Mazzini (1805–72). Perhaps the clearest expression of classical nationalism is found in US President Woodrow Wilson's (see p. 445) 'Fourteen Points'. Drawn up in 1918, these were proposed as the basis for the reconstruction of Europe after WWI, and provided a blueprint for the sweeping territorial changes that were implemented by the Treaty of Versailles (1919).

Classical nationalism has been strongly associated with liberal ideas and values. Indeed, in nineteenth-century Europe, to be a nationalist meant to be a liberal, and *vice versa*. In common with all forms of nationalism, classical nationalism is based on the fundamental assumption that humankind is naturally divided into a collection of nations, each possessed of a separate identity. Nations are therefore genuine or organic communities, not the artificial creation of political leaders or ruling classes. The characteristic theme of classical nationalism, however, is that it links the idea of the nation with a belief in popular sovereignty (see p. 4), ultimately derived from Jean-Jacques Rousseau's

CONCEPT

Nation-state

A nation-state is an autonomous political community bound together by the overlapping bonds of citizenship and nationality, meaning that political and cultural identity coincide. Nation-states thus reflect Mazzini's goal: 'Every nation a state, only one state for the entire nation'. Most modern states are nation-states, in that, thanks to classical nationalism, the nation has come to be accepted as the basic unit of political rule. However, the nation-state is more a political ideal than a reality, as all states are, to some degree, culturally and ethnically heterogeneous. However, the term 'nation-state' has (often incorrectly) become a synonym for the 'state' in much public, and some academic, discourse.

● National self-determination: The principle that the nation is a sovereign entity; self-determination implies both national independence and democratic rule.

(1712–78) idea of the 'general will'. This fusion was brought about because the multinational empires against which nineteenth-century European nationalists fought were also autocratic and oppressive. Mazzini, for example, wished not only to unite the Italian states, but also to throw off the influence of autocratic Austria. Woodrow Wilson, for his part, wished not only that the constituent nations of Europe should achieve statehood but also that they should be reconstructed on the basis of US-style liberal republicanism. The central theme of this form of nationalism is therefore a commitment to the principle of **national self-determination**. Its goal is therefore the construction of a nation-state.

This form of nationalism has had profound implications for world politics. From the early nineteenth century onwards, the seemingly irresistible process of nation-state formation transformed the state-system, reconfiguring political power, ultimately across the globe, and giving states an internal cohesion and sense of purpose and identity they had previously lacked. This was, nevertheless, a complex process. Although primordialists, such as Anthony Smith (1986, 1991), tend to view pre-modern ethnic communities as a kind of template for modern states, nation-state formation changed nationalism every bit as much as nationalism changed the state-system. Nationalism was an important component of the 1848 revolutions that spread across Europe, from the Iberian peninsula to the borders of Russia (see p. 181). However, nationalist movements were nowhere strong enough to accomplish the process of nation-building alone. Where nationalist goals were realized, as in Italy and Germany (both were finally unified in 1871), it was because nationalism coincided with the ambitions of powerful states, in this case Piedmont and Prussia. The character of nationalism also changed. Nationalism had previously been associated with liberal and progressive movements, but was increasingly taken up by conservative and reactionary politicians and used to promote social cohesion, order and stability, or, as discussed in the next section, projects of imperial expansion.

During the twentieth century, the process whereby multinational empires were replaced by territorial nation-states was extended into Africa and Asia. Indeed, in a sense, nineteenth-century European imperialism (see p. 28) turned nationalism into a genuinely global creed by generating anti-colonial or 'national liberation' movements across much of the developing world. The independence movements that sprang up in the inter-war period gained new impetus from the conclusion of WWII. The over-stretched empires of the UK, France, the Netherlands and Portugal crumbled in the face of rising nationalism. India was granted independence in 1947. China (see p. 238) achieved genuine unity and independence only after the 1949 communist revolution. During the 1950s and early 1960s, the political map of Africa was entirely redrawn through the process of decolonization. Africa's last remaining colony, Southwest Africa, finally became independent Namibia in 1990. The last stage in this process was the collapse of the world's final major empire, the Russian empire, which was brought about by the fall of communism and the disintegration of the Soviet Union in 1991.

The image of a world of sovereign nation-states nevertheless remains misleading. In the first place, despite the collapse of major empires, significant unresolved nationalist tensions persist. These range from those in Tibet and the predominantly Muslim province of Xinjiang in China to Chechnya and elsewhere in the Russian Caucasus, the Kurds in the Middle East and the Basques in Spain. Second,

KEY THEORISTS IN NATIONALISM

Ernest Gellner (1925–95)

A UK social philosopher and anthropologist, Gellner made major contributions to a variety of academic fields, including social anthropology, sociology and political philosophy. The most prominent figure in the modernist camp in the study of nationalism, Gellner explained the rise of nationalism in terms of the need of industrial societies, unlike agrarian ones, for homogeneous languages and cultures in order to work efficiently. Gellner's major writings include *Legitimation of Belief* (1974), *Nations and Nationalism* (1983), *Culture, Identity and Politics* (1987) and *Reason and Culture* (1992).

Anthony D. Smith (born 1933)

A UK academic and one of the founders of the interdisciplinary field of nationalism studies, Smith has been particularly concerned to transcend the debate between crude primordialism and modernism. Although his work does not contain a comprehensive explanation for the emergence and character of nationalism, it explores the ethnic origins of nations as well as the historical forces that help to fashion nationalism's various forms. Smith's key works include *Theories of Nationalism* (1972), *The Ethnic Origin of Nations* (1986) and *Nations and Nationalism in a Global Era* (1995).

Benedict Anderson (born 1936)

An Irish academic who was brought up mainly in California, Anderson's main publication on nationalism is the celebrated *Imagined Communities* (1983). He views nationalities and nationalism as cultural artefacts of a particular kind, defining the nation as an 'imagined community', in the sense that it generates a deep, horizontal comradeship regardless of actual inequalities within the nation and despite the fact that it is not a face-to-face community. Anderson's other publications in the field include *The Spectres of Comparison* (1998) and *Under Three Flags* (2005).

nation-states are inherently imperfect, as none is ethnically and culturally 'pure' and all rely, to some degree, on political circumstances to maintain themselves in existence. This can be illustrated by the rise and fall of Yugoslavia. Finally, given that nation-states are, and are destined to remain, unequal in terms of their economic and political power, genuine national self-determination remains elusive for many. This is a tendency that has been further compounded by the advance of globalization (see p. 8) and the erosion of state sovereignty.

Nationalism, war and conflict

However, nationalism has not merely supported liberating causes, related to the achievement of national unity and independence. Nationalism has also been

Debating . . .
Is nationalism inherently aggressive and oppressive?

Is nationalism as a whole, in principle, defensible? While some argue that its association with expansionism and oppression exposes deep and dark forces that are intrinsic to nationalism itself, others suggest that nationalism, in the right circumstances, can be peaceful and socially enlightened.

YES

Nationalism as narcissism. All forms of nationalism are based on partisanship, a preference for one's own nation over other nations, underpinned by the belief that it has special or unique qualities. Nationalism is thus the enemy of universal values and global justice. In promoting self-love within the nations of the world, it encourages each nation to restrict its moral concerns to its own people, and to believe that their interests somehow outrank those of any other people. Nationalism is thus inherently chauvinistic and embodies, at minimum, a *potential* for aggression. The only question is whether national chauvinism is explicit or implicit, and therefore whether aggression is overt or latent.

Negative integration. National identity is forged not only through the belief that one's own nation is unique or 'special', but also through negative integration, the portrayal of another nation or race as a threat or an enemy. Nationalism therefore breeds off a clear distinction between 'them' and 'us'. There has to be a 'them' to deride or hate in order to forge a sense of 'us'. This tendency to divide the world into an 'in group' and an 'out group' means that nationalism is always susceptible to dark and pathological forces. As a necessarily homogenizing force, all forms of nationalism harbour intolerance, hostility and racist tendencies. 'True' nationalism is therefore ethnic nationalism.

Nationalism and power. Nationalism is invariably associated with the quest for power and therefore leads to rivalry and conflict rather than cooperation. The nationalism of the weak draws from a sense of powerlessness and subjugation, a desire to assert national rights and identities in the context of perceived injustice and oppression. However, it is a delusion to believe that the quest for power is assuaged once a nation achieves sovereign statehood. In established states and even great powers, nationalism is strongly linked to self-assertion, as national identity is remodelled around aggrandizement and the quest for 'greatness'.

NO

Nationalism and freedom. Nationalism is a chameleon ideology. Its character is determined by the circumstances in which nationalist aspirations arise and the (highly diverse) political causes that it articulates. When nationalism is a reaction against the experience of foreign domination or colonial rule, it tends to have a liberating character and is linked to the goals of liberty, justice and democracy. Committed to the principle of self-determination, nationalism has been an anti-expansionist and anti-imperialist force that has expanded freedom worldwide. Moreover, self-determination has powerful implications for the domestic organization of political power, implying equal citizenship and democratic accountability.

Civic nationalism. Nationalism only becomes intolerant and oppressive when the nation is defined in narrowly ethnic or racial terms. Some nations, however, are very clearly 'political' nations, constructed out of allegiances to particular values and civic ideals rather than on the basis of cultural homogeneity. The forms of nationalism that develop in such cases are typically tolerant and democratic, managing to sustain a remarkable degree of social harmony and political unity against a background of sometimes profound religious, linguistic, cultural and racial diversity. National identity can therefore be inclusive, flexible and always evolving, adapting itself to changing political and social circumstances.

Cultural belonging. The central benefit of nationalism is that it gives people a sense of cultural inheritance, a sense of who or what they are, binding them together and promoting sociability. Nationalism's success in this respect helps to explain why citizenship and nationality are invariably overlapping ideas. The 'inner' benefits of nationalism, which help to promote political stability and social cohesion, are not always, or necessarily, associated with projects of expansionism, conquest and war. The link between nationalism and militarism is therefore strictly conditional, and tends to occur in particular when nationalist sentiments are generated by international rivalry and conflict.

expressed through the politics of aggression, militarism and war. In many ways, expansionist nationalism is the antithesis of the principled belief in equal rights and self-determination that is the core of classical nationalism. National rights, in this context, imply, not respect for the rights of all nations, but the rights of a particular nation *over* other nations. The recurrent, and, many would argue, defining, theme of expansionist nationalism is therefore the idea of national chauvinism. Derived from the name of Nicholas Chauvin, a (possibly apocryphal) French soldier noted for his fanatical devotion to Napoleon and the cause of France, chauvinism is underpinned by the belief that nations have particular characteristics and qualities, and so have very different destinies. Some nations are suited to rule; others are suited to be ruled. Typically, this form of nationalism is articulated through doctrines of ethnic or racial superiority, thereby fusing nationalism and racialism (see p. 172). The chauvinist's own people are seen as unique and special, in some way a 'chosen people', while other peoples are viewed either as weak and inferior, or as hostile and threatening. An extreme example of this can be found in the case of the German Nazis, whose 'Aryanism' portrayed the German people (the Aryan race) as a 'master race' destined for world domination, backed up by virulent anti-Semitism.

From this perspective, the advance of nationalism is associated not so much with balance or harmony amongst independent nation-states as with deepening rivalry and ongoing struggle. Some, indeed, argue that nationalism from its inception was infected with chauvinism and has always harboured at least implicit racist beliefs, based on the assumption that it is 'natural' to prefer one's own people to others. In this light, nationalism may appear to be inherently oppressive and expansionist. All forms of nationalism may thus exhibit some form of xenophobia. The aggressive face of nationalism became increasingly prominent from the late nineteenth century onwards, as European powers indulged in the 'scramble for Africa' in the name of national glory and their 'place in the sun'. Aggression and expansion were also evident in the forms of pan-nationalism that developed in Russia and Germany in the years leading up to WWI. The build up to WWII was similarly shaped by nationalist-inspired programmes of imperial expansion pursued by Germany, Japan and Italy. Nationalism can therefore be seen as a major contributory factor explaining the outbreak of both world wars of the twentieth century. Neither was this form of nationalism extinguished in 1945. The break-up of Yugoslavia in the early 1990s, for example, led to a quest by Bosnian Serbs to construct a 'Greater Serbia' which was characterized by militarism and an aggressive programme of 'ethnic cleansing'.

NATIONS IN AN AGE OF MIGRATION

One of the ironies of nationalism is that just as it was completing its greatest accomplishment – the destruction of the world's final remaining empires – the nation-state was being undermined by forces within and without. This has led some to talk of a 'crisis of the nation-state', or even the 'twilight of the nation-state'. These forces are many and various. They include the tendency for economic globalization (see p. 98) to diminish the state's capacity to function as an

● **Militarism:** The achievement of ends by military means; or the spread of military ideas and values throughout civilian society.

● **Chauvinism:** An irrational belief in the superiority or dominance of one's own group or people; it can be applied to a nation, an ethnic group, a gender and so on.

● **Anti-Semitism:** Prejudice or hatred towards Jewish people; Semites are by tradition the descendants of Shem, son of Noah.

● **Xenophobia:** A fear or hatred of foreigners; pathological ethnocentrism.

● **Pan-nationalism:** A style of nationalism dedicated to unifying a disparate people through either expansionism or political solidarity ('pan' means all or every).

● **Ethnic cleansing:** A euphemism that refers to the forcible expulsion of an ethnic group or groups in the cause of racial purity, often involving genocidal violence.

CONCEPT

Racialism

Racialism is, broadly, the belief that political or social conclusions can be drawn from the idea that humankind is divided into biologically distinct races. Racialist theories are thus based on two assumptions. The first is that there are fundamental genetic, or species-type, differences amongst the peoples of the world (a highly unlikely claim in the light of modern scientific knowledge). The second is that these genetic or racial differences are reflected in cultural, intellectual and/or moral differences, making them politically and socially significant. In political terms, racialism is manifest in calls for racial segregation (such as apartheid, or 'apartness', in South Africa), and in doctrines of 'blood' superiority or inferiority (for example, Aryanism and anti-Semitism).

● **Hybridity**: A condition of social and cultural mixing; the term derives from cross-breeding between genetically unalike plants or animals.

● **Migration**: The movement of a person or group of persons, either across an international border, or within a state.

autonomous economic unit (examined in Chapter 4) and the trend for cultural globalization (see p. 151) to weaken the cultural distinctiveness of the nation-state (discussed in Chapter 6). However, some argue that the most potent threat to the nation stems from the upsurge in international migration and the growth, as a result, of transnational communities and **hybridity** generally. Population movement has thus had major implications for modern world politics.

A world on the move

Migration has been part of human experience throughout history. Indeed, settlement (which was brought about by the emergence of agriculture, some 8,000 years ago) is of relatively recent origin, human societies having been fluid communities of hunters and gatherers that can now be traced back for over three million years. The development of substantial villages, and subsequently towns and cities, did not put an end to migration, however. The early empires of the Hittites, the Phoenicians and the Greeks, for example, reshaped the culture of much of Europe, parts of North Africa, the Near East and Central Asia between the third and the first millennia BCE. This process is reflected most strikingly in the distribution of the closely related languages of the Indo-European group, which embraces both Sanskrit and Persian at one end, and such European languages as Greek, Latin, French, German and English at the other. The Vikings, Magyars and Saracens invaded much of northern and central Europe in the ninth and tenth centuries, the Vikings also establishing settlements in Iceland, Greenland and Newfoundland. European expansion overseas started in the sixteenth century with the Spanish invasion of Mexico and Peru, followed by the colonization of North America, mainly by the British. Hardly any nation in the world, in short, can claim always to have lived where it does now.

Migration has occurred for a variety of reasons. Until early modern times, as the examples above demonstrate, migration was usually a consequence of conquest and invasion, followed by settlement and colonization. In cases such as the USA (see p. 46), Canada, Australia and throughout Latin America, conquest and settlement led to the emergence of nations of immigrants, as native peoples were reduced to the status of marginalized minorities through the combined impact of disease, repression and discrimination. Mass migration has also been a forcible process, the best examples of which were the slave trade and the system of indentured labour. An estimated 40 million people in the Americas and the Caribbean are descended from slaves, who, between the mid-sixteenth and mid-eighteenth centuries, were captured in Africa and transported, via Europe, to work in the expanding sugar and tobacco plantations of the 'New World'. Indentured workers, derogatorily known as 'Coolies' and living in conditions little different from slavery, were taken from China and India in the nineteenth century to work in the various British, French, German and Dutch colonies around the world. Some 37 million people were sent abroad under such circumstances, and, although many of those who had left India returned once slavery was abolished, modern-day Indian communities in the Caribbean, East Africa and the Pacific are mainly composed of descendants of indentured labourers.

Other migrants, however, have travelled by choice for economic reasons, albeit ones that have sometimes involved considerable privation and hardship. This applies to the voluntary mass migration from Europe to the Americas from

Focus on . . .

International migration: are people pulled or pushed?

Theories of migration can be divided into those that emphasize the role of the individual and those that highlight the importance of structural factors. In practice, it is highly likely that these factors interact, as individual decision-making cannot be understood separately from the structural context in which it takes place.

Individual theories stress the role of individual calculation in making migration decisions, influenced by the pursuit of rational self-interest. This is an economic model of migration, which relies on a kind of cost–benefit analysis. It implies that migration occurs because people are 'pulled' by an awareness on the part of potential migrants that its likely benefits will outweigh its possible costs. In this view, migration can be contained by increasing the cost of migration (for example, through the imposition of immigration quotas and controls) or by reducing its benefits (for example, by restricting immigrants' access to social security and imposing work restrictions).

Structural theories stress the degree to which social, economic or political factors influence, or determine, individuals' actions. Migrants are therefore either 'pushed' from their country of origin (by factors such as chronic and acute poverty, political unrest and civil strife), or they are 'pulled' to their country of settlement (by the need of expanding economies for additional labour, particularly in relation to jobs the domestic population is unwilling, or, through lack of skills, unable to fill). From this perspective, migration can best be contained by strategies such as a reduction in global inequality and the spread of stable governance.

● **Diaspora**: (from the Hebrew) literally, dispersion; implies displacement or dispersal by force, but is also used to refer to the transnational community that arose as a result of such dispersal.

● **Emigration**: A process whereby people leave their native country, to settle in another.

● **Internally displaced person**: A person forced to flee from his or her habitual residence by the effects of armed conflict, generalized violence or natural or man-made disaster.

● **Refugee**: A person compelled to leave his or her country because their life, security or freedom have been threatened.

the mid-nineteenth century until the outbreak of WWI, which involved, for example, the migration of about a million Irish people escaping the potato famine of 1845–47 and over 3 million people from the German territories fleeing from rural poverty and periodic crop failures. A final reason for migration has been religious or political persecution. The classic example of this was the Jewish **diaspora**, which was initiated by Roman repression in Judea and involved the expulsion of Jews in the Middle Ages from England, France, Spain, Portugal and many of the German cities. **Emigration** from Europe to North America, both in the colonial period and in the late nineteenth century, also often reflected a desire to escape from religious persecution on the part of groups of Puritans, Nonconformists of various kinds, Catholics and Jews.

The bulk of migration has always been, and continues to be, internal. For instance, the number of **internally displaced persons** (28.8 million in 2012) consistently exceeds the number of **refugees** (15.4 million); and labour migration is more commonly associated with urbanization than with globalization (over 260 million people have moved from the countryside to urban areas since the 1990s in China alone). However, international migration has become an increasingly important feature of the modern world. The number of international migrants (never an easy figure to calculate in view of the proportion of irregular (or 'undocumented' or 'illegal') migrants) rose from 81 million in 1970 to 214 million in 2010, or 3.1 per cent of the world's population. If international migrants lived together, they would constitute the fifth most populous country in the world. The idea that the modern period is an 'age of migration' highlights not only the intensification of cross-border migration in what has come to be a hyper-mobile planet, but also the growing significance of migration in economic, social, cultural and political terms (Castles *et al.* 2013). Above all, the age of migration is characterized by the challenges posed by international migration to the sovereignty of states, seemingly unable to regulate the movements of people across their borders effectively, despite increasing efforts to do so. Transnational and trans-border population flows, just like flows of money, goods and other economic resources, thus underline how far the divide between the domestic and international spheres has been undermined.

Why and how have migratory patterns changed in recent years? In addition to the acceleration of migration, international migration has become increasingly differentiated. One dimension of modern migration is clearly linked to economic globalization. The onset of globalization has intensified pressures for international migration in a variety of ways. These include the development of genuinely global labour markets for a small but growing number of high-paid and high-profile jobs, and the fact that the restructuring that globalization has fostered both creates a range of skills needs that the domestic population cannot meet and, where turbulence has caused insecurity and hardship, enlarges the ranks of those looking for, or needing to find, new economic opportunities. Such trends also serve to explain the 'globalization of migration'; that is, the tendency both for more countries to be affected by migratory movements at the same time, and for immigration to come from a larger number of source countries. This contrasts markedly with the pattern of labour migration in the early post-1945 period, when migratory flows were predominantly from poorer countries to either their richer neighbours or their former colonial rulers. In the latter case, this was sometimes orchestrated by a deliberate policy of recruiting workers from abroad.

A further dimension of modern migration is linked to refugees, and has been the result of war, ethnic conflict and political upheaval in areas ranging from Algeria, Rwanda and Uganda to Bangladesh, Afghanistan and Syria. The political upheavals associated with the collapse of communism in eastern Europe in 1989–91 created, almost overnight, a new group of migrants, having, later, even greater impact due to the rise of ethnic conflict in former Yugoslavia. Although the number of refugees has declined since reaching a peak of 18 million in 1993, mass and sudden refugee flows continue to provoke humanitarian emergencies. The large-scale displacement of people across borders remains a major issue in many developing countries, which, together, host about 80 per cent of the world's refugees. A final dimension of modern migration is human trafficking. Although it is very difficult to assess the real extent of human trafficking, the UN has put the number of victims at any one time at 2.5 million, a disproportionate number of whom are women. The most commonly identified form of human trafficking is sexual exploitation (79 per cent), followed by forced labour (18 per cent). Almost always a form of organized crime, trafficking usually takes place from less-developed countries to more-developed countries, people being rendered vulnerable to trafficking by virtue of poverty, conflict or other conditions.

● **Immigration**: A process whereby non-nationals move into a country for the purpose of settlement.

● **Human trafficking**: The recruitment and harbouring of persons for the purpose of exploitation, brought about by the threat or use of coercion or force.

Transnational communities and diasporas

Modern migration flows have had significant implications for the domestic politics of states. These include the development in many societies of communities bound together by transnational, rather than national, allegiances. There is, of

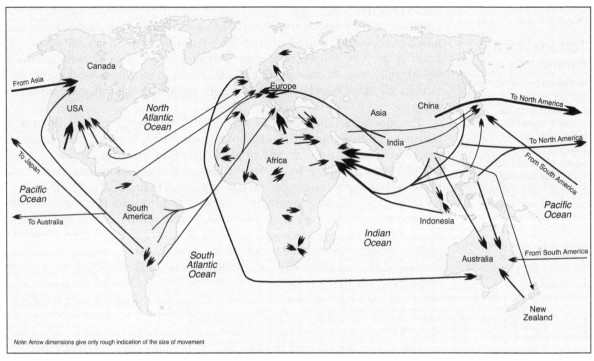

Map 10.1 **Global migratory flows since 1973**
Source: Castles *et al.* (2013).

course, nothing new about scattered communities that have nevertheless maintained their cultural distinctiveness and resisted pressure for **assimilation**. The
Jewish diaspora, which can be traced back to the eighth century BCE, is the
classic example of a transnational community. Ironically, the remarkable
resilience of Judaism and the Hebrew language in the absence of a Jewish homeland can be significantly explained by a history of discrimination and persecution through various forms of anti-Semitism. Other examples include the
Armenians, many of whom have been forced into exile by successive invasions
and conquests, dating back to the Byzantine Empire. However, many argue that
the emergence of transnational communities is one of the chief features of the
modern, globalized world (Basch *et al.* 1994).

An increase in international migration does not in itself create new, transnational social spaces: for transnational communities to be established, immigrant
groups must forge and, crucially, sustain relations that link their societies of
origin and of settlement. This is made easier in the modern world by a variety of
developments. Whereas, say, Irish emigrants to the USA in the nineteenth
century had little prospect of returning home and only a postal service to keep
them in touch with friends and family, modern communities of Filipinos in the
Gulf states, Indonesians in Australia and Bangladeshis in the UK benefit from
cheaper transport and improved communications. Air travel enables people to
return 'home' on a regular basis, creating fluid communities that are bound
neither by their society of origin nor their society of settlement. The near-ubiquitous mobile phone has also become a basic resource for new immigrants,

● **Assimilation**: The process
through which immigrant
communities lose their cultural
distinctiveness by adjusting to
the values, allegiances and
lifestyles of the host society.

CONCEPT

Transnational community

A transnational community is a community whose cultural identity, political allegiances and psychological orientations cut across or transcend national borders. In that sense, they challenge the nation-state ideal, which clearly links politico-cultural identity to a specific territory or 'homeland'. Transnational communities can therefore be thought of as 'deterritorialized nations' or 'global tribes'. However, not every diasporic community is a transnational community, in the sense that its members retain allegiances to their country of origin. Transnational communities typically have multiple attachments, as allegiances to their country of origin do not preclude the formation of attachments to their country of settlement.

helping to explain, amongst other things, its increasing penetration in the developing world, including the rural parts of Asia and Africa. Transnational communities, moreover, are bound together by a network of family ties and economic flows. Migration, for example, may maintain rather than weaken extended kinship links, as early immigrants provide a base and sometimes working opportunities for other members of their families or village who may subsequently emigrate.

The idea of a transition from territorial nation-states to deterritorialized transnational communities should not be over-stated, however. The impact of modern migration patterns, and of globalization in its various forms, is more complex than is implied by the simple notion of transnationalism. In the first place, the homogeneous nation that has supposedly been put at risk by the emergence of transnational communities is always, to some extent, a myth, a myth created by the ideology of nationalism itself. In other words, there is nothing new about cultural mixing, which long pre-dates the emergence of the hyper-mobile planet. Second, transnational communities are characterized as much by difference and division as they are by commonality and solidarity. The most obvious divisions within diaspora communities are those of gender and social class, but other divisions may run along the lines of ethnicity, religion, age and generation. Third, it is by no means clear that transnational loyalties are as stable and enduring as nationalism. Quite simply, social ties that are not territorially rooted and geographically defined may not be viable in the long term. Doubts about the enduring character of transnational communities are raised by the phenomenon of return migration, often stimulated by improved political or economic circumstances in the country of origin. For example, there has been a general tendency for people to return to Asia, notably China and Taiwan, to take advantage of improving economic prospects since the 1980s. Finally, it is misleading to suggest that transnationalism has somehow displaced nationalism when, in reality, each has influenced the other, creating a more complex web of hybrid identities. Hybridity or 'creolization', has thus become one of the major features of modern society. It is examined in Chapter 8, in relation to multiculturalism (see p. 192).

Economic impact of migration

Assessments of the economic impact of migration are problematic for at least three reasons. First, debates about migration are often highly politically charged, meaning that *perceptions* about the extent and implications of migration commonly differ from 'hard' evidence on the matter. This applies particularly in 'receiving' countries, where the dominant political discourse about immigration tends to focus on issues of management and control. Since the early twentieth century, no country has permitted unchecked immigration, with pressure for tighter immigration controls being exerted from the 1970s onwards. This trend was markedly intensified in the aftermath of September 11. Indeed (as discussed in the final section of the chapter), anti-immigration sentiment is one of the factors that has contributed to the revival of nationalism in the modern period. Second, generalizations about the impact of migration are notoriously misleading. This occurs not only because migration has an uneven impact on host and 'sending' countries, but also because (as we shall see) what may be beneficial in one set of circumstances may be a serious drawback in other circumstances. Third, when it comes to the impact of migration, 'proof' may be very difficult to establish. For instance, although there is often a correlation between increased immigration and economic growth in receiving countries, it is less clear whether immigration is a cause or a consequence of economic growth, and, if it is a cause, how significant a factor it is.

From the point of view of sending countries, the clearest economic benefit of migration comes in the form of **remittances**. The World Bank estimated that, in 2011, global remittance flows stood at $501 billion, $372 billion of which went to developing countries. Not only do remittances dwarf international aid in their scale, being some three times the size of official development assistance, but, in sharp contrast to aid, remittances are largely unaffected by downturns in the world economy. Remittance levels thus rose during the global financial crisis of 2007–09 while levels of international aid shrank. In this light, remittances may be vital in reducing the extent and severity of poverty, lowering incidences of child labour (and thereby improving levels of literacy and education) and boosting business investment and entrepreneurship. On the other hand, remittances, like international aid, may entrench patterns of global inequality, discouraging initiative and self-reliance within sending countries and strengthening a culture of dependency. A further alleged advantage of migration is that it can act as a pressure valve, especially in countries such as Mexico, the Philippines and Morocco, which have fast-growing and youthful populations but high levels of unemployment. Emigration may therefore help to prevent an explosion in welfare spending and thus tax increases, to say nothing of the political and social benefits of avoiding rampant unemployment, particularly among the young. This helps to explain why emigration has sometimes been orchestrated and encouraged by governments, as has happened in Mexico.

Such advantages may nevertheless be offset by the damage caused to sending countries by the loss of workers with technical skills or knowledge, a phenomenon often called a '**brain drain**'. Critical theorists have therefore sometimes argued that the free movement of people within a global capitalist economy has a similar effect to the free movement of goods and capital, in that it serves to benefit wealthy or 'core' countries at the expense of poor or 'peripheral' ones.

However, how accurate is it to treat migration as a greater benefit for (usually wealthier) receiving countries than for sending countries? Certainly, allegations that immigrants 'steal' the jobs of local workers or 'sponge off' the welfare state would suggest otherwise. Such claims are based on the assumption that, because they are escaping from poverty, immigrants are prepared to accept lower wages and less attractive conditions of work than local workers, and that many migrants are 'pulled' by the prospect of accessing better-funded public services and more generous welfare provision. However, the former notion is based on what economists call the **lump of labour fallacy**, which implies that new entrants to the workforce can only find jobs by displacing those who already have them. In practice, this is misleading because immigration may stimulate economic growth, reducing, rather than increasing, unemployment. This applies especially if immigrants take jobs that local workers either cannot take (because they lack the necessary skills or training) or will not take (because they consider the work to be demeaning or too low paid). Immigration controls in wealthier countries invariably, therefore, make exceptions for certain categories of

● **Remittances**: Monies earned or acquired by non-nationals that are transferred back to their country of origin.

● **Brain drain**: The emigration of trained or talented individuals from their country of origin to another country, sometimes called 'human capital flight'.

●**Lump of labour fallacy**: The fallacious belief that there is a fixed amount of work to be done, suggesting that unemployment levels are determined simply by how work is shared out amongst the available labour force.

Mexican immigration into the USA

Events: With more than 10 per cent of its native population living abroad, over-whelmingly in the USA, Mexico is the country with the most emigrants in the world. In 2011, some 10.8 per cent of the US population were Mexican-Americans, over 35.5 million Americans having full or partial Mexican ancestry, not including an estimated 6.1 million 'undocumented' or 'illegal' Mexicans. Until the early twentieth century, Mexicans were free to move across the border with the USA, and even when immigration controls started to be applied, exceptions were often made in the case of Mexican immigrants. Special allowances for Mexican immigrants ended abruptly in the 1930s, as, fuelled by the Great Depression, anti-immigration sentiment spread across the USA. Tighter immigration control in the post-WWII period nevertheless failed to prevent the level of immigration from Mexico exceeding that from any other single country in US history. However, there are signs that this trend may have ceased: between 2005 and 2010, the net flow of Mexicans into the USA dwindled to a trickle and may have gone into reverse.

Significance: The high level of migration across the Mexican-US border – the most crossed border in the world – is easy to explain. The chief underlying factor has been the dramatic imbalance in the economic fortunes of Mexico and the USA. Powerful 'push' factors, including low pay, widespread unemployment, poor medical facilities and limited education prospects, encouraged generation after generation of Mexicans to seek better opportunities in *el Norte*. This was facilitated by relatively easy access from Mexico to the USA. Not only are Mexico and the USA neighbouring countries, but the length of the border between them (3,169 km) means that immigration control is, at best, imperfect, despite the efforts of over 20,000 border patrol agents. The main reason for the altered pattern of migration in recent years is that while the USA has suffered an economic downturn, particularly associated with the 2007–09 global financial crisis, the Mexican economy has been growing steadily. Other factors may include a crackdown on illegal immigrants under Obama since 2009, and increased violence in Northern Mexico associated with drugs cartels and organized crime.

It has widely been assumed that emigration has been a key factor inhibiting economic growth in Mexico. Persistent migratory flows have left the Mexican countryside with a shortage of economically active people, and social problems have emerged due to the fact that most migrants are males and relatively young, leaving fewer people to support the elderly and the very young. And yet, at $22.45 billion in 2012, remittances, overwhelmingly from the USA, constitute Mexico's second largest source of foreign revenue (after petroleum), and make a major contribution to improving domestic living standards. Over time, Mexico's formal policy of discouraging emigration has given way to an emphasis on supporting the integration of the Mexican emigrant community in the USA, largely through the Institute of Mexicans Abroad.

US policy on immigration from Mexico has tended to focus on a combination of efforts to reduce irregular immigration (both by increased border enforcement and strengthened legal sanctions on the employment of undocumented workers) and attempts to stimulate economic growth in Mexico, not least through the 1994 North American Free Trade Agreement (NAFTA). However, a recognition of the vital importance of workers of Mexican ancestry to certain sectors of the US economy, and, above all, the growing political significance of Latino voters in the USA, have dictated a more liberal approach to immigration. Although this has primarily affected the Democratic Party, encouraging, amongst other things, President Obama to support the DREAM Act (which would provide a conditional path to citizenship for a proportion of undocumented immigrants), it is difficult to see how the Republican Party can long remain immune from the same pressures.

workers, namely those whose aquisition would bring about a 'brain gain'. Supporters of immigration also argue that the allegation that immigrants are 'welfare scroungers' is undermined by evidence showing that immigrants are often less likely than the population at large to rely on the benefit system, in part because the act of migration demonstrates a strong commitment to finding work and making social progress. Finally, immigration may bring economic benefit to receiving countries by modifying, or even reversing, demographic trends in developed societies. In particular, an influx of predominantly young migrants, who also tend to have larger families than the local population, may help to solve the problem of an aging population, in which the growing ranks of elderly people are supported by a shrinking workforce.

NATIONALISM REVIVED

As the twentieth century progressed, there were growing predictions of the decline of nationalism, even of the construction of a 'post-national' world. Not only had the barbarism and destruction of WWII created a distaste for nationalism as an ideology seemingly inherently linked to expansionism and conflict, but increasing cross-border cultural, economic and population flows appeared to render the sovereign nation-state redundant. Surely political identity was in the process of being redefined, even though it was unclear whether the successor to nationalism would be multiculturalism, transnational communities, cosmopolitanism or whatever? The reality, however, has been very different. Nationalism has demonstrated remarkable resilience and durability: in the twenty-first century, the overwhelming mass of people across the globe accept that they belong to a nation, and nationality continues to retain an unrivalled position as the basis for political allegiance. Indeed, in a number of ways, there has been a resurgence of nationalism. How and why has this happened? Primordialists, of course, may argue that the survival of nationalism simply bears out the truth of their theories: nationalism cannot be a dying doctrine because ethnic communities have not, and cannot, die out. Modernists, for their part, follow Gellner in explaining the rise of nationalism since the late twentieth century in terms of the simultaneous spread of industrial capitalism around the globe. However, resurgent nationalism has a number of manifestations, and therefore a number of underlying causes. Its main manifestations are an increase in national self-assertion in the post-Cold War period, the rise of cultural and ethnic nationalism, and the emergence of anti-globalization nationalism.

National self-assertion in the post-Cold War period

The Cold War period certainly did not witness the eclipse of nationalism. However, during the Cold War, nationalist conflict took place within a context of East–West rivalry and the ideological antagonism between capitalism and communism. For example, the Vietnamese invasion and occupation of Cambodia in 1978–9 was the only large-scale conventional war waged between one revolutionary Marxist regime and another (Anderson 1983). The end of the Cold War, and the declining significance of ideology as an organizing principle of global politics, nevertheless provided opportunities for the resurgence of nationalism as a modernizing force. This certainly happened in East and South-east Asia, where 'tiger' states such as Singapore, South Korea and Taiwan very deliberately used nation-building as a strategy for economic success in a global context. Although globalization may provide new and challenging circumstances for nationalism, such examples also show how globalization can generate new opportunities for redefining nationhood and national identity. Singapore is a particular example of this. Lacking the ethnic and cultural unity of a conventional nation-state, Singapore has nevertheless become possibly the most globalized state in the world. Basic to this process have been attempts by the ruling People's Action Party (PAP) to inculcate civic nationalism by instilling a sense of pride in the public institutions of the state as well as patriotic pride in the populace itself, in part by generous investment in technologically glossy public amenities. Civic nationalism thus helps to legitimize authoritarian rule and ensure social control, which, in turn, attracts foreign capital, thereby maintaining the growth levels that underpin patriotic pride and state allegiance.

National self-assertion has also become a strategy of growing significance for emerging powers, especially in the light of the fluid nature of world order in the post-Cold War world. Nationalism has thus once again proved its capacity for investing the drive for economic and political development with an ideological impetus that emphasizes strength, unity and pride. For instance, China's remarkable economic revival has been accompanied by clear evidence of rising nationalism. This has been apparent in the greater pressure that has been brought to bear on Taiwan to prevent moves towards the declaration of formal independence, in a firm and sometime forcible response to independence movements in Tibet and Xinjiang, and sometimes in the growth of anti-Japanese sentiment. The 2008 Beijing Olympics, as well as a host of other engineering and technological achievements, have been used to instil patriotic pride at home and to project an image of China abroad as advanced and successful. Rising nationalism in India, particularly Hindu nationalism, led to the establishment of a Bharatiya Janata Party (BJP) government in 1998. The BJP government intensified pressures to develop nuclear weapons, achieved in 1998, which have since remained hugely popular within India as a symbol of great power status. In the case of Russia, nationalism has been significantly more prominent since the rise of Vladimir Putin in 1999. Most clearly demonstrated by the aggressive resurgence of the war in Chechnya, revived nationalism has also been evident in the form of so-called 'fuel nationalism' (the use of price adjustments and restrictions on the flow of Russian gas and oil to exert control over fuel-dependent neighbouring countries) and in a firmer and more combative stance adopted towards the West in general and the USA in particular, not least through the 2008 Georgian War.

Rise of cultural and ethnic nationalism

There is evidence that although globalization may have weakened forms of classical nationalism, based on a nation-state ideal that is increasingly difficult to sustain in an age of 'borderless' economic flows, it has strengthened cultural and ethnic forms of nationalism. If the conventional nation-state is no longer capable of generating meaningful collective identities, particularist nationalisms based on region, religion, ethnicity or race may develop to take its place. Such

GLOBAL ACTORS . . .

RUSSIA

Type: State • **Population:** 143.3 m • **GDP per capita:** $21,246 • **HDI ranking:** 55/187 • **Capital:** Moscow

The Russian federation was formed as a result of the break-up of the Soviet Union on 31 December 1991. This happened in the context of the collapse of communism across the Soviet bloc during 1989–91, strengthening nationalism within the non-Russian Soviet republics and growing opposition to communist rule within Russia itself. Under Yeltsin in the 1990s, drastic economic reforms led to a reduction in living standards, soaring inflation, industrial decline and financial instability. The rise of Vladimir Putin, first as prime minister in 1999, and later as president, prime minister and (since 2012) president, has been associated with strengthened political leadership, economic recovery and the emergence of 'electoral authoritarianism'. Russia is an illiberal democracy with the following major institutions:

- The State Duma, a 450-member lower house of the legislature, and the Federal Council, the upper chamber which contains 2 members from each of the 59 federal units.
- A semi-presidential executive, comprising the prime minister, who heads the Council of Ministers, working alongside a directly elected executive president.

Significance: Russian power stems, in large part, from its vast size. It is the largest country in the world, almost twice the size of the USA. By the eighteenth century, the Russian Empire had been established, the

third largest empire in history, stretching from Poland in Europe to Alaska in North America. Russia's ascendancy to world power dates from the 1917 Russian Revolution and the establishment of the Soviet Union (founded in 1922) as the world's first communist state. The Soviet Union played a decisive role in the allied victory in WWII, emerging in 1945 as a superpower, by virtue of its military might and control over the expanding communist world. The political basis for the revival of Russian power after the chaos and instability of the 1990s was laid by a combination of strong government, resurgent nationalism (linked not least to the Chechen War) and the use of the state as a modernizing tool. These developments have nevertheless been underpinned by economic recovery, based on Russia's abundant supply of natural gas, oil, coal and precious metals. This has been used both to boost industrial and agricultural investment and to exert leverage over neighbouring states (Russia's 'near abroad') and Europe generally. Russia's 2008 invasion of Georgia was widely interpreted as marking Russia's re-emergence as a global power. A further dimension of Russian influence is the fact that its enormous nuclear arsenal means that it is the only state capable of threatening the USA with destruction.

Nevertheless, Russian power should not be overstated. In the first place, Russia's emergence as a 'resource superpower' has been significantly linked to hikes in the price of oil, natural gas and minerals

which have been fuelled by globalization and the expansion of the world economy. This leaves the Russian economy vulnerable to a downturn in world commodity prices, especially as customs duties and taxes from the fuel and energy sector account for nearly half of the federal government's revenues. In some respects, commodity-driven growth has undermined the long-term prospects of the Russian economy, because it has slowed the pace of economic diversification and concealed other structural weaknesses. The 2007–09 global financial crisis hit Russia particularly hard because it led to a drop in oil prices, so reducing capital in-flows and leading to a 16 per cent fall in industrial production in 2008 alone. Further concerns about Russian power stem from the possibility that 'electoral authoritarianism' may ultimately prove to be an unreliable basis for modernization. In this view, if strong government persists it will be ultimately at the expense of economic flexibility and modernization, and if pressure for liberal democratic reform becomes irresistible, the result may be a long period of political and social instability. A final threat to Russia is the changing political and economic complexion of eastern Europe, due to the expansion of the EU (see p. 509) and NATO (see p. 259). Russia's strategic interests may thus remain more regional than global, focusing on attempts to ensure that its 'near abroad' and, in particular, countries such as Ukraine, Georgia and the former Soviet republics of central Asia do not fall outside its sphere of influence.

tendencies can be traced back to the 1960s when secessionist groups and forms of cultural nationalism sprang up in many parts of western Europe and North America. This was evident in Quebec in Canada, Scotland and Wales in the UK, Catalonia and the Basque area of Spain, Corsica in France and Flanders in Belgium. It created pressures for political decentralization, and sometimes precipitated major constitutional upheavals. Similar manifestations of ethnic assertiveness were found in the emergence of black nationalism in the USA and amongst the Native Americans in Canada in the USA, the Aboriginal peoples in Australia and the Maoris in New Zealand. In the latter two cases, at least, this has brought about a major reassessment of national identity.

Ethnic nationalism became significantly more prominent after the end of the Cold War. What is sometimes called 'new nationalism' (Kaldor 2007) led in the 1990s to a series of wars in former Yugoslavia, which also featured programmes of 'ethnic cleansing' and the worst massacres in Europe since WWII. A number of new nation-states were created but other states that have emerged from this process have been subject to deep ethnic rivalries and tensions. For example, Bosnia has effectively been divided into 'ethnically pure' Muslim, Serb and Croat areas, while Kosovo's declaration of independence in 2008 precipitated acute tensions between its Serb minority in northern Kosovo and the majority Muslim population. Other examples of ethnic assertiveness include secessionist uprisings in Chechnya and elsewhere in the Caucasus, and the genocidal bloodshed that broke out in Rwanda in 1994, when between 800,000 and 1 million Tutsis and moderate Hutus were slaughtered in an uprising by militant Hutus.

Rising ethnic nationalism in the post-Cold War period has been explained in terms of the tendency of communist rule and East–West rivalry to drive religious, ethnic and national identities underground, only for these to rise dramatically to the surface once the suppressing factors were removed. However, the process is more complex and, in some senses, deep-seated. Smith (1995) highlighted three components that explain why nationalism resurfaced in the late twentieth century. The first is what he called 'the uneven distribution of ethno-history', meaning that under-privileged or relatively deprived communities have been drawn to emulate more powerful nations who are able to celebrate their identity without fear. The second is the ability of nationalism to call on the 'deep resources' of religious belief to legitimize rule and mobilize populations, helping to explain the parallels that exist between ethnic nationalism and religious fundamentalism. Finally, the idea of an 'ancestral homeland' has remained, and will continue to remain, a potent symbol. This highlights the fact that the quest for self-determination can never be fully achieved in a world of unequally powerful nations. (Ethnic nationalism is examined further in Chapter 8 in connection with the rise of identity politics.)

Anti-globalization nationalism

● Cultural nationalism: A form of nationalism that places primary emphasis on the regeneration of the nation as a distinctive civilization rather than on self-determination.

While certain forms of nationalism have developed as a means of allowing states to manage the globalization process, nationalism has more commonly developed as a reaction against globalization, as a form of resistance. Nationalism has often prospered in conditions of fear, insecurity and social dislocation, its strength being its capacity to represent unity and certainty. The forms of nationalism that develop in such circumstances tend not to be orientated around established nation-states but, instead, provide opportunities for generally right-wing parties' movements to mount campaigns against conventional politics. This has been most apparent since the 1970s in the rise of far-right anti-immigration parties, which tend to define national identity in terms of a 'backward-looking' and culturally and perhaps ethnically 'pure' model.

Such parties have become a feature of politics in many European states. The National Front in France, led by Marine Le Pen, has attracted growing electoral support since the 1980s for a platform largely based on resistance to immigration. In 2002, Marine's father, Jean-Marie Le Pen, the founder of the party, gained 5.8 million votes (18 per cent) and got through to the run-off stage in the presidential election. In Austria in 2000, the Freedom Party, then under the leadership of Joerg Haider, won 27 per cent of the vote in the general election and became a member of the coalition government. The Northern League in Italy, which campaigns against immigration and advocates autonomy for that part of northern Italy they call Padania, served in a coalition government under Silvio Berlusconi. Vlaams Blok, which campaigns both against immigration and in favour of Flemish independence, has become a major force in Belgian politics. In the Netherlands, the Freedom Party (PVV), which was founded in 2005 and is headed by Geert Wilders, has called for a ban on immigration from Muslim countries and places a strong emphasis on cultural assimilation. The main anti-immigration parties in Scandinavia are the Progress Party in Norway and the Danish People's Party, which broke away from the Progress Party in 1995.

SUMMARY

- Nationalism is a complex and deeply contested political phenomenon. This stems in part from the fact that all nations comprise a blend of cultural and political, and objective and subjective, characteristics. Nationalism has also been a cross-cutting ideology, associated with a wide range of doctrines, movements and causes.

- From the perspective of primordialism, national identity has been seen to be rooted in a cultural heritage and language that may long predate statehood or the quest for independence. From the contrasting perspective of modernism, national identity is forged in response to changing social and historical circumstances, especially linked to industrialization.

- The liberating 'face' of nationalism is reflected in the reconfiguration of the world into a collection of nation-states, based on the principle of self-determination. However, it oppressive 'face; is evident in a common link to the politics of aggression, militarism and war. While some argue that nationalism is inherently aggressive and oppressive, others suggest that there are 'good' and 'bad' nationalisms.

- Nationalism in the modern world has been weakened by an upsurge in international migration which has led to the growth of hybridity and cultural mixing in most, if not all, societies. Migratory flows have led to the formation of transnational communities and the diasporas that some believe provide an alternative to conventional nations, and stimulated sometimes passionate debate about the economic impact of migration.

- Nations and nationalism have demonstrated remarkable resilience. Indeed, nationalism has revived in that it has been used to underpin state self-assertion in a 'de-ideologized' post-Cold War period. It has also re-emerged in the forms of cultural and ethnic nationalism, and it has provided a vehicle through which the transformations brought about through globalization can be challenged or resisted.

Questions for discussion

- How can nationality and ethnicity be distinguished?
- Are nations simply nothing more than 'invented' or 'imagined' communities?
- Why has the nation-state been such a successful political form?
- To what extent is nationalism a single doctrine?
- Is nationalism inherently oppressive and destructive?
- Is increased international migration an inevitable consequence of economic globalization?
- Do transnational communities constitute a viable alternative to conventional nations?
- Does population movement bring economic benefit, and if so, to whom?
- How and why has nationalism revived in the post-Cold War period?
- Does nationalism have a future in a globalizing world?

Further reading

Castles, S., H. de Haas and M. J. Miller, *The Age of Migration: International Population Movements in the Modern World* (2013). An up-to-date and comprehensive assessment of the nature, extent and dimensions of international population movements.

Pryke, S., *Nationalism in a Global World* (2009). An exploration of the complex relationship between globalization and nationalism.

Spencer, P. and H. Wollman, *Nationalism: A Critical Introduction* (2002). An accessible study of nationalism that surveys both classical and contemporary approaches to the subject.

Sutherland, C., *Nationalism in the Twenty-First Century* (2012). An insightful analysis of the continuing improtance of nationalism in contemporary global politics.

 ONLINE RESOURCES AVAILABLE

Links to relevant web resources can be found on the *Global Politics* website

CHAPTER 11

Multilevel Politics

'All politics is local.'

Favourite saying of former Speaker of the US House of Representatives
THOMAS ('TIP') O'NEILL JR

PREVIEW   The nation-state has traditionally been viewed as the natural, and perhaps only
legitimate, unit of political rule. Domestic politics therefore centred on the activities
of the national government, while, in international politics, nation-states have been
treated as discreet and unified entities. However, globalization and other developments have contributed to a process through which political authority has been
both 'sucked up' and 'drawn down', creating what is called 'multilevel governance'.
States have always incorporated a range of internal divisions and levels of power;
most significantly, territory-based divisions between central or national government
and various forms of provincial, city or local government. These divisions are
crucially shaped by a state's constitutional structure; that is, by whether it has a
federal or unitary system of government. Although each provides a distinct framework within which centre–periphery relationships can be conducted, both have
been subject in recent years to a combination of centrifugal and centripetal pressures. At the same time, a trend towards transnational regionalism has emerged out
of the fact that states are increasingly confronted by challenges that even the most
powerful state struggles to meet on its own. This has created the spectre of an
emerging 'world of regions'. In this view, regionalism is both the successor to the
nation-state and an alternative to globalization. Without doubt, the most advanced
example of regionalism found anywhere in the world is the European Union, but
this raises questions about whether the EU regional model is exportable and
whether it is viable.

KEY ISSUES
- Why does politics always have a territorial dimension?
- What is multilevel governance?
- How successfully do federal and unitary systems of government recon-
  cile territorial and other differences?
- Why has transnational regionalism grown in prominence?
- How does regionalism in Europe differ from regionalism in other parts
  of the world?

POLITICS, TERRITORY AND MULTILEVEL GOVERNANCE

Geopolitics

Geopolitics is an approach to foreign policy analysis that understands the actions, relationships and significance of states in terms of geographical factors such as location, climate, natural resources, physical terrain and population. Key exponents of geopolitics include Alfred Mahan (1840–1914), who argued that the state that controls the seas would control world politics, and Halford Mackinder (1861–1947), who suggested that control of the land mass between Germany and central Siberia is the key to controlling world politics. The advance of globalization is sometimes seen to have made geopolitics obsolete.

● **Territory**: A delimited geographical area that is under the jurisdiction of a governmental authority.

● **Centralization**: The concentration of political power or government authority at the national level.

● **Decentralization**: The expansion of local autonomy through the transfer of powers and responsibilities away from national bodies.

Politics has always had a spatial, or territorial, dimension. As political rule involves making and enforcing general rules over a particular population, this must imply taking account of where those people live, even if their location is imprecise or shifting (as in the case of a nomadic tribe). The association between politics and territory became more formalized and explicit from the sixteenth century onwards, as a result of the emergence of the modern state. For example, as the Peace of Westphalia (1648) defined sovereignty (see p. 58) in territorial terms, states were seen to be defined by their ability to exercise independent control over all the institutions and groups that live within their territorial borders. Two further developments consolidated the importance of territory. The first of these was the emergence of nationalism from the late eighteenth century onwards. As nationalist doctrines spread, so did the idea that national communities are, in part, forged by their sense of having a 'homeland'. As states evolved into nation-states, territory therefore became a matter not just of legal jurisdiction, but also one of identity and emotional attachment. The second development was the strengthened association between national power with territorial expansion that was brought about by imperialism.

Political power is always linked to the control of territory because it allows rulers both to extract resources and to control geographically-defined populations. However, the European 'struggle for colonies' in Africa and Asia during the nineteenth century was motivated by a heightened sense of this link, encouraging some to argue that the destiny of states is essentially determined by geographical factors. This gave rise to the discipline of 'geopolitics'.

Nevertheless, the unity and coherence of established nation-states, as well as their ability to maintain territorial sovereignty, have both been compromised in recent decades. Although the expansion of the state's economic and social responsibilities during much of the twentieth century had helped to fuel political centralization, during the 1960s and 1970s countervailing forces emerged, particularly through the tendency to redefine identity on the basis of culture or ethnicity (see p. 160), as discussed in Chapter 7. This was evident in the emergence of secessionist groups and forms of ethnic nationalism that sprang up places such as Quebec in Canada, Scotland and Wales in the UK, Catalonia and the Basque area in Spain, Corsica in France, and Flanders in Belgium. As the pressure for political decentralization grew, major constitutional upheavals were precipitated in a number of states (as discussed later in the chapter). In Italy, the process did not get under way until the 1990s with the rise of the Northern League in Lombardy. There have been similar manifestations of ethnic assertiveness amongst the Native Americans in Canada and the USA, the aboriginal peoples in Australia and the Maoris in New Zealand. In the latter two cases, at least, this has brought about a major reassessment of national identity, suggesting, perhaps, that nationalism was being displaced by multiculturalism (see p. 167).

The process through which political authority has been 'pulled down' within the state has been complemented by a tendency for political authority also to be 'sucked up' beyond the state, especially through the creation, or strengthening, of regional organizations. This has occurred, first, through a substantial growth in

Multilevel governance

Multilevel governance is a complex policy process in which political authority is distributed at different levels of territorial aggregation. The 'vertical' conception of multilevel governance takes account of the interdependence of actors in the policy process at subnational, national and transnational levels, creating a fluid process of negotiation. Much of the complexity of multilevel governance derives from 'horizontal' developments such as the growth of relationships between states and non-state actors, and the emergence of new forms of public-private partnership.

● **Transnational:** A configuration, which may apply to events, people, groups or organizations, that takes little or no account of national government or state borders.

● **Federal system:** A system of government in which sovereignty is shared between central and peripheral levels. (see p. 382).

● **Unitary system:** A system of government in which sovereignty is located in a single national institution, allowing the centre to control the periphery.

● **Confederation:** A qualified union of states in which each state retains its independence, typically guaranteed by unanimous decision-making.

cross-border, or transnational, flows and transactions – movements of people, goods, money, information and ideas. In other words, state borders have become increasingly 'porous', a development particularly associated with 'accelerated' globalization (see p. 142) since the 1980s. The second development, linked to the first, is that relations among states have come to be characterized by growing interdependence (see p. 433) and interconnectedness. Tasks such as promoting economic growth and prosperity, tackling global warming, halting the spread of weapons of mass destruction and coping with pandemic diseases are impossible for any state to accomplish on its own, however powerful it may be. States, in these circumstances, are forced to work together, relying on collective efforts and energies. The combination of these processes, through which an increasing burden of political decision-making has been made both 'above' and 'below' the national level, has helped to reshape territorial politics and generate interest in the phenomenon of multilevel governance. This could best be examined by looking, respectively, at the governance processes that operate at the subnational level and at the transnational level.

SUBNATIONAL POLITICS

All modern states are divided on a territorial basis between central (national) and peripheral (regional, provincial or local) institutions. The balance between centralization and decentralization is shaped by a wide range of historical, cultural, geographical, economic and political factors. The most prominent of these is the constitutional structure of the state, particularly the location of sovereignty in the political system. Although modified by other factors, the constitutional structure provides, as a minimum, the framework within which centre–periphery relationships are conducted. The two most common forms of territorial organization found in the modern world are the federal and unitary systems. A third form, confederation, has generally proved to be unsustainable. As confederations establish only the loosest and most decentralized type of political union by vesting sovereign power in peripheral bodies, it is not surprising that their principal advocates have been anarchists such as Pierre-Joseph Proudhon (see p. 381). The confederal principle is, in fact, most commonly applied in the form of intergovernmentalism (see p. 395), as embodied in international organizations such as the North Atlantic Treaty Organization (NATO), the United Nations (UN), the African Union (AU) and the Commonwealth of Nations. Examples of confederations at the nation-state level are, however, far rarer. The USA was originally a confederation, first in the form of the Continental Congresses (1774–81), and then under the Articles of Confederation (1781–89). The most important modern example of a confederal state is the Commonwealth of Independent States (CIS) which, in 1991, formally replaced the USSR. The CIS was established by 11 of the 15 former Soviet republics (only Georgia and the three Baltic states refused to join). However, it lacks executive authority and therefore constitutes little more than an occasional forum for debate and arbitration. Indeed, the evidence is that, in the absence of an effective central body, confederations either, as in the USA, transform themselves into federal states, or succumb to centrifugal pressures and disintegrate altogether, as has more or less occurred in the case of the CIS.

Pierre-Joseph Proudhon (1809–65)

French anarchist. A largely self-educated printer, Proudhon was drawn into radical politics in Lyons before settling in Paris in 1847. As a member of the 1848 Constituent Assembly, Proudhon famously voted against the constitution 'because it was a constitution'. He was later imprisoned for three years, after which, disillusioned with active politics, he concentrated on writing and theorizing. His best-known work, *What is Property?* ([1840] 1970), developed the first systematic argument for anarchism, based on the 'mutualist' principle; it also contained the famous dictum 'property is theft'. In *The Federal Principle* (1863), Proudhon modified his anarchism by acknowledging the need for a minimal state to 'set things in motion' (although by 'federal' he meant a political compact between self-governing communities – in effect, confederalism).

Federal systems

Federal systems of government have been more common than confederal systems. Over one-third of the world's population is governed by states that have some kind of federal structure. These states include the USA, Brazil, Pakistan, Australia, Mexico, Switzerland, Nigeria, Malaysia and Canada. Although no two federal structures are identical, the central feature of each is a sharing of sovereignty between central and peripheral institutions. This ensures, at least in theory, that neither level of government can encroach on the powers of the other (see Figure 11.1). In this sense, a federation is an intermediate form of political organization that lies somewhere between a confederation (which vests sovereign power in peripheral bodies) and a unitary state (in which power is located in central institutions). Federal systems are based on a compromise between unity and regional diversity, between the need for an effective central power and the need for checks or constraints on that power.

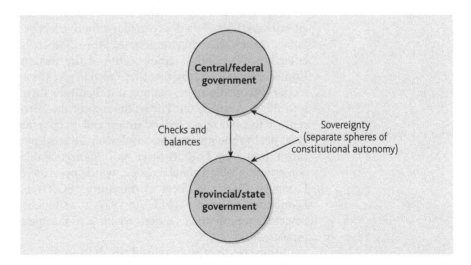

Figure 11.1   Federal states

Federalism

Federalism (from the Latin *foedus*, meaning 'pact', or 'covenant') usually refers to legal and political structures that distribute power territorially within a state. Nevertheless, in accordance with its original meaning, it has been taken to imply reciprocity or mutuality (Proudhon), or, in the writings of Alexander Hamilton and James Madison (see p. 319), to be part of a broader ideology of pluralism. As a political form, however, federalism requires the existence of two distinct levels of government, neither of which is legally or politically subordinate to the other. Its central feature is therefore shared sovereignty.

Why federalism?

When a list of federal states (or states exhibiting federal-type features) is examined, certain common characteristics can be observed. This suggests that the federal principle is more applicable to some states than to others. In the first place, historical similarities can be identified. For example, federations have often been formed by the coming together of a number of established political communities that nevertheless wish to preserve their separate identities and, to some extent, their autonomy. This clearly applied in the case of the world's first federal state, the USA. Although the 13 former British colonies in America quickly recognized the inadequacy of confederal organization, each possessed a distinctive political identity and set of traditions that it was determined to preserve within the new, more centralized, constitutional framework.

The reluctance of the former colonies to establish a strong national government was demonstrated at the Philadelphia Constitutional Convention of 1787, which drafted the US constitution, and by the ensuing debate over ratification. The 'nationalist' position, which supported ratification, was advanced in the so-called 'Federalist Papers', published between 1787 and 1789. They emphasized the importance of establishing a strong centralized government while, at the same time, preserving state and individual freedoms. Ratification was finally achieved in 1789, but only through the adoption of the Bill of Rights and, in particular, the Tenth Amendment, which guaranteed that powers not delegated to the federal government would be 'reserved to the states respectively, or to the people'. This provided a constitutional basis for US federalism. A similar process occurred in Germany. Although unification in 1871 reflected the growing might of Prussia, a federal structure helped to allay the fears of central control of the other 38 Germanic states that had long enjoyed political independence. This tradition of regional autonomy, briefly interrupted during the Nazi period, was formalized in the constitution of the Federal Republic of Germany, adopted in 1949, which granted each of the 11 *Länder* (provinces or states) its own constitution. Their number was increased to 16 as a result of the reunification of Germany in 1990.

A second factor influencing the formation of federations is the existence of an external threat, or a desire to play a more effective role in international affairs. Small, strategically vulnerable states, for instance, have a powerful incentive to enter broader political unions. One of the weaknesses of the US Articles of Confederation was, thus, that they failed to give the newly-independent US states a clear diplomatic voice, making it difficult for them to negotiate treaties, enter into alliances and so on. The willingness of the German states in the nineteenth century to enter into a federal union and accept effective 'Prussification' owed a great deal to the intensifying rivalry of the great powers, and, in particular, the threat posed by both Austria and France. Similarly, the drift towards the construction of a federal Europe, which began with the establishment of the European Coal and Steel Community (ECSC) in 1952 and the European Economic Community (EEC) in 1957, was brought about, in part, by a fear of Soviet aggression and by a perceived loss of European influence in the emerging bipolar world order.

A third factor is geographical size. It is no coincidence that many of the territorially largest states in the world have opted to introduce federal systems. This was true of the USA, and it also applied to Canada (federated in 1867), Brazil (1891), Australia (1901), Mexico (1917) and India (1947). Geographically large states tend to be culturally diverse and often possess strong regional traditions. This creates greater pressure for decentralization and the dispersal of power than can usually be accommodated within a unitary system. The final factor encouraging the adoption of federalism is cultural and ethnic heterogeneity. Federalism, in short, has often been an institutional response to societal divisions and diversities. Canada's ten provinces, for instance, reflect not only long-established regional traditions, but also language and cultural differences between English-speaking and French-speaking parts of the country. India's 25 self-governing states were defined primarily by language but, in the case of states such as Punjab and Kashmir, also take religious differences into account. Nigeria's 36-state federal system similarly recognizes major tribal and religious differences, particularly between the north and south-east of the country.

Features of federalism

Each federal system is unique, in the sense that the relationship between federal (national) government and state (regional) government is determined not just by constitutional rules, but also by a complex of political, historical, geographical, cultural and social circumstances. In some respects, for example, the party system is as significant a determinant of federal–state relationships as are the constitutionally allocated powers of each level of government. Thus, the federal structure of the USSR, which unlike the USA granted each of its 15 republics the right of secession, was entirely bogus given the highly centralized nature of the 'ruling' Communist Party, to say nothing of the rigidly hierarchical central-planning system. A similar situation was found in Mexico, where the once dominant Institutional Revolutionary Party (PRI) effectively counteracted a federal system that was consciously modelled on the US example. In the USA, Canada, Australia and India, on the other hand, decentralized party systems have safeguarded the powers of state and regional governments.

There is a further contrast between federal regimes that operate a 'separation of powers' (see p. 313) between the executive and legislative branches of government (typified by the US presidential system), and parliamentary systems in which executive and legislative power is 'fused'. The former tend to ensure that government power is diffused both territorially and functionally, meaning that there are multiple points of contact between the two levels of government. This leads to the complex patterns of interpenetration between federal and state levels of government that are found in the US and Swiss systems. Parliamentary systems, however, often produce what is called 'executive federalism', most notably in Canada and Australia.

Nevertheless, certain features are common to most, if not all, federal systems:

● **Two relatively autonomous levels of government:** Both central government (the federal level) and regional government (the state level) possess a range of powers on which the other cannot encroach. These include, at least, a measure of legislative and executive authority, and the capacity to raise revenue; thus enjoying a degree of fiscal independence. However, the specific fields of jurisdiction of each level of government, and the capacity

● **Executive federalism:** A style of federalism in which the federal balance is largely determined by the relationship between the executives of each level of government.

of each to influence the other, vary considerably. In Germany and Austria, for instance, a system of 'administrative federalism' operates in which central government is the key policy-maker, and provincial government is charged with the responsibility for the details of policy implementation.

- **Written constitution:** The responsibilities and powers of each level of government are defined in a codified or 'written' constitution. The relationship between the centre and the periphery is therefore conducted within a formal legal framework. The autonomy of each level is usually guaranteed by the fact that neither is able to amend the constitution unilaterally; for example, in Australia and Switzerland amendments to the constitution must also be ratified by an affirmative referendum.

- **Constitutional arbiter:** The formal provisions of the constitution are interpreted by a supreme court, which thereby arbitrates in the case of disputes between federal and state levels of government. In determining the respective fields of jurisdiction of each level, the judiciary in a federal system is able to determine how federalism works in practice, inevitably drawing the judiciary into the policy process. The centralization that occurred in all federal systems in the twentieth century was invariably sanctioned by the courts.

- **Linking institutions:** In order to foster cooperation and understanding between federal and state levels of government, the regions and provinces must be given a voice in the processes of central policy-making. This is usually achieved through a bicameral legislature, in which the second chamber or upper house represents the interests of the states. The 105 seats in the Canadian Senate, for example, are assigned on a regional basis, with each of the four major regions receiving 24 seats, the remainder being assigned to smaller regions.

Assessment of federalism

One of the chief strengths of federal systems is that, unlike unitary systems, they give regional and local interests a constitutionally guaranteed political voice. The states or provinces exercise a range of autonomous powers and enjoy some measure of representation in central government, usually, as pointed out above, through the second chamber of the federal legislature. On the other hand, federalism was not able to stem the general twentieth-century tendency towards centralization. Despite guarantees of state and provincial rights in federal systems, the powers of central government have expanded, largely as a result of the growth of economic and social intervention, and central government's own greater revenue-raising capacities.

The US system, for instance, initially operated according to the principles of 'dual federalism'. From the late nineteenth century onwards, this gave way to a system of 'cooperative federalism' that was based on the growth of 'grants in aid' from the federal government to the states and localities. State and local government therefore became increasingly dependent on the flow of federal funds, especially after the upsurge in economic and social programmes that occurred under the New Deal in the 1930s. From the mid-1960s, however, cooperative federalism, based on a partnership of sorts between federal government and the states, was replaced by what has been called 'coercive federalism'. This is a system through which federal government has increasingly brought about the compli-

● **Administrative federalism:** A style of federalism in which central government is the key policy-maker, and provincial government is charged with responsibility for policy implementation.

● **Dual federalism:** A style of federalism in which federal and state/provincial government occupy separate and seemingly indestructible spheres of policy power.

ance of the states by passing laws that pre-empt their powers, and imposing restrictions on the states and localities in the form of mandates.

A second advantage of federalism is that, in diffusing government power, it creates a network of checks and balances that helps to protect individual liberty. In James Madison's (see p. 319) words, 'ambition must be made to counteract ambition'. Despite a worldwide tendency towards centralization, federal systems such as those in the USA, Australia and Canada have usually been more effective in constraining national politicians than have been unitary systems. However, structures intended to create healthy tension within a system of government may also generate frustration and paralysis. One of the weaknesses of federal systems is that, by constraining central authority, they make the implementation of bold economic or social programmes more difficult. F. D. Roosevelt's New Deal in the USA, for example, was significantly weakened by Supreme Court decisions that were intended to prevent federal government from encroaching on the responsibilities of the states. In the 1980s, Ronald Reagan deliberately used federalism as a weapon against 'big' government, and specifically against the growing welfare budget. Under the slogan 'new federalism', Reagan attempted to staunch social spending by transferring responsibility for welfare from federal government to the less prosperous state governments. In contrast, the dominant pattern of cooperative federalism in Germany has facilitated, rather than thwarted, the construction of a comprehensive and well-funded welfare system. Nevertheless, since the 1990s the USA has increasingly relied on fiscal federalism, federal grants to state and local government having risen steadily under a succession of presidents.

Finally, federalism has provided an institutional mechanism through which fractured societies have maintained unity and coherence. In this respect, the federal solution may be appropriate only to a limited number of ethnically diverse and regionally divided societies but, in these cases, it may be absolutely vital. The genius of US federalism, for instance, was perhaps less that it provided the basis for unity amongst the 13 original states, and more that it invested the USA with an institutional mechanism that enabled it to absorb the strains that immigration exerted from the mid-nineteenth century onwards. The danger of federalism, however, is that by breeding governmental division it may strengthen centrifugal pressures and ultimately lead to disintegration. Some have argued, as a result, that federal systems are inherently unstable, tending either towards the guaranteed unity that only a unitary system can offer, or towards greater decentralization and ultimate collapse. Federalism in Canada, for example, can perhaps be deemed a failure, if its chief purpose were to construct a political union within which both French-speaking and English-speaking populations can live together in harmony (see p. 114).

Unitary systems

The vast majority of contemporary states have unitary systems of government. These vest sovereign power in a single, national institution. In the UK, this institution is Parliament, which possesses, at least in theory, unrivalled and unchallengeable legislative authority. Parliament can make or unmake any law it wishes; its powers are not checked by a codified or written constitution; there are no rival UK legislatures that can challenge its authority; and its laws outrank all other forms of English and Scottish law. Since constitutional supremacy is vested with

● Fiscal federalism: A style of federalism in which the federal balance is largely determined by funding arrangements, especially transfer payments from the centre to the periphery.

the centre in a unitary system, any system of peripheral or local government exists at the centre in a unitary system, any system of peripheral or local government exists at the pleasure of the centre (see Figure 11.2). At first sight, this creates the spectre of unchecked centralization. Local institutions can be reshaped, reorganized and even abolished at will; their powers and responsibilities can be contracted as easily as they can be expanded. However, in practice, the relationship between the centre and the periphery in unitary systems is as complex as it is in federal systems – political, cultural and historical factors being as significant as more formal constitutional ones. Nevertheless, two distinct institutional forms of peripheral authority exist in unitary states: local government and devolved assemblies. Each of these gives centre–periphery relationships a distinctive shape.

Local government

Local government, in its simplest sense, is government that is specific to a particular locality; for example, a village, district, town, city or county. More particularly, it is a form of government that has no share in sovereignty, and is thus entirely subordinate to central authority – or, in a federal system, to state or regional authority. This level of government is, in fact, universal, being found in federal and confederal systems, as well as in unitary systems. In the USA, for instance, there are over 86,000 units of local government that employ 11,000,000 people, compared with a total of fewer than 8,000,000 staff at federal and state levels. However, what makes local government particularly important in unitary systems is that, in most cases, it is the only form of government outside the centre.

It would, nevertheless, be a mistake to assume that the constitutional subordination of local government means that it is politically irrelevant. The very ubiquity of local government reflects the fact that it is both administratively necessary and, because it is 'close' to the people, easily intelligible. Moreover, elected local politicians have a measure of democratic legitimacy (see p. 81) that enables them to extend their formal powers and responsibilities. This often means that central–local relationships are conducted through a process of bargaining and negotiation, rather than by diktat from above. The balance between the centre and the periphery is further influenced by factors such as the political culture (particularly by established traditions of local autonomy and regional diversity) and the

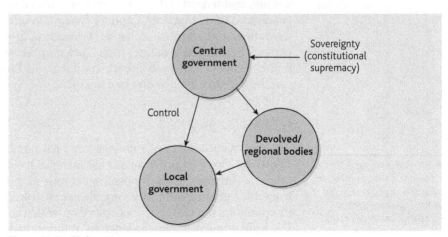

Figure 11.2   Unitary states

nature of the party system. For instance, the growing tendency for local politics to be 'politicized', in the sense that national parties have increasingly dominated local politics, has usually brought with it greater centralization. In the absence of the kind of constitutional framework that federalism provides, the preservation of local autonomy relies, to a crucial extent, on self-restraint by the centre. This tends to mean that the degree of decentralization in unitary systems varies significantly, both over time and from country to country. This can be illustrated by the contrasting experiences of the UK and France.

The UK traditionally possessed a relatively decentralized local government system, with local authorities exercising significant discretion within a legal framework laid down by Parliament. Indeed, respect for **local democracy** was long seen as a feature of the UK's unwritten constitution. However, the pattern of local–central relationships was dramatically restructured in the 1980s and 1990s, as the Conservative governments of that period saw local government as an obstacle to the implementation of their radical market-orientated policies. Central control was thus strengthened as local authorities were robbed of their ability to determine their own tax and spending policies. Local authorities that challenged the centre, such as the Greater London Council and the metropolitan county councils, were abolished – their functions being devolved to smaller district and borough councils, and a variety of newly-created **quangos**. The ultimate aim of these policies was fundamentally to remodel local government by creating 'enabling' councils, whose role is not to provide services themselves, but to supervise the provision of services by private bodies through a system of contracting-out and privatization. Although later governments re-established a London-wide council, in the form of the Greater London Authority (2000), and supported the introduction of elected mayors for towns and cities, the overall shift in power from local to central government in the UK has not been reversed. Very different policies were nevertheless adopted in France over the same period. During the 1980s, President Mitterrand sought to dismantle the strict administrative control in regional government that operated largely through prefects (appointed by, and directly accountable to, the Ministry of the Interior), who were the chief executives of France's 96 *départements*. The executive power of the prefects was transferred to locally elected presidents, and the prefects were replaced by *Commissaires de la République*, who are concerned essentially with economic planning. In addition, local authorities were absolved of the need to seek prior approval for administrative and spending decisions. The net result of these reforms was to give France a more decentralized state structure than it had had at any time since the 1789 revolution. Underpinning these developments was faith in the benefits of decentralization, reflecting the belief that political decisions should be made at the lowest possible level (see p. 388).

Devolution

Devolution (see p. 390), at least in its legislative form, establishes the greatest possible measure of decentralization in a unitary system of government – short, that is, of its transformation into a federal system. Devolved assemblies have usually been created in response to increasing centrifugal tensions within a state, and as an attempt, in particular, to conciliate growing regional, and sometimes nationalist, pressures. Despite their lack of entrenched powers, once devolved

● **Local democracy:** A principle that embodies both the idea of local autonomy and the goal of popular responsiveness.

● **Quango:** An acronym for quasi-autonomous non-governmental organization: a public body staffed by appointees, rather than politicians or civil servants (see p. 368).

Debating . . .
Should political decisions be made at the lowest possible level?

Although all modern states are divided on a territorial basis, there is considerable debate about where the balance should lie between centralization and decentralization. Supporters of decentralization tend to argue that it is a core principle of democratic rule. But may local power only be achieved at the cost of efficient government and, maybe, social justice?

YES	NO

Boosting participation. Local or provincial government is a more effective agent of participation than central government. This is because far more people hold office at the local level than the national level, and even more are involved in standing for election or campaigning generally. By making political participation more attractive, devolving decision-making responsibility to lower levels helps to narrow the gap between the politically 'active' few and the 'passive' many.

Greater responsiveness. By being, quite literally, 'closer' to the people, peripheral bodies are more sensitive to their needs. This both strengthens popular accountability and ensures that government responds not merely to the general interests of society, but also to the specific needs of particular communities. There is certainly a much greater chance that local or provincial politicians will have a personal knowledge of, and perhaps live in, the community they serve, bolstering their responsiveness.

Increased legitimacy. Physical distance from government affects the acceptability or rightfulness of political decisions. Decisions that are made at a local or provincial level are likely to be seen as intelligible, and therefore legitimate, whereas geographical remoteness engenders a sense of political remoteness, so weakening the binding character of political decisions. This is especially the case as centralized decision-making can only treat the public as an amorphous mass, rather than as a collection of different groups and different communities.

Upholding liberty. Decentralization and localism help to deter tyranny and, therefore, protect individual freedom. This happens because, as liberals emphasize, corruption increases as power becomes more concentrated, as there are fewer checks on politicians' self-seeking inclinations. As political decisions are devolved to lower and lower levels, power is more widely dispersed and a network of checks and balances emerges. Strong peripheral bodies are more effective in checking central government power, as well as one another.

National disunity. Central government alone articulates the interests of the whole of society, rather than its various parts. While a strong centre ensures that government addresses the common interests and shared concerns, a weak centre allows people to focus on what divides them, creating rivalry and discord. Shifting political decision-making to lower levels risks fostering parochialism and will make it more difficult for citizens to see the political 'big picture'.

Uniformity threatened. Only central governments can establish uniform laws and public services that, for instance, help people move more easily from one part of the country to another. Geographical mobility, and therefore social mobility, are likely to be restricted to the extent that political decentralization results in differing tax regimes and differing legal, educational and social-security systems across a country. A lack of uniformity may also threaten the nationwide growth of businesses.

Inhibiting social justice. Devolving political decisions from the centre has the disadvantage that it forces peripheral institutions increasingly to rely on the resources available in their locality or region. Only central government can rectify inequalities that arise from the fact that the areas with the greatest social needs are invariably those with the least potential for raising revenue, and only central government has the resources to devise and implement major programmes of welfare provision. Decentralization therefore puts social justice at risk.

Economic development. Centralization and economic development invariably go hand-in-hand. Because of its greater administrative capacity, central government can perform economic functions that are beyond the capacity of local bodies. These include managing a single currency, controlling tax and spending, and providing an infrastructure in the form of roads, railways, airports and so on. Centralization also promotes efficiency because it allows government to benefit from economies of scale.

assemblies have acquired a political identity of their own, and possess a measure of democratic legitimacy, they are very difficult to weaken and, in normal circumstances, impossible to abolish. Northern Ireland's Stormont Parliament was an exception. The Stormont Parliament was suspended in 1972 and replaced by direct rule from the Westminster Parliament, but only when it became apparent that its domination by predominantly Protestant Unionist parties prevented it from stemming the rising tide of communal violence in Northern Ireland that threatened to develop into civil war.

One of the oldest traditions of devolved government in Europe is found in Spain. Although it has been a unitary state since the 1570s, Spain is divided into 50 provinces, each of which exercises a measure of regional self-government. As part of the transition to democratic government following the death of General Franco in 1975, the devolution process was extended in 1979 with the creation of 17 autonomous communities. This new tier of regional government is based on elected assemblies invested with broad control of domestic policy, and was designed to meet long-standing demands for autonomy, especially in Catalonia and the Basque area. The French government has also used devolution as a means of responding to the persistence of regional identities, and, at least in Brittany and Occitania, to the emergence of forms of ethnic nationalism. As part of a strategy of 'functional regionalism', 22 regional public bodies were created in 1972 to enhance the administrative coordination of local investment and planning decisions. These, however, lacked a democratic basis and enjoyed only limited powers. In 1982, they were transformed into fully-fledged regional governments, each with a directly elected council. The tendency towards decentralization in Europe has, however, also been fuelled by developments within the European Union (EU), and especially by the emergence since the late 1980s of the idea of 'Europe of the Regions'. Regional and provincial levels of government have benefited from the direct distribution of aid from the European Regional Development Fund (1975), and have responded both by seeking direct representation in Brussels and by strengthening their involvement in economic planning and infrastructure development.

The UK was slower in embracing devolution. The revival of Scottish and Welsh nationalism since the late 1960s had put devolution on the political agenda, but devolved bodies were not established until 1999. A system of 'asymmetrical' devolution was established. Legislative devolution operated in Scotland, through the Scottish Parliament's ability to vary income tax by up to three pence in the pound and its **primary legislative power**; administrative devolution operated in Wales, as the Welsh Assembly had no control over taxation and only **secondary legislative power**; and so-called 'rolling' devolution was established in Northern Ireland, as the powers of the Northern Ireland Assembly were linked to progress in the province's 'peace process'. At the same time, England, with 84 per cent of the UK's population, remained entirely outside the devolution process. Nevertheless, devolution in the UK quickly developed into a form of '**quasi-federalism**', having gone beyond the simple handing down of power by a still sovereign Westminster Parliament. This has occurred because, although the Scottish, Welsh and Northern Irish bodies lack constitutional entrenchment, they enjoy a significant measure of democratic legitimacy by virtue of being popular assemblies that were set up following affirmative referendums. Moreover, the asymmetrical nature of UK devolution

● **Primary legislative power**: The ability to make law on matters which have been devolved from a central authority.

● **Secondary legislative power**: The ability to vary some laws devolved from a central authority that retains ultimate legislative control.

● **Quasi-federalism**: A division of powers between central and regional government that has some of the features of federalism without possessing a formal federal structure.

Devolution

Devolution is the transfer of power from central government to subordinate regional institutions. Devolved bodies thus constitute an intermediate tier of government between central and local government. However, devolution differs from federalism in that devolved bodies have no share in sovereignty. In *administrative* devolution, regional institutions implement policies that are decided elsewhere. In *legislative* devolution (sometimes called 'home rule'), devolution involves the establishment of elected regional assemblies that have policy-making responsibilities.

● Security regionalism: Forms of transnational regional cooperation that are designed primarily to protect states from their enemies, both neighbouring and distant ones.

● Political regionalism: Attempts by states in the same area to strengthen or protect shared values, thereby enhancing their image, reputation and diplomatic effectiveness.

creates pressures for the ratcheting-up of devolved powers: the Welsh and Northern Irish assemblies have aspired to the powers of the Scottish Parliament, and the Scottish Parliament has, in turn, been encouraged to expand its powers in order to maintain its superior status. The Welsh Assembly thus acquired primary legislative powers in 2011, and, when the Scottish National Party (SNP) gained majority control of the Scottish Parliament in 2011, it committed itself to holding a referendum on Scottish independence, due to take place in 2014.

TRANSNATIONAL REGIONALISM

Regionalism: its nature and growth

Types of regionalism

In general terms, regionalism is a process through which geographical regions become significant political and/or economic units. Regionalism has two faces, however. In the first place, it is a subnational phenomenon, a process of decentralization that takes place *within* countries, and is closely associated, as already discussed, with federalism and devolution. The second face of regionalism is transnational, rather than subnational. In this, regionalism refers to a process of cooperation or integration *between* countries in the same region of the world. An ongoing problem with regionalism has nevertheless been the difficulty in establishing the nature and extent of a region. What is a 'region'? On the face of it, a region is a distinctive geographical area. Regions can therefore be identified by consulting maps. This leads to a tendency to identify regions with continents, as applies in the case of Europe (through the EU), Africa (through the African Union, or AU) and America (through the Organization of American States). However, many regional organizations are sub-continental, such as the Association of Southeast Asian Nations (ASEAN), the Southern African Customs Unions and the Central American Common Market, while others are transcontinental, such as Asia-Pacific Economic Cooperation (APEC) and the North Atlantic Treaty Organization (NATO). An alternative basis for regional identity is socio-cultural, reflecting similarities of region, language, history, or even ideological belief amongst a number of neighbouring states. Cultural identity is particularly important in the case of bodies such as the Arab League and the Nordic Council, and it may also apply in the case of the EU, where membership requires an explicit commitment to liberal-democratic values.

Regionalism has taken a number of forms and been fuelled by a variety of factors. Security regionalism emerged in the early post-1945 period through the growth of regional defence organizations that gave expression to the new strategic tensions that were generated by the Cold War. NATO and the Warsaw Pact were the most prominent such organizations, although other bodies, such as the Southeast Asian Treaty Organization (SEATO), were also formed. Political regionalism has witnessed the construction of organizations such as the Arab League, which was formed in 1945 to safeguard the independence and sovereignty of Arab countries; the Council of Europe, which was established in 1949 with the aim of creating a common democratic and legal area throughout the continent of Europe; and the Organization of African Unity (OAU), which was

Regionalism

Regionalism is the theory or practice of coordinating social, economic and political activities within a geographical region, which may either be part of a state (subnational regionalism) or comprise a number of states (transnational regionalism). On an *institutional* level, regionalism involves the growth of norms, rules and formal structures through which coordination is brought about. On an *affective* level, regionalism implies a realignment of political identities and loyalties from the state to the region.

● Economic regionalism: Forms of cooperation amongst states in the same region that are designed to create greater economic opportunities, usually by fostering trading links.

● Pooled sovereignty: The sharing of decision-making authority by states within a system of international cooperation, in which certain sovereign powers are transferred to central bodies.

● Functionalism: The theory that social and political phenomena can be explained by their function within a larger whole, implying that regional integration occurs because it has functional advantages over state independence.

founded in 1963 to promote self-government and social progress throughout the African continent, and was replaced by the African Union (AU) in 2002. The most significant impetus towards transnational regionalism has undoubtedly been economic, however. Economic regionalism is therefore the primary form of regional integration and has become more so since the advent of so-called 'new' regionalism in the early 1990s.

Regionalism and globalization

'New' regionalism is manifest in the growth of regional trade blocs and the deepening of existing trade blocs (see p. 392). This surge has continued unabated, so that, by 2005, only one member of the World Trade Organization – Mongolia – was not party to a regional trade agreement. These agreements usually establish free trade areas through the reduction in internal tariffs and other barriers to trade; but, in other cases, they may establish customs unions, through the establishment of a common external tariff, or common markets (sometimes called 'single markets'), areas within which there is a free movement of labour and capital, and a high level of economic harmonization. The advent of 'new' regionalism has nevertheless highlighted the complex, and sometimes contradictory, relationship between regionalism and globalization. As Bhagwati (2008) put it, regional trade blocs can operate as both 'stumbling blocks' or 'building blocks' within the global system. Economic regionalism can be essentially defensive, in that regional organizations have sometimes embraced protectionism as a means of resisting the disruption of economic and, possibly, social life through the impact of intensifying global competition. This gave rise to the idea of the region as a fortress, as indeed evinced by the once-fashionable notion of 'fortress Europe'. Nevertheless, regional trade blocs have also been motivated by competitive impulses, and not merely protectionist ones. In these cases, countries have formed regional blocs not so much to resist global market forces but, rather, to engage more effectively with them. Although states have wished to consolidate or expand trade blocs in the hope of gaining access to more secure and wider markets, they have rarely turned their back on the wider global market, meaning that regionalism and globalization are usually interlocking, rather than rival, processes.

Explaining regionalism

Wider explanations have also been advanced for the rise of regionalism. The earliest theory of regional, or even global, integration was federalism, drawing inspiration from its use in domestic politics. As an explanation for transnational regionalism, federalism relies on a process of conscious decision-making by political elites, attracted, in particular, by the desire to avoid war by encouraging states to transfer at least a measure of their sovereignty to a higher, federal body. This is often referred to as 'pooled' sovereignty. However, although a federalist vision is often said to have inspired the early process of European integration, federalism has had relatively little impact on the wider process of regional integration. Instead, even in the case of the European project, federalist thinking has had less impact than a functionalist road to integration. In the functionalist view, regional cooperation reflects the recognition that specific activities can be performed more effectively through collective action than by states acting indi-

Focus on . . .
Regional economic blocs

- **North American Free Trade Agreement (NAFTA):** This was signed in 1993 by Canada, Mexico and the USA. NAFTA was formed, in part, as a response to the growing pace of European integration, and is intended to provide the basis for a wider economic partnership covering the whole western hemisphere.

- **European Union (EU):** This was formed in 1993, developing out of the European Economic Community (founded in 1957). The EU has expanded from 6 to 27 members, and now includes many former communist states. It is the most advanced example of regional integration at an economic and political level.

- **Asia-Pacific Economic Cooperation (APEC):** This informal forum was created in 1989 and has expanded from 12 member states to 21 (including Australia, China, Russia, Japan and the USA); collectively, these states account for 40 per cent of the world's population and over 50 per cent of global GDP.

- **Association of South-East Asian Nations (ASEAN):** This was established in 1967 by Brunei, Indonesia, Malaysia, Philippines, Singapore and Thailand, with Brunei, Vietnam, Laos, Myanmar and Cambodia joining subsequently. ASEAN has attempted to promote a free-trade zone that would help south-east Asian states maintain their economic independence.

- **Mercosur:** The Mercosur agreement (1991) links Argentina, Brazil, Venezuela, Paraguay and Uruguay with Chile, Colombia, Ecuador, Peru and Bolivia as associate members. It is Latin America's largest trade bloc, and operates as a free-trade union.

- **Free Trade Area of the Americas (FTAA):** This is an agreement made at the 1994 Miami Summit of the Americas to build a free-trade area to extend across the Americas, as a proposed extension to NAFTA. The FTAA has 34 provisional members, but it is dominated by the USA and Canada.

vidually. This also helps to explain why regional integration has a predominantly economic character, as this is the area in which the functional benefits of co-operation are most evident. The weakness of functionalism is, however, that it overemphasizes the willingness of states to hand over responsibilities to functional bodies, especially in areas that are political, rather than technical. Furthermore, there is little evidence that regional bodies are capable of acquiring a level of political allegiance that rivals that of the nation-state, regardless of their functional importance. As a result of these deficiencies, a growing emphasis has been placed what is called 'neofunctionalism'. Neofunctionalism has been particularly influential in explaining European integration, the most advanced example of regional integration found anywhere in the world.

● **Neofunctionalism:** A revision of functionalism that recognizes that regional integration in one area generates pressures for further integration in the form of 'spillover'.

European regionalism

What is the EU?

The 'European idea' (broadly, the belief that, regardless of historical, cultural and language differences, Europe constitutes a single political community) was born long before 1945. Before the Reformation in the sixteenth century, common alle-

Focus on . . .

How the European Union works

- **The European Commission:** This is the executive-bureaucratic arm of the EU. It is headed by 27 commissioners (one from each of the member states) and a president (José Manuel Barroso's term of office as president began in 2004). It proposes legislation, is a watchdog that ensures that EU treaties are respected, and is broadly responsible for policy implementation.
- **The Council:** This is the decision-making branch of the EU, and comprises ministers from the 27 states who are accountable to their own assemblies and governments. The presidency of the Council of Ministers rotates amongst member states every six months. Important decisions are made by unanimous agreement, and others are reached through qualified majority voting or by a simple majority.
- **The European Council:** Informally called the 'European Summit', this is a senior forum in which heads of government, accompanied by foreign ministers and two commissioners, discuss the overall direction of the Union's work. The Council

meets periodically and provides strategic leadership for the EU.
- **The European Parliament:** The EP is composed of 754 Members of the European Parliament (MEPs), who are directly elected every five years. Originally a scrutinizing assembly rather than a legislature, the passage of the Lisbon Treaty means that the EP now decides on the vast majority of EU legislation. The Parliament is a co-legislator with the Council over matters including agriculture, energy policy, immigration and EU funds, with the Parliament having the last say on the EU budget.
- **The European Court of Justice:** The ECJ interprets, and adjudicates on, European Union law. There are 27 judges, one from each member state, and 8 advocates general, who advise the court. As EU law has primacy over the national law of EU member states, the court can 'disapply' domestic laws. A Court of First Instance handles certain cases brought by individuals and companies.

giance to Rome invested the Papacy with supranational authority over much of Europe. Even after the European state-system came into existence, thinkers as different as Rousseau (see p. 97), Saint-Simon (1760–1825) and Mazzini (see p. 116) championed the cause of European cooperation and, in some cases, advocated the establishment of Europe-wide political institutions. However, until the second half of the twentieth century aspirations to achieve this through consent (as opposed to military power, as in the case of Charlemagne and Napolean) proved to be hopelessly utopian. Since World War II, Europe has undergone a historically unprecedented process of integration, aimed, some argue, at the creation of what Winston Churchill in 1946 called a 'United States of Europe'. Indeed, it is sometimes suggested that European integration provides a model of political organization that will eventually be accepted worldwide as the deficiencies of the nation-state become increasingly apparent.

It is clear that this process was precipitated by a set of powerful, and possibly irresistible, historical circumstances in post-1945 Europe. The most significant of these were the following:

- The need for economic reconstruction in war-torn Europe through cooperation and the creation of a larger market.

Jean Monnet (1888–1979)

French economist and administrator. Monnet was largely self-taught. He found employment during World War I coordinating Franco-British war supplies, and he was later appointed Deputy Secretary-General of the League of Nations. He was the originator of Winston Churchill's offer of union between the UK and France in 1940, which was abandoned once Pétain's Vichy regime had been installed. Monnet took charge of the French modernization programme under de Gaulle in 1945, and in 1950 he produced the Schuman Plan, from which the European Coal and Steel Community and the European Economic Community were subsequently developed. Although Monnet rejected intergovernmentalism in favour of supranational government, he was not a formal advocate of European federalism.

- The desire to preserve peace by permanently resolving the bitter Franco-German rivalry that caused the Franco-Prussian War (1870–71), and led to war in 1914 and 1939.
- The recognition that the '**German problem**' could be tackled only by integrating Germany into a wider Europe.
- The desire to safeguard Europe from the threat of Soviet expansionism, and to mark out for Europe an independent role and identity in a bipolar world order.
- The wish of the USA to establish a prosperous and united Europe, both as a market for US goods and as a bulwark against the spread of communism.
- The widespread acceptance, especially in continental Europe, that the sovereign nation-state was the enemy of peace and prosperity.

To some extent, the drift towards European integration was fuelled by an idealist commitment to internationalism (see p. 117) and the belief that international organizations embody a moral authority higher than that commanded by nation-states. However, more practical consideration, not least linked to economic matters, ultimately proved to be of greater significance. The European Coal and Steel Community (ECSC) was founded in 1952 on the initiative of Jean Monnet, adviser to the French foreign minister, Robert Schuman. Under the Treaty of Rome (1957), the European Economic Community (EEC) came into existence. The ECSC, EEC and Euratom (the body concerned with the peaceful use of nuclear energy) were formally merged in 1967, forming what became known as the European Community (EC). Although the community of the original 'Six' (France, Germany, Italy, the Netherlands, Belgium and Luxembourg) was expanded in 1973 with the inclusion of the UK, Ireland and Denmark, the 1970s was a period of stagnation. The integration process was relaunched, however, as a result of the signing in 1986 of the Single European Act (SEA), which envisaged an unrestricted flow of goods, services and people throughout Europe (a 'single market'), to be introduced by 1993. The Treaty of European Union (the TEU or Maastricht treaty), which became effective in 1993, marked the creation of the European Union (EU). This committed the EU's then-15 members (Greece, Portugal, Spain, Austria, Finland and Sweden having joined)

● **German problem:** The structural instability in the European state system caused by the emergence of a powerful and united Germany.

Inter-governmentalism, supranationalism

Intergovernmentalism refers to any form of interaction between states that takes place on the basis of sovereign independence. This includes treaties and alliances as well as leagues and confederations. Sovereignty is preserved through a process of unanimous decision-making that gives each state a veto, over vital national issues.

Supranationalism is the existence of an authority that is 'higher' than that of the nation-state and capable of imposing its will on it. It can therefore be found in international federations, where sovereignty is shared between central and peripheral bodies.

● **Political union**: Although the term lacks clarity, it refers to the coming together of a number of states under a common government; can imply supranational governance.

● **Monetary union**: The establishment of a single currency within an area comprising a number of states.

● **Veto**: The formal power to block a decision or action through the refusal of consent.

● **Qualified majority voting**: A system of voting in which different majorities are needed on different issues, with states' votes weighted (roughly) according to size.

to the principles of political union and monetary union (although Sweden, Denmark and the UK opted not to participate in monetary union). The centre-piece of this proposal was the establishment of a single European currency, the euro, which took place in 1999, with notes and coins being circulated in 2002. In 2004, the EU began its most radical phase of enlargement, as ten countries of Central and Eastern Europe and the Mediterranean joined, bringing about the reunification of Europe after decades of division by the Iron Curtain. Bulgaria and Romania joined in 2007, with negotiations for membership under way with Croatia, Macedonia and Turkey, and with Albania, Bosnia-Herzegovina, Montenegro and Serbia all potential candidate countries.

The EU is a very difficult political organization to categorize. In strict terms, it is no longer a confederation of independent states operating on the basis of intergovernmentalism (as the EEC and EC were at their inception). The sovereignty of member states was enshrined in the so-called 'Luxembourg compromise' of 1966. This accepted the general practice of unanimous voting in the Council, and granted each member state an outright veto on matters threatening vital national interests. As a result of the SEA and the TEU, however, the practice of qualified majority voting, which allows even the largest state to be outvoted, was applied to a wider range of policy areas, thereby narrowing the scope of the national veto. This trend has been compounded by the fact that EU law is binding on all member states, and that the power of certain EU bodies has expanded at the expense of national governments. The result is a political body that has both intergovernmental and supranational features; the former evident in the Council, and the latter primarily in the European Commission and the Court of Justice. The EU may not yet have created a federal Europe, but because of the superiority of European law over the national law of the member states, it is perhaps accurate to talk of a 'federalizing' Europe. An attempt was made to codify the EU's various constitutional rules, particularly in the light of enlargement, through the introduction of the Constitutional Treaty, commonly known as the 'EU Constitution'. This failed because of referendum defeats in the Netherlands and France in 2005 but, although many elements of the Constitutional Treaty were incorporated into the 2009 Lisbon Treaty, the episode highlights the extent to which, despite decades of institutional 'deepening', EU member states continue to function as states, still orientated around issues of national interest.

As an economic, monetary and, to a significant extent, political union brought about through voluntary cooperation amongst states, the EU is a unique political body: the world's only genuine experiment in supranational governance. The transition from Community to Union, achieved via the TEU, not only extended cooperation into areas such as foreign and security policy, home affairs and justice, and immigration and policing, but also established the notion of EU citizenship through the right to live, work and be politically active in any member state. This level of integration has been possible because of the powerful, and, some would argue, exceptional combination of pressures in post-1945 Europe that helped to shift public attitudes away from nationalism and towards cooperation, and to convince elites that national interests are ultimately better served by concerted action, rather than independence. Where such pre-requisites were weak, as in the case of the UK, often dubbed Europe's 'awkward partner', participation in the integration process has tended to be either reluctant

POLITICS IN ACTION . . .

The eurozone crisis: regionalism beyond its limits?

Events: The euro officially came into existence on 1 January 1999. Of the EU's then-15 members, only the UK, Sweden and Denmark chose not to join the currency. The eurozone subsequently expanded to 17 members. The new currency achieved parity with the US dollar by November 2002 and increased steadily thereafter, peaking at a value of $1.59 in July 2008. However, the onset of the 2007–09 global financial crisis and a global recession created deepening problems. As growth slowed and tax revenues contracted, concern built about the heavily-indebted countries in the eurozone; notably, Portugal, Ireland, Greece, Spain and, to some extent, Italy. The crisis in Greece was so severe that, in May 2010, it led to a massive German-led eurozone bailout, backed by the IMF, with a further bailout being agreed in July 2011. Similar bailouts were agreed for Ireland in November 2010 and Portugal in May 2011, amid fears that 'contagion' might spread to Spain, Italy and beyond. In each of these countries severe austerity measures were introduced in the hope that spending cuts and increased taxation would reduce budget deficits and so restore the confidence of financial markets.

Significance: A single European currency had been seen as an important way of bolstering growth and prosperity within the EU. The key attraction of the euro was that its introduction promised to boost trade by reducing the costs and risks involved in transactions. Cross-currency transactions incur costs because of the need to buy or sell foreign currency. Such transactions involve risk and uncertainty because unanticipated exchange rate movements may make trade either more expensive or less expensive than expected. A single currency would therefore complete the single market, and help to ensure unrestricted labour and capital mobility. What is more, much had been done already to ensure the success of the euro, as many barriers to the free movement of goods and peoples within the EU had been removed by the Single European Act (1986) and the Treaty of European Union (1993). This encouraged the view that the EU constituted an optimal currency area, with confidence that, over time, the workings of the single currency would foster greater economic harmonization. An additional advantage was that a single currency would bring with it helpful economic disciplines; notably, limits on the size of budget deficits and national debts, as laid out in the 1997 Stability and Growth Pact.

The eurozone crisis, nevertheless, highlights the limitations and flaws in the single currency project. Some even argue that monetary union was, in principle, economically unfeasible and stretched European regionalism beyond its proper limits. Any transnational currency area is likely to contain such disparate economies, operating according to different business cycles, that it may be doomed to fail. A particular concern is that monetary union prevents an underperforming eurozone member from using one of the three traditional strategies for boosting growth: devaluation, reducing interest rates, and Keynesian-style deficit budgeting. For some, the chief problem with the eurozone is that monetary union was established in the absence of fiscal union, or 'fiscal federalism'. A major step to rectifying this, acknowledging that the Stability and Growth Pact has simply proved to be unenforceable, was the Fiscal Stability Treaty, or 'fiscal pact', signed by 25 EU states in March 2012. However, the fiscal pact has at least two key drawbacks. First, in substantially strengthening political union it may precipitate a backlash once populations recognize that losing 'fiscal sovereignty' is more significant than losing 'monetary sovereignty'. Second, the terms of the fiscal pact are designed to restore the confidence of financial markets, but their net effect may be to generate EU-wide austerity and make economic growth impossible to achieve.

or faltering (the UK rejected an invitation to join the EEC in 1957, and negotiated an opt-out from monetary union in 1991).

Nevertheless, although the EU has done much to realize the Treaty of Rome's goal of establishing 'an ever closer union', moving well beyond Charles de Gaulle's vision of Europe as a confederation of independent states, it stops far short of realizing the early federalists' dream of a European 'superstate'. This has been ensured, partly, by respect for the principle of subsidiarity, embodied in the TEU, and by the pragmatic approach to integration adopted by key states such as France and Germany. Decision-making within the 'New Europe' is increasingly made on the basis of multilevel governance, in which the policy process has interconnected subnational, national, intergovernmental and supranational levels, the balance between them shifting in relation to different issues and policy areas. This image of complex policy-making is more helpful than the sometimes sterile notion of a battle between national sovereignty and EU domination.

The EU in crisis?

Despite the progress it has made, the EU is confronted by a number of problems. For some, the failure of the EU has just been a matter of time. In this view, the level of diversity within the EU, in terms of history, traditions, language and culture, means that the EU can never match the capacity of the nation-state to engender loyalty and a sense of civic belonging, or to act effectively on the world stage. Tensions have been particularly intense over the long-term viability of the euro, with some arguing that the eurozone crisis since 2010 has shown that Euro-regionalism has gone too far, while others believe that it has not gone far enough. (see p. 396).

Challenges have also arisen from the process of enlargement, especially the eastward expansion of the EU during 2004–07. This saw the EU grow from an organization of 15 members to one of 27 members. In some respects, the 2004–07 enlargements were the crowning achievement of the EU, in that they underpinned – and, in a sense, completed – the politico-economic transformation of Central and Eastern Europe, marking the Europe-wide triumph of liberal democracy (see p. 270). However, progressive enlargements have created tension between the EU's 'widening' and 'deepening' agendas. As a larger number of states and interests become involved in the EU policy process, decision-making becomes more difficult and threatens to become impossible. This created pressure for the adoption of an EU Constitution but, despite the resurrection of some of the elements of the rejected Constitutional Treaty through the Treaty of Lisbon, the EU continues to face the prospect of institutional sclerosis. Finally, there is the problem of the EU's so-called 'democratic deficit'. This is usually understood to mean the EU's lack of democratic accountability, resulting from the fact that its only directly elected body, the European Parliament, remains relatively weak, despite being bolstered by the Treaty of Lisbon. This, indeed, may merely highlight a deeper deficiency in all forms of transnational governance, which is that, as the locus of policy-making becomes more remote from the people, political legitimacy is compromised, perhaps fatally.

● Subsidiarity: The principle that decisions should be taken at the lowest appropriate level.

SUMMARY

- Politics has always had a spatial, or territorial, dimension, but this became more formalized and explicit with the emergence of the idea of territorial sovereignty. However, territorial politics have been reconfigured by a shift in political decision-making to bodies both 'above' and 'below' national government, giving rise to multi-level governance and the establishment of a complex policy process in which political authority is distributed vertically and horizontally.

- The most common forms of subnational territorial organization are federal and unitary systems. Federalism is based on the notion of shared sovereignty, in which power is distributed between the central and peripheral levels of government. Unitary systems, however, vest sovereign power in a single, national institution, which allows the centre to determine the territorial organization of the state.

- Other factors affecting territorial divisions include the party system and political culture; the economic system and level of material development; the geographical size of the state; and the level of cultural, ethnic and religious diversity. There has been a tendency towards centralization in most, if not all, systems. This reflects, in particular, the fact that central government alone has the resources and strategic position to manage economic life and deliver comprehensive social welfare.

- Regionalism is a process through which geographical regions become significant political and/or economic units, serving as the basis for cooperation and, possibly, identity. Transnational regionalism takes different forms depending on whether the primary areas for cooperation are economic, security related or political. The main theories of regional integration are federalism, functionalism and neofunctionalism.

- Regional integration has been taken furthest in Europe. The product of this process, the EU, is nevertheless a very difficult political organization to categorize, having both intergovernmental and supranational features. Amongst the challenges confronting the EU are tensions between the goals of 'widening' and 'deepening', continuing anxieties about the EU's 'democratic deficit' and the crisis in the eurozone which may threaten the long-term viability of monetary union.

Questions for discussion

- Why, and to what extent, is politics linked to territory?
- Is the federal principle applicable only to certain states, or to all states?
- What are the respective merits of federalism and devolution?
- Is the tendency towards centralization in modern states resistable?
- Why has economic regionalism made more progress than security regionalism or political regionalism?
- Does regionalism have the capacity to replace nationalism?
- What is the relationship between regionalism and globalization?
- What kind of political body is the EU?
- Is the process of European integration in danger of unravelling?

Further reading

Burgess, M., *Comparative Federalism: Theory and Practice* (2006). A comprehensive and accessible introduction to the study of federalism and federations.

Denters, B. and L. E. Rose (eds), *Comparing Local Governance: Trends and Developments* (2005). A useful examination of the nature and extent of transformation of local governance, which looks across Europe as well as at New Zealand, Australia and the USA.

Fawn, R. (ed.) *Globalising the Regional, Regionalising the Global* (2009). An authoritative collection of essays that examine theoretical and thematic approaches to regionalism, including six regional case studies.

McCormick, J., *Understanding the European Union: A Concise Introduction* (5th edn) (2011). A concise, lively and readable introduction to the workings and development of the EU, and the implications of European integration.

CHAPTER 12

Democracy and Legitimacy

'Democracy is the worst form of government except all the other forms that have been tried from time to time.'

WINSTON CHURCHILL, Speech, UK House of Commons (11 November, 1947)

PREVIEW

Although states may enjoy a monopoly of coercive power, they seldom remain in existence through the exercise of force alone. As Jean-Jacques Rousseau put it, 'The strongest is never strong enough unless he turns might into right and obedience into duty'. This is why all systems of rule seek legitimacy or 'rightfulness', allowing them to demand compliance from their citizens or subjects. Legitimacy is thus the key to political stability; it is nothing less than the source of a regime's survival and success. In modern politics, debates about legitimacy are dominated by the issue of democracy, so much so that 'democratic legitimacy' is sometimes viewed as the only meaningful form of legitimacy. However, the link between legitimacy and democracy is both a relatively new idea and one that is culturally specific. Until well into the nineteenth century, the term 'democracy' continued to have pejorative implications, suggesting a form of 'mob rule'; and, in parts of the developing world, democracy promotion continues to be associated with 'westernization'. Nevertheless, there is a sense in which we are all now democrats. Liberals, conservatives, socialists, communists, anarchists and even fascists are eager to proclaim the virtues of democracy and to demonstrate their own democratic credentials. Indeed, as the major ideological systems have faltered or collapsed since the late twentieth century, the flame of democracy has appeared to burn yet more strongly. As the attractions of socialism have faded, and the merits of capitalism have been called into question, democracy has emerged as perhaps the only stable and enduring principle in the postmodern political landscape.

KEY ISSUES

- How do states maintain legitimacy?
- Are modern societies facing a crisis of legitimation?
- Why is political legitimacy so often linked to the claim to be democratic?
- What are the core features of democratic rule?
- What models of democratic rule have been advanced?
- How do democratic systems operate in practice?

CONCEPT

Legitimacy

Legitimacy (from the Latin *legitimare*, meaning 'to declare lawful') broadly means 'rightfulness'. Legitimacy therefore confers on an order or command an authoritative or binding character, thus transforming power (see p. 5) into authority (see p. 4). Political philosophers treat legitimacy as a moral or rational principle; that is, as the grounds on which governments may demand obedience from citizens. The *claim* to legitimacy is thus more important than the *fact* of obedience. Political scientists, however, usually see legitimacy in sociological terms; that is, as a willingness to comply with a system of rule regardless of how this is achieved.

LEGITIMACY AND POLITICAL STABILITY

The issue of legitimacy, the rightfulness of a regime or system of rule, is linked to the oldest and one of the most fundamental of political debates, the problem of political obligation. Why should citizens feel obliged to acknowledge the authority of government? Do they have a duty to respect the state and obey its laws? In modern political debate, however, legitimacy is usually understood less in terms of moral obligations, and more in terms of political behaviour and beliefs. In other words, it addresses not the question of why people *should* obey the state, in an abstract sense, but the question of why they *do* obey a particular state or system of rule. What are the conditions or processes that encourage them to see authority as rightful, and therefore underpin the stability of a regime? This reflects a shift from philosophy to sociology, but it also highlights the contested nature of the concept of legitimacy.

Legitimizing power

The classic contribution to the understanding of legitimacy as a sociological phenomenon was provided by Max Weber (see p. 82). Weber was concerned to categorize particular 'systems of domination', and to identify in each case the basis on which legitimacy was established. He did this by constructing three ideal types (see p. 20), or conceptual models, which he hoped would help to make sense of the highly complex nature of political rule. These ideal types amount to three kinds of authority:

- traditional authority
- charismatic authority
- legal–rational authority.

Each of these is characterized by a particular source of political legitimacy and, thus, different reasons that people may have for obeying a regime. In the process, Weber sought to understand the transformation of society itself, contrasting the systems of domination found in relatively simple traditional societies with those typically found in industrial and highly bureaucratic ones.

Weber's first type of political legitimacy is based on long-established customs and traditions (see p. 82). In effect, *traditional* authority is regarded as legitimate because it has 'always existed': it has been sanctified by history because earlier generations have accepted it. Typically, it operates according to a body of concrete rules: that is, fixed and unquestioned customs that do not need to be justified because they reflect the way things have always been. The most obvious examples of traditional authority are found amongst tribes or small groups in the form of patriarchalism (the domination of the father within the family, or the 'master' over his servants) and gerontocracy (the rule of the aged, normally reflected in the authority of village 'elders'). Traditional authority is closely linked to hereditary systems of power and privilege, as reflected, for example, in the survival of dynastic rule in Saudi Arabia, Kuwait and Morocco. Although it is of marginal significance in advanced industrial societies, the survival of monarchy, (see p. 292), albeit in a constitutional form, in the UK, Belgium, the Netherlands

Max Weber (1864–1920)

German political economist and sociologist. Following a breakdown in 1898, Weber withdrew from academic teaching, but he continued to write and research until the end of his life. He was one of the founders of modern sociology, and he championed a scientific and value-free approach to scholarship. He also highlighted the importance to social action of meaning and consciousness. Weber's interests ranged from social stratification, law, power and organization to religion. He is best known for the thesis that the Protestant ethic encourages the development of capitalism, and for his analysis of bureaucracy. Weber's most influential works include *The Protestant Ethic and the Spirit of Capitalism* (1902), *The Sociology of Religion* (1920) and *Economy and Society* (1922).

CONCEPT

Tradition

Tradition may refer to anything that is handed down or transmitted from the past to the present (long-standing customs and practices, institutions, social or political systems, values and beliefs, and so on). Tradition thus denotes continuity with the past. This continuity is usually understood to link the generations, although the line between the traditional and the merely fashionable is often indistinct. 'Traditional' societies are often contrasted with 'modern' ones, the former being structured on the basis of status (see p. 152) and by supposedly organic hierarchies, and the latter on the basis of contractual agreement and by democratic processes.

and Spain, for example, helps to shape political culture by keeping alive values such as deference, respect and duty.

Weber's second form of legitimate domination is *charismatic* authority. This form of authority is based on the power of an individual's personality; that is, on his or her 'charisma' (see p. 83). Owing nothing to a person's status, social position or office, charismatic authority operates entirely through the capacity of a leader to make a direct and personal appeal to followers as a kind of hero or saint. Although modern political leaders such as de Gaulle, Kennedy and Thatcher undoubtedly extended their authority through their personal qualities and capacity to inspire loyalty, this did not amount to charismatic legitimacy, because their authority was essentially based on the formal powers of the offices they held. Napoleon, Mussolini, Hitler (see p. 47), Ayatollah Khomeini (see p. 167), Fidel Castro and Colonel Gaddafi are more appropriate examples.

However, charismatic authority is not simply a gift or a natural propensity; systems of personal rule are invariably underpinned by 'cults of personality' (see p. 302), the undoubted purpose of which is to 'manufacture' charisma. Nevertheless, when legitimacy is constructed largely, or entirely, through the power of a leader's personality, there are usually two consequences. The first is that, as charismatic authority is not based on formal rules or procedures, it often has no limits. The leader is a Messiah, who is infallible and unquestionable; the masses become followers or disciples, who are required only to submit and obey. Second, so closely is authority linked to a specific individual, that it is difficult for a system of personal rule to outlive its founding figure. This certainly applied in the case of the regimes of Napoleon, Mussolini and Hitler.

Weber's third type of political legitimacy, *legal–rational* authority, links authority to a clearly and legally defined set of rules. In Weber's view, legal–rational authority is the typical form of authority operating in most modern states. The power of a president, prime minister or government official is determined in the final analysis by formal, constitutional rules, which constrain or limit what an office holder is able to do. The advantage of this form of authority over both traditional and charismatic authority is that, as it is attached to an office rather than a person, it is far less likely to be abused or to give rise to injustice. Legal–rational authority therefore maintains limited government and, in

CONCEPT

Charisma

Charisma was originally a theological term meaning the 'gift of grace'. This was supposedly the source of the power that Jesus exerted over his disciples. As a sociopolitical phenomenon, charisma refers to charm or personal power: the capacity to establish leadership (see p. 300) through psychological control over others. Charismatic authority therefore includes the ability to inspire loyalty, emotional dependence and even devotion. Although it is usually seen as a 'natural' capacity, all political leaders cultivate their charismatic qualities through propaganda, practised oratory and honed presentational skills.

addition, promotes efficiency through a rational division of labour. However, Weber also recognised a darker side to this type of political legitimacy. The price of greater efficiency would, he feared, be a more depersonalized and inhuman social environment typified by the relentless spread of bureaucratic forms of organization.

Although Weber's classification of types of legitimacy is still seen as relevant, it also has its limitations. One of these is that, in focusing on the legitimacy of a political regime or system of rule, it tells us little about the circumstances in which political authority is challenged as a result of unpopular policies, or a discredited leader or government. More significantly, as Beetham (1991) pointed out, to see legitimacy, as Weber did, as nothing more than a 'belief in legitimacy' is to ignore how it is brought about. This may leave the determination of legitimacy largely in the hands of the powerful, who may be able to 'manufacture' rightfulness through public-relations campaigns and the like.

Beetham suggested that power can only be said to be legitimate if three conditions are fulfilled. First, power must be exercised according to established rules, whether these are embodied in formal legal codes or in informal conventions. Second, these rules must be justified in terms of the shared beliefs of the government and the governed. Third, legitimacy must be demonstrated by an expression of consent on the part of the governed. This highlights two key features of the legitimation process. The first is the existence of elections and party competition, a system through which popular consent can be exercised (as discussed below in connection with democratic legitimacy). The second is the existence of constitutional rules that broadly reflect how people feel they should be governed.

Legitimation crises and revolutions

An alternative to the Weberian approach to legitimacy has been developed by neo-Marxist (see p. 64) theorists. While orthodox Marxists were inclined to dismiss legitimacy as bogus, seeing it as nothing more than a bourgeois myth, modern Marxists, following Gramsci (see p. 175), have acknowledged that capitalism is in part upheld by its ability to secure political support. Neo-Marxists such as Jürgen Habermas (see p. 84) and Claus Offe (1984) have therefore focused attention not merely on the class system, but also on the machinery through which legitimacy is maintained (the democratic process, party competition, welfare and social reform, and so on). Nevertheless, they have also highlighted what they see as the inherent difficulty of legitimizing a political system that is based on unequal class power. In *Legitimation Crisis* (1973), Habermas identified a series of 'crisis tendencies' within capitalist societies that make it difficult for them to maintain political stability through consent alone. At the heart of this tension, he argued, lie contradictions and conflicts between the logic of capitalist accumulation, on the one hand, and the popular pressures that democratic politics unleashes, on the other.

From this perspective, capitalist economies are seen to be bent on remorseless expansion, dictated by the pursuit of profit. However, the extension of political and social rights in an attempt to build legitimacy within such systems has stimulated countervailing pressures. In particular, the democratic process has led to escalating demands for social welfare, as well as for increased popular

Jürgen Habermas (born 1929)

German philosopher and social theorist. After growing up during the Nazi period, Habermas was politicized by the Nuremburg trials and the growing awareness after the war of the concentration and death camps. Drawn to study with Adorno (1903–69) and Horkheimer (1895–1973), he became the leading exponent of the 'second generation' of the Frankfurt School of critical theory. Habermas work ranges over epistemology, the dynamics of advanced capitalism, the nature of rationality, and the relationship between social science and philosophy. During the 1970s, he developed critical theory into what became a theory of 'communicative action'. Habermas' main works include *Towards a Rational Society* (1970), *Theory and Practice* (1974) and *The Theory of Communicative Competence* (1984, 1988).

participation and social equality. The resulting expansion of the state's responsibilities into economic and social life, and the inexorable rise of taxation and public spending, nevertheless constrain capitalist accumulation by restricting profit levels and discouraging enterprise. In Habermas' view, capitalist democracies cannot permanently satisfy both popular demands for social security and welfare rights, and the requirements of a market economy based on private profit. Forced either to resist popular pressures or to risk economic collapse, such societies would find it increasingly difficult, and eventually impossible, to maintain legitimacy. (The implications for political stability of economic and financial crises are discussed in Chapter 6.)

A very similar problem has been identified since the 1970s in the form of what is called government 'overload'. Writers such as Anthony King (1975) and Richard Rose (1980) argued that governments were finding it increasingly difficult to govern because they were subject to over-demand. This had come about both because politicians and political parties were encouraged to outbid one another in the attempt to get into power, and because pressure groups were able to besiege government with unrelenting and incompatible demands. Government's capacity to deliver was further undermined by a general drift towards corporatism (see p. 251) that created growing interdependence between government agencies and organized groups. However, whereas neo-Marxists believed that the 'crisis tendencies' identified in the 1970s were beyond the capacity of capitalist democracies to control, overload theorists tended to call for a significant shift of political and ideological priorities in the form of the abandonment of a 'big' government approach.

In many ways, the rise of the New Right since the 1980s can be seen as a response to this legitimation, or overload, crisis. Influenced by concerns about a growing **fiscal crisis of the welfare state**, the New Right attempted to challenge and displace the theories and values that had previously legitimized the progressive expansion of the state's responsibilities. In this sense, the New Right amounted to a 'hegemonic project' that tried to establish a rival set of pro-individual and pro-market values and theories. This constituted a public philosophy that extolled rugged individualism, and denigrated the 'nanny state'. The success of this project is demonstrated by the fact that socialist parties in states as differ-

● **Fiscal crisis of the welfare state**: The crisis in state finances that occurs when expanding social expenditure coincides with recession and declining tax revenues.

Focus on . . .
Why do revolutions occur?

Why do regimes collapse? Should revolutions be understood primarily in political terms, or are they more a reflection of deeper economic or social developments? Contrasting theories of revolution have been advanced by Marxists and non-Marxists. In Marxist theory, revolution emerges out of contradictions that exist at a socio-economic level. Marx (see p. 41) believed that revolution marks the point at which the class struggle develops into open conflict, leading one class to overthrow and displace another. Just as the French Revolution was interpreted as a 'bourgeois' revolution, the Russian Revolution was later seen as a 'proletarian' revolution that set in motion a process that would culminate in the establishment of socialism and, eventually, full communism. However, revolutions have not come about as Marx forecast. Not only have they tended to occur in relatively backward societies, not (as he predicted) in the advanced capitalist countries, but Marxist revolutions were often *coup d'états* rather than popular revolutions.

A variety of non-Marxist theories of revolution have been advanced. Systems theorists have argued that revolution results from 'disequilibrium' in the political system, brought about by economic, social, cultural or international changes to which the system itself is incapable of responding – the 'outputs' of government become structurally out of line with the 'inputs'. The idea of a 'revolution of rising expectations' suggests that revolutions occur when a period of economic and social development is abruptly reversed, creating a widening gap between popular expectations and the capabilities of government. The classic statement of this theory is found in Ted Gurr's *Why Men Rebel* (1970), which links rebellion to 'relative deprivation'.

The social-structural theory of revolution implies that regimes usually succumb to revolution when, through international weakness and/or domestic ineffectiveness, they lose their ability, or the political will, to maintain control through the exercise of coercive power. Theda Skocpol (1979) explained the outbreak of the French, Russian and Chinese revolutions in these terms, but they could equally be applied to the swift and largely bloodless collapse of the Eastern European communist regimes in the autumn and winter of 1989 (see p. 44).

● **Revolution:** A popular uprising, involving extra-legal mass action, which brings about fundamental change (a change in the political system itself) as opposed to merely a change of policy or governing elite.

● **Reform:** Change brought about within a system, usually by peaceful and incremental measures; reform implies improvement.

ent as the UK, France, Spain, Australia and New Zealand have accommodated themselves to broadly similar goals and values. As this happened, a political culture that once emphasized social justice, welfare rights and public responsibilities gave way to one in which choice, enterprise, competition and individual responsibility are given prominence.

However, legitimation crises may have more dramatic consequences. When faltering support for a regime can no longer be managed by adjustments in public policy or a change in leadership, legitimacy may collapse altogether, leading either to a resort to repression, or to revolution. While evolutionary change is usually thought of as reform, revolution involves root-and-branch change. Revolutions recast the political order entirely, typically bringing about an abrupt and often violent break with the past. Although there is considerable debate about the causes of revolution, there is little doubt that revolution has played a crucial role in shaping the modern world. The American Revolution (1776) led to the creation of a constitutional republic independent from Britain and gave practical expression to the principle of representation. The French Revolution (1789) set out to destroy the old order under the banner of 'liberty, equality and fraternity', advancing democratic ideals and sparking an 'age of revolution' in early nineteenth-century Europe. The Russian Revolution (1917), the first 'communist' revolution, provided a model for subsequent twentieth-century revolutions, including the Chinese Revolution (1949), the Cuban Revolution (1959), the Vietnamese Revolution (1975) and the Nicaraguan Revolution (1979). The Eastern European Revolutions (1989-91) and the rebellions of the Arab Spring (2011) (see p. 88) nevertheless re-established the link between revolution and the pursuit of political democracy.

Democratic legitimacy

Modern discussions about legitimacy are dominated by its relationship to democracy, so much so that democratic legitimacy is now widely accepted as the only meaningful form of legitimacy. The claim that a political organization is legitimate is therefore intrinsically linked to its claim to be democratic. The next main section examines competing models of democratic rule and debates how democracy operates in practice, but this section considers the nature of the link between democracy and legitimacy. Democracy can be seen to promote legitimacy in at least three ways. In the first place, it does so through consent. Although citizens do not explicitly give their consent to be governed, thereby investing political authority with a formal 'right to rule', they do so implicitly each time they participate in the political process. In this respect, democracy underpins legitimacy by expanding the opportunities for political participation, most importantly though the act of voting, but also through activities such as joining a political party or interest group or by engaging in protests or demonstrations. Political participation, in this sense, binds government and the people, encouraging the latter to view the rules of the political game as rightful and so to accept that they have an obligation to respect and obey those in authority.

Second, the essence of democratic governance is a process of compromise, conciliation and negotiation, through which rival interests and groups find a way of living together in relative peace, rather than resorting to force and the use of naked power. The mechanisms through which this non-violent conflict resolution takes place, notably elections, assembly debates, party competition and so forth, thus tend to enjoy broad popular support as they ensure that power is widely dispersed, each group having a political voice of some kind or other. Third, democracy operates as a feedback system that tends towards long-term political stability, as it brings the 'outputs' of government into line with the 'inputs' or pressures placed upon it. As democracy provides a mechanism through which governments can be removed and public policy changed, it tends to keep 'disequilibrium' in the political system to a minimum, enabling legitimation crises to be managed effectively and substantially undermining the potential for civil strife, rebellion or revolution.

Nevertheless, the notion of an intrinsic link between legitimacy and democracy has also been questioned. Some, for example, argue that the high levels of political stability and low incidence of civic strife and popular rebellion in democratic societies can be explained more persuasively by factors other than democracy. These include the fact that, having in the main advanced capitalist economies, democratic societies tend to enjoy widespread prosperity and are effective in 'delivering the goods'. Democratic legitimacy

● **Consent**: Assent or permission; in politics, usually an agreement to be governed or ruled.

Trust

Trust means faith, a reliance on, or confidence in, the honesty, worth and reliability of another person. It is therefore based on expectations of others' future actions. Political trust consists in the level of confidence people have in one another in discharging their civic responsibilities and, crucially, the confidence citizens have that politicians generally, and leaders in particular, will keep their promises and carry out their public duties honestly and fairly. In liberal theory, trust arises through voluntary contracts that we uphold through mutual self-interest. In communitarian theory, trust is grounded in a sense of social duty and a common morality.

may therefore be less significant than 'capitalist legitimacy'. A further factor is that democratic societies tend to be liberal as well as democratic, liberal democracy (see p. 270) being the dominant form of democracy worldwide. Liberal societies offer wide opportunities for personal freedom, self-expression and social mobility, and these may be as important, or perhaps more important, in maintaining legitimacy than the opportunities that democracy offers for political participation.

Even if democracy is accepted as the principal mechanism through which legitimacy is promoted, there are reasons for thinking that its effectiveness in this respect may be faltering. In particular, mature democratic societies appear to be afflicted by growing political disenchantment or disaffection. This has been most evident in declining electoral turnouts and in the falling membership of mainstream political parties. For some, this 'democratic malaise' is a product of the tendency within democratic systems for politicians to seek power by promising more than they can deliver, thereby creating an expectations gap. As this gap widens, trust in politicians declines and healthy scepticism about the political process threatens to turn into corrosive cynicism. The issue of political disenchantment is examined in greater detail.

Non-democratic legitimacy?

If democracy is taken to be the only genuine basis for legitimacy, this implies that non-democratic regimes are, by their nature, illegitimate. Nevertheless, some authoritarian regimes survive for many decades with relatively little evidence of mass political disaffection, still less concerted opposition. Clearly, this can very largely be explained through the use of coercion and repression, fear rather than consent being the principal means through which citizens are encouraged to obey the state. However, non-democratic regimes rarely seek to consolidate their hold on power through coercion alone. They typically adopt a two-pronged approach in which political control is exercised alongside claims to legitimacy. But, in the absence of democracy, what means of legitimation are available to such regimes?

Three key forms of non-democratic legitimation have been used. First, elections, albeit one-party, sometimes non-competitive or 'rigged' elections, have been used to give a regime a democratic façade, helping both to create the impression of popular support and to draw people into a ritualized acceptance of the regime. This legitimation device was used in Nazi Germany and Fascist Italy, and has also been used African one-party states and communist regimes. Second, non-democratic regimes have sought performance legitimation based on their ability to deliver, amongst other things, rising living standards, public order, improved education and health care, and so forth. Communist regimes thus emphasize the delivery of a package of socio-economic benefits to their citizens, a strategy that continues to be practised by China through its ability to generate high levels of economic growth.

Third, ideological legitimation has been used, either in an attempt to uphold the leader's, military's or party's right to rule, or to establish broader goals and principles that invest the larger regime with a sense of rightfulness. Examples of the former include Gamal Abdel Nasser's portrayal of the Egyptian military as the 'vanguard of the revolution' after its 1952 *coup*, and Colonel Gaddafi's proclama-

POLITICS IN ACTION . . .

The Arab Spring: democracy comes to the Arab world?

Events: The 'Arab Spring' (also known as the 'Arab revolutions' or the 'Arabic rebellions') was a revolutionary wave of demonstrations and protests that swept through North Africa and parts of the Middle East during 2011, toppling four dictators. The process was initiated by Tunisia's 'Jasmine' revolution, in which a growing wave of anti-government rallies in early January turned into a nationwide revolt due to incidents of police repression. On 14 January, President Ben Ali fled the country, bringing an end to his 23-year rule. Inspired by events in Tunisia, Egyptian demonstrators took to the streets on January 25, calling for the removal of President Hosni Mubarak; Tahrir Square, in Cairo, becoming the centre of protests. Under growing pressure from the Egyptian military and after 18 days of protests, Mubarak resigned on 11 February. In Libya, the 42-year rule of President Muammar Gaddafi was brought to an end by an eight-month civil war, in which rebel forces were supported by NATO aerial attacks, thanks to a no-fly zone imposed by the UN Security Council. Gaddafi's death on October 22 signalled the final collapse of his regime. Other significant popular uprisings in the Arab world occurred in Yemen (where President Saleh was forced from power in November 2011), in Syria (against President Assad) and in Bahrain.

Significance: There are significant debates about both the causes and consequences of the Arab Spring. Why did the uprisings occur? Clearly, as with the 1989 East European Revolutions, demonstrators were inspired, inflamed or emboldened by developments elsewhere, creating a chain reaction of protest, in this case often facilitated by the internet and social networking sites such as Facebook. The underlying factors were nevertheless common to much of the Arab world: poor living standards, widening inequality, rampant unemployment (particularly affecting the young), police violence and a lack of human rights. Ethnic and religious tensions were also significant in countries such as Syria, Libya and Bahrain. Nevertheless, such circumstances did not always translate into successful revolutions, or even, as in cases such as Sudan and Saudi Arabia, popular uprisings. Where these revolutions succeeded, three factors were significant. A broad section of the population, spanning ethnic and religious groups, and socio-economic classes, were mobilized; the loyalty of key elites, and especially in the military, started to fracture; and international powers either refused to defend embattled governments or gave moral and, in the case of Libya, military support to opponents of the regime.

What kind of political change will the Arab Spring bring about? Three possibilities offer themselves. The first is a transition to democratic rule, giving the lie to the view that, being mired in 'backward' cultural and religious beliefs, the Arab world is not ready for democracy. Certainly, the key demands of protestors were for the introduction of western-style democratic reforms, notably free and competitive elections, the rule of law and protections for civil liberties. Moreover, where regimes collapsed, this was invariably accompanied by the promise to hold free elections, as duly occurred during 2011 in Tunisia in October and in Egypt in November–December. The second possibility is that the hope for a smooth transition to stable democracy will be disappointed as some kind of recast authoritarianism emerges once the post-revolutionary honeymoon period ends. This scenario is supported by the crucial role still played by the military, especially in Egypt, and by the likelihood that, as divisions start to surface within the former-opposition, a perhaps lengthy period of political instability and policy reversals may develop. The third possibility is that, although the revolutions were strongest in the relatively secular Arab republics of North Africa, the long-term beneficiaries of the Arab Spring will be Islamist radicals, who initially appeared to play a marginal role. Not only are Islamist groups, such as the Muslim Brotherhood, generally better organized than their rivals, but post-revolutionary chaos and uncertainty offer fertile ground for advancing the politics of religious regeneration.

tion of a 'Green revolution' after seizing power in Libya in 1969. Examples of the latter include the emphasis on Marxism-Leninism in communist states and the use of Wahhabism to support monarchical rule in Saudi Arabia. However, when such strategies fail, all semblance of legitimation evaporates and non-democratic regimes are forced either to resort to progressively more draconian means of survival, or else they collapse in the face of popular uprisings. This can be seen in the case of the so-called 'Arab Spring' of 2011.

DEMOCRACY

Understanding democracy

Debates about democracy extend well beyond its relationship to legitimacy. These stem, most basically, from confusion over the nature of democracy. The origins of the term 'democracy' can be traced back to Ancient Greece. Like other words ending in 'cracy' (for example, autocracy, aristocracy and bureaucracy), democracy is derived from the Greek word *kratos*, meaning power, or rule. Democracy thus means 'rule by the *demos*' (the *demos* referring to 'the people', although the Greeks originally used this to mean 'the poor' or 'the many'). However, the simple notion of 'rule by the people' does not get us very far. The problem with democracy has been its very popularity, a popularity that has threatened the term's undoing as a meaningful political concept. In being almost universally regarded as a 'good thing', democracy has come to be used as little more than a 'hurrah! word', implying approval of a particular set of ideas or system of rule. In Bernard Crick's (1993) words, 'democracy is perhaps the most promiscuous word in the world of public affairs'. A term that can mean anything to anyone is in danger of meaning nothing at all. Amongst the meanings that have been attached to the word 'democracy' are the following:

- a system of rule by the poor and disadvantaged
- a form of government in which the people rule themselves directly and continuously, without the need for professional politicians or public officials
- a society based on equal opportunity and individual merit, rather than hierarchy and privilege
- a system of welfare and redistribution aimed at narrowing social inequalities
- a system of decision-making based on the principle of majority rule
- a system of rule that secures the rights and interests of minorities by placing checks upon the power of the majority
- a means of filling public offices through a competitive struggle for the popular vote
- a system of government that serves the interests of the people regardless of their participation in political life.

Perhaps a more helpful starting point from which to consider the nature of democracy is Abraham Lincoln's Gettysburg Address (1863). Lincoln extolled the virtues of what he called 'government of the people, by the people, and for

Political equality

Political equality means, broadly, an equal distribution of political power and influence. Political equality can thus be thought of as the core principle of democracy, in that it ensures that, however 'the people' is defined, each individual member carries the same weight: all voices are equally loud. This can be understood in two ways. In liberal-democratic theory, political equality implies an equal distribution of political rights: the right to vote, the right to stand for election and so on. In contrast, socialists, amongst others, link political influence to factors such as the control of economic resources and access to the means of mass communication.

● **Majority rule**: The rule that the will of the majority, or numerically strongest, overrides the will of the minority, implying that the latter should accept the views of the former.

● **Cosmopolitan democracy**: A form of democracy that operates at supranational levels of governance and is based on the idea of transnational or global citizenship.

the people'. What this makes clear is that democracy links government to the people, but that this link can be forged in a number of ways: government *of*, *by* and *for* the people. This section explores the implications of these links by considering three questions. Who are the people? In what sense should the people rule? And how far should popular rule extend?

Who are the people?

One of the core features of democracy is the principle of political equality, the notion that political power should be distributed as widely and as evenly as possible. However, within what body or group should this power be distributed? In short, who constitutes 'the people'? On the face of it, the answer is simple: 'the *demos*', or 'the people', surely refers to *all* the people; that is, the entire population of the country. In practice, however, every democratic system has restricted political participation, sometimes severely.

As noted, early Greek writers usually used *demos* to refer to 'the many': that is, the disadvantaged and usually propertyless masses. Democracy therefore implied not political equality, but a bias towards the poor. In Greek city-states, political participation was restricted to a tiny proportion of the population, male citizens over the age of 20, thereby excluding all women, slaves and foreigners. Strict restrictions on voting also existed in most western states until well into the twentieth century, usually in the form of a property qualification or the exclusion of women. Universal suffrage was not established in the UK until 1928, when women gained full voting rights. In the USA, it was not achieved until the early 1960s, when African-American people in many Southern states were able to vote for the first time, and in Switzerland universal suffrage was established in 1971 when women were eventually enfranchised. Nevertheless, an important restriction continues to be practised in all democratic systems in the form of the exclusion of children from political participation, although the age of majority ranges from 21 down to as low as 15 (as in Iranian presidential elections up to 2007). Technical restrictions are also often placed on, for example, the certifiably insane and imprisoned criminals.

Although 'the people' is now accepted as meaning virtually all adult citizens, the term can be construed in a number of different ways. The people, for instance, can be viewed as a single, cohesive body, bound together by a common or collective interest: in this sense, the people are one and indivisible. Such a view tends to generate a model of democracy that, like Rousseau's (see p. 97) theory, examined in the next main section, focuses upon the 'general will' or collective will, rather than the 'private will' of each individual. Alternatively, as division and disagreement exist within all communities, 'the people' may in practice be taken to mean 'the majority'. In this case, democracy comes to mean the strict application of the principle of majority rule. This can, nevertheless, mean that democracy degenerates into the 'tyranny of the majority'. Finally, there is the issue of the body of people within which democratic politics should operate. Where should be the location or 'site' of democracy? Although, thanks to the potency of political nationalism, the definition 'the people' is usually understood in national terms, the ideas of local democracy and, in the light of globalization (see p. 142), cosmopolitan democracy (discussed in the final section of the chapter) have also been advanced.

How should the people rule?

Most conceptions of democracy are based on the principle of 'government *by* the people'. This implies that, in effect, people govern themselves – that they participate in making the crucial decisions that structure their lives and determine the fate of their society. This participation can take a number of forms, however. In the case of direct democracy, popular participation entails direct and continuous involvement in decision-making, through devices such as referendums (see p. 201), mass meetings, or even interactive television. The alternative and more common form of democratic participation is the act of voting, which is the central feature of what is usually called 'representative democracy'. When citizens vote, they do not so much make the decisions that structure their own lives as choose who will make those decisions on their behalf. What gives voting its democratic character, however, is that, provided that the election is competitive, it empowers the public to 'kick the rascals out', and it thus makes politicians publicly accountable.

There are also models of democracy that are built on the principle of 'government *for* the people', and that allow little scope for public participation of any kind, direct or indirect. The most grotesque example of this was found in the so-called 'totalitarian democracies' that developed under fascist dictators such as Mussolini and Hitler. The democratic credentials of such regimes were based on the claim that the 'leader', and the leader alone, articulated the genuine interests of the people, thus implying that a 'true' democracy can be equated with an absolute dictatorship. In such cases, popular rule meant nothing more than ritualized submission to the will of an all-powerful leader, orchestrated through rallies, marches and demonstrations. This was sometimes portrayed as plebiscitary democracy. Although totalitarian democracies have proved to be a travesty of the conventional notion of democratic rule, they demonstrate the tension that can exist between 'government *by* the people' (or popular participation), and 'government *for* the people' (rule in the public interest). Advocates of representative democracy, for example, have wished to confine popular participation in politics to the act of voting, precisely because they fear that the general public lack the wisdom, education and experience to rule wisely on their own behalf.

How far should popular rule extend?

Now that we have decided who 'the people' are, and how they should rule, it is necessary to consider how far their rule should extend. What is the proper realm of democracy? What issues is it right for the people to decide, and what should be left to individual citizens? In many respects, such questions reopen the debate about the proper relationship between the public realm and the private realm that was discussed in Chapter 1. Models of democracy that have been constructed on the basis of liberal individualism have usually proposed that democracy be restricted to political life, with politics being narrowly defined. From this perspective, the purpose of democracy is to establish, through some process of popular participation, a framework of laws within which individuals can conduct their own affairs and pursue their private interests. Democratic solutions, then, are appropriate only for matters that specifically relate to the

● **Totalitarian democracy:** An absolute dictatorship that masquerades as a democracy, typically based on the leader's claim to a monopoly of ideological wisdom.

Focus on . . .

Direct democracy or representative democracy?

Direct democracy (sometimes 'classical', 'participatory', or 'radical' democracy) is based on the direct, unmediated and continuous participation of citizens in the tasks of government. Direct democracy thus obliterates the distinction between government and the governed, and between the state and civil society; it is a system of popular self-government. It was achieved in ancient Athens through a form of government by mass meeting; its most common modern manifestation is the use of the referendum (see p. 201). The merits of direct democracy include the following:

- It heightens the control that citizens can exercise over their own destinies, as it is the only pure form of democracy.
- It creates a better-informed and more politically sophisticated citizenry, and thus it has educational benefits.
- It enables the public to express their own views and interests without having to rely on self-serving politicians.
- It ensures that rule is legitimate, in the sense that people are more likely to accept decisions that they have made themselves.

Representative democracy is a limited and indirect form of democracy. It is limited in that popular participation in government is infrequent and brief, being restricted to the act of voting every few years. It is indirect in that the public do not exercise power themselves; they merely select those who will rule on their behalf. This form of rule is democratic only insofar as representation (see p. 197) establishes a reliable and effective link between the government and the governed. This is sometimes expressed in the notion of an electoral mandate (see p. 200). The strengths of representative democracy include the following:

- It offers a practicable form of democracy (direct popular participation is achievable only in small communities).
- It relieves ordinary citizens of the burden of decision-making, thus making possible a division of labour in politics.
- It allows government to be placed in the hands of those with better education, expert knowledge and greater experience.
- It maintains stability by distancing ordinary citizens from politics, thereby encouraging them to accept compromise.

---

community; used in other circumstances, democracy amounts to an infringement of liberty. Not uncommonly, this fear of democracy is most acute in the case of direct or participatory democracy.

However, an alternative view of democracy is often developed by, for example, socialists and radical democrats. In **radical democracy**, democracy is seen not as a means of laying down a framework within which individuals can go about their own business but, rather, as a general principle that is applicable to all areas of social existence. People are seen as having a basic right to participate in the making of *any* decisions that affect their lives, with democracy simply being the collective process through which this is done. This position is evident in socialist demands for the collectivization of wealth and the introduction of workers' self-management, both of which are seen as ways of democratizing economic life. Instead of endorsing mere political democracy, socialists have therefore called for 'social democracy' or 'economic democracy'. Feminists, similarly, have demanded the democratization of family life, understood as the right of all to

● **Radical democracy:** A form of democracy that favours decentralization and participation, the widest possible dispersal of political power.

● **Economic democracy:** A broad term that covers attempts to apply democratic principles to the workplace, ranging from profit-sharing and the use of workers' councils to full workers' self-management.

CONCEPT

Plebiscitary democracy

Plebiscitary democracy is a form of democratic rule that operates through an unmediated link between the rulers and the ruled, established by plebiscites (or referendums). These allow the public to express their views on political issues directly. However, this type of democracy is often criticized because of the scope it offers for demagoguery (rule by political leaders who manipulate the masses through oratory, and appeal to their prejudices and passions). This type of democracy may amount to little more than a system of mass acclamation that gives dictatorship a populist (see p. 307) gloss.

participate in the making of decisions in the domestic or private sphere. From this perspective, democracy is regarded as a friend of liberty, not as its enemy. Only when such principles are ignored can oppression and exploitation flourish.

Models of democracy

All too frequently, democracy is treated as a single, unambiguous phenomenon. It is often assumed that what passes for democracy in most western societies (a system of regular and competitive elections based on a universal franchise) is the only, or the only legitimate, form of democracy. Sometimes this notion of democracy is qualified by the addition of the term 'liberal', turning it into liberal democracy. In reality, however, there are a number of rival theories or models of democracy, each offering its own version of popular rule. This highlights not merely the variety of democratic forms and mechanisms, but also, more fundamentally, the very different grounds on which democratic rule can be justified. Even liberal democracy is a misleading term, as competing liberal views of democratic organization can be identified. Four contrasting models of democracy can be identified as follows:

- classical democracy
- protective democracy
- developmental democracy
- people's democracy.

Classical democracy

The classical model of democracy is based on the *polis*, or city-state, of Ancient Greece, and particularly on the system of rule that developed in the largest and most powerful Greek city-state, Athens. The form of direct democracy that operated in Athens during the fourth and fifth centuries BCE is often portrayed as the only pure or ideal system of popular participation. Nevertheless, although the model had considerable impact on later thinkers such as Rousseau and Marx (see p. 41), Athenian democracy (see p. 95) developed a very particular kind of direct popular rule, one that has only a very limited application in the modern world. Athenian democracy amounted to a form of government by mass meeting.

What made Athenian democracy so remarkable was the level of political activity of its citizens. Not only did they participate in regular meetings of the Assembly, but they were also, in large numbers, prepared to shoulder the responsibility of public office and decision-making. The most influential contemporaneous critic of this form of democracy was the philosopher Plato (see p. 13). Plato attacked the principle of political equality on the grounds that the mass of the people possess neither the wisdom nor the experience to rule wisely on their own behalf. His solution, advanced in *The Republic*, was that government be placed in the hands of a class of philosopher kings, Guardians, whose rule would amount to a kind of enlightened dictatorship. On a practical level, however, the principal drawback of Athenian democracy was that it could operate only by excluding the mass of the population from political activity. Participation was restricted to Athenian-born males who were over 20 years of age. Slaves (the majority of the population), women and foreigners had no political rights

Debating...
Is democracy always the best form of government?

In modern politics, democracy has come to be so widely accepted that it appears to be almost politically incorrect to question it. The 'right' solution to a political problem is thus the democratic solution; that is, one made either by the people themselves or, more commonly, by politicians who are accountable to the people. But why is democracy so widely revered? And are there circumstances in which democratic rule is inappropriate or undesirable?

YES	NO

The highest form of politics. The unique strength of democracy is that it is able to address the central challenge of politics – the existence of rival views and interests within the same society – while containing the tendency towards bloodshed and violence. In short, democratic societies are stable and peaceful. This occurs because democracy relies on open debate, persuasion and compromise. People with rival views or competing interests are encouraged to find a way of living together in relative harmony because each has a political voice. Democracy is therefore a kind of political safety valve, democratic participation preventing the build up of anger and frustration and, thereby, containing political extremism.

Democracy as a universal value. It is now widely argued that democracy is a human right: a fundamental and absolute right that belongs to all people, regardless of nationality, religion, gender and other differences. Rights of political participation and access to power, especially the right to vote, are universally applicable because they stem from the basic entitlement to shape the decisions that affect one's own life – the right to self-rule. Indeed, an equal access to power and the right to political participation could be viewed not simply as virtues in their own right, but as preconditions for the maintenance of all other rights and freedoms.

Keeping tyranny at bay. All systems of rule are apt to become tyrannies against the people, reflecting the fact that those in power (and, for that matter, all people) are inclined to place self-interest before the interests of others. Governments and leaders therefore need to be checked or constrained, and there is no more effective constraint on power than democracy. This is because democratic rule operates through a mechanism of accountability, which ultimately allows the public to 'kick the rascals out'. Democratic societies are therefore not only the most stable societies in the world, but also the societies in which citizens enjoy the widest realm of freedom.

The disharmony of democracy. Far from being a guarantee of stability, democracy is biased in favour of conflict and disharmony. This is because democracy sets up an ongoing electoral battle between opponents who are encouraged to condemn one another, exaggerating their faults and denying their achievements. Democratic politics is often, as a result, noisy and unedifying. While the disharmony of democracy is unlikely to threaten structural breakdown in mature and relatively prosperous societies, democracy in the developing world may make things worse rather than better (Hawksley, 2009). 'Democratization' may therefore deepen tribal, regional or ethnic tensions, and strengthen the tendency towards charismatic leadership, thereby breeding authoritarianism.

Democracy as westernization. Rather than being universally applicable, democracy is based on values and assumptions that betray the cultural biases of its western heartland. Democracy is rooted in ideas such as individualism, notably through the principle of equal citizenship and 'one person, one vote', and notions of pluralism and competition that are intrinsically liberal in character. The dominant form of democracy is therefore western-style democracy, and its spread, sometimes imposed and always encouraged, to the non-western world can therefore be viewed as a form of cultural imperialism.

Good government not popular government. Democratic solutions to problems are often neither wise nor sensible. The problem with democracy is that the dictates of wisdom and experience tend to be ignored because the views of the well-educated minority are swamped by those of the less well-educated majority. Being committed to the principle of political equality, democracy cannot cope with the fact that the majority is not always right. This is a particular concern for economic policy, where options, such as raising taxes or cutting government spending, which may best promote long-term economic development, may be ruled out simply because they are unpopular.

CONCEPT

Athenian democracy

Athenian democracy is characterized by the high level of citizen involvement in the affairs of the city-state. Major decisions were made by the Assembly, or *Ecclesia*, to which all citizens belonged. When full-time public officials were needed, they were chosen on a basis of lot or rota to ensure that they constituted a microcosm of the larger citizenry. A Council, consisting of 500 citizens, acted as the executive or steering committee of the Assembly, and a 50-strong Committee, in turn, made proposals to the Council. The President of the Committee held office for only a single day, and no Athenian could hold this honour more than once in his lifetime.

● **Natural rights**: God-given rights that are fundamental to human beings and are therefore inalienable (they cannot be taken away).

whatsoever. Indeed, Athenian citizens were able to devote so much of their lives to politics only because slavery relieved them of the need to engage in arduous labour, and the confinement of women to the private realm freed men from domestic responsibilities. Nevertheless, the classical model of direct and continuous popular participation in political life has been kept alive in, for instance, the township meetings of New England in the USA, the communal assemblies that operate in the smaller Swiss cantons and in the wider use of referendums.

Protective democracy

When democratic ideas were revived in the seventeenth and eighteenth centuries, they appeared in a form that was very different from the classical democracy of Ancient Greece. In particular, democracy was seen less as a mechanism through which the public could participate in political life, and more as a device through which citizens could protect themselves from the encroachments of government, hence 'protective democracy'. This view appealed particularly to early liberal thinkers whose concern was, above all, to create the widest realm of individual liberty. The desire to protect the individual from over-mighty government was expressed in perhaps the earliest of all democratic sentiments, Aristotle's response to Plato: 'who will guard the Guardians?'.

This same concern with unchecked power was taken up in the seventeenth century by John Locke (see p. 31), who argued that the right to vote was based on the existence of natural rights and, in particular, on the right to property. If government, through taxation, possessed the power to expropriate property, citizens were entitled to protect themselves by controlling the composition of the tax-setting body: the legislature. In other words, democracy came to mean a system of 'government by consent' operating through a representative assembly. However, Locke himself was not a democrat by modern standards, as he believed that only property owners should vote, on the basis that only they had natural rights that could be infringed by government. The more radical notion of universal suffrage was advanced from the late eighteenth century onwards by utilitarian theorists such as Jeremy Bentham and James Mill (1773–1836). The utilitarian (see p. 353) case for democracy is also based on the need to protect or advance individual interests. Bentham came to believe that, since all individuals seek pleasure and the avoidance of pain, a universal franchise (conceived in his day as manhood suffrage) was the only way of promoting 'the greatest happiness for the greatest number'.

However, to justify democracy on protective grounds is to provide only a qualified endorsement of democratic rule. In short, protective democracy is but a limited and indirect form of democracy. In practice, the consent of the governed is exercised through voting in regular and competitive elections. This thereby ensures the accountability of those who govern. Political equality is thus understood in strictly technical terms to mean equal voting rights. Moreover, this is, above all, a system of constitutional democracy that operates within a set of formal or informal rules that check the exercise of government power. If the right to vote is a means of defending individual liberty, liberty must also be guaranteed by a strictly enforced separation of powers via the creation of a separate executive, legislature and judiciary, and by the maintenance of basic rights and freedoms, such as freedom of expression, freedom of movement, and freedom

Jeremy Bentham (1748–1832)

UK philosopher, legal reformer and founder of utilitarianism. Bentham developed a moral and philosophical system that was based on the idea that human beings are rationally self-interested creatures or utility maximizers, which he believed provided a scientific basis for legal and political reforms. Using the 'greatest happiness' principle, his followers, the Philosophic Radicals, were responsible for many of the reforms in social administration, law, government and economics in the UK in the nineteenth century. A supporter of *laissez-faire* economics, in later life Bentham also became a firm advocate of political democracy. His utilitarian creed was developed in *Fragments on Government* ([1776] 1948), and more fully in *Principles of Morals and Legislation* (1789).

from arbitrary arrest. Ultimately, protective democracy aims to give citizens the widest possible scope to live their lives as they choose. It is therefore compatible with *laissez-faire* capitalism (see p. 132) and the belief that individuals should be entirely responsible for their economic and social circumstances. Protective democracy has therefore particularly appealed to classical liberals and, in modern politics, to supporters of the New Right.

Developmental democracy

Although early democratic theory focused on the need to protect individual rights and interests, it soon developed an alternative focus: a concern with the development of the human individual and the community. This gave rise to quite new models of democratic rule that can broadly be referred to as systems of developmental democracy. The most novel, and radical, such model was developed by Jean-Jacques Rousseau. In many respects, Rousseau's ideas mark a departure from the dominant, liberal conception of democracy, and they came to have an impact on the Marxist and anarchist traditions as well as, later, on the New Left. For Rousseau, democracy was ultimately a means through which human beings could achieve freedom (see p. 339) or autonomy, in the sense of 'obedience to a law one prescribes to oneself'. In other words, citizens are 'free' only when they participate directly and continuously in shaping the life of their community. This is an idea that moves well beyond the conventional notion of electoral democracy and offers support for the more radical ideal of direct democracy. Indeed, Rousseau was a strenuous critic of the practice of elections used in England, arguing in *The Social Contract* ([1762] 1913) as follows:

> The English people believes itself to be free, it is gravely mistaken; it is only free when it elects its member of parliament; as soon as they are elected, the people are enslaved; it is nothing. In the brief moment of its freedom, the English people makes such use of its freedom that it deserves to lose it.

● **General will**: The genuine interests of a collective body, equivalent to the common good; the will of all, provided each person acts selflessly.

However, what gives Rousseau's model its novel character is his insistence that freedom ultimately means obedience to the **general will**. Rousseau believed the

Jean-Jacques Rousseau (1712–78)

Geneva-born French moral and political philosopher, perhaps the principal intellectual influence upon the French Revolution. Rousseau was entirely self-taught. He moved to Paris in 1742, and became an intimate of leading members of the French Enlightenment, especially Diderot. His writings, ranging over education, the arts, science, literature and philosophy, reflect a deep belief in the goodness of 'natural man' and the corruption of 'social man'. Rousseau's political teaching, summarized in *Émile* (1762) and developed in *The Social Contract* ([1762] 1913), advocates a radical form of democracy that has influenced liberal, socialist, anarchist and, some would argue, fascist thought. His autobiography, *Confessions* (1770), examines his life with remarkable candour and demonstrates a willingness to expose weaknesses.

general will to be the 'true' will of each citizen, in contrast to his or her 'private' or selfish will. By obeying the general will, citizens are therefore doing nothing more than obeying their own 'true' natures, the general will being what individuals would will if they were to act selflessly. In Rousseau's view, such a system of radical developmental democracy required not merely political equality, but a relatively high level of economic equality. Although not a supporter of common ownership, Rousseau nevertheless proposed that 'no citizen shall be rich enough to buy another and none so poor as to be forced to sell himself' ([1762] 1913).

Rousseau's theories have helped to shape the modern idea of participatory democracy taken up by New Left thinkers in the 1960s and 1970s. This extols the virtues of a 'participatory society', a society in which each and every citizen is able to achieve self-development by participating in the decisions that shape his or her life. This goal can be achieved only through the promotion of openness, **accountability** and decentralization within all the key institutions of society: within the family, the workplace and the local community just as much as within 'political' institutions such as parties, interest groups and legislative bodies. At the heart of this model is the notion of 'grass-roots democracy'; that is, the belief that political power should be exercised at the lowest possible level. Nevertheless, Rousseau's own theories have been criticized for distinguishing between citizens' 'true' wills and their 'felt' or subjective wills. The danger of this is that, if the general will cannot be established by simply asking citizens what they want (because they may be blinded by selfishness), there is scope for the general will to be defined from above, perhaps by a dictator claiming to act in the 'true' interests of society. Rousseau is therefore sometimes seen as the architect of so-called 'totalitarian democracy' (Talmon, 1952).

However, a more modest form of developmental democracy has also been advanced that is compatible with the liberal model of representative government. This view of developmental democracy is rooted in the writings of John Stuart Mill (see p. 198). For Mill, the central virtue of democracy was that it promotes the 'highest and harmonious' development of individual capacities. By participating in political life, citizens enhance their understanding, strengthen their sensibilities and achieve a higher level of personal development. In short, democracy is essentially an educational experience. As a result, Mill proposed the

● **Accountability**: Answerability; a duty to explain one's conduct and be open to criticism by others.

CONCEPT

Parliamentary democracy

Parliamentary democracy is a form of democratic rule that operates through a popularly elected deliberative assembly, which mediates between government and the people. Democracy, in this sense, means responsible and representative government. Parliamentary democracy thus balances popular participation against elite rule: government is accountable not directly to the public but to the public's elected representatives. The alleged strength of such a system is that representatives are, by virtue of their education and experience, better able than citizens themselves to define their best interests.

● Deliberative democracy: A form of democracy that emphasizes the need for discourse and debate to help to define the public interest.

broadening of popular participation, arguing that the franchise should be extended to all but those who are illiterate. In the process, he suggested (radically, for his time) that suffrage should also be extended to women. In addition, he advocated strong and independent local authorities in the belief that this would broaden the opportunities available for holding public office.

On the other hand, Mill, in common with all liberals, was also aware of the dangers of democracy. Indeed, Mill's views are out of step with mainstream liberal thought in that he rejected the idea of formal political equality. Following Plato, Mill did not believe that all political opinions are of equal value. Consequently, he proposed a system of plural voting: unskilled workers would have a single vote, skilled workers two votes, and graduates and members of the learned professions five or six votes. However, his principal reservation about democracy was derived from the more typical liberal fear of what Alexis de Tocqueville (see p. 245) famously described as 'the tyranny of the majority'. In other words, democracy always contains the threat that individual liberty and minority rights may be crushed in the name of the people. Mill's particular concern was that democracy would undermine debate, criticism and intellectual life in general by encouraging people to accept the will of the majority, thereby promoting uniformity and dull conformism. Quite simply, the majority is not always right; wisdom cannot be determined by the simple device of a show of hands. Mill's ideas therefore support the idea of deliberative democracy or parliamentary democracy.

People's democracy

The term 'people's democracy' is derived from the orthodox communist regimes that sprang up on the Soviet model in the aftermath of World War II. It is here used, however, to refer broadly to the various democratic models that the Marxist tradition has generated. Although they differ, these models offer a clear contrast to the more familiar liberal democratic ones. Marxists have tended to be dismissive of liberal or parliamentary democracy, seeing it as a form of 'bourgeois' or 'capitalist' democracy. Nevertheless, Marxists were drawn to the concept or ideal of democracy because of its clear egalitarian implications. The term was used, in particular, to designate the goal of social equality brought about through the common ownership of wealth ('social democracy' in its original sense), in contrast to 'political' democracy, which establishes only a facade of equality.

Marx believed that the overthrow of capitalism would be a trigger that would allow genuine democracy to flourish. In his view, a fully communist society would come into existence only after a transitionary period characterized by 'the revolutionary dictatorship of the proletariat'. In effect, a system of 'bourgeois' democracy would be replaced by a very different system of 'proletarian' democracy. Although Marx refused to describe in detail how this transitionary society would be organized, its broad shape can be discerned from his admiration for the Paris Commune of 1871, which was a short-lived experiment in what approximated to direct democracy.

The form of democracy that was developed in twentieth-century communist states, however, owed more to the ideas of V. I. Lenin (see p. 99) than it did to those of Marx. Although Lenin's 1917 slogan 'All power to the Soviets' (the workers' and soldiers' and sailors' councils) had kept alive the notion of

Vladimir Ilyich Lenin (1870–1924)

Russian Marxist theorist and active revolutionary. As leader of the Bolsheviks, Lenin masterminded the 1917 Russian Bolshevik Revolution, and became the first leader of the USSR. His contributions to Marxism were his theory of the revolutionary (or vanguard) party, outlined in *What is to be Done?* ([1902] 1968); his analysis of colonialism as an economic phenomenon, described in *Imperialism, the Highest Stage of Capitalism* ([1916] 1970); and his firm commitment to the 'insurrectionary road to socialism', developed in *State and Revolution* (1917). Lenin's reputation is inevitably tied up with the subsequent course of Soviet history; he is seen by some as the father of Stalinist oppression, but by others as a critic of bureaucracy and a defender of debate and argument.

commune democracy, in reality power in Soviet Russia quickly fell into the hands of the Bolshevik party (soon renamed the 'Communist Party'). In Lenin's view, this party was nothing less than 'the vanguard of the working class'. Armed with Marxism, the party claimed that it was able to perceive the genuine interests of the proletariat and thus guide it to the realization of its revolutionary potential. This theory became the cornerstone of 'Leninist democracy', and it was accepted by all other orthodox communist regimes as one of the core features of Marxism–Leninism. However, the weakness of this model is that Lenin failed to build into it any mechanism for checking the power of the Communist Party (and, particularly, its leaders), and for ensuring that it remained sensitive and accountable to the proletarian class. To rephrase Aristotle, 'who will guard the Communist Party?'

Democracy in practice: rival views

Although there continues to be controversy about which is the most desirable form of democracy, much of contemporary debate revolves around how democracy works in practice and what 'democratization' (see p. 272) implies. This reflects the fact that there is broad, even worldwide, acceptance of a particular model of democracy, generally termed liberal democracy. Despite the existence of competing tendencies within this broad category, certain central features are clear:

● Liberal democracy is an indirect and representative form of democracy, in that political office is gained through success in regular elections that are conducted on the basis of formal political equality.
● It is based on competition and electoral choice. These are achieved through political pluralism, tolerance of a wide range of contending beliefs, and the existence of conflicting social philosophies and rival political movements and parties.
● It is characterized by a clear distinction between the state and civil society. This is maintained through the existence of autonomous groups and interests, and the market or capitalist organization of economic life.

● Leninist democracy: A form of democracy in which the communist party, organized on the basis of 'democratic centralism', articulates the interest of the proletariat.

CONCEPT

Pluralism

In its broad sense, pluralism is a belief in, or a commitment to, diversity or multiplicity (the existence of many things). As a descriptive term, pluralism may be used to denote the existence of party competition (political pluralism), a multiplicity of moral values (ethical pluralism), or a variety of cultural norms (cultural pluralism). As a normative term, it suggests that diversity is healthy and desirable, usually because it safeguards individual liberty and promotes debate, argument and understanding. More narrowly, pluralism is a theory of the distribution of political power. It holds that power is widely and evenly dispersed in society.

● **Madisonian democracy:** A form of democracy that incorporates constitutional protections for minorities that enable them to resist majority rule.

It provides protection for minorites and individuals, particularly through the allocation of basic rights that safeguard them from the will of the majority.

Nevertheless, there is a considerable amount of disagreement about the meaning and significance of liberal democracy. Does it, for instance, ensure a genuine and healthy dispersal of political power? Do democratic processes genuinely promote long-term benefits, or are they self-defeating? Can political equality coexist with economic inequality? In short, this form of democracy is interpreted in different ways by different theorists. The most important of these interpretations are advanced by:

- pluralism
- elitism
- corporatism
- the New Right
- Marxism.

Pluralist view

Pluralist ideas can be traced back to early liberal political philosophy, and notably to the ideas of Locke and Montesquieu (see p. 312). Their first systematic development, however, is found in the contributions of James Madison (see p. 319) to *The Federalist Papers* (Hamilton *et al.*, [1787–89] 1961). In considering the transformation of America from a loose confederation of states into the federal USA, Madison's particular fear was the 'problem of factions'. In common with most liberals, Madison argued that unchecked democratic rule might simply lead to majoritarianism, to the crushing of individual rights and to the expropriation of property in the name of the people. What made Madison's work notable, however, was his stress upon the multiplicity of interests and groups in society, and his insistence that, unless each such group possessed a political voice, stability and order would be impossible. He therefore proposed a system of divided government based on the separation of powers (see p. 313), bicameralism and federalism (see p. 382), that offered a variety of access points to competing groups and interests. The resulting system of rule by multiple minorities is often referred to as '**Madisonian democracy**'. Insofar as it recognizes both the existence of diversity or multiplicity in society, and the fact that such multiplicity is desirable, Madison's model is the first developed statement of pluralist principles.

The most influential modern exponent of pluralist theory is Robert Dahl (see p. 250). As described in *Who Governs? Democracy and Power in an American City* (1961), Dahl carried out an empirical study of the distribution of power in New Haven, Connecticut, USA. He concluded that, although the politically privileged and economically powerful exerted greater power than ordinary citizens, no ruling or permanent elite was able to dominate the political process. His conclusion was that 'New Haven is an example of a democratic system, warts and all'. Dahl recognized that modern democratic systems differ markedly from the classical democracies of Ancient Greece. With Charles Lindblom, he coined the term 'polyarchy' (see p. 273) to mean rule by the many, as distinct from rule by all citizens. The key feature of such a system of pluralist democracy (see p. 101) is that

Pluralist democracy

The term pluralist democracy is sometimes used interchangeably with liberal democracy. More specifically, it refers to a form of democracy that operates through the capacity of organized groups and interests to articulate popular demands and ensure responsive government. The conditions for a healthy pluralist democracy include: (1) a wide dispersal of political power amongst competing groups, specifically the absence of elite groups; (2) a high degree of internal responsiveness, group leaders being accountable to members; and (3) a neutral governmental machine that is sufficiently fragmented to offer groups a number of points of access.

competition between parties at election time, and the ability of interest or pressure groups to articulate their views freely, establishes a reliable link between the government and the governed, and creates a channel of communication between the two. While this may fall a long way short of the ideal of popular self-government, its supporters nevertheless argue that it ensures a sufficient level of accountability and popular responsiveness for it to be regarded as democratic.

However, the relationship between pluralism and democracy may not be a secure one. For instance, one of the purposes of the Madisonian system was, arguably, to constrain democracy in the hope of safeguarding property. In other words, the system of rule by multiple minorities may simply have been a device to prevent the majority (the propertyless masses) from exercising political power. A further problem is the danger of what has been called 'pluralist stagnation'. This occurs as organized groups and economic interests become so powerful that they create a log jam, resulting in the problem of government 'overload'. In such circumstances, a pluralist system may simply become ungovernable. Finally, there is the problem identified by Dahl in later works, such as *A Preface to Economic Democracy* (1985); notably, that the unequal ownership of economic resources tends to concentrate political power in the hands of the few, and deprive the many of it. This line of argument runs parallel to the conventional Marxist critique of pluralist democracy, and has given rise to neopluralism (see p. 63).

Elitist view

Elitism (see p. 102) developed as a critique of egalitarian ideas such as democracy and socialism. It draws attention to the fact of elite rule, either as an inevitable and desirable feature of social existence, or as a remediable and regrettable one. Classical elitists, such as Vilfredo Pareto (1848–1923), Gaetano Mosca (1857–1941) and Robert Michels (1876–1936), tended to take the former position. For them, democracy was no more than a foolish delusion, because political power is always exercised by a privileged minority: an elite. For example, in *The Ruling Class* ([1896] 1939), Mosca proclaimed that, in all societies, 'two classes of people appear – a class that rules and a class that is ruled'. In his view, the resources or attributes that are necessary for rule are always unequally distributed, and, further, a cohesive minority will always be able to manipulate and control the masses, even in a parliamentary democracy. Pareto suggested that the qualities needed to rule conforms to one of two psychological types: 'foxes' (who rule by cunning and are able to manipulate the consent of the masses), and 'lions' (whose domination is typically achieved through coercion and violence). Michels developed an alternative line of argument based on the tendency within all organizations, however democratic they might appear, for power to be concentrated in the hands of a small group of dominant figures who can organize and make decisions. He termed this 'the iron law of oligarchy' (see p. 232).

Whereas classical elitists strove to prove that democracy was always a myth, modern elitist theorists have tended to highlight how far particular political systems fall short of the democratic ideal. An example of this can be found in C. Wright Mills' influential account of the power structure in the USA. In contrast to the pluralist notion of a wide and broadly democratic dispersal of power, Mills, in *The Power Elite* (1956), offered a portrait of a USA dominated by a nexus of leading groups. In his view, this 'power elite' comprised a triumvirate of

Elitism

Elite originally meant, and can still mean, 'the highest', 'the best', or 'the excellent'. Used in an empirical sense, it refers to a minority in whose hands power, wealth or privilege is concentrated. Elitism is a belief in, or practice of, rule by an elite or minority. *Normative* elitism suggests that political power should be vested in the hands of a wise or enlightened minority. *Classical* elitism claimed to be empirical (although normative beliefs often intruded), and saw elite rule as an unchangeable fact of social existence. *Modern* elitism is also empirical, but it is more critical and discriminating about the causes of elite rule.

big business (particularly defence-related industries), the US military and political cliques surrounding the President. Drawing on a combination of economic power, bureaucratic control and access to the highest levels of the executive branch of government, the power elite is able to shape key 'history-making' decisions, especially in the fields of defence and foreign policy, as well as strategic economic policy. The power-elite model suggests that liberal democracy in the USA is largely a sham. Elitists have, moreover, argued that empirical studies have supported pluralist conclusions only because Dahl and others have ignored the importance of non-decision-making as a manifestation of power (see p. 9).

Certain elite theorists have nevertheless argued that a measure of democratic accountability is consistent with elite rule. Whereas the power-elite model portrays the elite as a cohesive body, bound together by common or overlapping interests, competitive elitism (sometimes called 'democratic elitism') highlights the significance of elite rivalry (see Figure 12.1). In other words, the elite, consisting of the leading figures from a number of competing groups and interests, is fractured. This view is often associated with Joseph Schumpeter's (see p. 141) 'realistic' model of democracy outlined in *Capitalism, Socialism and Democracy* (1942):

> The democratic method is that institutional arrangement for arriving at political decisions in which individuals acquire the power to decide by means of a competitive struggle for the people's vote.

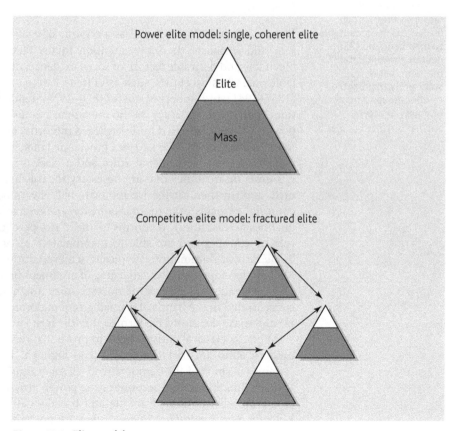

Figure 12.1 Elite models

The electorate can decide which elite rules, but cannot change the fact that power is always exercised by an elite. This model of competitive elitism was developed by Anthony Downs (1957) into the 'economic theory of democracy'. In effect, electoral competition creates a political market in which politicians act as entrepreneurs bent upon achieving government power, and individual voters behave like consumers, voting for the party with the policies that most closely reflect their own preferences. Downs argued that a system of open and competitive elections guarantees democratic rule because it places government in the hands of the party whose philosophy, values and policies correspond most closely to the preferences of the largest group of voters. As Schumpeter put it, 'democracy is the rule of the politician'. As a model of democratic politics, competitive elitism at least has the virtue that it corresponds closely to the workings of the liberal-democratic political system. Indeed, it emerged more as an attempt to *describe* how the democratic process works than through a desire to *prescribe* certain values and principles – political equality, popular participation, freedom or whatever.

Corporatist view

The origins of corporatism (see p. 251) date back to the attempt in Fascist Italy to construct a so-called 'corporate state' by integrating both managers and workers into the processes of government. Corporatist theorists, however, have drawn attention to parallel developments in the world's major industrialized states. In the form of **neocorporatism**, or liberal corporatism, this gave rise to the spectre of 'tripartite government', in which government is conducted through organizations that allow state officials, employers' groups and unions to deal directly with one another. To a large extent, this tendency to integrate economic interests into government (which was common in the post-1945 period, and particularly prominent in, for example, Sweden, Norway, the Netherlands and Austria) was a consequence of the drift towards economic management and intervention. As government sought to manage economic life and deliver an increasingly broad range of public services, it recognized the need for institutional arrangements designed to secure the cooperation and support of major economic interests. Where attempts have been made to shift economic policy away from state intervention and towards the free market (as in the UK since 1979), the impact of corporatism has markedly diminished.

The significance of corporatism in terms of democratic processes is clearly considerable. There are those who, like the British guild socialists, argue that corporatism makes possible a form of functional representation, in that individuals' views and interests are articulated more by the groups to which they belong than through the mechanism of competitive elections. What is called 'corporate pluralism' thus portrays tripartism as a mechanism through which the major groups and interests in society compete to shape government policy. Some commentators, however, see corporatism as a threat to democracy. In the first place, corporatism only advantages groups that are accorded privileged access to government. 'Insider' groups therefore possess a political voice, while 'outsider' groups are denied one. Second, corporatism can work to the benefit of the state, rather than major economic interests, in that the **peak associations** that the government chooses to deal with can be used to exert discipline over their

● **Neocorporatism**: A tendency found in western polyarchies for organized interests to be granted privileged and institutionalized access to policy formulation.

● **Peak association**: A group recognized by government as representing the general or collective interests of businesses or workers.

members and to filter out radical demands. Finally, corporatism threatens to subvert the processes of electoral or parliamentary democracy. Policy is made through negotiations between government officials and leaders of powerful economic interests, rather than through the deliberations of a representative assembly. Interest-group leaders may thus exert considerable political power, even though they are in no way publicly accountable and their influence is not subject to public scrutiny.

New Right view

The emergence of the New Right from the 1970s onwards has generated a very particular critique of democratic politics. This has focused on the danger of what has been called 'democratic overload': the paralysis of a political system that is subject to unrestrained group and electoral pressures. One aspect of this critique has highlighted the unsavoury face of corporatism. New Right theorists are keen advocates of the free market, believing that economies work best when left alone by government. The danger of corporatism from this perspective is that it empowers sectional groups and economic interests, enabling them to make demands on government for increased pay, public investment, subsidies, state protection and so on. In effect, corporatism allows well-placed interest groups to dominate and dictate to government. The result of this, according to the New Right, is an irresistible drift towards state intervention and economic stagnation (Olson, 1982).

Government 'overload' can also be seen to be a consequence of the electoral process. This was what Brittan (1977) referred to as 'the economic consequences of democracy'. In this view, electoral politics amounts to a self-defeating process in which politicians are encouraged to compete for power by offering increasingly unrealistic promises to the electorate. Both voters and politicians are held to blame here. Voters are attracted by promises of higher public spending because they calculate that the cost (an increased tax burden) will be spread over the entire population. Politicians, consumed by the desire to win power, attempt to outbid one another by making ever more generous spending pledges to the electorate. According to Brittan, the economic consequences of unrestrained democracy are high levels of inflation fuelled by public borrowing, and a tax burden that destroys enterprise and undermines growth. As characterized by Marquand (1988), the New Right view is that 'democracy is to adults what chocolate is to children: endlessly tempting; harmless in small doses; sickening in excess'. New Right theorists therefore tend to see democracy in strictly protective terms, regarding it essentially as a defence against arbitrary government, rather than a means of bringing about social transformation.

Marxist view

As pointed out in relation to people's democracy, the Marxist view of democratic politics is rooted in class analysis. In this view, political power cannot be understood narrowly in terms of electoral rights, or in terms of the ability of groups to articulate their interests by lobbying and campaigning. Rather, at a deeper level, political power reflects the distribution of economic power and, in particular, the unequal ownership of productive wealth. The Marxist critique of liberal democracy thus focuses upon the inherent tension between democracy and capitalism; that is, between the political equality that liberal democracy proclaims and the social inequality that a capitalist economy inevitably generates. Liberal democracies are thus seen as 'capitalist' or 'bourgeois' democracies that are manipulated and controlled by the entrenched power of a **ruling class**.

Marxism thus offers a distinctive critique of pluralist democracy. Power cannot be widely and evenly dispersed in society as long as class power is unequally distributed. Indeed, in many respects, the Marxist view parallels the elitist critique of pluralism. Both views suggest that power is ultimately concentrated in the hands of the few, the main difference being whether the few is conceived of as a 'power elite' or as a 'ruling class'. However, significant differences can also be identified. For instance, whereas elitists suggest that power derive from a variety of sources (education, social status, bureaucratic position, political connections, wealth and so on), Marxists emphasize the decisive importance of economic factors; notably, the ownership and control of the means of production. Modern Marxists, however, have been less willing to dismiss electoral democracy as nothing more than a sham. **Eurocommunists**, for example, abandoned the idea of revolution, embracing instead the notion of a peaceful, legal and democratic 'road to socialism'.

Towards cosmopolitan democracy?

The idea of cosmopolitan democracy has received growing attention due to the advance of globalization and the evident 'hollowing out' of domestic democratic processes focused on the nation-state. If global interconnectedness means that policy-making authority has shifted from national governments to international organizations, surely democracy should be recast in line with this? However, what would cosmopolitan democracy look like, and how would it operate? Two basic models have been advanced. The first would involve the construction of a world parliament, a body whose role would be to introduce greater scrutiny and openness to the process of global decision-making by calling to account established international organizations, such as the United Nations, the World Trade Organization, the International Monetary Fund and so forth. Very few advocates of such an idea contemplate the creation of a fully-fledged world government or global state; most, instead, favour a multilevel system of post-sovereign governance in which no body or level is able to exercise final authority. Held (1995) proposed a package of measures, including the establishment of a 'global parliament', reformed and more accountable international organizations, and the 'permanent shift of a growing proportion of a nation state's coercive capacity to regional and global institutions'. Monbiot (2004), for his part, backed the creation of a popularly elected world parliament, composed of 600 representatives, each with a constituency of about 10 million people, many of which would straddle national borders.

The alternative model of cosmopolitan democracy is less ambitious and formalized, relying less on the construction of new bodies and more on the reform of existing international organizations, often linked to the strengthening of global civil society (see p. 106). This model places its faith in non-governmental organizations (NGOs) (see p. 248) to reconfigure global power by offering an alternative to top-down corporate globalization. This idea of 'globalization from

● **Ruling class:** A Marxist term, denoting a class that dominates other classes and society at large by virtue of its ownership of productive wealth.

● **Eurocommunism:** A form of deradicalized communism that attempted to blend Marxism with liberal-democratic principles.

CONCEPT

Global civil society

Global civil society refers to a realm in which transnational non-governmental groups and associations interact. These groups are typically voluntary and non-profitmaking, setting them apart from TNCs. (see p. 149). However, the term 'global civil society' is complex and contested. In its 'activist' version, transnational social movements are the key agents of global civil society, giving it an 'outsider' orientation, and a strong focus on cosmopolitan ideals. In its 'policy' version, NGOs are the key agents of global civil society, giving it an 'insider' orientation and meaning that it overlaps with global governance.

below' amounts to a bottom-up democratic vision of a civilizing world order. Such an approach would be effective to the extent that NGOs and transnational social movements could introduce an element of public scrutiny and accountability to the working of international bodies, conferences, summits and the like, meaning that global civil society functions as a channel of communications between the individual and global institutions.

However, the prospects for cosmopolitan democracy are far from rosy. In the first place, states, and especially major states, are likely to block any trend towards global democracy, or ensure that any 'alternative' bodies that may be created will lack credibility and remain peripheral to global decision-making. In a wider sense, the egalitarian thrust implicit in the idea of cosmopolitan democracy is simply out of step with the deep economic, political and military disparities of the existing global system. Aside from the obstacles confronting the transition to cosmopolitan democracy, critics have argued that the project itself may be profoundly misconceived. In the first place, however structured and composed, any global institution that is tasked with ensuring public accountability is doomed to failure. The inevitable 'gap' between popularly-elected global political institutions and ordinary citizens around the world would mean that any claim that these institutions are democratic would be mere pretence. Democracy, in this light, is perhaps only meaningful if it is local or national, and all international organizations, whether these are regional or global, are destined to suffer from a debilitating 'democratic deficit'. Second, the democratic credentials of NGOs and, for that matter, social movements may be entirely bogus. Large memberships, committed activists and the ability to mobilize popular protests and demonstrations undoubtedly give social movements and NGOs political influence, but they do not invest them with democratic authority. Quite simply, there is no way of testing the weight of their views against those of the population at large.

SUMMARY

- Legitimacy maintains political stability because it establishes a regime's right to rule, and so underpins the regime's authority over its people. Legitimacy may be based on traditional, charismatic or legal–rational authority. Nevertheless, structural imbalances in modern society may make it increasingly difficult to maintain legitimacy. Legitimation crises may arise from the conflict between the pressure for social and economic interventionism generated by democracy on the one hand, and the pressure generated by market economy on the other.

- Democratic legitimacy is now widely accepted as the only meaningful form of legitimacy. However, it has been suggested that economic and other factors may be more effective than democracy in maintaining legitimacy, that evidence of growing political disengagement in mature democracies indicates that democracy's capacity to deliver legitimacy is declining, and that non-democratic regimes may enjoy at least a measure of legitimacy.

- There are a number of rival models of democracy, each offering its own version of popular rule. Classical democracy, which is based on the political system of Ancient Athens, is defended on the grounds that it alone guarantees government by the people. Protective democracy gives citizens the greatest scope to live their lives as they choose. Developmental democracy has the virtue that, in extending participation, it widens liberty and fosters personal growth. People's democracy aims to achieve economic emancipation, rather than merely the extension of political rights.

- There is considerable controversy about how liberal-democratic systems work in practice. Pluralists praise the system's capacity to guarantee popular responsiveness and public accountability. Elitists highlight the tendency for political power to be concentrated in the hands of a privileged minority. Corporatists draw attention to the incorporation of groups into government. The New Right focuses on the dangers of 'democratic overload'. And Marxists point to tensions between democracy and capitalism.

- Growing global interdependence has stimulated interest in whether democracy can, and should, operate at a global or cosmopolitan level, either through the construction of some kind of world parliament, or through a global civil society. However, major obstacles stand in the way of cosmopolitan democracy, with many rejecting the idea as unfeasible in principle.

Questions for discussion

- Why does power need legitimation?
- Are capitalist societies inevitably prone to legitimation crises?
- Is democratic legitimacy the only meaningful form of legitimacy?
- Is direct democracy in any way applicable to modern circumstances?
- Have the virtues of democracy been overstated?
- Which model of democracy is the most attractive, and why?
- Do modern forms of representative democracy deserve to be described as democratic?
- What are the major threats to democracy in modern society?
- Is cosmopolitan democracy possible, or desirable?

Further reading

Beetham, D., *The Legitimation of Power* (1991). A clear and authoritative introduction to the idea of legitimacy, which also considers the role of democracy and other factors in legitimizing power.

Dahl, R., *Democracy and its Critics* (1991). A wide-ranging and thorough discussion of the democratic ideal and democratic practices.

Gill, G., *The Dynamics of Democratization: Elite, Civil Society and the Transition Process* (2000). A clear and accessible overview of the scale, scope and character of democratization in the contemporary world.

Held, D., *Models of Democracy* (3rd edn) (2006). A rigorous and stimulating examination of rival models of democracy and the present state of democratic theory.

CHAPTER 13

Political Ideas and Ideologies

'The philosophers have only interpreted the world in various ways: the point is to change it.'

KARL MARX, *Theses on Feuerbach* (1845)

PREVIEW   All people are political thinkers. Whether they know it or not, people use political ideas and concepts whenever they express their opinions or speak their mind. Everyday language is littered with terms such as freedom, fairness, equality, justice and rights. In the same way, words such as conservative, liberal, fascist, socialist or feminist are regularly employed by people either to describe their own views, or those of others. However, even though such terms are familiar, even commonplace, they are seldom used with any precision or a clear grasp of their meaning. What, for instance, is 'equality'? What does it mean to say that all people are equal? Are people born equal, should they be treated by society as if they are equal? Should people have equal rights, equal opportunities, equal political influence, equal wages? Similarly, words such as communist or fascist are commonly misused. What does it mean to call someone a 'fascist'? What values or beliefs do fascists hold, and why do they hold them? How do communist views differ from those of, say, liberals, conservatives or socialists? This chapter examines political ideas from the perspective of the key ideological traditions. It focuses, in particular, on the 'classical' ideologies (liberalism, conservatism and socialism), but it also considers a range of other ideological traditions, which have arisen either out of, or in opposition to, the classical ones. Each ideological tradition constitutes a distinctive intellectual framework or paradigm, and so offers a particular 'lens' on political world. However, before examining the various ideological traditions, it is necessary to consider the nature of political ideology itself.

KEY ISSUES
- What is political ideology?
- Is politics intrinsically linked to ideology? Can ideology come to an end?
- What are the key ideas and theories of the major ideological traditions?
- What internal tensions do each of the major ideologies encompass?
- How has ideological thought changed over time?
- How can the rise and fall of ideologies be explained?

Ideology

From a social-scientific viewpoint, an ideology is a more or less coherent set of ideas that provides a basis for organized political action, whether this is intended to preserve, modify or overthrow the existing system of power relationships. All ideologies therefore (1) offer an account of the existing order, usually in the form of a 'world-view', (2) provide a model of a desired future, a vision of the Good Society, and (3) outline how political change can and should be brought about. Ideologies are not, however, hermetically sealed systems of thought; rather, they are fluid sets of ideas that overlap with one another at a number of points.

WHAT IS POLITICAL IDEOLOGY?

Ideology is one of the most controversial concepts encountered in political analysis. Although the term now tends to be used in a neutral sense, to refer to a developed social philosophy or world-view, it has in the past had heavily negative or pejorative connotations. During its sometimes tortuous career, the concept of ideology has commonly been used as a political weapon to condemn or criticize rival creeds or doctrines.

The term 'ideology' was coined in 1796 by the French philosopher Destutt de Tracy (1754–1836). He used it to refer to a new 'science of ideas' (literally, an idea-ology) that set out to uncover the origins of conscious thought and ideas. De Tracy's hope was that ideology would eventually enjoy the same status as established sciences such as zoology and biology. However, a more enduring meaning was assigned to the term in the nineteenth century in the writings of Karl Marx (see p. 41). For Marx, ideology amounted to the ideas of the 'ruling class', ideas that therefore uphold the class system and perpetuate exploitation. In their early work *The German Ideology*, Marx and Engels wrote the following:

> The ideas of the ruling class are in every epoch the ruling ideas, i.e. the class which is the ruling material force in society, is at the same time the ruling intellectual force. The class which has the means of mental production at its disposal, has control at the same time over the means of mental production. (Marx and Engels, [1846] 1970:64)

The defining feature of ideology in the Marxist sense is that it is false: it mystifies and confuses subordinate classes by concealing from them the contradictions on which all class societies are based. As far as capitalism is concerned, the ideology of the property-owning bourgeoisie (bourgeois ideology) fosters delusion or 'false consciousness' amongst the exploited proletariat, preventing them from recognizing the fact of their own exploitation. Nevertheless, Marx did not believe that all political views had an ideological character. He held that his own work, which attempted to uncover the process of class exploitation and oppression, was scientific. In his view, a clear distinction could be drawn between science and ideology, between truth and falsehood. This distinction tended, however, to be blurred in the writings of later Marxists such as Lenin (see p. 99) and Gramsci (see p. 175). These referred not only to 'bourgeois ideology', but also to 'socialist ideology' or 'proletarian ideology', terms that Marx would have considered absurd.

Alternative uses of the term have also been developed by liberals and conservatives. The emergence of totalitarian dictatorships in the interwar period encouraged writers such as Karl Popper (1902–94), J. L. Talmon and Hannah Arendt (see p. 7) to view ideology as an instrument of social control to ensure compliance and subordination. Relying heavily on the examples of fascism and communism, this Cold War liberal use of the term treated ideology as a 'closed' system of thought, which, by claiming a monopoly of truth, refuses to tolerate opposing ideas and rival beliefs. In contrast, liberalism, based as it is on a fundamental commitment to individual freedom, and doctrines such as conservatism and democratic socialism that broadly subscribe to liberal principles are clearly not ideologies. These doctrines are 'open' in the sense that they permit, and even insist on, free debate, opposition and criticism.

Debating...
Can politics exist without ideology?

The term 'ideology' has traditionally carried pejorative implications, often expressed through predictions of its imminent (and usually welcome) demise. Nevertheless, despite its varied obituaries, political ideology has stubbornly refused to die: while particular ideologies may rise or fall, ideological forms of politics seem to be an enduring feature of world history. Is politics intrinsically linked to ideology? Or may politics finally be able to emerge from the shadow cast by ideological belief?

YES

Overcoming falsehood and delusion. Most critiques of ideology associate it with falsehood and manipulation, implying that reason and critical understanding can, and will, emancipate us from ideological politics. In this view, ideologies are, in effect, political religions, sets of values, theories and doctrines that demand faith and commitment from 'believers', who are then unable to think outside or beyond their chosen world-view. If ideologies are intellectual prisons, the solution is to see the world 'as it is', something that can be achieved through the application of value-free scientific method. The purpose of political science is thus to disengage politics from ideology.

Rise of technocratic politics. Political ideology arose in the form of contrasting attempts to shape emergent industrial society. The left/right divide and the struggle between socialism and capitalism has always been at the heart of ideological debate. However, the collapse of communism and the near worldwide acceptance of market capitalism means that this rivalry has become irrelevant to modern politics. Politics has therefore come to revolve not around ideological questions to do with ownership and the distribution of wealth, but around 'smaller' questions to do with the effective management of the capitalist system. Ideological politics has given way to technocratic politics.

Rise of consumerist politics. Ideology has little place in modern democratic systems due to the logic of electoral competition. Elections force political parties to behave like businesses in the marketplace, formulating 'products' (policies) in the hope of attracting the largest number of 'consumers' (voters). Parties thus increasingly respond to consumer/voter demands, rather than trying to reshape these demands in the light of a pre-existing ideological vision. Whether parties have historically been left-wing, right-wing or centrist in orientation, they recognise the electoral value of 'travelling light' in ideological terms. Electoral politics therefore contributes to a process of party de-ideologization.

NO

Ideology as an intellectual framework. Political ideology will always survive because it provides politicians, parties and other political actors with an intellectual framework which helps them to make sense of the world in which they live. Ideologies are not systematic delusions but, rather, rival visions of the political world, each illuminating particular aspects of a complex and multifaceted reality. Ideologies are therefore neither, in a simplistic sense, true nor false. Perhaps the most dangerous delusion is the notion of a clear distinction between science and ideology. Science itself is constructed on the basis of paradigms that are destined to be displaced over time (Kuhn, 1962).

Ideological renewal. The secret of ideology's survival and continued relevance is its flexibility, the fact that ideological traditions go through a seemingly endless process of redefinition and renewal. As old ideologies fade, new ones emerge, helping to preserve the relevance of political ideology. The world of ideologies does not stand still, but changes in response to changing social and historical circumstances. The declining relevance of the left/right divide has not led to the 'end of ideology' or the 'end of history'; it has merely opened up new ideological spaces that have been filled by the likes of feminism, green politics, multiculturalism and cosmopolitanism.

The 'vision thing'. As the principal source of meaning and idealism in politics, ideology touches those aspects of politics that no other political form can reach. Ideology gives people a reason to believe in something larger than themselves, because people's personal narratives only make sense when they are situated within a broader historical narrative. A post-ideological age would therefore be an age without hope, without vision. If politicians cannot cloak their pursuit of power in ideological purpose, they risk being seen simply as power-seeking pragmatists, and their policy programmes will appear to lack coherence and direction.

A distinctively conservative use of the term 'ideology' has been developed by thinkers such as Michael Oakeshott (see p. 177). This view reflects a characteristically conservative scepticism about the value of rationalism, born out of the belief that the world is largely beyond the capacity of the human mind to fathom. As Oakeshott put it, in political activity 'men sail a boundless and bottomless sea'. From this perspective, ideologies are seen as abstract 'systems of thought'; that is, as sets of ideas that distort political reality because they claim to explain what is, frankly, incomprehensible. This is why conservatives have traditionally dismissed the notion that they subscribe to an ideology, preferring instead to describe conservatism as a disposition, or an 'attitude of mind', and placing their faith in pragmatism, tradition (see p. 82) and history.

The drawback of each of these usages, however, is that, as they are negative or pejorative, they restrict the application of the term. Certain political doctrines, in other words, are excluded from the category of 'ideologies'. Marx, for instance, insisted that his ideas were scientific, not ideological, liberals have denied that liberalism should be viewed as an ideology, and conservatives have traditionally claimed to embrace a pragmatic rather than ideological style of politics. Moreover, each of these definitions is loaded with the values and orientation of a particular political doctrine. An inclusive definition of 'ideology' (one that applies to all political traditions) must therefore be neutral: it must reject the notion that ideologies are 'good' or 'bad', true or false, or liberating or oppressive. This is the virtue of the modern, social-scientific meaning of the term, which treats ideology as an action-orientated belief system, an interrelated set of ideas that in some way guides or inspires political action.

However, much of the debate about ideology since the mid-twentieth century has focused on predictions of its demise, or at least of its fading relevance. This came to be known as the 'end of ideology' debate. It was initiated in the 1950s, stimulated by the collapse of fascism at the end of World War II and the decline of communism in the developed West. In *The End of Ideology* (1960), the US sociologist Daniel Bell (1919–2011) declared that the stock of political ideas had been exhausted. In his view, ethical and ideological questions had become irrelevant because in most western societies parties competed for power simply by promising higher levels of economic growth and material affluence. This debate was revived in the aftermath of the collapse of communism by 'end of history' theorists, such as Fukuyama (see p. 271), who suggested that a single ideology, liberal democracy, had triumphed over all its rivals, and that this triumph was final (see p. 44). At the heart of such debates lies questions about the relationship between politics and ideology, and specifically about whether politics can exist without ideology (see p. 29).

CLASSICAL IDEOLOGICAL TRADITIONS

Political ideology arose out of the transition from feudalism to industrial capitalism. In simple terms, the earliest, or 'classical' ideologies – liberalism, conservatism and socialism – developed as contrasting attempts to shape emerging industrial society. This meant that the central theme in ideological debate and argument during this period and beyond was the battle between two rival economic philosophies: capitalism (see p. 131) and socialism. Political ideology

● **Rationalism**: The belief that the world can be understood and explained through the exercise of human reason, based on assumptions about its rational structure.

● **Pragmatism**: A theory or practice that places primary emphasis on practical circumstances and goals; pragmatism implies a distrust of abstract ideas.

John Locke (1632–1704)

English philosopher and politician. Locke studied medicine at Oxford University before becoming secretary to Anthony Ashley Cooper, First Earl of Shaftsbury, in 1661. His political views were developed against the backdrop of the English Revolution, and are often seen as providing a justification for the 'Glorious Revolution' of 1688, which ended absolutist rule and established a constitutional monarchy in Britain. Locke was a key thinker of early liberalism, placing particular emphasis on 'natural' or God-given rights, identified as the rights to life, liberty and property. An exponent of representative government and toleration, Locke's views had a considerable impact on the American Revolution. His most important political works are *A Letter Concerning Toleration* (1689) and *Two Treatises of Government* ([1690] 1965).

thus had a strong economic focus. The battle lines between capitalism and socialism were significantly sharpened by the 1917 Russian Revolution, which created the world's first socialist state. Indeed, throughout what is sometimes called the 'short' twentieth century (from the outbreak of World War I to the fall of communism, 1989–91), and particularly during the Cold War period (1945–90), international politics was structured along ideological lines, as the capitalist West confronted the communist East. Although ideological debate has became richer and certainly progressively more diverse since the 1960s, not least as a result of the rise of so-called 'new' ideologies such as feminism and green politics, the classical ideologies have retain their central importance. In large part, this has been because of their capacity to reinvent themselves. In the process of doing so, the dividing lines between them have often been blurred.

Liberalism

Any account of political ideologies must start with liberalism. This is because liberalism is, in effect, the ideology of the industrialized West, and is sometimes portrayed as a **meta-ideology** that is capable of embracing a broad range of rival values and beliefs. Although liberalism did not emerge as a developed political creed until the early nineteenth century, distinctively liberal theories and principles had gradually been developed during the previous 300 years. Early liberalism certainly reflected the aspirations of a rising industrial middle class, and liberalism and capitalism have been closely linked (some have argued intrinsically linked) ever since. In its earliest form, liberalism was a political doctrine. As relected in the ideas of thinkers such as John Locke, it attacked absolutism (see p. 268) and feudal privilege, instead advocating constitutional and, later, representative government. By the early nineteenth century, a distinctively liberal economic creed had developed that extolled the virtues of *laissez-faire* (see p. 132) and condemned all forms of government intervention. This became the centrepiece of classical, or nineteenth-century, liberalism. From the late nineteenth century onwards, however, a form of social liberalism emerged that looked more favourably on welfare reform and economic intervention. Such an emphasis became the characteristic theme of modern, or twentieth-century, liberalism.

● Meta-ideology: A higher or second-order ideology that lays down the grounds on which ideological debate can take place.

Liberalism: key ideas

◆ **Individualism:** Individualism (see p. 158) is the core principle of liberal ideology. It reflects a belief in the supreme importance of the human individual as opposed to any social group or collective body. Human beings are seen, first and foremost, as individuals. This implies both that they are of equal moral worth and that they possess separate and unique identities. The liberal goal is therefore to construct a society within which individuals can flourish and develop, each pursuing 'the good' as he or she defines it, to the best of his or her abilities. This has contributed to the view that liberalism is morally neutral, in the sense that it lays down a set of rules that allow individuals to make their own moral decisions.

◆ **Freedom:** Individual freedom, (see p. 339), or liberty (the two terms are interchangeable), is the core value of liberalism; it is given priority over, say, equality, justice or authority. This arises naturally from a belief in the individual and the desire to ensure that each person is able to act as he or she pleases or chooses. Nevertheless, liberals advocate 'freedom under the law', as they recognize that one person's liberty may be a threat to the liberty of others; liberty may become licence. They therefore endorse the ideal that individuals should enjoy the maximum possible liberty consistent with a like liberty for all.

◆ **Reason:** Liberals believe that the world has a rational structure, and that this can be uncovered through the exercise of human reason and by critical enquiry. This inclines them to place their faith in the ability of individuals to make wise judgements on their own behalf, being, in most cases, the best judges of their own interests. It also encourages liberals to believe in progress and the capacity of human beings to resolve their differences through debate and argument, rather than bloodshed and war.

◆ **Equality:** Individualism implies a belief in foundational equality: that is, the belief that individuals are 'born equal', at least in terms of moral worth. This is reflected in a liberal commitment to equal rights and entitlements, notably in the form of legal equality ('equality before the law') and political equality ('one person, one vote; one vote, one value'). However, as individuals do not possess the same levels of talent or willingness to work, liberals do not endorse social equality or an equality of outcome. Rather, they favour equality of opportunity (a 'level playing field') that gives all individuals an equal chance to realize their unequal potential. Liberals therefore support the principle of meritocracy, with merit reflecting, crudely, talent plus hard work.

◆ **Toleration:** Liberals believe that toleration (that is, forbearance: the willingness of people to allow others to think, speak and act in ways of which they disapprove) is both a guarantee of individual liberty and a means of social enrichment. They believe that pluralism (see p. 100), in the form of moral, cultural and political diversity, is positively healthy: it promotes debate and intellectual progress by ensuring that all beliefs are tested in a free market of ideas. Liberals, moreover, tend to believe that there is a balance or natural harmony between rival views and interests, and thus usually discount the idea of irreconcilable conflict.

◆ **Consent:** In the liberal view, authority and social relationships should always be based on consent or willing agreement. Government must therefore be based on the 'consent of the governed'. This is a doctrine that encourages liberals to favour representation (see p. 197) and democracy, notably in the form of liberal democracy (see p. 270). Similarly, social bodies and associations are formed through contracts willingly entered into by individuals intent on pursuing their own self-interest. In this sense, authority arises 'from below' and is always grounded in legitimacy (see p. 81).

◆ **Constitutionalism:** Although liberals see government as a vital guarantee of order and stability in society, they are constantly aware of the danger that government may become a tyranny against the individual ('power tends to corrupt' (Lord Acton)). They therefore believe in limited government. This goal can be attained through the fragmentation of government power, by the creation of checks and balances amongst the various institutions of government, and by the establishment of a codified or 'written' constitution embodying a bill of rights that defines the relationship between the state and the individual.

Classical liberalism

The central theme of classical liberalism is a commitment to an extreme form of individualism. Human beings are seen as egoistical, self-seeking and largely self-reliant creatures. In what C. B. Macpherson (1962) termed 'possessive individualism', they are taken to be the proprietors of their own persons and capacities, owing nothing to society or to other individuals. This **atomist** view of society is underpinned by a belief in 'negative' liberty, meaning non-interference, or the absence of external constraints on the individual. This implies a deeply unsympathetic attitude towards the state and all forms of government intervention.

In Tom Paine's (see p. 199) words, the state is a 'necessary evil'. It is 'necessary' in that, at the very least, it establishes order and security, and ensures that contracts are enforced. However, it is 'evil' in that it imposes a collective will on society, thus limiting the freedom and responsibilities of the individual. The classical liberal ideal is therefore the establishment of a minimal or 'nightwatchman' state, with a role that is limited to the protection of citizens from the encroachments of fellow citizens. In the form of **economic liberalism**, this position is underpinned by a deep faith in the mechanisms of the free market and the belief that the economy works best when left alone by government. *Laissez-faire* capitalism is thus seen as guaranteeing prosperity, upholding individual liberty, and, as this allows individuals to rise and fall according to merit, ensuring social justice.

Modern liberalism

Modern liberalism is characterized by a more sympathetic attitude towards state intervention. Indeed, in the USA, the term 'liberal' is invariably taken to imply support for **'big' government** rather than 'minimal' government. This shift was born out of the recognition that industrial capitalism had merely generated new forms of injustice and left the mass of the population subject to the vagaries of the market. Influenced by the work of J. S. Mill (see p. 198), the so-called New Liberals' (figures such as T. H. Green (1836–82), L. T. Hobhouse (1864–1929) and J. A. Hobson (1858–1940)) championed a broader, 'positive' view of freedom. From this perspective, freedom does not just mean being left alone, which might imply nothing more than the freedom to starve. Rather, it is linked to personal development and the flourishing of the individual; that is, the ability of the individual to gain fulfilment and achieve self-realization.

This view provided the basis for social or welfare liberalism. This is characterized by the recognition that state intervention, particularly in the form of social welfare, can enlarge liberty by safeguarding individuals from the social evils that blight individual existence. These evils were identified in the UK by the 1942 Beveridge Report as the 'five giants': want, ignorance, idleness, squalor and disease. In the same way, modern liberals abandoned their belief in *laissez-faire* capitalism, largely as a result of J. M. Keynes' (see p. 137) insight that growth and prosperity could be maintained only through a system of managed or regulated capitalism, with key economic responsibilities being placed in the hands of the state. Nevertheless, modern liberals' support for collective provision and government intervention has always been conditional. Their concern has been with the plight of the weak and vulnerable, those who are literally not able to help themselves. Their goal is to raise individuals to the point where they are able, once

● **Progress**: Moving forwards; the belief that history is characterized by human advancement based on the accumulation of knowledge and wisdom.

● **Meritocracy**: Rule by the talented; the principle that rewards and positions should be distributed on the basis of ability.

● **Atomism**: The belief that society is made up of a collection of largely self-sufficient individuals who owe little or nothing to one another.

● **Economic liberalism**: A belief in the market as a self-regulating mechanism tending naturally to deliver general prosperity and opportunities for all.

● **Big government**: Interventionist government, usually understood to imply economic management and social regulation.

again, to take responsibility for their own circumstances and make their own moral choices. The most influential modern attempt to reconcile the principles of liberalism with the politics of welfare and redistribution was undertaken by John Rawls (see p. 45). (The liberal approach to international politics is examined in Chapter 18.)

Conservatism

Conservative ideas and doctrines first emerged in the late eighteenth century and early nineteenth century. They arose as a reaction against the growing pace of economic and political change, which was in many ways symbolized by the French Revolution. In this sense, conservatism harked back to the *ancien régime*. In trying to resist the pressures unleashed by the growth of liberalism, socialism and nationalism, conservatism stood in defence of an increasingly embattled traditional social order. However, from the outset, divisions in conservative thought were apparent. In continental Europe, a form of conservatism emerged that was characterized by the work of thinkers such as Joseph de Maistre (1753–1821). This conservatism was starkly autocratic and reactionary, rejecting out of hand any idea of reform. A more cautious, more flexible and, ultimately, more successful form of conservatism nevertheless developed in the UK and the USA, characterized by Edmund Burke's belief in 'change in order to conserve'. This stance enabled conservatives in the nineteenth century to embrace the cause of social reform under the paternalistic banner of 'One Nation'. The high point of this tradition in the UK came in the 1950s as the Conservative Party came to accept the postwar settlement and espouse its own version of Keynesian social democracy. However, such ideas increasingly came under pressure from the 1970s onwards as a result of the emergence of the New Right. The New Right's radically antistatist and antipaternalist brand of conservatism draws heavily on classical liberal themes and values.

Paternalistic conservatism

The paternalistic strand in conservative thought is entirely consistent with principles such as organicism, hierarchy and duty, and it can therefore be seen as an outgrowth of traditional conservatism. Often traced back to the early writings of Benjamin Disraeli (1804–81), paternalism draws on a combination of prudence and principle. In warning of the danger of the UK being divided into 'two nations: the Rich and the Poor', Disraeli articulated a widespread fear of social revolution. This warning amounted to an appeal to the self-interest of the privileged, who needed to recognize that 'reform from above' was preferable to 'revolution from below'. This message was underpinned by an appeal to the principles of duty and social obligation rooted in neofeudal ideas such as *noblesse oblige*. In effect, in this view, duty is the price of privilege; the powerful and propertied inherit a responsibility to look after the less well-off in the broader interests of social cohesion and unity. The resulting One-Nation principle, the cornerstone of what since the early nineteenth century has been termed a Tory position, reflects not so much the ideal of social equality as a cohesive and stable hierarchy that arises organically.

● **Redistribution**: A narrowing of material inequalities brought about through a combination of progressive taxation and welfare provision.

● *Ancien régime*: (French) Literally, 'old order'; usually linked with the absolutist structures that predated the French Revolution.

● **Paternalism**: An attitude or policy that demonstrates care or concern for those unable to help themselves, as in the (supposed) relationship between a father and a child.

● *Noblesse oblige*: (French) Literally, the 'obligations of the nobility'; in general terms, the responsibility to guide or protect those less fortunate or less privileged.

● **Toryism**: An ideological stance within conservatism characterized by a belief in hierarchy, an emphasis on tradition, and support for duty and organicism.

● **Natural aristocracy**: The idea that talent and leadership are innate or inbred qualities that cannot be acquired through effort or self-advancement.

Conservatism: key ideas

◆ **Tradition:** The central theme of conservative thought, 'the desire to conserve', is closely linked to the perceived virtues of tradition, respect for established customs, and institutions that have endured through time. In this view, tradition reflects the accumulated wisdom of the past, and institutions and practices that have been 'tested by time', and it should be preserved for the benefit of the living and for generations yet to come. Tradition also has the virtue of promoting a sense of social and historical belonging.

◆ **Pragmatism:** Conservatives have traditionally emphasized the limitations of human rationality, which arise from the infinite complexity of the world in which we live. Abstract principles and systems of thought are therefore distrusted, and instead faith is placed in experience, history and, above all, pragmatism: the belief that action should be shaped by practical circumstances and practical goals, that is, by 'what works'. Conservatives have thus preferred to describe their own beliefs as an 'attitude of mind' or an 'approach to life', rather than as an ideology, although they reject the idea that this amounts to unprincipled opportunism.

◆ **Human imperfection:** The conservative view of human nature is broadly pessimistic. In this view, human beings are limited, dependent, and security-seeking creatures, drawn to the familiar and the tried and tested, and needing to live in stable and orderly communities. In addition, individuals are morally corrupt: they are tainted by selfishness, greed and the thirst for power. The roots of crime and disorder therefore reside within the human individual rather than in society. The maintenance of order (see p. 400) therefore requires a strong state, the enforcement of strict laws, and stiff penalties.

◆ **Organicism:** Instead of seeing society as an artefact that is a product of human ingenuity, conservatives have traditionally viewed society as an organic whole, or living entity. Society is thus structured by natural necessity, with its various institutions, or the 'fabric of society' (families, local communities, the nation and so on), contributing to the health and stability of society. The whole is more than a collection of its individual parts. Shared (often 'traditional') values and a common culture are also seen as being vital to the maintenance of the community and social cohesion.

◆ **Hierarchy:** In the conservative view, gradations of social position and status are natural and inevitable in an organic society. These reflect the differing roles and responsibilities of, for example, employers and workers, teachers and pupils, and parents and children. Nevertheless, in this view, hierarchy and inequality do not give rise to conflict, because society is bound together by mutual obligations and reciprocal duties. Indeed, as a person's 'station in life' is determined largely by luck and the accident of birth, the prosperous and privileged acquire a particular responsibility of care for the less fortunate.

◆ **Authority:** Conservatives hold that, to some degree, authority is always exercised 'from above', providing leadership (see p. 300), guidance and support for those who lack the knowledge, experience or education to act wisely in their own interests (an example being the authority of parents over children). Although the idea of a natural aristocracy was once influential, authority and leadership are now more commonly seen as resulting from experience and training. The virtue of authority is that it is a source of social cohesion, giving people a clear sense of who they are and what is expected of them. Freedom must therefore coexist with responsibility; it therefore consists largely of a willing acceptance of obligations and duties.

◆ **Property:** Conservatives see property ownership as being vital because it gives people security and a measure of independence from government, and it encourages them to respect the law and the property of others. Property is also an exteriorization of people's personalities, in that they 'see' themselves in what they own: their houses, their cars, and so on. However, property ownership involves duties as well as rights. In this view, we are, in a sense, merely custodians of property that has either been inherited from past generations ('the family silver'), or may be of value to future ones.

Edmund Burke (1729–97)

Dublin-born UK statesman and political theorist who is often seen as the father of the Anglo-American conservative tradition. Burke's enduring reputation is based on a series of works, notably *Reflections on the Revolution in France* ([1790] 1968), that were critical of the French Revolution. Though sympathetic to the American Revolution, Burke was deeply critical of the attempt to recast French politics in accordance with abstract principles such as liberty, equality and fraternity, arguing that wisdom resided largely in experience, tradition and history. Nevertheless, he held that the French monarchy was, in part, responsible for its own fate since it had obstinately refused to 'change in order to conserve'. Burke had a gloomy view of government, recognizing that it could prevent evil but rarely promote good. He supported free market economics on the grounds that it reflects 'natural law'.

The One-Nation tradition embodies not only a disposition towards social reform, but also an essentially pragmatic attitude towards economic policy. This is clearly seen in the 'middle way' approach adopted in the 1950s by UK Conservatives. This approach eschewed the two ideological models of economic organization: *laissez-faire* capitalism on the one hand, and state socialism and central planning on the other. The former was rejected on the grounds that it results in a free for all, which makes social cohesion impossible, and penalizes the weak and vulnerable. The latter was dismissed because it produces a state monolith and crushes all forms of independence and enterprise. The solution therefore lies in a blend of market competition and government regulation – 'private enterprise without selfishness' (H. Macmillan).

Very similar conclusions were drawn after 1945 by continental European conservatives, who embraced the principles of **Christian democracy**, most rigorously developed in the 'social market' philosophy (see p. 133) of the German Christian Democrats (CDU). This philosophy embraces a market strategy, insofar as it highlights the virtues of private enterprise and competition; but it is social, in that it believes that the prosperity so gained should be employed for the broader benefit of society. Such a position draws from Catholic social theory, which advances an organic view of society that stresses social harmony. Christian democracy thus highlights the importance of intermediate institutions, such as churches, unions and business groups, bound together by the notion of 'social partnership'. The paternalistic strand of modern conservatism thought is often linked to the idea of 'compassionate conservatism'.

The New Right

● **Christian democracy:** An ideological tendency within European conservatism, characterized by commitment to social market principles and qualified interventionism.

The New Right represents a departure in conservative thought that amounted to a kind of counter-revolution against both the post-1945 drift towards state intervention and the spread of liberal or progressive social values. New Right ideas can be traced back to the 1970s and the conjunction between the apparent failure of Keynesian social democracy, signalled by the end of the postwar boom, and growing concern about social breakdown and the decline of authority. Such

Friedrich von Hayek (1899–1992)

Austrian economist and political philosopher. An academic who taught at the London School of Economics and the Universities of Chicago, Freiburg and Salzburg, Hayek was awarded the Nobel Prize for Economics in 1974. As an exponent of the so-called 'Austrian School', he was a firm believer in individualism and market order, and an implacable critic of socialism. *The Road to Serfdom* (1948) was a pioneering work that attacked economic interventionism. In later works such as *The Constitution of Liberty* (1960) and *Law, Legislation and Liberty* (1979) Hayek developed themes in political philosophy. Hayek's writings fused liberal and conservative elements, and had a considerable impact on the emergent New Right.

ideas had their greatest impact in the UK and the USA, where they were articulated in the 1980s in the form of Thatcherism and Reaganism, respectively. They have also had a wider, even worldwide, influence in bringing about a general shift from state- to market-orientated forms of organization. However, the New Right does not so much constitute a coherent and systematic philosophy as attempt to marry two distinct traditions, usually termed 'neoliberalism' and 'neoconservatism'. Although there is political and ideological tension between these two, they can be combined in support of the goal of a strong but minimal state: in Andrew Gamble's (1981) words, 'the free economy and the strong state'.

Neoliberalism

Neoliberalism (see p. 144) is an updated version of classical political economy that was developed in the writings of free-market economists such as Friedrich Hayek and Milton Friedman (see p. 138), and philosophers such as Robert Nozick (see p. 68). The central pillars of neoliberalism are the market and the individual. The principal neoliberal goal is to 'roll back the frontiers of the state', in the belief that unregulated market capitalism will deliver efficiency, growth and widespread prosperity. In this view, the 'dead hand' of the state saps initiative and discourages enterprise; government, however well-intentioned, invariably has a damaging effect on human affairs. This is reflected in the liberal New Right's concern with the politics of ownership, and its preference for private enterprise over state enterprise or nationalization: in short, 'private, good; public, bad'. Such ideas are associated with a form of rugged individualism, expressed in Margaret Thatcher's famous assertion that 'there is no such thing as society, only individuals and their families'. The '**nanny state**' is seen to breed a culture of dependence and to undermine freedom, which is understood as freedom of choice in the marketplace. Instead, faith is placed in self-help, individual responsibility and entrepreneurialism. Such ideas are widely seen to be advanced through the process of globalization (see p. 142), viewed by some as neoliberal globalization.

● **Nanny state**: A state with extensive social responsibilities; the term implies that welfare programmes are unwarranted and demeaning to the individual.

Neoconservatism

Neoconservatism reasserts nineteenth-century conservative social principles. The conservative New Right wishes, above all, to restore authority and return to traditional values, notably those linked to the family, religion and the nation. Authority is seen as guaranteeing social stability, on the basis that it generates discipline and respect, while shared values and a common culture are believed to generate social cohesion and make civilized existence possible. The enemies of neoconservatism are therefore **permissiveness**, the cult of the self and 'doing one's own thing', thought of as the values of the 1960s. Indeed, many of those who style themselves neoconservatives in the USA are former liberals who grew disillusioned with the progressive reforms of the Kennedy–Johnson era. Another aspect of neoconservatism is the tendency to view the emergence of multicultural and multireligious societies with concern, on the basis that they are conflict-ridden and inherently unstable. This position also tends to be linked to an insular form of nationalism that is sceptical about both multiculturalism (see p. 167) and the growing influence of supranational bodies such as the UN and the EU. Neoconservatism also developed into a distinctive approach to foreign policy, particularly in the USA under George Bush Jr, linked to attempts to consolidate US global domination, in part through militarily imposed 'regime change'.

Socialism

Although socialist ideas can be traced back to the Levellers and Diggers of the seventeenth century, or to Thomas More's *Utopia* ([1516] 1965), or even Plato's *Republic*, socialism did not take shape as a political creed until the early nineteenth century. It developed as a reaction against the emergence of industrial capitalism. Socialism first articulated the interests of artisans and craftsmen threatened by the spread of factory production, but it was soon being linked to the growing industrial working class, the 'factory fodder' of early industrialization. In its earliest forms, socialism tended to have a fundamentalist, utopian and revolutionary character. Its goal was to abolish a capitalist economy based on market exchange, and replace it with a qualitatively different socialist society, usually to be constructed on the principle of common ownership. The most influential representative of this brand of socialism was Karl Marx, whose ideas provided the foundations for twentieth-century communism.

From the late nineteenth century onwards, however, a reformist socialist tradition emerged that reflected the gradual integration of the working classes into capitalist society through an improvement in working conditions and wages, and the growth of trade unions and socialist political parties. This brand of socialism proclaimed the possibility of a peaceful, gradual and legal transition to socialism, brought about through the adoption of the 'parliamentary road'. Reformist socialism drew on two sources. The first was a humanist tradition of ethical socialism, linked to thinkers such as Robert Owen (1771–1858), Charles Fourier (1772–1837) and William Morris (1834–96). The second was a form of **revisionist** Marxism developed primarily by Eduard Bernstein (see p. 43).

During much of the twentieth century, the socialist movement was thus divided into two rival camps. Revolutionary socialists, following the example of Lenin and the Bolsheviks, called themselves 'communists', while reformist socialists, who practised a form of constitutional politics, embraced what increasingly came to be called 'social democracy'. This rivalry focused not only on the most appropriate means of achieving socialism, but also on the nature of the socialist

● **Permissiveness:** The willingness to allow people to make their own moral choices; permissiveness suggests that there are no authoritative values.

● **Revisionism:** The modification of original or established beliefs; revisionism can imply the abandonment of principle or a loss of conviction.

Socialism: key ideas

Community: The core of socialism is the vision of human beings as social creatures linked by the existence of a common humanity. As the poet John Donne put it, 'no man is an Island entire of itself; every man is a piece of the Continent, a part of the main'. This refers to the importance of community, and it highlights the degree to which individual identity is fashioned by social interaction and membership of social groups and collective bodies. Socialists are inclined to emphasize nurture over nature, and to explain individual behaviour mainly in terms of social factors, rather than innate qualities.

Fraternity: As human beings share a common humanity, they are bound together by a sense of comradeship or fraternity (literally meaning 'brotherhood', but broadened in this context to embrace all humans). This encourages socialists to prefer cooperation to competition, and to favour collectivism over individualism (see p. 158). In this view, cooperation enables people to harness their collective energies and strengthens the bonds of community, while competition pits individuals against each other, breeding resentment, conflict and hostility.

Social equality: Equality (see p. 454) is the central value of socialism. Socialism is sometimes portrayed as a form of egalitarianism, the belief in the primacy of equality over other values. In particular, socialists emphasize the importance of social equality, an equality of outcome as opposed to equality of opportunity. They believe that a measure of social equality is the essential guarantee of social stability and cohesion, encouraging individuals to identify with their fellow human beings. It also provides the basis for the exercise of legal and political rights. However, socialists disagree about the extent to which social equality can and should be brought about. While Marxists have believed in absolute social equality, brought about by the collectivization of production wealth, social democrats have favoured merely narrowing material inequalities, often being more concerned with equalizing opportunities than outcomes.

Need: Sympathy for equality also reflects the socialist belief that material benefits should be distributed on the basis of need, rather than simply on the basis of merit or work. The classic formulation of this principle is found in Marx's communist principle of distribution: 'from each according to his ability, to each according to his need'. This reflects the belief that the satisfaction of basic needs (hunger, thirst, shelter, health, personal security and so on) is a prerequisite for a worthwhile human existence and participation in social life. Clearly, however, distribution according to need requires people to be motivated by moral incentives, rather than just material ones.

Social class: Socialism has often been associated with a form of class politics. First, socialists have tended to analyse society in terms of the distribution of income or wealth, and they have thus seen social class (see p. 153) as a significant (usually the most significant) social cleavage. Second, socialism has traditionally been associated with the interests of an oppressed and exploited working class (however defined), and it has traditionally regarded the working class as an agent of social change, even social revolution.
Nevertheless, class divisions are remediable: the socialist goal is either the eradication of economic and social inequalities, or their substantial reduction.

Common ownership: The relationship between socialism and common ownership has been deeply controversial. Some see it as the *end* of socialism itself, and others see it instead simply as a *means* of generating broader equality. The socialist case for common ownership (in the form of either Soviet-style state collectivization, or selective nationalization (a 'mixed economy')) is that it is a means of harnessing material resources to the common good, with private property being seen to promote selfishness, acquisitiveness and social division. Modern socialism, however, has moved away from this narrow concern with the politics of ownership.

goal itself. Social democrats turned their backs on fundamentalist principles such as common ownership and planning, and recast socialism in terms of welfare, redistribution and economic management. Both forms of socialism, however, experienced crises in the late twentieth century that encouraged some to proclaim the 'death of socialism' and the emergence of a postsocialist society. The most dramatic event in this process was the collapse of communism brought about by the Eastern European revolutions of 1989–91, but there was also a continued retreat of social democracy from traditional principles, making it, some would argue, indistinguishable from modern liberalism.

Marxism

As a theoretical system, Marxism has constituted the principal alternative to the liberal rationalism that has dominated western culture and intellectual enquiry in the modern period. As a political force, in the form of the international communist movement, Marxism has also been seen as the major enemy of western capitalism, at least in the period 1917–91. This highlights a central difficulty in dealing with Marxism: the difference between Marxism as a social philosophy derived from the classic writings of Karl Marx and Friedrich Engels (1820–95), and the phenomenon of twentieth-century communism, which in many ways departed from and revised classical principles. Thus, the collapse of communism at the end of the twentieth century need not betoken the death of Marxism as a political ideology; indeed, it may give Marxism, now divorced from the vestiges of **Leninism** and **Stalinism**, a fresh lease of life.

Marx's ideas and theories reached a wider audience after his death, largely through the writings of his lifelong collaborator Engels, the German socialist leader Karl Kautsky (1854–1938) and the Russian theoretician Georgi Plekhanov (1856–1918). A form of orthodox Marxism, usually termed '**dialectical materialism**' (a term coined by Plekhanov, not Marx), came into existence that was later used as the basis for Soviet communism. This 'vulgar' Marxism undoubtedly placed a heavier stress on mechanistic theories and historical determinism than did Marx's own writings.

Classical Marxism

The core of classical Marxism – the Marxism of Marx – is a philosophy of history that Engels described as the 'materialist conception of history', or **historical materialism**. This highlights the importance of economic life and the conditions under which people produce and reproduce their means of subsistence. Marx held that the economic 'base', consisting essentially of the 'mode of production, or economic system, conditions or determines the ideological and political 'superstructure'. Following Hegel (see p. 59), Marx believed that the driving force of historical change was the dialectic, a process of interaction between competing forces that results in a higher stage of development. In its materialist version, this model implies that historical change is a consequence of internal contradictions within a 'mode of production', reflected in class conflict. Like all earlier class societies, capitalism is therefore doomed to collapse; in this case, as a result of conflict between the bourgeoisie or capitalist class, the owners of productive wealth, and the proletariat, who are, in effect, 'wage slaves'. This conflict is irreconcilable, because the proletariat is necessarily and systematically exploited

• **Leninism**: Lenin's theoretical contributions to Marxism, notably his belief in the need for a 'vanguard' party to raise the proletariat to class consciousness.

• **Stalinism**: The structures of Stalin's USSR, especially a centrally placed economy linked to systematic and brutal political oppression.

• **Dialectical materialism**: The crude and deterministic form of Marxism that dominated intellectual life in orthodox communist states.

• **Historical materialism**: The Marxist theory that holds that economic conditions ultimately structure law, politics, culture and other aspects of social existence.

Karl Marx (1818–83)

German philosopher, economist and political thinker, usually portrayed as the father of twentieth-century communism. After a brief career as a university teacher, Marx took up journalism and became increasingly involved with the socialist movement. He settled in London after being expelled from Prussia, and worked for the rest of his life as an active revolutionary and writer, supported by his friend and lifelong collaborator Friedrich Engels. In 1864, Marx helped to found the First International, which collapsed in 1871 because of growing antagonism between Marx's supporters and anarchists led by Bakunin. Marx's classic work was the three-volume *Capital* ([1867, 1885, 1894] 1970). His best-known and most accessible work is the *Communist Manifesto* ([1848] 1967).

under capitalism, the bourgeoisie living by extracting 'surplus value' from its labour.

According to Marx, the inevitable proletarian revolution will occur once a series of deepening crises have brought the proletariat to full class consciousness. This would allow the working masses to recognize the fact of their own exploitation and so become a revolutionary force. The proletarian revolution would usher in a transitionary 'socialist' period of development, characterized by the '**dictatorship of the proletariat**'. However, as class antagonisms fade and a fully communist society comes into existence, this proletarian state will 'wither away', meaning that a communist society will be both classlessness and statelessness. As a system of 'commodity production' gives rise to one based on 'production for use' and geared to the satisfaction of genuine human needs, 'the free development of each would become the precondition for the free development of all' (Marx).

Orthodox communism

Marxism in practice is inextricably linked to the experience of Soviet communism, (see p. 275), and especially to the contribution of the first two Soviet leaders, V. I. Lenin and Joseph Stalin (1879–1953). Indeed, twentieth-century communism is best understood as a form of Marxism–Leninism: that is, as orthodox Marxism modified by a set of Leninist theories and doctrines. Lenin's central contribution to Marxism was his theory of the revolutionary or vanguard party. This reflected Lenin's fear that the proletariat, deluded by bourgeois ideas and beliefs, would not realize its revolutionary potential because it could not develop beyond 'trade-union consciousness': a desire to improve working and living conditions rather than to overthrow capitalism. A revolutionary party, armed with Marxism, was therefore needed to serve as the 'vanguard of the working class'. In due course, this 'vanguard' or 'Leninist' party, composed of professional and dedicated revolutionaries, became the model for communist parties across the globe.

The USSR was, however, more profoundly affected by Stalin's 'second revolution' in the 1930s than it had been by the 1917 Bolshevik Revolution. In reshaping Soviet society, Stalin created a model of orthodox communism that was followed in the post-1945 period by states such as China, North Korea and Cuba, and throughout Eastern Europe. What may be called 'economic Stalinism' was

● **Dictatorship of the proletariat**: A temporary proletarian state, established to prevent counter-revolution and oversee the transition from capitalism to communism.

Herbert Marcuse (1898–1979)

German political philosopher and social theorist, and co-founder of the Frankfurt School. A refugee from Hitler's Germany, Marcuse lived in the USA from 1934. He developed a form of neo-Marxism that drew heavily on Hegel and Freud. Marcuse came to prominence in the 1960s as a leading thinker of the New Left and a 'guru' of the student movement. He portrayed advanced industrial society as an all-encompassing system of repression that subdued argument and debate, and absorbed opposition. His hopes rested not on the proletariat, but on marginalized groups such as students, ethnic minorities, women and workers in the developing world. His most important works include *Reason and Revolution* (1941), *Eros and Civilization* (1958) and *One-Dimensional Man* (1964).

initiated with the launch in 1928 of the first Five Year Plan, which brought about the swift and total eradication of private enterprise. This was followed in 1929 by the collectivization of agriculture. All resources were brought under the control of the state, and a system of central planning dominated by the State Planning Committee (*Gosplan*) was established. Stalin's political changes were no less dramatic. During the 1930s, Stalin transformed the USSR into a personal dictatorship through a series of purges that eradicated all vestiges of opposition and debate from the Communist Party, the state bureaucracy and the military. In effect, Stalin turned the USSR into a totalitarian dictatorship, operating through systematic intimidation, repression and terror.

Although the more brutal features of orthodox communism did not survive Stalin's death in 1953, the core principles of the Leninist party (hierarchical organization and discipline) and of economic Stalinism (state collectivization and central planning) stubbornly resisted pressure for reform. This was highlighted by Gorbachev's *perestroika* reform process (1985–91), which merely succeeded in exposing the failings of the planning system, and in releasing long-suppressed political forces. These eventually consigned Soviet communism to what Trotsky (see p. 369) had, in very different circumstances, called 'the dustbin of history'. However, political Stalinism survives in China, despite the embrace of market reforms, and North Korea remains a thoroughgoing orthodox communist regime. The collapse of communism during the 1989–91 period is widely seen as the most significant ideological event of the modern period.

Neo-Marxism

A more complex and subtle form of Marxism developed in western Europe. By contrast with the mechanistic and avowedly scientific notions of Soviet Marxism, western Marxism or neo-Marxism (see p. 64) tended to be influenced by Hegelian ideas and by the stress on 'Man the creator' found in Marx's early writings. In other words, human beings were seen as makers of history, and not simply as puppets controlled by impersonal material forces. By insisting that there was an interplay between economics and politics, between the material

● *Perestroika*: (Russian) Literally, 'restructuring'; a slogan that refers to the attempt to liberalize and democratize the Soviet system within a communist framework.

Eduard Bernstein (1850–1932)

German socialist politician and theorist. An early member of the German SPD, Bernstein became one of the leading advocates of revisionism, the attempt to revise and modernize orthodox Marxism. Influenced by British Fabianism and the philosophy of Kant (see p. 410), Bernstein developed a largely empirical critique that emphasized the absence of class war, and proclaimed the possibility of a peaceful transition to socialism. This is described in *Evolutionary Socialism* ([1898] 1962). He left the SPD over his opposition to World War I, although he subsequently returned and served as the secretary of state for the economy and finance in the Ebert government (1918–19). Bernstein is often seen as one of the founding figures of modern social democracy.

circumstances of life and the capacity of human beings to shape their own destinies, neo-Marxists were able to break free from the rigid 'base–superstructure' straitjacket. This indicated an unwillingness to treat the class struggle as the beginning and end of social analysis.

The Hungarian Marxist Georg Lukács (1885–1971) was one of the first to present Marxism as a humanistic philosophy. He emphasized the process of 'reification', through which capitalism dehumanizes workers by reducing them to passive objects or marketable commodities. In his *Prison Notebooks*, written in 1929–35, Antonio Gramsci emphasized the degree to which capitalism was maintained not merely by economic domination, but also by political and cultural factors. He called this ideological 'hegemony' (see p. 174). A more overtly Hegelian brand of Marxism was developed by the so-called 'Frankfurt School', the leading members of which were Theodor Adorno (1903–69), Max Horkheimer (1895–1973) and Herbert Marcuse (see p. 42). Frankfurt theorists developed what was called 'critical theory', a blend of Marxist political economy, Hegelian philosophy and Freudian psychology, which had a considerable impact on the New Left in the 1960s. A later generation of Frankfurt members included Jürgen Habermas (see p. 84).

While early critical theorists were primarily concerned with the analysis of discrete societies, later theorists have tended to give greater attention to uncovering inequalities and asymmetries in world affairs. This has been evident in an emphasis on the hegemonic power of the USA (Cox, 1987) and the analysis of capitalism as a 'world-system' (Wallerstein, 1984).

Social democracy

● Fundamentalist socialism: A form of socialism that seeks to abolish capitalism and replace it with a qualitatively different kind of society.

Social democracy lacks the theoretical coherence of, say, classical liberalism or fundamentalist socialism. Whereas the former is ideologically committed to the market, and the latter champions the cause of common ownership, social democracy stands for a balance between the market and the state, a balance between the individual and the community. At the heart of social democracy there is a compromise between, on the one hand, an acceptance of capitalism as

Fall of communism: the triumph of liberal democracy?

Events: The collapse of communism was precipitated by a series of revolutions that took place during the momentous year of 1989. The first popular challenge to a communist regime in 1989 was the Tiananmen Square protests in Beijing, China, which began in April, but were suppressed by a military crackdown on 4 June. Events in Eastern Europe nevertheless gathered momentum the following day, as Solidarity, the newly-legalized independent trade union movement, swept the board in parliamentary elections, leading, by September, to the formation of the first non-communist government in the Eastern bloc. In October, the Hungarian parliament adopted legislation providing for multiparty elections and, eventually, the establishment of a second non-communist government. Pressure for political change built up in East Germany, the USSR's firmest Eastern bloc ally, as thousands of East Germans escaped to West Germany, via Hungary, and a growing wave of demonstrations eventually culminated on the night of 9/10 November in the fall of the Berlin Wall, the chief symbol of the Cold War and of Europe's East–West divide. Whereas peaceful protest led to the collapse of communist rule in Czechoslovakia (the 'velvet revolution') in December, and in Bulgaria in February 1990, the process was more violent in Romania, where the communist leader Ceaușescu and his wife Elena were summarily executed on Christmas Day 1989. The period of revolutionary upheaval eventually culminated in December 1991 with the official dissolution of the USSR, the world's first communist state, following a succession of nationalist uprisings across the multinational Soviet state.

Significance: The ideological significance of the fall of communism has been profound and far-reaching, and, in some senses, it remains a continuing process. The dominant early interpretation of the collapse of communism was advanced by so-called 'end of history' theorists such as Fukuyama (see p. 271). In this view, the collapse of orthodox communist regimes across Eastern Europe and beyond indicated the death of Marxism as an ideology of world-historical importance, revealing western-style, and more specifically US-style, liberal democracy as the determinant end-point of human history. The events of 1989–91 therefore merely illustrate the irresistible fact that human societies are destined to converge around an essentially liberal model of economic and social development, as only western liberalism can offer the benefits of social mobility and material security, on the one hand, and the opportunity for personal self-development without the interference of the state, on the other hand. Such an analysis suggests not only that communism is a spent ideological force, but also that socialism in its wider forms has been seriously compromised by the dramatic failure of the world's only significant non-capitalist economic systems. Social-democratic parties have, as a result, gone through a process of de-radicalization, encouraging some to proclaim that socialism, as a distinctive ideology, is dead.

However, there are reasons for thinking that the 'end of history' thesis was at best premature and at worst wholly misconceived. In the first place, the period since 1989–91 has certainly not witnessed worldwide ideological convergence around the principles of liberal democracy. Indeed, in the non-western world, liberalism has sometimes been contested more ferociously than ever before, not least by the forces of ethnic nationalism and religious fundamentalism, especially in the Muslim world. In China, and across much of East and Southeast Asia, Confucian and other indigenous ideas have gained renewed political currency, gaining strength in large part from the desire to resist the spread of atomistic and rights-orientated liberal thinking. Similarly, in its western heartland, liberalism's ascendancy has been challenged by an array of ideological forces, ranging from green politics and certain strains within feminism to communitarianism, multiculturalism and postmodernism. Finally, despite its undoubted resilience, it is difficult to see how liberal capitalism will ever achieve a universal appeal, given its inherent tendency towards social inequality and instability.

John Rawls (1921–2002)

US academic and political philosopher. His major work, *A Theory of Justice* (1970), is regarded as the most important work of political philosophy written in English since World War II. It has influenced modern liberals and social democrats alike. Rawls proposed a theory of 'justice as fairness' that is based on the belief that social inequality can be justified only if it is of benefit to the least advantaged. This presumption in favour of equality is rooted in Rawls' belief that most people, deprived of knowledge about their own talents and abilities, would choose to live in an egalitarian society, rather than an inegalitarian one. As, for most people, the fear of being poor outweighs the desire to be rich, redistribution and welfare can be defended on grounds of fairness. Rawls' other works include *Political Liberalism* (1993) and *The Laws of People* (1999).

the only reliable mechanism for generating wealth and, on the other, a desire to distribute wealth in accordance with moral, rather than market, principles. For socialists, this conversion to the market was a difficult, and at times painful, process that was dictated more by practical circumstances and electoral advantage than by ideological conviction.

The chief characteristic of modern social democratic thought is a concern for the underdog in society, the weak and vulnerable. There is a sense, however, in which social democracy cannot simply be confined to the socialist tradition. It may draw on a socialist belief in compassion and a common humanity, a liberal commitment to positive freedom and equal opportunities, or, for that matter, a conservative sense of paternal duty and care. Whatever its source, it has usually been articulated on the basis of principles such as welfarism, redistribution and social justice. In the form of Keynesian social democracy, which was widely accepted in the early period after World War II, it was associated with a clear desire to 'humanize' capitalism through state intervention. It was believed that Keynesian economic policies would secure full employment, a mixed economy would help government to regulate economic activity, and comprehensive welfare provision funded via progressive taxation would narrow the gap between rich and poor.

Since the 1980s, a further process of revisionism has taken place within social democracy. This occurred for a variety of reasons. In the first place, changes in the class structure, and particularly the growth of professional and clerical occupations, meant that social-democratic policies orientated around the interests of the traditional working class were no longer electorally viable. Second, globalization appeared to render all specifically national forms of economic management, such as Keynesianism, redundant. Third, nationalized industries and economic planning proved to be inefficient, at least in developed states. Fourth, the collapse of communism undermined the intellectual and ideological credibility not just of state collectivization, but of all 'top-down' socialist models. In this context, it became increasingly fashionable for politicians and political parties to rethink or revise 'traditional' social democracy.

Third way

The term the third way encapsulates the idea of an alternative to both capitalism and socialism. Initially used by fascists, the term is now firmly linked to 'new' or modernized social democracy. In this context the third way is an alternative to old-style social democracy and neoliberalism. The former is rejected because it is wedded to statist structures that are inappropriate to the modern knowledge-based and market-orientated economy. The latter is rejected because it generates a free-for-all that undermines the moral foundations of society.

'New' social democracy

'New' social democracy (sometimes called 'neo-revisionism' or the 'third way') is a term that refers to a variety of attempts by social-democratic parties, in countries ranging from Germany, Italy and the Netherlands to the UK and New Zealand, to reconcile old-style social democracy with, at least, the electorally-attractive aspects of neoliberalism. Although 'new' social democracy is imprecise and subject to a number of interpretations, certain characteristic themes can nevertheless be identified. The first of these is the belief that socialism, at least in the form of 'top-down' state intervention, is dead: there is no alternative to what Clause 4 of the UK Labour Party's constitution, rewritten in 1995, refers to as 'a dynamic market economy'. With this goes a general acceptance of globalization and the belief that capitalism has mutated into a 'knowledge economy', which places a premium on information technology, individual skills, and both labour and business flexibility. In this light, the state came to be seen not as a vehicle for wholesale social restructuring, but as a means of promoting international competitiveness; particularly by building up education and skills.

A further feature of 'new' social-democratic politics is that it has broken with socialist egalitarianism (which is seen as a form of 'levelling') and embraced, instead, the liberal ideas of equality of opportunity and meritocracy. Neorevisionist politicians typically endorse welfare reform. They reject both the neoliberal emphasis on 'standing on your own two feet' and the 'traditional' social-democratic commitment to 'cradle to grave' welfare in favour of an essentially modern liberal belief in 'helping people to help themselves', or, as the former US president Bill Clinton put it, giving people 'a hand up, not a hand out'. This has led to support for what has been called a 'workfare state', in which government provision in terms of benefits or education is conditional on individuals seeking work and becoming self-reliant. Critics of 'new' social democracy, on the other hand, argue either that it is contradictory, in that it simultaneously endorses the dynamism of the market and warns against its tendency to social disintegration, or that, far from being a centre-left project, it amounts to a shift to the right.

OTHER IDEOLOGICAL TRADITIONS

Liberalism, conservatism and socialism by no means exhaust the field of ideological politics. Other ideological traditions have nevertheless tended to develop either out of, or in opposition to, these core ideologies. Where they have drawn, to a significant extent, on liberal, conservative and/or socialist thinking, these other ideologies have a 'cross-cutting' character, in that they incorporate elements from 'bigger' ideological traditions. This applies, albeit in different ways, to anarchism, feminism, green politics and cosmopolitanism, as well as to nationalism and multiculturalism; ideological traditions that are examined, respectively, in Chapters 5 and 7. Where other ideological traditions have emerged largely in opposition to liberalism, conservatism and socialism, they have been marked by an attempt to challenge and overturn core features of the western political tradition itself. This applies in the case of

Adolf Hitler (1889–1945)

German Nazi dictator. Hitler was the son of an Austrian customs official. He joined the German Worker's Party (later the Nationalsozialistische Deutsche Arbeiterpartei (NSDAP), or Nazi Party) in 1919, becoming its leader in 1921. He was appointed Chancellor of Germany in 1933, and declared himself *Führer* (Leader) the following year, by which time he had established a one-party dictatorship. The central feature of Hitler's world-view, outlined in *Mein Kampf* ([1925] 1969), was his attempt to fuse expansionist German nationalism and virulent anti-Semitism into a theory of history in which there was an endless battle between the Germans and the Jews, who represented, respectively, the forces of good and evil. Hitler's policies contributed decisively to both the outbreak of World War II and the Holocaust.

fascism and certain trends in non-western ideological thought, notably political Islam.

Fascism

Whereas liberalism, conservatism and socialism are nineteenth-century ideologies, fascism is a child of the twentieth century. Some would say that it is specifically an interwar phenomenon. Although fascist beliefs can be traced back to the late nineteenth century, they were fused together and shaped by World War I and its aftermath and, in particular, by the potent mixture of war and revolution that characterized the period. The two principal manifestations of fascism were Mussolini's Fascist dictatorship in Italy in 1922–43, and Hitler's Nazi dictatorship in Germany in 1933–45. Forms of neofascism and neo-Nazism have also resurfaced in recent decades, taking advantage of the combination of economic crisis and political instability that often followed the collapse of communism or, more widely, of increased anxieties over immigration and multiculturalism (see p. 167).

In many respects, fascism constituted a revolt against the ideas and values that had dominated western political thought since the French Revolution: in the words of the Italian Fascist slogan, '1789 is dead'. Values such as rationalism, progress, freedom and equality were thus overturned in the name of struggle, leadership, power, heroism and war. In this sense, fascism has an 'anticharacter'. It is defined largely by what it opposes: it is a form of anticapitalism, antiliberalism, anti-individualism, anticommunism, and so on. A core theme that, nevertheless, runs throughout fascism is the image of an organically unified national community. This is reflected in a belief in 'strength through unity'. The individual, in a literal sense, is nothing; individual identity must be absorbed entirely into that of the community or social group. The fascist ideal is that of the 'new man', a hero, motivated by duty, honour and self-sacrifice, prepared to dedicate his life to the glory of his nation or race, and to give unquestioning obedience to a supreme leader.

Not all fascists, however, think alike. Italian Fascism was essentially an extreme form of statism (see p. 71) that was based on unquestioning respect and absolute loyalty towards a 'totalitarian' state. As the Fascist philosopher Gentile (1875–1944) put it, 'everything for the state; nothing against the state; nothing outside the state'. German National Socialism (or Nazism), on the other hand, was constructed largely on the basis of racialism (see p. 120). Its two core theories were Aryanism (the belief that the German people constitute a 'master race' and are destined for world domination), and a virulent form of anti-Semitism (see p. 121) that portrayed the Jews as inherently evil, and aimed at their eradication. This latter belief found expression in the 'Final Solution'.

Anarchism

Anarchism is unusual amongst political ideologies in that no anarchist party has ever succeeded in winning power, at least at national level. Nevertheless, anarchist movements were powerful in, for example, Spain, France, Russia and Mexico through to the early twentieth century, and anarchist ideas continue to fertilize political debate by challenging the conventional belief that law, government and the state are either wholesome or indispensable. Anarchist thinking has also been influential within the modern anti-capitalist, or anti-globalization, movement. The central theme within anarchism is the belief that political authority in all its forms, and especially in the form of the state, is both evil and unnecessary (anarchy literally means 'without rule'). Nevertheless, the anarchist preference for a stateless society in which free individuals manage their own affairs through voluntary agreement and cooperation has been developed on the basis of two rival traditions: liberal individualism, and socialist communitarianism. Anarchism can thus be thought of as a point of intersection between liberalism and socialism: a form of both 'ultraliberalism' and 'ultrasocialism'.

> ● **Anarcho-capitalism:** An ararchist tradition which holds that unregulated market competition can and should be applied to all social arrangements, making the state unnecessary.

The liberal case against the state is based on individualism, and the desire to maximize liberty and choice. Unlike liberals, individualist anarchists such as William Godwin (1756–1836) believed that free and rational human beings would be able to manage their affairs peacefully and spontaneously, government being merely a form of unwanted coercion. Modern individualists have usually looked to the market to explain how society would be regulated in the absence of state authority, developing a form of **anarcho-capitalism**, an extreme version of free-market economics. The more widely-recognized anarchist tradition, however, draws on socialist ideas such as community, cooperation, equality and common ownership. Collectivist anarchists (sometimes called social anarchists) stress the capacity for social solidarity that arises from our sociable, gregarious and essentially cooperative natures. On this basis, the French anarchist Pierre-Joseph Proudhon (see p. 381), for instance, developed what he called '**mutualism**'. Other anarchists, such as the Russian Peter Kropotkin (1842–1921), advanced a form of **anarcho-communism**, the central principles of which were common ownership, decentralization and workers' self-management. Modern thinkers influenced by anarchism include Noam Chomsky (see p. 181) and the US libertarian and social ecologist Murray Bookchin (1921–2006).

> ● **Mutualism:** A system of fair and quitable exchange, in which individuals or groups trade goods and services with one another without profiteering or exploitation.

> ● **Anarcho-communism:** An anarchist tradition which takes common ownership to be the sole reliable basis for social solidarity, thereby linking statelessness to classlessness.

Feminism

Although feminist aspirations have been expressed in societies dating back to Ancient China, they were not underpinned by a developed political theory until the publication of Mary Wollstonecraft's (see p. 50) *A Vindication of the Rights of Women* ([1792] 1985). Indeed, it was not until the emergence of the women's suffrage movement in the 1840s and 1850s that feminist ideas reached a wider audience, in the form of so-called 'first-wave feminism'. The achievement of female suffrage in most western countries in the early twentieth century deprived the women's movement of its central goal and organizing principle. 'Second-wave feminism', however, emerged in the 1960s. This expressed the more radical, and sometimes revolutionary, demands of the growing Women's Liberation Movement (WLM). Feminist theories and doctrines are diverse, but their unifying feature is a common desire to enhance, through whatever means, the social role of women. The underlying themes of feminism are therefore, first, that society is characterized by sexual or gender inequality and, second, that this structure of male power can, and should be, overturned.

Feminist thinking has traditionally been analysed in terms of a division between liberal, socialist and radical schools of thought. Liberal feminists, such as Wollstonecraft and Betty Friedan (see p. 263), have tended to understand female subordination in terms of the unequal distribution of rights and opportunities in society. This 'equal-rights feminism' is essentially reformist. It is concerned more with the reform of the 'public' sphere; that is, with enhancing the legal and political status of women, and improving their educational and career prospects, than with reordering 'private' or domestic life. In contrast, socialist feminists typically highlight the links between female subordination and the capitalist mode of production, drawing attention to the economic significance of women being confined to a family or domestic life where they, for example, relieve male workers of the burden of domestic labour, rear and help to educate the next generation of capitalist workers, and act as a reserve army of labour.

However, the distinctive flavour of second-wave feminism results mainly from the emergence of a feminist critique that is not rooted in conventional political doctrines; namely, radical feminism. Radical feminists believe that gender divisions are the most fundamental and politically significant cleavages in society. In their view, all societies, historical and contemporary, are characterized by patriarchy (see p. 65), the institution whereby, as Kate Millett (1969) put it, 'that half of the population which is female is controlled by that half which is male'. Radical feminists therefore proclaim the need for a sexual revolution, a revolution that will, in particular, restructure personal, domestic and family life. The characteristic slogan of radical feminism is thus 'the personal is the political'. Only in its extreme form, however, does radical feminism portray men as 'the enemy', and proclaim the need for women to withdraw from male society, a stance sometimes expressed in the form of political lesbianism. However, since the 1970s feminism has, in many ways, moved beyond the three-fold division into liberal, socialist and radical traditions. Although 'new feminism' or 'third-wave feminism' are disparate, they tend to be characterized by doubts about the conventional goal of gender equality, placing an emphasis

● **Liberal feminism:** A feminist tradition whose core goal is equal access for women and men to the public realm, based on a belief of genderless personhood.

● **Socialist feminism:** A feminist tradition that seeks to restructure economic life to achieve gender equality, based in links between patriarchy and capitalism.

● **Radical feminism:** A feminist tradition that aims to overthrow patriarchy through a radical transformation of all spheres of life, but especially 'the personal'.

Mary Wollstonecraft (1759–97)

UK social theorist and feminist. Deeply influenced by the democratic radicalism of Rousseau, Wollstonecraft developed the first systematic feminist critique some 50 years before the emergence of the female-suffrage movement. Her most important work, *A Vindication of the Rights of Women* ([1792] 1985), was influenced by Lockean liberalism, and it stressed the equal rights of women, especially the right to education, on the basis of the notion of 'personhood'. However, the work developed a more complex analysis of womanhood itself that is relevant to the concerns of contemporary feminism. Wollstonecraft was married to the anarchist William Godwin, and she was the mother of Mary Shelley, the author of *Frankenstein*.

instead on differences, both between women and men and between women themselves.

Green politics

Although green politics, or ecologism (see p. 51), is usually seen as a new ideology that is linked to the emergence of the environmental movement since the late twentieth century, its roots can be traced back to the nineteenth-century revolt against industrialization. Green politics therefore reflects concern about the damage done to the natural world by the increasing pace of economic development (exacerbated since the second half of the twentieth century by the advent of nuclear technology, acid rain, ozone depletion, global warming and so on), and anxiety about the declining quality of human existence and, ultimately, the survival of the human species. Such concerns are sometimes expressed through the vehicle of conventional ideologies. For instance, ecosocialism explains environmental destruction in terms of capitalism's rapacious desire for profit. Ecoconservatism links the cause of conservation to the desire to preserve traditional values and established institutions. And ecofeminism locates the origins of the ecological crisis in the system of male power, reflecting the fact that men are less sensitive than women to natural processes and the natural world.

However, what gives green politics its radical edge is the fact that it offers an alternative to the **anthropocentric**, or human-centred, stance adopted by all other ideologies; it does not see the natural world simply as a resource available to satisfy human needs. By highlighting the importance of ecology, green politics develops an ecocentric world-view that portrays the human species as merely part of nature. One of the most influential theories in this field is the Gaia hypothesis, advanced by James Lovelock (1979, 2006). This portrays the planet Earth as a living organism that is primarily concerned with its own survival. Others have expressed sympathy for such radical **holism** by drawing on the ideas of Eastern religions that emphasize the oneness of life, such as Taoism and Zen Buddhism (Capra, 1983). 'Shallow' or humanist ecologists, such as those in some environmental pressure groups, believe that an appeal to self-interest and common sense will persuade humankind to adopt ecologically sound policies and lifestyles, usually in line with the principle of sustainable development (see

● Anthropocentrism: The belief that human needs and interests are of overriding moral and philosophical importance; the opposite of ecocentrism.

● Holism: The belief that the whole is more imortant than its parts, implying that understanding is gained only by studying relationships among its parts.

Ecologism

Ecology (a term first used by Ernst Haeckel in 1873) is the study of the relationship between living organisms and their environment. It thus draws attention to the network of relationships that sustain all forms of life. Ecologism is a political doctrine or ideology that is constructed on the basis of ecological assumptions, notably about the essential link between humankind and the natural world: humans are part of nature, not its 'masters'. Ecologism is sometimes distinguished from environmentalism, in that the former implies the adoption of a biocentric perspective, while the latter is concerned with protecting nature, ultimately for human benefit.

Figure 13.1   As ecologists argue, human-centredness poses a threat to both nature and, ultimately, human survival (Ferrybridge, UK).

p. 140). 'Deep' ecologists, on the other hand, insist that nothing short of a fundamental reordering of political priorities, and a willingness to place the interests of the ecosystem before those of any individual species, will ultimately secure planetary and human survival. Members of both groups can be found in the 'anti-party' green parties that have sprung up in Germany, Austria and elsewhere in Europe since the 1970s.

Cosmopolitanism

Although cosmopolitan ideas can be traced back to the Cynics of Ancient Greece and the Stoics of Ancient Rome, cosmopolitanism has only been treated as an ideological tradition in its own right since the 1990s. This occurred as the moral, political and cultural implications of growing global interconnectedness became increasingly apparent. In that sense, cosmopolitanism can be viewed as the ideological expression of globalization (although the relationship between the two is complex, cosmopolitans often calling for radical changes in the currently dominant forms of globalization). In a literal sense, cosmopolitanism means a belief in a *cosmopolis* or 'world state'. However, such 'political' cosmopolitanism, which is reflected in the quest to establish global political institutions, has limited relevance to modern cosmopolitan thinking, due to its association with the unfashionable idea of **world government**. Modern cosmopolitanism therefore tends to have a moral or cultural character.

'Moral' cosmopolitanism, the notion that underpins much anti-globalization activism, is the belief that the world constitutes a single moral community. This implies that people have obligations (potentially) towards all other people in the world, regardless of nationality, religion, ethnicity and so forth. Such ethical thinking is based on the core idea that the individual, rather than any political community, is the principal focus of moral concern. Most commonly, this is asserted through the doctrine of human rights (see p. 342). Nevertheless, moral cosmopolitanism has taken contrasting liberal and socialist forms.

● **World government:** The idea of all of humankind united under one common political authority, whether a unitary world state with supranational authority or a federal body that shares sovereignty with nation-states.

CONCEPT

Postcolonialism

Postcolonialism is a trend in literary, cultural and political studies that seeks to expose and overturn the cultural and psychological dimensions of colonial rule. As such, it recognizes that 'inner' subjugation can persist long after the political structures of colonialism have been removed. A major thrust of postcolonialism has been to establish the legitimacy of non-western, and sometimes anti-western, political ideas and traditions. Postcolonialism has nevertheless taken a variety of forms. These range from Gandhi's attempt to fuse Indian nationalism with ideas rooted in Hinduism to forms of religious fundamentalism.

Liberal cosmopolitanism has been expressed in two ways. The first is the attempt to universalize civic and political rights, especially classic 'liberal' rights such as the right to life, liberty and property, freedom of expression and freedom from arbitrary arrest. This form of cosmopolitanism has been associated with, amongst other things, support for humanitarian intervention (see p. 424) and attempts to strengthen the framework of international law, notably through international courts and tribunals. The second form of liberal cosmopolitanism derives from economic liberalism, and places particular stress on attempts to universalize market society, seen as a means of widening individual freedom and promoting material advancement. In marked contrast, socialist cosmopolitanism is rooted in the Marxist belief that proletarian class solidarity has a transnational character, graphically expressed in the famous final words of the *Communist Manifesto*: 'Working men of all countries, unite!' Modern versions of such thinking are, nevertheless, more likely to be based on the idea of economic and social rights, than on Marxist analysis. The key theme in this form of cosmopolitanism is the quest for global social justice, implying both a substantial redistribution of wealth from the global North to the global South and a radical reform of the system of global economic governance (discussed in Chapter 19).

Such thinking is often associated with 'cultural' cosmopolitanism, which highlights the extent to which people's values and lifestyles have been reconfigured as a result of intensified global interconnectedness. In this sense, political community is in the process of being redefined as people come to think of themselves as 'global citizens', rather than merely citizens of a particular state. The supposed evidence for this is the shift from nationalism to multiculturalism, or, at least, a form of multiculturalism that emphasizes hybridity and cultural mixing, or 'mongrelization' (Waldron, 1995). However, although cosmopolitanism has had a growing impact on ethical thinking, it has had only a limited impact in terms of cultural restructuring. Nationalism may be under growing pressure from forces both within and without, but (as discussed in Chapter 5) the nation remains the pre-eminent basis for political community, with no international body, including the European Union, coming close to rivalling its ability to foster affection and civic allegiance.

Non-western ideological trends

In origin, political ideology was a distinctively western construct. The major ideological traditions developed as contrasting attempts to shape emergent industrial society, their ideas and theories being indelibly shaped by historical experience in Europe and North America. Moreover, in the case of liberalism and socialism in particular, political ideology drew from an Enlightenment tradition that emphasized the ideas of reason and progress, and helped to shape wider intellectual and cultural developments in the West. As political ideology spread, it therefore exported to the rest of the world an essentially western model of modernity, or, more accurately, competing western models of modernity. Ideological trends such as 'Arab nationalism', 'African socialism' or 'Chinese communism' therefore amounted to attempts to apply western ideas in non-western contexts, although, at times, western doctrines were also entangled with indigenous values and ideas. As Julius Nyerere, president of Tanzania, 1964-85,

CONCEPT

Fundamentalism

Fundamentalism refers to a style of thought in which certain principles are recognized as essential 'truths' which have unchallengeable and overriding authority. Substantive fundamentalisms have little or nothing in common, except that their supporters tend to evince an earnestness or fervour born out of doctrinal certainty. Although it is usually associated with religion and the literal truth of sacred texts, fundamentalism can also be found in political creeds. The term is controversial because it is often used pejoratively, to imply inflexibility, dogmatism and authoritarianism.

● **Non-Aligned Movement:** An organization of countries, founded in Belgrade in 1961, that sought to avoid formal political and economic affiliation with either the capitalist West or the communist East.

● *Jihad:* (Arabic) Conventionally translated as 'holy war' but, more correctly, as 'holy struggle' or 'effort'; intense and all-consuming devotion to Islamic goals.

pointed out, 'We, in Africa, have no more real need to be "converted" to socialism, than we have of being "taught" democracy'. He therefore described his own views as 'tribal socialism'.

Postcolonialism

Nevertheless, more explicit attempts to give political ideology a non-western identity emerged out of trends associated with postcolonialism (see p. 52). The characteristic feature of postcolonialism is that it sought to give the non-western world a distinctive political voice separate from, in particular, the universalist pretensions of liberalism and socialism. An early but influential attempt to do this was undertaken at the Bandung Conference of 1955, when 29 mostly newly-independent African and Asian countries, including Egypt, Ghana, India and Indonesia, initiated what later became known as the **Non-Aligned Movement**. They saw themselves as an independent power bloc, offering a 'Third World' perspective on global political, economic and cultural priorities. This 'third-worldism' defined itself in contradistinction to both western and Soviet models of development.

However, postcolonial ideological trends have been highly disparate. They have been reflected in Gandhi's (see p. 54) political philosophy, which was based on a religious ethic of non-violence and self-sacrifice that was ultimately rooted in Hinduism. In this view, violence, 'the doctrine of the sword', was a western imposition on India. In contrast, the Martinique-born French revolutionary theorist Franz Fanon (1926–61) highlighted the extent to which colonial rule operates at a psycho-political level through the asymmetrical relationship between 'whites' and 'blacks', and that this could only be destroyed through the purifying force of 'absolute violence' (Fanon, 1968).

Religious fundamentalism

Postcolonialism has, nevertheless, been expressed most forcibly through the upsurge, especially since the late 1970s, in religious fundamentalism and, most importantly, Islamic fundamentalism, or political Islam. The idea that an intense and militant faith that Islamic beliefs constitute the overriding principles of social life and politics first emerged in the writings of thinkers such as Sayyid Qutb (1906–66) and through the activities of the Muslim Brotherhood. Their goal was the establishment of an Islamic state based on the principles of *shari'a* law. Political Islam was brought to prominence by the Iranian revolution of 1979, which led to the founding of the world's first Islamic state, under Ayatollah Khomeini (see p. 164). It subsequently spread throughout the Middle East, across North Africa, and into parts of Asia. Although the Shi'a fundamentalism of Iran has generated the fiercest commitment and devotion, Islamism (see p. 165) in general has been a vehicle for expressing anti-westernism, reflecting both antipathy towards the neo-colonial policies of western powers and anxiety about the 'imposition' of permissive and materialist values. This was clearly reflected in the Taliban regime of Afghanistan (1997–2001), and also in the growth of **jihadist** groups such as al-Qaeda, for whom the spiritual quest became synonymous with militant politics, armed struggle and possibly martyrdom.

Mohandas Karamchand Gandhi (1869–1948)

An Indian spiritual and political leader (called *Mahatma*, 'Great Soul'), Gandhi trained as a lawyer in the UK and worked in South Africa, where he organized protests against discrimination. After returning to India in 1915, he became the leader of the nationalist movement, campaigning tirelessly for independence, finally achieved in 1947. Gandhi's ethic of non-violent resistance, *satyagraha*, reinforced by his ascetic lifestyle, gave the movement for Indian independence enormous moral authority. Derived from Hinduism, Gandhi's political philosophy was based on the assumption that the universe is regulated by the primacy of truth, or *satya*, and that humankind is 'ultimately one'. Gandhi was assassinated in 1948 by a fanatical Hindu, becoming a victim of the ferocious Hindu-Muslim violence which followed independence.

Asian values

Other non-western ideological trends have had no connection with fundamentalist religion, however. During the 1980s and 1990s, for example, the idea of so-called 'Asian values' gained growing currency, fuelled by the emergence of Japan as an economic superpower and the success of the 'tiger' economies of Hong Kong, South Korea, Thailand and Singapore. While not rejecting the idea of universal human rights, Asian values drew attention to supposed differences between western and Asian value systems, highlighting the extent to which human rights had traditionally been constructed on the basis of culturally-biased western assumptions. Asian values had sought to rectify this by offering a vision of social harmony and cooperation grounded in loyalty, duty and respect for authority. Although their influence declined markedly following the 1997–98 Asian financial crisis, they have resurfaced through their association with Confucianism (see p. 278), bolstered by the rise of China.

Beyond dualism

An alternative non-western ideological trend has contrasted the non-dualistic emphasis found in some non-western philosophical traditions with the resolute **dualism** of conventional western philosophy. Aristotle's (see p. 6) insistence that everything has a distinctive essence that it cannot lack, expressed through the idea that 'everything must either be or not be', can thus be contrasted with the Buddhist philosopher Nagarjuna's (*ca.* 150–250 CE) doctrine of *sunyata* or 'emptiness'. According to this, all concepts and objects lack 'own-being', highlighting intrinsic interdependence. Such thinking, often influenced by Buddhism or Taoism, was also been expressed by Kyoto School philosophers in Japan such as Nishada Kitaro (1870–1945), who asserted that the world is characterized by the 'absolute unity of opposites'. If western 'either/or' thinking is set aside in favour of a world-view that stresses integration and oneness, all other forms of dualism – mind/body, good/evil, subject/object, humankind/nature and so on – begin to collapse. Non-dualistic thinking has had its greatest ideological impact in relation to green politics, where it provides the philosophical foundation for many forms of deep ecology.

● **Asian values**: Values that supposedly reflect the history, culture and religious backgrounds of Asian societies; examples include social harmony, respect for authority and a belief in the family.

● **Dualism**: The belief that reality consists of two basic principles, often taken to be mind and matter but it may extend to other dualities.

SUMMARY

- Ideology is a controversial political term that has often carried pejorative implications. In the social-scientific sense, a political ideology is a more or less coherent set of ideas that provides a basis for organized political action. Its central features are an account of existing power relationships, a model of a desired future, and an outline of how political change can and should be brought about.

- Ideologies link political theory with political practice. On one level, ideologies resemble political philosophies, in that they constitute a collection of values, theories and doctrines; that is, a distinctive world-view. On another level, however, they take the form of broad political movements, and are articulated through the activities of political leaders, parties and groups.

- Every ideology can be associated with a characteristic set of principles and ideas. Although these ideas 'hang together', in the sense that they interlock in distinctive ways, they are systematic or coherent only in a relative sense. All ideologies thus embody a range of rival traditions and internal tensions. Conflict within ideologies is thus sometimes more passionate than that between ideologies.

- Ideologies are by no means hermetically sealed and unchanging systems of thought. They overlap with one another at a number of points, and they sometimes have shared concerns and a common vocabulary. They are also always subject to political or intellectual renewal, both because they interact with, and influence the development of, other ideologies, and because they change over time as they are applied to changing historical circumstances.

- The significance of particular ideologies rises and falls in relation to the ideology's relevance to political, social and economic circumstances, and its capacity for theoretical innovation. Development during the twentieth century and beyond have forced major ideologies such as liberalism, conservatism and socialism to re-examine their traditional principles. Since around the 1960s, the ideological landscape has been transformed by the emergence of so-called 'new' ideologies, such as feminism, green politics and cosmopolitanism, and by a growing recognition of the ideological significance of a range of non-western ideas and theories.

Questions for discussion

- Why has the concept of ideology so often carried negative associations?
- Is it any longer possible to distinguish between liberalism and socialism?
- To what extent do New Right ideas conflict with those of traditional conservatism?
- Is 'new' social democracy a meaningful and coherent ideological stance?
- Has Marxism a future?
- What circumstances are most conducive to the rise of fascism?
- Do anarchists demand the impossible?
- Why have feminism, green politics and comopolitanism grown in significance?
- To what extent do non-western ideological trends challenge western ideologies?

Further reading

Freedman, M., *Ideology: A Very Short Introduction* (2003). A brief (as promised) but authoritative guide to the nature of ideology and its place in the modern world.

Heywood, A., *Political Ideologies: An Introduction* (5th edn) (2012). An accessible, up-to-date and comprehensive guide to the major ideological traditions.

Good introductions to particular ideologies include the following: Arblaster (1984) on liberalism, O'Sullivan (1976) on conservatism, Wright (1987) on socialism, Giddens (2001) on the 'third way', Marshall (1991) on anarchism, Laqueur (1979) on fascism, Bryson (2003) on feminism, Dobson (1990) on green politics, Appiah (2007) on cosmopolitanism, and Marty and Appleby (1993) on religious fundamentalism.

CHAPTER 14

Parties and Party Systems

'In politics, shared hatreds are almost always the basis of friendships.'

ALEXIS DE TOCQUEVILLE, *Democracy in America* (1835)

PREVIEW So fundamental are political parties to the operation of modern politics that their role and significance are often taken for granted. It is forgotten, for instance, that parties are a relatively recent invention. As political machines organized to win elections and wield government power, parties came into existence only in the early nineteenth century. Now, however, they are virtually ubiquitous. The only parts of the world in which they do not exist are those where they are suppressed by dictatorship or military rule. Quite simply, the political party has become the major organizing principle of modern politics. Political parties are the vital link between the state and civil society, between the institutions of government and the groups and interests that operate within society. However, parties are by no means all alike. Not only do they differ in terms of matters such as organizational structure and ideological orientation, but they also carry out different roles within the larger political system. Political parties have thus been both lauded as the great tools of democracy and criticized as a source of tyranny and repression. Their impact, moreover, is crucially influenced by what is known as the party system, the network of relationships between and among parties, structured in particular by the number of parties in existence. One-party systems operate very differently from competitive party systems, but there are also important contrasts between two-party and multiparty systems. Nevertheless, parties and party systems have increasingly come under attack. They have been blamed for failing to articulate the new and more diverse aspirations that have emerged in modern societies, and for failing to solve, or perhaps even to address, many of their most troubling problems.

KEY ISSUES
- What is a political party? How can parties be classified?
- What are the key functions of political parties?
- How are parties organized, and where is power located within them?
- What kinds of party system are there?
- How does the party system shape the broader political process?
- Are parties in decline, and is this decline terminal?

Political party

A political party is a group of people that is organized for the purpose of winning government power, by electoral or other means. Parties typically exhibit the following characteristics (1) They aim to exercise government power by winning political office (small parties may nevertheless use elections more to gain a platform than to win power). (2) They are organized bodies with a formal 'card carrying' membership. (3) They typically adopt a broad issue focus, addressing each of the major areas of government policy (small parties, however, may have a single-issue focus). (4) To varying degrees, they are united by shared political preferences and a general ideological identity.

PARTY POLITICS

Political parties are found in the vast majority of countries and in most political systems. Parties may be authoritarian or democratic; they may seek power through elections or through revolution; and they may espouse ideologies of the left, right or centre, or, indeed, disavow political ideas altogether. However, parties of some kind exist from Brazil to Burundi and from Norway to New Zealand. The development of political parties and the acquisition of a party system came to be recognized as a mark of political modernization. By the late 1950s, some 80 per cent of the world's states were ruled by political parties. During the 1960s and early 1970s, however, a decline set in with the spread of military rule in the developing world. Political parties were accused of being divisive, and of failing to solve overriding problems of poverty, and ethnic and tribal rivalry. They also proved to be inconvenient for economic and military elites. The upsurge of democratization (see p. 272) since the 1980s has, nevertheless, led to a renewed flourishing of parties. In Asia, Africa and Latin America, the relaxation or collapse of military rule was invariably accompanied by the re-emergence of parties. In former communist states, one-party rule was replaced by the establishment of competitive party systems.

It would be a mistake, however, to assume that parties have always been with us. Political parties are part of the structures of mass politics, ushered in by the advent of representative government and the progressive extension of the franchise during the nineteenth century. Until then, what were called 'factions' (see p. 223) or 'parties' were little more than groups of like-minded politicians, usually formed around a key leader or family. So-called 'court' parties, for instance, often developed within autocratic monarchies as a result of the struggle for influence amongst notables and advisers. Thus, when Edmund Burke (see p. 36) in the late eighteenth century described a party as 'a body of men united . . . upon some particular principle upon which they all agree', he was thinking about fluid and informal groupings such as the Whigs and the Tories, and not about the organized and increasingly disciplined machines into which they were to develop.

Parties of the modern kind first emerged in the USA. Despite the abhorrence of parties felt by the 'founding fathers' who created the US constitution, the Federalist Party (later the Whigs and, from 1860, the Republican Party) appeared as a mass-based party during the US presidential election of 1800. Many conservative and liberal parties started life as legislative factions. Only later, forced to appeal to an ever-widening electorate, did they develop an extraparliamentary machinery of constituency branches, local agents and so on. In contrast, socialist parties and parties representing religious, ethnic and language groups were invariably born as social movements, or interest groups, operating outside government. Subsequently, they developed into fully-fledged parliamentary parties in the hope of winning formal representation and shaping public policy. By the beginning of the twentieth century, parties and party systems had, in effect, become the political manifestation of the social and other cleavages that animated society at large. However, the resulting party forms varied considerably.

Types of party

A variety of classifications have been used for political parties. The most important of these are the following:

Faction, factionalism

A faction is a section or group within a larger formation, usually a political party. Its aims and organizational status must therefore be compatible with those of its host party; otherwise the group is a 'party within a party'. A distinction is sometimes drawn between 'factions' and 'tendencies', the latter being looser and more informal groups, distinguished only by a common policy or ideological disposition. Factionalism refers either to the proliferation of factions, or to the bitterness of factional rivalry. The term faction is often used pejoratively; the term factionalism is always pejorative, implying debilitating infighting.

- cadre and mass parties
- representative and integrative parties
- constitutional and revolutionary parties
- left-wing and right-wing parties.

The most common distinction is that between cadre parties and mass parties. The term *cadre* party originally meant a 'party of notables', dominated by an informal group of leaders who saw little point in building up a mass organization. Such parties invariably developed out of parliamentary factions or cliques at a time when the franchise was limited. However, the term 'cadre' is now more commonly used (as in communist parties) to denote trained and professional party members who are expected to exhibit a high level of political commitment and doctrinal discipline. In this sense, the Communist Party of the Soviet Union (CPSU), the Nazi Party in Germany, and the Fascist Party in Italy were cadre parties, as are the Chinese Communist Party (CCP) and, in certain respects, the Indian Congress Party in the modern period. The distinguishing feature of cadre parties is their reliance on a politically active elite (usually subject to quasi-military discipline) that is capable of offering ideological leadership to the masses. Although strict political criteria are laid down for party membership, careerism and simple convenience are often powerful motives for joining such parties, as both the CPSU and the Nazis found out.

A *mass* party, on the other hand, places a heavy emphasis on broadening membership and constructing a wide electoral base. Although the extension of the franchise forced liberal and conservative parties to seek a mass appeal, the earliest examples of mass parties were European socialist parties, such as the German Social Democratic Party (SPD) and the UK Labour Party, which constructed organizations specifically designed to mobilize working-class support. The key feature of such parties is that they place heavier stress on recruitment and organization than on ideology and political conviction. Although such parties often have formally democratic organizations, except for a minority of activists, membership usually entails little in the way of participation and only general agreement about principles and goals.

Most modern parties fall into the category of what Otto Kirchheimer (1966) termed 'catch-all parties'. These are parties that drastically reduce their ideological baggage in order to appeal to the largest possible number of voters. Kirchheimer particularly had in mind the Christian Democratic Union (CDU) in Germany, but the best examples of catch-all parties are found in the USA in the form of the Republicans and the Democrats. Modern de-ideologized socialist parties such as the German Social Democrats and the Labour Party in the UK also fit this description. These parties differ from the classic model of a mass party in that they emphasize leadership and unity, and downgrade the role of individual party members in trying to build up broad coalitions of support, rather than relying on a particular social class or sectional group.

The second party distinction, advanced by Sigmund Neumann (1956), is that between so-called parties of representation and parties of integration. Representative parties see their primary function as being the securing of votes in elections. They thus attempt to reflect, rather than shape, public opinion. In this respect, representative parties adopt a catch-all strategy and therefore place pragmatism before principle and market research before popular mobilization.

The prevalence of such parties in modern politics gave considerable force to arguments based on rational choice models of political behaviour, such as those of Joseph Schumpeter (see p. 202) and Anthony Downs (1957), which portray politicians as power-seeking creatures who are willing to adopt whatever policies are likely to bring them electoral success.

Integrative parties, in contrast, adopt proactive, rather than reactive, political strategies; they wish to mobilize, educate and inspire the masses, rather than merely respond to their concerns. Although Neumann saw the typical mobilizing party as an ideologically disciplined cadre party, mass parties may also exhibit mobilizing tendencies. For example, until they became discouraged by electoral failure, socialist parties set out to 'win over' the electorate to a belief in the benefits of public ownership, full employment, redistribution, social welfare and so on. This approach was also, rather ironically, adopted by the UK Conservatives under Margaret Thatcher in the 1980s. Abandoning the party's traditional distaste for ideology (see p. 28) and abstract principle, Thatcher embraced 'conviction politics' in pursuing a mobilizing strategy based on firm support for cutting taxes, encouraging enterprise, promoting individual responsibility, tackling trade union power and so forth.

The third type of classification distinguishes between constitutional parties and revolutionary parties. *Constitutional* parties acknowledge the rights and entitlements of other parties and, thus, operate within a framework of rules and constraints. In particular, they acknowledge that there is a division between the party and the state, between the party in power (the government of the day) and state institutions (the bureaucracy, judiciary, police and so on) that enjoy formal independence and political neutrality. Above all, constitutional parties acknowledge and respect the rules of electoral competition. They recognize that they can be voted out of power as easily as they can be voted in. Mainstream parties in liberal democracies all have such a constitutional character.

Revolutionary parties, on the other hand, are antisystem or anticonstitutional parties, either of the left or of the right. Such parties aim to seize power and overthrow the existing constitutional structure using tactics that range from outright insurrection and popular revolution to the quasi-legalism practised by the Nazis and the Fascists. In some cases, revolutionary parties are formally banned by being classified as 'extremist' or 'anti-democratic', as has been the case in post-World War II Germany. When such parties win power, however, they invariably become 'ruling' or regime parties, suppressing rival parties and establishing a permanent relationship with the state machinery. In one-party systems, whether established under the banner of communism, fascism, nationalism or whatever, the distinction between the party and the state is so weakened that the 'ruling' party, in effect, substitutes itself for the government, creating a fused 'party–state' apparatus. It was common in the USSR, for instance, for the General Secretary of the CPSU to act as the chief executive or head of government without bothering to assume a formal state post.

The final way of distinguishing between parties is on the basis of ideological orientation, specifically between those parties labelled left-wing and those labelled right-wing (see p. 225). Left-wing parties (progressive, socialist and communist parties) are characterized by a commitment to change, in the form of either social reform or wholesale economic transformation. These have traditionally drawn their support from the ranks of the poor and disadvantaged

● **Rational choice**: An approach to politics based on the assumption that individuals are rationally self-interested actors; an 'economic' theory of politics (see p. 14–15).

Focus on . . .

The left/right divide

The left–right political spectrum is a shorthand method of describing political ideas and beliefs, summarizing the ideological positions of politicians, parties and movements. Its origins date back to the French Revolution and the positions that groups adopted at the first meeting of the French Estates-General in 1789. The terms 'left' and 'right' do not have exact meanings, however. In a narrow sense, the *linear* political spectrum (see Figure 14.1) summarizes different attitudes to the economy and the role of the state: left-wing views support intervention and collectivism, right-wing views favour the market and individualism. This supposedly reflects deeper ideological or value differences, as listed below:

An alternative, *horseshoe-shaped* political spectrum (see Figure 14.2) was devised in the post-World War II period to highlight the totalitarian and monistic (anti-pluralist) tendencies of both fascism and communism, by contrast with the alleged tolerance and openness of mainstream creeds. Those, like Hans Eysenck (1964), who have developed a two-dimensional political spectrum (see Figure 14.3) have tried to compensate for the crudeness and inconsistencies of the conventional left–right spectrum by adding a vertical authoritarian–libertarian one. This enables positions on economic organization to be disentangled from those related to civil liberty.

Left			**Right**
	Liberty	Authority	
	Equality	Hierarchy	
	Fraternity	Order	
	Rights	Duties	
	Progress	Tradition	
	Reform	Reaction	
	Internationalism	Nationalism	

(in urban societies, the working classes). Right-wing parties (conservative and fascist parties, in particular) generally uphold the existing social order and are, in that sense, a force for continuity. Their supporters usually include business interests and the materially-contented middle classes. However, this notion of a neat left–right party divide is, at best, simplistic and, at worst, deeply misleading. Not only are both the left and the right often divided along reformist/revolutionary and constitutional/insurrectionary lines, but also all parties, especially constitutional ones, tend to be 'broad churches', in the sense that they encompass their own left and right wings. Moreover, electoral competition has the effect of blurring ideological identities, once-cherished principles commonly being discarded in the search for votes. The definitions of left and right have also changed over time, and often differ from one political system to the next. Finally, the shift away from old class polarities and the emergence of new political issues such as the environment, animal rights and feminism has perhaps rendered the conventional ideas of left and right redundant (Giddens, 1994).

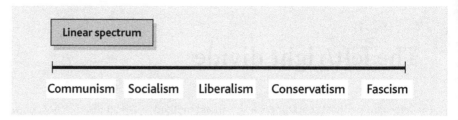

Figure 14.1   Linear political spectrum

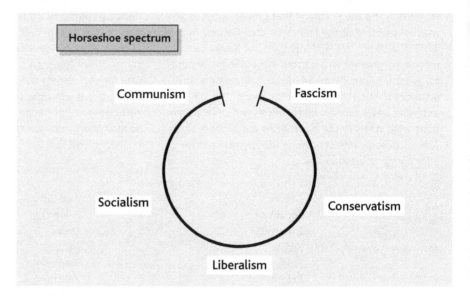

Figure 14.2   Horseshoe political spectrum

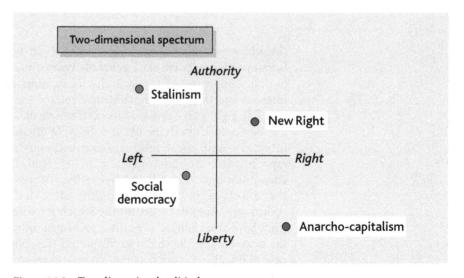

Figure 14.3   Two-dimensional political spectrum

Thomas Jefferson (1743–1826)

US political philosopher and statesman. A wealthy Virginian planter who was Governor of Virginia 1779–81, Jefferson served as the first US Secretary of State, 1789–94. He was the third president of the USA, 1801–09. Jefferson was the principal author of the Declaration of Independence, and wrote a vast number of addresses and letters. He developed a democratic form of agrarianism that sought to blend a belief in rule by a natural aristocracy with a commitment to limited government and *laissez-faire*, sometimes called Jeffersonianism. He also demonstrated sympathy for social reform, favouring the extension of public education, the abolition of slavery and greater economic equality.

Functions of parties

Although political parties are defined by a central function (the filling of political office and the wielding of government power), their impact on the political system is substantially broader and more complex. It goes without saying that there are dangers in generalizing about the functions of parties. Constitutional parties operating in a context of electoral competition tend to be portrayed as bastions of democracy; indeed, the existence of such parties is often seen as the litmus test of a healthy democratic system. On the other hand, regime parties that enjoy a monopoly of political power are more commonly portrayed as instruments of manipulation and political control. Moreover, controversy continues to surround the wider impact of political parties. For instance, Thomas Jefferson and the other 'founding fathers' of the US constitution – and, in the modern period, supporters of so-called 'anti-party parties' – have portrayed parties in deeply negative terms, seeing them as a source of discord and political regimentation (see p. 230). A number of general functions of parties can nevertheless be identified. The main functions are as follows:

- representation
- elite formation and recruitment
- goal formulation
- interest articulation and aggregation
- socialization and mobilization
- organization of government.

Representation

Representation (see p. 197) is often seen as the primary function of parties. It refers to the capacity of parties to respond to and articulate the views of both the members and the voters. In the language of systems theory, political parties are major 'inputting' devices that ensure that government heeds the needs and wishes of the larger society. Clearly, this is a function that is best carried out, some would say only carried out, in an open and competitive system that forces parties to respond to popular preferences. Rational-choice theorists, following

● **Anti-party party**: Parties that set out to subvert traditional party politics by rejecting parliamentary compromise and emphasizing popular mobilization.

CONCEPT

Primary election

A primary election is an intraparty election in which candidates are selected to contest a subsequent 'official' election. During the twentieth century, primaries became the principal nominating device used in the USA, also being used to choose convention delegates and party leaders. Most US states hold 'closed' primaries, in which participation is restricted to registered supporters of the party; 'open' primaries allow all voters to participate, regardless of party affiliation. Primary elections give rank-and-file voters more of a voice in party affairs and lead to a more candidate-orientated and less party-orientated style of politics.

Anthony Downs (1957), explain this process by suggesting that the political market parallels the economic market, in that politicians act essentially as entrepreneurs seeking votes, meaning that parties behave very much like businesses. Power thus ultimately resides with the consumers, the voters. This 'economic model' can, however, be criticized on the grounds that parties seek to 'shape' or mobilize public opinion, as well as respond to it; that the image of voters as well-informed, rational and issue-orientated consumers is questionable; and that the range of consumer (or electoral) choice is often narrow.

Elite formation and recruitment

Parties of all kinds are responsible for providing states with their political leaders. Exceptions to this include parties that are, effectively, the creation of powerful politicians and are used as political vehicles to mobilize support for them, such as Silvio Berlusconi's Forza Italia, established in 1993 but rebranded as the People of Freedom party in 2009, and Vladimir Putin's United Russia party, founded in 2001. Much more commonly, however, politicians achieve office by virtue of their party post: contestants in a presidential election are usually party leaders, while in parliamentary systems the leader of the largest party in the assembly normally becomes prime minister. Cabinet and other ministerial posts are usually filled by senior party figures, though exceptions are found in presidential systems such as the USA's, which allow non-party ministers to be appointed.

In most cases, parties therefore provide a training ground for politicians, equipping them with skills, knowledge and experience; and offering them some form of career structure, albeit one that depends on the fortunes of the party. On the other hand, the stranglehold that parties exert over government offices can be criticized for ensuring that political leaders are drawn from a relatively small pool of talent: the senior figures in a handful of major parties. In the USA, however, this stranglehold has been weakened by the widespread use of primary elections, which reduce the control that a party has over the process of candidate selection and nomination.

Goal formulation

Political parties have traditionally been one of the means through which societies set collective goals and, in some cases, ensure that they are carried out. Parties play this role because, in the process of seeking power, they formulate programmes of government (through conferences, conventions, election manifestos and so on) with a view to attracting popular support. Not only does this mean that parties are a major source of policy initiation, it also encourages them to formulate coherent sets of policy options that give the electorate a choice amongst realistic and achievable goals.

This function is most clearly carried out by parties in parliamentary systems that are able to claim a mandate (see p. 200) to implement their policies, if they are elected to power. However, it can also occur in presidential systems with usually non-programmic parties, as in the case of the Republicans' 'Contract with America' in the US congressional elections of 1994. Nevertheless, the tendency towards de-ideologized catch-all parties, and the fact that electoral campaigns increasingly stress personality and image over policies and issues, has generally reduced the impact that parties have on policy formulation. Party programmes, moreover, are almost certain to be modified by pressure from the civil service and interest groups, as well as in the light of domestic and international circumstances. Policy implementation, on the other hand, is usually carried out by bureaucracies rather than parties, except in one-party systems such as those in orthodox communist states, where the 'ruling' party supervises the state apparatus at every level.

Interest articulation and aggregation

In the process of developing collective goals, parties also help to articulate and aggregate the various interests found in society. Parties, indeed, often develop as vehicles through which business, labour, religious, ethnic or other groups advance or defend their various interests. The UK Labour Party, for instance, was created by the trade union movement with the aim of achieving working-class political representation. Other parties have, effectively, recruited interests and groups in order to broaden their electoral base, as the US parties did in the late nineteenth and early twentieth centuries with immigrant groups.

The fact that national parties invariably articulate the demands of a multitude of groups forces them to aggregate these interests by drawing them together into a coherent whole, balancing competing interests against each other. Constitutional parties are clearly forced to do this by the pressures of electoral competition, but even monopolistic parties articulate and aggregate interests through their close relationship with the state and the economy, especially in centrally planned systems. However, not even in competitive party systems are all interests articulated, those of the poor being most vulnerable to exclusion.

Socialization and mobilization

Through internal debate and discussion, as well as campaigning and electoral competition, parties are important agents of political education and socialization. The issues that parties choose to focus on help to set the political agenda, and the values and attitudes that they articulate become part of the larger political culture (see p. 172). In the case of monopolistic parties, the propagation of an 'official' ideology (be it Marxism–Leninism, National Socialism, or simply the ideas of a charismatic leader) is consciously acknowledged to be a central, if not its supreme, function.

Mainstream parties in competitive systems play no less significant a role in encouraging groups to play by the rules of the democratic game, thus mobilizing support for the regime itself. For example, the emergence of socialist parties in the late nineteenth and early twentieth centuries was an important means of integrating the working class into industrial society. Nevertheless, the capacity of parties to mobilize and socialize has been brought into doubt by evidence in many countries of partisan dealignment (see p. 217) and growing disenchantment with conventional pro-system parties. The problem that parties have is that, to some extent, they themselves are socialized (some would say corrupted) by the experience of government, making them, it appears, less effective in engaging partisan sympathies and attracting emotional attachments. (These issues are discussed more fully.)

Debating . . .
Do parties breed discord and constrain political debate?

So common are parties in modern politics that it is often forgotten how controversial they were when they first emerged. Although some welcomed them as the agents of a new age of mass politics, others warned that they would deepen conflict and subvert the politics of individual consciousness. The trend towards falling party membership and declining party identification in the modern period has served to revive such criticisms.

YES

Sacrificing personal conscience. By their nature, parties are collective entities, groups of people who agree a common platform, and advance shared views and opinions. Without unity and cohesion, parties have very little reason to exist. And yet this unity comes at the price of personal conscience, as it is inconceivable that any member would genuinely support all of a party's policies in all circumstances. Over matter small and sometimes large, parties therefore come to 'think for' their members, whether this comes about through party discipline and the fear of punishment (including expulsion from the party) or, more insidiously, through an emotional or ideological attachment to the party and its goals.

Disharmony and adversarialism. Party politics is based on partisanship, adherence and, maybe, even devotion to a particular cause or group. This inevitably breeds a tribal mentality in which the flaws and failings of other parties are exaggerated, while those of one's own party are consistently denied. Parties thus promote a one-sided view of politics in which political issues and debates are constantly distorted by considerations of party advantage. This tendency towards mindless adversarialism – disagreement for the sake of disagreement – is hardly a sound basis for advancing the public good.

Domination by the cunning and ambitious. Parties serve to concentrate political power rather than disperse it. In the 'iron law of oligarchy',   this tendency is explained in terms of organization. However, elite rule also reflects the fact that, within parties, 'foot soldiers' are required to do little other than obey and follow, encouraged by the knowledge that loyalty and discipline will be rewarded, while dissent and, in particular, criticism of the leadership will be punished. Those who climb the 'greasy pole' and gain advancement within the party are therefore likely, in George Washington's words, to be 'cunning, ambitious and unprincipled men'. Political parties are, in this sense, a particular example of the corruption of power.

NO

Forums of debate. The image of parties as austere, monolithic bodies, in which free debate is sacrificed in the cause of party unity, is accurate only in the context of authoritarianism. In other circumstances, parties are vibrant and multifarious; indeed, the existence of rival factions and tendencies ensures unending debate about policy issues and strategic concerns. Rather than requiring members to sacrifice personal conscience, parties provide their members with an education in politics, helping them to strengthen their knowledge and skills and making them more engaged citizens. Party membership is therefore an important vehicle for the aspect of personal self-development.

Engaging the people. Parties provide a channel of communication through which political leaders both mobilize citizens and respond to their needs and concerns. This applies most clearly when the electoral process forces parties to compete for the popular vote in order to win or retain government power, but it can also occur (albeit to a limited extent) in authoritarian systems, through attempts by 'ruling' parties to maintain legitimacy. The need to engage with the ideas and interests of the people generates pressure within parties to permit, even encourage, internal debate and argument among their members, rather than uncritical obedience.

Cross-party interaction. Bipartisanship is more common than is often supposed. For instance, the use of proportional electoral systems typically creates a bias in favour of consensus-building and alliances amongst parties based on the fact that no single party is likely to have parliamentary strength to rule on its own. The resulting coalition governments are held together by the fact that conflicts between the parties involved are resolved through a process of ongoing cross-party dialogue. A similar dynamic can develop in presidential systems due to the phenomenon of cohabitation, whereby the executive is in the hands of one party while the assembly is dominated by another party.

CONCEPT

Party democracy

Party democracy is a form of popular rule that operates through the agency of a party. There are two models of party democracy. In the first (intraparty democracy), parties are democratic agents, in that power within them is widely and evenly dispersed. This implies, for instance, that there should be broad participation in the election of leaders and selection of candidates. In the second model, democracy dictates that policy-making power should be concentrated in the hands of party members who are elected and, therefore, publicly accountable. In this view, the first model may lead to the tyranny of non-elected constituency activists.

Organization of government

It is often argued that complex modern societies would be ungovernable in the absence of political parties. In the first place, parties help with the formation of governments, in parliamentary systems, to the extent that it is possible to talk of 'party government' (see p. 236). Parties also give governments a degree of stability and coherence, especially if the members of the government are drawn from a single party and are, therefore, united by common sympathies and attachments. Even governments that are formed from a coalition of parties are more likely to foster unity and agreement than those that consist of separate individuals each with his or her own priorities.

Parties, furthermore, facilitate cooperation between the two major branches of government: the assembly and the executive. In parliamentary systems, this is effectively guaranteed by the fact the government is usually formed from the party or parties that have majority control of the assembly. However, even in presidential systems the chief executive can wield some influence, if not control, through an appeal to party unity. Finally, parties provide, in competitive systems at least, a vital source of opposition and criticism, both inside and outside government. As well as broadening political debate and educating the electorate, this helps to ensure that government policy is more thoroughly scrutinized and, therefore, more likely to be workable.

Party organization: where does power lie?

Because of the crucial role that political parties play, considerable attention has been focused on where power lies within parties. The organization and structure of parties thus provides vital clues about the distribution of power within society as a whole. Can parties function as democratic bodies that broaden participation and access to power? Or do they simply entrench the dominance of leaders and elites?

One of the earliest attempts to investigate internal party democracy was undertaken in Mosei Ostrogorski's *Democracy and the Organization of Political Parties* (1902), which argued that the representation of individual interests had lost out to the growing influence of the party machine and control exerted by a caucus of senior party figures. This view was more memorably expressed by Robert Michels in *Political Parties* ([1911] 1962) in the form of the 'iron law of oligarchy' (see p. 232), or, as Michels put it, 'he who says organization says oligarchy'. Michels (1876–1936), a prominent elite theorist, wished to analyse the power structure of the German SPD; he argued that, despite the party's formally democratic organization, power was concentrated in the hands of a small group of party leaders.

For Michels, the 'law' explained the inevitable failure of democratic socialism and, indeed, exploded the myth of political democracy. Critics, however, point out that Michels' observations are generalizations made on the basis of a single political party at a particular moment in time, and also rest on questionable psychological theories. In practice, party elites have often proved to be more faction-ridden, and mass memberships less deferential and quiescent, than Michels suggested.

Attempts have been made to strengthen the democratic and participatory features of parties through reform. One of the clearest examples of this occurred

Focus on . . .

The iron law of oligarchy

Oligarchy is government or domination by the few. The 'iron law of oligarchy', formulated by Robert Michels ([1911] 1962), suggests that there is an inevitable tendency for political organizations, and by implication all organizations, to be oligarchic. Participatory or democratic structures cannot check oligarchic tendencies; they can only disguise them.

Michels advanced a number of arguments in support of his law:

- Elite groups result from the need for specialization. Elite members have greater expertise and better organizational skills than those possessed by ordinary members.
- Leaders form cohesive groups because they recognize that this improves their chances of remaining in power.
- Rank-and-file members of an organization tend to be apathetic and are, therefore, generally disposed to accept subordination and venerate leaders.

in the USA in the 1970s and 1980s. US parties differ in many respects from their European counterparts. Being loose coalitions of sometimes conflicting interests held together by little more than the need to contest presidential elections, they are highly decentralized and generally non-programmic. Traditionally, state-based or city-based party bosses (a legacy of the **machine politics** of the early twentieth century) acted as power brokers and exercised a decisive influence at nominating conventions. Following protests and clashes at the 1968 Democratic national convention in Chicago, however, a reform movement sprang up aimed at weakening the power of local party leaders and strengthening the role of rank-and-file members.

This was accomplished largely through the wider use of nominating primaries and **caucuses**. These, first with the Democrats and later with the Republicans, attracted a growing number of issue and candidate activists into party politics, leading to the nomination of more ideological candidates such as George McGovern for the Democrats in 1972 and Ronald Reagan for the Republicans in 1980. Such tendencies have, nevertheless, generated concern, particularly amongst Democrats, who feared that more open and participatory structures could simply result in the nomination of unelectable 'outsider' candidates. Both the main US parties have responded to this by modernizing and strengthening their committee structures, especially at national, congressional and senatorial levels. Although this has been portrayed as a process of 'party renewal', it is evidence of the parties' desire to provide better electoral support for individual candidates, rather than of the emergence of European-style, party-focused elections.

The existence of factions and tendencies is as important as formal organization in determining the location of power within a party. While all parties, even those with an apparently monolithic character, embrace some measure of political and ideological rivalry, the degree to which this rivalry is reflected in conflict between organized and coherent groups is crucial in determining the degree of authority of party leaders. In some cases, factions can break away from parties in the manner that European communist parties often emerged out of socialist

● **Machine politics**: A style of politics in which party 'bosses' control a mass organization through patronage and the distribution of favours.

● **Caucus**: A meeting of party members held to nominate election candidates, or to discuss legislative proposals in advance of formal proceedings.

parties in the years following the 1917 Russian Revolution. Factionalism is often linked to the weight that parties place on political ideas and ideological direction. Whereas pragmatic right-wing parties usually merely have to balance or conciliate rival tendencies, more ideological parties of the left often have to deal with open disagreement and institutionalized rivalry. Together with their inclination to endorse internal democracy, this has generally made socialist parties more difficult to lead than liberal or conservative parties.

Perhaps a more significant consideration, however, is the extent to which parties have a secure hold on power. Factionalism is, in a sense, a luxury that only long-time parties of government can afford. This is why monopolistic communist parties were able to keep factionalism at bay only by exercising ruthless discipline enforced through the strictures of **democratic centralism**. It also explains the deeply factional nature of 'dominant' parties such as the Liberal Democratic Party (LDP) in Japan and the Italian Christian Democratic Party (DC). The UK Conservative Party is an example of a party with an ethos that once stressed, above all, deference and loyalty. However, the Party became increasingly factionalized in the 1980s and 1990s through a combination of its more ideological character and its prolonged electoral success after 1979. Bottom-up pressures thus gave the Conservative Party a more democratic character than its formal leader-dominated structure suggested was possible. The most conspicuous casualty of this process was Margaret Thatcher, who was forced to stand down as party leader in 1990 despite having won three successive general elections. Albeit to different degrees, all subsequent Conservative leaders have experienced difficulties in confronting factional resistance inside and outside of Parliament.

PARTY SYSTEMS

Political parties are important not only because of the range of functions they carry out (representation, elite recruitment, aggregation of interests and so on), but also because the complex interrelationships between and among parties are crucial in structuring the way political systems work in practice. This network of relationships is called a **party system**. The most familiar way of distinguishing between different types of party system is by reference to the number of parties competing for power. On this basis, Duverger (1954) distinguished between 'one-party', 'two-party' and 'multiparty' systems. Although such a typology is commonly used, party systems cannot simply be reduced to a 'numbers game'.

As important as the number of parties competing for power is their relative size, as reflected in their electoral and legislative strength. As Sartori (1976) pointed out, what is vital is to establish the 'relevance' of parties in relation to the formation of governments and, in particular, whether their size gives them the prospect of winning, or at least sharing, government power. This approach is often reflected in the distinction made between 'major', or government-orientated, parties and more peripheral, 'minor' ones (although neither category can be defined with mathematical accuracy). A third consideration is how these 'relevant' parties relate to one another. Is the party system characterized by cooperation and consensus, or by conflict and polarization? This is closely linked to the ideological complexion of the party system, and the traditions and history of the parties that compose it.

● **Democratic centralism:** The Leninist principle of party organization, based on a supposed balance between freedom of discussion and strict unity of action.

● **Party system:** A relatively stable network of relationships between parties that is structured by their number, size and ideological orientation.

The mere presence of parties does not, however, guarantee the existence of a party system. The pattern of relationships amongst parties constitutes a system only if it is characterized by stability and a degree of orderliness. Where neither stability nor order exists, a party system may be in the process of emerging, or a transition from one type of party system to another may be occurring. For instance, this can be said of early postcommunist Russia. The collapse of communist rule in 1991 and the initial banning of the CPSU was always going to make the emergence of a competitive party system a difficult, perhaps tortuous, business. Russia's problem was a proliferation of parties and political groupings, none of which came close to establishing a mass membership or a nationwide organization. No fewer than 43 parties contested the 1995 parliamentary elections, with the largest of these, the Russian Communist Party, gaining just 22 per cent of the vote. The subsequent introduction of measures such as electoral **thresholds** and registration on the basis of petitions greatly reduced the number of parties, meaning, for instance, that just seven parties contested the 2011 Russian Duma elections. However, some have argued that, in an age of partisan dealignment and volatile voting patterns, party systems are generally losing their 'systematic' character, making it more difficult to distinguish one system from another. Moreover, where subnational bodies exert significant influence, different party systems may operate at different levels within the political system.

The major party systems found in modern politics are, nevertheless, as follows:

- one-party systems
- two-party systems
- dominant-party systems
- multiparty systems.

One-party systems

Strictly speaking, the term one-party system is contradictory since 'system' implies interaction amongst a number of entities. The term is, nevertheless, helpful in distinguishing between political systems in which a single party enjoys a monopoly of power through the exclusion of all other parties (by political or constitutional means) and those systems characterized by a competitive struggle amongst a number of parties. Because monopolistic parties effectively function as permanent governments, with no mechanism (short of a *coup* or revolution) through which they can be removed from power, they invariably develop an entrenched relationship with the state machine. This allows such states to be classified as 'one-party states', their machinery being seen as a fused 'party–state' apparatus. Two rather different types of one-party system can be identified, however.

The first type has been found in state socialist regimes where 'ruling' communist parties have directed and controlled virtually all the institutions and aspects of society. Such parties are subject to strict ideological discipline, traditionally linked tenets of Marxism–Leninism, and they have highly-structured internal organizations in line with the principles of democratic centralism. These are cadre parties, in the sense that membership is restricted on political and ideological grounds. Almost 6 per cent of the Chinese population are members of the

● **Threshold**: A minimum level of electoral support needed for a party to be eligible to win seats.

Chinese Communist Party (CCP), and around 9 per cent of the Soviet population belonged to the CPSU. In this type of party, the party core consists of well-paid full-time officials, the *apparatchiki*, who run the party *apparat*, or apparatus, and exercise supervision over both the state machine and social institutions.

A central device through which communist parties control the state, economy and society, and ensure the subordination of 'lower' organs to 'higher' ones, is the *nomenklatura* system. This is a system of vetted appointments in which, effectively, all senior posts are filled by party-approved candidates. The justification for both the party's monopoly of power, and its supervision of state and social institutions, lies in the Leninist claim that the party acts as the 'vanguard of the proletariat' in providing the working masses with the ideological leadership and guidance needed to ensure that they fulfil their revolutionary destiny. **Vanguardism** has, however, been criticized for being deeply elitist and providing the seed from which Stalinism later grew. Trotsky (1937), on the other hand, offered an alternative interpretation by suggesting that, far from the 'ruling' party dominating Soviet development, its formal monopoly of power merely concealed the burgeoning influence of the state bureaucracy.

The second type of one-party system is associated with anticolonial nationalism and state consolidation in the developing world. In Ghana, Tanzania and Zimbabwe, for example, the 'ruling' party developed out of an independence movement that proclaimed the overriding need for nation-building and economic development. In Zimbabwe, one-party rule developed only in 1986 (six years after independence) through the merger of the two major parties, ZANU and ZAPU, both former guerrilla groups. In other cases, such parties have developed as little more than vehicles through which a national leader has tried to consolidate power, as with General Ershad's People's Party in Bangladesh in the 1980s and President Mobutu's Popular Movement of the Revolution in Zaire, 1965–97.

One-party systems in Africa and Asia have usually been built around the dominant role of a charismatic leader and drawn whatever ideological identity they have possessed from the views of that leader. Kwame Nkrumah, the leader of the Convention People's Party (CPP) in Ghana until his overthrow in 1966, is often seen as the model such leader, but other examples have been Julius Nyerere in Tanzania and Robert Mugabe in Zimbabwe. Not uncommonly, these parties are weakly organized (very different from the tight discipline found in communist one-party states), and they play, at best, only a peripheral role in the process of policy-making. Their monopolistic position, nevertheless, helps to entrench authoritarianism (see p. 277) and to keep alive the danger of corruption.

Two-party systems

A two-party system is duopolistic in that it is dominated by two 'major' parties that have a roughly equal prospect of winning government power. In its classical form, a two-party system can be identified by three criteria:

- Although a number of 'minor' parties may exist, only two parties enjoy sufficient electoral and legislative strength to have a realistic prospect of winning government power.

● **Vanguardism**: The Leninist belief in the need for a party to lead and guide the proletariat towards the fulfilment of its revolutionary destiny.

CONCEPT

Party government

Party government is a system through which single parties are able to form governments and carry through policy programmes. Its key features are as follows. (1) Major parties possess a clear programmic character and thus offer the electorate a meaningful choice between potential governments. (2) The governing party enjoys sufficient ideological and organizational unity to deliver on its manifesto commitments. (3) Responsibility is maintained by the government's accountability to the electorate through its mandate, and by the existence of a credible opposition that acts as a balancing force.

- The larger party is able to rule alone (usually on the basis of a legislative majority); the other provides the opposition.
- Power alternates between these parties; both are 'electable', the opposition serving as a 'government in the wings'.

The UK and the USA are the most frequently cited examples of states with two-party systems, though others have included Canada, Australia and, until the introduction of electoral reform in 1993, New Zealand. Archetypal examples of two-party politics are, nevertheless, rare. The UK, for instance, often portrayed as the model two-party system, has conformed to its three defining criteria only for particular (and, some would argue, untypical) periods of its history. Even the apparent Labour–Conservative two-partyism of the early post-World War II period (power alternating four times between 1945 and 1970) was punctuated by 13 years of continuous Conservative rule (1951–64), a period during which time Labour's electability was called into question. Moreover, despite persistent major party domination of the House of Commons in the UK, it is more doubtful that a two-party system has existed 'in the country' since 1974. This is suggested by the decline of combined Labour–Conservative support (down from over 95 per cent in the early 1950s to consistently below 75 per cent since 1974).

Even the seemingly incontrovertible two-partyism of the USA – which, for instance, sees the Republicans and Democrats usually holding between them all the seats in the House of Representatives and the Senate – can be questioned. On the one hand, the presidential system allows one party to capture the White House (the presidency) while the other controls one or both houses of Congress, as, for instance, occurred between 1984 and 2000, meaning that it may not be possible to identify a clear government–opposition divide. On the other hand, 'third' party candidates are sometimes of significance. Ross Perot's 16 per cent of the vote in the 1992 presidential election not only highlighted the decline of the Republican and Democratic parties, but also, arguably, proved decisive in securing victory for Bill Clinton.

Two-party politics was once portrayed as the surest way of reconciling responsiveness with order, representative government with effective government. Its key advantage is that it makes possible a system of party government, supposedly characterized by stability, choice and accountability. The two major parties are able to offer the electorate a straightforward choice between rival programmes and alternative governments. Voters can support a party knowing that, if it wins the election, it will have the capacity to carry out its manifesto promises without having to negotiate or compromise with coalition partners. This is sometimes seen as one of the attractions of majoritarian electoral systems that exaggerate support for large parties. Two-party systems have also been praised for delivering strong but accountable government based on relentless competition between the governing and opposition parties. Although government can govern, it can never relax or become complacent because it is constantly confronted by an opposition that acts as a government in waiting. Two-partyism, moreover, creates a bias in favour of moderation, as the two contenders for power have to battle for 'floating' votes in the centre ground. This was, for example, reflected in the so-called 'social-democratic consensus' that prevailed in the UK from the 1950s to the 1970s.

However, two-party politics and party government have not been so well regarded since the 1970s. Instead of guaranteeing moderation, two-party systems such as the UK's have displayed a periodic tendency towards adversary politics (see p. 324). This is reflected in ideological polarization and an emphasis on conflict and argument, rather than consensus and compromise. In the UK in the early 1980s, this was best demonstrated by the movement to the right by a 'Thatcherized' Conservative Party and the movement to the left by a radicalized Labour Party, although a new, post-Thatcherite consensus soon emerged. Adversarial two-partyism has often been explained by reference to the class nature of party support (party conflict being seen, ultimately, as a reflection of the class struggle), or as a consequence of party democratization and the influence of ideologically committed grass-roots activists.

A further problem with the two-party system is that two evenly-matched parties are encouraged to compete for votes by outdoing each other's electoral promises, perhaps causing spiralling public spending and fuelling inflation. This amounts to irresponsible party government, in that parties come to power on the basis of election manifestos that they have no capacity to fulfil. A final weakness of two-party systems is the obvious restrictions they impose in terms of electoral and ideological choice. While a choice between just two programmes of government was perhaps sufficient in an era of partisan alignment and class solidarity, it has become quite inadequate in a period of greater individualism (see p. 158) and social diversity.

Dominant-party systems

Dominant-party systems should not be confused with one-party systems, although they may at times exhibit similar characteristics. A dominant-party system is competitive in the sense that a number of parties compete for power in regular and popular elections, but is dominated by a single major party that consequently enjoys prolonged periods in power. This apparently neat definition, however, runs into problems, notably, in relation to determining how 'prolonged' a governing period must be for a party to be considered 'dominant'. Japan is usually cited as the classic example of a dominant-party system. Until its defeat in 2009, the Liberal Democratic Party (LDP) had been in power almost continuously for 54 years, only having been in opposition for a brief 11-month period between 1993 and 1994. LDP dominance had been underpinned by the Japanese 'economic miracle'. It also reflected the powerful appeal of the party's neo-Confucian principles of duty and obligation in the still-traditional Japanese countryside, and the strong links that the party had forged with business elites. However, economic stagnation and internal divisions have meant that the LDP has lost members and supporters to a number of newly-formed, smaller parties, its decline being underlined in 2009 when the Democratic Party of Japan became the first opposition party since 1945 to win a parliamentary majority.

The Congress Party in India enjoyed an unbroken spell of 30 years in power commencing with the achievement of independence in 1947. Until 1989 it had endured only three years in opposition, following Indira Gandhi's 1975–77 state of emergency. The African National Congress (ANC) has similarly been the dominant party in South Africa since the ending of apartheid in 1993, its position being based on its pre-eminent role in the long struggle against white rule (see p. 238). The best European examples of a dominant-party system are Sweden, where the Social Democratic Labour Party (SAP) held power for 65 of the previous 74 years

The African National Congress: a liberation movement or a 'ruling' party?

Events: In April 1994, South Africa held its first non-racial election. The African National Congress (ANC) won the election, gaining 63 per cent of both votes and seats. The following month, Nelson Mandela was inaugurated as the president of South Africa. The ANC subsequently developed into the ruling party of post-apartheid South Africa. It has had a succession of comfortable majorities in the National Assembly, based on electoral support that has ranged from 70 per cent in 2004 to 62 per cent in 2014. This has been a remarkable achievement for a political movement that had been banned until 1990, and whose leadership had mostly been either in prison or in exile since the early 1960s.

Significance: What accounts for the ANC's predominant position in South African politics? The key explanation is the leading role the party played in the campaign against extreme Afrikaner nationalism and in helping to promote resistance to the policies of apartheid. In describing itself as a 'liberation movement', rather than a conventional political party, the ANC continues to portray itself as the leader of South Africa's 'national democratic revolution'. This position has been bolstered by two factors. First, the ANC responds to and accommodates a broad diversity of interests and voices. Of particular significance in this respect have been the 'tripartite' alliance the ANC forged with the Congress of South African Trade Unions (COSATU) and the South African Communist Party (SACP), and the ANC's willingness in 1994 to form not a single-party government but a government of national unity, including the (New) National Party (which had abandoned its support for apartheid) and the Inkatha Freedom Party (historically, the voice of Zulu nationalism). Second, the ANC has placed a heavy stress on national reconciliation, seeking to forge a single South African identity and sense of purpose amongst a diverse and splintered population. Made possible by the ANC's long-standing commitment to non-racialism, this was reflected in the establishment in 1995 of the Truth and Reconciliation Commission, which sought to heal the wounds of the apartheid era by exposing the crimes and injustices committed by all sides of the struggle, rather than by handing down punishments.

However, the ANC faces at least three major challenges. First, the party's ability to define itself in terms of the struggle for liberation is certain to decline over time. Not only is the proportion of the ANC's membership (and, in due course, leadership, which has direct experience of anti-apartheid activism) steadily diminishing; in people's wider perceptions, the ANC is certain to be viewed progressively more as a vehicle for government than as a vehicle for liberation. Second, and in common with other dominant parties, the ANC has been afflicted by factionalism and, at times, tumultuous internal conflicts. The most dramatic of these was between supporters of Thabo Mbeki, who became South Africa's second post-apartheid president, serving from 1999 to 2008, and supporters of Jacob Zuma, who defeated Mbeki in 2007 in the contest for the presidency of the ANC and went on to become the president of South Africa in 2009. Third, even though post-apartheid South Africa has clearly embraced liberal-democratic principles and structures, the ANC's dominance has fostered developments more commonly associated with one-party states. In particular, the ANC's apparent electoral invulnerability has blurred the distinction between the party and the state, creating scope for corruption. The most high profile corruption scandal in post-apartheid South Africa emerged in 2005 and led to the conviction of Jacob Zuma's financial advisor, Schabir Shaik, over his role in a 1999 arms deal. Zuma himself was dismissed as deputy president by President Mbeki and was subsequently charged with corruption, although these developments did nothing to diminish Zuma's power base within the ANC, or to damage his subsequent career.

CONCEPT

Coalition

A coalition is a grouping of rival political actors brought together either through the perception of a common threat, or through a recognition that their goals cannot be achieved by working separately. *Electoral* coalitions are alliances through which parties agree not to compete against one another, with a view to maximizing their representation. *Legislative* coalitions are agreements between two or more parties to support a particular bill or programme. *Governing* coalitions are formal agreements between two or more parties that involve a cross-party distribution of ministerial portfolios. A 'grand coalition' or 'national government' comprises all major parties.

until its defeat in 2006; and Italy, where the Christian Democratic Party (DC) dominated every one of the country's 52 post-World War II governments until the party's effective collapse amidst mounting allegations of corruption in 1992–94.

The most prominent feature of a dominant-party system is the tendency for the political focus to shift from competition between parties to factional conflict within the dominant party itself. The DC in Italy, for example, functioned as little more than a coalition of privileged groups and interests in Italian society, the party acting as a broker to these various factions. The most powerful of these groups were the Catholic Church (which exercised influence through organizations such as Catholic Action), the farming community and industrial interests. Each of these was able to cultivate voting loyalty and exert influence on DC's members in the Italian parliament.

Factions were also an integral institution in the Japanese political process. Within the LDP, which, until its defeat in 2009, had enjoyed 54 years of virtually unbroken rule, a perennial struggle for power took place, as various subgroups coalesced around rising or powerful individuals. Such factionalism was maintained at the local level by the ability of faction leaders to provide political favours for their followers, and at the parliamentary level through the allocation of senior government and party offices. Although the resulting infighting may have been seen as a means of guaranteeing argument and debate in a system in which small parties were usually marginalized, in Japan factionalism tended to revolve more around personal differences than policy or ideological disagreement. One example of this was the conflict between the Fukuda and Tanaka factions during the 1970s and 1980s, which continued long after the two principals had left the scene.

Whereas other competitive party systems have their supporters, or at least apologists, few are prepared to come to the defence of the dominant-party system. Apart from a tendency towards stability and predictability, dominant-partyism is usually seen as a regrettable and unhealthy phenomenon. In the first place, it tends to erode the important constitutional distinction between the state and the party in power. When governments cease to come and go, an insidious process of politicization takes place through which state officials and institutions adjust to the ideological and political priorities of the dominant party. Second, an extended period in power can engender complacency, arrogance and even corruption in the dominant party. The course of Italian and Japanese politics has, for example, regularly been interrupted by scandals, usually involving allegations of financial corruption. Third, a dominant-party system is characterized by weak and ineffective opposition. Criticism and protest can more easily be ignored if they stem from parties that are no longer regarded as genuine rivals for power. Finally, the existence of a 'permanent' party of government may corrode the democratic spirit by encouraging the electorate to fear change and to stick with the 'natural' party of government.

Multiparty systems

A multiparty system is characterized by competition amongst more than two parties, reducing the chances of single-party government and increasing the likelihood of coalitions. However, it is difficult to define multiparty systems in terms of the number of major parties, as such systems sometimes operate through coalitions including smaller parties that are specifically designed to exclude larger parties from government. This is precisely what happened to the French Communist Party (PCF) in the 1950s, and to the Italian Communist Party (PCI) throughout its existence. If the likelihood of coalition government is the index of multipartyism, this classification contains a number of subcategories.

Germany, for example, tends to have a 'two-and-a-half-party' system, in that the CDU and SDP typically have electoral strengths roughly equivalent to those of the Conservative and Labour parties in the UK. However, they were forced into coalitions with the small Free Democrat Party by the workings of the mixed-member proportional electoral system (see p. 211). Italian multipartyism traditionally involves a larger number of relatively small parties. Thus, even the DC rarely came close to achieving 40 per cent of the vote. Sartori (1976) distinguished between two types of multiparty system, which he termed the 'moderate' and 'polarized' pluralist systems. In this categorization, moderate pluralism exists in countries such as Belgium, the Netherlands and Norway, where ideological differences between major parties are slight, and where there is a general inclination to form coalitions and move towards the middle ground. Polarized pluralism, on the other hand, exists when more marked ideological differences separate major parties, some of which adopt an anti-system stance. The existence of electorally strong communist parties (as in France, Italy and Spain until the 1990s), or of significant fascist movements (such as the Movimento Sociale Italiano (MSI) – reborn in 1995 as the 'post-Fascist' Alleanza Nazionale), provided evidence of polarized pluralism.

The strength of multiparty systems is that they create internal checks and balances within government and exhibit a bias in favour of debate, conciliation and compromise. The process of coalition formation and the dynamics of coalition maintenance ensure a broad responsiveness that cannot but take account of competing views and contending interests. Thus, in Germany, the liberal Free Democrats act as a moderating influence on both the conservative CDU and the socialist SPD. Where SPD–Green coalitions have been formed in the *Länder* (provinces), the Green presence has helped to push environmental issues up the political agenda. Similarly, the multiparty features of the Swedish system, which make coalition government more common than not, have encouraged the SAP to build a broad welfare consensus, and to pursue moderate policies that do not alienate business interests.

The principal criticisms of multiparty systems relate to the pitfalls and difficulties of coalition formation. The post-election negotiations and horsetrading that take place when no single party is strong enough to govern alone can take weeks, or (as in Israel and Italy) sometimes months, to complete. More seriously, coalition governments may be fractured and unstable, paying greater attention to squabbles amongst coalition partners than to the tasks of government. Italy is usually cited as the classic example of this, its post-1945 governments having lasted, on average, only 10 months. It would, nevertheless, be a mistake to suggest that coalitions are always associated with instability, as the record of stable and effective coalition government in Germany and Sweden clearly demonstrates. In some respects, in fact, the Italian experience is peculiar, owing as much to the country's political culture and the ideological complexion of its party system as to the dynamics of multipartyism.

A final problem is that the tendency towards moderation and compromise may mean that multiparty systems are so dominated by the political centre that they are unable to offer clear ideological alternatives. Coalition politics tends, naturally, to be characterized by negotiation and conciliation, a search for common ground, rather than by conviction and the politics of principle. This process can be criticized as being implicitly corrupt, in that parties are encouraged to abandon policies and principles in their quest for power. It can also lead to the over-representation of centrist parties and centrist interests, especially when, as in Germany, a small centre party is the only viable coalition partner for both of the larger conservative and socialist parties. Indeed, this is sometimes seen as one of the drawbacks of proportional representation electoral systems, which, by ensuring that the legislative size of parties reflects their electoral strength, are biased in favour of multiparty politics and coalition government.

DECLINE OF PARTIES?

Modern concerns about parties principally stem from evidence of their decline as agents of representation, and as an effective link between government and the people. Evidence of a 'crisis of party politics' can be found in a decline of both party membership and partisanship, reflected in partisan dealignment. For example, by 2007 fewer than 1 per cent of people across the UK belonged to political parties, down from 7 per cent some 50 years before. Membership of the Labour Party fell from more than 1 million in 1956 to around 166,000 in 2009, while Conservative Party membership fell from an estimated 2.8 million to around 250,000 in the same period. A seemingly inexorable rise in the age of party members is as significant, the average age of Conservative Party members in 1998 having risen to 63. Dramatic electoral swings against governing parties have intensified such concerns. Notable examples of this include the slump of the French Socialists in 1993 from 282 seats to just 70, and the virtual annihilation in the same year of the Canadian Progressive Conservatives, who were swept out of office retaining only two seats. Falling voter turnout also illustrates the declining capacity of parties to mobilize electoral support. For instance, Wattenberg (2000) found that, in 19 liberal democracies, turnout had declined on average by 10 per cent between the 1950s and the 1990s, the trend having been particularly prominent in the USA, Western Europe, Japan and Latin America.

Alongside these changes, there is evidence of what has been called 'antipolitics'; that is, the rise of political movements and organizations the only common feature of which appears to be antipathy towards conventional centres of power and opposition to established parties of government. This has been reflected in the emergence of new political movements, the principle attraction of which is that they are untainted by having held power. Good examples have been the dramatic success of Berlesconi's Forza Italia in 1994, and the emergence in the USA since 2008 of the Tea Party movement. The rise of new social movements (see p. 260), such as the women's movement, peace movement and environmental movement, is also part of the same phenomenon. Even when they articulate their views through party organization, as in the case of green parties, these movements tend to assume the mantle of antiparty parties. (The role of such parties and movements in expressing forms of 'anti-politics' is examined in Chapter 20.)

How can the decline of parties be explained? One of the problems that parties suffer from is their real or perceived oligarchical character. Parties are seen as bureaucratized political machines, whose grass-roots members are either inactive, or engaged in dull and routine tasks (attending meetings, sitting on committees and so on). In contrast, single-issue protest groups have been more successful in attracting membership and support, particularly from amongst the young, partly because they are more loosely organized and locally based, and partly because they place a heavier emphasis on participation and activism. The public image of parties has been further tarnished by their links to government and to professional politicians. As political 'insiders', parties are tainted by the power, ambition and corruption that is often associated with high office. In other words, parties are not seen as being 'of the people'; too often, they appear to be consumed by political infighting and the scramble for power, so becoming divorced from the concerns of ordinary people.

An alternative way of explaining party decline is to see it as a symptom of the fact that complex, modern societies are increasingly difficult to govern. Disillusionment and cynicism grow as parties seek power by proclaiming their capacity to solve problems and improve conditions, but fail to deliver once in government. This reflects the mounting difficulties that confront any party of government in the form of the expanding power of interest groups and an increasingly globalized economy. A final explanation is that parties may be declining because the social identities and traditional loyalties that gave rise to them in the first place have started to fade. This can certainly be seen in the decline of class politics, linked to the phenomenon of post-Fordism.

In addition, with the decline of old social, religious and other solidarities, new aspirations and sensibilities have come onto the political agenda; notably, those associated with postmaterialism (see p. 177). Whereas broad, programmic parties once succeeded in articulating the goals of major sections of the electorate, issues such as gender equality, nuclear power, animal rights and pollution may require new and different political formations to articulate them. Single-issue groups and social movements may thus be in the process of replacing parties as the crucial link between government and society.

SUMMARY

- A political party is a group of people organized for the purpose of winning government power, and usually displays some measure of ideological cohesion. The principal classifications of parties have distinguished between cadre and mass or, later, catch-all parties, parties of representation and parties of integration, constitutional or 'mainstream' parties and revolutionary or anti-system ones, and left-wing parties and right-wing parties.

- Parties have a number of functions in the political system. These include their role as a mechanism of representation, the formation of political elites and recruitment into politics, the formulation of social goals and government policy, the articulation and aggregation of interests, the mobilization and socialization of the electorate, and the organization of governmental processes and institutional relationships.

- The organization and structure of parties crucially influence the distribution of power within society at large. Party democracy can be promoted either by a wide dispersal of power within the party, or by the concentration of power in the hands of the party's elected and publicly accountable members. Oligarchic tendencies may be an inevitable consequence of organization, or they may arise from the need for party unity and electoral credibility.

- A party system is a network of relationships through which parties interact and influence the political process. In one-party systems, a 'ruling' party effectively functions as a permanent government. In two-party systems, power alternates between two 'major' parties. In dominant-party systems, a single 'major' party retains power for a prolonged period. In multiparty systems, no party is large enough to rule alone, leading to a system of coalition government.

- Party systems shape the broader political process in various ways. They influence the range and nature of choice available to the electorate, and affect the cohesion and stability of governments. They structure the relationship between the executive and the assembly, establish a bias in favour of either conflict or consensus, and shape the general character of the political culture.

- Evidence of a crisis in party politics can be found in the decline in party membership and partisanship, as well as in the rise of 'antiparty' groups and movements. This can be explained by the perception that parties are tainted by power, ambition and corruption, and that they have suffered as a result of general disillusionment caused by the growing inability of governments to deliver on their promises. They are also seen to have failed to articulate the aspirations and sensibilities associated with postmaterialism, or generated within post-industrial societies.

Questions for discussion

- Are all modern political parties essentially catch-all parties?
- Is it possible to have 'post-ideological' parties?
- Could government function in contemporary circumstances without political parties?
- In what ways, and to what extent, do parties promote democracy?
- Why do political parties so often tend to be leader-dominated?
- By what criteria should party systems be judged?
- How have modern parties adjusted to the decline of class and other loyalties?
- Is the age of party politics over?

Further reading

Dalton, R. and D. Farrell, *Political Parties and Democratic Linkage: How Parties Organize Democracy* (2011). An examination of the link between parties and representative government that focuses on their impact on the electoral process and on government.

Katz, R. and W. Crotty (eds), *Handbook of Party Politics* (2006). A wide-ranging collection of articles that discuss the nature, functions and organization of parties and their relationship to society and the state.

Sartori, G., *Parties and Party Systems: A Framework for Analysis* (2005). A classic, if challenging, analysis of the role of parties and the nature of party systems.

Wolinetz, S. (ed.), *Political Parties* (1997). A comprehensive set of articles that examines all aspects of the workings and significance of political parties.

CHAPTER 15

Representation, Elections and Voting

'If voting changed anything they'd abolish it.'

Anarchist slogan

PREVIEW

Elections are often thought of as the heart of the political process. Perhaps no questions in politics are as crucial as 'Do we elect the politicians who rule over us?', and 'Under what rules are these elections held?' Elections are seen as nothing less than democracy in practice. They are a means through which the people can control their government, ultimately by 'kicking the rascals out'. Central to this notion is the principle of representation. Put simply, representation portrays politicians as servants of the people, and invests them with a responsibility to act for or on behalf of those who elect them. When democracy, in the classical sense of direct and continuous popular participation, is regarded as hopelessly impractical, representation may be the closest we can come to achieving government by the people. There is, nevertheless, considerable disagreement about what representation means and how it can be achieved in practice. Although it is widely accepted that elections play a pivotal role in the process of representative democracy, electoral systems are many and various and debate has long raged over which system is the 'best'. Not only do different systems have different strengths or advantages, but there is no consensus over the criteria that should be used for assessing them. Finally, elections need voters, but there is little agreement about why voters vote as they do, and especially about the extent to which their behaviour is rationally-based, as opposed to being influenced by underlying psychological, social or ideological forces.

KEY ISSUES

- What is representation? How can one person 'represent' another?
- How can representation be achieved in practice?
- What do elections do? What are their functions?
- How do electoral systems differ? What are their strengths and weaknesses?
- What do election results mean?
- Why do people vote as they do? How can voting behaviour be explained?

REPRESENTATION

The issue of representation has generated deep and recurrent political controversy. Even the absolute monarchs of old were expected to rule by seeking the advice of the 'estates of the realm' (the major landed interests, the clergy, and so on). In this sense, the English Civil War of the seventeenth century, fought between King and Parliament, broke out as a result of an attempt to deny representation to key groups and interests. Similarly, debate about the spread of democracy in the nineteenth and twentieth centuries centred largely on the question of who should be represented. Should representation be restricted to those who have the competence, education and, perhaps, leisure to act wisely and think seriously about politics (variously seen as men, the propertied, or particular racial or ethnic groups), or should representation be extended to all adult citizens?

Such questions have now largely been resolved through the widespread acceptance of the principle of political equality (see p. 90), at least in the formal sense of universal suffrage and 'one person, one vote'. Plural voting, for example, was abolished in the UK in 1949, women were enfranchised in one canton in Switzerland in 1971, and racial criteria for voting were swept away in South Africa in 1994. However, this approach to representation is simplistic, in that it equates representation with elections and voting, politicians being seen as 'representatives' merely because they have been elected. This ignores more difficult questions about how one person can be said to represent another, and what it is that he or she represents. Is it the views of the represented, their best interests, the groups from which they come, or what?

Theories of representation

There is no single, agreed theory of representation. Rather, there are a number of competing theories, each of which is based on particular ideological and political assumptions. For example, does representative government imply that government 'knows better' than the people, that government has somehow 'been instructed' by the people what to do and how to behave; or that the government 'looks like' the people, in that it broadly reflects their characteristics or features? Such questions are not of academic interest alone. Particular models of representation dictate very different behaviour on the part of representatives. For instance, should elected politicians be bound by policies and positions outlined during an election and endorsed by the voters, or is it their job to lead public opinion and thereby help to define the public interest? Moreover, it is not uncommon for more than one principle of representation to operate within the same political system, suggesting, perhaps, that no single model is sufficient in itself to secure representative government.

Four principal models of representation have been advanced:

- trusteeship
- delegation
- the mandate
- resemblance.

CONCEPT

Representation

Representation is, broadly, a relationship through which an individual or group stands for, or acts on behalf of, a larger body of people. Representation differs from democracy in that, while the former acknowledges a distinction between government and the governed, the latter, at least in its classical form, aspires to abolish this distinction and establish popular *self*-government. Representative democracy may nevertheless constitute a limited and indirect form of democratic rule, provided that the representation links government and the governed in such a way that the people's views are articulated, or their interests secured.

John Stuart Mill (1806–73)

UK philosopher, economist and politician. Mill was subject to an intense and austere regime of education by his father, the utilitarian theorist James Mill (1773–1836). This resulted in a mental collapse at the age of 20, after which he developed a more human philosophy influenced by Coleridge and the German Idealists. His major writings, including *On Liberty* (1859), *Considerations on Representative Government* (1861) and *The Subjection of Women* (1869), had a powerful influence on the development of liberal thought. In many ways, Mill's work straddles the divide between classical and modern liberalism. His distrust of state intervention was firmly rooted in nineteenth-century principles, but his emphasis on the quality of individual life (reflected in a commitment to 'individuality') looked forward to later developments.

Trustee model

A **trustee** is a person who acts on behalf of others, using his or her superior knowledge, better education or greater experience. The classic expression of representation as trusteeship is found in Edmund Burke's (see p. 36) speech to the electors of Bristol in 1774:

> You choose a member indeed; but when you have chosen him he is not member of Bristol, but he is a member of parliament . . . Your representative owes you, not his industry only, but his judgement; and he betrays, instead of serving you, if he sacrifices it to your opinion (Burke, 1975).

For Burke, the essence of representation was to serve one's constituents by the exercise of 'mature judgement' and 'enlightened conscience'. In short, representation is a moral duty: those with the good fortune to possess education and understanding should act in the interests of those who are less fortunate. This view had strongly elitist implications, since it stresses that, once elected, representatives should think for themselves and exercise independent judgement on the grounds that the mass of people do not know their own best interests. A similar view was advanced by John Stuart Mill in the form of the liberal theory of representation. This was based on the assumption that, although all individuals have a right to be represented, not all political opinions are of equal value. Mill therefore proposed a system of plural voting in which four or five votes would be allocated to holders of learned diplomas or degrees, two or three to skilled or managerial workers, and a single vote to ordinary workers. He also argued that rational voters would support politicians who could act wisely on their behalf, rather than those who merely reflected the voters' own views. Trustee representation thus portrays professional politicians as representatives, insofar as they are members of an educated elite. It is based on the belief that knowledge and understanding are unequally distributed in society, in the sense that not all citizens know what is best for them.

This Burkean notion of representation has also attracted severe criticism, however. For instance, it appears to have clearly antidemocratic implications. If

● **Trustee:** A person who is vested with formal (and usually legal) responsibilities for another's property or affairs.

Thomas Paine (1737–1809)

UK-born writer and revolutionary. Paine was brought up in a Quaker family and spent his early years as an undistinguished artisan. He went to America in 1774 and fought for the colonists in the War of Independence. He returned to England in 1789, but, after being indicted for treason, fled to France as a supporter of the republican cause, where he narrowly escaped the guillotine during the Terror. Paine's radicalism fused a commitment to political liberty with a deep faith in popular sovereignty, providing inspiration for both liberal republicanism and socialist egalitarianism. He was an important figure in revolutionary politics in the USA, the UK and France. His most important writings include *Common Sense* ([1776] 1987), *The Rights of Man* (1791/92) and *The Age of Reason* (1794).

politicians should think for themselves because the public is ignorant, poorly educated or deluded, then surely it is a mistake to allow the public to elect their representatives in the first place. Second, the link between representation and education is questionable. Whereas education may certainly be of value in aiding the understanding of intricate political and economic problems, it is far less clear that it helps politicians to make correct moral judgements about the interests of others. There is little evidence, for example, to support Burke's and Mill's belief that education breeds **altruism** and gives people a broader sense of social responsibility. Finally, there is the fear traditionally expressed by radical democrats such as Thomas Paine that, if politicians are allowed to exercise their own judgement, they will simply use that latitude to pursue their own selfish interests. In this way, representation could simply become a substitute for democracy. In his pamphlet *Common Sense* ([1776] 1987), Paine came close to the rival ideal of delegate representation in insisting that 'the elected should never form to themselves an interest separate from the electors'.

Delegate model

A **delegate** is a person who acts as a conduit conveying the views of others, while having little or no capacity to exercise his or her own judgement or preferences. Examples include sales representatives and ambassadors, neither of whom are, strictly speaking, authorized to think for themselves. Similarly, a trade-union official who attends a conference with instructions on how to vote and what to say is acting as a delegate, not as a Burkean representative. Those who favour this model of representation as delegation usually support mechanisms that ensure that politicians are bound as closely as possible to the views of the represented. These include what Paine referred to as 'frequent interchange' between representatives and their constituents in the form of regular elections and short terms in office. In addition, radical democrats have advocated the use of **initiatives** and the right of **recall** as means of giving the public more control over politicians. Although delegation stops short of direct democracy, its supporters nevertheless usually favour the use of referendums (see p. 201) to supplement the representative process.

● **Altruism**: A concern for the welfare of others, based on either enlightened self-interest, or a recognition of a common humanity.

● **Delegate**: A person who is chosen to act for another on the basis of clear guidance and instruction; delegates do not think for themselves.

● **Initiative**: A type of referendum through which the public is able to raise legislative proposals.

● **Recall**: A process whereby the electorate can call unsatisfactory public officials to account and ultimately remove them.

CONCEPT

Mandate

A mandate is an instruction or command from a higher body that demands compliance. The idea of a *policy* mandate arises from the claim on behalf of a winning party in an election that its manifesto promises have been endorsed, giving it authority to translate these into a programme of government. The doctrine of the mandate thus implies that the party in power can only act within the mandate it has received. The more flexible notion of a *governing* mandate, or, for an individual leader, a *personal* mandate, has sometimes been advanced, but it is difficult to see how this in any way restricts politicians once they are in power.

● Popular sovereignty: The principle that there is no higher authority than the will of the people (the basis of the classical concept of democracy).

● Manifesto: A document outlining (in more or less detail) the policies or programme a party proposes to pursue if elected to power.

The virtue of what has been called 'delegated representation' is that it provides broader opportunities for popular participation and serves to check the self-serving inclinations of professional politicians. It thus comes as close as is possible in representative government to realizing the ideal of **popular sovereignty**. Its disadvantages are, nevertheless, also clear. In the first place, in ensuring that representatives are bound to the interests of their constituents, it tends to breed narrowness and foster conflict. This is precisely what Burke feared would occur if members of the legislature acted as ambassadors who took instructions from their constituents, rather than as representatives of the nation. As he put it, 'Parliament is a deliberative assembly of one nation, with one interest, that of the whole'. A second drawback is that, because professional politicians are not trusted to exercise their own judgement, delegation limits the scope for leadership (see p. 300) and statesmanship. Politicians are forced to reflect the views of their constituents or even pander to them, and are thus not able to mobilize the people by providing vision and inspiration.

Mandate model

Both the trustee model and the delegate model were developed before the emergence of modern political parties, and therefore view representatives as essentially independent actors. However, individual candidates are now rarely elected mainly on the basis of their personal qualities and talents; more commonly, they are seen, to a greater or lesser extent, as foot soldiers for a party, and are supported because of its public image or programme of policies. New theories of representation have therefore emerged. The most influential of these is the so-called 'doctrine of the mandate'. This is based on the idea that, in winning an election, a party gains a popular mandate that authorizes it to carry out whatever policies or programmes it outlined during the election campaign. As it is the party, rather than individual politicians, that is the agent of representation, the mandate model provides a clear justification for party unity and party discipline. In effect, politicians serve their constituents not by thinking for themselves or acting as a channel to convey their views, but by remaining loyal to their party and its policies.

The strength of the mandate doctrine is that it takes account of the undoubted practical importance of party labels and party policies. Moreover, it provides a means of imposing some kind of meaning on election results, as well as a way of keeping politicians to their word. Nevertheless, the doctrine has also stimulated fierce criticism. First, it is based on a highly questionable model of voting behaviour, insofar as it suggests that voters select parties on the grounds of policies and issues. Voters are not always the rational and well-informed creatures that this model suggests. They can be influenced by a range of 'irrational' factors, such as the personalities of leaders, the images of parties, habitual allegiances and social conditioning.

Second, even if voters are influenced by policies, it is likely that they will be attracted by certain **manifesto** commitments, but be less interested in, or perhaps opposed to, others. A vote for a party cannot therefore be taken to be an endorsement of its entire manifesto or, indeed, of any single election promise. Third, the doctrine imposes a straitjacket. It limits government policies to those positions and proposals that the party took up during the election, and leaves no

Focus on . . .

Referendums: for or against?

A referendum is a vote in which the electorate can express a view on a particular issue of public policy. It differs from an election in that the latter is essentially a means of filling a public office and does not provide a direct or reliable method of influencing the content of policy. The referendum is therefore a device of direct democracy (see p. 92). It is typically used not to replace representative institutions, but to supplement them. Referendums may be either advisory or binding; they may also raise issues for discussion (initiatives), or be used to decide policy questions (propositions or plebiscites).

Amongst the advantages of referendums are the following:

- They check the power of elected governments, ensuring that they stay in line with public opinion.
- They promote political participation, thus helping to create a more educated and better-informed electorate.

- They strengthen legitimacy by providing the public with a way of expressing their views about specific issues.
- They provide a means either of settling major constitutional questions, or of gauging public opinion on issues not raised in elections because major parties agree on them.

The disadvantages of referendums include the following:

- They leave political decisions in the hands of those who have the least education and experience, and are most susceptible to media and other influences.
- They provide, at best, only a snapshot of public opinion at one point in time.
- They allow politicians to manipulate the political agenda and absolve themselves of responsibility for making difficult decisions.
- They tend to simplify and distort political issues, reducing them to questions that have a yes/no answer.

scope to adjust policies in the light of changing circumstances. What guidance do mandates offer in the event of, say, international or economic crises? Finally (as discussed in the next main section of this chapter), the doctrine of the mandate can be applied only in the case of majoritarian electoral systems, and its use even there may appear absurd if the winning party fails to gain 50 per cent of the popular vote.

Resemblance model

- **Microcosm**: Literally, a little world; a miniature version of a larger body, but exact in its features and proportions.

- **Descriptive representation**: A model of representation that takes account of politicians' social and other characteristics, usually based on the idea that they should be a 'representative sample' of the larger society.

The final theory of representation is based less on the manner in which representatives are selected than on whether they typify or resemble the group they claim to represent. This notion is embodied in the idea of a 'representative cross-section', as used by market researchers and opinion pollsters. By this standard, a representative government would constitute a microcosm of the larger society, containing members drawn from all groups and sections in society (in terms of social class, gender, age and so on), and in numbers that are proportional to the size of the groups in society at large. The idea of descriptive representation, or as it has been called 'microcosmic representation', has traditionally been endorsed by socialist, feminist and other radical thinkers. They argue that the 'under-representation' of groups such as the working class, women and racial

Joseph Schumpeter (1883–1950)

Moravian-born US economist and sociologist. Following an early academic career and a brief spell as Minister of Finance in post-First-World-War Austria, Schumpeter became professor of economics at Harvard University in 1932. His economic thought, developed in *Theory of Economic Development* (1912) and *Business Cycles* (1939), centred on the long-term dynamics of the capitalist system and in particular the role of 'risk-loving' entrepreneurs. In *Capitalism, Socialism and Democracy* (1942), Schumpeter drew on economic, sociological and political theories to advance the famous contention that western capitalism was, impelled by its very success, evolving into a form of socialism.

minorities at senior levels in key institutions ensures that their interests are marginalized, or ignored altogether.

The resemblance model suggests that only people who come from a particular group, and have shared the experiences of that group, can fully identify with its interests. This is the difference between 'putting oneself in the shoes of another' and having direct and personal experience of what other people go through. A 'new man' or a 'pro-feminist' male may, for instance, sympathize with women's interests and support the principle of gender equality, but will never take women's problems as seriously as women do themselves, because they are not his problems. On the other hand, the idea that representatives should resemble the represented undoubtedly causes a number of difficulties.

One of these is that this model portrays representation in exclusive or narrow terms, believing that only a woman can represent women, only a black person can represent other black people, only a member of the working class can represent the working classes and so on. If all representatives simply advanced the interests of the groups from which they come, the result would be social division and conflict, with no one being able to defend the common good or advance a broader public interest. Moreover, a government that is a microcosm of society would reflect that society's weaknesses as well as its strengths. What would be the advantage, for example, of government resembling society if the majority of the population are apathetic, ill-informed and poorly educated? Finally, the microcosmic ideal can be achieved only by imposing powerful constraints on electoral choice and individual freedom. In the name of representation, political parties may be forced to select quotas of female and minority candidates, constituencies may be set aside for candidates from particular backgrounds, or, more dramatically, the electorate might have to be classified on the basis of class, gender, race and so on, and only be allowed to vote for candidates from their own group.

ELECTIONS

Although controversy continues to rage about the nature of representation, there is one point of universal agreement: the representative process is intrinsically linked to elections and voting. Elections may not, in themselves, be a sufficient condition for political representation but, in modern circumstances, there is little doubt that they are a necessary condition. Indeed, some thinkers have gone further and portrayed elections as the very heart of democracy. This was the view developed by Joseph Schumpeter (see p. 202) in *Capitalism, Socialism and Democracy* (1942), which portrayed democracy as an 'institutional arrangement', as a means of filling public office by a competitive struggle for the people's vote. As he put it, 'democracy means only that the people have the opportunity of accepting or refusing the men [*sic*] who are to rule them'. In interpreting democracy as nothing more than a political method, Schumpeter, in effect, identified it with elections, and specifically with competitive elections. While few modern democratic theorists are prepared to reduce democracy simply to competitive elections, most nevertheless follow Schumpeter in understanding democratic government in terms of the rules and mechanisms that guide the conduct of elections. This focuses attention on the very different forms that elections can take.

First, which offices or posts are subject to the elective principle? Although elections are widely used to fill those public offices whose holders have policy-making responsibilities (the legislature and executive, in particular), key political institutions are sometimes treated as exceptions. This applies, for instance, to the second chambers of legislature in states such as the UK and Canada, and where constitutional monarchs still serve as heads of state. Second, who is entitled to vote, how widely is the franchise drawn? As pointed out, restrictions on the right to vote based on factors such as property ownership, education, gender and racial origin have been abandoned in most countries. Nevertheless, there may be informal restrictions, as in the practice in most US states of leaving electoral registration entirely in the hands of the citizen, with the result that non-registration and non-voting are widespread. On the other hand, in Australia, Belgium and Italy, for instance, voting is compulsory.

Third, how are votes cast? Although public voting was the norm in the USSR until 1989, and it is still widely practised in small organizations in the form of a show of hands, modern political elections are generally held on the basis of a secret ballot (sometimes called an 'Australian ballot', as it was first used in South Australia in 1856). The secret ballot is usually seen as the guarantee of a 'fair' election, in that it keeps the dangers of corruption and intimidation at bay. Nevertheless, electoral fairness cannot simply be reduced to the issue of how people vote. It is also affected by the voters' access to reliable and balanced information, the range of choice they are offered, the circumstances under which campaigning is carried out, and, finally, how scrupulously the vote is counted.

Fourth, are elections competitive or non-competitive? This is usually seen as the most crucial of distinctions, as, until the 1990s, only about half of the countries that used elections offered their electorates a genuine choice of both candidates and parties. Single-candidate elections, for example, were the rule in orthodox communist states. This meant that public office was effectively filled through a nomination process dominated by the communist party. Electoral competition is a highly complex and often controversial issue. It concerns not merely the right of people to stand for election and the ability of political parties to nominate candidates and campaign legally, but also broader factors that affect party performance, such as their sources of funding and their access to the media. From this point of view, the nature of the party system may be as crucial

Debating...
Should voting be compulsory?

In 2005, some 33 countries operated a system of compulsory voting for some or all elected bodies, although only in a minority of cases was this enforced through the threat of punishment (usually by a small fine, or community service). However, while some argue that compulsory voting strengthens democracy, even seeing it as a civic duty, others point out that 'non-voting' is a basic civil right, whose infringement may make a mockery of the democratic process.

YES	NO
Increased participation. The almost certain consequence of introducing compulsory voting would be that turnout rates will increase. Voter turnout in Australia has thus been consistently around 94–96 per cent since the introduction of nationwide compulsory voting in 1924, having previously been as low as 47 per cent. Compulsory voting would, at a stroke, resolve the 'participation crises' that afflict so many mature democracies, in the process counteracting longer-term trends against voting in modern, individualized and consumerist societies.	***Abuse of freedom.*** Compulsion, even in the name of democracy, remains compulsion: a violation of individual freedom. The right *not* to vote may, in some senses, be as important as the right to choose for whom to vote. Non-voting may thus be a conscientious act, a product of rational and considered reflection, an attempt to draw attention to, amongst other things, the lack of choice among mainstream political parties or, perhaps, to express a principled rejection of the political system itself.
Greater legitimacy. Governments formed on the basis of compulsory voting would be much more likely to rest on a popular majority (a majority of those eligible to vote), not just an electoral majority (a majority of those who actually vote). Declining turnout in the UK's non-compulsory system meant that, in 2005, the Labour Party was able to gain a comfortable parliamentary majority with the support of just 22 per cent of the electorate. Compulsory voting would therefore strengthen democratic legitimacy and ensure that governments do not neglect sections of society that are less active politically.	***Cosmetic democracy.*** Compulsory voting addresses the symptoms of the problem but not the cause. Making voting compulsory would undoubtedly increase the electoral turnout, but it would not address the deeper problems that account for a growing decline in civic engagement. Higher turnout levels brought about through compulsion may therefore simply mask deeper problems, making it less likely, rather than more likely, that issues such as the decline in trust in politicians, and a lack of effective responsiveness and accountability, will be properly addressed.
Civic duty. Citizenship is based on reciprocal rights and responsibilities. The right to vote therefore involves a duty to exercise that right, and legal compulsion simply ensures that that duty is fulfilled (treating it like paying taxes, jury service and (possibly) military conscription). Moreover, enforcing the responsibility to vote has educational benefits, in that it will stimulate political activism and create a better informed citizenry.	***Worthless votes.*** Generally, those who do not vote have the least interest in and understanding of politics. Forcing would-be non-voters to vote would therefore simply increase the number of random and unthinking votes that are cast. This may particularly be the case when some voters, because they only turn up through a fear of punishment, may feel resentful and aggrieved. This is an especially worrying prospect as such 'worthless' votes may, ultimately, determine the outcome of an election.
Countering social disadvantage. Voluntary voting effectively disadvantages the most vulnerable elements in society, the poor and less-educated – those who are, as research consistently shows, least likely to vote. Non-compulsion therefore means that the interests of the educated, articulate and better-off prevail over those of other groups. Genuine political equality requires not only that all *can* vote, but that all *do* vote. Only then can political equality serve the interests of social equality.	***Distorted political focus.*** A final problem with compulsory voting is that it may distort the strategies adopted by political parties. Instead of focusing on the interests of the mass of the electorate, parties may be encouraged to frame policies designed to attract more volatile 'marginal' voters (that is, would-be non-voters), thereby leading to a decline in coherence and an increase in polarization.

to the maintenance of genuine competition as are rules about who can stand and who can vote. Finally, how is the election conducted? As will be discussed later, there is a bewildering variety of electoral systems, each of which has its own particular political and constitutional implications.

Functions of elections

Because of the different kinds of elections, and the variety of electoral systems, generalization about the roles or functions of elections is always difficult. Nevertheless, the advance of democratization (see p. 272) in the 1980s and 1990s, stimulated in part by the collapse of communism, has usually been associated with the adoption of liberal-democratic electoral systems, characterized by universal suffrage, the secret ballot and electoral competition. The significance of such systems is, however, more difficult to determine. As Harrop and Miller (1987) explained, there are two contrasting views of the function of competitive elections.

The conventional view is that elections are a mechanism through which politicians can be called to account and forced to introduce policies that somehow reflect public opinion. This emphasizes the bottom-up functions of elections: political recruitment, representation, making government, influencing policy and so on. On the other hand, a radical view of elections, developed by theorists such as Ginsberg (1982), portrays them as a means through which governments and political elites can exercise control over their populations, making them more quiescent, malleable and, ultimately, governable. This view emphasizes top-down functions: building legitimacy, shaping public opinion and strengthening elites. In reality, however, elections have no single character; they are neither simply mechanisms of public accountability, nor a means of ensuring political control. Like all channels of political communication, elections are a 'two-way street' that provides the government and the people, the elite and the masses, with the opportunity to influence one another. The central functions of elections include the following:

- **Recruiting politicians**: In democratic states, elections are the principal source of political recruitment, taking account also of the processes through which parties nominate candidates. Politicians thus tend to possess talents and skills that are related to electioneering, such as charisma, oratorical skills and good looks, not necessarily those that suit them to carrying out constituency duties, serving on committees, running government departments and so on. Elections are typically not used to fill posts that require specialist knowledge or experience, such as those in the civil service or judiciary.
- **Making governments**: Elections make governments directly only in states such as the USA, France and Venezuela, in which the political executive is directly elected. In the more common parliamentary systems, elections influence the formation of governments, most strongly when the electoral system tends to give a single party a clear parliamentary majority. The use of proportional representation (see p. 207) may mean that governments are formed through post-election deals, and that governments can be made and unmade without the need for an election.

- **Providing representation:** When they are fair and competitive, elections are a means through which demands are channelled from the public to the government. Short of the use of initiatives and the recall, however, the electorate has no effective means of ensuring that mandates are carried out, apart from its capacity to inflict punishment at the next election. Moreover, nowhere do elected governments constitute a microcosm of the larger society.
- **Influencing policy:** Elections certainly deter governments from pursuing radical and deeply unpopular policies; however, only in exceptional cases, when a single issue dominates the election campaign, can they be said to influence policy directly. It can also be argued that the range of policy options outlined in elections is typically so narrow that the result can be of only marginal policy significance. Others suggest that government policy is, in any case, shaped more by practical dictates, such as the state of the economy, than it is by electoral considerations.
- **Educating voters:** The process of campaigning provides the electorate with an abundance of information, about parties, candidates, policies, the current government's record, the political system and so on. However, this leads to education only if the information that is provided, and the way it is provided, engages public interest and stimulates debate, as opposed to apathy and alienation. As candidates and parties seek to persuade, rather than to educate, they also have a strong incentive to provide incomplete and distorted information.
- **Building legitimacy:** One reason why even authoritarian regimes bother to hold elections, even if they are non-competitive, is that elections help to foster legitimacy (see p. 81) by providing justification for a system of rule. This happens because the ritual involved in campaigning somehow confers on an election a ceremonial status and importance. Most importantly, by encouraging citizens to participate in politics, even in the limited form of voting, elections mobilize active consent.
- **Strengthening elites:** Elections can also be a vehicle through which elites can manipulate and control the masses. This possibility encouraged of proportional representation (see p. 207) may mean that governments are tion'. Political discontent and opposition can be neutralized by elections that channel them in a constitutional direction, and allow governments to come and go while the regime itself survives. Elections are particularly effective in this respect because, at the same time, they give citizens the impression that they are exercising power over the government.

Electoral systems: debates and controversies

An electoral system is a set of rules that governs the conduct of elections. Not only do these rules vary across the world; they are also, in many countries, the subject of fierce political debate and argument. These rules vary in a number of ways:

- Voters may be asked to choose between candidates or between parties.
- Voters may either select a single candidate, or vote preferentially, ranking the candidates they wish to support in order.

Proportional representation

Proportional representation is the principle that parties should be represented in an assembly or parliament in direct proportion to their overall electoral strength, their percentage of seats equalling their percentage of votes. The term is generally used to refer not to a single method of election but to a variety of electoral mechanisms, those able to secure proportional outcomes, or at least a high and reliable degree of proportionality. The best known PR systems are the party-list system, the single-transferable-vote system and the additional member system.

- The electorate may or may not be grouped into electoral units or constituencies.
- Constituencies may return a single member or a number of members.
- The level of support needed to elect a candidate varies from a plurality to an overall or 'absolute' majority, or a quota of some kind.

For general purposes, however, the systems available can be divided into two broad categories on the basis of how they convert votes into seats. On the one hand, there are majoritarian systems, in which larger parties typically win a higher proportion of seats than the proportion of votes they gain in the election. This increases the chances of a single party gaining a parliamentary majority and being able to govern on its own. In the UK, for example, single-party government prevailed between 1945 and 2010 despite the fact that no party achieved an electoral majority during this period. On the other hand, there are proportional systems, which guarantee an equal (or, at least, more equal) relationship between the seats won by a party and the votes gained in the election. In a pure system of proportional representation (PR), a party that gains 45 per cent of the votes would win exactly 45 per cent of the seats. PR systems therefore make single-party majority rule less likely, and are commonly associated with multiparty systems and coalition government. The electoral systems described in the following Focus boxes range from the most majoritarian type of system to the purest type of proportional system.

Although in some countries the electoral system provokes little debate or interest, in others it is an issue of pressing political and constitutional significance. France, for instance, has changed its electoral system so many times that any statement about it runs the risk of being out of date. The second ballot (see p. 209) was abandoned for parliamentary elections in 1985, when France switched to a regional-list system (see p. 213), but it was reintroduced for the 1993 election. In the UK, although the majoritarian single-member plurality (SMP) system (see p. 208) continues to be used for general elections, since 1999 a number of more proportional systems have been introduced for elections to the devolved bodies in Scotland, Wales and Northern Ireland, the Greater London Authority and the European Parliament. The confusing thing about the electoral reform debate is that the shifts that have occurred reflect no consistent pattern. In 1993, while New Zealand adopted proportional representation in place of the SMP system (see p. 214), Italy moved in the opposite direction, replacing the party list with the less proportional additional member system, before, in 2005, returning to the list system.

Electoral systems attract attention, in part, because they have a crucial impact on party performance and, particularly, on their prospects of winning (or, at least, sharing) power. It would be foolish, then, to deny that attitudes towards the electoral system are shaped largely by party advantage. President Mitterrand's twists and turns in France in the 1980s and 1990s were dictated mainly by his desire to strengthen Socialist representation in the National Assembly. Similarly, the UK Labour Party's interest in electoral reform since the 1980s has waxed and waned according to whether it appeared that the party could win under SMP rules. The party's conversion to PR for devolved bodies and its commitment in 1997 to holding a referendum on electoral reform for the House of Commons were, in part, a consequence of spending 18 years in opposition. It is notable that Labour's

- **Plurality**: The largest number out of a collection of numbers, not necessarily an absolute majority (50 per cent or more of all the numbers combined).

Focus on . . .

Electoral systems: single-member plurality (SMP) system ('first past the post')

Used: The UK (House of Commons), the USA, Canada and India, for example. **Type:** Majoritarian.

Features:
- The country is divided into single-member constituencies, usually of equal size.
- Voters select a single candidate, usually marking his or her name with a cross on the ballot paper.
- The winning candidate needs only to achieve a plurality of votes (the 'first past the post' rule).

Advantages:
- The system establishes a clear link between representatives and constituents, ensuring that constituency duties are carried out.
- It offers the electorate a clear choice of potential parties of government.
- It allows governments to be formed that have a clear mandate from the electorate, albeit often on the basis of plurality support amongst the electorate.
- It keeps extremism at bay by making it more difficult for small radical parties to gain seats and credibility.
- It makes for strong and effective government in that a single party usually has majority control of the assembly.

- It produces stable government, in that single-party governments rarely collapse as a result of disunity and internal friction.

Disadvantages:
- The system 'wastes' many (perhaps most) votes, those cast for losing candidates and those cast for winning ones over the plurality mark.
- It distorts electoral preferences by 'under-representing' small parties and ones with geographically evenly distributed support (the 'third-party effect').
- It offers only limited choice because of its duopolistic (two-major-parties) tendencies.
- It undermines the legitimacy of government, in that governments often enjoy only minority support, producing a system of plurality rule.
- It creates instability because a change in government can lead to a radical shift of policies and direction.
- It leads to unaccountable government in that the legislature is usually subordinate to the executive, because the majority of its members are supporters of the governing party.
- It discourages the selection of a socially broad spread of candidates in favour of those who are attractive to a large body of voters.

landslide victories in 1997 and 2001 coincided with declining interest in the party in changing Westminster elections. However, other less cynical and more substantial considerations need to be taken into account. The problem, though, is that there is no such thing as a 'best electoral system'.

The electoral reform debate is, at heart, a debate about the desirable nature of government and the principles that underpin 'good' government. Is representative government, for instance, more important than effective government? Is a bias in favour of compromise and consensus preferable to one that favours conviction and principle? These are normative questions that do not permit objective answers. Moreover, in view of the complex role they play, elections can be judged according to a diverse range of criteria, which not uncommonly contradict one another. Electoral systems therefore merit only a qualified

Focus on . . .

Electoral systems: second ballot system

Used: Traditionally in France, but it is used for presidential elections in countries such as Austria, Chile and Russia. **Type**: Majoritarian.

Features:

- There are single-candidate constituencies and single-choice voting, as in the single-member plurality (SMP) system.
- To win on the first ballot, a candidate needs an overall majority of the votes cast.
- If no candidate gains a first-ballot majority, a second, run-off ballot is held between the leading two candidates.

Advantages:

- The system broadens electoral choice: voters can vote with their hearts for their preferred candidate in the first ballot, and with their heads for the least-bad candidate in the second.
- As candidates can win only with majority support, they are encouraged to make their appeal as broad as possible.
- Strong and stable government is possible, as with SMP systems.

Disadvantages:

- As the system is little more proportional than the SMP system, it distorts preferences and is unfair to 'third' parties.
- Run-off candidates are encouraged to abandon their principles in search of short-term popularity, or as a result of deals with defeated candidates.
- The holding of a second ballot may strain the electorate's patience and interest in politics.

endorsement, reflecting a balance of advantages over disadvantages and their strength relative to other systems. These criteria fall into two general categories: those related to the quality of representation, and those linked to the effectiveness of government.

Majoritarian systems are usually thought to be at their weakest when they are evaluated in terms of their representative functions. To a greater or lesser extent, each majoritarian system distorts popular preferences, in the sense that party representation is not commensurate with electoral strength. This is most glaringly apparent in their 'unfairness' to small parties and parties with evenly distributed geographical support, and their 'over-fairness' in relation to large parties and those with geographically concentrated support. For example, in 2010 in the UK, the Conservative Party gained 47 per cent of the parliamentary seats with 36 per cent of the vote, the Labour Party won 40 per cent of the seats with 29 per cent of the vote, and the Liberal Democrats gained merely 9 per cent representation with 23 per cent of the vote. Such biases are impossible to justify in representative terms, especially since the unfortunate 'third' parties are often centrist parties, and not the extremist parties of popular image.

Two-party systems and single-party government are thus 'manufactured' by the majoritarian bias of the electoral system, and do not reflect the distribution of popular preferences. Moreover, the fact that parties can come to power with barely two-fifths of the popular vote (in 2005 in the UK, for example, the Labour Party gained a House of Commons majority with 35.3 per cent of the vote) strains the legitimacy of the entire political system, and creates circumstances in which radical,

Focus on . . .

Electoral systems: alternative vote (AV) system; supplementary vote (SV)

Used: Australia (House of Representatives (AV)), and the UK (London mayor (SV)). **Type:** Majoritarian.

Features:
- There are single-member constituencies.
- There is preferential voting. In AV, voters rank the candidates in order of preference: 1 for their first preference, 2 for their second preference and so on. In SV, there is only a single 'supplementary' vote.
- Winning candidates must gain 50 per cent of all the votes cast.
- Votes are counted according to the first preferences. If no candidate reaches 50 per cent, the bottom candidate is eliminated and his or her votes are redistributed according to the second (or subsequent) preferences. This continues until one candidate has a majority. In SV, all candidates drop out except the top two.

Advantages:
- Fewer votes are 'wasted' than in the SMP system.
- Unlike the second-ballot system, the outcome cannot be influenced by deals made between candidates.
- Although winning candidates must secure at least 50 per cent support, single-party majority government is not ruled out.

Disadvantages:
- The system is not much more proportional than the SMP system, and so is still biased in favour of large parties.
- The outcome may be determined by the preferences of those who support small, possibly extremist, parties.
- Winning candidates may enjoy little first-preference support, and have only the virtue of being the least unpopular candidate available.

ideologically-driven parties can remain in power for prolonged periods under little pressure to broaden their appeal. The Conservatives in the UK were thus able to implement a programme of market-orientated reforms in the 1980s and 1990s while never gaining more than 43 per cent of support in general elections. When the majority of voters oppose the party in power, it is difficult to claim that that party has a popular mandate for anything.

Looked at in this light, proportional electoral systems seem to be manifestly more representative. Nevertheless, it may be naive simply to equate electoral fairness with **proportionality**. For instance, much of the criticism of PR systems stems from the fact that they make coalition government (see p. 239) much more likely. Although it can be argued that, unlike single-party governments, coalitions enjoy the support of at least 50 per cent of the electors, their policies are typically thrashed out in post-election deals, and thus are not endorsed by any set of electors. An additional danger is that parties within a coalition government may not exert influence in line with their electoral strength. The classic example of this is when small centre parties (such as the Free Democrats in Germany) can dictate to larger parties (for example, the CDU or the SPD in Germany) by threatening to switch their support to another party. Then, in effect, 'the tail wags the dog'.

The defence of majoritarian systems is more commonly based on government functions, and specifically on the capacity of such systems to deliver stable

● **Proportionality**: The degree to which the allocation of seats amongst parties reflects the distribution of the popular vote.

Focus on . . .

Electoral systems: mixed-member proportional (MMP) system; additional member system (AMS)

Used: Germany, Italy, New Zealand and the UK (Scottish Parliament and Welsh Assembly).

Type: Proportional.

Features:

- A proportion of seats (50 per cent in Germany, but more in Italy, Scotland and Wales, for instance) are filled by the SMP system using single-member constituencies.
- The remaining seats are filled using the party-list system.
- Electors cast two votes: one for a candidate in the constituency election, and the other for a party.

Advantages:

- The hybrid nature of this system balances the need for constituency representation against the need for electoral fairness. The party-list process ensures that the whole assembly is proportionally representative.
- Although the system is broadly proportional in terms of its outcome, it keeps alive the possibility of single-party government.

- It allows electors to choose a constituency representative from one party and yet support another party to form a government.
- It takes account of the fact that representing constituents and holding ministerial office are very different jobs that require very different talents and experience.

Disadvantages:

- The retention of single-member constituencies prevents the achievement of high levels of proportionality.
- The system creates two classes of representative, one burdened by insecurity and constituency duties, the other having higher status and the prospect of holding ministerial office.
- Constituency representation suffers because of the size of constituencies (generally, twice as large as in SMP systems).
- Parties become more centralized and powerful under this system, as they decide not only who has the security of being on the list and who has to fight constituencies, but also where on the list candidates are placed.

and effective rule. In other words, a lack of proportionality may simply be the price that is paid for strong government. In these systems, the bias in favour of single-party rule means that the electorate can usually choose between two parties, each of which has the capacity to deliver on its election promises by translating its manifesto commitments into a programme of government. Supported by a cohesive majority in the assembly, such governments are usually able to survive for a full term in office. In contrast, coalition governments are weak and unstable, in the sense that they are endlessly engaged in a process of reconciling opposing views, and are always liable to collapse as a result of internal splits and divisions. The classic example here is post-1945 Italy which, up to 2012, had had no fewer than 63 governments.

Supporters of PR argue, on the other hand, that having a strong government, in the sense of a government that is able to push through policies, is by no means an unqualified virtue, tending as it does to restrict scrutiny and parliamentary accountability. Instead, they suggest that 'strong' government should be understood

Focus on . . .

Electoral systems: single-transferable-vote (STV) system

Used: The Republic of Ireland and the UK (Northern Ireland Assembly). **Type:** Proportional.

Features:

- There are multimember constituencies, each of which usually returns between three and eight members.
- Parties may put forward as many candidates as there are seats to fill.
- Electors vote preferentially, as in the alternative vote system.
- Candidates are elected, if they achieve a quota. This is the minimum number of votes needed to elect the stipulated number of candidates, calculated according to the Droop formula:

$$\text{quota} 5 \ \frac{\text{total number of votes cast}}{(\text{number of seats to be filled} + 1)} + 1$$

For example, if 100,000 votes are cast in a constituency that elects four members, the quota is 100,000/(4 + 1) + 1 = 20,001.

- The votes are counted according to first preferences. If not all the seats are filled, the bottom candidate is eliminated. His or her votes are redistributed according to second preferences and so on, until all the seats have been filled.

Advantages:

- The system is capable of achieving highly proportional outcomes.
- Competition amongst candidates from the same party means that they can be judged on their records and on where they stand on issues that cut across party lines.
- The availability of several members means that constituents can choose to whom to take their grievances.

Disadvantages:

- The degree of proportionality achieved varies, largely on the basis of the party system.
- Strong and stable single-party government is unlikely.
- Intra-party competition may be divisive, and may allow members to evade their constituency responsibilities.

in terms of popular support, and the willingness of citizens to obey and respect the government. Broadly-based coalitions may possess these qualities in greater abundance than do single-party governments. By the same token, 'stable' government could mean a consistent development of government policies over a number of governments, rather than a government with the ability to survive for a single electoral term. This is more likely to be achieved by coalition governments (in which one or more parties may remain in power over a number of governments, albeit reshuffled) than by single-party governments, in which more sweeping changes in personnel and priorities are unavoidable when power changes hands.

The electoral reform debate, however, constantly risks overestimating the importance of electoral systems. In practice, elections are only one amongst a variety of factors that shape the political process, and may not be the most crucial. Indeed, the impact of particular electoral systems is conditioned largely by other circumstances; namely, the political culture, the nature of the party system, and the economic and social context within which politics is conducted. Generalizations about the nature of coalition government are always highly

Focus on . . .
Electoral systems: party-list system

Used: Israel, and in countries throughout Europe, including Belgium, Luxembourg and Switzerland, and the European Parliament. **Type**: Proportional.

Features:
- Either the entire country is treated as a single constituency, or, in the case of regional party lists, there are a number of large multimember constituencies.
- Parties compile lists of candidates to place before the electorate, in descending order of preference.
- Electors vote for parties, not for candidates.
- Parties are allocated seats in direct proportion to the votes they gain in the election. They fill these seats from their party list.
- A 'threshold' may be imposed (5 per cent in Germany) to exclude small, possibly extremist, parties from representation.

Advantages:
- This is the only potentially pure system of proportional representation, and is therefore fair to all parties.
- The system promotes unity by encouraging electors to identify with their nation or region, rather than with a constituency.
- The system makes it easier for women and minority candidates to be elected, provided, of course, they feature on the party list.
- The representation of a large number of small parties ensures that there is an emphasis upon negotiation, bargaining and consensus.

Disadvantages:
- The existence of many small parties can lead to weak and unstable government.
- The link between representatives and constituencies is entirely broken.
- Unpopular candidates who are well-placed on a party list cannot be removed from office.
- Parties become heavily centralized, because leaders draw up party lists, and junior members have an incentive to be loyal in the hope of moving up the list.

suspect, for instance. Whereas coalitions in Italy have typically been weak and short-lived, in Germany they have usually produced stable and effective government. Similarly, although majoritarian systems can produce significant shifts in policy as one government follows another, broad policy consensuses are also not uncommon. In the 1950s and 1960s, despite an alternation in power between the Conservative and the Labour parties, UK government policy displayed a remarkable consistency of policy direction, rooted in a cross-party commitment to Keynesian social democracy. Furthermore, it is far from clear what damage electoral systems can cause. Despite Italy's famed political instability, often blamed on its now-abandoned party-list electoral system, in the post-World War II period the north of the country at least experienced steady economic growth, making Italy, by the 1990s, the third most prosperous state in the EU.

What do elections mean?

The importance of elections cannot be doubted. At the very least, they provide the public with its clearest formal opportunity to influence the political process, and also help, directly or indirectly, to determine who will hold government

POLITICS IN ACTION . . .

Electoral reform in New Zealand: politics renewed?

Events: In a non-binding referendum in New Zealand in 1992, 85 per cent of electors voted to change the established single-member plurality (SMP) electoral system, (popularly known as 'first past the post') with 71 per cent of voters backing the mixed-member proportional (MMP) system as their preferred alternative. In a binding second referendum the following year, MMP gained the support of 54 per cent in a straight contest against SMP. The first election using MMP was held in 1996, and it has been used in each of the subsequent elections. The issue of electoral reform had gained growing prominence in New Zealand after two successive elections (in 1978 and 1981) had been won by the 'wrong' party (the National Party won parliamentary majorities even though the Labour Party gained more votes). Other factors included growing discontent with the electoral system amongst Labour supporters, due to the National Party being in power for all but six years during 1949–84, and the belief that proportional representation would boost Maori representation.

Significance: Has electoral reform in New Zealand been a success? As ever with electoral reform, the debate turns on how 'success' is defined. Supporters of electoral reform have argued that MMP in New Zealand has brought about greater responsiveness and accountability. The clearest evidence of this has been a significant widening of the representation of parties, both in the House of Representatives and in government. The Labour-National two-party system has undoubtedly been broken, giving way to a multiparty system. The average number of parties represented in the House under MMP has increased from 2.4 during the period 1946–93 to 7. Most tellingly, since reform, neither National nor Labour has been able to govern alone on the basis of a parliamentary majority. The succession of coalition governments that has resulted from reform has shifted the focus of New Zealand politics away from simple rivalry between National and Labour towards a more complex process of consensus-building, as both major parties look to forge alliances with smaller parties. After the 2011 election, for instance, National formed a coalition government through an agreement with ACT, United Future and the Maori

Party. Moreover, since 1996, New Zealand governments have been minority governments for all but two years, a situation that allows parties outside of government, such as the Green Party, to exert a measure of policy influence.

However, criticisms of MMP continue to be voiced in New Zealand, not least by the National Party, which remains committed to a return to SMP. Critics claim that the two-vote system causes voter confusion and leads to the 'contamination effect', whereby views about constituency candidates affect the distribution of party-list votes. It is also far from clear that the introduction of MMP has had a beneficial impact on voter turnout, the second election under MMP, in 1999, having recorded the lowest turnout of any twentieth-century New Zealand election. Two, deeper concerns about MMP continue to be voiced, however. First, MMP has been portrayed as the enemy of strong government, in that, being divided, coalition governments are often unable to deliver decisive leadership. Second, misgivings have been expressed about the power of so-called 'pivotal parties', small parties whose policy influence greatly exceeds their electoral strength because they are able to do deals with both major parties. Concerns such as these encouraged National to call a further electoral reform referendum which coincided with the 2011 general election and offered voters a straight choice between MMP and a return to SMP. However, the resulting 58 per cent in favour of keeping MMP (a 4 per cent increase on the vote in 1993) indicated broad satisfaction with the new system and suggests that it is unlikely to be abandoned in the near future.

Public interest

The public interest consists of the general or collective interests of a community; that is, that which is good for society as a whole. Two contrasting notions of the public interest can be identified. Strong versions distinguish clearly between the interests of the public as a collective body and the selfish or personal interests of each individual. In the view of Rousseau and many socialists, the interests of the public are 'higher' than, or morally superior to, those of the individual. Weak versions recognize only private interests, and therefore see the public interest as nothing more than the sum of private interests.

power. From this perspective, elections are about results – in other words, who wins and who loses. This view is encouraged by media coverage, which, with the aid of opinion polls, increasingly turns elections into horseraces. Nevertheless, politicians are not backward in claiming that elections have a broader and more profound meaning. Elections are, in this sense, seen as nothing less than a visible manifestation of the public interest; in short, 'the public has spoken'. Political commentators also express their opinions, proclaiming, for instance, that elections reflect a 'shift in the popular mood'. The problem, however, is that all such claims and interpretations have a strongly arbitrary character; any attempt to invest an election with 'meaning' is fraught with dangers. The people may have spoken, but it is frustratingly difficult to know what they have said.

Many of these problems stem from the difficult notion of the 'public interest'. If such a thing as a 'public' interest exists, it surely reflects the common or collective interests of all citizens. This is precisely what Rousseau (see p. 97) implied in the idea of the 'general will', which he understood to mean the will of all citizens, provided each of them acts selflessly. The difficulty with this view is obvious. Quite simply, individuals do not, in practice, act selflessly in accordance with a general or collective will; there is no such thing as an indivisible public interest. All generalizations about 'the public' or 'the electorate' must therefore be treated with grave suspicion. There is no electorate as such, only a collection of electors who each possess particular interests, sympathies, allegiances and so on. At best, election results reflect the preferences of a majority, or perhaps a plurality, of voters. However, even then there are perhaps insuperable problems in deciding what these votes 'mean'.

The difficulty in interpreting election results lies in the perhaps impossible task of knowing why voters vote as they do. As is made clear in the next section, generations of political scientists have grappled with the question of electoral behaviour, but have failed to develop a universally accepted theory of voting. Voting, on the surface a very simple act, is shaped by a complex of factors, conscious and unconscious, rational and irrational, selfish and selfless. All theories are therefore partial and must be qualified by a range of other considerations. This can be seen in relation to the so-called 'economic theory of democracy', advanced by Anthony Downs (1957). This theory suggests that the act of voting reflects an expression of self-interest on the part of voters, who select parties in much the same way as consumers select goods or services for purchase. On this basis, the winning party in an election can reasonably claim that its policies most closely correspond to the interests of the largest group of voters.

On the other hand, it can be argued that, rather than 'buying' policies, voters are typically poorly-informed about political issues and are influenced by a range of 'irrational' factors such as habit, social conditioning, the image of the parties and the personalities of their leaders. Moreover, the ability of parties to attract votes may have less to do with the 'goods' they put up for purchase than with the way those goods are 'sold' through advertising, political campaigning, propaganda and so on. To the extent that this is true, election results may reflect not so much the interests of the mass of voters, as the resources and finances available to the competing parties.

A further – and, some would argue, more intractable – problem is that no elective mechanism may be able reliably to give expression to the multifarious preferences of voters. This is a problem that the US economist Kenneth Arrow described in terms of his 'impossibility theorem'. In *Social Choice and Individual Values* (1951) Arrow drew attention to the problem of 'transitivity' that occurs when voters are allowed to express a range of preferences for candidates or policy options, rather than merely cast a single vote. The drawback of casting but a single vote is not only that it is a crude all-or-nothing device, but also that no single candidate or option may gain majority support. For instance, candidate A may gain 40 per cent of the vote, candidate B 34 per cent, and candidate C 26 per cent. The situation could, nevertheless, become more confused if second preferences were taken into account.

Let us assume, for the sake of argument, that the second preferences of all candidate A's supporters go to candidate C, the second preferences of candidate B favour candidate A, and the second preferences of candidate C go to candidate B. This creates a situation in which each candidate can claim to be preferred by a majority of voters. The first and second preferences for candidate A add up to 74 per cent (40 per cent plus B's 34 per cent). Candidate B can claim 60 per cent support (34 per cent plus C's 26 per cent), and candidate C can claim 66 per cent support (26 per cent plus A's 40 per cent). This problem of 'cyclical majorities' draws attention to the fact that it may not be possible to establish a reliable link between individual preferences and collective choices. In other words, election results cannot speak for themselves, and politicians and political commentators who claim to find meaning in them are, to some extent, acting arbitrarily. Nevertheless, the latitude that this allows politicians is not unlimited, because they know that they will be called to account at the next election. In this light, perhaps the most significant function of elections is to set limits to arbitrary government by ensuring that politicians who claim to speak for the public must ultimately be judged by the public.

VOTING BEHAVIOUR

The growth of academic interest in voting behaviour coincided with the rise of behavioural political science. As the most widespread and quantifiable form of political behaviour, voting quickly became the focus for new techniques of sample surveying and statistical analysis. *The American Voter* (Campbell *et al.*, 1960), the product of painstaking research by the University of Michigan, became the leading work in the field and stimulated a wealth of similar studies, such as Butler and Stokes' *Political Change in Britain* (1969). At the high point of the behavioural revolution, it was thought that voting held the key to disclosing all the mysteries of the political system, perhaps allowing for laws of mass political psychology to be developed. Even though these lofty hopes have not been fulfilled, psephology (the scientific study of voting behaviour) still commands a central position in political analysis. This is because voting provides one of the richest sources of information about the interaction between individuals, society and politics. By investigating the mysteries of voting behaviour, we are thus able to learn important lessons about the nature of the political system, and gain insight into the process of social and political change.

Voting behaviour is clearly shaped by short-term and long-term influences. Short-term influences are specific to a particular election and do not allow conclusions to be drawn about voting patterns in general. The chief short-term influence is the state of the economy, which reflects the fact that there is usually a link

CONCEPT

Partisan dealignment

Partisan dealignment is a decline in the extent to which people align themselves with a party by identifying with it. This implies that the 'normal' support of parties falls, and a growing number of electors become 'floating' or 'swing' voters. As party loyalties weaken, electoral behaviour becomes more volatile, leading to greater uncertainty and, perhaps, the rise of new parties, or the decline of old ones. The principal reasons for partisan dealignment are the expansion of education, increased social mobility, and growing reliance on television as a source of political information.

between a government's popularity and economic variables such as unemployment, inflation and disposable income. Optimism about one's own material circumstances (the so-called 'feel-good' factor) appears to be particularly crucial here. Indeed, it is often alleged that governments attempt to create pre-election booms in the hope of improving their chances of gaining re-election. The chances that political and business cycles can be brought into conjunction are clearly strengthened by flexible-term elections that allow the government to choose when to 'go to the country'.

Another short-term influence on voting is the personality and public standing of party leaders. This is particularly important, because media exposure portrays leaders as the brand image of their party. This means that a party may try to rekindle popular support by replacing a leader who is perceived to be an electoral liability. Another factor is the style and effectiveness of the parties' electoral campaigning. The length of the campaign can vary from about three weeks for flexible-term elections to up to two years in the case of fixed-term elections, such as those for the US president. Opinion polls are usually thought to be significant in this respect, either giving a candidate's or party's campaign momentum, or instilling disillusionment, or even complacency, amongst voters.

A final short-term influence, the mass media (see p. 179), may also be of long-term significance if biased or partisan coverage reflects structural, and therefore continuing, factors such as press ownership. However, the pattern of media coverage may change from election to election. For instance, under Tony Blair's leadership, the UK Labour Party made concerted attempts to court the Murdoch press in particular, helping to explain the party's longest period in power, between 1997 and 2010. All such considerations, nevertheless, operate within a context of psychological, sociological, economic and ideological influences on voting. These are best examined in relation to rival models of voting. The most significant of these are the following:

- the party-identification model
- the sociological model
- the rational-choice model
- the dominant-ideology model.

Theories of voting

Party-identification model

The earliest theory of voting behaviour, the party-identification model, is based on the sense of psychological attachment that people have to parties. Electors are seen as people who identify with a party, in the sense of being long-term supporters who regard the party as 'their' party. Voting is therefore a manifestation of partisanship, not a product of calculation influenced by factors such as policies, personalities, campaigning and media coverage. This model places heavy stress on early political socialization (see p. 178), seeing the family as the principal means through which political loyalties are forged. These are then, in most cases, reinforced by group membership and later social experiences.

In this model, attitudes towards policies and leaders, as well as perceptions about group and personal interests, tend to be developed on the basis of party

CONCEPT

Class dealignment

Class dealignment is the weakening of the relationship between social class and party support. Social class may nevertheless remain a significant (even the most significant) factor influencing electoral choice. The impact of dealignment has been to undermine traditional class-based parties (notably, working class parties of the left), often bringing about a realignment of the party system. Explanations of class dealignment usually focus on changes in the social structure that have weakened the solidaristic character of class identity, such as post-industrialism.

identification. Events are thus interpreted to fit with pre-existing loyalties and attachments. This partisan alignment tends to create stability and continuity, especially in terms of habitual patterns of voting behaviour, often sustained over a lifetime. From this point of view, it should be possible to calculate the 'normal' vote of a party by reference to partisanship levels. Deviations from this 'normal' level presumably reflect the impact of short-term factors. One of the weaknesses of this model is the growing evidence from a number of countries of partisan dealignment (see p. 217). This indicates a general fall in party identification and a decline in habitual voting patterns. In the USA, partisan dealignment is reflected in a decline in the number of registered Democrats and Republicans, and a rise in the number of Independents (up from 6 per cent in 1952 to 36 per cent in 2009). In the UK, it is demonstrated by a decline in the strength of allegiance to the Conservative Party and the Labour Party, 'very strong' identification with either party having fallen from 43 per cent in 1966 to 9 per cent in 2005.

Sociological model

The sociological model links voting behaviour to group membership, suggesting that electors tend to adopt a voting pattern that reflects the economic and social position of the group to which they belong. Rather than developing a psychological attachment to a party on the basis of family influence, this model highlights the importance of a social alignment, reflecting the various divisions and tensions within society. The most significant of these divisions are class, gender, ethnicity, religion and region. Although the impact of socialization is not irrelevant to this model, social-base explanations allow for rationality insofar as group interests may help to shape party allegiances. For many analysts, the sociological model is best understood as an 'interest plus socialization' approach to voting (Denver, 2012). This has perhaps been clearest in relation to social class.

Not uncommonly, party systems have been seen to reflect the class system, with the middle classes providing the electoral base for right-wing parties, and the working classes providing the electoral base for left-wing parties. The Labour–Conservative two-party system in the UK was traditionally understood in precisely this light. Peter Pulzer (1967) was able to declare, famously, 'class is the basis of British party politics; all else is embellishment and detail'. The sociological model, however, has been attacked on the grounds that, in focusing on social groups, it ignores the individual and the role of personal self-interest. Moreover, there is growing empirical evidence that the link between sociological factors and party support has weakened in modern societies. In particular, attention has been paid to the phenomenon of class dealignment. Evidence of class dealignment can be found in most western societies. For example, absolute class voting (the proportion of voters who support their 'natural' class party) fell in the UK from 66 per cent in 1966 to 47 per cent in 1983. In 1997, the Labour Party, for the first time, received more votes from non-manual workers than from manual workers.

Rational-choice model

Rational-choice models of voting shift attention onto the individual, and away from socialization and the behaviour of social groups. In this view, voting is seen as a rational act, in the sense that individual electors are believed to decide their party preference on the basis of personal self-interest. Rather than being habitual, a manifestation of broader attachments and allegiances, voting is seen as essentially instrumental; that is, as a means to an end. Rational-choice models differ in that some, following the example of V. O. Key (1966), see voting as a retrospective comment on the party in power and how its performance has influenced citizen's choice. Others, such as Himmelveit *et al.*, (1985), portray voters as active, in the sense that they behave like consumers expressing a choice amongst the available policy options.

The latter view stresses the importance of what is called 'issue voting', and suggests that parties can significantly influence their electoral performance by revising and reshaping their policies. It is generally accepted that this has been one of the consequences of partisan and class dealignment. This has also been encouraged by the pluralism and individualism that postmodernism has fostered. The weakness of rational-choice theories is that they abstract the individual voter from his or her social and cultural context. In other words, to some extent, the ability to evaluate issues and calculate self-interest (the essence of instrumental voting) is structured by broader party attachments and group loyalties.

Dominant-ideology model

Radical theories of voting tend to highlight the degree to which individual choices are shaped by a process of ideological manipulation and control. In some respects, such theories resemble the sociological model, in that voting is seen to reflect a person's position in a social hierarchy. Where these theories differ from the sociological model, however, is in emphasizing that how groups and individuals interpret their position depends on how it has been presented to them through education, by the government and, above all, by the mass media. (The influence of the media on political debate and party competition is examined in greater detail in Chapter 8.)

In contrast to the earlier view that the media merely reinforce pre-existing preferences, this suggests that the media are able to distort the flow of political communications, both by setting the agenda for debate and by structuring preferences and sympathies. The consequence of this is that, if voters' attitudes conform to the tenets of a dominant ideology, parties will not be able to afford to develop policies that fall outside that ideology. In this way, far from challenging the existing distribution of power and resources in society, the electoral process tends to uphold it. The weakness of the dominant-ideology model is that, by overstating the process of social conditioning, it takes individual calculation and personal autonomy out of the picture altogether.

● **Issue voting:** Voting behaviour that is shaped by party policies and (usually) a calculation of personal self-interest.

SUMMARY

- Representation is a relationship in which an individual or group stands for, or acts on behalf of, a larger body of people. This may be achieved through the exercise of wisdom by an educated elite, through guidance or instructions given to a delegate, through the winning of a popular mandate, or through representatives being drawn from the groups they represent.

- In modern politics, representation is invariably linked with elections. Elections may not be a sufficient condition for political representation, but are certainly a necessary condition. For elections to serve representative purposes, however, they must be competitive, free and fair, and conducted on the basis of universal adult suffrage.

- Elections have a variety of functions. On the one hand, they have 'bottom-up' functions, such as political recruitment, representation, making government and influencing policy. On the other hand, radical theorists emphasize their 'top-down' functions, which include that they build legitimacy, shape public opinion and help to strengthen elites.

- Electoral systems are often classified as either majoritarian systems or proportional systems. In majoritarian systems, large parties typically win a higher proportion of seats than votes, thereby increasing the chances of single-party government. In proportional systems, there is an equal (or at least, more equal) relationship between the percentages of seats and votes won, increasing the likelihood of coalition government.

- Majoritarian systems are usually defended on the grounds that they offer the electorate a clear choice of potential governments, invest winning parties with a policy mandate, and help to promote strong and stable government. In contrast, proportional systems are defended on the grounds that they usually give government a broader electoral base, promote consensus and cooperation amongst a number of parties, and establish a healthy balance between the executive and the assembly.

- The meaning of elections is closely linked to the factors that shape voting behaviour. Amongst the various theories of voting are models that highlight the importance of party identification and habitual attachments, those that emphasize the importance of group membership and social alignment, those that are based on rational choice and calculations of self-interest, and those that suggest that individual choices are shaped by ideological manipulation and control.

Questions for discussion

- Is representation merely a substitute for democracy?
- What conditions best promote representative government?
- Are elections more significant in calling politicians to account, or in ensuring the survival of a regime?
- Is there inevitably a trade-off between electoral fairness and strong and stable government?
- Should electoral systems seek to deliver proportionality?
- Is there a 'best' electoral system?
- How successful are elections in defining the public interest?
- To what extent is voting behaviour a rational and issue-based activity?

Further reading

Birch, A. H., *The Concepts and Theories of Democracy* (3rd edn) (2007). A clear and thorough discussion of the concept of representation and the theory of representative democracy.

Farrell, D., *Electoral Systems: A Comparative Introduction* (2nd edn) (2011). A clear introduction to the six principal types of election system currently used.

Gallagher, M. and P. Mitchell (eds), *The Politics of Electoral Systems* (2008). An analysis of the operation of electoral systems in 22 states that highlights the complex relationship between electoral systems and the larger political process.

LeDuc, L., R. Niemi and P. Norris (eds), *Comparing Democracies 3: Elections and Voting in the 21st Century* (2010). A wide-ranging collection of essays that examine the nature and health of electoral democracy and the significance of electoral systems.

CHAPTER **16** # Groups, Interests and Movements

'Ten persons who speak make more noise than ten thousand who are silent.'

NAPOLEON, *Maxims*

PREVIEW

Patterns of political interaction were transformed in the twentieth century by the growing prominence of organized groups and interests. Indeed, in the 1950s and 1960s, at the high point of enthusiasm about 'group politics', it was widely asserted that business interests, trade unions, farm lobbies and the like had displaced assemblies and parties as the key political actors. The interest group universe was further expanded, particularly from the 1960s onwards, by the growth of single-issue protest groups taking up causes ranging from consumer protection to animal rights and from sexual equality to environmental protection. Such groups were often associated with broader social movements (the women's movement, the civil-rights movement, the green movement and so on) and were characterized by the adoption of new styles of activism and campaigning, sometimes termed 'new politics'. Considerable debate, nevertheless, surrounds the nature and significance of groups, interests and movements, especially in relation to their impact on the democratic process. Groups come in all shapes and sizes, and carry out a wide range of functions, being, for instance, agents of citizen empowerment as well as cogs within the machinery of government. There is particular disagreement about political implications of group politics. While some believe that organized groups serve to distribute political power more widely and evenly in society, others argue that groups empower the already powerful and subvert the public interest. These issues are related to questions about how groups exert influence and the factors that allow them to exert political influence. Finally, so-called 'new' social movements have been both praised for stimulating new forms of decentralized political engagement and criticized for encouraging people to abandon the formal representative process.

KEY ISSUES

- What are interest groups, and what different forms do they take?
- What have been the major theories of group politics?
- Do groups help or hinder democracy and effective government?
- How do interest groups exert influence?
- What determines the success or failure of interest groups?
- Why have new social movements emerged, and what is their broader significance?

Alexis de Tocqueville (1805–59)

French politician, political theorist and historian. Following the July Revolution of 1830 in France, Tocqueville visited the USA, ostensibly to study its penal system. This resulted in his epic two-volume *Democracy in America* (1835/40), which developed an ambivalent critique of US democracy with its equality of opportunity, but warned against the 'tyranny of the majority'. His political career was ended by Louis Napoleon's *coup* in 1849, leaving him free to devote his time to historical work such as *The Old Regime and the French Revolution* ([1856] 1947). A friend and correspondent of J. S. Mill, de Tocqueville's writings reflect a highly ambiguous attitude to the advance of political democracy. His ideas have influenced both liberal and conservative theorists, as well as academic sociologists.

GROUP POLITICS

Interest groups (see p. 247), like political parties (see p. 222), constitute one of the major linkages between government and the governed in modern societies. In some respects, their origins parallel those of parties. They were the children of a new age of representativegovernment and came into existence to articulate the increasingly complex divisions and cleavages of an emerging industrial society. While political parties, concerned with winning elections, sought to build coalitions of support and broaden their appeal, interest groups usually staked out a more distinct and clear-cut position, in accordance with the particular aspirations or values of the people they represented.

It is difficult to identify the earliest such group. Some groups predated the age of representative government; for example, the Abolition Society, which was founded in Britain in 1787 to oppose the slave trade. The Anti-Corn Law League, established in 1839, is often seen as the model for later UK groups, in that it was set up with the specific purpose of exerting pressure on government. After visiting the USA in the 1830s, Alexis de Tocqueville reported that what he called association had already become a 'powerful instrument of action'. Young Italy, set up in 1831 by the Italian patriot Giuseppe Mazzini (see p. 116), became the model for sister nationalist organizations that later sprang up throughout Europe. Similarly, the Society for Women's Rights, founded in France in 1866, stimulated the formation of a worldwide women's suffrage movement. By the end of the nineteenth century powerful farming and business interests operated in most industrial societies, alongside a growing trade-union movement. However, most of the interest groups currently in existence are of much more recent origin. They are, in the main, a product of the explosion in pressure and protest politics that has occurred since the 1960s. As such they may be part of a broader process that has seen the decline of political parties and a growing emphasis on organized groups and social movements (see p. 260) as agents of mobilization and representation.

● **Cleavage:** A social division that creates a collective identity on both sides of the divide.

● **Association:** A group formed by voluntary action, reflecting a recognition of shared interests or common concerns.

Types of group

The task of defining and classifying groups is fraught with danger, given the imprecise nature of groups and their multiplicity of forms. Are we, for instance, concerned with groups or with **interests**? In other words, do we only recognize groups as associations that have a certain level of cohesion and organization, or merely as collections of people who happen to share the same interest but may lack consciousness of the fact? Similarly, are interest groups only concerned with selfish and material interests, or may they also pursue broader causes or public goals? There is also the difficult issue of the relationship between interest groups and government. Are interest groups always autonomous, exerting influence from outside, or may they operate in and through government, perhaps even being part of the government machine itself?

This confusion is compounded by the lack of agreed terminology amongst political scientists active in this field. For instance, whereas the term 'interest group' is used in the USA and elsewhere to describe all organized groups, it tends to be used in the UK to refer only to those groups that advance or defend the interests of their members. The term 'pressure group' is therefore usually preferred in the UK, 'interest group' tending to be used as a subcategory of the broader classification.

Groups can nevertheless be classified into three types:

- communal groups
- institutional groups
- associational groups.

Communal groups

The chief characteristic of communal groups is that they are embedded in the social fabric, in the sense that membership is based on birth, rather than recruitment. Examples of such groups are families, tribes, castes and ethnic groups. Unlike conventional interest groups, to which members choose to belong, and which possess a formal structure and organization, communal groups are founded on the basis of a shared heritage and traditional bonds and loyalties. Such groups still play a major role in the politics of developing states. In Africa, for instance, ethnic, tribal and kinship ties are often the most important basis of interest articulation. Communal groups also continue to survive and exert influence in advanced industrial states, as the resurgence of ethnic nationalism and the significance of Catholic groups in countries like Italy and Ireland demonstrate.

Institutional groups

Institutional groups are groups that are part of the machinery of government and attempt to exert influence in and through that machinery. They differ from interest groups in that they enjoy no measure of autonomy or independence. Bureaucracies and the military are the clearest examples of institutional groups, and, not uncommonly, each of these contains a number of competing interests. In the case of authoritarian or totalitarian states, which typically

● **Interest**: That which benefits an individual or group; interests (unlike wants or preferences) are usually understood to be objective or 'real'.

CONCEPT

Interest group

An interest group (or pressure group) is an organized association that aims to influence the policies or actions of government. Interest groups differ from political parties in the following way. (1) They seek to exert influence from outside, rather than to win or exercise government power. (2) They typically have a narrow issue focus, in that they are usually concerned with a specific cause or the interests of a particular group. (3) They seldom have the broader programmic or ideological features that are generally associated with political parties. Interest groups are distinguished from social movements by their greater degree of formal organization.

● **Direct action**: Political action taken outside the constitutional and legal framework; direct action may range from passive resistance to terrorism.

suppress autonomous groups and movements, rivalry amongst institutional groups may become the principal form of interest articulation. The highly centralized Stalinist system in the USSR, for instance, was driven largely by entrenched bureaucratic and economic interests, in particular those centred around heavy industry. Similarly, the apparently monolithic character of the Hitler state in Germany (1933–45), concealed a reality of bureaucratic infighting as Nazi leaders built up sprawling empires in an endless struggle for power.

Institutional groups are not only of significance in non-democratic regimes. Some go so far as to argue that the bureaucratic elites and vested interests that develop in the ministries, departments and agencies of democratic systems in effect shape the policy process: they serve to constrain, some would say dictate to, elected politicians and elected governments. Such groups certainly also form alliances with conventional interest groups, as in the case of the celebrated 'military–industrial complex'. The significance of the bureaucracy and the military, and the importance of the interests that operate in and through them, discussed in Chapters 16 and 18, respectively.

Associational groups

Associational groups are ones that are formed by people who come together to pursue shared, but limited, goals. Groups as associations are characterized by voluntary action and the existence of common interests, aspirations or attitudes. The most obvious examples of associational groups are thus what are usually thought of as interest groups or pressure groups. However, the distinction between these and communal groups may sometimes be blurred. For example, when class loyalties are strong and solidaristic, membership of an associational group such as a trade union may be more an expression of social identity than an instrumental act aimed at furthering a particular goal. Although associational groups are becoming increasingly important in developing states, they are usually seen as a feature of industrial societies. Industrialization both generates social differentiation, in the form of a complex web of competing interests, and, in a capitalist setting at least, encourages the growth of self-seeking and individualized patterns of behaviour in the place of ones shaped by custom and tradition. When their primary function is to deal with government and other public bodies, such groups are usually called interest groups.

Interest groups appear in a variety of shapes and sizes. They are concerned with an enormous array of issues and causes, and use tactics that range from serving on public bodies and helping to administer government programmes to organizing campaigns of civil disobedience (see p. 259) and popular protest. Similarly, they may operate at a local, national, or (as discussed later) international level, or at a combination of these. However, anti-constitutional and paramilitary groups are excluded from this classification. Groups such as the Black Panthers and the Irish Republican Army (IRA) may not be categorized as interest groups because they sought fundamentally to restructure the political system, not merely to influence it, and used the tactics of terrorism (see p. 416) and **direct action** instead of pressure politics. Structure must, however, be imposed on the apparently shapeless interest group universe by the attempt to identify the different types of group. The two most common classifications are:

- sectional and promotional groups
- insider and outsider groups.

Sectional groups (sometimes called protective or functional groups) exist to advance or protect the (usually material) interests of their members. Trade unions, business corporations, trade associations and professional bodies are the prime examples of this type of group. Their 'sectional' character is derived from the fact that they represent a section of society: workers, employers, consumers, an ethnic or religious group, and so on. Strictly speaking, however, only groups engaged in the production, distribution and exchange of goods and services can be seen as 'functional' groups. In the USA, sectional groups are often classified as 'private interest groups', to stress that their principal concern is the betterment and well-being of their members, not of society in general.

In contrast, *promotional* groups (sometimes termed cause or attitude groups) are set up to advance shared values, ideals or principles. These causes are many and diverse. They include 'pro-choice' and 'pro-life' lobbies on abortion, campaigns in favour of civil liberties or against sex and violence on television, protests about pollution and animal cruelty or in defence of traditional or religious values. In the USA, promotional groups are dubbed 'public interest groups', to emphasize that they promote collective, rather than selective, benefits. When involved in international politics, these groups are often call non-governmental organizations, or NGOs. Promotional groups are therefore defined by the fact that they aim to help groups other than their own members. Save the Whale, for instance, is an organization for whales, not one of whales. Some organizations, of course, have both sectional and promotional features. The National Association for the Advancement of Coloured People (NAACP) addresses the sectional interests of American black people (by opposing discrimination and promoting employment opportunities), but is also concerned with causes such as social justice and racial harmony.

The alternative system of classification is based on the status that groups have in relation to government and the strategies they adopt in order to exert pressure. *Insider* groups enjoy regular, privileged and usually institutionalized access to government through routine consultation or representation on government bodies. In many cases there is an overlap between sectional and insider classifications. This reflects the ability of key economic interests, such as business groups and trade unions, to exert powerful sanctions if their views are ignored by government. Government may also be inclined to consult groups that possess specialist knowledge and information that assists in the formulation of workable policy. Insider status, however, is not always an advantage, since it is conferred only on groups with objectives that are broadly compatible with those of the government and which have a demonstrable capacity to ensure that their members abide by agreed decisions.

Outsider groups, on the other hand, are either not consulted by government or consulted only irregularly and not usually at a senior level. In many cases outsider status is an indication of weakness, in that, lacking formal access to government, these groups are forced to 'go public' in the hope of exercising indirect influence on the policy process. Ironically, then, there is often an inverse relationship between the public profile of an interest group and the political influence it exerts. Radical protest groups in fields such as environmental protection and animal rights may have little choice about being outsiders. Not only are their goals frequently out of step with the priorities of government, but their members and supporters are often attracted by the fact that such groups are untainted by close links with government. In that sense, groups may choose to remain outsiders, both to preserve their ideological purity and independence, and to protect their decentralized power structures.

Models of group politics

Some commentators believe that the pattern and significance of group politics are derived entirely from factors that are specific to each political system. The role of groups thus reflects a particular political culture (see p. 172), party system, set of institutional arrangements, and so on. This means that general conclusions cannot be drawn about the nature of group politics. On the other hand, the understanding of group politics is often shaped by broader assumptions about both the nature of the political process and the distribution of power in society. These assumptions are closely linked to the rival theories of the state examined in Chapter 3. The most influential of these as models of interest group politics are the following:

- pluralism
- corporatism
- the New Right.

Pluralist model

Pluralist theories offer the most positive image of group politics. They stress the capacity of groups to both defend the individual from government and promote democratic responsiveness. The core theme of pluralism (see p. 100) is that political power is fragmented and widely dispersed. Decisions are made through a complex process of bargaining and interaction that ensures that the views and interests of a large number of groups are taken into account. One of the earliest and most influential attempts to develop a pluralist 'group theory' was undertaken by Arthur Bentley in *The Process of Government* ([1908] 1948). Bentley's emphasis on organized groups as the fundamental building blocks of the political process is neatly summed up in his famous dictum: 'when the groups are adequately stated, everything is stated'. David Truman's *The Governmental Process* (1951) is usually seen to have continued this tradition, even if his conclusions were more narrowly focused on the US political process.

Enthusiasm for groups as agents of interest articulation and aggregation was strengthened by the spread of behaviouralism in the 1950s and early 1960s. Systems analysis, for example, portrayed interest groups as 'gatekeepers' that filtered the multiple demands made of government into manageable sets of claims. At the same time, community power studies carried out by analysts such as Robert Dahl (1961) and Nelson Polsby (1963) claimed to find empirical support for the pluralist assertion that no single local elite is able to dominate community decision-making.

From the pluralist perspective, group politics is the very stuff of the democratic process. Indeed, it became common in the 1960s to argue that a form of

Robert Dahl (born 1915)

US political scientist. Appointed professor of political science at Yale University in 1946, Dahl subsequently became one of the USA's most eminent political analysts. In 1953 (with Charles Lindblom) he coined the term 'polyarchy' (rule by the many) to distinguish modern societies from classical democracy. Dahl's early writings reflect the impact of positivist and behaviouralist doctrines and, in the 1950s and early 1960s, he developed a conventional pluralist position. From the late 1960s, however, together with Lindblom and Galbraith (see p. 155), he developed a radicalized form of liberalism, 'neopluralism', that revealed an increasing concern with the power of major capitalist corporations. His major works include *A Preface to Democratic Theory* (1956), *Who Governs?* (1961) and *Dilemmas of Pluralist Democracy* (1982).

pluralist democracy (see p. 101) had superseded more conventional electoral democracy, in that groups and organized interests had replaced political parties as the principal link between government and the governed. The central assumptions of this theory are that all groups and interests have the potential to organize and gain access to government, that they are internally responsive in the sense that leaders broadly articulate the interests or values of their members, and that their political influence is roughly in line with their size and the intensity of their support. One way in which this was demonstrated was by evidence that political power is fragmented in such a way that no group or interest can achieve dominance for any period of time. As Dahl (1956) put it, 'all the active and legitimate groups in the population can make themselves heard at some crucial stage in the process of decision'. The alternative idea of 'countervailing powers', developed in J. K. Galbraith's (see p. 155) early writings, suggests that a dynamic equilibrium naturally emerges amongst competing groups, as the success of, say, business merely encourages opponents, such as labour or consumers, to organize to counter that success. Group politics is thus characterized by a rough balance of power.

This highly optimistic view of group politics has been heavily criticized by elitists and Marxists. Elitists challenge the empirical claims of pluralism by suggesting that they recognize only one 'face' of power: the ability to influence decision-making (see p. 9). In contrast to the notion that power is widely and evenly distributed, elite theorists draw attention to the existence of a 'power elite', comprising the heads of business corporations, political leaders and military chiefs (Mills, 1956). Marxists, for their part, have traditionally emphasized that political power is closely linked to the ownership of productive wealth, which suggests the existence of a capitalist 'ruling class'. For neo-Marxists such as Ralph Miliband (2009) this is reflected in 'unequal competition' between business and labour groups, the former enjoying a control of economic resources, a public status, and a level of access to government that the latter cannot match. The rise of globalization (see p. 142) has renewed such arguments, leading some to suggest that the increased mobility of capital and a free-trade international system has resulted in the 'corporate takeover' of government (Hertz, 2001). In the face of such criticism, a more critical or qualified form of pluralism, neopluralism (see

p. 63), emerged. This has perhaps been most clearly expressed in Charles Lindblom's *Politics and Markets* (1980), which highlighted the privileged position that business groups enjoy in western polyarchies, while acknowledging that this seriously compromises the claim that such societies are democratic.

Corporatist model

Corporatist models of group politics differ from pluralism in that they attempt to trace the implications of the closer links that have developed in industrialized societies between groups and the state. Corporatism is a social theory that emphasizes the privileged position that certain groups enjoy in relation to government, enabling them to influence the formulation and implementation of public policy. Some commentators regard corporatism as a state-specific phenomenon, shaped by particular historical and political circumstances. They thus associate it with countries such as Austria, Sweden, the Netherlands and, to some extent, Germany and Japan, in which the government has customarily practised a form of economic management.

Others, however, see corporatism as a general phenomenon that stems from tendencies implicit in economic and social development, and thus believe that it is manifest, in some form or other, in all advanced industrial states. Even the USA, usually portrayed as the model of pluralist democracy, has invested its regulatory agencies with quasi-legislative powers, thereby fostering the development of formal bonds between government and major interests. From this perspective, corporatist tendencies may merely reflect the symbiotic relationship that exists between groups and government. Groups seek 'insider' status because it gives them access to policy formulation, which enables them better to defend the interests of their members. Government, on the other hand, needs groups, both as a source of knowledge and information, and because the compliance of major interests is essential if policy is to be workable. In increasingly differentiated and complex industrial societies the need for consultation and bargaining continues to grow, with the result that, perhaps inevitably, institutional mechanisms emerge to facilitate it.

The drift towards corporatism in advanced capitalist states, particularly pronounced in the 1960s and 1970s, provoked deep misgivings about the role and power of interest groups. In the first place, corporatism considerably cut down the number and range of groups that enjoyed access to government. Corporatism invariably privileges economic or functional groups, because it leads to a form of **tripartitism** that binds government to business and organized labour. However, it may leave consumer or promotional groups out in the cold, and institutionalized access is likely to be restricted to so-called 'peak' associations that speak on behalf of a range of organizations and groups. In Austria this role is carried out by the Chamber of Commerce and the Trade Union Federation, in the UK by the Confederation of British Industry (CBI) and the Trades Union Congress (TUC), and in the USA by the National Association of Manufacturers and the American Federation of Labor–Congress of Industrial Organizations (AFL–CIO).

A second problem is that, in contrast to the pluralist model, corporatism portrays interest groups as hierarchically ordered and dominated by leaders who are not directly accountable to members. Indeed, it is sometimes argued that the

---

CONCEPT

Corporatism

Corporatism, in its broadest sense, is a means of incorporating organized interests into the processes of government. There are two faces of corporatism. *Authoritarian* corporatism ('state' corporatism) is an ideology or economic form closely associated with Italian Fascism. It was characterized by the political intimidation of industry and the destruction of independent trade unions. *Liberal* corporatism ('societal' corporatism or 'neocorporatism') refers to the tendency found in mature liberal democracies for organized interests to be granted privileged and institutional access to the process of policy formulation.

● **Tripartitism:** The construction of bodies that represent government, business and the unions, designed to institutionalize group consultation.

CONCEPT

Public choice

Public-choice theory is a subfield of rational-choice theory (see pp. 14–15) The 'public' character of public-choice theory stems from its concern with the provision of so-called 'public goods'. These are goods that are delivered by government rather than the market, because (as with clean air) their benefit cannot be withheld from individuals who choose not to contribute to their provision. Public-choice theorists have generally highlighted the failures and defects of government in this respect, focusing on issues such as the policy impact of self-serving bureaucrats, and the consequences of interest-group politics.

price that group leaders pay for privileged access to government is a willingness to deliver the compliance of their members. From this point of view, 'government by consultation' may simply be a sham concealing the fact that corporatism acts as a mechanism of social control. Third, concern has been expressed about the threat that corporatism poses to representative democracy. Whereas pluralism suggests that group politics supplements the representative process, corporatism creates the spectre of decisions being made outside the reach of democratic control and through a process of bargaining in no way subject to public scrutiny. Finally, corporatism has been linked to the problem of government 'overload', in which government may effectively be 'captured' by consulted groups and thus be unable to resist their demands. This critique has been advanced most systematically by the New Right.

New Right model

The antipathy of the New Right towards interest groups is derived, ideologically, from the individualism that lies at the heart of neoliberal economics. Social groups and collective bodies of all kinds are therefore viewed with suspicion. This is clearly reflected in the New Right's preference for a market economy driven by self-reliance and entrepreneuralism. However, the New Right has expressed particular concern about the alleged link between corporatism and escalating public spending and the associated problems of over-government. New Right anticorporatism has been influenced by public-choice theory, notably Mancur Olson's *The Logic of Collective Action: Public Goods and the Theory of Groups* (1974). Olson argued that people join interest groups only to secure 'public goods': that is, goods that are to some extent indivisible in that individuals who do not contribute to their provision cannot be prevented from enjoying them.

A pay increase is thus a public good in that workers who are not union members, or who choose not to strike in furtherance of the pay claim, benefit equally with union members and those who did strike. This creates opportunities for individuals to become 'free riders', reaping benefits without incurring the various costs that group membership may entail. This analysis is significant because it implies that there is no guarantee that the existence of a common interest will lead to the formation of an organization to advance or defend that interest. The pluralist assumption that all groups have some kind of political voice therefore becomes highly questionable. Olson also argued that group politics may often empower small groups at the expense of large ones. A larger membership encourages free riding because individuals may calculate that the group's effectiveness will be little impaired by their failure to participate.

This analysis was further developed in Olson's later work, *The Rise and Decline of Nations* (1984), which advanced a trenchant critique of interest group activity, seeing it as a major determinant of the prosperity or economic failure of particular states. The UK and Australia, for example, were seen as suffering from 'institutional sclerosis'. This occurred as strong networks of interest groups emerged that were typically dominated by coalitions of narrow, sectional interests, including trade unions, business organizations and professional associations. The message that there is an inverse relationship between strong and well-organized interest groups, on the one hand, and economic growth and

Debating...
Do interest groups enhance democracy?

Controversy about interest groups largely centres on their impact on democracy and the distribution of political power. While pluralists view group politics as the very stuff of democracy, elitists and others claim that it weakens or undermines the democratic process. Do interest groups empower citizens and widen access to government, or do they strengthen special interests and narrow the distribution of power?

YES	NO
Dispersing power. Interest groups empower groups of people who would otherwise be marginalized and lack political representation. Organized interests, for instance, give a political voice to minorities that tend to be ignored by political parties, which, because of electoral pressures, are more concerned about the views of numerically-strong groups. Few people, moreover, exist outside the interest group universe. Promotional groups are thus formed to act on behalf of people (such as the poor, the elderly or consumers) who find it difficult, for various reasons, to organize themselves, and the use of 'outsider' tactics enables groups to exert influence even though they may lack wealth and institutional power.	***Entrenching political inequality***. Interest groups typically empower the already powerful. Interest groups that possess money, expertise, institutional leverage and privileged links to government are substantially more powerful than other groups, helping to create a 'power elite'. At the heart of this elite are major corporations, whose influence, in most cases, greatly exceeds the influence of, say, trade unions, charities or environmental groups. By the same token, there are significant, and sometimes large, sections of society that benefit little from interest group representation. This is usually because they lack resources and are difficult, or impossible, to organize.
Political education. Groups stimulate debate and discussion, helping to create a better-informed and more educated electorate. Not only do interest groups provide citizens with alternative sources of information, but their specialist knowledge and level of technical expertise may even, at times, rival those of government. This is particularly important when it means that radical or critical views (which are inconvenient to the political establishment) can be expressed. Further, interest groups do not support a single viewpoint but rival viewpoints; the most stimulating political debate often takes place between interest groups rather than between interest groups and government.	***Non-legitimate power***. Unlike conventional politicians, interest group leaders are not popularly elected. Interest groups are therefore not publicly accountable, meaning that the influence they wield is not democratically legitimate. This problem is compounded by the fact that very few interest groups operate on the basis of internal democracy. Leaders are rarely elected by their members and, when they are (as, sometimes, in the case of trade unions), turnout levels are typically low. Indeed, there has been a growing trend for interest groups to be dominated by a small number of senior professionals.
Boosting participation. While party membership and voter turnout decline, the number of groups and their membership size has steadily increased, meaning that organized interests have become the principal agents of participation in modern political systems. In particular, there has been an explosion of cause or promotional groups, as well as of NGOs. Not only has single-issue politics proved to be popular, but the grass-roots activism and decentralized organization embraced by many campaigning groups have often proved to be attractive to young people and to those who are disillusioned with conventional politics.	***Subverting representative democracy***. Interest groups exert influence in ways that are democratically questionable. Insider groups operate 'behind closed doors', their meetings with ministers and government officials being unseen by the public, the media or democratic representatives. No one knows (apart from occasional leaks) who said what to whom, or who influenced whom, and how. Groups subvert representative democracy by both circumventing assemblies and forging direct links with executives, and exerting control over parties and politicians through the provision of campaign finance. Protest groups also undermine democracy when they achieve their objectives through the use of direct action, operating outside the established legal and constitutional framework.

national prosperity on the other had a powerful impact on New Right policies and priorities. The clearest demonstration of this was the backlash against corporatism from the 1980s onwards, spearheaded in the USA by Reagan and in the UK by Thatcher. In the USA, this took the form of an attempt to deregulate the economy by weakening regulatory agencies; in the UK, it was evident in the marginalization and later abolition of corporatist bodies such as the National Economic Development Council (NEDC or Neddy) and a determined assault on trade union power.

Patterns of group politics

How important are interest groups?

It is widely accepted that interest group activity is closely linked to economic and social development. Whereas agrarian or traditional societies tend to be dominated by a small number of interests, advanced industrial ones are complex and highly differentiated. Interest groups thus come to assume a central importance in mediating between the state and a more fragmented society, especially as the spread of education extends political awareness and organizational skills. However, the roles and significance of organized interests vary from system to system, from state to state, and over time. The principal factors determining group influence are the following:

- the political culture
- the institutional structure
- the nature of the party system
- the nature and style of public policy.

The *political culture* is crucial for two reasons. First, it determines whether interest groups are viewed as legitimate or non-legitimate actors, whether their formation and influence is permitted and encouraged, or otherwise. Second, it affects the willingness of people to form or join organized interests or to engage in group politics. At one extreme, regimes can practise **monism**, suppressing all forms of voluntary associational activity in order to ensure a single, unchallengeable centre of state power. This typically occurs in military regimes and one-party states. Although no contemporary or historical state has succeeded in stamping out all forms of group or factional activity, monistic regimes at least push group activity underground or ensure that it is expressed through the party–state apparatus and is thus entangled with the political and ideological goals of the regime. In the case of China, despite the persistence of formal political monolithicism, market reforms and over three decades of relentless economic growth have led to the emergence of new social actors, such as entrepreneurs and migrant workers, creating a form of state corporatism.

Pluralist regimes, on the other hand, not only permit group politics, but encourage and even, in some cases, require it. Groups may be asked to participate in policy formulation or to be represented on public bodies or quangos (see p. 368). One of the reasons for the generally high level of group activity found in the USA, for instance, is the recognition in US political culture of the right of private groups to be heard. This is enshrined in constitutional guarantees of free

● **Monism**: A belief in only one theory or value; monism is reflected politically in enforced obedience to a unitary power and is, thus, implicitly totalitarian.

speech, freedom of the press, freedom of assembly, and so forth. In Japan, the absence of clear distinctions between the public and private realms has created a political culture in which, in predemocratic and democratic periods alike, a close relationship between government and business has been taken for granted.

In contrast, in some European states, organized interests are regarded with suspicion. This has traditionally been the case in France, where, influenced by Jacobin ideology, groups have been seen to both undermine the 'general will' of the people and challenge the strength and unity of the French state. At its high point in 1975, for instance, only 24 per cent of the French workforce belonged to a union, a figure that had fallen to 8 per cent by 2008. However, French political culture also embodies a tradition of direct action, demonstrated by the use by French farmers of road blocks and even lorry hijacks, and by the rebellion of students and trade unionists during the political troubles of May 1968.

The *institutional structure* of government is clearly significant in terms of interest group activity in that it establishes points of access to the policy process. Unitary and centralized political systems, such as the UK's, tend to narrow the scope of group politics and concentrate it around the executive branch of government. Although this does not condemn groups to a marginal existence, it places heavy emphasis on 'insider' status and broadens the capacity of the government of the day to choose whether or not to respond to group pressure. This was most clearly demonstrated in the UK since the 1980s in the downgrading of corporatist bodies and the marginalization of the trade unions. Interest-group activity in France is similarly focused on direct consultation with the administration, particularly since the strengthening of presidential government and the weakening of the National Assembly in the Fifth Republic.

US government, on the other hand, is fragmented and decentralized. This reflects the impact of bicameralism, the separation of powers, federalism and judicial review. The range of 'access points' that this offers interest groups makes the US system peculiarly vulnerable to group pressures. Groups know, for instance, that battles lost in Congress can be refought in the courts, at the state or local level, and so on. Although this undoubtedly acts as a stimulus to group formation, and enlarges the number of influential groups, it may also be self-defeating, in that the activities of groups can end up cancelling each other out. Organized interests may thus act only as 'veto groups'.

The relationship between political parties and interest groups is always complex. In some senses, they are clearly rivals. While parties seek to aggregate interests and form political programmes typically based on broad ideological goals, interest groups are concerned with a narrower and more specific range of issues and objectives. Nevertheless, interest groups often seek to exert influence in and through parties, in some cases even spawning parties in an attempt to gain direct access to power. Many socialist parties, such as the UK Labour Party, were effectively created by the trade unions, and institutional and financial links, albeit modified, endure to this day.

The pattern of interest group politics is also influenced by the *party system*. Dominant-party systems tend, quite naturally, to narrow the focus of group politics, concentrating it on the governing party. Major industrial and commercial interests in Italy and Japan therefore traditionally tried to exert pressure through 'ruling' parties such as the Christian Democrats and the Liberal-Democratic Party, which, in the process, did much to entrench the factional tendencies within these parties. Multiparty systems, on the other hand, are fertile ground for interest group activity, because they broaden the scope of access. The legislative influence of interest groups is perhaps greatest in party systems like the USA's, in which political parties are weak in terms of both organization and discipline. This was demonstrated in the late 1970s by the capacity of business interests effectively to destroy President Carter's energy programme, despite the existence of Democrat majorities in both the House of Representatives and the Senate.

Finally, the level of group activity fluctuates in relation to shifts in *public policy*, particularly the degree to which the state intervenes in economic and social life. As a general rule, interventionism goes hand-in-hand with corporatism, although there is a debate about which is the cause and which is the effect. Do interventionist policies force government into a closer relationship with organized interests in the hope of gaining information, advice and cooperation? Or do groups exploit their access to government to extract subsidies, supports and other benefits for their members? Whatever the answer is, it is clear that, amongst western states, the integration of organized interests, particularly functional interests, into public life has been taken furthest where social-democratic policies have been pursued.

The Swedish system is the classic example of this. Interest groups constitute an integral part of the Swedish political scene at every level. There are close, if not institutional, links between the trade unions and the Social Democratic Labour Party (SAP). The legislative process in the *Riksdag* is geared to wide consultation with affected interests, and state officials recognize 'peak' associations such as the Swedish Trade Union Confederation and the Employers' Confederation as 'social partners'. A similar pattern of corporate representation has developed in the Austrian 'chamber' system, which provides statutory representation for major interests such as commerce, agriculture and labour. In Germany, key economic groups such as the Federation of German Employers' Associations, the Federation of German Industry and the German Trades Union Federation are so closely involved in policy formulation that the system has been described as one of 'polyarchic elitism'.

How do groups exert influence?

Interest groups have at their disposal a broad range of tactics and political strategies. Indeed, it is almost unthinkable that a group should confine itself to a single strategy or try to exert influence through just one channel of influence. The methods that groups use vary according to a number of factors. These include the issue with which the group is concerned and how policy in that area is shaped. For instance, in the UK, since most policies relating to civil liberties and political rights are developed by the Ministry of Justice, a group such as Liberty is compelled to seek 'insider' status, which it does by emphasizing itsspecialist knowledge and political respectability. Similarly, the nature of the group and the resources at its disposal are crucial determinants of its political strategy. These resources include the following:

- public sympathy for the group and its goals
- the size of its membership or activist base
- its financial strength and organizational capabilities

● Interventionism:
Government policies designed to regulate or manage economic life; more broadly, a policy of engagement or involvement.

Lobby

The term lobby is derived from the areas in parliaments or assemblies where the public may petition legislators, or politicians meet to discuss political business. In modern usage, the term is both a verb and a noun. The verb 'to lobby' means to make direct representations to a policy-maker, using argument or persuasion. Broadly, 'a lobby' (noun) is equivalent to an interest group, in that both aim to influence public policy, as in the case of the farm lobby, the environmental lobby and the roads lobby. Narrowly, following US practice, a lobbyist is a 'professional persuader': that is, a person hired to represent the arguments of interest group clients.

● **Peak group:** A hierarchically organized group that coordinates the work of a collection of groups in the same area of interest, usually formed to strengthen links to government.

● its ability to use sanctions that in some way inconvenience or disrupt government
● personal or institutional links it may have to political parties or government bodies.

Business groups are more likely than, say, trade unions or consumer groups to employ professional lobbyists or mount expensive public-relations campaigns, because, quite simply, they have the financial capacity to do so. The methods used by interest groups are shaped by the channel of access through which influence is exerted. The principal channels of access available are:

● the bureaucracy
● the assembly
● the courts
● political parties
● the mass media
● international organizations.

In all states, interest group activity tends to centre on the *bureaucracy* as the key institution in the process of policy formulation. Access via this channel is largely confined to major economic and functional groups, such as large corporations, employers' associations, trade unions, farming interests and key professions. In Austria, the Netherlands and the Scandinavian states, for example, corporatist institutions have been developed specifically to facilitate group consultation, usually giving **'peak' groups** representing employers' and employees' interests a measure of formal representation. More commonly, the consultative process is informal yet institutionalized, taking place through meetings and regular contacts that are rarely publicized and are beyond the scope of public scrutiny.

The crucial relationship here is usually that between senior bureaucrats and leading business or industrial interests. The advantages that business groups enjoy in this respect include the key role they play in the economy as producers, investors and employers, the overlap in social background and political outlets between business leaders and ministers and senior officials, and the widely held public belief that business interests coincide with the national interest ('what is good for General Motors is good for America'). This relationship is often consolidated by a 'revolving door' through which bureaucrats, on retirement, move into well-paid jobs in private business. In Japan this practice is so clearly established that it is known as *amakudari*, literally meaning 'descent from heaven'. Two factors that have further strengthened big business' control over ministers and bureaucrats are the greater ease with which corporations can relocate production and investment in a global economy, and the advent of the 'new' public management in which governments become increasingly dependent on the private sector for investment in, and sometimes the delivery of, public services (Monbiot, 2001).

Influence exerted through the *assembly*, often called lobbying, is another important form of interest group activity. One manifestation of this is the growth in the number of professional lobbyists, nearly 15,000 of whom were registered in Washington DC in 2009. The significance of the assembly or legislature in this respect depends on two factors: first, the role it plays in the political system and the degree to which it can shape policy, and second, the strength and discipline of the party system. Interest group activity surrounding the US Congress is usually seen as the most intense in the world. This reflects the strength of Congress in terms of its constitutional independence and powerful committee system, and the fact that its decentralized party system allows individual representatives to be easily recruited by groups and causes. Much of this influence is exerted through financial contributions made to election campaigns by political action committees (PACs). However, since the 1990s and as a result of tighter campaign finance laws, 'hard money' donated by PACs has tended to be displaced by 'soft money' (indirect and unregulated donations).

Policy networks (see p. 358) have also developed through institutionalized contacts between legislators (particularly key figures on legislative committees) and 'affected' groups and interests. In the USA these form two 'legs' (executive agencies being the third leg) of the so-called 'iron triangles' that dominate much of domestic policy-making. Lobbying activities focused on the assembly are less extensive and less significant in states like Canada and the UK in which party discipline is strong and parliaments are usually subject to executive control. Nevertheless, a US-style lobbying industry developed in the UK in the 1980s, with a trebling of the amount of money spent on professional lobbying, usually by parliamentary consultancies. This was in part a consequence of the dismantling of corporatism in the UK. However, it created growing concern about the spectre of 'MPs for hire' and led to the establishment in 1995 of the Committee on Standards in Public Life.

In systems in which the *courts* are unable to challenge legislation and rarely check executive actions, interest group activity focused on the judiciary is of only limited significance. This applies in states like the UK and New Zealand, despite a general tendency since the 1990s towards judicial activism, which has encouraged civil liberties and environmentalist groups in particular to fight campaigns through the courts. Where codified constitutions invest judges with the formal power of judicial review, however, as in Australia and the USA, the court system attracts far greater attention from interest groups. The classic example of this in the USA was the landmark *Brown v Board of Education* Supreme Court ruling in 1954, which rejected the constitutionality of segregation laws. The NAACP had lobbied the US legal community for several years in an attempt to shift attitudes on issues such as race and segregation, and helped to sponsor the case. Similarly, since the 1980s the energies of the US pro-life (anti-abortion) lobby have been largely directed at the Supreme Court, specifically in an attempt to overturn the 1973 *Roe v Wade* judgment, which established the constitutionality of abortion.

Interest group pressure is often also exerted through *political parties*. In some cases, parties and groups are so closely linked by historical, ideological and even institutional ties that they are best thought of as simply two wings of the same social movement. The UK and Australian Labour parties began in this way, and still function, if to a lesser extent, as part of a broader labour movement. Agrarian parties such as the Centre parties in Sweden and Norway are still part of a broad farmers' movement, and even Christian Democratic parties in central Europe can be seen as part of a broad Catholic movement. In other cases, however, the relationship between parties and groups is more pragmatic and instrumental.

The principal means through which groups influence parties is via campaign finance, and the benefits they hope to achieve are clear: 'he who pays the piper

● **Iron triangle**: A closed, mutually supportive relationship in US politics between an executive agency, a special interest group and a legislative committee or subcommittee.

CONCEPT

Civil disobedience

Civil disobedience is law-breaking that is justified by reference to 'higher' religious, moral or political principles. Civil disobedience is an overt and public act; it aims to break a law in order to 'make a point', not to get away with it. Indeed, its moral force is based largely on the willing acceptance of the penalties that follow from law-breaking. This both emphasizes the conscientious or principled nature of the act and provides evidence of the depth of feeling or commitment that lies behind it. The moral character of civil disobedience is normally demonstrated by the strict avoidance of violence.

plays the tune'. Throughout the world, conservative or right-wing parties and candidates are funded largely by business contributions, while support for socialist or left-wing ones traditionally came mainly from organized labour. Spending levels are higher in the USA, where President Obama and his Republican challenger Mitt Romney together spent almost six billion dollars during the 2012 presidential election campaign, mainly donated by business or corporate interests. However, groups may also have good reasons for avoiding too close an association with parties. For one thing, if 'their' party is in opposition, the government of the day may be less sympathetic to their interests; for another, open partisanship may restrict their ability to recruit members from amongst supporters of other parties. As a result, groups such as Shelter and the Child Poverty Action Group in the UK have assiduously guarded their non-partisan status. There are, in addition, examples of political parties that have sought to 'divorce' themselves from interest groups. In the 1990s, the UK Labour Party thus reduced the influence of affiliated trade unions at every level in the party in an attempt to destroy the image that the Labour Party is merely a puppet of the union movement. However, as this was being achieved, the party was also engaged in a 'charm offensive' to attract business backers, the success of which helped to consolidate its shift to the ideological middle ground.

Very different methods are employed by groups that seek to influence government indirectly via the *mass media* (see p. 179) and public opinion campaigns. Tactics here range from petitions, protests and demonstrations to civil disobedience and even the tactical use of violence. Interest groups use such methods for one of two reasons. They may either reflect the group's outsider status and its inability to gain direct access to policy-makers, or they may follow from the nature of the group's activist base or the character of its ideological goals. The traditional practitioners of this form of politics were trade unions, which utilized their 'industrial muscle' in the form of strikes, pickets and marches.

However, the spectacular rise of promotional and cause groups since the 1960s has seen the emergence of new styles of activist politics practised by peace campaigners, environmental lobbyists, animal rights groups, anti-roads protesters, and so on. A common aim of these groups is to attract media attention and stimulate public awareness and sympathy. Greenpeace and Friends of the Earth, for example, have been particularly imaginative in devising protests against nuclear testing, air and water pollution, deforestation, and the use of non-renewable energy sources. The nature and significance of such activities in relation to new social movements are examined in the next main section of the chapter.

Finally, since the closing decades of the twentieth century, interest group activity has increasingly adjusted to the impact of globalization and the strengthening of *international organizations*. Amongst the groups best suited to take advantage of such shifts are charities and environmental campaigners that already possess transnational structures and an international membership. Since its creation in 1961, Amnesty International has developed into a global organization with 52 sections worldwide and a presence in about 100 more countries, and over 3 million members and supporters. Many NGOs enjoy formal representation on international bodies or at international conferences; some 2,400 representatives of NGOs were, for instance, present at the 1992 Rio 'Earth Summit'. The better-funded NGOs now have permanent offices in New York and Brussels, which monitor the work of the UN and EU respectively, and conduct regular lobbying campaigns.

Social movement

A social movement is a particular form of collective behaviour in which the motive to act springs largely from the attitudes and aspirations of members, typically acting within a loose organizational framework. Being part of a social movement requires a level of commitment and political activism, rather than formal or card-carrying membership: above all, movements move. A movement is different from spontaneous mass action (such as an uprising or rebellion), in that it implies a level of intended and planned action in pursuit of a recognized social goal.

Sectional interest groups in EU member states have adjusted to the fact that, in a number of policy areas, key decisions are increasingly made by EU institutions rather than national ones. This particularly applies in relation to agriculture, trade agreements, competition policy and social and workers' rights. The most financially powerful and best-organized groups operating at the EU level are undoubtedly business interests. Their influence is exerted in various ways: through direct lobbying by large corporations, national trade bodies and peak groups, and through the activities of a new range of EU peak groups such as the European Round Table of Industrialists and the Union of Industrial and Employers' Confederations of Europe (UNICE). The style of lobbying that has developed in the EU focuses primarily on the Commission in Brussels, and, unlike the aggressive lobbying found in the USA and some other domestic contexts, tends to depend on building up long-term relationships based on trust (see p. 87) and reciprocity.

SOCIAL MOVEMENTS

Interest in social movements has been revived by the emergence of so-called 'new' social movements since the 1960s: the women's movement, the environmental or green movement, the peace movement, and so on. However, social movements can be traced back to the early nineteenth century. The earliest were the labour movement, which campaigned for improved conditions for the growing working class, various national movements, usually struggling for independence from multinational European empires, and, in central Europe in particular, a Catholic movement that fought for emancipation through the granting of legal and political rights to Catholics. In the twentieth century it was also common for fascist and right-wing authoritarian groups to be seen as movements rather than as conventional political parties.

New social movements

What is 'new' about the social movements that emerged in the final decades of the twentieth century? In the first place, whereas their more traditional counterparts were movements of the oppressed or disadvantaged, contemporary social movements have more commonly attracted the young, the better-educated and the relatively affluent. This is linked to the second difference: new movements typically have a postmaterial (see p. 177) orientation, being more concerned with 'quality of life' issues than with social advancement. Although the women's movement, for example, addresses material concerns such as equal pay and equal opportunities, it draws from a broader set of values associated with gender equality and opposition to patriarchy. Third, while traditional movements had little in common and seldom worked in tandem, new social movements subscribe to a common, if not always clearly defined, ideology.

In broad terms, their ideological stance is linked to New Left (see p. 261) ideas and values. Such a stance challenges prevailing social goals and political styles, and embraces libertarian aspirations such as personal fulfilment and self-expression. It is therefore not surprising that there is a significant membership overlap, as well as mutual sympathy, amongst the women's, environmental, animal rights, peace, anti-roads, 'anti-capitalist' or anti-globalization and other movements.

Naomi Klein (born 1970)

Canadian journalist, author and anticorporate activist. Klein's *No Logo: Taking Aim at the Brand Bullies* (2000) is a wide-ranging critique of lifestyle branding and labour abuses, and discusses emerging forms of resistance to globalization and corporate domination. It has been described as 'the book that became part of the movement', but has had wider significance in provoking reflection on the nature of consumer capitalism and the tyranny of brand culture. Klein is a frequent and influential media commentator. She lives in Toronto but travels throughout North America, Asia, Latin America and Europe tracking the rise of anticorporate activism and supporting movements campaigning against the negative effects of globalization. Her writings also include *The Shock Doctrine* (2007), which analyses the rise of 'disaster capitalism'.

CONCEPT

New Left

The New Left comprises the thinkers and intellectual movements (prominent in the 1960s and early 1970s) that sought to revitalize socialist thought by developing a radical critique of advanced industrial society. The New Left rejected both 'old' left alternatives: Soviet-style state socialism and de-radicalized western social democracy. Common themes within the New Left include a fundamental rejection of conventional society ('the system') as oppressive, disillusionment with the role of the working class as the revolutionary agent, and a preference for decentralization and participatory democracy.

● **Mass society**: A society characterized by atomism and by cultural and political rootlessness; the concept highlights pessimistic trends in modern societies.

A final difference between traditional and new social movements is that the latter tend to have organizational structures that stress decentralization and participatory decision-making and have also developed new forms of political activism. They thus practise what is sometimes called the 'new politics', which turns away from 'established' parties, interest groups and representative processes towards a more innovative and theatrical form of protest politics. The most dramatic examples of this have been the so-called 'Battle of Seattle' in 1999, in which mass demonstrations against the World Trade Organization degenerated into violent clashes between the police and groups of protesters, and other similar 'anti-capitalist' or anti-globalization protests, for example, in the Occupy movement that sprang up in 2011 (see p. 262). Such demonstrations involve a disparate range of environmental, development, ethnic nationalist, anarchist and revolutionary socialist groups, with the internet and mobile phones providing the principal means of communications. The ideas of the emergent anti-globalization movement have been articulated in the writing of authors such as Noam Chomsky (see p. 181) and Naomi Klein.

The emergence of a new generation of social movements practising new styles of activism has significantly shifted views about the nature and significance of movements themselves. The experience of totalitarianism (see p. 269) in the period between the two world wars encouraged mass society theorists such as Erich Fromm (1900–80) and Hannah Arendt (see p. 7) to see movements in distinctly negative terms. From the mass society perspective, social movements reflect a 'flight from freedom' (Fromm, 1941), an attempt by alienated individuals to achieve security and identity through fanatical commitment to a cause and obedience to a (usually fascist) leader. In contrast, new social movements are usually interpreted as rational and instrumental actors, whose use of informal and unconventional means merely reflects the resources available to them (Zald and McCarthy, 1987). The emergence of new social movements is widely seen as evidence of the fact that power in postindustrial societies is increasingly dispersed and fragmented. The class-based politics of old has thus been replaced by a new politics based on what Laclau and Mouffe (2001) called 'democratic pluralism'. Not only do new movements offer new and rival centres of power, but they also diffuse power more effectively by resisting bureaucratization and developing more spontaneous, affective and decentralized forms of organization.

The Occupy movement: a counter-hegemonic force?

Events: On 17 September 2011, about 5,000 people – carrying banners, shouting slogans and banging drums – gathered in New York and started to make their way to Zuccotti Park, located in the Wall Street financial district. There they erected tents, set up kitchens and established peaceful barricades. The Occupy movement was thus born with Occupy Wall Street (OWS), and quickly developed into a truly global wave of protest. On 15 October, tens of thousands of protestors took to the streets in some 82 countries around the world, affecting over 750 towns and cities, many demonstrators following the example of 'the Zuccottis' in setting up semi-permanent protest camps in parks or other prominent public spaces, usually close to financial centres. Although protests in different countries were often shaped by local issues and concerns, the common goals of the Occupy movement were to highlight social and economic inequality, and to condemn as unfair and unstable the dominance of the world economy by big corporations and the global financial system.

Significance: On one level, the Occupy movement is merely a further manifestation of anti-capitalist activism that dates back to the 1999 'Battle of Seattle'. However, the upsurge in Occupy protests was particularly significant in at least two respects. First, and most importantly, it was a response to the global financial crisis of 2007–09 and its aftermath, and thus constituted an attempt to challenge the values and redress the power imbalances that supposedly underpinned the crisis. This was evident in the movement's recurrent focus on the vulnerabilities and injustices that flow from the dominant position that banks and financial institutions have acquired as a result of three decades of neoliberal globalization. Across much of southern Europe and elsewhere, Occupy activism expressed anger at the politics of austerity. In this respect, the Occupy movement expressed anxieties and frustrations that mainstream political parties and conventional interest groups clearly struggled to articulate. Second, the Occupy movement drew inspiration from the Arab Spring, (see p. 88), with OWS sometimes being portrayed as the 'Tahir moment' of the Occupy movement (harking back to the waves of demonstrations in Cairo's Tahir Square that helped to bring about the fall of President Mubarak in May 2011). As such, the Occupy protestors were seeking to take advantage of what was seen as a major shift in global politics in favour of 'people power'.

How effective were the Occupy protests? This is a difficult question to answer as new social movements typically seek to raise political consciousness, and to shift values and attitudes, rather than affect specific public policies. In the case of Occupy, it looked to precipitate a 'global spiritual insurrection', a very difficult thing to quantify. The movement also attracted criticism, however. In the first place, it appeared to go little further than previous incarnations of the anti-capitalist movement in developing a systematic and coherent critique of neoliberal globalization, or in outlining a viable alternative. This, in part, reflects the political and ideological diversity within the movement itself. While some Occupy protestors were genuinely 'anti-capitalist', adopting a Marxist-style analysis of capitalism, many within the movement merely wished to remove the 'worst excesses' of capitalism. Second, although radical decentralization and participatory decision-making structures may have been part of Occupy's appeal, especially as far as the young and marginalized are concerned, it is difficult to transform a collection of 'anarchist swarms' into a sustainable mass movement. Finally, Occupy's tactic of establishing protest camps had clear drawbacks, not least because it was highly unlikely that such camps would be allowed to become permanent, meaning that the focus of the protest would be lost. Over time, the Occupy movement has thus become more tactically flexible, placing less emphasis on semi-permanent protest camps, and adopting wider and more innovative forms of protest.

Betty Friedan (1921–2006)

US feminist and political activist, sometimes seen as the 'mother' of women's liberation. Betty Friedan's *The Feminine Mystique* (1963) is often credited with having stimulated the emergence of 'second wave' feminism. In it, she examined 'the problem
with no name': the sense of frustration and despair afflicting suburban American
women. In 1966, she helped to found the National Organization of Women (NOW),
becoming its first president. In *The Second Stage* (1983), Friedan drew attention to
the danger that the pursuit of 'personhood' might encourage women to deny the
importance of children, the home, and the family. Her later writings include *The
Fountain of Age* (1993).

Nevertheless, the impact of social movements is more difficult to assess than
that of political parties or interest groups. This is because of the broader nature
of their goals, and because, to some extent, they exert influence through less
tangible cultural strategies. However, it is clear that in cases like the women's
movement and the environmental movement profound political changes have
been achieved through shifts in cultural values and moral attitudes brought
about over a number of years. For example, the Women's Liberation Movement
(WLM) emerged in the 1960s as a collection of groups and organizations mobilized by the emerging ideas of 'second wave' feminism, as expressed in the writings of such as Betty Friedan, Germaine Greer (1970) and Kate Millett (1970).
Despite the achievement by the women's movement of advances in specific
areas, such as equal pay and the legalization of abortion, perhaps its most significant achievement is an increasing general awareness of gender issues and the
eroding of support for patriarchal attitudes and institutions. This is a cultural
change that has had a deep, if unquantifiable, impact on public policy at many
levels.

The environmental movement has brought about similar politico-cultural
shifts. Not only have governments been confronted by interest group campaigns
mounted by the likes of Greenpeace, Friends of the Earth and the Worldwide
Fund for Nature, but they have also been influenced by broader anxieties about
the environment that extend well beyond those expressed by the formal
membership of such organizations. Since the 1970s these concerns have also
been articulated by green parties. Typically, these parties have embraced the idea
of 'new politics', styling themselves as 'anti-system' parties or even 'anti-party'
parties, and placing a heavy emphasis on decentralization and popular activism.
The impact of the environmental movement has also extended to conventional
or 'grey' parties, many of which have responded to new popular sensibilities by
trying to establish their green credentials. By contrast, the 'anti-capitalist' movement, or, more accurately, the loose coalition of groups that has been brought
together by resistance to globalization and its associated consumerist values and
free-trade practices, has as yet been less successful. Although international
summit meetings have become much more difficult to arrange, there is little sign
of governments or mainstream parties revising their support for free trade (see
p. 437) and economic deregulation.

SUMMARY

- An interest or pressure group is an organized association that aims to influence the policies or actions of government. Sectional groups advance or protect the (usually material) interests of their members, while promotional ones are concerned with shared values, ideals or principles. Whereas insider groups enjoy privileged access to policy formulation, outsider groups lack access to government and so are forced to 'go public'.

- Group politics has been understood in a number of ways. Pluralism emphasizes the dispersal of power and the ability of groups to guarantee democratic accountability. Corporatism highlights the privileged position that certain groups enjoy in relation to government. The New Right draws attention to the threat that groups pose in terms of over-government and economic inefficiency.

- Organized groups benefit the political system by strengthening representation, promoting debate and discussion, broadening political participation and acting as a check on government power. They may, nevertheless, pose a threat, in that they entrench political inequality, are socially and politically divisive, exercise nonlegitimate and unaccountable power, and make the policy process more closed and secretive.

- Interest groups exert influence through a variety of channels, including the bureaucracy, the assembly, the courts, the mass media, the parties and international bodies. The level of influence that groups have in a particular system, however, relates to how accommodating that system is to group activity in general, and to what access points it offers groups in terms of the distribution of policy-making power.

- Interest groups have at their disposal a wide range of tactics and political strategies. Their resources may include public sympathy for the group and its goals, the size of its membership or activist base, its financial strength and organizational capabilities, its ability to use sanctions against government and its personal or institutional links with political parties or government bodies.

- A social movement is a collective body in which there is a high level of commitment and political activism not necessarily based on a formal organization. New social movements are distinguished by their capacity to attract the young, better-educated and relatively affluent; their generally postmaterial orientation; and their commitment to new forms of political activism, sometimes called the 'new politics'.

Questions for discussion

- Why is it sometimes difficult to distinguish between interest groups and political parties?
- Does group politics allow private interests to prevail over the public good?
- Are organized groups the principal means through which interests are articulated in modern societies?
- Does corporatism work more to the benefit of groups, or more to the benefit of government?
- Do interest groups promote democracy, or undermine it?
- Why are some interest groups more powerful than others?
- In what sense are new social movements 'new'?
- To what extent have new social movements had an impact on public policy?

Further reading

Cigler, C. and B. Loomis (eds), *Interest Group Politics* (2011). A wide-ranging examination of various aspects of group politics that focuses primarily on the USA.

Jordan, G. and W. Maloney, *Democracy and Interest Groups: Enhancing Democracy?* (2007). An analysis of the ways and extent to which interest groups promote democracy, taking account of concerns about growing civic disengagement.

Tarrow, S., *Power in Movement: Social Movements and Contentious Politics* (2011). A useful introduction to the nature and significance of social movements.

Wilson, G., *Interest Groups* (1990). A clear and concise discussion of the role of groups in liberal democracies that remains a useful introduction to the subject.

CHAPTER 17

Global Environmental Issues

There are no passengers on Spaceship Earth. We are all crew.'

MARSHALL MCLUHAN, *Understanding Media* (1964)

PREVIEW   The environment is often viewed as the archetypal example of a global issue. This is because environmental processes are no respecters of national borders; they have an intrinsically transnational character. As countries are peculiarly environmentally vulnerable to the activities that take place in other countries, meaningful progress on environmental issues can often only be made at the international or even global level. Nevertheless, international cooperation on such matters has sometimes been very difficult to bring about. This has occurred for a number of reasons. In the first place, the environment has been an arena of particular ideological and political debate. Disagreements have emerged about both the seriousness and nature of environmental problems and about how they can best be tackled, not least because environmental priorities tend to conflict with economic ones. Can environmental problems be dealt with within the existing socio-economic system, or is this system the source of those problems? Such debates have been especially passionate over what is clearly the central issue on the global environmental agenda, climate change. Despite sometimes catastrophic predictions about what will happen if the challenge of climate change is not addressed, concerted international action on the issue has been frustratingly slow to emerge. What have been the obstacles to international cooperation over climate change, and what would concerted international action on the issue involve? Finally, climate change is not the only issue on the global environmental agenda. Another issue of major concern is energy security, with some talking in terms of a new international energy order in which a country's ranking in the hierarchy of states is being increasingly determined by the vastness of its oil and natural gas reserves, or its ability to acquire them. To what extent has energy security reshaped global order, and are natural resources always a blessing?

KEY ISSUES
- How and why has the environment developed into a global issue?
- Do modern environmental problems require reformist or radical solutions?
- What are the causes and major consequences of climate change?
- How far has international action over climate change progressed?
- What obstacles stand in the way of international cooperation over climate change?
- How has energy security shaped conflict both between states and within states?

CONCEPT

Ecology

The term 'ecology' was coined by the German zoologist Ernst Haeckel in 1866. Derived from the Greek *oikos*, meaning household or habitat, he used it to refer to 'the investigations of the total relations of the animal both to its organic and its inorganic environment'. Ecology developed as a distinct branch of biology through a growing recognition that plants and animals are sustained by self-regulating natural systems – ecosystems – composed of both living and non-living elements. Simple examples of an ecosystem are a field, a forest or, as illustrated in Figure 17.1, a pond. All ecosystems tend towards a state of harmony or equilibrium through a system of self-regulation, referred to by biologists as homeostasis.

● **Ecologism**: A political ideology that is based on the belief that nature is an interconnected whole, embracing humans and non-humans, as well as the inanimate world.

● **Fossil fuels**: Fuels that are formed through the decomposition of buried dead organisms, making them rich in carbon; examples include oil, natural gas and coal.

THE RISE OF GREEN POLITICS
The environment as a global issue

Although forms of environmental politics can be traced back to the industrialization of the nineteenth century, ecologism or green politics having always been, in a sense, a backlash against industrial society, the environment did not become a significant national or international issue until the 1960s and 1970s. This occurred through the emergence of an environmental movement that sought to highlight the environmental costs of increased growth and rising affluence, at least in the developed West, drawing attention also to a growing divide between humankind and nature. Influenced in particular by the idea of ecology (see Figure 17.1), the pioneering works of early green politics included Rachel Carson's *The Silent Spring* (1962), a critique of the damage done to wildlife and the human world by the increased use of pesticides and other agricultural chemicals, and Murray Bookchin's *Our Synthetic Environment* ([1962] 1975) which examined how pesticides, food additives and X-rays cause a range of human illnesses, including cancer. This period of the 1960s and 1970s also saw the birth of a new generation of activist NGOs (see p. 10) – ranging from Greenpeace and Friends of the Earth to animal liberation activists and so-called 'eco-warrior' groups – campaigning on issues such as the dangers of pollution, the dwindling reserves of fossil fuels, deforestation and animal experiments. From the 1980s onwards, environmental questions were kept high on the political agenda by green parties, which now exist in most industrialized countries, often modelling themselves on the pioneering efforts of the German Greens. The environmental movement addresses three general problems. These are:

● *Resource* problems – attempts to conserve natural materials through reducing the use of non-renewable resources (coal, oil, natural gas and so on), increasing the use of renewable resources (such as wind, wave and tidal power), and reducing population growth, thereby curtailing resource consumption.
● *Sink* problems – attempts to reduce the damage done by the waste products of economic activity, through, for example, reducing pollution levels, increasing recycling, and developing greener (less polluting) technologies.
● *Ethical* problems – attempts to restore the balance between humankind and nature through wildlife and wilderness conservation, respect for other species (animal rights and animal welfare), and changed agricultural practices (organic farming).

During the 1970s, environmental politics focused particularly on resource issues. This reflected a growing awareness that humankind lives in a world of 'global finiteness', an awareness reinforced by the oil crisis of 1973. A particularly influential metaphor for the environmental movement was the idea of 'spaceship Earth', because this emphasized the notion of limited and exhaustible wealth. Kenneth Boulding (1966) argued that human beings had traditionally acted as though they lived in a 'cowboy economy', an economy with unlimited opportunities, like the American West during the frontier period. However, as a spaceship

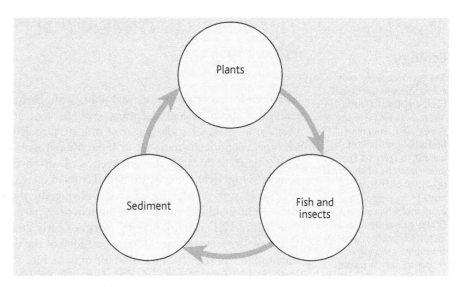

Figure 17.1 **A pond as an ecosystem**

is a capsule, it is a closed system and all closed systems tend to exhibit evidence of **entropy** in that they decay because they are not sustained by external inputs. Ultimately, however wisely and carefully human beings behave, the Earth, the sun and indeed all planets and stars are destined to be exhausted and die. Similar concerns about global finiteness were also highlighted by the unofficial UN report *Only One Earth* (Ward and Dubois 1972) and the report of the Club of Rome, *The Limits to Growth* (Meadows *et al.* 1972). The latter work had a stunning impact, in that it appeared to predict by extrapolating five variables – world population, industrialization, pollution, food production and resource depletion – that the world's oil supplies would run out by 1992. Although such predictions were subsequently revealed to be gross exaggerations, and despite widespread criticism of the methodology used, the idea of limits to growth dominated thinking about the environment for a decade or more.

Environmental issues also became an increasingly major focus of international concern. This reflected a growing awareness that environmental problems have an intrinsically transnational character: they are no respecters of borders. States are therefore environmentally vulnerable to the economic activities that take place in other states, a lesson that was reinforced during the 1970s by a growing concern about the regional impact of **acid rain** and by the truly global consequences of **ozone depletion** caused by emissions of man-made chemicals such as chlorofluorocarbons (CFCs) and halons. The first major international conference to be held on environmental issues was the 1972 UN Conference on the Human Environment (UNCHE) at Stockholm. The Stockholm conference also led to the establishment of the United Nations Environment Programme (UNEP), which is responsible for coordinating the environmental activities of states and international organizations to promote better regional and global environmental protection. However, the global recession of the 1970s and onset of the 'second Cold War' in the early 1980s subsequently pushed environmental issues down the international agenda. They were

● **Entropy**: A tendency towards decay or disintegration, a characteristic exhibited, sooner or later, by all closed systems.

● **Acid rain**: Rain that is contaminated by sulphuric, nitric and other acids that are released into the atmosphere by the burning of fossil fuels.

● **Ozone depletion**: A decline in the total amount of ozone in the Earth's stratosphere, particularly the development of a so-called 'ozone hole' over the Antarctic.

revived, in part, through the impact of environmental catastrophes such as the 1984 Bhopal chemical plant disaster and the 1986 Chernobyl nuclear disaster, but also by a growing recognition that environmental degradation was closely associated with the advance of globalization (see p. 8), encouraging many, particularly in the South, to link environmental and development issues. The 1987 Brundtland Commission Report, *Our Common Future*, exemplified this through its emphasis on 'sustainable development' (see p. 397), which subsequently provided the dominant mainstream framework for understanding and addressing environmental issues. The Brundtland Report prepared the way for the 1992 Rio 'Earth Summit' (officially, the UN Conference on Environment and Development, or UNCED), which was held twenty years after the landmark Stockholm conference.

From the 1990s onwards, environmental debate increasingly focused on the issue of 'climate change' brought about through **global warming**. Initial concerns about climate change had focused on CFC emissions, but this shifted over time to the impact of so-called '**greenhouse gases**'. One of the consequences of the Earth Summit was the establishment of the UN Framework Convention on Climate Change (FCCC), the first attempt to stabilize greenhouse gas concentrations at a level that would prevent dangerous anthropogenic (human-induced) climate change. Responsibility for reporting on the implementation of the FCCC was invested in the International Panel on Climate Change (IPCC) (see p. 403), established in 1988. Nevertheless, it took until the 1997 Kyoto Protocol to the FCCC to agree measures to control emissions of greenhouse gases. Under the Kyoto Protocol, developed countries agreed to cut their emissions by an average of 5 per cent, usually against 1990 levels, during the 'commitment period', 2008–12. Subsequent conferences were convened in Copenhagen (2009), Durban (2011) and Doha (2012) in an attempt to formulate a successor to Kyoto. However, in their different ways, these conferences demonstrated the difficulty of achieving concerted and effective action on the issue of climate change (see p. 409). These difficulties relate, most basically, to the mismatch between state interests and the collective interests of the international community, as illustrated by the idea of the 'tragedy of the commons' (see p. 395). Potentially, this problem applies to all environmental issues.

Green politics: reformism or radicalism?

The environment is an arena of particular ideological and political debate. Disagreements about the seriousness and nature of environmental problems, and about how they can best be tackled, are rooted in deeper, often philosophical debates about the relationship between humankind and the natural world. Conventional political thought has subscribed to a human-centred approach to understanding, often called **anthropocentrism**. Moral priority has therefore been given to the achievement of human needs and ends, with nature being seen merely as a way of facilitating these needs and ends. In the words of the early liberal English philosopher John Locke (1632–1704), human beings are 'the masters and possessors of nature'. Environmental thought, by contrast, is based on the principle of ecology, which stresses the network of relationships that sustain all forms of life including human life. However, green politics encompasses two broad traditions, which can be called 'reformist' ecology and 'radical' ecology.

● **Global warming:** An increase in the Earth's temperature, widely believed to be due to heat trapped by greenhouse gases, such as carbon dioxide.

● **Greenhouse gases:** Gases (such as carbon dioxide, water vapour, methane, nitrous oxide and ozone) that trap heat in the Earth's lower atmosphere (see The greenhouse effect.

● **Anthropocentrism:** A belief that human needs and interests are of overriding moral and philosophical importance.

Major international initiatives on the environment

1946	International Convention for the Regulation of Whaling. This set up the International Whaling Commission (IWC) which attempts to preserve Great Whales by upholding an international moratorium on whaling.
1950	World Meteorological Organization (WMO) established as a specialized agency of the UN for meteorology (weather and climate) and related geophysical sciences.
1959	Antarctic Treaty, which set aside Antarctica, Earth's only continent without a native human population, as a scientific preserve.
1972	United Nations Conference on the Human Environment (UNCHE) in Stockholm, which laid the foundations for environmental action at an international level and prepared the way for the launch of the UN's Environmental Programme (UNEP).
1973	Convention on International Trade in Endangered Species (CITES), which aimed to ensure that international trade in wildlife and plants does not threaten their survival.
1982	UN Convention on the Law of the Sea, which defined the rights and responsibilities of countries in their use of the world's oceans and established guidelines for businesses, the environment and the management of marine natural resources (entered into force in 1994).
1985	Vienna Convention for the Protection of the Ozone Layer, which confirmed the existence of the Arctic 'ozone hole', and attempted to reduce the use of CFC gasses (entered into force in 1987).
1987	Brundtland Commission Report, which highlighted the idea of sustainable development.
1987	Montreal Protocol on Substances that Deplete the Ozone Layer, which provided for the phasing out of CFCs with the goal of the ozone layer having recovered by 2050.
1988	International Panel on Climate Change (IPCC) (see p. 403) established, which reports on the implementation of the UN Framework Convention on Climate Change (FCCC).
1992	UN Conference on Environment and Development (UNCED) held in Rio de Janeiro and commonly called the 'Earth Summit', which included conventions on climate change and biodiversity and established the Commission on Sustainable Development (CSD).
1997	Kyoto Protocol to the FCCC, which established a legally binding commitment by developed states to limit greenhouse gas emissions in a phased process. (Entered into force in 2005 with the first commitment period being 2008–12).
2009–12	The UN Climate Change Conferences held in Copenhagen, Durban and Doha to formulate a successor to the Kyoto Protocol (see p. 409).

Focus on . . .
The tragedy of the commons?

Will shared resources always be misused or overused? Does community ownership of land, forests and fisheries lead to inevitable ruin, and what does this imply about modern environmental problems? Garrett Hardin (see p. 411) used the idea of the 'tragedy of the commons' to draw parallels between global environmental degradation and the fate of common land before the introduction of enclosures. He argued that if pasture is open to all, each herder will try to keep as many cattle as possible on the commons. However, sooner or later, the inherent logic of the commons will remorselessly generate tragedy, as the number of cattle exceeds the carrying capacity of the land. Each herder calculates that the *positive* benefit of adding one more animal (in terms of the proceeds from its eventual sale) will always exceed the *negative* impact on the pasture, as this is relatively slight and, anyway, shared by all herders. As Hardin put it, 'Freedom in a commons brings ruin to all'. The idea of the 'tragedy of the commons' draws attention to the importance of the 'global commons', sometimes seen as 'common pool resources', and of threats posed to these by overpopulation (a particular concern for Hardin), pollution, resource depletion, habitat destruction and over-fishing.

Is the 'tragedy of the commons' an unsolvable problem? Hardin himself argued in favour of strengthened political control, especially to restrict population growth, even showing sympathy for the idea of world government (see p. 464). Liberals, nevertheless, argue that the solution is, in effect, to abolish the commons by extending property rights, allowing the disciplines of the market (the price mechanism) to control resource usage. Although, as capitalism expanded, common land gradually became privately owned, it is more difficult to see how privatization could be applied to the global commons. Ostrom (1990) nevertheless argued that some societies have succeeded in managing common pool resources through developing diverse, and often bottom-up, institutional arrangements. However, others, particularly socialists and anarchists, reject the 'tragedy of the commons' altogether. Not only does historical evidence suggest that common land was usually successfully managed by communities (Cox 1985), as is borne out by examples such as the Aboriginal peoples of Australia, but the argument is also circular: its conclusions are implicit in the assumption that human nature is selfish and unchanging (Angus 2008). Indeed, ecosocialists would argue that selfishness, greed and the wanton use of resources are a consequence of the system of private ownership, not their cause. Community ownership, by contrast, engenders respect for the natural environment.

Reformist ecology

● **Carrying capacity**: The maximum population that an ecosystem can support, given the food, habitat, water and other necessities available.

● **Global commons**: Areas and natural resources that are unowned and so beyond national jurisdiction, examples including the atmosphere, the oceans and, arguably, Antarctica.

Reformist ecology seeks to reconcile the principle of ecology with the central features of capitalist modernity (individual self-seeking, materialism, economic growth and so on), which is why it sometimes called 'modernist' ecology. It is clearly a form of humanist or 'shallow' ecology. The key feature of reformist ecology is that recognition that there are 'limits to growth', in that environmental degradation (in the form of, for instance, pollution or the use of non-renewable resources) ultimately threatens prosperity and economic performance. The watchword of this form of ecologism is sustainable development, especially what is called 'weak' sustainability. In economic terms, this means 'getting rich more slowly'. From the reformist perspective, damage to the environment is an **externality**, or 'social cost'. By taking account of such costs, modernist ecologists attempted to develop a balance between modernization and **sustainability**.

The chief ideological influence on reformist ecology is **utilitarianism**, which is based on classical liberal thinking. In that sense, reformist ecology practises what can be called 'enlightened' anthropocentrism, encouraging individuals to take account of long-term, not merely short-term, interests. The British utilitarian philosopher and politician John Stuart Mill (1806–73) thus justified a steady-state economy (one without economic growth) on the grounds that the contemplation of nature is a 'higher' pleasure. Peter Singer (1993) justified animal rights on the grounds that all species, and not just humans, have a right to avoid suffering. More generally, utilitarian thinking acknowledges the impact on the quality of human life of environmental degradation by recognizing the interests of future generations (see p. 398). The most straightforward case for conserving resources is therefore that it maximises the welfare or happiness of people, taking account of both the living and of people who have yet to be born. Finally, reformist ecology is defined by the means through which it would deal with environmental problems, as typified by the mainstream environmental movement. It tends to advocate three main solutions to environmental degradation:

- 'Market ecologism' or 'green capitalism'. This involves attempts to adjust markets to take account of the damage done to the environment, making externalities internal to the businesses or organizations that are responsible for them. Examples of this include **green taxes**.
- Human ingenuity and the development of green technologies (such as drought resistant crops, energy-efficient forms of transport and 'clean' coal). The capacity for invention and innovation that created industrial civilization in the first place can also be used to generate an environmentally-friendly version of industrialization.
- International regimes (see p. 71) and systems of transnational regulation. Global governance (see p. 462) offers the prospect that the impact of 'tragedy of the commons' can be reduced, even though it can never be removed.

Radical ecology

Radical ecology, by contrast, encompasses a range of green perspectives that call, in their various ways, for more far-reaching, and in some cases even revolutionary, change. Rather than seeking to reconcile the principle of ecology with the central features of capitalist modernity, these theories view capitalist modernity, and its values, structures and institutions, as the root cause of environmental degradation. A variety of these perspectives can collectively be categorized as forms of **social ecology**, in that they each explain the balance between humankind and nature largely by reference to social structures. The advance of ecological principles therefore requires a process of radical social change. However, this social change is understood in at least three quite different ways:

- *Ecosocialism* advances an environmental critique of capitalism. For ecosocialists, capitalism's anti-ecological bias stems from the institution of private property and its tendency towards '**commodification**'. These reduce nature to mere resources and suggest that the only hope for ecological sustainability is the construction of a socialist society.

● **Shallow ecology**: A green ideological perspective that harnesses the lessons of ecology to human needs and ends, and is associated with values such as sustainability and conservation.

● **Externality**: A cost of an economic activity that has wider impact but does not feature on the balance sheet of a business or form part of the GDP of a country.

● **Sustainability**: The capacity of a system to maintain its health and continuing existence over a period of time.

● **Utilitarianism**: A moral philosophy that equates 'good' with pleasure or happiness, and 'evil' with pain or unhappiness, and aims to achieve 'the greatest happiness for the greatest number' (the principle of general utility).

● **Green taxes**: Taxes that penalize individuals or businesses for, for instance, the waste they generate, the pollution they cause, the emissions they generate or the finite resources they consume.

● **Social ecology**: The idea that ecological principles can and should be applied to social organization, a term originally used mainly by eco-anarchists.

● **Commodification**: Turning something into a commodity that can be bought and sold, having only an economic value.

Focus on ...
Sustainable development: reconciling growth with ecology?

Can development be ecologically sustainable? Is there an inevitable tension between economic growth and protecting the environment? The idea of 'sustainable development' has dominated thinking on environmental and development issues since it was highlighted by the 1987 Brundtland Report. The Brundtland Report's highly influential definition of the term is: 'Sustainable development is development that meets the needs of the present without compromising the ability of future generations to meet their own needs. It contains two key concepts: (1) the concept of need, in particular the essential needs of the world's poor, to which overriding priority should be given, and (2) the concept of limitations, imposed by the state of technology and social organization on the environment's ability to meet present and future needs.'

However, there is debate about what sustainable development means in practice, and about how growth and ecology can be reconciled. What is sometimes called 'weak' sustainability accepts that economic growth is desirable but simply recognizes that growth must limited to ensure that ecological costs do not threaten its long-term sustainability. This means, in effect, getting richer slower. Supporters of this view, moreover, argue that human capital can be substituted for natural capital, implying, for example, that better roads or a new airport could compensate for a loss of habitat or agricultural land. In this view, the key requirement of sustainability is that the net sum of natural and human capital available to future generations should not be less than that available to present generations. However, 'strong' sustainability, favoured by radical ecologists, rejects the pro-growth implications of weak sustainability. It focuses just on the need to preserve and sustain natural capital, seeing human capital as little more than a blight on nature. This is sometimes reflected in the belief that natural capital should be evaluated in terms of people's ecological footprint, an idea that has radically egalitarian implications.

● **Ecological footprint:** A measure of ecological capacity based on the hectares of biologically productive land that are needed to supply a given person's consumption of natural resources and absorb their waste.

● **Deep ecology:** A green ideological perspective that rejects anthropocentrism and gives priority to the maintenance of nature; it is associated with values such as bioequality, diversity and decentralization.

● **Ecocentrism:** A theoretical orientation that gives priority to the maintenance of ecological balance rather than the achievement of human ends.

● *Eco-anarchism* advances an environmental critique of hierarchy and authority. For eco-anarchists, domination over people leads to domination over nature. This implies that a balance between humankind and nature can only be restored through the abolition of the state and the establishment of decentralized, self-managing communities (Bookchin 1982).

● *Ecofeminism* advances an environmental critique of patriarchy (see p. 424). For ecofeminists, domination over women leads to domination over nature (Merchant 1983, 1992). As men are the enemy of nature because of their reliance on instrumental reason and their inclination to control or subjugate, respect for nature requires the creation of a post-patriarchal society.

While social ecology views radical social change as the key to ecological sustainability, so-called 'deep' ecology goes further in emphasizing the need for paradigm change, a change in our core thinking and assumptions about the world. This involves rejecting all forms of anthropocentrism, and embracing ecocentrism instead. Deep ecology therefore advocates a radical holism that implies that the world should be understood strictly in terms of interconnectedness and interdependence (see p. 7). The human species is merely part of nature,

Focus on ...
Obligations to future generations?

Do we have obligations towards future generations? In deciding how we should act, should we take account of the interest of people who have not yet been born? These questions are of relevance because it is in the nature of environmental matters that many of the consequences of our actions may not be felt for decades or even centuries. Industrialization, for instance, had advanced for some two hundred years before concerns were raised about the depletion of finite oil, gas or coal resources, or about greenhouse gas emissions. This has forced ecologists to develop ideas about inter-generational justice, suggesting that our obligations extend beyond the present generation to future genera-tions, encompassing the living and the yet to be born.

Such 'futurity' has been justified in different ways. Care for and obligations towards future generations have sometimes been seen as a 'natural duty', an extension of a moral concern for our children and, by extension,

their children, and so on. A concern for future genera-tions has also been linked to the idea of 'ecological stewardship'. This is the notion that the present genera-tion is merely the custodian of the wealth that has been generated by past generations and should conserve it for the benefit of future generations. However, the idea of cross-generational justice has also been criticized. Some argue that all rights depend on reciprocity (see p. 344) (rights are respected because of something that is done, or not done, in return), in which case it is absurd to endow people who have yet to be born with rights that impose duties on people who are currently alive. Moreover, in view of the poten-tially unlimited size of future generations, the burdens imposed by 'futurity' are, in practical terms, incalcula-ble. Present generations may either be making sacri-fices for the benefit of future generations that may prove to be much better off, or their sacrifices may be entirely inadequate to meet future needs.

neither more important, nor more special, than any other part. Such ecocentric thinking has been constructed on a variety of bases, ranging from the new physics (particularly quantum mechanics) and systems theory to Eastern mysti-cism (especially Buddhism and Taoism) (Capra 1975, 1982, 1997) and pre-Christian spiritual ideas, notably ones that stress the notion of 'Mother Earth', as advanced in the so-called Gaia hypothesis (see p. 399). Deep ecologists have radi-cally revised conventional ethical thinking, arguing that morality springs not from human beings, but from nature itself, and supporting the idea of 'biocen-tric equality'. They are also fiercely critical of consumerism and materialism, believing that these distort the relationship between humankind and nature.

CLIMATE CHANGE

Climate change is not only the most prominent global environmental issue, but it is also, some argue, the most urgent and important challenge currently confronting the international community. However, the issue is bedevilled by controversies and disagreements. The most important of these are over:

● **Biocentric equality**: The principle that all organisms and entities in the ecosphere are of equal moral worth, each being part of an interrelated whole.

- The *cause* of climate change: is climate change happening, and to what extent is it a result of human activity?

Focus on ...

The Gaia hypothesis: a living planet?

The Gaia hypothesis was developed by James Lovelock (1979, 1989 and 2006). It advances the idea that the Earth is best understood as a living entity that acts to maintain its own existence. At the suggestion of the novelist William Golding, Lovelock named the planet Gaia, after the Greek goddess of the Earth. The basis for the Gaia hypothesis is that the Earth's biosphere, atmosphere, oceans and soil exhibit precisely the same kind of self-regulating behaviour that characterizes other forms of life. Gaia has maintained 'homeostasis', a state of dynamic balance, despite major changes that have taken place in the solar system. The most dramatic evidence of this is the fact that although the sun has warmed up by more than 25 per cent since life began, the temperature on Earth and the composition of its atmosphere have remained virtually unchanged.

The idea of Gaia has developed into an ecological ideology that conveys the powerful message that human beings must respect the health of the planet, and act to conserve its beauty and resources. It also contains a revolutionary vision of the relationship between the animate and inanimate world. However, the Gaia philosophy has also been condemned as a form of 'misanthropic ecology'. This is because Gaia is non-human, and Gaia theory suggests that the health of the planet matters more than that of any individual species presently living on it. Lovelock has suggested that those species that have prospered have been ones that have helped Gaia to regulate its own existence, while any species that poses a threat to the delicate balance of Gaia, as humans currently do, is likely to be extinguished.

- The *significance* of climate change: how serious are the consequences of climate change likely to be?
- The *cures* for climate change: how can climate change best be tackled?

Causes of climate change

What is climate? Climate is different from weather: climate refers to the long-term or prevalent weather conditions of an area. As the US writer Mark Twain noted: 'Climate is what we expect; weather is what we get'. However, this certainly does not imply that the Earth's climate is stable and unchanging. Indeed, it has experienced wild swings throughout it 4.6 billion-year history. There have been numerous ice ages, interspersed with warmer interglacial periods. The last ice age occurred during the Pleistocene epoch, which ended about 10,000 years ago, during which glaciers on the North American continent reached as far south as the Great Lakes and an ice sheet spread over Northern Europe, leaving its remains as far south as Switzerland. By contrast, some 55 million years ago, at the end of the Palaeocene epoch and the beginning of the Eocene epoch, the planet heated up in one of the most extreme and rapid global warming events in geological history. Such changes resulted from a variety of developments: changes in the radiation output of the sun; changes in the Earth's attitude in relation to the sun (as the Earth's orbit alters from elliptical to circular and changes occur in its tilt and how it wobbles on its axis); variations in the composition of the Earth's atmosphere, and so forth. Over the past century, and particularly during the last few decades, a new period of rapid climate change has been initi-

APPROACHES TO . . .

NATURE

Realist view

Realism has traditionally paid little attention to environmental thinking and it would be highly questionable to suggest that realism can be associated with a particular conception of nature. Realism is certainly more concerned with survival than with sustainability. Nevertheless, it has addressed the issue of the relationship between humankind and the natural world in at least two senses. First, classical realists have often explained human behaviour and propensities in terms of those found in other animals and, indeed, in nature itself. Selfishness, greed and aggression have commonly been viewed as innate features of human nature, reflecting tendencies that are found in all species (Lorenz 1966). On a larger scale, the struggle and conflict that realists believe is an ineradicable feature of human existence has sometimes been traced back to the fact that nature itself is 'red in tooth and claw'. Conflict and war have thus been seen as a manifestation of 'the survival of the fittest', a kind of social Darwinism. Second, realists have acknowledged the importance of nature, in recognizing the role that scarcity, and therefore conflict over resources, often plays in generating international tensions. Such thinking has been particularly evident in the ideas of geopolitics (see p. 414), which is itself a form of environmentalism. It is also reflected in the idea that many, and perhaps most, wars are 'resource wars'.

Liberal view

In the liberal view, nature is viewed as a resource to satisfy human needs. This explains why liberals have rarely questioned human dominion over nature. Lacking value in itself, nature is invested with value only when it is transformed by human labour, or when it is harnessed to human ends. This is reflected in Locke's theory that property rights derived from the fact that nature has, in effect, been mixed with labour. Nature is thus 'commodified', assigned an economic value, and it is drawn into the processes of the market economy. Indeed, in emphasizing the virtues of free-market capitalism, classical liberals have endorsed self-interested materialism and economic growth, a position that many ecologists have linked to the rapacious exploitation of nature. The anti-nature or anti-ecological biases of liberalism can be seen to stem from two main sources. First, liberalism is strongly anthropocentric, by virtue of its belief in individualism (see p. 154). Second, liberals have a strong faith in scientific rationality and technology, encouraging them to adopt a problem-solving approach to nature and to place a heavy reliance on human ingenuity. Nevertheless, alternative traditions within liberalism reflect a more positive approach to nature. These include a modern liberal stress on human flourishing, which may be facilitated through the contemplation of nature, and a utilitarian emphasis on maximizing happiness and minimizing suffering, a stance that may be applied to other species or to future generations of humans (Singer 1993).

Critical views

The two critical theories that address the issue of nature most explicitly are feminism and green politics. Feminists generally hold nature to be creative and benign. This is a view that is most closely associated with ecofeminism. For most ecofeminists, there is an essential or natural bond between women and nature. The fact that women bear children and suckle babies means that they cannot live separated from natural rhythms and processes and this, in turn, means that traditional 'female' values (reciprocity, cooperation, nurturing and so on) have a 'soft' or ecological character. While women are creatures of nature, men are creatures of culture: their world is synthetic or man-made, a product of human ingenuity rather than natural creativity. Environmental degradation is therefore an inevitable consequence of patriarchal power. From the perspective of green politics, nature is an interconnected whole which embraces humans and non-humans as well as the inanimate world. Nature thus embodies the principles of harmony and wholeness, implying that human fulfilment comes from a closeness to nature, not from attempts to dominate it. This holistic view is embraced most radically by deep ecologists, for whom nature is the source of all value. Nature is thus an ethical community, meaning that human beings are nothing more than 'plain citizens' who have no more rights and are no more deserving of respect than any other member of the community (Leopold 1968).

ated, with temperatures climbing quickly from normal interglacial levels. This time, however, climate change has been largely, and perhaps entirely, the result of human activity.

During the 1990s, the issue of global warming due to climate change achieved a higher and higher profile on the international environmental agenda. This was due to the fact that environmental groups, such as Greenpeace and Friends of the Earth, increasingly made efforts to stop global warming the primary focus of their activities and because the establishment of the International Panel on Climate Change (IPCC) meant that there was, for the first time, a source of authoritative scientific statements on the issue. This latter development largely put paid to the first and most basic debate about climate change: is it actually happening? Until about 2004–5, a 'denial lobby', sometimes funded by US oil companies, challenged the very idea of global warming, claiming that the data on temperature changes in the Earth's atmosphere was either inconclusive or contradictory. However, in 2005, a series of articles in the journal *Science* highlighted serious flaws in the data that had been used by 'denial lobbyists', helping to establish a new consensus: the world was getting hotter, and this was an incontrovertible fact. According to the IPCC's 2013 Fifth Assessment Report, eleven out of the twelve years between 1995 and 2006 ranked among the twelve warmest years since records began on global surface temperatures in 1850. It also pointed out that the so-called 'pause' in temperature increases since 1998 is too short to reflect a long-term trend. It is more significant that the linear warming trend over the fifty years from 1956 to 2005 was nearly twice that for the 100 years from 1906 to 2005. However, while the fact of global warming was becoming more difficult to deny, the factors accounting for it remained a matter of sometimes passionate dispute.

Climate change 'sceptics' (as opposed to 'deniers') have called into question the link between global warming and human activity, specifically the emission of 'greenhouse gases'. They had done this by emphasizing that the Earth's climate is naturally variable even during an interglacial period. For example, during the so-called 'little ice age', which lasted until the second half of the nineteenth century, Europe and North America suffered from bitterly cold winters and Iceland was frequently ice-locked. Others attempted to establish links between temperatures on Earth and factors such as solar sun spot activity. In the USA, the Bush administration (2001–9), while not denying the fact of global warming or that a proportion of it was anthropogenic, skilfully exploited scientific disagreement over the exact relationship between greenhouse gases and climate change to cast doubt on the value of the larger project of tackling climate change. While climate change sceptics exploited uncertainty and scientific disagreement to justify political inertia, committed environmentalists did precisely the opposite in applying the **precautionary principle**. Nevertheless, over time, the relationship between the emission of greenhouse gases and climate change became more difficult to question. This occurred both as the science of climate change was better understood in terms of the 'greenhouse effect' (see p. 404) and because of an increasingly clear correlation between the rate of global warming and the level of greenhouse gas emissions. Whereas in its Third Assessment Report in 2001, the IPCC stated that it was '*likely*' that temperature increases were due to the observed increase in anthropogenic greenhouse gas concentrations, in its Fourth Assessment Report in 2007, it declared that such a causal link was '*very likely*', meaning that it was more than 90 per cent certain. Needless to say, the debate

● Precautionary principle: The presumption in favour of action in relation to major ecological and other issues over which there is scientific uncertainty, based on the fact that the costs of inaction vastly exceed the cost of (possibly unnecessary) action.

● The term 'climate change' has gradually replaced 'global warming' in official discussions about the phenomenon, at national and international levels. For instance, whereas UN reports had previously used both terms, by the establishment of the 1992 FCCC, only one reference was made to the idea of 'warming' and none to 'global warming'.

Deconstructing . . .

'CLIMATE CHANGE'

● Although there may be scientific reasons to prefer the term 'climate change' (for example, it allows for the possibility that temperatures may fall as well as rise), it is also a less frightening term than 'global warming'. The latter is more emotionally charged and has perhaps catastrophic connotations attached to it. The blander and seemingly neutral 'climate change' has thus been preferred by politicians and states reluctant to take urgent action on the issue.

● 'Climate change' has the advantage of being vague, specifically about its origins, in that it seems to cover both natural and human-induced changes to the climate. This vagueness, in turn, has tended to support the idea that there is uncertainty and controversy about the causes and consequences of the phenomenon. By contrast, 'warming' implies that there is an agent doing the warming, thus suggesting that human activity is the likely cause of the problem.

about the causes of climate change was politically vital because this affected not only whether the problem could be addressed, but also how this should be done.

Consequences of climate change

The prominence of the issue of climate change is linked to the idea that, if unaddressed, it will have catastrophic implications for human welfare and, possibly, for the future of humankind. How serious will the consequences of global warming be? What will be the impact of long-term climate change? The consequences of living on a warmer planet have, at times, been as keenly disputed as whether global warming is actually taking place and whether it is linked to human activity. This was particularly true in the early period of climate change research, when the impact of increased greenhouse gas emissions was thought to lie many decades into the future, the case for addressing the issue being linked more to our obligations towards future generations than to a concern about the present generation. However, the impact of climate change has occurred earlier

GLOBAL ACTORS . . .

INTERGOVERNMENTAL PANEL ON CLIMATE CHANGE

Type: Intergovernmental organization • **Founded:** 1988 • **Location:** Geneva, Switzerland

The Intergovernmental Panel on Climate Change (IPCC) is an international panel of scientists and researchers that provide advice on climate change to the international community. The IPCC was established in 1988 by the World Meteorological Organization (WMO) and the United Nations Environment Programme (UNEP) to provide decision-makers and others interested in climate change with an objective source of information about an issue that had become increasingly complex and controversial. The IPCC does not conduct any research, neither does it monitor climate change-related data or parameters. Its role is to assess on a comprehensive, open and transparent basis the latest scientific, technical and socio-economic literature produced worldwide, with a view to better understanding (1) the risks of anthropocentric climate change, (2) its observed and projected impacts, and (3) options for adaptation and mitigation.

Significance: The most significant work of the IPCC is in publishing reports, the most important being Assessment Reports. Hundreds of scientists all over the world contribute to these reports as authors, contributors and reviewers, drawing mainly on reviewed and published scientific literature. Five Assessment Reports have been produced to date:

- *IPCC First Assessment Report* (1990). This played a

decisive role in leading to the FCCC.
- *IPCC Second Assessment Report* (1995). This provided a key input for the negotiations that led to the Kyoto Protocol in 1997.
- *IPCC Third Assessment Report* (2001). This provided further information relevant to the development of the FCCC and the Kyoto Protocol.
- *IPCC Fourth Assessment Report* (2007). This provided more evidence of the link between climate change and anthropogenic greenhouse gas concentrations.
- *IPCC Fifth Assessment Report* (2013). This concluded that it is 95 per cent certain that humans are the 'dominant cause' of global warming.

The wide membership of the IPCC, its reputation for objectivity and its reliance on worldwide scientific expertise gives the IPCC unrivalled influence in shaping how the international community understands, and responds to, the issue of climate change. In this respect, it has played the leading role in building a consensus amongst scientists and national politicians about the existence of climate change and the fact that it is a consequence of anthropogenic greenhouse gas emissions, and is therefore linked to the burning of fossil fuels. Its influence can thus be seen in the growing acceptance that climate change is an issue that demands the attention of the international

community, making it increasingly difficult for countries such Russia, Australia, the USA, China and India to remain outside the climate change regime. The IPCC was awarded the Nobel Peace Prize in 2006, together with Al Gore, the former US Vice President.

The IPCC has also attracted criticism, however. Some argue that its emphasis on already published scientific data and on exacting reviews (the Fourth Assessment Report took six years to produce) means that its judgements and conclusions are dangerously out of date, and therefore tend to underestimate the seriousness of the climate change challenge. The Summary for Policy Makers, the only bit of an Assessment Report that is read by most politicians and journalists, is a politically negotiated document that sometimes omits controversial judgements found in the larger report. Some scientists also challenge the basis on which IPCC projections and conclusions are developed; for example, IPCC projections about global warming are founded on assumptions about the capacity of the oceans to absorb carbon dioxide that many environmentalists dismiss as unsound. The IPCC has also been criticized for overstating its claims (not least the claim, found in the 2007 Report but retracted in 2010, that the Himalayan glaciers would disappear by 2035) and for sacrificing its reputation for scientific neutrality by being seen to campaign for radical cuts in emissions.

Focus on ...
The greenhouse effect

The concepts behind the greenhouse effect were first discussed in the nineteenth century by scientists such as the British physicist John Tyndall (1820–93) and the Swedish chemist Svante Arrhenius (1859–1927). The sun is the only source of external heat for the Earth. Sunlight passes through the atmosphere during the day, heating up the surface of the Earth and releasing heat in the form of long-wave, infrared radiation. However, the presence in the atmosphere of greenhouse gases means that this radiation is absorbed and trapped in the lower atmosphere, thereby heating the Earth's surface (see Figure 17.2). In effect, our world is a natural greenhouse. The impact of the greenhouse effect can be demonstrated by comparing temperatures on the Earth to those on the moon, which does not have an atmosphere and on which night-time temperatures fall as low as -173˚C. By contrast, on Venus, which has a thick, carbon dioxide atmosphere, surface temperatures reach a blistering 483˚C.

Needless to say, the greenhouse effect is not necessarily a bad thing: were it not for heat-trapping gases such as carbon dioxide, solar radiation would be reflected straight back into space, leaving the world in the iron grip of frost. However, it is widely accepted that the increased emission of anthropogenic greenhouse gases – carbon dioxide, methane and nitrous oxide, the gases recognized in the Kyoto Protocol – is contributing to a significant trend of global warming. These gas emissions are a direct consequence of industrial activity and specifically the burning of fossil fuels. Atmospheric levels of carbon dioxide, the most important greenhouse gas, have risen from 280 parts per million (ppm) in pre-industrial times to 384 ppm in 2007.

and more dramatically than was anticipated, meaning that it can no longer be treated merely as a 'future generations' issue. Nevertheless, anxieties about climate change continue to have a marked future-looking character, as, even if robust action were to be taken shortly, its effects are certain to be felt more severely by today's children and their children.

In its 2013 Assessment Report, the IPCC noted a range of changes to climatic conditions, including following:

- It is *likely* (66–100 per cent certainty) that 1983–2013 was the warmest 30-year period in the Northern Hemisphere for at least 1,400 years.
- It is *virtually certain* (99 to 100 per cent) that the upper 700 m of the Earth's oceans have warmed during the period 1971–2010.
- It can be said with *high confidence* that the Greenland and Antarctic ice sheets have been losing mass in the last two decades, and that glaciers have continued to shrink almost worldwide.
- It is *very likely* (90–100 per cent) that heatwaves will occur with higher frequency and duration, although occasional winter extremes will continue.

The human impact of climate change has been significant and is very likely to increase. Although more warmer days and nights and fewer colder days and nights over most land areas is likely to reduce human mortality from decreased cold exposure, most of the effects of climate change are negative. Increased tropical cyclone activity creates a greater risk of death and injury from flooding and

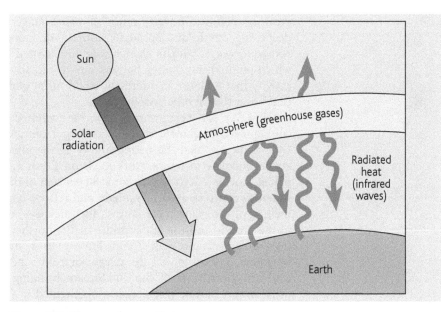

Figure 17.2 **The greenhouse effect**

from water- and food-borne diseases, and also leads to major displacement of populations. Since the mid-1990s, there has been a 40 per cent increase in Atlantic hurricane activities and, according to some scientists, the most powerful tropical cyclones now occur twice as often as they did thirty years ago. China has been particularly badly affected by flooding on the Yangtze, the Yellow River and on other rivers. The increased incidence of extreme high sea levels also causes a greater risk of death and injury by drowning, especially in the world's great river deltas, such as the Bengal delta in Bangladesh, the Mekong delta in Vietnam, the Nile delta in Egypt and the Yangtze delta in China. If current increases in sea level persist, one-sixth of the land area of Bangladesh could be lost to the sea by the middle of this century, if not earlier, leaving 13 per cent of the country's population with nowhere to live or farm. The prospects for people living in low-lying island groups, such as the Maldives, may be even bleaker, as these may disappear altogether. The greater incidence of drought and the advance of desertification will lead to an increased risk of food and water shortages, malnutrition and, once again, a greater risk of water- and food-borne diseases.

Climate change has affected all parts of the world, but it has not done so evenly. Africa and the Arctic (where sea-ice is shrinking by 2.7 per cent per decade) are likely to bear the brunt of climate impacts, along with low-lying small islands and the Asian river deltas. The IPCC estimates that by 2080, if current trends continue, anything from 1.2 to 3.2 billion people will be experiencing water scarcity, 200–600 million people will be malnourished or hungry and between 2 and 7 million people each year will be subject to coastal flooding. However, the effects of climate change will be truly global, not least through its impact on migration trends and economic development. An estimated 200–850 million people could be forced to move to more temperate zones by 2050 due to water shortages, sea level crises, deteriorating pasture land, conflict and famine, all linked to climate change. Together with widening gaps in birth rates and growing wealth-to-poverty ratios, climate change could therefore also lead to deepening ethnic and social tensions in developed societies. The economic consequences of climate change were highlighted by the Stern Review (2006), which pointed out that global warming could so disrupt economic and social activity that a failure to address it could mean global GDP being up to 20 per cent lower than it otherwise might be.

However, some environmentalists have painted still more dire images of the consequence of climate change, creating a number of 'catastrophe scenarios'. One of these is that the disappearance of the polar icecaps could result in an abrupt increase in temperature levels on Earth as white ice helps to keep the planet cool by reflecting back some 80 per cent of the sunlight that falls on it. Sea water, by contrast, absorbs sunlight and reflects back little. A second is that the melting of the planet's permafrost, the thick level of frozen soil covering much of the ground in the high latitudes of the northern hemisphere, could release trapped greenhouse gases, contributing to a major acceleration in global warming. A third is that the release of cold water through melting Artic ice could, in effect, 'turn off' the Gulf Stream, bringing freezing conditions to much of Northern Europe (the scenario highlighted in the 2004 Hollywood disaster movie *The Day After Tomorrow*). Others, however, have dismissed these catastrophe scenarios as scaremongering. The IPCC, for example, rates the likelihood of the Gulf Stream faltering during the twenty-first century as *'very unlikely'* (a probability of less than 10 per cent).

How should climate change be tackled?

The task of tackling climate change is notoriously difficult; some even fear that it may be impossible. It is instructive, in this respect, to compare efforts to deal with climate change with the response to the problem of ozone depletion. In the case of ozone depletion, there was little scientific disagreement about its cause (the emission of CFC gases from aerosols and other sources); there was general agreement that its consequences were negative and a recognition that they affected developed and developing states alike; and, most importantly, there was a straightforward solution available at an acceptable price – banning CFCs and switching to alternatives that could be developed economically. The Montreal Protocol of 1987 thus demonstrated how effective international cooperation on environmental matters can be. CFC emissions were reduced from the mid-1990s onwards, with a view to being completely phased out by 2030, allowing the ozone layer to recover completely by 2050. Climate change, by contrast, is profoundly difficult because its origins lie not in the use of particular substances or a specific productive process or set of commodities, but, arguably, in the process of industrialization itself. The burning of fossil fuels (coal, oil and natural gas) has not only been the basis for industrialization and thus the key to economic growth for the last 200 years or more, but it has also been the basis for greenhouse gas emissions that have resulted in global warming. Any serious attempt to address the problem of climate change must therefore either recast the nature of industrial society, providing an alternative to 'carbon industrialization', or make significant sacrifices in terms of economic growth and therefore material prosperity. How far has international cooperation on climate change progressed, and what obstacles stand in the way of effective international action?

International cooperation over climate change

The Rio 'Earth Summit' of 1992 was the first international conference to give significant attention to the issue of climate change. It did so by establishing the FCCC as a 'framework convention', calling for greenhouse gases to be stabilized at safe levels on the basis of equity and in accordance with states' 'common but differentiated responsibilities and respective capabilities'. The clear implication was that developed states should take the lead, committing themselves to restoring 1990 levels of emissions by the year 2000. However, although it was accepted by 181 governments, the FCCC was no more than a framework for further action and it contains no legally binding targets. This was just as well for developed states, whose carbon emissions continued to rise during the 1990s. The exclusion of developing states meant, in fact, that the rate of increase got steeper, particularly due to the economic emergence of China and India.

The most significant international agreement on climate change was the Kyoto Protocol to the FCCC, negotiated in 1997. The significance of the Kyoto Protocol was that it set binding targets for developed states to limit or reduce their greenhouse gas emissions by 2012. The targets were designed to reduce total emissions from the developed world to at least 5.2 per cent below their 1990 levels. National targets varied, however, with the EU and the USA being set targets for reductions of 8 per cent and 7 per cent, respectively, while other states, such as Australia, were allowed to exceed their 1990 levels. These targets were accompanied by 'flexibility mechanisms' that introduced a system of carbon trading that was designed to assist countries in meeting their targets. This established a 'cap and trade' approach to climate change, which has since become the dominant strategy for addressing the issue. Kyoto's strengths included that it introduced, for the first time, legally binding targets on greenhouse gas emissions, and by applying these targets to 37 developed states (so-called 'Annex 1' countries) it prepared the way for later participation of developing states, 137 of which ratified the Protocol. Furthermore, in providing a mechanism for **emissions trading**, it helped to promote the idea of carbon as a commodity and introduced a vital element of flexibility that made binding targets appear more acceptable. For example, emissions trading allows developed states to meet their targets in part through technology transfers and investment in the developing world, thereby, at least in theory, contributing to reducing their emissions levels. Critics of carbon trading nevertheless argue that it is a loophole that allows countries to exceed their targets and not take climate change sufficiently seriously, especially as the system is difficult to police and has given rise to many allegations of abuse.

However, the Kyoto Protocol also had significant limitations. In the first place, the targets set at Kyoto were, arguably, inadequate in terms of achieving the Protocol's goals of preventing 'dangerous anthropogenic interference with the climate system'. For example, the EU, which has taken a leading role in the campaign to address climate change, had called for greenhouse gas cuts of 15 per cent by 2010, almost three times greater than the Kyoto cuts and over a shorter time span. Second, the USA's failure to ratify the treaty, first through the Clinton administration's fear that the US Senate would not ratify the treaty and later through the Bush administration's outright opposition, dealt Kyoto a fatal blow and set the process of tackling climate change back for over a decade. This was

● **Emissions trading**: A mechanism that allows parties to the Kyoto Protocol to buy or sell emissions from or to other parties, while keeping within overall emissions targets.

not only because the USA, then the world's largest emitter, accounted for about 25 per cent of all greenhouse gas emissions, but also because US non-participation ensured that developing states, and especially China and India, would remain outside the Kyoto process. Third, the decision to restrict binding targets to developed states alone seriously compromised the Kyoto process from the outset. The USA consistently used the exclusion of China and India as a justification for its non-participation. Moreover, China's carbon emissions continued to rise steeply, and have exceeded those of the USA since 2008, meaning that climate change could no longer be seen merely as a developed world problem.

While the Kyoto Protocol was never going to be the solution to climate change, it provided a perhaps necessary first step along the road. Nevertheless, the faltering progress associated with Kyoto meant that, by 2005, global carbon dioxide emissions were rising four times faster than they were in the 1990s. One consequence of this has been a shift in emphasis away from 'mitigation' towards 'mitigation and adaptation'. Key 'mitigation' technologies and practices identified in the 2007 IPCC Assessment Report include the following:

- Fuel switching from coal to gas
- The wider use of nuclear power
- The greater use of renewable heat and power (hydropower, solar, wind, geothermal and bio-energy)
- Early applications of carbon dioxide capture and storage (e.g. storage of CO_2 removed from natural gas)
- More fuel-efficient vehicles, such as hybrid and cleaner diesel vehicles
- Shifts from road transport to rail, public transport and non-motorized transport (cycling, walking).

The same report nevertheless highlights a range of 'adaptation' strategies, including the following:

- The relocation of settlements, especially coastal zones
- Improved sea walls and storm surge barriers
- Expanded rainwater harvesting and improved water storage and conservation techniques
- Adjustment of planting dates and crop varieties
- Crop relocation and improved land management (e.g. erosion control and soil protection through tree planting)
- Improved climate-sensitive disease surveillance and control.

● **Mitigation**: Moderating or reducing the impact of something; in particular, reducing greenhouse gas emissions in order to limit climate change.

● **Adaptation**: Changing in the light of new circumstances; in particular, learning to live with climate change.

Nevertheless, there were signs that greater scientific agreement on the existence, causes and implications of climate change, together with shifting public attitudes, in part through the work of environmental NGOs, had strengthened international cooperation on the issue. Russia ratified the Kyoto Protocol in 2004, as did Australia in 2007 (although Russia, together with Canada, Japan and New Zealand withdrew from the Kyoto process in 2012). Most significantly, the election of Barack Obama in 2008, together with Democrat control of both houses of Congress (until 2011), appeared to mark a key shift in US policy, creating a willingness to participate in formulating a successor to the Kyoto Protocol, which was due to run out in 2012. What is more, despite China's unapologetic

GLOBAL POLITICS IN ACTION . . .

Climate change after the Kyoto Protocol

Events: The 1997 Kyoto Protocol (to the UNFCCC) marked the first use of binding targets to reduce greenhouse gas emissions. The Protocol entered into force in 2005, and its first commitment period ended in 2012. The principal attempt to construct a post-Kyoto Protocol climate change framework was undertaken at the 2009 UN Climate Change Conference in Copenhagen. However, the Copenhagen conference failed to create any new legally-binding obligations on any country to cut its emissions, even failing to establish any non-legal targets for national or global emissions reductions. The 2011 United Nations Climate Change Conference in Durban, South Africa, nevertheless appeared to get the post-Kyoto process back on track, by supporting a plan for a new treaty to be agreed in Paris in late 2015, and to come into force in 2020, with the Kyoto Protocol continuing to operate until then. Although the 2012 United Nations Climate Change Conference in Doha, Qatar, did not consider the shape of the new treaty, agreement was reached on extending the life of the Kyoto Protocol until 2020.

Significance: Pessimists view this catalogue of failure, delay and obfuscation as a stark abandonment of responsibility on the part of the international community. Extending the life of the Kyoto Protocol achieves little because the treaty is so clearly flawed. Not only did the USA (then the world's largest carbon emitter) never ratify the treaty, and the entire developing world including China (which, in 2008, overtook the USA as the world's largest emitter) remained outside Kyoto's target regime, but, through its 'flexible mechanisms', Kyoto provided a range of loopholes which parties could exploit to fulfil their targets. Thus, although most of the parties to Kyoto met their commitments easily, worldwide emissions have surged by 50 per cent since 1990, driven by economic growth in China and other parts of Asia, South America and Africa. Optimists, nevertheless, questioned this bleak assessment, pointing to a record of slow, but meaningful, progress. For all its limitations, Kyoto was a vital first step, both marking the first use of legally binding emissions targets and introducing the 'cap and trade' systems and carbon taxes that have subsequently been taken up in Europe, Australia, Japan, China, California and parts of Canada. Copenhagen moved beyond Kyoto, in that the USA and China were full participants in the climate change process. Durban formally

endorsed the idea of a post-Kyoto treaty, and Doha established the principle that rich countries should compensate poor countries for 'loss and damage' due to climate change, while resisting the idea of legal liability.

Nevertheless, the task of developing a successor to Kyoto remains fraught with problems. These include conflict between the developed world and the developing world over burden sharing. The former emphasizes the need for targets to reflect current emissions levels, as developing countries have, since 2012, been responsible for more than half the world's carbon emissions. The latter argues that targets should reflect the historic responsibility of developed countries for the carbon emitted since the beginning of the industrial revolution. Progress at Copenhagen, Durban, Doha and elsewhere has also been made more difficult by great power rivalries, particularly between the USA and China. Perhaps the most fundamental problem, nevertheless, is that reductions in greenhouse gas emissions that are sufficient to mitigate the effect of climate change are both costly (because of the need to develop alternatives to carbon-based production) and threaten to impede growth and therefore prosperity. Short- and medium-term economic self-interest therefore tend to be given priority over longer-term environmental concerns (despite growing evidence of the economic costs associated with climate change). States thus have an incentive to do as little as possible about climate change, in the hope that others will shoulder the burden, especially in the context of the 2007–09 global financial crisis and its aftermath.

emphasis on largely coal-based industrial growth, the environmental costs of carbon industrialization have become increasingly apparent, through, for instance, heavily polluted cities (eight out of ten of the world's most polluted cities are in China), shrinking glaciers on the Tibet-Qinghai plateau and falling water tables across the country. This created a growing likelihood that China and other developing countries would be more willing to address the issue of climate change and recognize that they have an interest in tackling it. This was the context in which the UN began to consider the shape of the post-Kyoto climate change regime, starting with the 2009 Climate Change Conference in Copenhagen. However, the outcomes of this process have widely been seen as disappointing, highlighting yet again the difficulties of achieving international agreement on the issue of climate change.

Why is international cooperation so difficult to achieve?

Effective international action to tackle climate change will only occur if solutions are found to a series of obstacles to international cooperation. The most significant of these obstacles are the following:

- Conflict between the collective good and national interests
- Tensions between developed and developing states
- Economic obstacles
- Ideological obstacles.

The issue of climate change can be seen as a classic example of the 'tragedy of the commons'. What countries accept would be generally beneficial to all of them may not be the same as what benefits each of them individually. Clean air and a healthy atmosphere are therefore **collective goods**, key elements of the 'global commons'. However, tackling global warming imposes costs on individual states in terms of investment in sometimes expensive mitigation and adaptation strategies, as well as accepting lower levels of economic growth. In such circumstances, states are encouraged to be 'free riders', enjoying the benefits of a healthier atmosphere without having to pay for them. It is entirely rational, therefore, for each actor to try to 'pay' as little as possible to overcome the problem of climate change. This creates a situation in which states are either unwilling to agree to binding targets, or if targets, binding or otherwise, are developed, these are likely to be set below the level needed to deal effectively with the problem. Moreover, the more economically developed a state is, the greater will be the costs incurred in tackling climate change, and the more reluctant such states will be to undertake concerted action. Democracy, in such a context, may create further problems, particularly as party competition tends to be orientated around rival claims about the ability to deliver growth and prosperity.

The second problem is that the issue of climate change exposes significant divisions between the developed world and the developing world. Climate change, in other words, serves to widen the North–South divide (see p. 367). One source of tension is that current emissions levels arguably provide an unfair guide for setting targets because of 'outsourcing'. The transfer of much of manu-

● **Collective good**: A general benefit from which individuals cannot be excluded and, as a result, for which beneficiaries have no incentive to pay.

KEY THEORISTS IN GREEN POLITICS

Ernst Friedrich Schumacher (1911–77)

A German-born UK economist and environmental thinker, Schumacher championed the cause of human-scale production and advanced a 'Buddhist' economic philosophy (economics 'as if people mattered') that stresses the importance of morality and 'right livelihood'. His key work is *Small is Beautiful* (1973).

Arne Naess (1912–2009)

A Norwegian philosopher who was influenced by the teachings of Spinoza, Gandhi and Buddha, Naess was the leading advocate of 'deep ecology', arguing that ecology should be concerned with every part of nature on an equal basis, because natural order has an intrinsic value. His writings include *Ecology, Community and Lifestyle* (1989).

Garrett Hardin (1915–2003)

A US ecologist and microbiologist, Hardin is best known for the idea of the 'tragedy of the commons', which calls attention to 'the damage that innocent actions by individuals can inflict on the environment'. He developed an uncompromising form of ecologism that warned against the dangers of population growth and excessive freedom. Hardin's chief works include *The Tragedy of the Commons* (1968) and *Lifeboat Ethics* (1974).

Murray Bookchin (1921–2006)

A US libertarian socialist, Bookchin highlighted parallels between anarchism and ecology through the idea of 'social ecology', and was also strongly critical of the 'mystical' ideas of deep ecology, which he dubbed 'eco-la-la'. His major works in this field include *The Ecology of Freedom* ([1982]) and *Re-Enchanting Humanity* (1995).

Carolyn Merchant (born 1936)

A US ecofeminist philosopher and historian of science, Merchant portrays female nature as the benevolent mother of all undermined by the 'dominion' model of nature that emerged out of the scientific revolution and the rise of market society. Her main works include *The Death of Nature* (1983) and *Radical Ecology* (1992).

Vandana Shiva (born 1952)

An Indian ecofeminist activist and nuclear physicist, Shiva is a trenchant critic of the biotechnology industry. She argues that the advance of globalization has threatened biodiversity and deepened poverty, particularly among women. Her writings include *Monocultures of the Mind* (1993) and *Stolen Harvest* (1999).

See also James Lovelock

facturing industry to the developing world means that over one-third of carbon dioxide emissions associated with the consumption of goods and services in many developed countries are actually emitted outside their borders. Deeper divisions nevertheless stem from rival approaches to the problem of burden-sharing in the area of climate change. From a Southern perspective, the developed world has a historic responsibility for the accumulated stock of carbon emitted since the beginning of the industrial age. In effect, developed countries have used up a large part of the safe carbon-absorbing capacity of the atmosphere, and made substantial gains in terms of economic growth and prosperity as a result. Developing countries, by contrast, are both disproportionately badly affected by climate change and have the fewest capabilities to tackle it, whether through mitigation or adaptation. This implies either that emissions targets should not be imposed on developing countries (as at Kyoto), or that any such targets should take account of historic responsibilities and be structured accordingly, imposing significantly heavier burdens on developed countries than on developing ones.

From a Northern perspective, however, countries cannot be held responsible for actions whose consequences were quite unknown at the time they were carried out, and, anyway, those who were responsible are largely dead and gone. In this view, targets should be set in line with *current* emission levels alone, in which case developed and developing countries would be treated alike. Apart from anything else, the growing importance of emerging economies such as China, India and Brazil means that unless the developing world plays a significant role in cutting emissions global targets will be impossible to meet. Nevertheless, tensions between developed and developing countries are even more acute if population size and per capita income are taken into account. For instance, although China has overtaken the USA as the world's foremost emitter, per capita emissions in the USA remain almost four times higher than in China (19.2 tons against 4.9 tons in 2010). Southern thinking on the matter tends to be rights-based, reflecting both the idea that each human being has an equal right to the world's remaining carbon space and the idea of a right to development (already exercised by the developed North). This suggests that emissions targets should clearly favour the developing world, where most of the world's people live, as well as most of the world's poor. Critics of the rights-based approach to tackling climate change nevertheless argue that it introduces egalitarian assumptions that do not apply to other aspects of life. For example, why should the use of the world's remaining carbon space be allocated equally when there is no agreement on the wider issue that natural resources should be equally shared?

Radical ecologists, including both social ecologists and deep ecologists, tend to argue that inadequate progress in responding to climate change has much deeper, and perhaps structural, roots. The problem is not simply a manifestation of the difficulty of bringing about international cooperation but, rather, is about the underlying economic and ideological forces that have shaped capitalist modernity. As far as economic factors are concerned, criticism usually focuses on the anti-ecological tendencies of the capitalist system, at both national and global levels. In particular, profit-maximizing businesses will always be drawn towards the most easily available and cheapest source of energy: fossil fuels. Short-term profitability will dominate their thinking, rather than issues to do

Debating...
Can only radical action tackle the problem of climate change?

The divide in green politics between radicals and reformists is clearly reflected in competing approaches to tackling climate change. While some argue in favour of structural economic and ideological change, others champion less radical, and less painful, options.

YES

Dangerous delays. There is a wide and growing gap between the recognition of the problem of global warming and the introduction of effective international action. The failings of Rio, Kyoto and Copenhagen therefore mean that modest emissions cuts are no longer adequate. The general consensus is that global temperature rises of more than 2°C would mark the 'tipping point' in terms of dangerous human impact, while, according to the IPCC's 2013 prediction, these may increase by up to 4.8°C.

Myth of 'easy' solutions. Sadly, the strategies that are the least economically and politically problematical are also the least effective. Renewable energy sources are likely to make only a minor contribution to reducing the use of fossil fuels. Carbon trading has failed to produce significant emissions reductions. Technological 'fixes' for climate change, such as the use of so-called bio-fuels, carbon storing, 'clean' coal and nuclear power, have often proved to be expensive, ineffective or are associated with other environmental costs.

Economic restructuring. It is difficult to see how global warming can be addressed without changes being introduced to the economic system that has caused it. Market capitalism has proved to be a highly effective way of generating wealth, but it is, arguably, the enemy of ecological sustainability. Although ecosocialists' ideas have been increasingly derided, many environmentalists call for a radical restructuring of capitalism, in particular through the strengthening of state intervention to impose sustainable practices.

Post-material society. Economic restructuring is impossible if the values and appetites that sustain industrial society and 'growthism' go unchallenged. Concerted action on climate change thus has to have a cultural and psychological dimension. Materialism must be overthrown as the demand for 'more and more' is displaced by a steady-state economy based on 'enough'. Only if values and sensibilities alter will policy-makers at national and international levels have the political space to develop meaningful solutions to the problem.

NO

Exaggerated fears. Concern about climate change has been driven by a kind of environmental hysteria. Environmental NGOs try to grab public attention and shift attitudes by highlighting 'doomsday scenarios'. The mass media often conspire in this process to make the coverage of current affairs 'sexy' and attention-grabbing. Policy-makers may therefore adopt radical strategies, not so much to deal with the problem of climate change, but rather to allay public anxieties about the issue.

Adapt to change. Most environmentalists view global warming simply as something that must be stopped, based on the assumption that all of its impacts are negative. However, climate change may bring opportunities (new tourist destinations, improved plant viability and so on), as well as challenges. Moreover, the cost of stopping its negative impact may be unacceptably high. In these circumstances, it may be easier and more cost-effective to understand the implications of global warming and find ways of living with it.

Market solutions. Capitalism is resolutely not anti-green. Capitalism's environmental credentials are reflected in its responsiveness to more eco-sensitive consumer pressures, and the recognition that long-term corporate profitability can only be ensured in the context of sustainable development. Further, carbon usage is best discouraged not through strictures and prohibitions, but by market mechanisms that disincentivize carbon usage and incentivize the development of low-carbon or carbon-neutral technologies.

Human ingenuity. The capacity for innovation and creativity that lay behind carbon industrialization can surely be harnessed to build carbon-neutral businesses, industries and societies. Although investment in renewable energy sources is currently insufficient, its potential is enormous, especially if technology such as super-efficient wind turbines is utilized. Solar power plants, using solar cells, are becoming increasingly common in many parts of the world, and zero-carbon 'eco-cities' are being built in China, Abu Dhabi and elsewhere.

CONCEPT

Geopolitics

Geopolitics is an approach to foreign policy analysis that understands the actions, relationships and significance of states in terms of geographical factors, such as location, climate, natural resources, physical terrain and population. The field of geopolitics was significantly shaped by Alfred Mahan (1840–1914), who argued that the state that controls the seas would control world politics, and Halford Mackinder (1861–1947), who suggested, by contrast, that control of the land mass between Germany and central Siberia is the key to controlling world politics. Critics of geopolitics have usually objected to its geographical determinism, which appears to imply that in international politics 'geography is destiny'. The rise of globalization is sometimes seen to have made geopolitics obsolete.

● **Resource security:** Security understood in terms of access to energy and other resources sufficient to meet a state's economic and military needs.

● **Resource war:** A war that is fought to gain or retain control of resources which are important to economic development and political power.

with ecological sustainability. In this view, 'green capitalism' is merely a contradiction in terms. At an ideological level, countries' attachment to carbon industrialization may, in the final analysis, be a manifestation of the materialist values that dominate modern society, creating, deep ecologists argue, a profound disjuncture between humankind and nature. Materialism and consumerism mean that the economic and political systems are geared towards economic growth and the quest for rising living standards. From this perspective, the difficulties of tackling climate change stem not only from the problem of persuading people to forego at least a measure of their material prosperity, but, more challengingly, from the task of encouraging people to revise their values.

RESOURCE SECURITY

Although climate change has tended, since the late 1980s, to be the pre-eminent issue on the global environmental agenda, it is by no means the only important issue. Indeed, over very much the same period, non-renewable resources, and particularly energy resources, have come to be seen as having a growing bearing on matters such as security, development and conflict. In fact, in many ways, climate change and **resource security** have become counter-balancing priorities for states. For example, while climate change encourages states to reduce their use of fossil fuels, the quest for resource security encourages them to seek and to exploit new fossil fuel reserves. On the other hand, environmentalists have presented investment in renewable resources and non-carbon technologies as a 'green' road to resource security, although this only applies if such alternatives genuinely have the capacity to generate the same energy levels as fossil fuels. What is clear, though, is that concerns over the adequacy of natural resources to sustain human populations and ensure national power long predate concerns over climate change. They can be traced back to Thomas Malthus' (see p. 415) gloomy prediction that, due to the 'principle of population', living standards in any country would always return to subsistence levels. Although technological innovation and the discovery of new resources have tended to keep Malthusian pessimism at bay, history has been characterized by periods of anxiety, sometimes bordering on panic, over scarce resources. For example, in the nineteenth century the earliest industrial powers scrambled for control over sources of iron and coal, while after WWI the major European powers engaged in a desperate search for foreign sources of petroleum.

Anxieties about resources, nevertheless, subsided during the 1970s and 1980s, due both to the discovery of new, and seemingly abundant, fossil fuel supplies and because accelerated globalization appeared to have created larger and more responsive markets for energy and other resources. However, they have revived with particular force since the 1990s, moving the issue especially of energy security significantly up the international agenda. A growing number of wars, for example, appeared to be **resource wars** (Klare 2001). Geopolitics, once thought dead, had suddenly revived. Why did this happen? At least three developments help to explain it. First, the demand for energy, particularly oil, gas and coal, rose sharply through the arrival of new contenders on the global resources playing-field, notably China and India, but also, to a lesser extent, Brazil and other emerging economies. Second, the world's leading energy consumer, the USA, became increasingly concerned about its dwindling

Thomas Malthus (1766–1834)

A UK political economist and clergyman. Malthus was brought up according to the Enlightenment ideas of thinkers such as Jean-Jacques Rousseau (1712–78) and David Hume (1711–76). He became a Church of England minister in 1788. Malthus is best known for the views set out in his pamphlet, later expanded into a book in many editions, the *Essay on Population* (1798). Its key argument was that (unchecked) population growth will always exceed the growth of the means of subsistence, because population growth is exponential (or geometric) while the growth in the supply of food and other essentials is merely arithmetical. Population growth would therefore always result in famine, disease and war. While some have argued that Malthus' predictions were fundamentally flawed, as they took no account of improvements in agricultural and other technologies, others have suggested that his predictions have merely been postponed.

supplies of cheap domestic oil and its growing reliance on increasingly expensive, and less secure, foreign oil. Third, just as demand pressures intensified, anxieties concerns resurfaced. Fears grew generally that the world's stockpile of essential commodities had started to shrink, and these focused particularly on oil (Deffeyes 2005). Concern was raised not only by the seeming failure of new oil supplies to keep pace with burgeoning demand, but also, more alarmingly, by predictions (debunked by some) that the moment of **peak oil** may soon be reached. The world's oil may be running out, without any alternative energy source, renewable or non-renewable, appearing to be capable of replacing it. Such developments have both contributed to important shifts in global power, as well as created turbulence and often conflict in countries 'blessed' by abundant supplies of oil and other resources.

Resources, power and prosperity

The link between resources and global power can be seen in the emergence of a new international energy order. In this, a state's ranking in the hierarchy of states may no longer be measured by conventional economic and military capabilities (see Elements of national power, p. 219), but by the vastness of its oil and gas reserves and its ability to mobilize other sources of wealth in order to purchase (or otherwise acquire) the resources of energy-rich countries (Klare 2008). This notion divides the world into energy-surplus and energy-deficit states, and further divides them on the basis of the level of their surplus and deficit. The key players in this international energy order are the USA, China and India, all energy-deficit countries, and Russia, an energy-surplus country. As far as the USA is concerned, a context of dwindling domestic reserves of oil and rising international prices has encouraged it to strengthen its geopolitical influence in the area with the most abundant oil supplies, the Gulf region. Many have thus argued that the 1991 Gulf War and the 2003 invasion of Iraq were, in significant ways, motivated by such considerations about oil. One dimension of the 'war on terror' (see p. 230) may therefore have been the USA's concerns about energy security (Heinberg 2006).

● **Peak oil:** The point at which the maximum rate of petroleum extraction is reached.

Focus on ...
The paradox of plenty: resources as a curse?

Are resources a blessing or a curse? Why are countries and areas that are richly endowed with natural resources often amongst the poorest and most troubled in the world? In the first place, natural resources can be seen to create a number of economic imbalances and difficulties. These include increased volatility in government revenues, which can lead to inflation and boom-and-bust cycles in government spending. Damage can be caused to other economic sectors as revenues from natural resource exports push up wages and the exchange rate (this is sometimes called the 'Dutch disease', from the fact that the discovery of natural gas in the Netherlands the 1960s led to declines in manufacturing industries). There can also be a dangerous lack of economic diversification, as other industries fail to develop because they cannot match the profitability levels of natural resources.

Second, natural resources can also have a damaging impact on the nature and quality of governance. This occurs both because huge flows of money from natural resources tend to fuel political corruption and because, as resource-rich countries have less need to raise revenue from the general public, they often pay little attention to popular pressures. There is therefore a link between abundant natural resources and authoritarianism. Third, natural resources can, and often do, breed conflict and civil strife. Conflict tends to occur over the control and exploitation of resources as well as over the allocation of their revenues, meaning that resource-rich societies are more prone to ethnic conflict, separatist uprisings and general warlordism. While 'diamond wars' have been common, if usually relatively brief, in Africa, oil-related conflicts, ranging from low-level secessionist struggles to full-blown civil wars, have occurred in countries as different as Algeria, Colombia, Sudan, Indonesia, Nigeria and Equatorial Guinea.

The economic emergence of China and India, sometimes collectively referred to in this context as 'Chindia', has transformed the world markets for oil, natural gas, coal, uranium and other primary sources of energy, as well as industrial commodities such as iron ore, copper, aluminium and tin. As far as China is concerned, the search for energy security has had implications for both domestic and foreign policy. Domestically, it has encouraged China to crack down on separatist movements and strengthen political control over western and southwestern provinces such as Xinjiang and Tibet, which may provide access to central Asia and its rich supplies of oil and other resources. China's burgeoning external influence has focused on strengthening diplomatic ties with oil-rich countries such as Iran and, most clearly, undertaking massive investment in Africa, the home of the world's largest untapped energy and mineral supplies. China leads the modern 'scramble for resources' in Africa which, in some respects, resembles the late nineteenth-century 'scramble for colonies'. The new international energy order has particularly favoured Russia as the world's foremost energy-surplus state. Russia thus emerged from the collapse of communism and a decade of post-communist turmoil as an energy superpower. It now operates as a key power broker of Eurasian energy supplies, being able to exert substantial leverage through the growing dependency of EU and other states on Russian oil and natural gas. However, the quest for energy security has also encouraged Russia to strengthen its control over its 'near abroad' and especially

● **Resource curse:** The tendency for countries and regions with an abundance of natural resources to experience low growth, blocked development and, sometimes, civil strife.

over the oil-rich Caucasus region. This, for example, may have been one of the factors contributing to Russia's 2008 invasion of Georgia.

Natural resources, finally, are generally considered to be an unmixed blessing, widely being seen as one of the key components of national power. Energy, mineral and other resources provide a country not only with the basis for long-term economic development, but also with a means of gaining income from, and exercising influence over, other countries. Examples such as Saudi Arabia and other oil-rich Gulf states, Venezuela, Kazakhstan and, of course, Russia appear to bear this out. However, in practice, natural resources often bring as many problems as they bring blessings. This can be seen in the fact that many of the poorest and most troubled parts of the world are also characterized by abundant supplies of energy and minerals, with sub-Saharan Africa and the Middle East being obvious examples. This has lead to the idea of the 'resource curse', sometimes called the 'paradox of plenty' (see p. 416).

SUMMARY

- The environment is often seen as the archetypal example of a global issue. The intrinsically transnational character of environmental processes means that countries are peculiarly environmentally vulnerable to the environmental activities that take place in other countries. Meaningful progress on environmental issues can therefore often only be made at the international or even global level.

- Disagreements about the seriousness and nature of environmental problems, and about how they can best be tackled, are rooted in deeper, often philosophical debates about the relationship between humankind and the natural world. Reformist and radical strategies are influenced by contrasting views about whether human needs (anthropocentrism) or larger ecological balances (ecocentrism) should take precedence.

- Climate change has dominated the international environmental agenda since the early 1990s. Although some disagreement persists, there has been a growing consensus that climate change is happening, and that it is the product of human activity, notably the emission, since the beginning of the industrial age, of greenhouse gases. However, substantial disagreement persists both about its consequences (and so the seriousness of the problem) and, most particularly, about how it should be tackled.

- Effective international action to tackle climate change is hampered by a variety of obstacles to international cooperation. The most significant of these are: (perhaps fundamental) conflict between national self-interest and the common good; tensions of various kinds between developed and developing states; biases within capitalism in favour of growth; and a deeply-rooted ethic of materialism and consumerism.

- Energy resources have come to be seen as having a growing bearing on matters such as security, development and conflict, particularly as access to oil, gas and coal has become a crucial factor in determining the shape of twenty-first-century world order. However, it is by no means clear that natural resources are always a source of national power, in that resources may be a 'curse' when they, for instance, create economic imbalances and attract unwanted foreign interference.

Questions for discussion

- Why have environmental issues become an increasingly major focus of international concern?
- How does 'shallow' ecology differ from 'deep' ecology?
- What are the implications of the idea of sustainable development?
- Do we have obligations towards future generations and, if so, what does this imply?
- Can it any longer be doubted that climate change stems from human activity?
- Have the negative consequences of climate change been exaggerated?
- Should developed countries take primary responsibility for tackling climate change?
- Should greenhouse gas emissions targets be set on a per capita basis?
- Do concerns about resource security always conflict with those about climate change?
- To what extent are natural resources a 'curse'?

Further reading

Betsill, M., K. Hochstetler and D. Stevis (eds), *International Environmental Politics* (2006). An authoritative collection of essays that review the key debates in international environmental politics.

Dessler, A. and E. Parson, *The Science and Politics of Global Climate Change* (2010). A clear and accessible introduction to the nature of global climate change and the challenges it poses.

Elliott, L., *The Global Politics of the Environment* (2004). A comprehensive and detailed examination of the nature and development of global environmental issues.

Laferrière, E. and P. Stoett, *International Relations Theory and Ecological Thought: Towards a Synthesis* (1999). A stimulating examination of the overlaps between international relations theory and ecophilosophy.

ONLINE RESOURCES AVAILABLE

Links to relevant web resources can be found on the *Global Politics* website

CHAPTER 18

Introducing Global Politics

> *'Only connect!'*
>
> E. M. FORSTER, *Howards End* (1910)

PREVIEW How should we approach the study of world affairs? How is the world best understood? World affairs have traditionally been understood on the basis of an *international* paradigm. In this view, states (often understood as 'nations', hence 'international') are taken to be the essential building blocks of world politics, meaning that world affairs boil down, essentially, to the relations between states. This suggests that once you understand the factors that influence how states interact with one another, you understand how the world works. However, since the 1980s, an alternative *globalization* paradigm has become fashionable. This reflects the belief that world affairs have been transformed in recent decades by the growth of global interconnectedness and interdependence. In this view, the world no longer operates as a disaggregated collection of states, or 'units', but rather as an integrated whole, as 'one world'. Global politics, as understood in this book, attempts to straddle these rival paradigms. It accepts that it is equally absurd to dismiss states and national government as irrelevant in world affairs as it is to deny that, over a significant range of issues, states now operate in a context of global interdependence. However, in what sense is politics now 'global'? And how, and to what extent, has globalization reconfigured world politics? Our understanding of global politics also needs to take account of the different theoretical 'lenses' though which the world has been interpreted; that is, different ways of *seeing* the world. What, in particular, is the difference between mainstream perspectives on global politics and critical perspectives? Finally, the world stubbornly refuses to stand still. Global politics is therefore an arena of ongoing and, many would argue, accelerating change. And yet, certain aspects of global politics appear to have an enduring character. What is the balance between continuity and change in global politics?

KEY ISSUES
- How do 'the global' and 'the international' complement one another?
- How have the contours of world politics changed in recent years?
- What have been the implications of globalization for world politics?
- How do mainstream approaches to global politics differ from critical approaches?
- How has global politics changed in recent years in relation to the issues of power, security and justice?

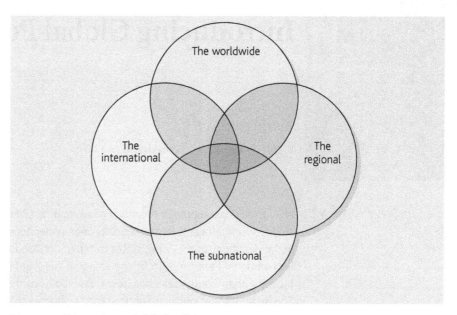

Figure 18.1 **Dimensions of global politics**

FROM 'THE INTERNATIONAL' TO 'THE GLOBAL'?

The aim of this book is to provide an up-to-date, integrated and forward-looking introduction to international relations/ global politics.(see p. 3). It seeks to be genuinely global while not ignoring the international dimension of world affairs, accepting that 'the global' and 'the international' complement one another and are not rival or incompatible modes of understanding. In this view, global politics encompasses not just politics at the 'global' level – that is, world-wide processes, systems and institutional frameworks – but politics at, and, crucially, across, *all* levels – the worldwide, the regional, the national and the subnational (see Figure 18.1). Such an approach reflects the fact that while, over an increasing range of issues, **states** interact with one another in conditions of global interdependence, they nevertheless remain the key actors on the world stage.

However, if the international paradigm, in which world affairs boil down, essentially, to relations between and among states, no longer constitutes an adequate basis for understanding, what has changed, and how profound have these changes been? How have the contours of world politics changed in recent years? The most significant changes have been the following:

- The emergence of new global actors
- The growth of interdependence and interconnectedness
- The erosion of the domestic/international divide
- The rise of global governance.

● **State**: A political association that enjoys sovereign jurisdiction within defined territorial borders.

Focus on . . .
Defining global politics?

What does it mean to suggest that politics has 'gone global'? How does 'global' politics differ from 'international' politics? The term 'global' has two meanings. In the first, global means *worldwide*, having planetary (not merely regional or national) significance. The globe is, in effect, the world. Global politics, in this sense, refers to politics that is conducted at a global rather than a national or regional level. It therefore focuses primarily on the work of organizations such as the United Nations (UN) and the World Trade Organization (WTO), which have a near universal membership, and on issues (such as the environment and the economy) where interconnectedness has gone so far that events and developments affect, actually or potentially, all parts of the world and so all people on the planet.

In the second meaning (the one used in this book), global means *comprehensive*; it refers to *all* elements within a system, not just to the system as a whole. While such an approach acknowledges that a significant (and, perhaps, growing) range of political interactions now takes place at the global level, it rejects the idea that the global level has, in any sense, *transcended* politics at the national, local or, for that matter, any other level. In particular, the advent of global politics does not imply that international politics should be consigned to the dustbin of history. This is important because the notion that politics has been caught up in a swirl of interconnectedness that effectively absorbs all of its parts, or 'units', into an indivisible, global whole, is difficult to sustain.

From state-centrism to the mixed-actor model?

World politics has conventionally been understood in international terms. Although the larger phenomenon of patterns of conflict and cooperation between and among territorially-based political units has existed throughout history, the term 'international relations' was not coined until the UK philosopher and legal reformer, Jeremy Bentham (1748–1832), used it in his *Principles of Morals and Legislation* ([1789] 1968). Bentham's use of the term acknowledged a significant shift: that, by the late eighteenth century, territorially-based political units were coming to have a more clearly national character, making relations between them appear genuinely 'inter-national'. However, although most modern states are either nation-states (see p. 168) or aspire to be nation-states, it is their possession of statehood rather than nationhood that allows them to act effectively on the world stage. 'International' politics should thus, more properly, be described as 'inter-state' politics. But what is a state? As defined by the 1933 Montevideo Convention on the Rights and Duties of States, a state must possess four qualifying properties: a defined territory, a permanent population, an effective government, and the 'capacity to enter into relations with other states'. In this view, states, or countries (the terms can be used interchangeably in this context); are taken to be the key actors on the world stage, and perhaps the only ones that warrant serious consideration. This is why the conventional approach to world politics is seen as **state-centric**, and why the international system is often portrayed as a **state-system**. The origins of this view of international politics are usually traced back to the Peace of Westphalia (1648), which established sovereignty (see p. 4) as the distinguishing feature of

● **State-centrism**: An approach to political analysis that takes the state to be the key actor in the domestic realm and on the world stage.

● **State-system**: A pattern of relationships between and amongst states that establishes a measure of order and predictability.

CONCEPT

Sovereignty

Sovereignty is the principle of supreme and unquestionable authority, reflected in the claim by the state to be the sole author of laws within its territory. *External* sovereignty (sometimes called 'state sovereignty' or 'national sovereignty') refers to the capacity of the state to act independently and autonomously on the world stage. This implies that states are legally equal and that the territorial integrity and political independence of a state are inviolable. *Internal* sovereignty refers to the location of supreme power/authority within the state. The institution of sovereignty is nevertheless developing and changing, both as new concepts of sovereignty emerge ('economic sovereignty', 'food sovereignty' and so on) and as sovereignty is adapted to new circumstances ('pooled sovereignty', 'responsible sovereignty' and so forth).

● **Mixed-actor model:** The theory that, while not ignoring the role of states and national governments, international politics is shaped by a much broader range of interests and groups.

● **Security:** To be safe from harm, the absence of threats; security may be understood in 'national', 'international', 'global' or 'human' terms.

the state. State sovereignty thus became the primary organizing principle of international politics.

However, the state-centric approach to world politics has become increasingly difficult to sustain. This has happened, in part, because it is no longer possible to treat states as the only significant actors on the world stage. Transnational corporations (TNCs) (see p. 94), non-governmental organizations (NGOs) (see p 10) and a host of other non-state bodies have come to exert influence. In different ways and to different degrees, groups and organizations ranging from al-Qaeda (see p. 301), the anti-capitalist movement (see p. 74) and Greenpeace to Google (see p. 146), General Motors and the Papacy contribute to shaping world politics. Since the 1970s, indeed, pluralist theorists have advocated a **mixed-actor model** of world politics. However, although it is widely accepted that states and national governments are merely one category of actor amongst many on the world stage, they may still remain the most important actors. No TNC or NGOs, for instance, can rival the state's coercive power, either its capacity to enforce order within its borders or its ability to deal militarily with other states. (The changing role and significance of the state are examined in depth in Chapter 5.)

From independence to interdependence?

To study international politics traditionally meant to study the implications of the international system being divided into a collection of states. Thanks to sovereignty, these states were, moreover, viewed as independent and autonomous entities. This state-centric approach has often been illustrated through the so-called 'billiard ball model', which dominated thinking about international relations in the 1950s and later, and was particularly associated with realist theory. This suggested that states, like billiard balls, are impermeable and self-contained units, which influence each other through external pressure. Sovereign states interacting within the state-system are thus seen to behave like a collection of billiard balls moving over the table and colliding with each other, as in Figure 18.2. In this view, interactions between and amongst states, or 'collisions', are linked, in most cases to military and **security** matters, reflecting the assumption that power and survival are the primary concerns of the state. International politics is thus orientated mainly around issues of war and peace,

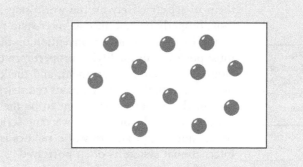

Figure 18.2 **Billiard ball model of world politics**

Focus on ...
The Westphalian state-system

The Peace of Westphalia (1648) is commonly said to mark the beginning of modern international politics. The Peace was a series of treaties that brought an end to the Thirty Years War (1618–48), which consisted of a series of declared and undeclared wars throughout central Europe involving the Holy Roman Empire and various opponents, including the Danes, the Dutch and, above all, France and Sweden. Although the transition occurred over a much longer period of time, these treaties helped to transform a medieval Europe of overlapping authorities, loyalties and identities into a modern state-system. The so-called 'Westphalian system' was based on two key principles:

- States enjoy sovereign jurisdiction, in the sense that they have independent control over what happens within their territory (all other institutions and groups, spiritual and temporal, are therefore subordinate to the state).
- Relations between and among states are structured by the acceptance of the sovereign independence of all states (thus implying that states are legally equal).

with **diplomacy** and possibly military action being the principal forms of state interaction.

The billiard ball model of world politics implies that patterns of conflict and cooperation within the international system are largely determined by the distribution of power among states. Thus, although state-centric theorists acknowledged the formal, legal equality of states, each state being a sovereign entity, they also recognized that some states are more powerful than others, and, indeed, that strong states may sometimes intervene in the affairs of weak ones. In effect, not all billiard balls are the same size. This is why the study of international politics has conventionally given particular attention to the interests and behaviour of so-called 'great powers'.

The billiard ball model has nevertheless come under pressure as a result of growing interdependence (see p. 7) and interconnectedness. Tasks such as promoting economic growth and prosperity, tackling global warming, halting the spread of weapons of mass destruction and coping with pandemic diseases are impossible for any state to accomplish on its own, however powerful it might be. States, in these circumstances, are forced to work together, relying on collective efforts and energies. For Keohane and Nye (1977), such a web of relationships has created a condition of 'complex interdependence', in which states are drawn into cooperation and integration by forces such as closer trading and other economic relationships. This is illustrated by what has been called the 'cobweb model' of world politics (see Figure 18.3). Nevertheless, such thinking can be taken too far. For one thing, there are parts of the world, not least the Middle East, where states clearly remain enmeshed in military-strategic conflict, suggesting both that the billiard ball model is not entirely inaccurate and that levels of interdependence vary greatly across the globe. For another, interdependence is by no means always associated with trends towards peace, cooperation and integration. Interdependence may be asymmetrical rather than

● **Diplomacy:** A process of negotiation and communication between states that seeks to resolve conflict without recourse to war; an instrument of foreign policy.

CONCEPT

Great power

A great power is a state deemed to rank amongst the most powerful in a hierarchical state-system. The criteria that define a great power are subject to dispute, but four are often identified. (1) Great powers are in the first rank of military prowess, having the capacity to maintain their own security and, potentially, to influence other powers. (2) They are economically powerful states, although (as Japan shows) this is a necessary but not a sufficient condition for great power status. (3) They have global, and not merely regional, spheres of interest. (4) They adopt a 'forward' foreign policy and have actual, and not merely potential, impact on international affairs (during its isolationist phase, the USA was thus not a great power).

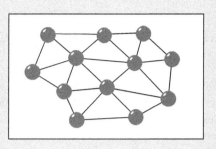

Figure 18.3 **Cobweb model of world politics**

symmetrical, in which case it can lead to domination and conflict rather than peace and harmony.

From the domestic/international divide to transnationalism?

One of the key implications of approaching study from the perspective of 'the international' is that politics has a distinct spatial or territorial character. In short, borders and boundaries matter. This applies especially in the case of the distinction between *domestic* politics, which is concerned with the state's role in maintaining order and carrying out regulation within its borders, and *international* politics, which is concerned with relations between and among states. In that sense, sovereignty is a 'hard shell' that divides the 'inside' of politics from the 'outside'. This domestic/international, or 'inside/outside', divide also separates what have conventionally been seen as two quite different spheres of political interaction. Whereas politics 'inside' has an orderly and regulated character, stemming from the ability of the state within the domestic sphere to impose rule from above, order of this kind is absent from politics 'outside', in that there is no authority in the international sphere higher than the sovereign state. According to John Agnew (1994), such thinking had created a 'territorial trap' within the discipline of international relations, reflected in three assumptions. First, the state is a clearly bounded territorial space. Second, domestic and foreign affairs are entirely different realms. Third, states are 'containers' of society, implying that the boundaries of the state coincide with the boundaries of society.

Such an emphasis on borders and clear territorial divisions have nevertheless come under pressure as a result of recent trends and developments, not least those associated with **globalization**, as discussed in the next main section. In particular, there has been a substantial growth in cross-border flows and transactions – movements of people, goods, money, information and ideas. This has created the phenomenon of **transnationalism**. As state borders have become increasingly 'porous', the conventional domestic/international, or 'inside/outside' divide has become more difficult to uphold. This can be illustrated by both the substantially greater vulnerability of domestic economies to events that take place elsewhere in the world (as demonstrated by the wide-ranging impact

● **Globalization:** The emergence of a complex web of interconnectedness that means that our lives are increasingly shaped by events that occur, and decisions that are made, at a great distance from us.

● **Transnationalism:** Political, social, economic or other forms that transcend or cut across national borders

Interdependence

Interdependence refers to a relationship between two parties in which each is affected by decisions that are taken by the other. Interdependence implies mutual influence, even a rough equality between the parties in question, usually arising from a sense of mutual vulnerability. Interdependence, then, is usually associated with a trend towards cooperation and integration in world affairs. Keohane and Nye (1977) advanced the idea of 'complex interdependence' as an alternative to the realist model of international politics. This highlighted the extent to which (1) states have ceased to be autonomous international actors; (2) economic and other issues have become more prominent in world affairs; and (3) military force has become a less reliable and less important policy option.

● **Anarchy:** Literally, without rule; the absence of a central government or higher authority, sometimes, but not necessarily, associated with instability and chaos.

● **Self-help:** A reliance on internal or inner resources, often seen as the principal reason states prioritize survival and security.

● **Balance of power:** A condition in which no one state predominates over others, tending to create general equilibrium and curb the hegemonic ambitions of all states.

of the 2007–09 global financial crisis) and by the wider use of digital technologies that enable people to communicate with one another through means (such as mobile phones and the Internet) that national governments find difficult to control. It is also notable that issues that are becoming more prominent in world affairs, such as environmental politics and human rights (see p. 311), tend to have an intrinsically transnational character. However, claims that the modern world is effectively 'borderless' are manifestly absurd, and, in some ways, territorial divisions are becoming more important, not less important. This is evident, for instance, in the greater emphasis on national or 'homeland' security in many parts of the world since the terrorist attacks of September 11, and in attempts to constrain international migration by strengthening border and other immigration controls.

From international anarchy to global governance?

A key assumption of the traditional approach to international politics has been that the state-system operates in a context of **anarchy**. This reflects the notion that there is no higher authority than the state, meaning that external politics operates as an international 'state of nature', a pre-political society. The implications of international anarchy are profound. Most importantly, in the absence of any other force attending to their interests, states are forced to rely on **self-help**. If international politics operates as a 'self-help system', the power-seeking inclinations of one state are only tempered by competing tendencies in other states, suggesting that conflict and war are inevitable features of the international system. In this view, conflict is only constrained by a **balance of power**, developed either as a diplomatic strategy by peace-minded leaders or occurring through a happy coincidence. This image of anarchy has been modified by the idea that the international system operates more like an 'international society' (see p. 9). Hedley Bull ([1977] 2012) thus advanced the notion of an 'anarchical society', in place of the conventional theory of international anarchy.

However, the idea of international anarchy, and even the more modest notion of an 'anarchical society', have become more difficult to sustain because of the emergence, especially since 1945, of a framework of global governance (see p. 462) and sometimes regional governance. This is reflected in the growing importance of organizations such as the United Nations, the International Monetary Fund (IMF) (see p. 475), the World Trade Organization (WTO) (see p. 537), the European Union (see p. 509) and so on. The growing number and significance of international organizations has occurred for powerful and pressing reasons. Notably, they reflect the fact that states are increasingly confronted by **collective dilemmas**, issues that are particularly taxing because they confound even the most powerful of states when acting alone. This first became apparent in relation to the development of technologized warfare and particularly the invention of nuclear weapons, but has since been reinforced by challenges such as financial crises, climate change, terrorism, crime, migration and development. Such trends, nevertheless, have yet to render the idea of international anarchy altogether redundant. While international organizations have undoubtedly become significant actors on the world stage, competing, at times, with states and other non-state actors, their impact should not be exaggerated. Apart from anything else, they are, to a greater or lesser extent, the creatures of their members: they

CONCEPT

Globalization

Globalization is the emergence of a complex web of interconnectedness that means that our lives are increasingly shaped by events that occur, and decisions that are made, at a great distance from us. The central feature of globalization is therefore that geographical distance is of declining relevance and that territorial borders, such as those between nation-states, are becoming less significant. By no means, however, does globalization imply that 'the local' and 'the national' are subordinated to 'the global'. Rather, it highlights the *deepening* as well as the *broadening* of the political process, in the sense that local, national and global events (or perhaps local, regional, national, international and global events) constantly interact.

● **Collective dilemma**: A problem that stems from the interdependence of states, meaning that any solution must involve international cooperation rather than action by a single state.

● **Globality**: A totally interconnected whole, such as the global economy; the end-state of globalization.

● **Globalism**: An ideological project committed to the spread of globalization, usually reflecting support for the values and theories of free-market capitalism.

can do no more than their member states, and especially powerful states, allow them to do.

GLOBALIZATION AND ITS IMPLICATIONS

No development has challenged the conventional state-centric image of world politics more radically than the emergence of globalization. Globalization, indeed, can be seen as the buzz word of our time. Amongst politicians, for instance, the conventional wisdom is that the twenty-first century will be the 'global century'. But what actually is 'globalization'? Is it actually happening, and, if so, what are its implications?

Explaining globalization

Globalization is a complex, elusive and controversial term. It has been used to refer to a process, a policy, a marketing strategy, a predicament or even an ideology. Some have tried to bring greater clarity to the debate about the nature of globalization by distinguishing between globalization as a *process* or set of processes (highlighting the dynamics of transformation or change, in common with other words that end in the suffix '-ization', such as modernization) and **globality** as a *condition* (indicating the set of circumstances that globalization has brought about, just as modernization has created a condition of modernity) (Steger 2003). Others have used the term **globalism** to refer to the *ideology* of globalization, the theories, values and assumptions that have guided or driven the process (Ralston Saul 2009). The problem with globalization is that it is not so much an 'it' as a 'them': it is not a single process but a complex of processes, sometimes overlapping and interlocking but also, at times, contradictory and oppositional. It is therefore difficult to reduce globalization to a single theme. Nevertheless, the various developments and manifestations that are associated with globalization, or indeed globality, can be traced back to the underlying phenomenon of interconnectedness. Globalization, regardless of its forms or impact, forges connections between previously unconnected people, communities, institutions and societies. Held *et al.* (1999) thus defined globalization as 'the widening, intensifying, speeding up, and growing impact of world-wide interconnectedness'.

The interconnectedness that globalization has spawned is multidimensional and operates through distinctive economic, cultural and political processes. In other words, globalization has a number of dimensions or 'faces'. Although globalization theorists have championed particular interpretations of globalization, these are by no means mutually exclusive. Instead, they capture different aspects of a complex and multifaceted phenomenon. Globalization has been interpreted in three main ways:

● *Economic* globalization (see p. 98) is the process through which national economies have, to a greater or lesser extent, been absorbed into a single global economy (examined in greater depth in).

● *Cultural* globalization (see p. 151) is the process whereby information, commodities and images that have been produced in one part of the world enter into a global flow that tends to 'flatten out' cultural differences

CONCEPT

International society

The term 'international society' suggests that relations between and amongst states are conditioned by the existence of norms and rules that establish the regular patterns of interaction that characterize a 'society'. Such a view modifies the realist emphasis on power politics and international anarchy by suggesting the existence of a 'society of states' rather than simply a 'system of states'. This implies both that international relations are rule-governed, and that these rules help to maintain international order. The chief institutions that generate cultural cohesion and social integration are international law (see p. 399), diplomacy and the activities of international organizations (see p. 440).

● **Hyperglobalism:** The view that new, globalized economic and cultural patterns became inevitable once technology such as computerized financial trading, satellite communications, mobile phones and the Internet became widely available.

between nations, regions and individual (discussed more fully in Chapter 6).

● *Political* globalization (see p. 122) is the process through which policy-making responsibilities have been passed from national governments to international organizations (considered in greater detail in Chapter 5).

Globalization: myth or reality?

Is globalization actually happening? Although globalization may be the buzz word of our time, there has been intense debate about its impact and significance. No sooner had (roughly by the mid-1990s) academics and other social commentators seemed to agree that globalization was 'changing everything', than it became fashionable (in the early 2000s) to proclaim the 'end of globalization', or the 'death of globalism' (Bisley 2007). The most influential attempt to outline the various positions on this globalization debate was set out by Held *et al.* (1999). They distinguished between three positions:

● The hyperglobalists
● The sceptics
● The transformationalists.

The hyperglobalizers are the chief amongst 'the believers' in globalization. **Hyperglobalism** portrays globalization as a profound, even revolutionary set of economic, cultural, technological and political shifts that have intensified since the 1980s. Particular emphasis, in this view, is placed on developments such as the digital revolution in information and communications, the advent of an integrated global financial system and the emergence of global commodities that are available almost anywhere in the world. Indeed, hyperglobalism is often based on a form of technological determinism, which suggests that the forces creating a single global economy became irresistible once the technology that facilitates its existence was available. The chief image of hyperglobalism is captured in the notion of a 'borderless world' (discussed in more detail in Chapter 22), which suggests that national borders and, for that matter, states themselves have become irrelevant in a global order increasingly dominated by transnational forces. 'National' economic strategies are therefore virtually unworkable in a global context. Resistance to the dictates of global markets is both damaging – countries prosper to the extent that their economies are integrated into the global economy – and ultimately futile. Hyperglobalizers therefore have a strongly positive attitude towards globalization, usually assuming that, in marking the triumph of markets over the state, it is associated with economic dynamism and growing worldwide prosperity.

Nevertheless, hyperglobalism offers an unbalanced and exaggerated view of globalization, in at least two senses. First, it overstates the extent to which policy-makers have been dominated by 'irresistible' economic and technological forces, underestimating the importance of values, perceptions and ideological orientations. Second, the images of the 'end of sovereignty' and the 'twilight of the nation-state' can be said to feature amongst the myths of globalization (sometimes called 'globalony'). Although states may increasingly operate in post-sovereign conditions, in a context of interdependence and permeability, their role

GLOBAL ACTORS . . .

NON-GOVERNMENTAL ORGANIZATIONS

A non-governmental organization (NGO) is a private, non-commercial group or body which seeks to achieve its ends through non-violent means. The World Bank (see p.380) defines NGOs as 'private organizations that pursue activities to relieve suffering, promote the interests of the poor, protect the environment, provide basic social services, or undertake community development'. Very early examples of such bodies were the Society for the Abolition of the Slave Trade (formed by William Wilberforce in 1787) and the International Committee of the Red Cross, founded in 1863. The first official recognition of NGOs was by the United Nations (UN) in 1948, when 41 NGOs were granted consultative status following the establishment of the Universal Declaration of Human Rights (indeed, some NGO activists believe that only groups formally acknowledged by the UN should be regarded as 'true' NGOs). A distinction is often drawn between operational NGOs and advocacy NGOs:

- *Operational* NGOs are those whose primary purpose is the design and implementation of development-related projects; they may be either relief-orientated or development-orientated, and they may be community-based, national or international.
- *Advocacy* NGOs exist to promote or defend a particular cause; they are sometimes termed 'promotional pressure groups' or 'public interest groups'.

Significance: Since the 1990s, the steady growth in the number of NGOs has become a veritable explosion. By 2012, over 3,500 groups had been granted consultative status by the UN, with estimates of the total number of international NGOs usually exceeding 40,000. If national NGOs are taken into account, the number grows enormously: the USA has an estimated 2 million NGOs; Russia has 65,000 NGOs; and Kenya, to take one developing country alone, has about 2,400 NGOs coming into existence each year. The major international NGOs have developed into huge organizations. For example, Care International, dedicated to the worldwide reduction of poverty, controls a budget worth more than 100m dollars, Greenpeace has a membership of 2.5m and a staff of over 1,200, and Amnesty International is better resourced than the human rights arm of the UN.

There can be little doubt that major international NGOs and the NGO sector as a whole now constitute significant actors on the global stage. Although lacking the economic leverage that TNCs can exert, advocacy NGOs have proved highly adept at mobilizing 'soft' power and popular pressure. In this respect, they have a number of advantages. These include that leading NGOs have cultivated high public profiles, often linked to public protests and demonstrations that attract eager media attention; that their typically altruistic and humanitarian objectives enable them to mobilize public support and exert moral pressure in a way that conventional politicians and political parties struggle to rival; and that, over a wide range of issues, the views of NGOs are taken to be both authoritative and disinterested, based on the use of specialists and academics. Operational NGOs, for their part, have come to deliver about 15 per cent of international aid, often demonstrating a greater speed of response and level of operational effectiveness than governmental bodies, national or international, can muster. Relief- and development-orientated NGOs may also be able to operate in politically sensitive areas where national governments, or even the UN, would be unwelcome.

Nevertheless, the rise of the NGO has provoked considerable political controversy. Supporters of NGOs argue that they benefit and enrich global politics. They counter-balance corporate power, challenging the influence of TNCs; democratize global politics by articulating the interests of people and groups who have been disempowered by the globalization process; and act as a moral force, widening people's sense of civic responsibility and even promoting global citizenship. In these respects, they are a vital component of emergent global civil society (see p.156). Critics, however, argue that NGOs are self-appointed groups that have no genuine democratic credentials, often articulating the views of a small group of senior professionals. In an attempt to gain a high media profile and attract support and funding, NGOs have been accused of making exaggerated claims, thereby distorting public perceptions and the policy agenda. Finally, in order to preserve their 'insider' status, NGOs tend to compromise their principles and 'go mainstream', becoming, in effect, deradicalized social movements. (The impact and significance of NGOs is examined further in Chapter 6.)

Focus on . . .
Definitions of globalization

- '[T]he intensification of worldwide social relations that link distant localities in a way that local happenings are shaped by events occurring many miles away and vice versa' (Giddens 1990)
- 'The integration of national economies into the international economy through trade, direct foreign investment, short-term capital flows, international flows of workers and humanity generally, and flows of technology' (Bhagwati 2004)

- 'The processes through which sovereign nation-states are criss-crossed and undermined by transnational actors with varying prospects of power, orientations, identities and networks' (Beck 2000)
- 'A process (or set of processes) which embody the transformation of the spatial organization of social relations and transactions' (Held et al. 1999)
- 'A reconfiguration of social geography marked by the growth of transplanetary and supraterritorial connections between people' (Scholte 2005)

and significance has altered rather than become irrelevant. States, for example, have become 'entrepreneurial' in trying to develop strategies for improving their competitiveness in the global economy, notably by boosting education, training and job-related skills. They are also more willing to 'pool' sovereignty by working in and through international organizations such as regional training blocs and the WTO. Finally, the advent of global terrorism and intensifying concern about migration patterns has re-emphasized the importance of the state in ensuring homeland security and in protecting national borders. (The implications of globalization for the state are examined more fully in Chapter 5.)

The sceptics, by contrast, have portrayed globalization as a fantasy and dismissed the idea of an integrated global economy. They point out that the overwhelming bulk of economic activity still takes place within, not across, national boundaries, and that there is nothing new about high levels of international trade and cross-border capital flows (Hirst and Thompson 1999). Sceptics have, further, argued that globalization has been used as an ideological device by politicians and theorists who wish to advance a market-orientated economic agenda. The globalization thesis has two major advantages in this respect. In the first place, it portrays certain tendencies (such as the shift towards greater flexibility and weaker trade unions, controls on public spending and particularly welfare budgets, and the scaling down of business regulation) as inevitable and therefore irresistible. Second, it suggests that such shifts are part of an impersonal process, and not one linked to an agent, such as big business, whose interests might be seen to be served by globalizing tendencies. However, although such scepticism has served to check the over-boiled enthusiasm of earlier globalization theorists, it is difficult to uphold the idea of 'business as normal'. Goods, capital, information and people do move around the world more freely than they used to, and this has inevitable consequences for economic, cultural and political life.

Falling between the hyperglobalizers and the sceptics, the 'transformationalist' stance offers a middle-road view of globalization. It accepts that profound changes have taken place in the patterns and processes of world politics without

APPROACHES TO . . .

GLOBALIZATION

Realist view

Realists have typically adopted a sceptical stance towards globalization, seeing it more in terms of intensifying economic interdependence (that is, 'more of the same') rather than the creation of an interlocking global economy. Most importantly, the state continues to be the dominant unit in world politics. Instead of being threatened by globalization, the state's capacity for regulation and surveillance may have increased rather than decreased. However, realists are not simply globalization deniers. In assessing the nature and significance of globalization, they emphasize that globalization and the international system are not separate, still less rival, structures. Rather, the former should be seen as a manifestation of the latter. Globalization has been made *by* states, *for* states, particularly dominant states. Developments such as an open trading system, global financial markets and the advent of transnational production were all put in place to advance the interests of western states in general and the USA in particular. Furthermore, realists question the notion that globalization is associated with a shift towards peace and cooperation. Instead, heightened economic interdependence is as likely to breed 'mutual vulnerability', leading to conflict rather than cooperation.

Liberal view

Liberals adopt a consistently positive attitude towards globalization. For economic liberals, globalization reflects the victory of the market over 'irrational' national allegiances and 'arbitrary' state borders. The miracle of the market is that it draws resources towards their most profitable use, thus bringing prosperity to individuals, families, companies and societies. The attraction of economic globalization is therefore that it allows markets to operate on a global scale, replacing the 'shallow' integration of free trade and intensified interdependence with the 'deep' integration of a single global economy. The increased productivity and intensified competition that this produces benefits all the societies that participate within it, demonstrating that economic globalization is a positive-sum game, a game of winners and winners. Liberals also believe that globalization brings social and political benefits. The freer flow of information and ideas around the world both widens opportunities for personal self-development and creates more dynamic and vigorous societies. Moreover, from a liberal standpoint, the spread of market capital-

ism is invariably associated with the advance of liberal democracy, economic freedom breeding a demand for political freedom. For liberals, globalization marks a watershed in world history, in that it ends the period during which the nation-state was the dominant global actor, world order being determined by an (inherently unstable) balance of power. The global era, by contrast, is characterized by a tendency towards peace and international cooperation as well as by the dispersal of global power, in particular through the emergence of global civil society (see p. 156) and the growing importance of international organizations.

Critical views

Critical theorists have adopted a negative or oppositional stance towards globalization. Often drawing on an established socialist or specifically Marxist critique of capitalism, this portrays the essence of globalization as the establishment of a global capitalist order. (Indeed, Marx (see p. 72) can be said to have prefigured much 'hyperglobalist' literature, in having highlighted the intrinsically transnational character of the capitalist mode of production.) Like liberals, critical theorists usually accept that globalization marks a historically significant shift, not least in the relationship between states and markets. States have lost power over the economy, being reduced to little more than instruments for the restructuring of national economies in the interests of global capitalism. Globalization is thus viewed as an uneven, hierarchical process, characterized both by the growing polarization between the rich and the poor, explained by world-systems theorists in terms of a structural imbalance between 'core' and 'peripheral' areas in the global economy, and by a weakening of democratic accountability and popular responsiveness due to burgeoning corporate power. Feminist analysts have sometimes linked globalization to growing gender inequalities, associated, for example, with the disruption of small-scale farming in the developing world, largely carried out by women, and growing pressure on them to support their families by seeking work abroad, leading to the 'feminization of migration'. Postcolonial theorists, for their part, have taken particular exception to cultural globalization, interpreted as a form of western imperialism which subverts indigenous cultures and ways of life and leads to the spread of soulless consumerism.

its established or traditional features having been swept away altogether. In short, much has changed, but not everything. This has become the most widely accepted view of globalization, as it resists both the temptation to over-hype the process and to debunk it. Major transformations have nevertheless taken place in world politics. These include the following:

- The *breadth* of interconnectedness has not only stretched social, political, economic and cultural activities across national borders, but also, potentially, across the globe. Never before has globalization threatened to develop into a *single* worldwide system.
- The *intensity* of interconnectedness has increased with the growing magnitude of transborder or even transworld activities, which range from migration surges and the growth of international trade to the greater accessibility of Hollywood movies or US television programmes.
- Interconnectedness has *speeded up*, not least through the huge flows of electronic money that move around the world at the flick of a computer switch, ensuring that currency and other financial markets react almost immediately to economic events elsewhere in the world.

LENSES ON GLOBAL POLITICS

However, making sense of global politics also requires that we understand the theories, values and assumptions through which world affairs have been interpreted. How do different analysts and theorists *see* the world? What are the key 'lenses' on global politics? The theoretical dimension of the study of global politics has become an increasingly rich and diverse arena in recent decades. The substantive ideas of the growing range of theoretical traditions are examined in, Chapter 3, while issues to do with the nature and purpose of theory are considered in Chapter 21. This introduction, nevertheless, attempts to map out broad areas of debate among the traditions, in particular by distinguishing between 'mainstream' perspectives and 'critical' perspectives.

Mainstream perspectives

The two mainstream perspectives on global politics are realism and liberalism. What do they have in common, and in what sense are they 'mainstream'? Realism and liberalism can be viewed as mainstream perspectives in the sense that they, in their various incarnations, have dominated conventional academic approaches to the field of international politics since its inception. Realist and liberal theories have two broad things in common. In the first place, they are both grounded in **positivism**. This suggests that it is possible to develop objective knowledge, through the capacity to distinguish 'facts' from 'values'. In short, it is possible to compare theories with the 'real world', the world 'out there'. Robert Cox (1981) thus describes such theories as 'problem-solving theories', in that they take the world 'as it is' and endeavour to think through problems and offer prudent advice to policy-makers trying to negotiate the challenges of the 'real world'. (These issues are discussed in greater detail in pp. 527–30.) Second, realist and liberal theorists share similar concerns and address similar issues, meaning that they, in effect, talk to, rather than past, one another. In particular,

● **Positivism:** The theory that social and indeed all forms of enquiry should conform to the methods of the natural sciences (see p. 526).

Thomas Hobbes (1588–1679)

English political philosopher. Hobbes was the son of a minor clergyman who subsequently abandoned his family. Writing at a time of uncertainty and civil strife, precipitated by the English Revolution, Hobbes developed the first comprehensive theory of nature and human behaviour since Aristotle. His classic work, *Leviathan* (1651) discussed the grounds of political obligation and undoubtedly reflected the impact of the Civil War. Based on the assumption that human beings seek 'power after power', it provided a realist justification for absolutist government as the only alternative to the anarchy of the 'state of nature', in which life would be 'solitary, poor, nasty, brutish and short'. Hobbes' emphasis on the state as an essential guarantor of order and security has led to a revived interest in his ideas since 9/11.

the core concern of both realism and liberalism is the balance between conflict and cooperation in state relations. Although realists generally place greater emphasis on conflict, while liberals highlight the scope for cooperation, neither is unmindful of the issues raised by the other, as is evidenced in the tendency, over time, for differences between realism and liberalism to have become blurred (see Closing the realist–liberal divide? p. 68). Nevertheless, important differences can be identified between the realist and liberal perspectives.

How do realists see global politics? Deriving from ideas that can be traced back to thinkers such as Thucydides (see p. 249), Sun Tzu, author of *The Art of War*, Machiavelli (see p. 58) and Thomas Hobbes, the realist vision is pessimistic: international politics is marked by constant power struggles and conflict, and a wide range of obstacles standing in the way of peaceful cooperation. Realism is grounded in an emphasis on **power politics**, based on the following assumptions:

- Human nature is characterized by selfishness and greed.
- Politics is a domain of human activity structured by power and coercion.
- States are the key global actors.
- States pursue self-interest and survival, prioritizing security above all else.
- States operate in a context of anarchy, and thus rely on self-help.
- Global order is structured by the distribution of power (capabilities) among states.
- The balance of power is the principal means of ensuring stability and avoiding war.
- Ethical considerations are (and should be) irrelevant to the conduct of foreign policy.

By contrast, how do liberals see global politics? Liberalism offers a more optimistic vision of global politics, based, ultimately, on a belief in human rationality and moral goodness (even though liberals also accept that people are essentially self-interested and competitive). Liberals tend to believe that the principle of balance or harmony operates in all forms of social interaction. As far as world politics is concerned, this is reflected in a general commitment to **internationalism**, as reflected in Immanuel Kant's (see p 15) belief in the possibility of

● **Power politics:** An approach to politics based on the assumption that the pursuit of power is the principal human goal; the term is sometimes used descriptively.

● **Internationalism:** The theory or practice of politics based on cooperation or harmony among nations, as opposed to the transcendence of national politics.

Immanuel Kant (1724–1804)

German philosopher. Kant spent his entire life in Königsberg (which was then in East Prussia), becoming professor of logic and metaphysics at the University of Königsberg in 1770. His 'critical' philosophy holds that knowledge is not merely an aggregate of sense impressions; it depends on the conceptual apparatus of human understanding. Kant's political thought was shaped by the central importance of morality. He believed that the law of reason dictated categorical imperatives, the most important of which was the obligation to treat others as 'ends', and never only as 'means'. Kant's most important works include *Critique of Pure Reason* (1781), *Idea for a Universal History with a Cosmopolitan Purpose* (1784) and *Metaphysics of Morals* (1785).

'universal and perpetual peace'. The liberal model of global politics is based on the following key assumptions:

- Human beings are rational and moral creatures.
- History is a progressive process, characterized by a growing prospect of international cooperation and peace.
- Mixed-actor models of global politics are more realistic than state-centric ones.
- Trade and economic interdependence make war less likely.
- International law helps to promote order and fosters rule-governed behaviour among states.
- Democracy is inherently peaceful, particularly in reducing the likelihood of war between democratic states.

Critical perspectives

Since the late 1980s, the range of critical approaches to world affairs has expanded considerably. Until that point, Marxism had constituted the principal alternative to mainstream realist and liberal theories. What made the Marxist approach distinctive was that it placed its emphasis not on patterns of conflict and cooperation between states, but on structures of economic power and the role played in world affairs by international capital. It thus brought international political economy, sometimes seen as a sub-field within IR, into focus. However, hastened by the end of the Cold War, a wide range of 'new voices' started to influence the study of world politics, notable examples including social constructivism, critical theory, poststructuralism, postcolonialism, feminism and green politics. What do these new critical voices have in common, and in what sense are they 'critical'? In view of their diverse philosophical underpinnings and contrasting political viewpoints, it is tempting to argue that the only thing that unites these 'new voices' is a shared antipathy towards mainstream thinking. However, two broad similarities can be identified. The first is that, albeit in different ways and to different degrees, they have tried to go beyond the positivism of mainstream theory, emphasizing instead the role of consciousness in shaping social conduct and, therefore, world affairs. These so-called post-positivist theories are therefore 'critical' in that they not only take issue with the conclusions of mainstream theory, but also subject these theories themselves to critical scrutiny, exposing biases that operate within them and examining their implications. The second similarity is linked to the first: critical persepectives are 'critical' in that, in their different ways, they oppose the dominant forces and interests in modern world affairs, and so contest the global status quo by (usually) aligning themselves with marginalized or oppressed groups. Each of them, thus, seeks to uncover inequalities and asymmetries that mainstream theories tend to ignore.

However, the inequalities and asymmetries to which critical theorists have drawn attention are many and various:

- Neo-Marxists (who encompass a range of traditions and tendencies that in fact straddle the positivist–post-positivist divide) highlight inequalities in the global capitalist system, through which developed countries or areas, sometimes operating through TNCs or linked to 'hegemonic' powers such as the USA, dominate and exploit developing countries or areas.
- Constructivism is not so much a substantive theory as an analytical tool. In arguing that people, in effect, 'construct' the world in which they live, suggesting that the world operates through a kind of 'inter-subjective' awareness, constructivists have thrown mainstream theory's claim to objectivity into question.
- Poststructuralists emphasize that all ideas and concepts are expressed in language which itself is enmeshed in complex relations of power. Influenced particularly by the writings of Michel Foucault, poststructuralists have drawn attention to the link between power and systems of thought using the idea of a 'discourse of power'.
- Feminists have drawn attention to systematic and pervasive structures of gender inequality that characterize global and, indeed, all other forms of politics. In particular, they have highlighted the extent to which mainstream, and especially realist, theories are based on 'masculinist' assumptions about rivalry, competition and inevitable conflict.
- Postcolonialists have emphasized the cultural dimension of colonial rule, showing how western cultural and political hegemony over the rest of the world has been preserved despite the achievement of formal political independence across almost the entire developing world.
- Green politics, or ecologism, has focused on growing concerns about environmental degradation, highlighting the extent to which this has been a by-product of industrialization and an obsession with economic growth, supported by systems of thought that portray human beings as 'masters over nature'.

CONTINUITY AND CHANGE IN GLOBAL POLITICS

Finally, global politics is an ever-shifting field, with, if anything, the pace of change accelerating over time. Recent decades have witnessed momentous

Michel Foucault (1926–84)

French philosopher and radical intellectual. The son of a prosperous surgeon, Foucault had a troubled youth in which he attempted suicide on several occasions and struggled to come to terms with his homosexuality. His work, which ranged over the history of madness, of medicine, of punishment, of sexuality and of knowledge itself, was based on the assumption that the institutions, concepts and beliefs of each period are upheld by 'discourses of power'. This suggests that power relations can largely be disclosed by examining the structure of 'knowledge', since 'truth serves the interests of a ruling class or the prevailing power-structure'. Foucault's most important works include *Madness and Civilization* (1961), *The Order of Things* (1966) and *The History of Sexuality* (1976).

events such as the end of the Cold War, the collapse of the Soviet Union, the September 11 terrorist attacks on the USA and the global financial crisis of 2007–09. While these and other events have changed the contours of global politics, sometimes radically, certain features of world affairs have proved to be of more enduring significance. This can be illustrated by examining the balance between continuity and change in three key aspects of world politics:

- Power
- Security
- Justice.

Power

All forms of politics are about power. Indeed, politics is sometimes seen as the study of power, its core theme being: who gets what, when, how? Modern global politics raises two main questions about power. The first is about where power is located: who has it? During the Cold War era, this appeared to be an easy question to answer. Two 'superpowers' (see p 38) dominated world politics, dividing the global system into rival 'spheres of influence'. East–West conflict reflected the existence of a bipolar world order, marked by the political, ideological and economic ascendancy, respectively, of the USA and the Soviet Union. The end of the Cold War has precipitated a major debate about the shifting location of global power. In one view, the fall of communism and the disintegration of the Soviet Union left the USA as the world's sole superpower, meaning that it had been transformed into a global **hegemon**. Such a view also took account of the extent to which the USA was the architect, and chief beneficiary, of the process of globalization, as well as the possessor of enormous 'structural' power (see pp. 218–20), its pivotal position within institutions such as the UN, the WTO, IMF and World Bank giving it disproportional influence over the frameworks within which states relate to one another and decide how things shall be done.

However, alternative views about the shifting configuration of global power suggest that it is becoming more fragmented and pluralized. For example, power

● **Hegemon**: A leading or paramount power.

may have shifted away from states generally through the growing importance of non-state actors and the increased role played by international organizations. Furthermore, globalization may have made power more diffuse and intangible, increasing the influence of global markets and drawing states into a web of economic interdependence that substantially restricts their freedom of manoeuvre. A further dimension of this traces the implications for global power of the rise of emerging states, such as China, India and Brazil, as well as the impact of a resurgent Russia, sometimes collectively known as the BRICs (see p. 463). In this view, the bipolar Cold War world order is in the process of being replaced by a multipolar world order. (The changing nature of global order is examined more closely in Chapter 9.) Power has also been pluralized through the capacity of new technology to alter power balances both within society and between societies, often empowering the traditionally powerless. For example, advances in communications technology, particularly the use of mobile phones and the Internet, have improved the tactical effectiveness of loosely organized groups, ranging from terrorist bands to protest groups and social movements. Al-Qaeda's influence on world politics since September 11 has thus been out of all proportion to its organizational and economic strength, because modern technology, in the form of bombs and airplanes, has given its terrorist activities a global reach.

The second debate is about the changing nature of power. This has, arguably, occurred because, due to new technology and in a world of global communications and rising literacy rates and educational standards, 'soft' power is becoming as important as 'hard' power in influencing political outcomes. As discussed in Chapter 9, soft power is power as *attraction* rather than *coercion*, the ability to influence others by persuading them to follow or agree to norms and aspirations, as opposed to using threats or rewards. This has, for instance, stimulated a debate about whether military power is now redundant in global politics, especially when it is not matched by 'hearts and minds' strategies. In addition, the near-ubiquitous spread of television and the wider use of satellite technology mean that pictures of devastation and human suffering, whether caused by warfare, famine or natural disaster, are shared across the globe almost instantly. This means, amongst other things, that the behaviour of governments and international organizations is influenced as never before by public opinion around the world.

Security

Security is the deepest and most abiding issue in politics. At its heart is the question: how can people live a decent and worthwhile existence, free from threats, intimidation and violence? Security has usually been thought of as a particularly pressing issue in international politics because, while the domestic realm is ordered and stable, by virtue of the existence of a sovereign state, the international realm is anarchical and therefore threatening and unstable. For realists, as the most important actors in the international system are states, security is primarily understood in terms of 'national' security. As, in a world of self-help, all states are under at least potential threat from all other states, each state must have the capacity for self-defence. National security therefore places a premium on military power, reflecting the assumption that the more militarily powerful

CONCEPT

Security dilemma

Security dilemma describes a condition in which actions taken by one actor to improve national security are interpreted as aggressive by other actors, thereby provoking military counter-moves. This reflects two component dilemmas (Booth and Wheeler 2008). First, there is a dilemma of *interpretation* – what are the motives, intentions and capabilities of others in building up military power? As weapons are inherently ambiguous symbols (they can be either defensive or aggressive), there is irresolvable uncertainty about these matters. Second, there is a dilemma of *response* – should they react in kind, in a militarily confrontational manner, or should they seek to signal reassurance and attempt to defuse tension?

● **International security**: Conditions in which the mutual survival and safety of states is secured through measures taken to prevent or punish aggression, usually within a rule-governed international order.

● **Security regime**: A framework of cooperation amongst states and other actors to ensure the peaceful resolution of conflict (see international regime, p. 71).

a state is, the more secure it is likely to be. This focus on military security nevertheless draws states into dynamic, competitive relationships with one another, based on what is called the 'security dilemma'. This is the problem that a military build-up for defensive purposes by one state is always liable to be interpreted by other states as potentially or actually aggressive, leading to retaliatory military build-ups and so on. The security dilemma gets to the very heart of politics amongst states, making it the quintessential dilemma of international politics (Booth and Wheeler 2008). Permanent insecurity between and amongst states is therefore the inescapable lot of those who live in a condition of anarchy.

However, the state-centric ideas of national security and an inescapable security dilemma have also been challenged. There is, for example, a long-established emphasis within liberal theory on collective security (see p. 447), reflecting the belief that aggression can best be resisted by united action taken by a number of states. Such a view shifts attention away from the idea of 'national' security towards the broader notion of 'international' security (Smith 2010). Furthermore, the security agenda in modern global politics has changed in a number of ways. These include, on the one hand, the expansion of 'zones of peace' in which the tensions and incipient conflicts implied by the security dilemma appear to be absent. Thus 'security regimes' or 'security communities' have developed to manage disputes and help to avoid war, a trend often associated with growing economic interdependence (linked to globalization) and the advance of democratization. On the other hand, September 11 and the wider threat of terrorism has highlighted the emergence of new security challenges that are particularly problematical because they arise from non-state actors and exploit the greater interconnectedness of the modern world. International security may therefore have given way to 'global' security. A further development has been the trend to rethink the concept of security at a still deeper level, usually linked to the notion of 'human security' (see p. 430). Interest in human security has grown both because the decline of inter-state war in the post-Cold War means that the threat from violent conflict now usually occurs *within* states, coming from civil war, insurrection and civic strife, and because of the recognition that in the modern world people's safety and survival is often put at risk more by non-military threats (such as environmental destruction, disease, refugee crises and resource scarcity), than it is by military threats.

Justice

Realist theorists have traditionally viewed justice as a largely irrelevant issue in international or global politics. Relations between states should be determined by hard-headed judgements related to the national interest, not by ethical considerations. Liberals, by contrast, insist that international politics and morality should go hand in hand, amoral power politics being a recipe for egoism, conflict and violence. Traditionally, however, they have defended the idea of 'international' justice based on principles that set out how nation-states should behave towards one another. Respect for state sovereignty and the norm of non-interference in the affairs of other states, seen as guarantees of national independence and therefore political freedom, are clearly an example of this. Such thinking is also reflected in 'just war' theory (see p. 264). This is the idea that the

September 11 and global security

Events: On the morning of 11 September 2001, a coordinated series of terrorist attacks were launched against the USA using four hijacked passenger jet airliners (the events subsequently became known as September 11, or 9/11). Two airliners crashed into the Twin Towers of the World Trade Centre in New York, leading to the collapse first of the North Tower and then the South Tower. The third airliner crashed into the Pentagon, the headquarters of the Department of Defence in Arlington, Virginia, just outside Washington DC. The fourth airliner, believed to be heading towards either the White House or the US Capitol, both in Washington DC, crashed in a field near Shanksville, Pennsylvania, after passengers on board tried to seize control of the plane. There were no survivors from any of the flights. A total of 2,995 people were killed in these attacks, mainly in New York City. In a videotape released in October 2001, responsibility for the attacks was claimed by Osama bin Laden, head of the al-Qaeda (see p. 301) organization, who praised his followers as the 'vanguards of Islam'.

Significance: September 11 has sometimes been described as 'the day the world changed'. This certainly applied in terms of its consequences, notably the unfolding 'war on terror' and the invasions of Afghanistan and Iraq and their ramifications. It also marked a dramatic shift in global security, signalling the end of a period during which globalization and the cessation of superpower rivalry appeared to have been associated with a diminishing propensity for international conflict. Globalization, indeed, appeared to have ushered in new security threats and new forms of conflict. For example, 9/11 demonstrated how fragile national borders had become in a technological age. If the world's greatest power could be dealt such a devastating blow to its largest city and its national capital, what chance did other states have? Further, the 'external' threat in this case came not from another state, but from a terrorist organization, and one, moreover, that operated more as a global network than a nationally-based organization. The motivations behind the attacks were also not conventional ones. Instead of seeking to conquer territory or acquire control over resources, the 9/11 attacks were carried out in the name of a religiously-inspired ideology, militant Islamism (see p. 205), and aimed at exerting a symbolic, even psychic, blow against the cultural, political and ideological domination of the West. This led some to see 9/11 as evidence of an emerging 'clash of civilization', (see p. 196), even as a struggle between Islam and the West.

However, rather than marking the beginning of a new era in global security, 9/11 may have indicated more a return to 'business as normal'. In particular, the advent of a globalized world appeared to underline the vital importance of 'national' security, rather than 'international' or 'global' security. The emergence of new security challenges, and especially transnational terrorism, re-emphasized the core role of the state in protecting its citizens from external attack. Instead of becoming progressively less important, 9/11 gave the state a renewed significance. The USA, for example, responded to 9/11 by undertaking a substantial build-up of state power, both at home (through strengthened 'homeland security') and abroad (through increased military spending and the invasions of Afghanistan and Iraq). A unilateralist tendency also became more pronounced in its foreign policy, as the USA became, for a period at least, less concerned about working with or through international organizations of various kinds. Other states affected by terrorism have also exhibited similar tendencies, marking a renewed emphasis on national security sometimes at the expense of considerations such as civil liberties and political freedom. In other words, 9/11 may demonstrate that state-based power politics is alive and kicking.

CONCEPT

Cosmopolitanism

Cosmopolitanism literally means a belief in a *cosmopolis* or 'world state'. *Moral* cosmopolitanism is the belief that the world constitutes a single moral community, in that people have obligations (potentially) towards all other people in the world, regardless of nationality, religion, ethnicity and so forth. All forms of moral cosmopolitanism are based on a belief that every individual is of equal moral worth, most commonly linked to the doctrine of human rights. *Political* cosmopolitanism ('legal' or 'institutional' cosmopolitanism) is the belief that there should be global political institutions, and possibly a world government (see p. 464). However, most modern political cosmopolitans favour a system in which authority is divided between global, national and local levels (Brown and Held 2010).

use of violence through war can only be justified if the reasons for war and the conduct of war conform to principles of justice.

However, the growth of interconnectedness and interdependence has extended thinking about morality in world affairs, particularly through an increasing emphasis on the notion of 'global' or 'cosmopolitan' justice. The idea of global justice is rooted in a belief in universal moral values, values that apply to all people in the world regardless of nationality and citizenship. The most influential example of universal values is the doctrine of international human rights. Such cosmopolitanism has shaped thinking on the issue of global distributive justice, suggesting, for instance, that rich countries should give more foreign aid, and that there should be a possibly substantial redistribution of wealth between the world's rich and the world's poor. The utilitarian philosopher Peter Singer (1993) argued that the citizens and governments of rich countries have a basic obligation to eradicate absolute poverty in other countries on the grounds that (1) if we can prevent something bad without sacrificing anything of comparable significance, we ought to do it, and (2) absolute poverty is bad because it causes suffering and death. For Pogge (2008), the obligation of rich countries to help poor countries stems not from the simple existence of poverty and our capacity to alleviate it, but from the *causal* relationship between the wealth of the rich and the poverty of the poor. The rich have a duty to help the poor because the international order is structured so as to benefit some people and areas at the expense of others. Similar ideas are implied by neo-colonial and world-system theories of global poverty, as examined in.

Similarly, ideas have been developed about global environmental justice. These, for instance, reflect on issues such as protecting the natural environment for the benefit of future generations, the disproportionate obligation of rich countries to tackle climate change because they largely created the problem in the first place, and the idea that any legally binding emissions targets should be structured on a per capita basis, rather than a country basis, so as not to disadvantage states with large populations (and therefore the developing world generally). These ideas are discussed further in.

USING THIS BOOK

Global politics is, by its nature, an overlapping and interlocking field. The material encountered in this book stubbornly resists compartmentalization, which is why, throughout, there is regular cross-referencing to related discussions that occur in other chapters and particularly to relevant boxed material found elsewhere. Nevertheless, the book develops by considering what can be thought of as a series of broad issues or themes.

The first group of chapters is designed to provide background understanding for the study of global politics.

- This chapter has examined the nature of global politics and considered the developments that make a global politics approach to world affairs appropriate, as well as providing an introduction to contrasting mainstream and critical perspectives on global politics.
- Chapter 2 examines the historical context of modern global politics, particularly by looking at key developments in world history during the twentieth and twenty-first centuries.

● Chapter 3 provides an account of the key theoretical approaches to global politics, thus considering mainstream perspectives and critical perspectives in greater depth, as well as the implications of global thinking.

The next group of chapters discusses the various transformations that have occurred, and are occurring, as a result of the globalization of world politics.

● Chapter 4 discusses the nature, extent and implications of economic globalization, and considers, amongst other things, the crisis tendencies within modern global capitalism.
● Chapter 5 examines the role and significance of the state in a global age, as well as the nature of foreign policy and how foreign policy decisions are made.
● Chapter 6 considers the social and cultural implications of globalization and whether or not it is possible to talk of an emergent global civil society.
● Chapter 7 examines the ways in which nations and nationalism have been shaped and reshaped in a global world, focusing on ways in which nationalism has been both weakened and strengthened.
● Chapter 8 examines the politics of identity and the growth of cultural conflict in a global age, particularly in the form of challenges to the politico-cultural domination of the West, especially from political Islam.

The following group of chapters considers the broad themes of global order and conflict.

● Chapter 9 looks at the nature of global power and the changing shape of twenty-first century global order, as well as at the implications of such changes for peace and stability.
● Chapter 10 examines how and why wars occur, the changing nature of warfare, and how, and how successfully, war has been justified.
● Chapter 11 considers the nature and implications of nuclear proliferation, and examines the prospects for non-proliferation and nuclear disarmament.
● Chapter 12 discusses the nature of terrorism, the various debates that have sprung up about its significance and the strategies that have been used to counter it.

The next group of chapters focuses on various issues to do with the theme of global justice.

● Chapter 13 considers the nature and significance of international human rights, how, and how effectively, they have been protected, and debates about humanitarian intervention and its implications.
● Chapter 14 addresses the issue of international law, in particular examining the changing nature and significance of international law in the modern period.
● Chapter 15 considers the issues of global poverty and inequality, and also looks at development and the politics of international aid.
● Chapter 16 focuses on global environmental issues, and examines the challenge of climate change in depth.

- Chapter 17 discusses feminist approaches to global politics and how gender perspectives have changed thinking about war, security and other matters.

The following group of chapters considers attempts to address global or transnational issues through the construction of intergovernmental or supranational institutions.

- Chapter 18 examines the nature and growth of international organizations, and looks in particular at the role and effectiveness of the United Nations.
- Chapter 19 discusses the idea of global governance and examines its development in the economic sphere through the evolution of the Bretton Woods system.
- Chapter 20 focuses on the causes and significance of regionalism, focusing especially on the nature and significance of the European Union.

The final group of chapters reflects on broad themes that have been addressed at various points in the book.

- Chapter 21 considers how, and how far, theory contributes to our understanding of global politics, and, in the process, examines key debates about the nature and purpose of theory.
- Chapter 22 provides a conclusion to the book by reviewing and evaluating various images of the global future and reflecting on whether attempts to predict the future are ultimately futile.

SUMMARY

- Global politics is based on a comprehensive approach to world affairs that takes account not just of political developments at a global level, but also at and, crucially, across, all levels – global, regional, national, sub-national and so on. In that sense, 'the global' and 'the international' complement one another and should not be seen as rival or incompatible modes of understanding.

- 'International' politics has been transformed into 'global' politics through a variety of developments. New actors have emerged from the world stage alongside states and national governments. Levels of interconnectedness and interdependence in world politics have increased, albeit unevenly. And international anarchy has been modified by the emergence of a framework of regional and global governance.

- Globalization is the emergence of a complex web of interconnectedness that means that our lives are increasingly shaped by events that occur, and decisions that are made, at a great distance from us. Distinctions are commonly drawn between economic globalization, cultural globalization and political global-ization. However, there are significant debates about whether globalization is actually happening and how far it has transformed world politics.

- The two mainstream perspectives on global politics are realism and liberalism; these are both grounded in positivism and focus on the balance between conflict and cooperation in state relations, even though they offer quite different accounts of this balance. Critical perspectives, by contrast, tend to adopt a post-positivist approach to theory and contest the global status quo by aligning themselves with the interests of marginal-ized or oppressed groups.

- Global politics is an ever-shifting field, with, if anything, the pace of change accelerating over time. Debates have emerged about the changing nature of power and the shifting configuration of global power, about whether national security has been displaced by international, global or even human security, and about the extent to which justice now has to be considered in cosmopolitan or global terms.

Questions for discussion

- How does 'global' politics differ from 'international' politics?
- In what ways is the international dimension of politics still important?
- To what extent have non-state actors come to rival states and national governments on the world stage?
- Does interdependence always lead to cooperation and peace, or can it generate conflict?
- Which definition of globalization is most persua-sive, and why?
- Has the impact and significance of globalization been exaggerated?
- What are the key differences between mainstream and critical approaches to global politics?
- Over what do realist and liberal theorists disagree?
- To what extent has global power become more diffuse and intangible in recent years?
- Why has there been growing interest in the notion of 'human' security?
- Does the idea of 'global' justice make sense?

Further reading

Brown, C. and K. Ainley, *Understanding International Relations* (2009). A highly readable and thought-provoking intro-duction to the theory and practice of international rela-tions.

Hay, C. (ed.), *New Directions in Political Science: Responding to the Challenges of an Interdependent World* (2010). A series of astute reflections on the nature, extent and implications of global interdependence.

Held, D. and A. McGrew, *Globalization/Anti-globalization: Beyond the Great Divide* (2007). A comprehensive and authoritative survey of contemporary political and intel-lectual debates over globalization.

Scholte, J. A., *Globalization: A Critical Introduction* (2005). An excellent and accessibly written account of the nature of globalization and of its various implications.

 **ONLINE RESOURCES AVAILABLE**   Links to relevant web resources can be found on the *Global Politics* website

Chapter 19

Introduction

What is Security?

Security is ultimately about life and death and therefore the things that ensure our continued existence. But as social animals, our security is not the same as that of animals and plants: basic biological functioning is not all we need to live and so not all it takes to be secure. Rather, security relates to the continuation of life and the protection and production of ways of life. To present our ways of life as merely a struggle for survival, in which all forms of social, political and economic organization are oriented to the prevention of death and the prolonging of life, would be to miss most of the experiences we have of living and seeking security. Security debates represent different views of what it is about life that is to be secured, how some deaths are to be avoided and other deaths deemed necessary or inevitable, and how the pursuit of life and prevention of death establish the ways in which both are organized.

The term 'security' has meant different things in different contexts and at different times (Rothschild, 1995). In common usage, 'security' relates to survival, to the protection from threats to existence, and being relatively free from harm inflicted by others. In academic usage, it generally relates to the protection of something that is valued, which may be physical life, the organization of political life in a particular nation-state, democracy, identity, language, property, territory and so on. Thus, for Arnold Wolfers (1952: 484), security means 'some degree of protection of values previously acquired'. This separates security from power and wealth, since wealth is a measure of material possessions and power is the 'ability to control the actions of others'. In contrast, security is characterized by other measures: 'security in an objective sense measures the absence of threats to acquired values, in a subjective sense, the absence of fear that such values will be attacked' (Wolfers, 1952: 485). Precise measurements of security are therefore impossible; clearly, we can have more security or less security. Perfect, complete security is unattainable.

The word 'security' derives from the Latin *securitas*, which comes from *sine cura* – *sine* (without), *cura/curio* (troubling). Thus, 'security' originally implied a condition of being without care, trouble or anxiety. This is not purely subjective. *Cura* relates to a state of mind and responsibilities – to be free from worries, but also from responsibilities – so that security is neither wholly positive (feeling secure in oneself) or negative (negligent, reckless) (Dillon, 1996). While etymology is important for understanding how the meaning of security came to be and came to change, it does not present us with a simple origin, a true meaning of security that we can return to. This is partly because it is always entwined with politics. Indeed, security is a foundational concept of the sovereign state and underlies what we conceive of as the political and how it works. Most understandings of security have not questioned security, but sought to explore how the state provides protection (to us and to itself), particularly in relations with other states; so security is often considered in terms of 'national security'. But while the invocation of security gives an issue the air of precision, distinguishing it from other issues, it remains, without further specification, an ambiguous term (Wolfers, 1952). Simply put, there is nothing within the term 'security' that sets the limits of that specification. For Barry Buzan (1991: 7), security issues 'encompass a whole domain, rather than just a fixed point, and for this reason cannot be defined in any general sense'. This domain used to be focused on the 'threat, use and control of military force' (Walt, 1991), but has expanded to include economic, societal and environmental issues, as well as political and military concerns. It has also moved beyond an exclusive focus on states as the 'referent object' to be secured to include the security of individuals, communities, regions or even the whole globe (see Chapter 1).

Understanding security is not a matter of definition but of understanding a concept in its living usage. There is little prospect of distilling the essence of security, since security is always related to other concepts. Security is better approached conceptually by asking questions: Security for whom? Security for which values? How much security can be expected or produced? From what threats? At what cost? In what time period? (Baldwin, 1997). These questions are linked, but they are not equivalent. Disagreement on such questions about security should not be viewed negatively (as a barrier to definition) but as the practice of debate that produces the concept. Some scholars refer to security as an 'essentially contested concept' (Buzan, 1991; Smith, 2005), indicating that not only are there many definitions of security, but that the differences between them contain an ideological element, which means that empirical analysis will never be sufficient to produce agreement. Similarly, Booth (1997) argues that security is a 'derivative concept', in that one's view of what security is derives from a philosophical and political perspective, complicated by the fact that security means nothing on its own. It is a term that is always used in (sometimes implied) conjunction with a threat or risk, an object to be made secure, and often in some balance or tension with other things, such as liberty, privacy, freedom of movement and so on. Without these relationships, definitions of security, such as freedom from threat, reveal very little about security's nature, scope, practice, ethics, dilemmas, purpose or possibilities.

Since security has no inherent meaning outside its relations with other concepts, there is no one 'security' but multiple securities. Perhaps the easiest way to begin to understand this is to look at the multiple meanings a single word, such as love, freedom and security, can have, depending on their usage as a noun, verb, adjective and so on. As such, security is a condition, a value and an indicator of the importance of other values; and a process through which that condition is achieved. Further, security, as a relational concept, always involves some concept of insecurity, such as threat, enemy, vulnerability and risk, that makes it understandable.

Security as a condition

The condition of security is being without threats to existence or something valued. While some say 'security is about survival' (Buzan et al., 1998: 21), others argue that it is about 'survival plus': 'the "plus" being some freedom from life-determining threats, and therefore [having] some life choices' (Booth, 2007: 104). While survival is an absolute, one either survives or perishes, security is a relative condition. The rich person, with security guards, alarms, fences, insurance policies, food, heat, water and luxurious accommodation, and the poor person, with meagre food and no protection from the elements or the violence of others, are both surviving but do not enjoy the same security.

As a condition, security may be viewed negatively, as the absence of threats, or positively, as the presence of something valued, which involves other concepts: order and stability, which render a given way of life relatively predictable and temporarily free from many cares, but do not eliminate all threats, and peace, which may denote an absence of war and violence, or the presence of justice, human dignity and emancipation (see Chapters 3 and 9).

As Wolfers (1952) argued, the condition of security is objective (actually being secure) and subjective (feeling or perceiving oneself to be secure). Clearly, one does not imply the other, as one might feel safe when one is in danger, or be afraid when there is no reason to be. However, these dual meanings of security are closely related: subjective security is integral to objective security, since perceptions of insecurity cause states to act in ways that may enhance or reduce their actual security. This relates to the limits of certainty in international relations: there are limits to knowing with certainty whether another actor intends to attack and, for some theorists, this lies at the heart of fear as a driving force of security politics (see Chapter 5). Indeed, in many understandings, the production of security is predicated on the elimination not of threats but uncertainties and the production not of safety but certainty and control (Der Derian, 1995; Dillon, 1996). This accords with the colloquial use of the term 'security' – to be secure in oneself is to be secure in the knowledge that the world is a particular way and can be understood, analysed, broken down, and optimal solutions and strategies identified. This condition is sometimes called 'ontological security' (Giddens, 1991). So, both security and understanding security are often a quest for certainty or at least for strategies of living with uncertainty.

Security as a value

Security is also a value. For many realists, it is the primary thing that states hold dear and seek in their interactions. It is also an indicator of the amount of value given to something else: to speak of 'state security' is to value the state, while to speak of the 'security of one's identity' is to attach a strong importance to particular characteristics and practices, such as language and social norms. Security, then, is one means of claiming something as particularly important, so central, in fact, that without securing that thing, many other valued things could not occur. While security is more than mere survival, not every value is something to be secured. For example, to value my right to drink Coke rather than Pepsi as a matter of security would be ludicrous, but to value my access to safe drinking water might not.

Security is a value among others (such as wealth) and the practice and analysis of security policy establishes the importance of that value. The classic 'guns or butter' debate, for example, poses two values, security and economic wellbeing, in competition with each other. When governments spend more money on military forces than health and education, as many do, they are implicitly valuing military security over developmental and welfare issues. But this relies on an understanding of security that is deeply questionable. Is not the economic wellbeing of people facing starvation or death from preventable diseases also a security issue for them? Security does not just compete with other values in the allocation of finite resources. Actions taken to ensure security may, in effect, conflict with other values. Notably, within Western societies, there is often a debate around the balance of security and liberty. The surveillance powers a government has to gather information on criminal groups or suspected terrorists may conflict with the right to privacy, the right to fair legal process, freedom of movement and so on. Here, Wolfers' claim that security relates to the protection of previously acquired values is somewhat problematic. To imply that values are acquired first and then made secure limits the questions that are asked about security. It does not ask how values are acquired (until critical approaches began to speak of intersubjective production of norms and values) or how the process of securing them affects what is valued and how. In other words, it separates the production of values from their protection in ways that have become deeply questioned.

Security as a good/commodity and a process

Security is also viewed as a public good – something that is provided for people on a relatively equal basis. This may be understood as founded on an imagined social contract with a higher authority and power, such as the sovereign state or even some international organization, to which states and peoples give authority to provide security. Increasingly, however, security is also seen as a commodity, a private good exchanged and distributed through a market. In practice, the status of security as a public or private good is becoming ever more complex.

Security also denotes the actions taken to achieve, distribute and protect the condition of security. It is thus a type of politics and practice. For many critical theorists, security gives a sense of urgency and importance to an issue (Buzan et al., 1998; Neocleous, 2008). This may mean that security is a realm in which the rules of 'normal', democratic politics are suspended and an 'exceptional' politics of secrecy, urgency and possible violence give interactions a different character (see Chapter 3). Thus, for many realist scholars, national security denotes a valuing of political institutions and territory and characterizes international relations about national security as inherently about power competition and modes of behaviour that exclude compromise (Morgenthau, 2006). In contrast, some critical scholars explore how invocations of security produce rather than just describe particular orders of relations. Security does not merely serve to protect but to create 'a particular way of organizing forms of life' (Huysmans, 1998: 231). This is most commonly understood as distinguishing different locations of security and politics; people group together in communities to protect themselves from others, and may invest security powers in a sovereign state. This splits the world into those to be feared (outsiders) and those to be trusted (insiders). So, security creates the foundational assumption of international relations: relations among peoples within a state are of a different character to the relations among states (Walker, 1993).

Insecurity: threat, enemies, vulnerabilities and risks

While security may be a condition, a value and a process, it is always such in relation to some sense of insecurity, which may be viewed through several concepts – threats, enemies, dangers, vulnerabilities and risks.

What is a threat? How are real threats distinguished from misperceived ones? Threats require an enemy, thus insecurity relates to the anticipation and actualization of harm inflicted by another. The understanding of who an enemy is, and why they may inflict harm, is integral to understanding security. For some, this limits what counts as a security issue: some things that can harm us, like natural disasters or accidents, are important but cannot be considered through the concept of security, as they lack the calculation of other actors' intentions and capabilities and cannot be responded to by deterring or persuading other actors not to engage in deliberately harmful behaviour (see Chapter 13). However, the issue is much deeper than that. For Schmitt (1996), the separating of friends from enemies is what constitutes the political. Political communities identify themselves by distinguishing between the self and the other on the basis of some particular characteristic (history, ethnicity, religion, language and so on). This is not just about asserting a difference, but establishing a relationship of threat between them so that the self and the other become the friend and the enemy. Enemies are not just different but dangerous. This Schmittian concept can mean that security is the defining feature of politics, which rather limits what politics can be (Aradau, 2006).

Danger is subjective, not merely a recognition of objective reality of someone who wishes to harm us. During the Cold War (1946–89), Western, and particularly US, national security practice was defined in terms of a struggle against communism, a difference in ideology that was deemed threatening to Western values and thus identity (Campbell, 1998a). In the post-Cold War era, similar arguments have been made about drug traffickers and terrorists. Threats to international order and stability are often explained on the basis of claims that power is the primary motive of states, or at least that power is the route to security that motivates states. Since states have unequal power, there is often a possibility that a state might seek to change its relative power position. Even if this does not threaten war, the physical destruction of a state's political infrastructure or the capture of its territory, it threatens the state in its valued international relations. For example, there are concerns among Western commentators that the growing economic and military power of China might challenge the position of the USA as the sole remaining superpower, and that its ongoing pursuit of greater influence in the global political sphere may threaten Western interests.

Two related concepts are vulnerability and risk. Threat relates to the actions, intentions and capabilities of other actors; vulnerability relates to those of the state being secured, particularly its capability to deter or defend itself against threats (Buzan, 1991). This is the second dimension of the condition of security: the absence of threats and thus particular relations with potential enemies, and the ability to defend against threats, which if inadequate are characterized as vulnerabilities. Importantly, vulnerabilities do not require a specific enemy, merely an anticipation of a future event that one is not sufficiently prepared for. For instance, a nation may be vulnerable because of inadequate military forces to counter those of an enemy, gaps in the security systems of computer networks, or poorly integrated emergency services unable to cope with natural disasters or terrorist attacks. A group of people may be vulnerable because their government persecutes them, or because they are poor and unable to prevent or respond to natural disasters or to ensure they have sustainable access to food and water. In the latter sense, vulnerability is now increasingly linked not just to threats but to risks. While threats are measured by calculating the intentions and capabilities of specific potential enemies, risks are found in the nature of general phenomena and are measured by the probability of these phenomena multiplied by their potential for harm. For example, there is much concern about the prospect of nuclear terrorism. While the probability of this is very low, the harm it could create would be very high, therefore it is seen as an important risk. In risk, vulnerability means the damage that might occur in a catastrophic event, so it relates to 'resilience', the ability to minimize the damage of an earthquake or terrorist attack and to ensure minimal disruption of daily life, rather than merely security as protection, which prevents the event in the first place (see Chapter 5).

Understanding security: logics and limits

How do we understand security amid all these differences and relationships? One useful device is to think about the logic and limits of security behaviours, that is, what sets in motion and what stops. These are interrelated: a car is set in motion by a combination of the driver's foot, an engine, petrol and internal combustion processes; what stops or limits that movement may be brakes, reaching a destination, or a wall. Both may result from the driver's intentions and capabilities, or from things external to the driver and the car, such as laws, road conditions or fuel shortages.

'Logic' means the dynamics and patterns of action, the driving forces of security behaviour. Some logics of behaviour developed in international relations scholarship also apply in security, which posits different logics:

- *the logic of consequences:* in which actions derive from assumed cost–benefit calculations made by states on the basis of anticipated consequences and prior preferences
- *the logic of appropriateness:* in which action derives from norms, values and identities
- *the logic of arguing:* where action comes from and within communication about norms and values
- *the logic of practicality:* more recently asserted, where the forms and habits of security practices establish the dynamics of security (March and Olsen, 1998; Risse, 2000; Pouliot, 2008).

These are, however, rather broad. More specifically, some theories articulate differing logics of power, such as realism, that views the pursuit of power as establishing the direction and form of action and the outcomes of interactions. This may follow a further logic of competition that is counterposed with a logic of cooperation. Both may arise from anticipated consequences but posit different patterns (as seen in the diversity of rationalist thought in Chapter 2). If, for instance, the primary logic of security is one of competition for power in a world full of power-hungry, selfish and violent actors, the condition of security is scarce. If, however, the logics of political life are set by evolving patterns of rule and order between states and within them, then cooperative logics may predominate in how and how much security is produced. In more fine-grained accounts, we find other forces – fear, violence, uncertainty, hatred, greed, ambiguity, a desire for control and so on.

'Limits' means what constrains or stops. What limits the amount of security that can be achieved, or for whom it can be realized? What restricts the degree to which states are able to cooperate with each other? As Walker claims (1995: 307), theories of international relations are a 'primary expression of the limits of modern politics'. The limits of security may relate to limits on violence imposed by laws, limits on the scope of political communities imposed by geography, anarchy or human nature and so on. A focus on limits alone is problematic: we do not understand something merely by its boundaries but by its content. Thus, we must speak of logics and limits together. Booth and Wheeler (2008) posit 'fatalist', 'mitigator' and 'transcender' logics, which relate to whether the conditions of anarchy and uncertainty that produce insecurity in the global order can merely be lived within (fatalist), whether their effects can be mitigated, and if real progress can be made that transcends them.

About this book

Security is not just a condition of freedom from objective threat or subjective fear, it is a mode of thinking and acting in the world. As such, much of what is discussed in the book goes beyond simple logics and limits, or even their complex relations. Given that security is multifaceted, can we really speak of one single logic and set of limits to security? No. But how this is the case will require the rest of this book to explore. This book seeks to understand security by exploring different approaches to security and how they play out in the multifarious agendas and practices that constitute contemporary security. It brings diverse theories, concepts and claims into conversation with each other and shows how security has been understood when those understandings encounter complex political issues and relationships.

Chapters 1–3 focus on the different theoretical perspectives in the study of security. Chapter 1 discusses the building blocks of understanding security. It looks at the debates on the scope of the field of security studies, and outlines the various components that are put together in particular understandings of security. Chapter 2 examines 'traditional' or 'rationalist' theories that posit various logics of consequences. Chapter 3 explores various critical approaches, including forms of constructivism, critical theory, feminism, poststructuralism and peace studies, and their concepts, such as securitization and emancipation, which offer a wider range of logics and limits to security.

Since a distinction between security in domestic affairs and international relations is foundational to the study of security, Chapter 4 examines the state, state formation and internal security practices, such as policing and surveillance. Chapter 5 explores the conditions of uncertainty and how this establishes different logics and limits to the strategies of action in security, internationally and domestically.

The book then moves into more in-depth coverage of states and their security practices. Chapter 6 looks at how states come together in different groupings to seek security, from alliances to regimes and security communities. It also explores how geographical factors establish different logics and limits of security relationships by looking at hopes for global collective security and regional security practices. Chapter 7 addresses the logics and limits of killing, particularly in war, its causes and its contemporary transformations and limitations. Chapter 8 discusses the logics and limits of cooperation on issues of weapons and military technology by an examination of the arms trade, proliferation, arms control and disarmament.

The remaining chapters are concerned with security issues and practices that, to some degree, move beyond the state as the central object to be made secure and the main actor that provides security. They address common themes of whether and how the significance of private/non-state actors and the transnational threaten and disrupt the international and national frames of reference for security and what implications this has for security politics, policy, practice and analysis. Chapter 9 focuses on human security as an attempt to define and practise security without centring on the state. Chapter 10 looks at how human security and state security have become integrated into discussions of the phenomenon of 'failed states' and the extent to which the range of practices of conflict intervention seek to reassert security as being for states, by states, and located within an interstate framework. Chapter 11 engages with the phenomena of terrorism and counterterrorism that pervade contemporary security logics. Chapter 12 addresses other transnational security issues that relate to particular global flows, including migration and transnational crime, and the strengthening of international policing, border controls and surveillance. Chapter 13 considers understandings of security practices related to the environment, such as conflict over resources, climate change, energy security, and the security of the basic needs for food and water. Chapter 14 concludes the book with some reflections on how understandings of security combine all these issues, and how these might develop.

Chapter 20

Understanding and Theorizing Security

Understanding the logics and limits of security requires that we first understand the logics and limits of theorizing about security. For issues as complex and multifaceted as security, innumerable 'facts' arise from the real world – for example the end of the Cold War (1989), the al-Qaeda attacks of 11 September 2001, or the 2003 US-led invasion of Iraq – which do not speak unambiguously to us but require interpretation. Different understandings of security are not simply opposing evaluations of real-world security problems, leaving the student of security with the task of judging which theory best fits the facts of security. Rather, they contain widely varying underlying assumptions about the scope of security, the purpose and practice of developing theories, and the building blocks of those theories – deeper questions of what the social and political world is made of (ontology), and how we know, understand and produce knowledge (epistemology). These assumptions are formative of the way the academic field of 'security studies' has produced different understandings of security. This field initially arose as a subset of the wider discipline of international relations (IR), itself part of the study of politics. It has therefore been concerned with the international politics of security. However, it has increasingly focused on wider sets of relations, including domestic and transnational relations, and has frequently engaged with or drawn on concepts from other disciplines, most notably economics, sociology, history, geography and psychology. Security studies is now a hybrid field, whose foundational assumptions, and the challenges to them, often derive from wider theoretical and practical endeavours. It has also undergone periods of great theoretical innovation, and periods of a narrowing of debate onto empirical questions. As it has done so, the scope of its concern has changed (Walt, 1991; Booth, 1994; Baldwin, 1997; Prins, 1998; Buzan and Hansen, 2009).

The scope of security (studies)?

As understandings of security have developed since the Second World War (1939–45), the scope and distinctiveness of the field of security studies has evolved, intimately linked to the changing global landscape of security threats. In the first postwar decade, security theorizing was vibrant and diverse, but indistinct from IR (Baldwin, 1997). From the mid-1950s to the mid-1960s, a more distinct field of 'strategic studies' emerged and underwent a 'golden age' as the growing threat of nuclear confrontation produced a focus on matters of military force, such as how nuclear weapons could be made useful and how nuclear stability could be achieved through deterrence. This early development of strategic thought occurred particularly in government-linked think tanks (Walt, 1991). From the late 1960s, the US–Soviet detente made the prospect of a superpower war seem more distant and the field declined in relative importance. This enabled more theoretical innovation through the introduction of psychological approaches and organizational theory, which drew attention to subjective aspects of security, misperception and decision making in crises (Nye and Lynn-Jones, 1988). By the late 1970s, a resurgence of scholarly concern with matters of war brought with it an expansion of the field of strategic studies (Walt, 1991; Baldwin, 1997). Here, there was some broadening of issues of concern as conventional military conflicts rose in importance as well as matters nuclear. It also became a more mature academic discipline rather than being concentrated in think tanks (Walt, 1991; Miller, 2010). As it matured, its name started to change from strategic studies to 'security studies'. While some view this as a nominal change, in which the focus and concepts of the field remain rooted in 'strategy', others view security studies as a wider set of concerns that incorporates but goes far beyond matters of war and strategy. The post-Cold War development of security studies can be characterized as two interrelated processes of broadening and deepening: first, the breadth of issues covered and the deepening of referent objects to be made secure; and second, a similar expansion of the theoretical engagements and foundations of the field.

Broadening and deepening: issues and objects

For much of the second half of the twentieth century, the study and practice of security were defined in terms of the 'national security' of states, and related to military threats from other states and the practice of planning, deploying, threatening, controlling and using military force. Indeed, defending this focus, Stephen Walt (1991: 212) claimed that:

> Security studies assumes that conflict between states is always a possibility and that the use of military force has far-reaching effects on states and societies ... Accordingly, security studies may be defined as the study of the threat, use, and control of military force ... It explores the conditions that make the use of force more likely, the ways that the use of force affects individuals, states, and societies, and the specific policies that states adopt in order to prepare for, prevent, or engage in war.

Here, limiting the scope of security studies to issues of military force between states is justified by the claim that the field has its own assumptions about the possibilities and consequences of war. Yet these are not neutral assumptions, they are a restatement of the basic tenets of realist theory that determines the parameters of security for everyone (see Chapter 3). Amid the decline and end of the Cold War, security practitioners expanded the scope of security agendas and scholars debated the parameters of what counts as a security issue.

In his well-known discussion of national security, Wolfers (1952: 484) claimed that the term 'covers a range of goals so wide that highly divergent policies can be interpreted as policies of security'. This has broadened further as economic, social, environmental and wider political issues have been added to the list of security issues. Early arguments for broadening the scope of security beyond military issues came from within realist thought, although most realists do not welcome such moves. Herz (1981) argued that realism should endorse a wider security politics that tackled issues such as the depletion of energy resources, food scarcity and environmental harm. Ullman (1983: 129) claimed that 'defining national security merely (or even primarily) in military terms conveys a profoundly false image of reality' and that doing so 'causes states to concentrate on military threats and to ignore other and perhaps even more harmful dangers. Thus it reduces their total security.' The most common way of broadening security was provided by Buzan (1991), who attempted to systematize the types of issues that may now be considered part of security. Buzan (1991: 19–20) outlined five 'sectors' of security:

- *Military security:* remains conceived in fairly traditional terms as the 'interplay of the armed offensive and defensive capabilities of states and states' perceptions of each other's intentions'.
- *Political security:* relates largely to stability in the way states are organized and governed and the ideologies from which they draw legitimacy.
- *Economic security:* sustaining populations' levels of welfare and the power of the state in relation to their access to resources, finance and foreign markets.
- *Societal security:* the sustainability (and some evolution) of national identity and customs, and the culture, language and religious identity of social groups.
- *Environmental security:* reflecting the rising global interest in environmental issues from the 1980s onwards, this relates to the maintenance of the biosphere, locally and globally, as it is 'the essential support system on which all other human enterprise depends'.

Many of these issues had previously been part of security only inasmuch as they affected military power. Now, issues such as poverty, migration, terrorism and some aspects of environmental security are prominent security concerns in their own right.

The deepening of security relates to changes in the 'referent object' of security – that which is to be made secure. The primary, and largely exclusive, referent object of approaches to security has been the state: 'security' has meant 'national security'. For realists like Hans Morgenthau (2006: 561), 'national security must be defined as integrity of the national territory and of its institutions'. This integrity is threatened particularly in times of war and the use of military force between states, or the potential for such use to occur, has made up much of the business of security policy and security studies. However, the position of the state as the sole referent object of security has been challenged. As noted in the Introduction, attaching primacy to the security of some 'referent object' is an ethical statement of what should be valued and protected. Focusing on the state has meant that it has been assumed that the survival and wellbeing of human beings within a community are assured by the state, such that to secure the state is to secure people. Yet many states engage in widespread human rights abuses, or even genocide against their own populations. So, if it is not possible to assume that the security of citizens can be taken for granted within a state, perhaps the study and practice of security should emphasize 'human security' rather than state security (see Chapter 9). However, individuals are not made secure on an individual basis but as part of social groups. Thus, one might deepen security beyond the state but prefer to speak of 'societal' security (Buzan et al., 1998). Also, much security practice is above the level of the state. Increasingly, for instance, security practices are tied to regional groupings of states, and practised through regional organizations as well as states (see Chapter 6). Further, for some, the key to human security and state security lies not just at those levels, but in the nature of the global system. Thus, it may be desirable to theorize not just national security or even international security but to think about 'world security' (Booth, 2007).

The broadening and deepening of security is not always an ethically, politically or analytically desirable move. Critics of broadening reverse Ullman's critique and argue that expanding security distracts attention from the still urgent problems of military force. Some claim that this broader range of issues could cause security academics and practitioners to lose the hard-won coherence of the field (Walt, 1991; Morgan, 1992). However, broadening security has not necessarily entailed significant adjustment in what constitutes security. For Buzan, 'security' in each sector still relates to protection, to ensuring the existence and sustainability of something valued, or of something foundational to other values, be that forms of political life, social life, or economic welfare. While some welcomed the broadening of security as enabling thinking and doing security differently (Kolodziej, 1999), others argue that attaching the word 'security' to an issue often simply extends the militarized and competitive logics of military security to other fields. If this occurs, it is potentially problematic, such as when it is applied to migration or poverty reduction (see Chapters 9 and 12). Similarly, if all that changes is the referent object, then we risk militarizing human rights or climate change in ways that are not conducive to tackling these problems appropriately (see Chapters 9 and 13).

Broadening and deepening: theoretical underpinnings

The broadening of security issues and the deepening of referent objects can be accommodated within some extension of the basic theoretical paradigms of security developed during the Cold War. However, approaches to security have diversified and undergone their own broadening and deepening. Security studies today is characterized by many more different theories and concepts than it used to be. Some of this broadening has occurred with the developments of new forms of traditional theories like realism and liberalism, and took place throughout the Cold War (see Chapter 3). Other 'critical' approaches, encompassing constructivism, critical theory, feminism, poststructuralism and others, have developed more recently and differ fundamentally from traditional theories (see Chapter 3). This broadening is related to another form of deepening: the deepening of engagement with the political and social theory that underlies security theory. Indeed, for Kenneth Booth (2007: 155), the deepening of security relates primarily to this theoretical 'drilling down' into the origins of understanding security in political thought. This deepening of engagement has been seen in how security itself has become a contested concept (Buzan, 1991; Rothschild, 1995; Baldwin, 1997; Huysmans, 1998). This exposing of the political theoretical foundations of understanding security poses understanding in much more creative and open terms. Understandings of security are not just axiomatic statements that seek to simplify the complex empirical picture, but a set of beliefs and assumptions that shape how and why we seek to understand security and what understandings can result. Much like the broadening of issues and deepening of referent objects, the broadening and deepening of theorization is sometimes criticized for producing overly philosophical debates disconnected from the real world.

Approaches to security differ on what the purpose of theorizing is. For some, theory is a tool; like a hammer or a car, it is the means to a greater end of 'explanation'. For others, theories, the ideas we have about the world, are part of that world: they are 'constitutive', in the sense that they don't just describe the world but make it (Zalewski, 1996). This leads us to three possibilities: pure explanation, pure constitution, and a combination of the two.

Explanatory approaches see theory as a tool that allows us to grasp why events, such as wars, occur and how they can be avoided, mitigated, or won, and to deduce what the drivers and limits of security are. They treat the world of security as part of nature and attempt to explain what happens through discovering laws (like the law of gravity) – invariable truths – and causal relations (X action leads to Y result) in order to make predictions and thereby add to the sum of our knowledge of how the world works (Hollis and Smith,

1990). In explanatory views, theorists merely respond to the real world, to events like the end of the Cold War or the rise of transnational terrorism, and seek to find useful explanations. This is sometimes called a separation of the 'subject' (the theorist) and the 'object' (the nature of security policy and so on). This separation is defended by many realists and liberals as an extension of the modern Enlightenment project of gaining mastery over the world through rationalism (Zalewski, 1996). Claiming to produce value-free scientific knowledge of how security works, such security theorists are 'children of the Enlightenment', who 'seek knowledge in order to improve the quality of human action' (Haftendorn, 1991: 3). As Walt (1991: 212) claimed, security studies have tended to 'address phenomena that can be controlled by national leaders' and 'concentrate on manipulable variables, on relationships that can be altered by deliberate acts of policy'. Thus, explanatory approaches also tend to view the purpose of theory as producing knowledge that is useful for the strategic actions of states that seek to manipulate their environment to make themselves secure. In practice, this has also given security studies a short-term focus and an often unreflective tendency to make recommendations on what particular decision should be taken and how it should be done (Nye and Lynn-Jones, 1988).

In contrast, those who see theory as a tool and as constitutive see the purpose of theorizing as one of critique. Some critical approaches to security see the world of the theorist and the 'real world' of security politics as deeply entwined. Theory is still a tool, but not a neutral one, it is also constitutive of the real world. Seeing theory as constitutive means that our ideas about the real world are part of the real world, they shape what happens in it. For example, realist theory assumes that war is an inevitable part of international politics. Thinking this means accepting that war is always a possibility and the task of theorizing is to explain why and when it occurs, and how it can be won or avoided, but not eradicated. For some critical theorists, for example, the character of the world is not naturally given, but has been produced through particular historical processes that could have been different. If theorizing is constitutive not just explanatory, the point of theorizing may be not only to explain the existing rules of the game of security and to do better within them, but also to see how these rules emerged and how they may be changed in better directions (see Chapter 3). Here, theorizing does not necessarily portray itself as seeking to give advice only to state leaders but also to human rights campaigners, local groups, environmental groups and so on (Eriksson, 1999; Booth, 2007). Further, since theories are constitutive, theorizing is not merely the means through which advice for future action is produced, it is a political action itself.

A final type of theorizing goes beyond theory as a tool, a noun, and takes the constitutive nature of theory further. Theory, for poststructuralists, some feminists and others, is theorizing, a verb, the practice of giving meaning to the world and ourselves (see Chapter 3). This is something we all do, academics and policy makers alike, and is not confined to grand ideas about theorizing as a means of discerning the single truth of nature but to all sorts of daily practices; that is, the intersubjective ways we give meaning to the world are what constitute the practices of security and its omissions and silences. The real world is not separate from the world of the theorist, but constituted by theorists (of all types). Such constitutive approaches often conflict with instrumental notions of producing predictive knowledge for policy makers since they do not seek to identify manipulable variables. For explanatory theorists, like Walt (1991: 223), this makes them a 'self-indulgent discourse that is divorced from the real world'.

Are we to view this theoretical deepening and broadening as potentially liberating, giving us a wider range of tools to look at the world, which enable us to grasp different bits of the truth of security? Or should we despair at the loss of unity in focus that arises, which draws our attention to abstract metatheoretical questions rather than the security issues that affect people's daily lives and the survival of our way of life? Certainly, it would be a mistake to take a fully relativist stance that all theories are complementary. For instance, realist Colin Gray (1999: 165) claimed that 'poor – which is to say impractical – theories are at best an irrelevance, and at worst can help get people killed'. Yet how do we know which is the better theory? One might claim, as many have done, that the best theory is that which provides the most compelling explanation for security practices, that which fits the greatest amount of evidence. This may seem obvious, but actually it reflects different (explanatory) understandings of the purposes of theory. Importantly, however, the deepening of theory is not just a broadening of interpretations of what theorizing is, but a stronger engagement with the building blocks of theory – metatheoretical perspectives on ontology and epistemology.

The building blocks of understanding security

Understandings of security, and the role of theorizing, are built on assumptions about what the world is made of, how it works and how we understand it. In other words, they combine some basic building blocks that relate to ontology (what the world is made of and how it is organized) and epistemology (how we know, how understanding develops). These issues have also been important in shaping debates in IR (Lapid, 1989; Smith, 1996; Keohane, 1998). Indeed, much of the debate between different understandings of security reflects deeper divisions on these questions rather than just differing interpretations of evidence.

Ontology

Ontology, like metaphysics of which it is part, is a theory of what exists, what is real. The main ontological division is between those who assume that there is a 'real' world outside our ideas about it (ontological realism), and those who see the real world as constituted by our ideas about it (ontological idealism). In understandings of security, *ontological realism* is sometimes associated with naturalism, in which the character of security relations is given in nature, such as in human nature or the nature of the anarchic international system. Here, the real world is characterized by regularities that imply causal laws that need to be uncovered and understood. In contrast, *ontological idealism* draws attention to the historical processes or social interactions that create the world of security relations in a particular way. From these assumptions, understandings of security derive their specific ontologies of what the nature, units and content of security relations are. For instance:

- the *realist* view of the world as an anarchic system composed of states as units and their relations consisting largely of power competition
- a *liberal* view of a world comprising states, international institutions and non-state actors comprising competitive and cooperative relationships
- a *constructivist* or *poststructuralist* world of norms, identities and meanings, of discourses formed intersubjectively among states and powerful actors
- a *critical theorist* world of historical processes constructing the present, of competition, cooperation and ethics among social groups including states.

These more specific differences in the ontological building blocks of understandings of security point to a more complex array of distinctions. In security studies, as in the social sciences broadly, ontological questions are often understood through parsing up the world into different dualisms: subject-object, fact-value, material-ideational, structure-agency, system-unit, domestic-foreign. The first three are basic distinctions that are foundational to metatheoretical claims and debates, while the latter three are more derivative assumptions and distinctions that have prompted more explicit debate within approaches to security. For each distinction, four broad arguments are made: one is more important than (and determines) the other, or vice versa; third, some form of mutually constitutive relationship often conceived as a dialectic; and fourth, a denial of the distinction itself.

Basic distinctions

Basic distinctions of subject and object and fact and value relate to the nature of theorizing. The existence and nature of the distinctions between subject (person, theorist) and object (the object of study, security politics) are debated. Explanatory approaches rely on a clear separation of subject and object that interpretive and normative approaches deny. This is further reflected in the distinction between fact and value. Values are seen as belonging to the realm of the subject. If there is a clear subject–object distinction, then values are excluded from the realm of the object. Values are personal to the theorist and have no place in the study of the object: to do so would be to introduce bias and confuse one's own values with descriptions of the facts about the real world. If, however, values are seen as part of the object of study, we may have a constructivist view of the world made of two types of facts: 'brute' or 'material' facts that derive from the nature of the object itself, and 'social facts' that become facts through agreement rather than residing inherently in the nature of the thing.

The third distinction, between material and ideational factors, relates to the nature of theorizing and the things that are studied. A prior ontological commitment to materialism and idealism sets particular theories on a path to explaining security in terms of one set of factors. What matters most in explaining war? Is it material things, the amount of weapons and soldiers a country has, as many realists claim, or is it ideational things, norms and values and the identities of friends and enemies, or even socially constructed assumptions that tell us that war is an inevitable feature of the world, as constructivists argue? This is not a simple either/or choice. Some theories are almost wholly materialist, some are predominantly idealist, while others view security behaviour as a product of a combination of both.

Structure vs agency

What shapes behaviours and their outcomes, such as starting a war, negotiating a peace, forming an alliance, engaging in terrorism, trafficking drugs and so on? Is security politics a world of pure agency, of choices made freely, or is it a world in which something in the nature of the international system, or the collective implications of values and choices affect future decisions? Answers to these questions articulate arguments about structure and agency (Doty, 1997; Bieler and Morton, 2001; Wight, 2006). Broadly speaking, structure is something external to actors that shapes their behaviour. Agency relates to what actors (individuals or collectives, states or groups of states) do when they act. One metaphor used in IR theory is the billiard table. What shapes the movement and interaction of the balls on the table? Is it what the balls (state actors) do or what the table's cushioned edges (structure) do? Perhaps a better metaphor is to ask: What affects the course of a river? The properties of water, the shape of the river beds and banks, the gradient of hills, the presence of dams and boulders, or the interactions of all these things? While these metaphors imply material structures, it is important to note that social and ideational structures also matter. We drive on one side of the road not because cars and roads only permit that, but because socially and legally produced rules shape behaviour. They are not natural structures (some countries drive on the right, some on the left), nevertheless they affect drivers.

Structures may shape behaviours and outcomes. In social thought, from Emile Durkheim's sociology to Kenneth Waltz's structural realist security studies, structures explain behaviours and outcomes. The classic notion of structure in security studies is that of anarchy (the absence of hierarchical government) in the international system. For many realists, this structure imposes limits on how much security can be achieved and creates a competitive logic to states' security interactions. If structures are largely unchanging, then change and variation in security relate to some change in or among actors within the confines of pre-existing structural forces: in realism, this is changes in the distribution of material power among states (see Chapter 2). If structures are historically or socially produced, then change is more possible and both change and regularity need explaining, but still actors cannot simply decide to act differently and easily produce a new structure: those existing structures still shape their choices. This is the classic dialectic, as Marx (2001: 7) put it: 'Men make their own history, but they do not make it just as they please … but under circumstances directly encountered, given and transmitted from the past.'

Agency relates to the extent and capacities of actors to act within a structure. How much choice do they really have? How could things have been different? There are two key elements to the dominant view of agency – power and rationality. Agency in much security theory is the 'faculty or state of acting or exerting power' (Buzan et al., 1993: 103). Power is defined in different ways by different theories of security. Some realists define it primarily in terms of material military capabilities (force levels, weapons), others view it in terms of the ability to persuade others, or to set the rules of the game. But agency also relates to the manner in which power is used. Many theories also assume that action is rational. Rationality is the assumption that actors act in accordance with particular interests they seek to maximize. This is really two assumptions. First, actors have a particular set of interests and are able to calculate which are more important (territory or trade for instance) and, for the purpose of theorizing, most actors of a given type (states) have similar basic interests (power, survival and so on). Second, having and knowing these interests, actors seek to pursue them through a rational (meaning calculating rather than sensible or wise) process of cost–benefit analysis. In deciding whether to go to war, for instance, a state will calculate whether war is the best approach to seeking its interests, what the costs of war would be, whether they would win and so on. However, this is an oversimplification. Many understandings of security do not posit pure rationality in which actors have perfect information and seek to make optimal choices, but a limited 'bounded' rationality, in which actors are constrained by imperfect information and may come under pressure to seek the easiest satisfactory strategy (known as 'satisficing behaviour') rather than the objectively optimal one. Further, some critical approaches to security emphasize that the interests states pursue are not pregiven but socially constructed, and so the subsequent cost–benefit analyses are shaped by different values, interests and identities.

The relationships between structure and agency can be viewed in four main ways: structuralism, in which structures determine outcomes; agency-centred approaches, in which the choices of individual actors matter more; some combination of structure and agency shapes behaviour and outcomes, for example Wendt's constructivism combines structure and agency in the concept of 'structuration' (see Chapter 3); or a questioning of the importance of the distinction – found in some poststructuralism. Beyond these foundational views, questions of structure and agency raise questions of where and what structures matter.

Levels of analysis: system, unit or more

Assumptions of structure and agency permeate questions of levels of analysis. Early in the development of IR, Singer (1961) posed the challenge of accounting for behaviour in terms of the units (states) or the nature of the system. This framed the structure and agency problem as one of a difficult choice between macro- and micro-levels. Waltz (1959) discerned three 'images' where the explanation of war was located. Is war explained by human nature (first image), as in classical realism; in the nature of the state (second image), as in bureaucratic politics models (Allison, 1971) and liberal claims that democratic states are less prone to war than nondemocratic states; or in the structure of the international system (third image), conceived particularly as anarchy for Waltz and many later theorists? While dividing up enquiry or explanation into distinct levels is useful for clarifying differences in explanations of war – as was Waltz's intent – one is not necessarily faced with an either/or choice and many approaches seek to combine second and third image explanations.

Questions of agency and level of analysis combine in the status given to states as the main security actors. Can we conceive of states as simple individual units, known as 'methodological individualism', where they are like people (or even are people) (Wendt, 1999; Wight, 2006)? States are complex entities made up of various government departments, private interest groups and so on. When a state acts, does this complexity matter? For some theorists, agency is only a property of individual human beings, and so when a state seems to act, it is really the actions of leaders or powerful people. Further, do we conceive of actors as having interests before they interact with each other? Waltz's structural realism assumes we do, but for others, states and their interests and calculations are formed in their relationships with each other. For instance, human beings exist physically before they interact socially (even if only in the womb), but what it means to be human, what interests an individual, has to emerge through interactions. If what it means to be a state is constituted through interactions being set beforehand, then the state has a different ontological status.

Domestic/foreign: political ontology and spatiality

Moving from social ontology – the nature of actors and their relations – to political ontology – the make-up of politics within that social universe – a further foundational distinction is that between domestic and international security relations. Spatial metaphors are common in security studies. Levels of analysis present a vertical differentiation from the small (individual) to the big (system); Buzan's security sectors present a metaphor of dividing issues into zones. The distinction between international and domestic politics and security is stronger than these, as it is less a metaphorical schema for clarifying different theories within the study of security and more a foundational assumption that legitimates the wider discipline of IR. As noted in the Introduction, this distinction pertains particularly to the limits of politics and security. Within states, supposedly, politics functions through the presence of a government that allows politics to pursue moral goals, justice, freedom and the rule of law because security is assured. Outside, or among, states, the possibilities of politics and security are seen as different when the organizing principle of international relations is commonly assumed to be anarchy rather than hierarchy (government). Here, security is not assured and politics itself is much weaker, baser and more limited (Walker, 1993). While much Cold War security studies adopted a strong inside-outside distinction, the emergence of transnational security issues and behaviours such as transnational crime, migration and terrorism have been argued to reduce the salience of this divide. (see Chapters 11 and 12). Transnational simply means processes and interactions that occur across national boundaries. They usually involve at least one non-state actor, and so challenge the primacy of the state and the derivative spatial imagination of clear inside-outside division or easily identifiable levels of analysis (Risse-Kappen, 1995; Overbeek, 2000).

Building on the inside-outside distinction, many understandings of security have fallen into what Agnew called the 'territorial trap'. This combines three related assumptions: states are units within which territory and peoples are governed by a sovereign; the boundary between the domestic and the foreign is the boundary that defines political and economic interaction; and territorial states are prior to and containers of social orders, such that no other form or shape of social interaction can be imagined (Agnew and Corbridge, 1995). Together, these mean that conceptions of security are trapped into modes of thought with the state at the centre. This closes down permissible ontological claims about the universe of actors and their relations that can be made when articulating approaches to security. In particular, it encourages students of security to place themselves in the position of a state and think about security from that perspective (Morgenthau, 2006). This makes defining and understanding security beyond a state-centric paradigm difficult, and attempts to do this in relation to human security or transnational threats often end up falling back onto asserting that the state is the most important provider of security and container of insecurity. That is, the state may be challenged in its ability or willingness to provide security but it remains the defining point of the spatiality of security.

Epistemology

Epistemologies are theories of knowledge that underlie understandings of security. Understanding how we know relates to the status we give to the knowledge presented by theories of security and how they are built. While there are numerous approaches to this question, a central distinction has been drawn between 'positivist' and 'postpositivist' approaches. The dominant epistemology in security studies is most commonly referred to as 'positivism', although some criticize this label and argue that in IR and security, the term is erroneously used to describe 'empiricism' (Smith, 1996). In the philosophy of science, positivism, especially logical positivism, asserts that all phenomena are observable (Hollis and Smith, 1990). This is a pure empiricism, in which the only things that exist (ontology) are observable, and if something is not observable, it cannot be granted 'real' ontological status. However, it is not this pure empiricism that we find in much IR or security theory (Nicholson, 1996). Many theories labelled 'positivist' offer a wider empiricist view that allows for phenomena that are not directly observable but are asserted on the basis of what they appear to do; for instance, anarchy or the international system are observable only through their effects. These are, however, given the status of organizing ideas rather than real-world entities, although the distinction is all too often lost in the practice of theorizing. This means two things. First, seeing is believing: we know the world through our senses. Second, it has a correspondence theory of truth: a claim is 'true' when it corresponds to the evidence we see in the real world.

Pure empiricism can be contrasted with rationalism and pragmatism. Rationalism argues that good knowledge is derived from reasoned thought about the world, not merely the evidence one finds: simply put, all knowledge derives through reasoned thought, the facts do not simply speak for themselves. In IR, for instance, Morgenthau (2006: 4) claimed that 'theory consists in ascertaining facts and giving them meaning through reason'. However, this can be criticized for assuming a single 'reason' that is at odds with what we know from psychology. Both empiricism and rationalism presuppose a 'real' world separate from our knowledge of it and therefore rely on a clear distinction between subject and object, in which the subject is prior to what they encounter in the real world. Pragmatism defines good knowledge in somewhat different terms: good knowledge is that which is practically useful. In practice, while empiricism is dominant, many empiricist security scholars, such as Waltz, also claim the validity of their knowledge on pragmatic grounds.

Empiricism is not the same as valuing empirical evidence. Theorists of all kinds use empirical evidence (examples from the practice of security politics) and validate their claims on this basis. Rather, empiricists hold that we gain knowledge through particular processes of hypothesis formation and empirical testing. There is further diversity here. In the social sciences, behaviouralism has a particularly 'austere' view of what is testable (Hollis and Smith, 1990, 12), while others are more open in their ontology and methods and emphasize that it is only by the rigorous application of hypothesis formation and empirical testing that theoretical knowledge can be tested against its correspondence with an external 'reality'.

In understanding security, and wider social sciences, 'positivism' is more than a pure empiricism. It also combines assumptions of scientism, naturalism and value neutrality. Scientism is the assumption that the natural sciences represent the strongest form of knowledge and should be emulated. This is underpinned by ontological realism, and often a naturalism: the world, including political and social relations, is naturally a certain way (as opposed to being constructed) and is characterized by regularities that allow the discernment of fixed law-like relationships. This means that 'human beings and societies belong to a single natural order, which yields its secrets to a single scientific method' (Hollis, 1996: 304). Explanatory approaches to theorizing emphasize this by seeking to uncover such regularities underneath the seemingly endless variation in political reality. Value neutrality means that the process of producing knowledge should be free of one's own personal perspective and values. This has been emphasized since the political theorist Max Weber, who influenced the founders of IR such as Morgenthau (Barkawi, 1998), claimed that 'whenever the man of science introduces his personal value judgement, a full understanding of the facts ceases' (cited in Smith, 2004: 500). Conjoining the distinctions between subject and object and between facts and values gives empirical evidence a particular status – as the legible face the real world presents to us. Values are from another realm and should not be included. On the basis of an empiricist epistemology, this makes some sense; since moral claims cannot be proved correct (or incorrect) through observation of empirical evidence, a value-free science is essential.

These basic assumptions are criticized by a range of 'postpositivist' views, held particularly by critical approaches to security (see Chapter 3). They argue that the apparent value neutrality of positivism is not achieved by those who claim it, and for some critics, it is not achievable at all. Rather, knowledge is not a neutral set of facts separate from values, but is 'situated knowledge'. Critical IR theorist Robert Cox (1981: 128) thus claimed that 'all theory is for someone and for some purpose': there is no such thing as value-neutral theoretical observation, as all observers are situated within a particular historical and geographical context that they cannot simply leave at the door when theorizing. Many values and assumptions are seen as natural, or are held subconsciously, and cannot be stripped away. This means that no social scientist is unbiased or neutral in their pursuit of knowledge, and thereby all knowledge is not neutral in the way positivists have claimed. If knowledge is not the correspondence of theories with facts but is socially (and/or historically) produced and situated, then knowledge claims are located within the realm of the subject and intersubjective relations rather than in a relationship between the subject and the object. For some critical approaches, the resultant focus has been on language or discourse: the way we discuss the world through language, visual representations and so on is not only a description of separate reality but also affects the way we see things (see Chapter 3). This means that the knowledge we have is not just about power, but is itself related to power – the power to say what is 'true'. Thus, some constructivists, feminists and critical security scholars seek alternative foundations for producing and judging knowledge that can never be neutral but can be better when justified on pragmatic and ethical lines: the seeking of a more cosmopolitan knowledge, reflective not of one culture's specific ways of thinking but one that could be agreed by a wider range of peoples. Others, like poststructuralists, deny the possibility of such foundations against which we can judge the 'truth' of something. For them, there is no single 'Archimedean' point, no 'view from nowhere' from which we can discern truth from falsehood. This is sometimes mistaken for a denial of the existence of the real world (an ontological claim) rather than a more nuanced claim that our knowledge of the world does not and cannot attain an indisputable truth about the real world. Truth is always defined in relation to other potential truths, not discerned by discovering an objective truth. Here, the basis of truth is acceptance not correspondence to independent reality, and so truth and power are inseparable. Indeed, for poststructuralists, claims of an eternal and supposedly objective truth are associated with power and violence.

Some non-positivist approaches retain a stronger subject-object distinction, in which the two are mutually constitutive. Drawing on recent philosophy of science, especially the work of Bhaskar, 'critical realist' perspectives maintain that there is a reality independent of our knowledge of it, but that does not mean that our knowledge is or can be politically neutral (Patomaki, 2002; Wight, 2006). This view licenses an eclectic position in which relations between the subject and object, the material and the ideational are not to be decided on a priori but must be chosen to fit with the multiple and complex realities of security on a case-by-case, empirical basis (Patomaki and Wight, 2000; Kurki and Wight, 2007).

How does understanding develop? Methodology and progress

Numerous methods are used to produce security knowledge. Data may be gathered from official documents, archives, or other historical accounts, by interviewing key people or using questionnaires and so on. Different methods arise in part from differing ontological and epistemological warrants, which license particular methods as the most appropriate for generating 'good' knowledge. Many approaches use qualitative analyses, such as case studies or wider historical methods. Some, particularly rationalist, approaches may use quantitative methods by using statistics to find correlations between variables or developing formal mathematical models that elaborate particular logics of behaviour often without testing them against empirical evidence. Different views on rationality shape methodological differences among traditional approaches. For some, the rationality assumption is so strong that behaviour can be modelled on the basis of fixed and pregiven interests and calculations, and so use forms of analysis based on formal mathematical modelling, statistical analysis or game theory. For others, a softer rationality assumption guides theorizing but does not require or allow the reductive and parsimonious methods of game theory (Walt, 1999; Smith, 2004).

Critical and postpositivist approaches are diverse in their methods but tend not to use quantitative methods or formal modelling, as these are often features of positivist enquiry (Salter and Mutlu, 2013). Instead, they may use genealogical methods (historical philosophical accounts of how truths come into being), immanent critique (historical analysis of how a current state of affairs was produced and how it could have been different), deconstruction (a poststructuralist method of showing how seemingly natural or logical assumptions are actually particular combinations of sets of assumptions that may be internally contradictory) and forms of discourse analysis and ethnography.

Epistemological questions also relate to how understandings of security change. For instance, Robert Keohane's (1988) criticism that postpositivist approaches fail to articulate a coherent research programme assumes that knowledge progresses by proving or disproving particular propositions and moving towards some stronger truth. A broadly positivist view is that knowledge progresses through the collective efforts of 'scientists' making propositions about the world that are tested empirically and on that basis become accepted as true. Another influential view, even among those who adopt broadly positivist approaches, is that advocated by Popper, who argued that science advanced not through propositions being proved true but by being proved false (or at least incomplete and unsatisfactory). A process of 'falsification' implies that final and complete knowledge is never attained but progress occurs through refining ideas by proving earlier ones insufficient in some way. Assuming that understanding progresses in these ways underlies the dismay and dismissal expressed by some critics of the deepening and broadening of security.

In contrast, some theorists adopt a different view associated with Kuhn's philosophy of science. Kuhn speaks of paradigms, in which general theories cannot be contrasted with each other in a way designed to prove or disprove them. Paradigms establish different grounds for the truth of their theories: they have different types of units and basic concepts and different questions, different languages and different criteria for evidence. As such, they do not compete on the same playing field, they are 'incommensurable'. Not all theories differ paradigmatically: neorealism and neoliberalism share many of the same units, questions and understandings of what constitutes a research programme and good evidence (see Chapter 2). A Kuhnian perspective implies that the discovery of new facts, the falsification of key concepts, often has little effect on the ways in which security is understood. Rather, understandings of security change through paradigm shifts. It is arguable that the development of postpositivist approaches to security constitute such a shift, at least in respect of the development of some critical approaches (see Chapter 3), but these have not supplanted prior paradigms based on positivism. Importantly, while Kuhnian perspectives emphasize internal developments within disciplines, Buzan and Hansen's (2009) 'post-Kuhnian' history of the evolution of security studies shows how understanding security has also developed in relation to wider political and technological developments and changes in other disciplines, such as the philosophy of science, sociology and geography.

Conclusion

The study of security has a complex history of disciplinary development, interdisciplinary engagements (and disengagements) and multiple divisions on the theoretical building blocks of perspectives on security. Amid this complexity, one might question whether different approaches to the study of security are really constitutive of a single field of 'security studies'. While the changing scope of security certainly diversifies the field, it is the combination of ontological and epistemological assumptions that have divided the field most profoundly. In particular, distinctions between positivist and postpositivist approaches (and their ontological foundations) demarcate two fields of security studies: an empiricist and rationalist mainstream of realism and liberalism found in the mainstream academic discipline in the USA, and the largely postpositivist field of security studies practised in Western Europe (and Canada and Australasia) (Waever, 2004). Many conversations on security occur within rather than across this geographical division (Shah, 2010; Miller, 2010). Beyond this, it is also notable that much of security studies has been strongly 'Western centric'; even when talking about non-Western states, the basic assumptions and questions have their origins in the West (Bilgin, 2010).

It is impossible to know how security is understood by adopting only one set of building blocks. Rather, from debates on the scope of security to debates on the foundations of understanding, theories of security assemble these elements in particular ways. This chapter has explored the various distinctions and differences, and the underlying dualistic assumptions (subject-object, fact-value, material-ideational, structure-agency, inside-outside), that have shaped understandings of security. Chapters 2 and 3 explore how these multifarious differences coalesce into (more or less) coherent theoretical perspectives.

CHAPTER 21

Why Theory Matters

'In theory, theory and practice are the same. In practice,
they are not.'

Attributed to ALBERT EINSTEIN

PREVIEW   Theory is unavoidable in the study of global politics. We have no choice about
engaging with theory because, put most simply, facts do not speak for themselves.
If we try to make sense of the world simply by looking at it, our understanding is
overwhelmed by the complexity and sheer weight of the information confronting
us. Theory thus invests apparently shapeless and confusing reality with meaning,
and it does so, most obviously, by highlighting how and why events happen.
However, theory is not just an explanatory tool; it can also be a simplifying device,
a means of uncovering prejudice or bias, a guide to action and so on. But none of
these uses of theory is straightforward. For instance, how does theory allow us to
analyze events, rather than merely describe them? In what ways does theory
uncover supposedly 'hidden' processes and structures? How far can, or should,
theory be used as a guide to political practice? Nevertheless, recognizing what
theory can do for us does not, in itself, help us to choose which theory to use. What
constitutes 'good' theory? On what grounds can one theory be preferred to another
theory? Finally, the growing prominence in recent years of theoretical frameworks
such as constructivism, critical theory, feminism and poststructuralism has intensified debate about the nature and role of theory. This has raised deeper and, at
times, philosophically challenging questions about matters such as the value of
theoretical frameworks or 'paradigms', the extent to which 'reality' exists separate
from our perception of it, the relationship between theorizing and political activity,
and the status and role of normative theory.

KEY ISSUES
- Why is theory important?
- How can theories be evaluated?
- Are theoretical paradigms enlightening or constraining?
- Do theories, in effect, 'construct' the world?
- Are theories always 'political'?
- How can theory link what *is* to what *ought to be*?

THE IMPORTANCE OF THEORY

The key substantive theories of global politics are examined in Chapter 3, as well as in the 'Approaches' boxes that can be found in each chapter. The present chapter returns to the issue of theory, but for a different purpose. Its aim is to examine how, and how far, theory contributes to our understanding of global politics. Why do we need theory, and what can it do for us? An indication of the role and importance of theory can be gained by reflecting on the difference between academic study and journalism. Journalism sets out to provide an account of what has happened; it aims, in effect, to answer the question: who did what to whom, when and how? Journalism can therefore be seen as, at best, the 'first rough draft of history'. Academic study, by contrast, seeks to be more reflective and analytical. It is concerned not just with the surface of events, but with the deeper layers of meaning that underlie them; and theory is the means through which these layers are uncovered and investigated. Theory thus allows us to analyse, explain, interpret and evaluate, and not just describe. But there is considerable debate about how theory can, and should, be used.

Uses of theory

The academic study of international politics has been defined, through its history, by theoretical developments. Born in the aftermath of WWI, the discipline's early years were dominated by liberal internationalism (see p. 67) and the attempt to change the world for the better by removing the blight of war. However, liberal internationalist theories were subject to a growing realist critique in the years leading up to WWII, creating the discipline's first 'great debate' between liberalism and realism (see p. 516). As the Cold War took shape during the 1950s, this debate was won decisively by realism. By the 1970s, the dominant realist paradigm (see p. 524) came under sustained attack from both liberals and radicals, mainly Marxists. The resulting debate, usually dubbed the 'inter-paradigm debate', stimulated developments within both realism and liberalism, giving rise to neorealism and neoliberalism, and thus the 'neo-neo debate'. Since the 1980s, often stimulated by the fall of communism and the end of the Cold War, international theory has been significantly enriched, but it has also become more deeply fragmented, due to growing interest in a series of theoretical 'new voices'. These included constructivism (see p. 75), postcolonialism (see p. 200), poststructuralism and green politics, as well as theoretical frameworks with a deeper history, such as critical theory and feminism. Nevertheless, as these developments have unfolded, theory has performed not a single function but, rather, a range of functions, the most important of which include the following:

- Analyzing and explaining events
- Simplifying the world
- Widening and/or sharpening our perceptual field
- Defining our ethical horizons
- Providing a guide to action.

Analyzing and explaining events

If we look at the world without the benefit of theory we are likely to see, as the historian Arnold Toynbee (1889–1975) is reputed to have said, just 'one damned

Focus on ...
International relations: the 'great debates'

The academic discipline of international relations (frequently shortened to IR) emerged in the aftermath of World War I (1914–18), an important impetus being the desire to find ways of establishing enduring peace. The central focus of the discipline was on the study of the relations of states, and those relations were traditionally understood primarily in diplomatic, military and strategic terms. However, the nature and focus of the discipline has changed significantly over time, not least through a series of so-called 'great debates'.

- The first 'great debate' took place between the 1930s and 1950s, and was between liberal internationalists, who emphasized the possibility of peaceful cooperation, and realists, who believed in inescapable power politics. By the 1950s, realism had gained ascendancy within the discipline.

- The second 'great debate' took place during the 1960s, and was between **behaviouralists** and traditionalists over whether it is possible to develop objective 'laws' of international relations.

- The third 'great debate', sometimes called the 'inter-paradigm debate', took place during the 1970s and 1980s, and was between realists and liberals, on the one hand, and Marxists on the other, who interpreted international relations in economic terms.

- The fourth 'great debate' started in the late 1980s, and was between positivists and so-called post-positivists over the relationship between theory and reality. This reflected the growing influence within IR of a range of 'new' critical perspectives, such as constructivism, critical theory, poststructuralism, postcolonialism, feminism and green politics.

---

thing after another'. In its most common use, theory is an analytical tool, a means not only of describing events, but also of explaining why they happened. Theory does this by providing an account of **causality**. By uncovering causal relationships, or 'chains of events', order and shape is imposed on a world that might otherwise seem to be made up of a series of random occurrences. For instance, the democratic peace thesis (see p. 69) alerts us to patterns in the occurrence of war and peace, whereby wars very rarely (and, some argue, never) take place between democratic states. *Who*, *what* and *when* questions then allow us to ask *why* questions; in this case, about the likely reasons for the absence of war between democracies. Do democracies not fight each other because they are democracies, or because of other factors (such as their level of economic development)? If democracy promotes peace (at least, among democracies themselves), what is it about democratic rule that deters war – the impact of public opinion, ingrained habits of non-violent conflict resolution, shared values between democratic states, or what? Or does the alleged link between democracy and peace merely reflect a tendency among states to define their enemies as non-democratic?

For theorists who emphasize structure rather than agency (see p. 76), causality is sometimes elaborated into 'laws' of social or political development, suggesting that the social sciences resemble the natural sciences in being characterized by inevitable and predictable patterns of behaviour. Such a tendency is most clearly associated with orthodox Marxism and the belief that, driven by contra-

● **Behaviouralism**: The belief that social theories should be constructed only on the basis of observable behaviour, providing quantifiable data for research.

● **Causality**: The relationship between an event or set of circumstances (the cause) and another event or set of circumstances (the effect), in which the latter is a consequence of the former.

dictions that are found in all class societies, history develops through a series of predictable stages, and is destined to culminate in the establishment of a classless communist society. Such **determinism** has nevertheless become distinctively unfashionable, not only because it is incompatible with the idea of free will, but also because of the growing recognition that, in an interdependent world in which 'everything affects everything else', linear causal relationships are increasingly unreliable.

Simplifying the world

The second role played by theory is to simplify the world by providing conceptual **models**. A model is generally thought of as a representation of something, usually on a smaller scale, as in a dolls house or a toy airplane. In this sense, the purpose of the model is to resemble the original object as faithfully as possible. However, conceptual models need not in any way resemble the object they are being used to understand. It would be absurd, for instance, to insist that a computer model of the economy should bear a physical resemblance to the economy itself. Rather, conceptual models are analytical tools; their value is that they are devices through which meaning can be imposed on what would otherwise be a bewildering and disorganized collection of facts. As such, the primary functions of theory are selection (choosing what to look at, and what to ignore) and prioritization (deciding what is more significant and what is less significant).

　　This can be illustrated by Kenneth Waltz's *Theory of International Politics* (1979), the seminal work of neorealism or 'structural realism'. Waltz sought to overcome the limitations of classical realism by placing realist theory on a firmer, scientific basis. He did this by constructing a conceptual model of international politics based on three key assumptions. First, in the absence of a supreme or unchallengeable power, the international system functions as a 'self-help' system, in which states are forced to prioritize survival and security over all other goals. Second, states are the most important actors in the international system. Third, states are rational actors, in the sense that they choose amongst alternative courses of action on the basis of which best corresponds to their consistent and ordered preferences. On this basis, Waltz argued, amongst other things, that great-power war would tend to be more frequent in an international system characterized by multipolarity (see p. 237) rather than bipolarity (see p. 223), as the latter is more likely to generate a stable balance of power that discourages risk-taking and adventurism amongst states. However, it is vital to remember that conceptual models are, at best, simplifications of the reality they seek to explain. They are simply devices for drawing out understanding; they do not constitute reliable knowledge, in themselves. For this reason, it is better to think of conceptual models not as being 'true' or 'false', but merely as more or less 'useful'.

Widening or sharpening our perceptual field

The first two roles of theory are associated with **explanatory theory**, sometimes called 'empirical' theory. Explanatory theories comprise causal propositions or conceptual models that can be tested against 'hard' evidence; that is, data that exists separately of our perception of it. By contrast, when theory is used as a means of widening or sharpening our perceptual horizons, the theory in ques-

● **Determinism**: The belief that human actions and choices are entirely conditioned by external factors; determinism implies that free will is a myth.

● **Model**: A theoretical representation of empirical data that aims to advance understanding by highlighting significant relationships and interactions.

● **Explanatory theory**: Theory that seeks to make sense of events, developments and issues in the 'real world', by advancing generalized causal propositions.

tion is **interpretive theory**, sometimes called 'constitutive' theory. Interpretive theory emphasizes that human reflection is a social process, and treats the 'real world' as a series of competing truths and interpretations. Is this sense, theories are 'lenses' on the world, sometimes referred to as 'world-views'. But why do we need theory to widen or sharpen our perceptual field? The first reason is that if we try to see the world simply 'as it is' – that is, without the benefit of theory – we see what we expect to see, what we think we will see. All observation is therefore selective. The benefit of theory is that it alerts us to relationships, processes and structures of which we may previously have been unaware. For example, looking at the world through a 'feminist lens' not only means recognizing the previously 'invisible' contribution women make to shaping world politics, but it also allows us to see how world affairs might look if women's values and concerns were treated as of central importance. This enables us to generate new insights into issues ranging from globalization and development to security, war and armed conflict.

The second way in which theory can sharpen our perceptual field is by making us aware of 'hidden' prejudices and **biases**. The choice between a view of the world that is informed by theory and one that is *a*theoretical is a myth: all perception involves interpretation. The question that remains is whether we are aware of these interpretations and consciously acknowledge them. Theory, in this sense, is a device for self-reflection and critique; it is a means of uncovering 'taken-for-granted' assumptions and understandings about world politics. Once again, feminism has been influential in this respect. Beyond seeking to make women visible in discussions about world affairs, feminists have tried to expose the degree to which mainstream thinking about such matters is '**gendered**'. Feminists have, for instance, argued that conventional conceptions of security, based as they are on realist assumptions about the need for 'national security' and the importance of military-based 'hard' power, are indicative of a 'masculinist' mindset.

Defining our ethical horizons

In its fourth function, theory relates less to our ability to 'make sense' of events, developments and circumstances, and more to how we should react to them in ethical or even emotional terms. This is the realm of **normative theory**. Although empirical and normative theorizing appear to be quite different from one another, the former dealing with *facts* (empirical evidence) while the latter deals with *values* (ethical beliefs), in practice they are closely connected. All major theories of international or global politics have important empirical *and* normative dimensions (Reus-Smit and Snidal 2010). Indeed, it is difficult to imagine how theorizing about world affairs could be purely empirical in character, lacking a normative dimension altogether (something that even applies to realist theory, as discussed later in the chapter). Social activity of any kind raises moral questions because it has consequences for other human beings, challenging us to reflect on whether an activity or set of social arrangements is right or wrong, good or bad. This is particularly the case in the study of global politics, because, in considering matters such as war and peace, global poverty, international aid, climate change, humanitarian intervention and terrorism, it addresses issues whose implications for human well-being are difficult to exaggerate. Nevertheless, there are significant debates about the prominence of, and the

● **Interpretive theory**: Theory that imposes meaning on events or issues, in an attempt to understand, rather than explain, the world.

● **Bias**: Sympathies or prejudices that (often unconsciously) affect human judgement; bias implies distortion..

● **Gendered**: The tendency to reflect the experiences, prejudices or orientations of one gender more than the other; bias in favour of one gender.

● **Normative theory**: Theory that prescribes values and standards of conduct, what 'ought to be' rather than what 'is'.

Focus on . . .

'Explaining' and 'understanding' the fall of communism

'Explaining' and 'understanding' have been portrayed as alternative ways of making sense of the world (Hollis and Smith 1991). Explaining refers to attempts to uncover the *cause* (or causes) of events, making use of methods derived from the natural sciences. As explaining focuses on facts, evidence that is external to the actors involved, it can be viewed as an 'outside' story. Understanding refers to attempts to uncover the *meaning* of events, from the perspective of the actors involved. As understanding focuses on perceptions, motivations and beliefs, it can be viewed as an 'inside' story. Despite their different emphasis, explaining and understanding both offer fertile ways of making sense of the events, and, arguably, should be used in combination.

In the case of the fall of communism in the revolutions of 1989–91 (see p. 43), one of the key 'outside' stories was the widening economic gulf, since the 1960s, between the US-led West and the Soviet-led East. This, in turn, may be explained by factors such as the (perhaps fatal) structural flaws of Soviet-style central planning, the chaotic nature of the Gorbachev's economic reforms, and the tendency of 'accelerated' globalization to bolster growth rates in the West. However, these 'outside' developments also had an important 'inside' component, particularly in the form of rising frustration and discontent across much of the communist world due to a growing desire for western-style living standards and political freedom.

An alternative 'outside' story of the fall of communism stresses how the dynamics of Cold War bipolarity generated recurrent tension between the USA and the Soviet Union, helping to explain why President Reagan initiated the 'Second' Cold War in the early 1980s. This forced the Soviet Union into an unsustainable increase in military spending, so putting its economy under further pressure. Nevertheless, account should also be taken of the 'inside' story of the launch of the 'Second' Cold War, focusing not least on Reagan's perception of the Soviet Union as an 'Evil Empire'.

status that should be accorded, normative theory within the field of global politics, as well as about the proper relationship between what 'is' and what 'ought to be'. These issues are discussed in the final section of the chapter.

Providing a guide to action

In its final function, theory is prescriptive: it sets out how we should act in the world, and so links theory firmly to practice. This use of theory relies on a combination of normative and explanatory theorizing. Normative theory is used to establish a desired outcome, based on an evaluation of the rightness or wrongness of an action, policy, institution or practice. Explanatory theory is then used to highlight, by drawing attention to causal relationships, how the desired outcome can most reliably be brought about. An emphasis on the practical implications of theory has been one of the distinguishing features of the discipline of international relations, which has long been concerned with the 'policy relevance' of academic research, even advocating the idea of theory-informed policy-making. International relations was born in the aftermath of WWI, predominantly committed to liberal internationalist thinking that was designed to prevent future wars. Classical realism took shape in the writings of E. H. Carr (see p. 34) and others, who criticized the liberal world order of the inter-war period, and especially the reliance on international bodies such as the League of Nations, arguing that such policies made future major wars more likely, if not inevitable. The onset of the Cold War gave realism greater prominence within the discipline, first through classical realism and later in the form of neorealism, its power-politics theories helping to legitimize the USA's nuclear build-up and the policy of containment.

However, attempts by theorists to intervene in policy debates have by no means always been successful, and theorists and policy-makers have sometimes openly disagreed with one another, as when a collection of prominent realist theorists publicly criticized the Bush administration's conduct of the 'war on terror' and, especially, the 2003 invasion of Iraq (see p. 521). Nevertheless, the gap between theorists and practitioners of international politics has grown noticeably since the end of the Cold War. This has occurred, in part, because the rise of 'new' voices such as constructivism, critical theory, feminism and post-structuralism has meant that the idea of theory-informed policy-making has become distinctly less fashionable. Not only has theory increasingly been seen as a device for interpreting, rather than explaining, the world, but theorists have also become more concerned that participation in policy networks may compromise their academic independence. Such a stance on policy-making should, nevertheless, not be taken to imply that critical theorists insist on a strict distinction between theory and practice. Many critical theorists, indeed, see this as a false dichotomy, emphasizing that research, study and theorising are, in themselves, forms of political practice. This is why they have sometimes been inclined to view theory as a form of **praxis**.

Which theory is best?

What is the nature of 'good' theory? Can theories be meaningfully compared with one another and, if so, on what basis? From the perspective outlined in Thomas Kuhn's pioneering *The Structure of Scientific Revolutions* (1962), any attempt to show that one theory is better than another is, ultimately, a pointless exercise. Kuhn argued that the history of science is characterized by alternating 'revolutionary' and 'normal' phases. In the former, competition between rival theories means that progress is not made in terms of the accumulation of knowledge because protagonists are primarily concerned with establishing theoretical dominance. In the latter, a single paradigm achieves ascendancy over its rivals, but, while the stock of knowledge is then able to increase, this only occurs within the parameters of the established paradigm. As the search for knowledge only takes place *within* a paradigm, there is no external or objective criteria against which rival intellectual frameworks can be evaluated. Rival theories are therefore **incommensurable**. They do not provide competing accounts of the *same* world; in effect, they 'see' *different* worlds, and use different languages to describe those worlds. Rival theories, therefore, 'talk past each other'.

● **Praxis**: Free creative activity; reflection and action that seek to transform the world by challenging oppression.

● **Incommensurability**: An inability to compare or judge between rival beliefs or propositions, because of the absence of common features.

Those who use theory in an interpretive or a normative sense generally agree with the above reservations. In the absence of a reliable, objective standpoint from which theories can be judged, the task of choosing a preferred theory is likely to have more to do with political belief or ideological commitment than it does with evidence-based analysis. However, those who use theory in an explanatory sense would profoundly disagree. For them, theories are commensurable and one theory can be shown to be better than another. But what criteria

GLOBAL POLITICS IN ACTION . . .

Theorists take on the White House

Events: On 26 September 2002, as the Bush administration in the USA was stepping up preparations for the invasion of Iraq, 33 international relations scholars, most of whom identified themselves as realists, signed a *New York Times* advertisement warning that 'War with Iraq is *not* in America's national interest'. The signatories included prominent figures such as Kenneth Waltz, (see p. 63), John Mearsheimer (see p. 241), Robert Jervis and Steven Walt. Their key point was that military force should not be used in these circumstances as Iraq posed no immediate threat to the USA. Other concerns that were raised included that the justifications being advanced for an invasion (that Iraq possessed WMD and that the Saddam Hussein regime had links to terrorist groups) were, at best, unproven; that an invasion could cause regional instability and would divert resources from the more important campaign against al-Qaeda; and that, without a plausible exit strategy, war against Iraq may involve significant costs for both invading forces and neighbouring states, whilst increasing anti-Americanism around the globe. Such warnings nevertheless came to nothing, as the Iraq invasion duly went ahead in March 2003.

Significance: On the face of it, the warnings issued by the realist scholars were remarkably prescient. Not only did the claims about WMD and terrorist links prove to be bogus, but, despite the speedy overthrow of the Saddam Hussein regime, hopes for the establishment of a non-sectarian democracy were soon abandoned as the Iraq War spiralled into a complex counter-insurrectionary struggle, becoming the largest, most costly and (apart from Afghanistan) the longest use of armed force by the USA since the Vietnam War. In addition to the 4,421 US service personnel who had been killed by August 2010, when the US combat mission ended, estimates of Iraqi deaths (both civilian and military) due to violence related to the war have been put as high as 600,000. Realist critics of the war nevertheless argued that even had it not proved to be so problematic, the Iraq War would still have been unnecessary. At a deeper level, realists used the Iraq War to draw attention to the danger that a hegemonic USA was over-reaching itself, risking provoking opposition by its heavy-handed use of power.

However, it is by no means clear that the Iraq War demonstrates that foreign policy-makers should listen more closely to advice from the academy. In the first place, the Iraq War may have been a product of too much theory, not too little theory. The military assertiveness of the Bush administration was influenced, in large part, by a form of republican liberalism (or 'hard' Wilsonianism) that suggested that the spread of US-style democracy across the Middle East was the surest way of bringing peace and stability to that troubled region, even if this occurred through 'regime change'. The charge against the Bush administration, then, was not that it ignored the advice of theorists, but that it listened to the *wrong* theorists; in particular, it listened to neoconservative politicians and advisors rather than to realist academics (Mearsheimer 2005). Second, even if it were possible to determine which is the 'best' theory, it would by no means be easy to derive clear-cut policy strategies from a particular theory. This is because, in view of their breadth and complexity, all theoretical traditions embody some measure of ambiguity. The Iraq War, for instance, could be said to have reflected, rather than clashed with, realist principles, insofar as it was designed to deter challenges to the USA by redressing the image of a weakened post-9/11 USA. Finally, as realists claim to see the world 'as it is', rather than as they would 'like it to be', it could be argued that such a stark gap between theory and practice raises questions about the value of the realist project itself.

CONCEPT

Pragmatism

Pragmatism refers
generally to a concern
with practical
circumstances rather
than with theoretical
beliefs, with what can be
achieved in the real
world, as opposed to
what should be achieved
in an ideal world. As a
philosophical doctrine
(most commonly
associated with
philosophers such as
William James (1842–
1910) and John Dewey
(1859–1952),
pragmatism holds that
the meaning of and
justification for beliefs
should be judged by their
practical consequences.
Though, by definition, a
pragmatic style of
politics is non-ideological,
it does not amount to
unprincipled
opportunism. As a
political doctrine,
pragmatism suggests a
cautious attitude towards
change that rejects
sweeping reforms and
revolution as a descent
into the unknown.

● **Correspondence theory of
truth**: The theory that
propositions are true if, and
only if, they correspond with
the facts.

● **Proposition**: A statement
that affirms or denies
something, which may be
either true or false; 'what is
asserted'.

characterize 'good' theory? The standard criteria that are used in the social
sciences include the following:

● Correspondence to reality
● Explanatory power
● Parsimony and elegance
● Logical coherence.

Correspondence to reality

The ultimate test of any theory is conventionally taken to be how well it explains
events in the real world, an idea often dubbed the **correspondence theory of
truth**. When they are constructed, theories amount to mere '**propositions**'.
Propositions only become fully-fledged theories when they have been tested
against a selected body of evidence. As global politics is clearly not a laboratory
science, this suggests that arguments should be tested against the historical
record. For example, neorealist stability theory (see p. 57) can be tested by,
amongst other things, examining whether there is historical evidence that
periods dominated by two great powers or power blocs are more peaceful and
stable than other periods. Explanatory theories also stand or fall on the basis of
future developments. The standing of neorealist stability theory will therefore be
crucially affected by whether or not, as the twenty-first century unfolds, emerging multipolarity is associated with fluidity and instability, with great powers
becoming increasingly restless and ambitious. Although correspondence with
historical evidence is sometimes said to verify a theory, the fact that subsequent
developments may always disprove it indicates that the scientific basis for any
theory is, as Karl Popper (1959) pointed out, that it is falsifiable. Quite simply, if
it is not possible to prove that a theory is incorrect, the theory has no value.
However, the correspondence theory of truth depends entirely on whether 'the
facts' can be reliably established, suggesting that they exist in an objective sense
separate from our values and assumptions. In this light, it is worth remembering
how far the 'historical record' is based on selection and prioritization, and the
extent to which history is written by the victors rather than the vanquished, to
say nothing about being rewritten by succeeding generations.

Explanatory power

Some theories are more effective in explaining events than other theories. But
what would great explanatory power consist of? Explanatory power is not a
single or straightforward attribute but refers, rather, to a variety of qualities.
These include the range and complexity of phenomena that a theory is capable
of explaining. Good theories are therefore usually taken to have a high level of
generality; they have greater value because they have a significant scope and do
not just apply to particular events or specific circumstances. Moreover, effective
explanations are often said to have predictive power, providing a fuller and more
detailed account of likely future developments. In that sense, explanations and
predictions parallel one another, both consisting of a set of causal relationships.
Apart from anything else, theories from which clear and detailed predictions can
be derived contain grounds on which they can also be falsified. Finally, explana-

tory power is sometimes linked to a theory's internal fertility, the ability of a theory to be refined and expanded to make it relevant to a wider range of phenomena, or its capacity to generate a flow of interesting questions.

Parsimony and elegance

Good theories are often taken to be spare or sparse, the oft-repeated advice to theorists being to 'keep it simple'. A parsimonious theory, especially one that is elegant, in the sense of being simple and intellectually pleasing, has the advantage that it is clear, concise and intelligible. By contrast, complex theories, ones that contain a significant number of variable factors or qualifying conditions, are not only more difficult to comprehend, but also, in a sense, say less. Examples of parsimonious theory include **rational choice theory** and neorealism. Both of these are based on first principles. In the case of rational choice theory, individual actors, seen as the basic units of analysis, are taken to be rational, efficient and instrumental utility-maximizers. In the case of neorealism, such thinking, largely derived from neo-classical economics, is used to explain the behaviour of states in the international system. And yet, parsimony in theorizing is by no means an unambiguous good. For one thing, although concision and elegance may make a theory more attractive as an explanatory device, they do so only by increasing the theory's level of abstraction and reducing its reference to the real world. For another, simplicity is only of value in theorizing if the reality we wish to analyze is itself simple, something that can very seldom be said to apply in the field of global politics. Simple theories are thus of limited value in explaining complex realities.

Logical coherence

A final feature of good theory is that its various parts should 'fit' together, in the sense of being internally consistent. If this is not the case, a theory risks contradicting itself, so providing for its own downfall. This, nevertheless, may be a difficult judgement to make as far as the main theoretical traditions, such as realism, liberalism and Marxism/critical theory, are concerned, as each of these consists of a range of sub-traditions and specific theories, each of which has its own emphasis and implications. Interdependence liberalism therefore differs, in certain respects, from republican liberalism and neoliberal institutionalism. In this light, it is perhaps better to think of theoretical traditions as being only *more or less* coherent, rather than as being rigorously consistent. Of greater concern, however, is that the drive for logical coherence is rooted in **rationalist** assumptions that may be unfounded. Traditional conservatives, for instance, challenge the notion that the world has a rational structure, arguing instead that it is 'boundless and bottomless', its deep complexity meaning that the world is largely beyond the capacity of the human mind to fathom (Oakeshott 1962). If this is the case, theory does little more than perpetuate the belief that we can explain what is, frankly, incomprehensible, leaving pragmatism (see p. 522) as the surest guide to action.

DEBATING THEORY

The arrival of theoretical 'new voices' in recent decades (constructivism, critical theory, feminism, poststructuralism and so on) has not merely created a broader

● **Rational choice theory**: An approach to analysis in which models are constructed based on procedural rule, usually about the rationally-self-interested behaviour of the individuals concerned.

● **Rationalism**: The belief that the world can be understood and explained through the exercise of human reason, based on the assumption that it has a rational structure.

CONCEPT

Paradigm

A paradigm is, in a general sense, a pattern or model that highlights relevant features of a particular phenomenon. As used by Kuhn (1962), however, it refers to an intellectual framework comprising interrelated values, theories and assumptions, within which the search for knowledge is conducted. 'Normal' science is therefore conducted within an established intellectual framework; in 'revolutionary' science, an attempt is made to replace the old paradigm with a new one. The radical implication of this theory is that 'truth' and 'falsehood' cannot be finally established. They are only provisional judgements operating within an accepted paradigm that will, eventually, be replaced.

● **Meta-theory**: Theory that reflects on the philosophical assumptions that underlie theories, dealing in particular with issues of ontology, epistemology and methodology.

● **Ontology**: The study of what the world consists of, and what its relevant features might be.

● **Epistemology**: (From the Greek episteme, meaning 'knowledge') The study of how we can come to have relevant insights about the world.

● **Methodology**: A mode of analysis or research, including the methods used to unearth data or evidence.

and more fragmented theoretical landscape for the study of world affairs, but it has also stimulated deeper reflection about the nature and role of theory itself. This is the realm of **meta-theory**, sometimes thought of a 'theory about theory'. Although meta-theory appears to be a highly abstract – threatening (some warn) to descend into a concern with theory *for its own sake* – in fact, it addresses some of the most interesting and important questions in political analysis. The most basic meta-theoretical concern is with the issue of **ontology**; that is, what exists in the world, what the world is made of. What do we think political reality looks like? Answering ontological questions is often seen to inform where we stand on the issue of **epistemology**; that is, what we can know about the world, and how we can know it. What is it possible to know about political reality? Answering epistemological questions, in turn, leads us to adopt a particular **methodology**; that is, a set of procedures for acquiring knowledge of the world, a way of knowing. How can we find out about political reality? In the study of world affairs, these and other issues have been raised by a series of debates. The most important debates include the following:

● Do paradigms enlighten or constrain?
● Is there a real world 'out there', or does everything exist, in a sense, in the mind?
● Can theories be neutral, or are they always *for* someone or some purpose?
● How should we link what *is* ('reality') to what *ought to be* ('utopia')?

Paradigms: enlightening or constraining?

As pointed out earlier, one of the implications of Thomas Kuhn's (1962) account of the history of science is that all knowledge is, and can only be, framed within a specific paradigm. As defined by Kuhn, a paradigm is 'the entire constellation of beliefs, values, techniques and so on shared by members of a given community'. Although Kuhn developed the concept of paradigm specifically in relation to the natural sciences, it has come to be widely applied to the social sciences. The major theoretical approaches to world affairs are thus commonly treated as paradigms, in the Kuhnian sense. The value of paradigms is that they help us to make sense of what would otherwise be an impenetrably complex reality. They define what is important to study and highlight significant trends, patterns and processes. In so doing, they draw attention to relevant questions and lines of enquiry, as well as indicate how the results of intellectual enquiry should be interpreted. What is more, as the limitations of an established paradigm are more widely recognized, not least through a growing recognition of anomalies that it is unable to explain, the search for knowledge can be dramatically reinvigorated by a **paradigm shift**, as the established paradigm breaks down and a new one is constructed in its place. This, for example, occurred in physics in the early twentieth century, through the transition from Newtonian mechanics to the ideas of quantum mechanics, made possible by the development of Einstein's theory of relativity. In economics, a similar process occurred during the 1970s and 1980s as Keynesianism was displaced by monetarism.

However, paradigms may also foster tunnel vision and hinder intellectual progress. Paradigms may limit our perceptual field, meaning that we 'see' only what our favoured paradigm shows us. Moreover, paradigms tend to generate

CONCEPT

Postmodernism

'Postmodernism' is a controversial and confusing term that was first used to describe experimental movements in western arts, architecture and cultural development in general. As a tool of social and political analysis, postmodernism highlights the shift away from societies structured by industrialization and class solidarity to increasingly fragmented and pluralistic 'information societies', in which individualism replaces class, religious and ethnic loyalties. In philosophical terms, postmodernism is distinguished, above all, by its rejection of the idea of absolute and universal truth. Postmodernists, instead, place an emphasis on discourse and debate, embracing pluralism and difference, rather than seeking to banish or overcome them.

● **Paradigm shift**: The process through which the dominant paradigm within a field of knowledge is displaced by a rival paradigm.

● **Metanarrative**: A creed or ideology that is based on a universal theory of history which views society as a coherent totality.

● **Empiricism**: The belief that experience is the only basis for knowledge and, therefore, that all hypotheses and theories should be tested by observation

conformity amongst students and scholars alike, unable, or unwilling, to think outside the currently dominant (or fashionable) paradigm. An example of this came with the end of the Cold War, which, although it was the most significant event in world politics since 1945, appeared to take international relations scholars as much by surprise as it did other commentators (see p. 225). This occurred, at least in part, because neorealist and neoliberal thinking failed to draw attention to how far Soviet perceptions of the national interest had changed under Gorbachev. Apart from anything else, this shift meant that, in contrast to earlier uprisings in Hungary (1956) and Czechoslovakia (1968), the Soviet Union refused in 1989 to intervene in Eastern Europe to prop up crumbling communist regimes.

The field of global politics accentuates the drawbacks of paradigms because it is, by its nature, multifaceted and multidimensional, straining the capacity of any paradigm, or, for that matter, any academic discipline, to capture it in its entirety. Such a critical approach to 'paradigm thinking' (thinking firmly rooted in an established paradigm) has perhaps been taken furthest by postmodern theorists. The central theme of postmodernism was summed up by Jean-François Lyotard (1984) as 'incredulity towards **metanarratives**', the clearest examples of which are liberalism and Marxism. Metanarratives (which can be thought of as highly systematic and developed paradigms) emerged out of the sense of solidity and certainty that was generated by 'modern' societies which were structured by industrialization and strong class identities. Postmodernists argue that the emergence of increasingly fragmented and pluralistic 'postmodern' societies means that metanarratives have been rendered irrelevant. In their view, all knowledge is partial and local.

If paradigms are intellectual prisons, where does this leave us? Can we think *across* paradigms, or perhaps *beyond* paradigms? Certainly, in view of 'globalizing' tendencies in modern world politics, it is highly unlikely that a single paradigm – be it realism, liberalism, constructivism, feminism or whatever – is going to constitute the final word on any particular theme or issue. These paradigms, anyway, will be more or less relevant, or more or less persuasive, in relation to some issues rather than others. In considering paradigms, then, it is as unhelpful merely to select a theoretical 'box' within which to think as it is to adopt an 'anything goes' approach to theorizing that simply leads to incoherence. If no paradigm is capable, on its own, of fully explaining the almost infinitely complex realities it purports to disclose, cross-paradigm dialogue may offer the prospect of a fuller and clearer picture of world affairs. In this light, Sil and Katzenstein (2010) championed the cause of 'analytic eclecticism', an approach to research that is problem-driven rather than paradigm-driven, and is grounded in a pragmatic theory of knowledge. However, as long as paradigms survive, dialogue between them is constructive only if two conditions are met. First, competing paradigms must share sufficient common ground that they are commensurable. Second, dialogue must be conducted with open-mindedness rather than as a contest, something that is difficult to achieve as it requires, from the outset, an acceptance that one's chosen paradigm may be wrong.

All in the mind?

The conventional approach to theorizing draws its philosophical underpinning from the doctrine of **empiricism** (also known as 'naturalism'), which spread

CONCEPT

Positivism

Positivism is an intellectual movement that originated in nineteenth-century social science and early twentieth-century philosophy. Its key ideas are that science is the only reliable means of establishing knowledge, and that science can only deal with observable entities which can be directly experienced. Positivists argue that the methodology of the natural sciences can be applied to the study of society, in particular because human behaviour can be observed and objectively measured. Although positivism is sometimes equated with neorealism, its influence on the study of world affairs has extended more broadly to any attempt to build explanatory theory, whether or not this involves quantification.

from the seventeenth century onwards through the work of thinkers such as John Locke (1632–1704) and David Hume (1711–76). The doctrine of empiricism advanced the belief that experience is the only basis of knowledge, and that therefore all hypotheses and theories should be tested by a process of observation and experiment. By the nineteenth century, such ideas had developed into what became known as positivism, an intellectual movement particularly associated with the writings of Auguste Comte (1798–1857). This proclaimed that the social sciences and, for that matter, all forms of philosophical enquiry should adhere strictly to the methods of the natural sciences. As a methodological tradition, positivism was thus based on the following ontological and epistemological positions:

- There is a real world 'out there', independent of our experience of it
- This world consists of regularities and patterns, rather than random events
- Knowledge of these regularities and patterns can be gained through observation and experiment, what Comte called 'positive perception'
- A clear distinction exists between facts and values, between empirical and normative beliefs
- Empirical knowledge accumulates over time, both through the acquisition of new knowledge and the refinement of existing knowledge.

However, since the 1980s, positivist thinking about world affairs has been subject to criticism from a range of 'post-positivist' approaches. These include constructivism, critical theory, poststructuralism, postcolonialism and, in certain respects, feminism. What these approaches have in common is that they question the idea that there is a 'real world', separate from the beliefs, ideas and assumptions of the observer. As we observe the world, we are also in the process of imposing meaning upon it: we only ever see the world as we *think* it exists. Such an approach leads to a more critical and reflective view of theory, which is taken, in a sense, to 'construct' the world, rather than merely explain the world. Greater attention is therefore paid to the biases and hidden assumptions that are embodied in theory, implying that dispassionate scholarship may be an unachievable ideal.

Constructivism has been particularly influential in this respect, in that it challenges the tendency within mainstream realist and liberal theory to treat political actors as though they have fixed or objective interests or identities. Constructivists, rather, believe that account must also be taken of the normative, institutional, historical and other factors that shape how states see themselves and how they see each other. An example of this would be the stark difference in the way the USA reacts to UK nuclear weapons and how it reacts to North Korean nuclear weapons, given the perception of the UK as a 'friend' and of North Korea as an 'enemy' (Wendt 1995). The position of constructivism in the debate between positivism and post-positivism is nevertheless unclear, as constructivism itself is divided into two camps (Hopf 1998). 'Conventional' constructivists (also called 'mainstream' constructivists), such as Alexander Wendt (see p. 77) and Martha Finnemore (see p. 527), stress the importance in world politics of social concepts (like 'friend' and 'enemy'), but continue to adopt a positivist epistemology and explain the world largely in terms of cause-and-effect relationships. By contrast, 'critical' constructivists (also called 'radical' or 'postmodern' constructivists) reject

Martha Finnemore (born 1959)

A US international relations scholar. Finnemore helped to pioneer the use of constructivist analysis in international relations, especially in works such as *National Interests in International Society* (1996) and *The Purpose of Intervention* (2003). In the former, Finnemore challenged the tendency of neorealism and neoliberalism to treat state interests as though they are both stable and roughly identical, consisting of some combination of power, security and wealth. Instead, she highlighted the extent to which state interests are defined and redefined by the dense network of transnational and international social relations of which they are a part. In the latter work, Finnemore examined how the purposes for which states use military intervention have changed over some four centuries, giving particular attention to the growing significance of new norms about who is human and how we should treat 'strangers'.

the idea of objective knowledge, and question the notion that social relationships can be explained in terms of discrete 'causes' and 'effects'.

Although the ontological divide between positivists and post-positivists is ultimately unbridgeable, as the two positions are based on mutually exclusive assumptions, the two approaches may nevertheless aspire to similar goals. For instance, post-positivists may agree with positivists that there is a real world 'out there', resisting the stark division between **objectivism** and **subjectivism**. The major difference between them may be epistemological rather than ontological, as it relates to the reliability of our knowledge of the world. While post-positivists may, like positivists, pursue objectivity, not least through attempts to expose bias, they insist that the search for unchallengeable, rock-solid foundations for knowledge will always be fruitless.

For some purpose?

Post-positivist theorizing about world affairs has acquired a distinctive emphasis within critical theory. Critical theorists reject the idea of value-free social science on the grounds that, as knowledge is inherently political, theoretical debates are basically political debates. This stance is reflected in Robert Cox's (1981) much quoted observation that 'theory is always *for* someone and *for* some purpose'. Such a position is rooted in Marx's (see p. 72) theory of ideology. Marx used the term 'ideology' to refer to the ideas of the economically dominant class (the bourgeoisie), emphasizing that the purpose of these ideas was to manipulate and delude the oppressed class (the proletariat), preventing them from recognizing the fact of their own exploitation. Ideology therefore promotes 'false consciousness'. Marx nevertheless believed that his own ideas (portrayed by his friend and collaborator Friedrich Engels (1820–95) as 'scientific socialism') peeled off these layers of manipulation by exposing the exploitative nature of the capitalist system, so helping to bring the proletariat to revolutionary **class consciousness**. From the Marxist perspective, our theories, ideas and beliefs are therefore always politically engaged because they are linked to class interests: they either serve to uphold the class system or to overthrow it.

● **Objectivism**: Judgements that pertain to objects, in which case truth can be independently distinguished from falsehood.

● **Subjectivism**: Judgements that pertain to subjects (persons), which are neither true or false but relate to feelings, taste or morality.

● **Class consciousness**: A Marxist term denoting an accurate awareness of class interests, transforming a class in-itself into a class for-itself.

THEORY

Realist view

In view of their core focus on 'reality' (the world 'as it is') and their deep scepticism towards ideals and principles (the world 'as it ought to be'), realists traditionally 'travelled light' in theoretical terms. Classical realism thus set out to explain recurrent patterns of state interaction largely in terms of an unsentimental view of human nature (even if this was sometimes portrayed less as a theory and more as a 'fact of life'). Within classical realism, theoretical belief has always been balanced against pragmatism, reflected in a stress on statecraft and on subjective evaluations of international relations made by state leaders. However, the advent of neorealism marked the emergence of a more systematic, rigorous and structural approach to theory within realism. Heavily influenced by positivist models, particularly as used in economics, its pioneering work, Waltz's (1979) *Theory of International Politics*, set out to produce nothing less than a science of world politics. In this, states are compelled to act in certain ways by the structure of the international system. Abiding realist concerns about normative theory reflect not so much a rejection of morality (after all, few realists question the moral priority of the national interest) but, rather, a distaste for 'moralism', which places respect for ethical principles above all other considerations and blinds state leaders to the messy realities of the world. For realists, not only should morality never be an absolute guide to political practice, but it should also always be judged in relation to a particular time, place and national context.

Liberal view

Liberalism's strong emphasis on theory reflects the fact that its origins in the Enlightenment imbued it with a faith in scientific rationality, freedom and progress. As liberals believe in universal moral and rational principles, the explanatory and normative dimensions of theory are usually taken to be intertwined, although the balance between them has varied over time. Early liberal theorizing about international relations, in the years following WWI, drew heavily on idealism (see p. 65), and was shaped, above all, by the attempt to find a solution to the problem of war. However, as liberal thinking about international relations was eclipsed by realist thinking during the Cold War period, liberalism progressively disengaged from idealism, its normative agenda being significantly narrowed in the process.

This became particularly apparent during the 1970s and 1980s with the rise of neoliberal institutionalism, which adopted a clearly social-scientific methodology. The 'neo-neo' debate was therefore conducted *within* a positivist framework, neorealists and neoliberals subscribing to common ontological and epistemological assumptions. The end of the Cold War nevertheless encouraged liberals to re-embrace normative theory more explicitly, notably though a stress on human rights (see p. 311). However, this 'normative turn' did not amount to a full return to idealism, as it was also accompanied by a greater emphasis within liberalism on the construction of explanatory theories grounded in testable propositions.

Critical views

Critical perspectives on world affairs have stimulated a major reappraisal of the nature and role of theory. This has happened, most importantly, through the attempt to go beyond the positivism of mainstream realist and liberal theory. By emphasizing the role of consciousness in shaping social conduct, post-positivist perspectives used theory not so much as a tool for explaining the world, in an objective sense, but as a device for broadening and/or sharpening our perception of the world, implying that theory has an essentially constitutive or interpretive role. The extent of ontological and epistemological agreement among (and, sometimes, within) critical perspectives should not be over-stated, however. For instance, while 'conventional' constructivists (such as Wendt (see p. 77)) seek to probe the inter-subjective content of events and episodes, but within a social-scientific methodology, 'critical' constructivists either (in common with postmodernists) deny the existence of a real world 'out there', or argue that it is buried under so many layers of conceptual and contextual meaning that we can never gain access to it. The shift to post-positivism has also allowed a greater emphasis to be placed on the normative dimension of theory, albeit in different ways. Thus, whereas constructivism has been used to show how states may transcend a narrow perception of self-interest, Frankfurt School critical theory has focused on uncovering structures of oppression and injustice in world politics; and feminism has attempted, among other things, to challenge an established gender order that excludes women from moral status.

Focus on . . .

Can the study of global politics be value-free and dispassionate?

Those who champion the cause of neutral and dispassionate scholarship in global politics advance at least three arguments. In the first place, they hold that there is a strict distinction between political analysis and political advocacy, the motive for the former being a desire to understand and explain the political world (to 'make sense' of things), rather than to reshape the world in line with one's values or personal preferences. Political convictions are therefore put to one side, recognizing how they can blind people to 'inconvenient' truths. Second, education and the rigour of academic study are themselves a training-ground in dispassionate scholarship, encouraging students to distance themselves, over time, from allegiances and biases that derive from social and family background, Third, and most important, the possibility of neutral scholarship is founded on a commitment to, and belief in, 'scientific' objectivity. In this view, scientific method (involving the use of observation, measurement and experimentation) is the only approach to knowledge that can reliably distinguish between truth and falsehood, and it does this by insisting that propositions are verified or falsified by comparing them with what we know of the 'real world'. Such an approach to knowledge is applicable not only to global politics, but to all fields of learning.

However, while natural scientists may be able to approach their studies from an objective and impartial standpoint, this may be impossible in global politics. Politics, at all levels, addresses questions about the society in which we live and have grown up. Family background, social experience, economic position, political sympathies and so on therefore build into each of us ingrained preconceptions about the political world we are seeking to study. Indeed, perhaps the greatest threat to reliable knowledge comes not from bias, as such, but from a failure to acknowledge bias, reflected in bogus claims to academic neutrality. Such concerns have been deepened by doubts about the possibility of scientific objectivity derived from an awareness that there may be more than one way in which the world can be understood. From this perspective, there is no single, overarching truth about the 'real world' out there, separate from the beliefs, ideas and assumptions of the observer. If the subject (the student of global politics) cannot in any reliable way be distinguished from the object (the political world), then dispassionate scholarship must be treated as, at best, an unachievable ideal.

Influenced by the work of Antonio Gramsci (see p. 73) and of leading figures from the Frankfurt School of critical theory, Cox (1981) developed this analysis into a distinction between 'critical theory' and what he called 'problem-solving theory'. Problem-solving theory tends to legitimize prevailing social and political structures, because, as Cox put it, it 'takes the world as it finds it'. As it does not establish a position outside of prevailing power structures from which they can be critically evaluated, it accepts, rather than questions, the global status quo. In being used to 'solve problems', such theory therefore serves to ensure the 'smooth working' of the existing order. The classic examples of problem-solving theory are neorealism and neoliberalism, both of which are used to diffuse conflicts, tensions and crises within the established world order. By contrast, all forms of critical theory tend to have an emancipatory orientation. They seek to oppose the dominant forces and structures in modern world affairs, and are usually aligned to the interests of marginalized or oppressed groups. For Cox (2008), the purpose of studying world politics is to bring about basic change in the structure of world power, in line with priorities such as ensuring the survival of the

CONCEPT

Utopianism

A utopia is literally an ideal or perfect society. Utopianism is often used as a pejorative term, implying deluded or fanciful thinking, a belief in an unrealistic and unachievable goal. Realists have referred to liberal internationalism as 'utopianism', in this sense. However, the term can be used in the positive sense to refer to a style of political theorizing that develops a critique of the existing order by constructing a model of an ideal or perfect alternative (examples including anarchism and Marxism). Utopian theories are usually based on (realistic or unrealistic) assumptions about the scope for human self-development. Utopias are usually characterized by the abolition of want, the absence of conflict and the avoidance of oppression and violence.

biosphere, avoiding nuclear war, moderating the gap between the rich and the poor, and protecting the most vulnerable people.

This view of theory has also attracted criticism, however. In the first place, there appears to be tension between critical theory's commitment to serving the interests of the marginalized and oppressed, which must surely be founded on the ability to uncover reliable, if not objective, knowledge, and the adoption of a post-positivist methodology that casts serious doubt over the notion of objective truth. This tension, indeed, may be traced back to Marx's assertion that all belief systems are ideological (and therefore false), except his own. Some critical theorists may nevertheless argue that their purpose is not so much to establish objective solutions to the problems of the marginalized, as to recognise their experience and perspective and to give them a political voice, enabling them to develop solutions of their own.

Second, even if it is accepted that all theory is entangled with politics, judgements about which political purposes are 'emancipatory' and which are 'oppressive' may, in the absence of agreed or objective standards, be little more than a matter of personal preference or subjective ideological orientation. This can be seen, for example, in debates about the benefits of free trade (see p. 480). Third, the project of changing the world 'for the good', especially through radical social upheavals, has, at best, a patchy record. It is notable, for instance, that the scholars of the Frankfurt School deliberately retreated from political activism and concentrated instead on theory, in large part because of their distaste for 'actually-existing' socialism, in the form of the Soviet Union and the communist bloc. In other words, emancipatory theory may not always lead to emancipatory practice.

Between utopia and reality?

The status and role of normative theory in the study of world affairs has long been a matter of dispute. Normative concerns dominated the academic study of world affairs in its early years, as attempts were made to find a solution to the problem of war, inspired by a tradition of 'idealist' (see p. 65) theorizing that derived from the ideas of thinkers such as Thomas Aquinas (see p. 261) and Immanuel Kant (see p. 15). In the aftermath of WW II, however, normative theory became distinctly unfashionable, being pushed to the margins of academic interest. This occurred, first, because the rise of realism was accompanied by a critique of normative theory, sometimes dubbed 'utopianism', which held that it had contributed to the resurgence of great-power rivalry that eventually led to war in 1939. In this view, an unrealistic faith in the capacity of states to cooperate through bodies such as the League of Nations had blinded policymakers to the threat posed by rising and ambitious powers. Second, attempts, since the 1960s, to develop a 'science' of international politics strengthened the idea that facts are firmly distinct from values, suggesting that the search for truth should not be 'contaminated' by ethical considerations. Since the 1980s, nevertheless, normative theory has once again gained prominence, partly as a result of frustration with the 'amoral' power-politics theories that had dominated the Cold War period. The prospect of radically re-orientating world order as the shadow of superpower rivalry faded also helped to generate growing interest in the doctrine of human rights (see p. 311) and associated ideas such as cosmopolitanism (see p. 21) and international justice.

CONCEPT

Communitarianism

Communitarianism is, broadly, the belief that the self or person is constituted through the community, in the sense that individuals are shaped by the communities to which they belong and owe them a debt of respect and consideration. As a school of thought, communitarianism emerged in the 1980s and 1990s as a critique of liberalism, highlighting the damage done to the public culture by an over-emphasis on individual rights and freedoms. In the study of world politics, communitarianism is usually linked with nationalism, and especially the idea that morality is fashioned by the distinctive history, culture and traditions of particular nations, rather than by universal principles such as human rights. Communitarianism and cosmopolitanism are thus rival normative theories.

● Realistic utopia: An ideal of a society whose members enjoy just and peaceful relations, but which is sufficiently close to the 'real' world to be attainable.

Nevertheless, as discussed earlier, the apparently strict divide between explanatory theory and normative theory is misleading. Empirical analysis is invariably motivated, at some level, by normative concerns, implying that the 'is' and the 'ought' are intertwined. If people were unconcerned about the level of violence and suffering in the world, why would they study, for instance, the causes of war or the incidence of poverty? All theoretical traditions within the field of global politics are therefore shaped by normative goals. For example, although realists have firmly rejected the idea that foreign policy should be guided by ethical objectives, they have done so largely because of their assessment that 'hard-headed' foreign policy better serves the national interest. The choice is thus not between embracing or rejecting normative theory, but between different models of ethics, in particular between those based on communitarianism and those based on cosmopolitanism. Moreover, ethical speculation about world affairs cannot but address issues related to political 'reality', implying that normative theory always has an empirical dimension. For example, the (normative) commitment to reduce global poverty is invariably linked to (empirical) attempts to understand the causes of poverty and how it can be reduced or ended.

However, debate has surrounded the exact nature of the link between normative and empirical thinking. While normative aspirations have to be sufficiently bold to be appealing and desirable, they must also be politically feasible. In that sense, 'utopia' must be linked to 'reality', but is the notion of a '**realistic utopia**' meaningful? In *The Laws of the People* (1999), John Rawls outlined what he claimed was a realistic utopia. This took the form of a peaceful and cooperative international order, in which moral ambition was limited to a number of specific goals, including the elimination of unjust war and oppression, the removal of religious persecution and restrictions on freedom of conscience, and an end to genocide and mass murder. Rawls claimed that this vision fell within the limits of 'practical political possibility' because it was based on minimal standards of human rights and involved no requirement for wholesale economic redistribution. For Jürgen Habermas (2010), a realistic utopia could be constructed in the form of a 'democratically constituted world society', in which human rights would be enforceable. Habermas nevertheless acknowledged that democracy cannot operate meaningfully at a level beyond the nation-state, and accepted that global governance (see p. 462) could never develop into anything more than a 'negotiating system' which ensures fair bargaining amongst interested parties and networks. However, the drawback of any supposed realistic utopia is that it can be criticized from both sides. Realistic utopias may be condemned for being so utopian they are politically unfeasible, or for being so realistic they are fatally morally compromised.

SUMMARY

● Theory has a range of uses and a number of dimensions. Its uses include analyzing and explaining events, simplifying the world, widening and/or sharpening our perceptual field, defining our ethical horizons, and providing a guide to action. Although distinct explanatory, interpretive and normative dimensions of theory can be identified, these sometimes overlap.

● Attempts to establish 'good' theory are sometimes dismissed as pointless, on the grounds that rival theories are incommensurable. However, others argue that theories can be evaluated using the standard criteria employed in the social sciences. These include a theory's correspondence to reality, its explanatory power, its parsimony and elegance, and its logical coherence.

● Paradigms aid understanding in that they define what is important to study, draw attention to significant trends, patterns and processes, and highlight relevant questions and lines of enquiry. However, paradigms may also limit our perceptual field, meaning that we 'see' only what our favoured paradigm shows us.

● Positivists proclaim that the social sciences should adhere strictly to the methods of the natural sciences, based on the possibility of establishing objective knowledge. Post-positivists question whether there is a real world 'out there', separate from our beliefs, ideas and assumptions about it. We therefore only see the world as we *think* it exists.

● Critical theorists reject the idea of value-free social science on the grounds that knowledge is inherently political, in which case theoretical debates are basically political debates. Such thinking has been criticized for, amongst other things, failing to show how we can make reliable judgements about the (alleged) political purposes of theory.

● The notion of a 'realistic utopia' may allow us to reconcile normative theory with empirically-based explanatory theory. However, realistic utopias may fall between two stools, being either so utopian they are politically unfeasible or so realistic they are fatally morally compromised.

Questions for discussion

● Why is theory unavoidable?

● How does theory allow us to analyze, rather than just describe, world affairs?

● How can theory be used to widen and deepen our perceptions?

● Does theory constitute a sound guide to action?

● Is it possible to 'prove' that one theory is better than another?

● Is all knowledge framed within a paradigm?

● Do the attractions of thinking 'across' paradigms outweigh the drawbacks?

● Is there a real world 'out there', and, if so, how do we know?

● Is neutral and dispassionate scholarship possible?

● How and why are empirical and normative theory intrinsically linked?

● Is the notion of a 'realistic utopia' meaningful or helpful?

Further reading

Jørgensen, K. E., *International Relations Theory: A New Introduction* (2010). An account of the main theoretical traditions of international relations, which introduces students to the activity of 'doing' theory.

Moses, J. W. and T. Knutsen, *Ways of Knowing: Competing Methodologies in Social and Politics Science* (2012). A clear and accessible introduction to competing naturalist (positivist) and constructivist methodologies in the social sciences

Reus-Smit, C. and D. Snidal, *The Oxford Handbook of International Relations* (2010). A stimulating collection of essays that both explore the complex links between theory, method and political practice, and provide a comprehensive overview of international theories.

Savigny, H. and L. Marsden, *Doing Political Science and International Relations: Theories in Action* (2011). An innovative text that examines how a wide range of theoretical perspectives illuminate key issues in global as well as domestic politics.

 ONLINE RESOURCES AVAILABLE

Links to relevant web resources can be found on the *Global Politics* website

22

Theories of International Relations

Enduring question: *How do theoretical traditions in international relations differ on how to understand actors and their behavior on the global stage*

Did you know that people have tried to understand the root causes of conflict and cooperation for more than two thousand years? Over the centuries, people have watched the great dramas of international relations unfold – the emergence of nation-states, war and rivalry among great powers, the rise and decline of states, the boom and bust of global commerce, the building of alliances and political communities, the clash of cultures, religions, and ideologies – and tried to make sense of it. They have asked simple yet fundamental questions: What explains war? Why do states trade with each other? Why do states cooperate or quarrel? Do democratic states act differently than autocratic states in the conduct of foreign policy? How does the global capitalist system impact relations among states? How have international relations changed over the centuries? Are countries around the world trapped in a global system of violence and insecurity or can they cooperate to build peace? Scholars have debated these and other enduring questions for centuries and continue to debate them today.

We noted in Chapter 1 that, with so much happening across places and time, international relations may appear hopelessly complex. How do we make sense of it all? As part of their ongoing effort to understand and explain international relations, scholars have developed a set of tools called theories. A theory, we noted in Chapter 1, is a simplified picture of the patterns of actions and interactions within some domain of interest, and an account of why we see those patterns. Individual theories may be very specific, but in the study of international relations they tend to be grouped within broader categories that we may call theoretical frameworks or traditions. These frameworks allow us to focus on factors essential in organizing our thinking about international relations. Five theoretical traditions are most important in this respect: realism, liberalism, Marxism, constructivism, and feminism.

Each of these theoretical traditions places different weight on what matters most in understanding international relations. Each makes a series of assumptions and then directs you to a different set of driving forces to make sense of the complexity of world politics. Realists and constructivists, or liberals and Marxists, look out at the same world, but they each urge you to focus on very different features or, more precisely, causal mechanisms in order to understand that world. In this chapter, we explore these five theoretical traditions, highlighting the assumptions, concepts, and patterns of behavior that each school finds most important.

Source: © Image Source.

Learning Objectives

By the end of this chapter, you will be able to:

→ Recognize why the struggle for national power and security in a world of anarchy characterizes the realist tradition.

→ Analyze the interests and impulses of democratic and market-oriented states, which inform the liberal tradition.

→ Discuss the impact of the industrial revolution on theoretical frameworks, which gave rise to the class conflict of Marxism.

→ Evaluate the effects of ideas and belief systems on individuals, groups, and states; this perspective describes the constructivist tradition.

→ Illustrate the role of gender as an influence on foreign policy decision makers and international relations scholars.

Chapter Contents

- The Realist Tradition
- The Liberal Tradition
- The Marxist Tradition
- The Constructivist Tradition
- The Feminist Tradition
- Comparing Traditions
- Revisiting the Enduring Question and Looking Ahead
- Study Questions
- Further Reading

The Realist Tradition

From ancient times to the present, people have puzzled over the pervasiveness of conflict and violence among human groups, such as tribes, city-states, kingdoms, empires, and nation-states. Some of the earliest insights about conflict between political groups reflect what we call the *realist tradition* of thinking about international relations. Realism sees international relations as a struggle for power and security among competing nation-states in a dangerous world. In a world of *anarchy*, in which nation-states must provide their own security, competition and conflict is inevitable according to the realist perspective. In international politics, the resolution of conflicts between states will be shaped by the distribution of power between them. We identify the core ideas of this tradition by beginning with realism's assumptions, and then turn to its main propositions about how the world works and its predictions for the future.

Realist Assumptions

Realism is a simple vision that sees competition for power among groups or states as the central and enduring feature of international relations. It is built on five assumptions.

First, realists start with the observation that groups – currently states – exist in a world where no higher authority can enforce rules or order. That is, states operate in a world of anarchy. Anarchy does not mean chaos; instead, states are left to their own devices to protect themselves. In such a world, power is the coin of the realm, or the currency with which states do business in international relations. States achieve security or realize their interests to the extent of their power. As realists argue, in a world of anarchy the powerful prevail and the weak submit. The archetypical statement in this respect, described in Chapter 1, is Thucydides' famous observation about the Greek conquest of Melios that 'the strong do what they wish while the weak suffer what they must' (Thucydides 1954). When realists look at the long history of international relations, they see competition and the struggle for power, and sometimes even war, as the central drama. States and diplomats come and go across the global stage, but a struggle for security and power has been the recurring theme in relations among states. For realism, this *sameness* of international politics across time is due not to the character of peoples or governments, but the result of international anarchy. With no higher governing authority to protect them, states tend to be fearful of other states, and seek to increase their power in order to protect themselves and get what they want from the international system.

The second assumption for realists is that states are the main actors in international relations. Because anarchy creates insecurity, people divide themselves into conflict groups. Today, the most common form these conflict groups take is the state. Governments offer their people protection from the ravages of an insecure international system. They tax, spend, and deploy power. Citizens are tied to the state and rely on it for their well-being. Other actors in international relations, such as international organizations, churches, and private corporations, may flourish. But they are decidedly secondary in the ways and means of world politics. States command center stage as the political units that harness power and compete with other states.

Third, realists assume that states are reasonably rational actors that are able to recognize the international circumstances in which they find themselves and risks and opportunities in the international domain. When states undertake actions they can perceive the prospective benefits and losses and can adjust their behavior when the

Realism and State Rationality – the Issue of State Self-Defeatism

Theory: *Realist Theory and the Rationality of States*

Realist theory argues that states are serious and sober calculators of costs and benefits. It is generally not in a state's interest to engage in ideological crusades to remake the world or pursue self-defeating acts of hubris. Leaders will want to take steps to increase the power of the state through its economic and military capabilities. But leaders will be careful not to go to war when they are certain to be defeated or expend the wealth of the nation on fruitless military campaigns. Rationality as understood by realist theorists dictates the prudent matching up of ends to means.

Practice: *Germany and Japan in the 1930s Threatened Others and Triggered Coalitions that Brought their Complete Defeat*

In Jack Snyder's 1993 *Myths of Empire*, he describes the way in which Nazi Germany and Imperial Japan built domestic military-industrial coalitions and pursued aggression within their regions, triggering the formation of overwhelming counter-coalitions that brought the states to utter and complete defeat.

> Great powers in the industrial age have shown a striking proclivity for self-inflicted wounds. Highly advanced societies with a great deal to lose have sacrificed their blood and treasure, sometimes risking the survival of their states, as a consequence of their overly aggressive foreign policies. Germany and Japan proved so self-destructive in the first half of this century that they ended up in receivership.

In theory, states are depicted as rational decision makers. In practice, they can be loose and dysfunctional coalitions of societal interests who together pursue self-destructive foreign policy.

Source: Jack Snyder, *Myths of Empire: Domestic Politics and International Ambition* (Ithaca: Cornell University Press, 1993), p. 1.

---

costs of actions exceed their benefits. Assuming that states in general act rationally is not the same as saying that every state always acts this way. As we note in Box 22.1, states sometimes persist over long periods of time in behaving in ways in which the costs vastly exceed the gains. One of the challenges for the realist theoretical framework is to explain such seemingly irrational behavior.

Fourth, security is the central problem of international politics. This follows from the reality of anarchy. States operate in an international system where war and violence always lurk. Foreign policy is first and foremost an exercise in national security. Leaders must constantly scan the horizon looking for threats and dangers. States may want to spread lofty values around the world and create open trading systems, but, in the final analysis, states must worry about being exploited or attacked by other states. In certain eras of world history – as during the world wars of the twentieth century – all pretense of civility is stripped away and states struggle for survival. In these times, the bare essentials of international relations are revealed, and the bare essentials are about power and survival.

Finally, realists argue that the search for security is a competitive endeavor, so they expect competition and conflict to be inherent in world politics. There are winners and losers. Power has a relational quality. If one state grows stronger, others necessarily grow weaker. Some states are richer than others, and since power and wealth go hand in hand, to be richer is to be more secure and prosperous. Because of this logic, realists expect competition to be a natural and enduring feature of the international system. Conflict is inherent in relations among states. Peace and cooperation can be achieved at least temporarily and in specific ways, but it is not a permanent condition. States are always looking out for themselves, so they aim to exploit opportunities to gain an advantage on other states.

Realist Propositions

Building on these assumptions about the nation-state, anarchy, and security competition, realists advance a variety of key propositions or concepts. In this discussion, we focus on the main propositions, such as those involving power balancing, alliances, security dilemmas, relative gains, power transitions, and nationalism.

For realists, a core proposition is that the balance of power is a basic dynamic that states have pursed across the centuries. As we discussed in Chapter 2, the balance of power is a strategy that states employ to protect themselves in a world of anarchy and danger. Faced with rising power and threats from other states, a state can attempt to protect itself by generating countervailing power. For example, if one state amasses military power by manufacturing tanks and fighter aircraft that threaten a neighboring state, that neighboring state can respond by amassing its own military power to defend itself. If the threatened state generates enough military capabilities, the threatening state is less likely to attack. In effect, power is used to neutralize or balance power.

The threatened state can also neutralize or balance power by forming a coalition of states with enough collective military power to counter-balance the threatening state. Indeed, one of the oldest tendencies in international relations is for the rise of a powerful state to trigger the formation of a coalition of states that seek protect themselves as a group through counter-balancing the rising state. For example, as discussed in Chapter 2, Napoleonic France in the late eighteenth century rose up, amassed overwhelming military capabilities, and marched its armies across Europe. The other countries in Europe, led eventually by Great Britain, formed a coalition with sufficient aggregated military power to defeat France and push it back into its borders. Likewise, during the Cold War, the United States and the Soviet Union built coalitions of states to balance against each other. Each sought to aggregate enough power through internal military mobilization and partnerships with other states to keep the other in check. Power was used to balance power.

The fact that states exist in anarchy means they can never be sure of each other's intentions. This has the potential to lead to a process we noted in Chapter 1, the security dilemma. A security dilemma exists between states when one state seeks to ensure its survivability in the international system by acquiring military power but, in doing so, triggers insecurity in another state, leading it to try to protect itself by acquiring military power – thus making both states less secure than when they started (Herz 1950; Jervis 1978). This situation can lead to a reciprocal dynamic of insecurity and an arms race. Defensive mustering of power triggers a counter-reaction which, in turn, triggers a counter-counterreaction. It is important to note that this is a dynamic driven by *defensive* steps undertaken by both states. In reality, each simply wants to protect itself, but what looks like protection or defense to one state may appear to be the means for aggression or offense in the eyes of its neighbor. Security dilemmas, then, are the result of the interplay of differences in the perspectives of states' motives, actions, and the absence of a centralized international government to which states can appeal for protection. For an example of how such differences in perspectives and understandings of states can lead to arms races and regional tension, see Box 22.2.

A companion proposition to the balance of power is that states will respond to threatening situations by forming alliances. Alliances, we saw, Chapter 2, are coalitions of states formed for mutual protection. The most famous and long-lasting alliance in the world is the North Atlantic Treaty Organization (NATO), which ties together the United States and its European partners. Originally established in 1949 at the beginning of the Cold War as an organization of joint protection against the Soviet Union, it has survived the end of the Cold War and remains an organization that combines American and European military capabilities to be used for various conflicts in and around Europe. For realists, alliances are the main form of cooperation among states. They are temporary associations that pool military power to guard against or deter a common foe.

The basic predicament of states operating in a world of anarchy leads realists to another important proposition: states care deeply about relative gains or relative position. As noted above, realists believe that it is a state's material power capacities that give it the ability to pursue its interests and protect itself in a dangerous world. The stronger a state is, the more likely it is to realize its goals and guard itself against enemies. But the critical point is that power is relative; for one state to get more of it necessarily means that other states will have less. So realists argue that states are in an ongoing and unending competitive game to enhance their power. In an anarchic world, states must be continuously making decisions on whether their actions increase power or not. That is, states care more about *relative* gains than absolute gains. Absolute gains would be the sum total of benefits that a particular agreement or action yields. Free trade, for example, may produce very large absolute gains for the system of states. But power considerations lead states to evaluate the benefits in relative terms. If free trade generates great absolute gains but leaves other potentially threatening states relatively better off, then realists believe a state will be reluctant to engage is free trade.

This question of absolute versus relative gains is very important in current debates about US policy towards China. Realists worry more than proponents of other theoretical traditions that by increasing trade with China, the United States is helping to increase China's *relative* power, and that may weigh against the national security of the United States in the future, even though the United States, in absolute terms, is gaining as well. In general, the realist worry for a state is that other states will *gain* more and, over time, this will give them power advantages. So realists argue that states

Alliances: Coalitions of states formed for mutual protection.

Relative gains: (1) The gains a state makes *relative* to other states. As opposed to absolute gains, which are simply the total materials gains made by a state, relative gains focus on the gains one state makes compared to a rival. Realists emphasize the importance of relative gains. (2) An important element of economic nationalism, relative gains is the idea that some gain more than others in economic interactions, and those who gain less lose out, even if they have positive absolute gains.

China's Perspective

Many people view China today as a powerful state rising to great power status. But Chinese leaders have reason to see the world differently. They view the United States as the most powerful state in international relations, and one that may be looking to diminish China's regional influence. The United States is allied with Japan, a neighbor of China that is technologically more advanced, and one with which China shares a history of animosity. America also has close military relationships with some Southeast Asian states, for example Singapore and Thailand, and it has a long-standing alliance relationship with Australia. For China, continuing to modernize its military capability is a prudent defensive step given the uncertainty of its region and the potential hostility of neighboring states and their great power ally.

Southeast Asian States' Perspective

States in Southeast Asia such as Singapore, Malaysia, Thailand, Vietnam, and Indonesia see it differently. They view China as a large and powerful neighbor, upon whom they are economically dependent, and who appears to have a strong interest in exercising regional influence even at the expense of smaller states. Rapid increases in Chinese defense spending, fueled by rapid economic growth, and China's claims to disputed territories in the South China Sea make the leaders of Southeast Asian states nervous. A natural and prudent response is to increase their military spending. Between 2005 and 2010, for example, Singapore and Malaysia more than doubled their defense spending. Smaller countries in the region have also enlisted the support of the United States, which has strengthened its defense relationships with Singapore, Thailand, and Vietnam and has announced plans to station more troops and ships in Australia and elsewhere in the region. These moves only reinforce China's anxieties, leading it to continue to grow its own defense spending and thereby perpetuating the action–reaction dynamic of insecurity that characterizes the security dilemma.

will exhibit a tendency to make choices based on the relative benefits that accrue to the various parties.

Realists also focus on the problem of power transitions. One of the great dramas of international relations is the long-term historical dynamics of the rise and decline of states. Germany rose up in the late nineteenth century to challenge Great Britain; in the current era, China is rising up to challenge the Western great powers. International change results when technological innovations and uneven economic growth lead to shifts in the relative power positions of states. The realist proposition is that power transition moments – when a rising state comes to equal or surpass an older powerful state – are fraught with danger. E.H. Carr, a British scholar, has called this the problem of peaceful change, or the problem of how the international system copes with the transition of order based on the domination of one state over another state (Carr 1939). Conflict is possible at these moments because as the rising state grows more powerful, it will become dissatisfied with the existing international order presided over by a dominant but declining state. It has more power and wants the international system to accommodate its interests and accord it the status and rights due to a rising state. On the other hand, the older and declining state will be threatened by the rising state and seek to preserve its declining dominance.

Power transitions do not inevitably end in war. Germany did rise up to challenge British dominance of the nineteenth-century international system. But the United States also grew more powerful than Britain during these decades; driven by indus-

Power transitions: When the relative power of two (or more) states changes, often due to technological innovations and uneven economic growth.

Peaceful change: The problem of how the international system copes with the transition of order based on the domination of one state over other states.

trialization, it became the world's leading economy and a soon to be unrivaled global power. Yet while the British–German power transition generated conflict and war, the British–American transition was peaceful. Realists argue that power transitions are moments of danger. Whether war and security competition tear the global order apart depends on how rising and declining states define their interests and the ways they decide to defend, overturn, or accommodate themselves to the existing international order.

Finally, realists offer the proposition that nationalism is a dynamic force that motivates states on the international stage. Nationalism is a term that describes the political identity a people share, or a sense of collective fate as a political community. To be part of a nation is to be part of a people with a common history and identity. Nationalism is a feeling people have that they are bound together as part of a natural political entity. The nation is a community of people who live in a world of many peoples, each with their own sense of shared identity. This sense of common identity, or a shared community of fate, gives special meaning to the nation-state. It is also what the state can rely on when it asks for sacrifices by the people on behalf of the nation, such as taxes, obedience to law, and service in the military. Realists emphasize that it is nationalism and loyalty to the nation-state which provide the foundation for dominance of the nation-state and the competitive states system. Nationalism is a potential source of conflict in that it encourages groups of people to emphasize the differences between themselves and other groups.

> **Nationalism:** A term that describes an intense political identity a people share, or a sense of collective fate as a political community.

Within the realist tradition there are a variety of specific arguments and theories, some of which contradict each other. For example, realists agree that anarchy is important, but some realists think that anarchy tends to make states bold and aggressive, while other realists believe that anarchy tends to encourage states to be cautious and defensive. Despite these differences, however, what realists agree on is that when they look out into the world, they see international relations as a struggle for power and security among nation-states. It is a world of anarchy where competition and conflict is ever present. Law, idealism, and morality are human aspirations that make an appearance in the relations among states. But realists argue that power and the search for security are more fundamental, and they will not yield or disappear despite the best efforts of enlightened leaders.

No one can deny the influence of power and security on states' behaviors toward one another. However, states also have the tendency to build cooperative relationships in the international system. We turn next to the English School and, after this, the liberal tradition, whose scholars attempt to explain this cooperation, based on the assumptions and concepts of the theoretical framework.

The English School of International Relations

A rich body of international relations theory with links to realism is called the English School. Emerging in Great Britain in the postwar era, this tradition acknowledges the realist view that states operate within anarchy. But scholars in the English School go on to emphasize that states have organized themselves into what is called a 'society' of states. In effect, states are more 'social' than realists tend to admit. They have developed rules, norms, and institutions to manage the states system and it anarchical character. This orientation has led English School scholars to explore the historical dynamics of the modern states system – its origins, spread, and evolving political relationships.

▲ Photo 22.2 Serbian Nationalist Rally

People wave Serbian flags during a rally in Belgrade, Serbia, Friday, May 10, 2013. More than 3,000 nationalists have rallied in Belgrade against a deal normalizing relations with breakaway Kosovo, accusing the Serbian government of treason for accepting the agreement in order to advance the country's EU bid. According to realists, nationalism is the critical force that drives the dominance of the nation-state and the competitive international system of states. Without this collective feeling of community centered on the concept of a natural political entity, the nation-state could not exist.

Source: PA Images.

The classic statement of the English School vision is Hedley Bull's *The Anarchical Society* (Bull, 1977). Bull begins with the realist view that states are independent and competitive actors in a world of power politics. But he goes on to argue that states have shared interests in managing their anarchical circumstances. States are self-interested, but they share an interest in a stable and rule-based environment. In particular, Bull claims that states share an interest in establishing rules of the game in three areas – restraints on the use of force, sanctity of international agreements, and the security of property rights. These interests mean that states have incentives to build relations with each other, to work together to establish mutual expectations about the terms of their interaction. It is in this way that Bull sees the rise of what he calls 'international society' within the context of the modern states system. International society refers to the wide array of norms, rules, and institutions that reflect and guide relations among states. As Bull and Watson argue, an international society exists when 'a group of states (or, more generally, a group of independent political communities) which not merely form a system, in the sense that the behavior of each is a necessary factor in the calculations of the others, but also have established by dialogue and consent common rules and institutions for the conduct of their relations, and recognize their common interest in maintaining these arrangements' (Bull and Watson 1985: 1).

The focus on the rise and operation of a society of states leads English School theorists to emphasize the importance of diplomacy and dialogue in international relations. What scholars illuminate are the manifold ways in which statesmen over the centuries have worked to establish rules and understandings to manage power politics. Some scholars have focused on the rise of international law as a core institution of international society. Others have focused on the accumulation of rules and norms that regulate the states system – rules and norms relating to sovereignty, self-determination, non-discrimination, and the use of force. Others have focused on the expansion of the nation-state and the states system from Europe to the wider world. In all these areas, scholars offer accounts of the ways states have built the rules and institutions of order and established common norms and expectations about power, property, and rights. The result is a portrait of the modern international system, illuminating the remarkable spread of the system of states and the deepening of its shared norms and rules. (Dunne 1998; Buzan 2004)

English School scholars do differ on how 'social' the system of states actually is. Some scholars emphasize the 'pluralistic' character of international society, where realist dynamics of power and competition remain central, while others emphasize the 'solidaristic' character of international society, arguing that shared rules and norms have progressively weakened the role of power and coercion in world politics, or at least made it less legitimate and tolerable by states. In these various ways, the English School tradition blends realist assumptions and ideas with other international relations traditions, particularly the liberal and constructivist traditions, which we now turn to.

👤 **Individual**	🛡 **State**	🌐 **International**	*Levels of Analysis* *The Realist Tradition*
In realist theory, state leaders are the most important decision makers, pursuing the national interest and maneuvering in a world of competing states.	States – large and small, powerful and weak – are all competing for survival and advantage.	Nationalism is a dynamic force which reinforces the centrality of the nation-state.	

The Liberal Tradition

War and conflict have been pervasive features of international relations. But so too has been the tendency of states to trade, settle disputes, and build cooperative relationships. The liberal tradition offers a variety of ideas about how and why such cooperation takes place in the global system. Liberalism, like realism, is a body of thought that reaches back into the distant past with assumptions and arguments about international relations. While realism sees anarchy and the struggle for power as the defining features of international relations, liberalism sees the internal character of states, particularly the interests and impulses of democratic and market-oriented states, as the most important feature of international relations.

Liberal international theory has three intellectual branches. The first focuses on trade and its impact on international relations. Liberals believe that the spread of capitalism and market relations creates economic interdependence, joint gains, shared interests, and incentives for international cooperation. A second branch focuses on democratic states and their interaction. Here, the view is that democratic polities have a tendency to seek affiliation with other democracies and build peaceful relations. The third branch focuses on the pacifying effects of law and institutions. Liberals view international law and institutions as outgrowths of liberal societies as they seek to establish rule-based relations between them (Doyle 1997). Wielding these ideas, liberal international theory foresees the spread and development of democracy and market relations that transform and soften, even if they do not fully eliminate, the anarchic struggle for power of importance to realism.

Liberal Assumptions

Liberal theory is based on a series of five important assumptions. First is the view that the world is in an ongoing process of modernization. That is, humankind is constantly inventing, innovating, improving, and creating. Out of this constant process, people and groups advance – they modernize. The process of modernization is pushed forward by the forces of science and technology, which people are constantly using to enhance human capabilities. These transforming human capabilities have vast implications for the ways in which power, communication, relationships, interests, community, and political possibilities are arrayed. For example, innovations and discoveries in the last two centuries in telegraph, telephone, and computer technologies have transformed the way people in distant places can communicate and cooperate, and new commercial possibilities and political relationships have followed as well. This vision of human development can be contrasted with realist thinking. Realists tend to view history in cyclical terms, seeing humans making the same mistakes over and over again. Liberals are more inclined to see progress in which political, eco-

Modernization: The idea that mankind is constantly inventing, innovating, improving, and creating.

As you can see from this table, the EU currently consists of 28 members. The European Union demonstrates the principles of liberal theorists, as the EU is a political community that attempts to transcend the nationalism and sovereignty of the old European states. The EU still faces issues of coordination, but the organization has learned from these past internal conflicts.

Source: © European Union.

Member Country	Year of EU Entry	Member Country	Year of EU Entry
Austria	1995	Italy	1952 (Founding Member)
Belgium	1952 (Founding Member)	Latvia	2004
Bulgaria	2007	Lithuania	2004
Croatia	2013	Luxembourg	1952 (Founding Member)
Cyprus	2004	Malta	2004
Czech Republic	2004	Netherlands	1952 (Founding Member)
Denmark	1973	Poland	2004
Estonia	2004	Portugal	1986
Finland	1995	Romania	2007
France	1952 (Founding Member)	Slovakia	2004
Germany	1952 (Founding Member)	Slovenia	2004
Greece	1981	Spain	1986
Hungary	2004	Sweden	1995
Ireland	1973	United Kingdom	1973

nomic, and social circumstances of people improve over time. Realists stress the reoccurrence of war; liberals try to find ways to transcend it.

Second, liberals believe that individuals and groups, not states, are the basic actors in international relations. Individuals, societal groups, firms, associations, and other types of groups operate in and across nation-states. Depending on their interests and inclinations, they can also be found building communities and political orders above and below the level of the nation-state. The specific size and character of human communities evolve and change over the eras. For example, liberals are not surprised to see the rise of the European Union in the decades after World War II – a project to build a political community within Europe that transcends the nationalism and sovereignty of the old European states.

Importantly, while liberals see individuals and groups as the building blocks of their theories, they also see nation-states and the states system as important. Individuals and groups build larger political groups – such as nation-states – and these larger political groups matter as well. The rise of modern liberal democracies that are based on popular sovereignty and the rule of law is an important historical breakthrough for liberal theory. It is the rise and spread of liberal democracy that has allowed individuals and groups to go beyond old forms of nationalism and empire to strengthen the rule of law and cooperation among nation-states. So individuals and groups are important to liberals, but precisely because they have the potential ability to transcend old forms of war and hostility between peoples to establish more peaceful and cooperative forms of world politics.

A third liberal assumption is that individuals have incentives and impulses embedded in the deep structures of society to trade, bargain, negotiate, and seek cooperation for joint gain. Liberals argue that individuals can move beyond 'relative gains' thinking and seize possibilities for 'joint gains' based on trade, exchange, and cooperation. Relations among states are not inherently peaceful. But, there is always ample room for individuals and groups to look for ways to advance their interests through cooperation with others within their society and across the global system.

A fourth assumption that liberals make is that modernization and advancement tend to take societies down a common path toward democracy and market society. Modernization across societies and cultures tends to produce similar sorts of chal-

Changing Character of Economic Doctrines

Then: *Diversity of Economic Systems in the 1930s*

In the first half of the twentieth century, the industrial and developing states exhibited a wide diversity of types of economic systems. As the Great Depression took hold and the world economy collapsed, countries went their own way. Germany under the Nazis became an authoritarian industrial state, Britain and France experimented with various sorts of social democracy, the United States remained more market oriented, and the Soviet Union under Stalin consolidated its state socialism system. No consensus existed on economic doctrine or the best model of economic development.'

Now: *The Washington Consensus of the 1990s*

By the 1990s, there was a widespread consensus among capitalist countries, particularly in the West and the developing world, that decontrol, deregulation, and open markets were the best way to promote growth and development. Here is Harvard University scholar Dani Rodrik's description of this consensus:

> Stabilize, privatize, and liberalize' became the mantra of a generation of technocrats who cut their teeth in the developing world and of the political leaders they counseled . . . [T]his advice inspired a wave of reforms in Latin America and sub-Saharan Africa that fundamentally transformed the policy landscape in these developing areas. With the fall of the Berlin Wall and the collapse of the Soviet Union, former socialist countries similarly made a bold leap toward markets. There was more privatization, deregulation, and trade liberalization in Latin America and Eastern Europe than probably anywhere else at any point in economic history. In Sub-Saharan Africa, governments moved with less conviction and speed, but there too a substantial portion of the new policy agenda was adopted: state marketing boards were dismantled, inflation reduced, trade opened up, and significant amounts of privatization undertaken.

The financial crisis that began in 2008, however, has called the Washington Consensus into question. The crisis began in the United States, the epicenter of the Consensus, and quickly spread around the world. To many observers and participants, the crisis resulted at least in part from the policies of deregulation and liberalization championed by the proponents of the Washington Consensus.

Source: Dani Rodrik, 'Goodbye Washington Consensus, Hello Washington Confusion? A Review of the World Bank's Economic Growth in the 1990s: Learning from a Decade of Reform', *Journal of Economic Literature*, XLIV (December 2006): 973–4.

lenges and responses; the most general movement is toward loosely convergent sorts of political-economic institutions. That is, liberals see the movement of history as more or less linear, with a pathway that takes developing and advanced societies in the direction of liberal democracy and capitalism. The advanced capitalist societies are at the vanguard of this movement. Through trade, exchange, innovation, and learning, all societies will tend to move in this direction.

Finally, out of all these modernizing changes, liberals assume that there is such a thing as progress. The human condition can and will get better. Liberals believe that individuals and groups do indeed learn. They respond to incentives to make their world better. They are sensitive to human rights and the moral correctness of the rule of law. As we have noted, liberals ground their theory of politics in the individual, and

▼ Photos 22.3 and 22.4 Trials for Crimes Against Humanity

The Nuremberg Trials

The Hague Convention of 1907 established a list of war crimes for which individuals could be held accountable. After the Second World War, the highly publicized Nuremberg Trials, a list of military tribunals, prosecuted prominent members of the Nazi Party for major war crimes and crimes against humanity. In 2012 the ex-President of Liberia, Charles Taylor, was sentenced by a special UN-backed court to 50 years in prison for aiding and abetting the butchering of women and children during the civil war in neighboring Sierra Leone. Currently, the International Criminal Court prosecutes individuals accused of genocide, crimes against humanity, war crimes, and the crime of aggression. There are limits, however, to the reach of the ICC as it can only prosecute crimes committed on or after 1 July 2002 – the date of the court's establishment.

Source: Historical and Special Collections, Harvard Law School Library.

The Trial of Charles Taylor

Former Liberian President Charles Taylor, left, waits for the start of his appeal judgment at the Special Court for Sierra Leone (SCSL) in Leidschendam, near The Hague, Netherlands, Thursday September 26, 2013. Judges at a UN-backed tribunal are delivering their judgment in Taylor's appeal against his convictions and 50-year sentence for planning and aiding atrocities by rebels in Sierra Leone's bloody civil war. Taylor, 65, became the first former head of state convicted by an international war crimes court since World War II when the SCSL found him guilty on April 26, 2012, of 11 counts of war crimes and crimes against humanity including terrorism, murder, rape and using child soldiers.

Source: PA Images.

individuals possess rights and are worthy of respect. This puts liberals in a position to see progress within and between societies based on mutual recognition of rights and conduct based on the rule of law. Liberals look out at the international system and see that progress has, in fact, occurred; slavery has been abolished, genocide is now a crime against humanity, and despotic rule is seen as deeply illegitimate.

Liberal Propositions

Based on these assumptions, liberals advance a variety of concepts or propositions about how individuals and groups operate within and between states to shape international relations. These propositions involve commercial liberalism, democratic peace, liberal institutionalism, transnationalism, and cosmopolitanism.

The first proposition centers on the concept of commercial liberalism, which dates back to the writings of Adam Smith, an eighteenth-century Scottish social philosopher and pioneer of political economy. Liberals argue that market society and economic interdependence tend to have a *pacifying* impact on relations among states. As the economic relations between two states increase, the interests of these states in stable and continuous relations grow. This is because each country depends on the ongoing

Commercial liberalism: The idea that market society and economic interdependence tend to have a pacifying impact on relations among states. As the economic relations between two states increase, the interests of these states in stable and continuous relations grow.

trade and exchange with the other for its own economic well-being. War and destabilizing political conflict between these commercial partners jeopardize profits and employment at home. As a result, liberals argue that as economic relations between nation-states intensify, *vested interests* will emerge in these countries that advocate continued open and cooperative relations.

More generally, Adam Smith argued that the pursuit of wealth could contribute to moral perfection. A free market system could lead the consumer 'by an invisible hand to promote an end which was no part of his intention' (Smith 1937). In so doing, Smith and other liberals hold that a market society will eliminate some of the causes of war by causing states to abandon colonization and tariff barriers as policy tools. With democracy and capitalism, citizens become more rational and materialistic, and more resistant to belligerent nationalism. Liberals have developed these insights, arguing that the evolving character of economic interdependence between states will shape the foreign and security policies they adopt toward each other. Economic prosperity fueled by growing interdependence will make security competition and war less likely because the costs of conflict, particularly to domestic interest groups, will be unacceptably high.

The second and related liberal proposition is that democracies tend not to fight each other. This argument about the democratic peace, which as we noted
is a leading example of a theory in the contemporary field of international relations, was first proposed by Immanuel Kant in an essay entitled 'Perpetual Peace' in 1795. The argument is that democracies, or what Kant called 'republics,' are unusually peaceful toward each other. Republics, or democracies, are understood as states that have elected governments, a free press, private property, and the rule of law. Kant's expectation was that as democracy spread around the world, so too would peace and stability. He foresaw a widening realm of peaceful relations among democracies, a sort of democratic federation or union of like-minded states that band together and cooperate to create a zone of peace. In this view, democracies are not necessarily more peaceful in their relations with non-democracies, but relations between democracies are special, and peace is to be expected.

Liberal scholars have proposed a variety of reasons why democracies do not fight each other. We will explore their reasoning in detail in Chapter 5, but here we highlight the main elements of their perspective. One reason is that democracies share common preferences; they have similar aspirations about how international relations should be organized. They all want open systems built around stable rules and institutions. In this way, democracies acknowledge each other as legitimate and worthy states whose interests and security must be honored and respected. It is hard for a democracy to declare war on another democracy when they have such strong bonds of shared values and interests. Another reason democracies do not fight each other is because in democracies, citizens bear the costs of war – the costly expenditures of blood and treasure – and they also choose their leaders. Leaders in democracies are held to account for their actions. Citizens are in a position to avoid the costs of war by voting for leaders who uphold the peace. Another reason for the democratic peace is that democracies tend to have transparent and accountable governments, and this makes it easier for these states to trust each other and cooperate (Russett 1993; Lipson 2003). In all these ways, liberals argue that democratic states have characteristics that allow them to transcend the insecurities of anarchy and build cooperative and integrated zones of peace.

► Figure 22.1 World
Trends in Governance,
1800–2010

This graph shows the
number of democratic,
anocratic, and auto-
cratic countries in the
world from 1800 to
2010. Notice that since
the end of the Cold
War, there has been an
explosion in the
number of democra-
cies in the world, while
the number of auto-
cratic states has greatly
decreased.

Source: Centre for
Systemic Peace, Polity IV
Project,
www.systemicpeace.org.

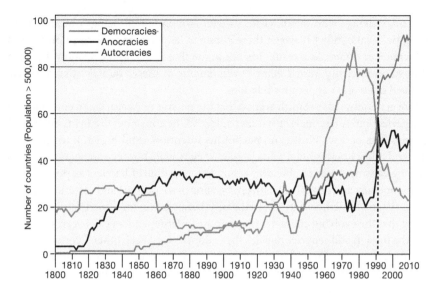

A third liberal proposition is that states will build international relations around international law and institutions. We explore the contributions that such laws and institutions can make to peace in Chapter 6. For now we emphasize that, in general, liberals argue that international rules and institutions can play an important role in shaping the operation of relations among states. This view dates back to seventeenth-century philosophers such as John Locke and early modern theorists of international law. Political thinking emerged in this era that argued in favor of legal and constitutional rights of individuals within Western polities. The power of the state – and autocratic and monarchical rule – must yield to the rule of law and the sovereignty of individuals. Rights of individuals were seen to be anchored in the appreciation of the fact that all people were equal members of the human community. It was but a small step to recognize that the laws that informed and constrained the exercise of power within liberal societies were also of some significance in relations among liberal democracies. Individuals in other states were also rights-bearing members of humanity, and so leaders of liberal states must also respect the laws that protected these individuals within their own countries.

Liberals have also developed more pragmatic arguments about why and how rules and institutions matter in international relations. In some circumstances, states simply have different interests, so institutions will not help foster cooperation. But in other circumstances, states do not cooperate because they do not trust each other. States do not cooperate because they worry the other states will not hold up their side of the bargain. They are not sure the other state will be a reliable partner. Under these circumstances, when the interests of two states do not inherently conflict with each other, international institutions may serve the important function of reconciling those interests by increasing the flow of information, transparency, and trust. This is function-alism; institutions are tools that allow states to develop more efficient and durable forms of cooperation (Keohane 1984).

When states agree to abide by a set of rules and institutions, they are agreeing to limit their freedom of action. Liberals argue that states agree to bind themselves to institutional agreements when doing so creates incentives and obligations of other

Functionalism: The liberal
idea that institutions are
tools that allow states to
develop more efficient and
durable forms of coopera-
tion.

states to do the same. These reciprocal agreements to operate according to rules and institutions create a predictable and functional environment in which all states can pursue their interests. Even powerful states may find a commitment to operate within mutually agreeable rules and institutions a way to protect their global interests and make their international leadership role acceptable to other states (Ikenberry 2001).

A fourth liberal proposition is that transnational relations provide important connections between states. Transnationalism refers to the tendency of groups within countries to build cooperative associations with groups in other countries. An extraordinary array of transnational groups operates across state borders. While realists argue that state-to-state interactions are most important, liberals stress that society-to-society interactions – that is, the interaction of individuals and groups across societies – can also shape patterns of cooperation and conflict within the global system. Transnational groups can come in many varieties, such as environmental groups, human rights organizations, religious sects, and scientific associations. In recent years, the world has also become aware of dangerous transnational groups, such as terrorist organizations, drug traffickers, and organized crime groups. Transnational groups can impact international relations in various ways. In some cases, the goal of these transnational organizations is to act as pressure groups seeking to alter state policies. Environmental groups such as Greenpeace and human rights organizations such as Amnesty International are of this sort. In other cases, transnational groups are associations of experts wielding scientific or other technical knowledge, and have an impact in informing the way in which states think about their interests. Some transnational business associations act as *private* governance institutions, facilitating cooperation between corporations on matters such as research and development, technical and regulatory standards, and so forth.

Finally, liberal theory stresses the importance of cosmopolitanism. Cosmopolitanism refers to the tendency of peoples in different countries to embrace each other as fellow global citizens. Cosmopolitanism can be contrasted with nationalism. If nationalism entails a shared identity of a particular national group expressed as an allegiance to others within the nation, cosmopolitanism involves the ability of people to identify with others in different lands and cultures. In emphasizing the cosmopolitan tendencies of mankind, liberals are suggesting that people are not trapped in their national identity. They can break out, seek people from other places, and build community between them.

Overall, liberal international theory offers a set of assumptions and propositions that stress the distinctive possibilities for cooperation among modern and advanced market democracies. The general claim is that these

Transnationalism: The tendency of groups within countries to build cooperative associations with groups in other countries.

Cosmopolitanism: The tendency of peoples in different countries to embrace each other as fellow global citizens. Cosmopolitanism can be contrasted with nationalism.

◀ Photo 22.5
Cosmopolitanism
This crowd is composed of people from different cultures and nations. It shows the principles of cosmopolitanism in action.
Source: Photoalto.

societies have incentives and capacities to build complex, stable, and mutually acceptable political relations. Liberal order is distinguished from other types of order, such as balance of power and imperial varieties, because of the way that state power is checked, restrained, and channeled. The problems of anarchy are reduced to such an extent that the distribution of power itself does not lead to balancing or coercive domination. Bargains, exchanges, reciprocity, specialization, and security cooperation are aspects of international relations that are captured by liberal theory.

But, not all people benefit equally from growing trade and cooperation, as liberal economic theory proposes. Rising inequality of wealth distribution during the industrial revolution gained support for the Marxist-Leninist theoretical framework, examined next.

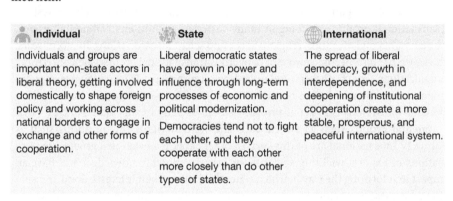

Levels of Analysis	👤 **Individual**	🏛️ **State**	🌐 **International**
The Liberal Tradition	Individuals and groups are important non-state actors in liberal theory, getting involved domestically to shape foreign policy and working across national borders to engage in exchange and other forms of cooperation.	Liberal democratic states have grown in power and influence through long-term processes of economic and political modernization. Democracies tend not to fight each other, and they cooperate with each other more closely than do other types of states.	The spread of liberal democracy, growth in interdependence, and deepening of institutional cooperation create a more stable, prosperous, and peaceful international system.

The Marxist Tradition

When the European states entered the industrial revolution in the early nineteenth century, observers puzzled over how the rise of capitalism would impact the politics and economics of countries around the world. Traditional economies based on agriculture were rapidly transforming into industrial economies with modern corporations, wage workers, steam engines, and new manufacturing technologies. During the nineteenth century, countries in Europe went from rural societies of farmers and villagers to modern urban societies with bankers, businessmen, and a growing industrial working class. The countries of Europe grew in prosperity and their relations with the rest of the world changed, but not in the way hoped by liberal economists such as Adam Smith. That is, as we point out in Box 22.4, according to liberal economic theory, all would gain from trade. But, at least in the nineteenth century, too often the rich European countries became the wealth core of an emerging world economy, while peoples and nations in less advanced areas became the poorer periphery. Within the countries of the industrializing West, economic inequality also increased. Great wealth was created by the industrial revolution but working people and the poor benefited the least.

As scholars puzzled over the implications of the industrial revolution for domestic and international politics, a school of thought pioneered by the political economist Karl Marx emerged in the mid-nineteenth century that focused on class and class conflict. Marx sought to understand how the industrial revolution – and the rise of capitalism as an economic system – worked. He sought to identify capitalism's winners and losers and how capitalism and economic change shaped politics and political life.

Liberal Visions of Shared Benefits of Economic Growth

Aspiration: *Adam Smith, The Wealth of Nations*

Adam Smith argued in his seminal statement of market economics that nations will grow and prosper if their people are free to use their skills and capital to productive ends. Workers and businesses would be most efficient when they specialized at what they did best, creating a division of labor within and between nations. Governments were to protect property rights, enforce laws, and provide public infrastructure such as roads. As Smith argued, the individual's pursuit of his or her self-interest would indirectly and unintentionally promote the wealth and advancement of the general public.

> As every individual, therefore, endeavors as much as he can both to employ his capital in support of domestic industry, and so to direct that industry that its produce may be of the greatest value; every individual necessarily labors to render the annual revenue of the society as great as he can. He generally, indeed, neither intends to promote the public interest, nor knows how much he is promoting it. By preferring the support of domestic to that of foreign industry, he intends only his own security; and by directing that industry in such a manner as its produce may be of the greatest value, he intends only his own gain, and he is on this, as in many other cases, led by an invisible hand to promote an end which was no part of his intention. Nor is it always the worse for the society that it was no part of it. By pursuing his own interest he frequently promotes that of the society more effectively than when he really intends to promote it.
>
> (Adam Smith, *The Wealth of Nations*, Book IV, Chapter II, paragraph IX)

Reality: *Wealth Inequality between States during the Industrial Revolution, and Today*

The nineteenth-century industrial revolution that Smith foresaw entailed the growth of great wealth in countries like Great Britain and continued poverty and squalor elsewhere, such as colonial India. A similar dynamic takes place today and informs the debate over the advantages and drawbacks of globalization. Proponents of globalization point to the overall growth in the world economy that has occurred as borders have opened to the flow of goods, services, capital, and technology. Critics of globalization point to the growing disparities in income and wealth within and across states. Inequality, based on the workings of global capitalism, is the core concern of the Marxist tradition.

In sum, this Marxist tradition focuses on conflict and revolution thought to be associated with economic change and the rise of rich and poor classes within and across countries.

Marxism is not explicitly a theory about international relations. It is a theory about capitalism – its logic and unfolding dynamics in world history. Marxist theory is premised on the notion of historical materialism. This is the idea that history – and the actors that operate on the global stage across eras and regions – are shaped and motivated by their underlying material or economic basis. As the material basis of society changes, so too does history. In effect, the Marxist claim is that the most fundamental fact about people and societies is their material or economic circumstance. Societies are shaped and reshaped around the need to produce the material requirements of life. In the modern era, capitalism has provided the organizing logic shaping the productive forces within and between societies. This deeply rooted and ever-changing system of capitalism provides the structural setting in which peoples, classes, and states operate. Importantly, in the view of Marxist theory, it is the owners of the productive forces of capitalism who ultimately control politics and society as well. As we shall see, it is from this perspective that Marxist scholars have been able to say a great deal about the interests and motivations of actors within the global arena.

Marxist Assumptions

Mode of production: The basic organization of the economy – the way in which people relate to one another and to the material world.

Relations of production: The system by which the people in a productive system are related, or the relations between those people. According to Marxism, these relations are shaped by the mode of production. In a capitalist industrial mode, the relations of production will be characterized by class conflict.

Marxist theory about international relations begins with five assumptions. First, political interests and relationships are determined by a person's position within the transforming economic system. Economics – or the material setting in which people are situated – shapes politics. Or to put it in Marxist terms, the economic *base* shapes the political *superstructure*. The mode of production, organized in the modern era according to a capitalist logic, shapes the relations of production. The relations of production are the social and political relationships that emerge in society – for example, between workers and owners of businesses. The mode of production is the basic organization of the economy. It refers to the deep logic of economic life. In Marx's account, human societies were for centuries organized according to feudal relations of production, where serfs and peasants worked on the land that was owned by nobles or an aristocratic class. It was in the early modern era that capitalism arose as a mode of production, and with it came modern industrial society. Under capitalism, an industrial and commercial class emerged as owners of factories and corporations, and workers emerged as wage laborers. With the rise of capitalism as the mode of production, the relations of productions pitted the owners of capital and workers against each other. The world of politics evolved to reflect shifts in the underlying system of production. In other words, in this view, politics is what happens on the surface level of societies, and it is shaped by the deep underlying forces of capitalism and industrial development.

Socioeconomic classes: Groupings of peoples based on their relationship to the economy.

Second, the important actors in societies are not individuals or states, but socio-economic classes, or groupings of peoples based on their relationship to the economy. With the rise of capitalism and the industrial revolution, the two most important classes are workers and capitalists. Workers are wage laborers and capitalists are the owners of the banks and businesses that make up the productive economy. While realists emphasize states as the key actors in the global system and liberals focus on individuals and groups, Marxist theory sees classes – within societies and between them – as the actors that directly or indirectly shape politics and international relations.

A third assumption is that the modern state is ultimately organized to serve the interests of the capitalist class – or what is sometimes called the ruling class. This is true even for constitutional democracies that elect their leaders. It is a fundamental claim of Marxist theory that modern states – despite their many differences around the world – have as their ultimate goal the protection and advancement of the capitalist class. Protecting and promoting the capitalist class is reflected in narrow instrumental ways when governments intervene to defend the property and profits of the capitalist class. But it is also manifest in a deeper and more structural way as the modern state upholds the rules, institutions, ideas, and privileges of the political order that support the capitalist system. Indeed, the capitalist class rules most effectively when its control over society is least visible.

A fourth Marxist assumption is that class conflict will increasingly define the relations among workers and capitalists. As capitalist industrialization unfolds, societies are expected to become increasingly divided between the two classes. The capitalist owners of wealth and industrial production will face off against workers. Class conflict is driven by their antagonistic economic interests. Workers are vulnerable to economic swings of boom and bust. They are exploited by the owners of capital who pay meager wages and keep the profits. For workers, unemployment and poverty always lurk around the corner. Capitalists, on the other hand, are enriched through economic growth. Moreover, these class relations are transnational. Workers share common interests across the industrial countries – a point captured in the old Marxist slogan, 'workers of the world unite!' Capitalists also tend to form transnational alliances, cooperating to protect their wealth, safeguard international trade and finance, and enforce the system of private property. Workers try to protect their interests by binding together in trade unions, such as the United Auto Workers, on the assumption that workers have more bargaining power if they act collectively rather than individually.

A final Marxist assumption is that revolution is the great source of political change. As class conflict grows more intense in the process of capitalist development, a breakpoint is eventually reached when the workers take control from the capitalist owners. The many overwhelm the few. Workers are expected to seize the ruling institutions of capitalist society – corporations, banks, and the state – and usher in a new political order. Society is to be transformed into a classless system. In Marx's ideal formulation, capitalism is to be turned into communism, a social system in which there is no private property or capitalist state, and workers collectively and harmoniously govern the economy and society. The Soviet Union, though characterized as a communist state, departed significantly from this Marxist ideal in that a small group of Communist Party officials, rather than the working class itself, took control of political power and the authority to allocate resources within society.

Marx foresaw a time when the conflicts and contradictions of modern capitalism would lead to revolution and a transformation in the mode of production – a transformation from capitalism to communism. But he also thought that capitalism was an extraordinarily dynamic and efficient system of production. Its powerful forces were transforming the world. Capitalist states would trade, invest, and expand outwards bringing the backward areas of the world into the arms of the capitalist system. In was in this sense that Marx was not an opponent of British or European colonialism. He saw it was part of the unfolding logic of capitalism, a process that would need to continue until capitalist societies were mature and ready for revolution.

In the twentieth century, Marxist theory of global capitalism evolved in various ways. The Russian revolutionary, Lenin, wrote perhaps the most influential Marxist-inspired treatise on the international politics of capitalism in his 1916 booklet, 'Imperialism: The Highest Stage of Capitalism'. Lenin argued that the capitalist class was becoming increasingly centralized in the major industrial countries, led by cartels of wealthy and powerful financial and industrial elites – what he called finance capitalism. To keep their workers peaceful, these elites in the advanced capitalist states were exporting their capital to poor underdeveloped countries to finance resources and cheap labor production. The poor and the backward regions of the world were being brought into the world capitalist system, and this was changing the relationship between capitalist states. This dynamic of finance capitalism allowed Lenin to explain

Class conflict: Conflict between the capitalist owners of wealth and industrial production and the workers they employ. Class conflict is driven by antagonistic economic interests and, according to Marxism, will increasingly define the relations between workers and capitalists.

Revolution: According to Marxism, in any instance of class conflict a breakpoint is eventually reached when the workers take control from the capitalist owners. Revolution is the dominant mode of political change in the Marxist school.

why revolution would not come – as Marx had predicted – in the most advanced countries but rather in the exploited less developed countries (Lenin 1917). With World War I as a backdrop, Lenin argued that the Western great powers, together with their finance capitalist elites, would be increasingly driven to compete with each other to divide up and exploit the undeveloped world. Thus it was imperialism and war – and not Marx's contradictions with the relations of production – that spelled the doom of advanced capitalism. Other Marxists during Lenin's time and later have continued to debate whether the global capitalist class would ultimately be divided into competing nation-states – reinforced by nationalism and geopolitics – or united in a global coalition to protect their shared interests.

In more recent decades, Marxist-inspired theory on international relations has explored the various ways in which global capitalism operates as a system of power. Some writings focus on the shifting winners and losers that emerge within global capitalism. Trade and open markets do not benefit all people in all places. The spread of capitalism worldwide has mobilized societies and raised many people up out of poverty. But the rich continue to get richer, while the poor – which is the vast majority of the people on earth – remain poor. Many non-Marxist scholars seek to explain these dynamics of inequality (see Stiglitz 2002), but Marxist theory is particularly committed as a theoretical tradition to identifying the divergent interests and outcomes that emerge from the expanding and transforming dynamics of capitalism. Other Marxist-inspired scholars have turned to the exploration of the ideologies and institutions that serve to preserve and protect the global capitalist system. Some scholars offer arguments about hegemony to explain the way in which leading capitalist states – most notably in the current era, the United States – dominate the resources and institutions of world politics (Cox 1987; Cox and Sinclair 1996; Gill 1992). Hegemony for Marxist scholars is a system of power where leading capitalist states exercise domination and control over weaker societies and peoples, often doing so indirectly through the influence of their ideologies and institutions.

Hegemony: The dominance of one state over other states. Many scholars believe that a hegemonic international system is most prone to peace.

Marxist Propositions

From these assumptions, Marxist theory offers a variety of insights about how capitalist states and international relations operate.

One proposition is that states – particularly those states in the advanced industrial countries – will act in ways that protect and advance the interests of capitalism and the capitalist class. This is not to argue that the governments of the leading capitalist countries will always promote the interests of specific businesses or banks. The proposition is that modern states will act to 'keep the world safe' for capitalism. This means that states will uphold property rights and the rules and institutions that support modern capitalism. In this regard, Marxist theory helps illuminate an entire history of state involvement in building, defending, and expanding the world capitalist system. This can be seen in the ways in which Western states over the last two centuries have pursed foreign policies that protect and advance the financial and commercial interests within their countries. The late nineteenth-century scramble for Africa, the partition of China, and the 'informal imperialism' pursued by Western capitalist states in Asia and Latin America were also episodes where states and capitalists worked together for economic and geopolitical advantage. While realists also expect to see states acting to advance the economic interests of their countries, they do so for national interest reasons. Marxists see states working on behalf of capitalism.

Marxists differ on precisely how business controls the state and argue that there are *structural* and *instrumental* capitalist influences on foreign policy. Structural influences of capitalism on foreign policy refer to the ways in which states automatically pursue policies that advance and protect the interests of capitalism. This is what Karl Marx himself argued when he said that 'the state is the handmaiden of capital.' Governments, after all, are dependent on a growing economy for taxes. They have an interest in making sure that the national economy is thriving. In this way, governments will protect the interests of capitalism. Governments will certainly not want to scare off businesses by imposing high taxes or expropriating their property. Governments will also seek to support rules and institutions within the global system that are supportive to trade and investment. In these ways, capitalism has a structural impact on what states do.

Marxists also point to instrumental influences of capitalism on foreign policy. In this case, it is the active lobbying of businesses that influences what states do. Capitalists are, in fact, well organized to influence government policy in most countries. Business associations have full-time representatives to lobby parliaments and presidents, and business elites are among the biggest donors to political campaigns. If 'money speaks' in politics, business groups use this advantage to influence governments. For example, in the United States, business groups with an interest in China have spoken loudly in favor of Sino-American trade and investment. More generally, the history of American foreign policy is full of episodes when business interests – oil companies or investment groups – pressure the government to intervene in the developing world on their behalf. Scholars continue to debate when and how these instrumental interests matter in international relations.

Another proposition is that transnational business will be a salient feature of world politics. As capitalism expands, businesses increasingly look outward into the international system for markets. In the nineteenth century and again in the decades after World War II, international trade grew rapidly. So, too, did international investment, where banks and corporations invest their money in foreign businesses. In recent decades, this *internationalization* of business has increased, and individual companies have established production operations in many different countries. These international businesses are called *multinational corporations* and include companies such as General Electric, Sony, Toyota, and Nestlé. Often, these companies become so internationalized that it is difficult to identify their home country; the world is their playing field.

Marxists argue that with the rise of transnational business, capitalists tend to win and workers tend to lose. That is, capitalists are able to cooperate to protect their wealth and maintain their privileged positions. International capitalists have options; they can establish operations in various countries and when conditions are not favorable to their business interests, they can shut down their operations and go elsewhere. National governments, therefore, have incentives to treat international business well, providing tax breaks and favorable deals so they will stay put. Workers, on the other hand, are not as mobile. They cannot move around as readily, and so their bargaining position is weaker. International capitalists are mobile. They fly around the world looking for business opportunities and they cooperate among themselves. Workers find it difficult to organize across countries. Marxists argue that international relations will bear the marks of this class conflict; national workers will press their governments for protection and international capitalists will lobby for an open world economy.

Taken together, Marxist theory sees the world in terms of class and economic interests. While realists see states struggling for power, Marxists see politics and

Transnational business: Businesses that operate across state lines. According to Marxism, as capitalism expands, businesses increasingly look outward into the international system for markets. This tendency enriches capitalists and impoverishes workers.

international relations as part of a deeper historical process of capitalist development. As the world capitalist system evolves, states and peoples organize and struggle accordingly. While liberals assert that economic interdependence is ultimately beneficial to all people and provides incentives for states to cooperate, Marxists believe that economic relations within and between countries are inherently unequal and exploitive. Economics does not breed peace – it generates conflict. Marxists do think that this conflict will someday be overcome through communist revolution. In the early decades of the twentieth century – before and after the Russian Revolution – some Marxists thought that the long-sought communist revolution had begun. But the Soviet Union ended up not establishing communism, but something very different – a despotic socialist state. Marxists believe that progress is possible, and class conflict can be overcome through revolution, but this dream for progressive change has yet to occur.

Marxism has enduring relevance as an analytic construct in international relations. In certain eras – such as the 'roaring 90s' – Marxism seems less relevant. Trade and investment expand and economic growth reaches around the world. Marxist ideas about class and class conflict give way to liberal ideas about mutual gain and the 'lifting of all ships.' But soon an economic crisis – such as the banking crisis and sharp economic downturn of 2008 – brings the insights of Marxism back into focus. The 2008 financial crisis highlights the tendency of capitalism to carry the seeds of its own destruction and to concentrate wealth – and by implication power – in the hands of fewer and fewer large actors, such as the large investment firms on Wall Street. Marxism also provides a useful counter-perspective to liberalism. Liberals tend to see globalization as a force for good, linking the world more closely together and generating economic gains for everyone. Marxism is more focused on the winners and losers in the global capitalist system. Globalization has drawn the world together, but it has also led to sharper divisions between haves and have nots. The United States and other advanced countries have seen their economies 'globalized' in recent decades. But globalization has led to concern in these countries over the hollowing out of their industrial sectors – the high-paying manufacturing jobs – leaving educated elites and those working low-wage service jobs to struggle within an increasingly unequal society.

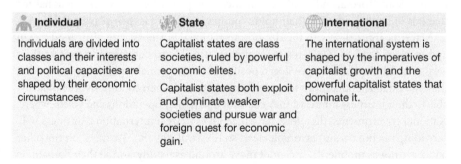

Levels of Analysis *The Marxist Tradition*	👤 **Individual**	🏛 **State**	🌐 **International**
	Individuals are divided into classes and their interests and political capacities are shaped by their economic circumstances.	Capitalist states are class societies, ruled by powerful economic elites. Capitalist states both exploit and dominate weaker societies and pursue war and foreign quest for economic gain.	The international system is shaped by the imperatives of capitalist growth and the powerful capitalist states that dominate it.

The Constructivist Tradition

In different ways, realists, liberals, and Marxists all make arguments about the impact of power and interests on international relations. Another theoretical perspective focuses on the role of ideas and the ways in which 'what people believe' shapes what individuals, groups, and states do. This constructivist perspective comes in several varieties, but it is unified by the view that ideas and beliefs matter in how actors define and pursue their interests. People do not simply act on self-evident interests or operate in a realist world of anarchy. International relations, according to constructivists, are 'socially constructed.' What people think and believe matters with regard to how they act in the world. While constructivism as a tradition in international relations is relatively new, the notion that ideas matter is an old notion reflected in a broader philosophical tradition known as idealism.

Idealism: The notion that ideas matter in international relations.

Constructivist Assumptions

Constructivist theory is built around four assumptions. First, the *interests* of individuals, groups, and states are not given or set in stone. Interests are shaped by the *identities* of actors. How people see themselves – for example, as a patriot, scientist, Christian, Muslim, Westerner, African, or citizen of the world – will shape how they think about their interests and what they want to achieve in politics. The realist, liberal, and Marxist theoretical traditions tend to see the interests of individuals as derived from specific social and political structures, such as anarchy, democracy, market society, or class position. In contrast, constructivists see much more diversity in the positions – and identities – of individuals.

Second, identities are molded by a variety of ideational factors – culture, religion, science, and normative beliefs. Constructivists do not fully discount the role of the material setting of individuals in shaping their identities. A steel worker or a bond trader operates within a setting that helps shape his or her thinking. But constructivists argue that identities emerge from interplay of these real world settings and the evolving ideas and beliefs inside the heads of people. Such differences in perspective on a given issue can be vitally important.

Third, elite individuals in both society and the state are the most important actors. The ideas and identities that these elites possess tend to shape the way the groups and states they lead take action within the international system. Thus, it is necessary to look closely at what leaders think and believe to explain what they do. Ideas shape the world.

Finally, communication plays an important role in shaping and changing identities. The interactions of elites and the networks they operate within are important in creating and reinforcing ideas and beliefs. Through communication and networking, elites tend to produce collective or shared world views that shape how interests are defined and pursued. The focus of constructivists is on critical historical moments when elites communicate and build consensus on who they are as groups and states, and how to think about problems. Interaction, process, networking, and communication all shape the way actors think and behave.

Constructivist Propositions

Four key concepts or propositions follow from this constructivist worldview. First, constructivists argue that 'the world is what you believe it is.' If people can be convinced and come to believe that the world is guided by universal moral standards, they will act that way. In a direct challenge to realism, one leading constructivist has argued: 'anarchy is what states make of it' (Wendt 1999). The world is anarchical, but this does not imply that inter-state relations will operate as realist theory predicts. Anarchy is shaped by how people think about it. As state elites learn more about each other, they

▶ **Photo 22.6 NATO Soldiers on a Humanitarian Mission in Afghanistan, 2007**

Since the end of the World Wars, and especially since the fall of the Soviet Union, new norms of humanitarian intervention have emerged to protect populations, especially minorities, within states. These norms give authority to the international community, including organizations such as NATO, to intervene in the domestic affairs of states to protect individuals from genocide or collective persecution. In the photo above, a soldier cuts webbing attached to a humanitarian aid-drop bundle in Parun, Afghanistan, June 27, 2007. The Nuristan Provincial Reconstruction Team worked side by side with the Afghan National Army to provide humanitarian aid and medical aid to Parun.

Source: ISAF, NATO.

Global civil society: The realm of private activity that lies outside the political system, where religious, ethnic, and civic groups flourish.. Civil society exists within countries but it also operates between countries, often manifest in transnational groups and associations. Global civil society is, in effect, the sum total of these transnational groups and activities.

can change their expectations and come to see each other as friends rather than foes. The United States does not worry about the United Kingdom's vast nuclear arsenal, but it frets that North Korea many have a small number of primitive nuclear bombs.

Indeed, anarchy can be manifest in several different ways. One type of anarchy is the harsh world that realists describe. This is a world in which states regard other states as enemies that deserve no respect, are not necessarily legitimate or sovereign, and can be conquered if circumstances allow. This is anarchy manifest as the law of the jungle. Another type of anarchy is where states view each other as rivals, but not enemies. States are not interested in conquering others simply because they can; instead, they seek to preserve the status quo, respect the rights of others to exist, and use force only for defensive purposes and in the name of stabilizing the system. The role of force is shaped by norms, absolute gains are often preferential to relative gains, and cooperation is possible. Yet another type of anarchy is one where states view other states as friends; states cooperate to maximize collective gains, the use of force is generally viewed as illegitimate, sovereignty is respected, and collective security replaces national security. According to the constructivist view, none of the types of anarchy is more natural or inevitable than the others, and through *learning* and *socialization*, which results from interaction between elites, the world can move toward more cooperative and collective security-oriented anarchy.

A second constructivist proposition is that states operate within a global civil society. In this sense, constructivism is compatible with liberalism's emphasis on cosmopolitanism. Civil society is the realm of private activity that lies outside the political system. It is the realm of private associations, where religious, ethnic, and civic groups flourish. Civil society exists within countries but it also operates between countries, often manifest in transnational groups and associations. Global civil society is, in effect, the sum total of these transnational groups and activities. Constructivists agree with liberal theorists that these transnational networks and exchanges are important mechanisms for spreading norms and ideas, and for building trust and consensus among countries. For constructivists, global civil society is what facilitates elite learning and socialization, providing the communication networks through which elites develop ideas and identities that shape state policy, and gives shape to the character of anarchy.

A third constructivist proposition is that normative change is a major way in which world politics evolved from era to era. Constructivists argue that the learning and socialization that takes place across the global system does tend to move the world in a progressive direction. Norms do change; often, although not always, for the better. The institution of slavery was outlawed by the end of the nineteenth century. The practice of apartheid was ended in South Africa in the 1980s. In the postwar era, as discussed in Chapter 11, new norms of humanitarian intervention emerged that give the international community the right and obligation to intervene in the domestic affairs of states to protect individuals from genocide or other forms of collective violence.

A final constructivist proposition is that state elites exist within and are influenced by strategic culture. As noted earlier, constructivists argue that states have *identities* that help shape how their leaders think about the nation's interests. Building on this view, constructivists go on to also argue that state leaders operate in a strategic culture that shapes foreign policy choices. Strategic culture refers to assumptions about the nature of the global system – for example, which states are friends and enemies – and strategies of action that are shared by government elites. Russia, Japan, Great Britain, France, China, and the United States all have different strategic cultures because of differences rooted in specific historical experiences and national security lessons crystallized in ideology and traditions of grand strategy (Johnston 1995). These differences in strategic culture give countries distinctive *personalities* as states, even as they operate in similar global situations. To understand how leading states will make choices, it is necessary to unpack the assumptions and ideational frameworks with which state leaders rank preferences and make grand strategic choices.

Recall our discussion in Chapter 2 of why the Cold War ended. Constructivists place great weight on the role of Gorbachev, and in particular on how he embraced a set of ideas to transform Soviet strategic culture. Gorbachev and his reformers believed war with the West was not inevitable, and there was greater room for cooperation with capitalism than traditional Soviet strategic culture had earlier believed. For constructivists, the world changed not because material power changed, but because ideas changed (Lebow and Risse-Kappen 1995).

In looking at the ways that ideas and identities shape the choices of states, some scholars have focused specifically on the role of gender as a shaping influence. We now turn to this emerging area of scholarship.

Normative change: The idea that as global learning and international socialization occur, ideas about what is or is not acceptable or 'normal' change. As normative change occurs, it can impact international relations.

Strategic culture: Strategic culture refers to assumptions about the nature of the global system – for example, which states are friends and enemies – and strategies of action that are shared by government elites.

👤 **Individual**	🏛️ **State**	🌐 **International**
Individuals are the most important actors in world politics. It is the ideas in their heads that shape what groups and societies do within the global system.	National political institutions and the reigning ideas and norms they embody shape the way states define their interests and act within the wider world.	The international system is composed of states and a global civil society. Anarchy does not necessarily breed conflict – it depends on what states make of it.

Levels of Analysis

The Constructivist Tradition

The Feminist Tradition

Alongside the theoretical approaches described above, feminist scholarship has emerged in recent decades to challenge traditional assumptions and visions of world politics, and it has developed its own distinctive theoretical tradition. Feminist thinking is wide ranging and offers provocative counter-points to old mainstream theoretical ideas about states, war, and power politics. The focus of feminist theory is on the role of gender – and the role of women – in society and world affairs. It seeks to illuminate biases and neglected ways of viewing international relations.

Feminist Assumptions

One of the groundbreaking feminist explorations of international relations is Cynthia Enloe's *Bananas, Beaches, Bases: Making Feminist Sense of International Politics* (Enloe 2000). The book provides a vivid historical account of the way women have been subordinated to men in various industries and institutions within the expanding global system such as tourism, agriculture, and the armed forces. In Enloe's portrait, women play a role in the world economy and geopolitical system primarily as subordinate and undervalued laborers – domestic workers, diplomatic wives, agricultural workers, and prostitutes outside military bases. Women are everywhere in international relations, but the lenses through which we view international relations tend to obscure and hide their presence. The great globalizing forces in world politics – multinational corporations, diplomatic relations, military alliances – are depicted as driven by the grand pursuits of men. In the background and with considerably less power, we find women playing undervalued and often demeaning supporting and subordinate roles. The important insight that Enloe advances – which is at the heart of the feminist critique – is that states and international relations have 'gendered' structures of domination and interaction. Feminism is similar to Marxism in that each emphasizes the structural inequality in political, economic, and social systems. Capitalism and the system of states is a system of domination, and women tend to be at the lower reaches and on the bottom. Traditional theories of international relations fail to acknowledge or analyze this hidden reality.

Building on this insight, beginning in the 1980s, scholars of international relations began thinking about the implications of gender for how we study world affairs. The focus was not just on the disadvantaged role of women in global affairs, but also the development of a feminist critique of traditional geopolitical and state power theories of world politics that have for the most part been constructed by men – that is, theories that look at the world from the perspective of state leaders, who also tend to be men. Scholar Robert Keohane poses the question that feminist theory asks: 'How have distinctively male values, and social structures in which male values are given priority, affected the concepts developed in international society?' (Keohane 1989). The goal of the feminist tradition in international relations is to expose the gender bias that pervades the traditional theories of states and power politics, and to offer alternative views of world affairs from the standpoint of the weak and powerless.

Two general lines of argument, or sets of propositions, have emerged most clearly and forcefully in the feminist tradition. One is a critique of male-oriented assumptions about world politics, challenging in particular the 'realist' orientation of prevailing theory. The other is the claim that gender bias has diminished the roles and capabilities of women in the actual conduct of international relations.

Feminist Propositions

In critiquing prevailing ideas and theories about international relations, feminist thinkers focus primarily on realist theory and its ideas about states, war, and power politics. Gender assumptions and biases are found at every level of this theoretical tradition. The language is male-oriented, sending the subtle or not-so-subtle message that world politics is a 'man's world'. After all, scholars talk of 'statesmen' and 'mankind'. The classic realist thinker, Hans Morgenthau, defines power as 'man's control over the minds and actions of other men' (Morgenthau 1967). The title of Kenneth Waltz's classic study is *Man, the State, and War*. The language of states and power – the 'high politics' of international relations that scholars focus on – suggests that the terrain of world politics is a man's terrain. The hidden assumption is that the rough and tumble 'public sphere' is a man's world, while the 'private sphere' of family and home is a woman's world.

Along these lines, in her influential feminist study, *Women and War*, Jean Bethke Elshtain argues that the great writings on war, by theorists from Thucydides to Machiavelli to modern realists, offer a vision of 'high politics' in which the public sphere is inhabited by men, wielding power and determining the fates of peoples and societies (Elshtain 1987). The scholarly study of international relations, Elshtain argues, has become a professionalized male-dominated world closed off from the wider values of society. 'Encumbered with lifeless jargon, systems and subsystems dominance, spirals of misperception, decision-making analysis, multipolar, intervening variables, dependence, interdependence, cost-effectiveness, IR specialists in the post-Second World War era began to speak exclusively to, or "at", one another or to their counterparts in government service' (Elshtain 1987). The discourse of international relations has become a closed intellectual system with deep assumptions about the masculinity of power and world politics. In making this feminist critique, Elshtain seeks to open up both the scholarly and political discussion of war and the exercise of power. By breaking down the gendered character of the study of international relations, the issues of war and peace can be seen and debated from more angles. More voices and sensibilities – including the voices and sensibilities of women – can be brought into the public debate over the great decisions of war and peace. The 'high politics' of international relations can become more open to a wider social and international conversation.

Feminist scholarship as a whole shares this aim of opening up and breaking down old gender-biased ways of thinking about international relations. If concepts such as state, power, anarchy, and war are masculine ideas, or at least ideas whose primacy in the study of international relations is reinforced by male gender biases, a feminine approach to international relations might emphasize cooperation, mutual gain, interdependence, and societal understanding. As Ann Tickner observes, 'Most feminists are committed to the emancipatory goal of achieving a more just society', which, for them, includes ending the subordinate position of women (Tickner 1997).

One implication is that if women are given more opportunities to hold power – to lead governments and make decisions about war and peace – they will do so with different priorities and sensibilities. Studies by anthropologists and biologists do give some evidence that males and females have different predispositions toward violence and aggression rooted in differences in their genetic and biological characteristics, such as the presence in males of the hormone testosterone. These biologically driven

US Secretary of State
Hillary Rodham
Clinton shakes hands
with a student at a
town hall meeting with
university students and
civil society represen-
tatives at the National
Theater in Sarajevo,
Bosnia and Herze-
govina, on October 12,
2010.

Source: US State
Department.

differences are seen by some experts to generate different social behaviors, including a greater tendency of males to engage in violence and aggressive actions. As we will, see in Chapter 5, there are even some experimental studies that test male and female students, finding that males are more likely to be overconfident and attack the enemy in simulated war games (Johnson 2006). Some experts see culture as more important in shaping differences between the genders in social behavior – and there certainly is a lot of variation across history and countries of the world in the role of women in war and as wielders of power (Goldstein 2001).[1]

A second line of feminist argument is that women have been systematically under-represented in both the study and practice of international relations. The basic insight starts with the observation that although gender relations differ from country to country, they are nonetheless almost always unequal. In this respect, the historian Joan Scott argues that gender has been a way for societies to signify relationships of power. The claim is not that women are different – that they embody different values or sensibilities – but that they are simply under-represented in the scholarly world of international relations and the governmental corridors of power.

Despite advances in education and the modernization of societies, such as in Western Europe and the United States, there remains deep-rooted inequality of opportunity and representation for women. Within the field of political science, a recent study indicates that only 26 percent of the 13,000 professors are women, and an even smaller percentage of professors who study international relations are women (Malinak 2008). Women also tend to study and teach different subjects than men. Woman are more likely to study transnational actors and international organizations, specialize in developing regions, such as Latin America and sub-Saharan Africa, and focus on the role of ideas and identities in their work. Men are more likely to study American foreign policy and issues of war and peace, specialize in the great powers, and use realist theories of world politics.

In the world of foreign policy and diplomacy, the under-representation of woman is also striking. In the United States there has never been a female President, and only

---

1. For a summary of the evidence, see Goldstein (2001).

recently – since the 1990s – has there been a female US Secretary of State. When heads of state travel each September to the United Nations for its annual opening, the overwhelming majority of these leaders are men. While there have been female leaders in countries such as India (Indira Gandhi), Israel (Golda Meir), the Philippines (Corazon Aquino), and others, only British Prime Minister Margaret Thatcher and German Chancellor Angela Merkel have been leaders of one of the great powers. Worldwide, women fill only 17 percent of parliamentary seats and 14 percent of ministerial-level positions (Hunt 2007).

Feminists focusing on the problem of inequality and under-representation are not arguing that women would make better leaders or that the world would be more peaceful if woman ran the planet. Their argument is not that women are somehow morally superior to men. Rather, these feminist thinkers argue simply that it is a question of justice – and, indeed, that it is a lost opportunity not to draw upon the talents and capacities of fully half of the human race. Some writers do argue that women might be better diplomats and state leaders. Francis Fukuyama argues in a famous essay that women are in fact more sensitive to a wider set of social values and, if in charge, would be more inclined to seek peaceful solutions to the world's problems (Fukuyama 1998). But this view has been challenged by some leading feminist scholars. Ann Tickner argues that in fact this thesis that associates women with peace and moral superiority has the effect of keeping women out of power. 'The association of women with peace can play into unfortunate gender stereotypes that characterize men as active, women as passive; men as agents, women as victims; men as rational, women as emotional', Tickner notes. 'Not only are these stereotypes damaging to women, particularly to their credibility as actors in matters of international politics and national security, but they are also damaging to peace' (Tickner 1999). The goal of feminist theory is not to seek the advance of women into positions of power because they bring more lofty values and aspirations. It is because their under-representation in positions of power stems from the social injustice and inequities that speak ill of today's economic and political systems.

Considering the five theoretical frameworks, how do the roles of actors and actions in each tradition differ? We offer a brief comparison next.

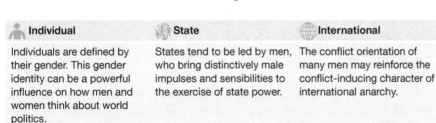

Individual	State	International	Levels of Analysis
Individuals are defined by their gender. This gender identity can be a powerful influence on how men and women think about world politics.	States tend to be led by men, who bring distinctively male impulses and sensibilities to the exercise of state power.	The conflict orientation of many men may reinforce the conflict-inducing character of international anarchy.	*The Feminist Tradition*

Comparing Traditions

These five theoretical traditions provide useful ways to look at international relations. It is not necessary to decide if one is right and the others are wrong. They each provide a window on the world. Each claims to capture the dynamics of world politics. In the chapters ahead, we will make use of these traditions. In doing so, we can make some comparisons between them based on what they think are the important actors and forces at work in the global system.

Realism: War is a major source of change in world politics. In every historical era, war – particularly among major states – has dramatically changed the geopolitical landscape. In the wake of war, powerful rising states have emerged to dominate the system, while defeated states have gone into decline. War has forced states to mobilize their economies and societies, leading to innovations and changes in government capacities. War and security competition between states has fueled arms races and efforts to build new and more destructive weapons. World War I is a good example of how a major war transformed politics, economics, and world affairs. It was a war that led to the destructions of vast empires, brought the United States to the center of world politics, and fueled changes in European politics that played out over the next half century.

Liberalism: Liberals argue that change in world politics comes from ongoing trade, exchange, innovation, and learning that occurs within and between countries. Through these processes, societies advance and modernize. World politics changes as the countries themselves become more advanced – liberal, capitalist, and democratic – and as the relations between these countries become more interdependent and cooperative. The post-1945 rise of the European Community – later called the European Union – is a major example of what liberals see as advancement.

Marxism: Marxists argue that change in world politics is generated by political conflict that is rooted in the capitalist system. Economic inequality and the divergent economic interests between classes provides the setting for struggle between peoples, classes, and states. Marx originally argued that these conflicts would result in revolution within capitalist societies, ushering in communism. Later Marxist scholars have focused on a wider array of conflicts, including clashes between wealthy and poor countries.

Constructivism: Constructivists argue that change in world politics emerges from the evolution in norms and world views that guide the behavior of people and societies – including the behavior of state leaders. The decline in the acceptability of slavery during the nineteenth century and empire in the twentieth century are examples of major shifts in normative orientations.

Feminism: Like constructivists, feminist theorists argue that dominant ideologies and orientations in world politics are formed over long periods of time. Feminists point in particular to the way gender roles and expectations get established, leading to the marginalization of women in world affairs. For change to occur, societies need to become more aware of these often hidden or unremarked upon biases. Change comes when people's ideas about gender change. Women who do rise to prominence in world politics – as foreign ministers or heads of states – can become role models, thereby helping to change ideas and expectations.

In terms of the actors that dominate world politics, realists argue that state leaders speak for the national interests. Liberals argue that foreign policy reflects the diversity of people and groups within society, as well as the ties they develop across states. Marxists trace the broad patterns of world politics to economic classes, particularly business elites. Constructivism tends to look to government and societal elites who are the carriers of ideas that influence the actions of states. Feminism focuses on the gender of leaders and citizens and the male bias in the way people think about international relations.

The traditions differ regarding the behavior of these actors as well. Realists see states acting primarily to advance the power and interests of the state, and this brings states into conflict with each other. In other words, world politics, according to realists, is a struggle for power defined by conflict between states. Liberals see states as more inclined toward cooperation. Individuals and groups in society are always looking for ways to advance their interests by working with others, a dynamic most consistently seen in relations among liberal democracies. Marxists see economic inequality and class conflict as the fundamental dynamics within and between states. Constructivists focus on the ways in which elites within and across states communicate with each other, interacting in ways that share knowledge and build consensus on important questions of peace, prosperity, stability, and order. Feminist theories seek to expose the biases in how scholars think about international relations, showing how masculine values often get emphasized at the expense of feminine values – and these theories also emphasize how gender inequality exists in the 'man's world' of international affairs.

Realists see world politics shaped and reshaped by war. It is war that ultimately serves to destroy the old relations between states, paving the way for newly powerful states. Liberals, in contrast, see learning as a much more powerful force of change in world politics. States are not doomed to repeat their mistakes. Societies can learn and make advancements in their relationships with others. Marxists see revolution as the master mechanism of change. Economic classes are fundamentally antagonistic. When class relations become so prone to conflict and violence, revolutions can erupt that serve to overturn the old political order and usher in new social relations. Constructivists see the spread of ideas as the most important mechanism of change, a process that is pushed forward by political activist groups, including social groups and international non-governmental organizations. Feminists stress the pathways by which gender can influence both how leaders act in world affairs and how scholars understand and interpret that action.

Finally, the traditions differ in regard to the direction of history. Realists see history as cyclical. States are ultimately caught up in continuous cycles of war and change, rise and fall. Liberals see the direction of history as more linear. Peoples and societies can cooperate and make their lives better. Marxists see class conflict ultimately leading to revolution that ushers in more equal and just social relations. Constructivists tend to see a progressive logic to change in world politics, but are usually less certain than liberals that the world can and will be made better. In this sense, they do not have explicit visions of the advancement of mankind. But they do see elites across the world engaged in dialogue and communication. This dialogue and communication can lead to conflict, of course. But it can also give states opportunities to find common ground and remake world politics. Feminists believe that history is shaped by gender and that the prospects for peace, war, conflict, and cooperation among states will be influenced by gender relations within those states.

👤 Individual	👥 State	🌐 International
Different theoretical perspectives place different weights on the importance of individuals; constructivism and feminism place the individual at the center of analysis; realism places the individual at the margins of its theory.	Realism, constructivism, and feminism downplay the significance of domestic institutions; liberalism and Marxism place them at the heart of their respective analyses, although the former stresses political institutions while Marxism-Leninism focuses on economic institutions.	Realism places its main emphasis on the international system; feminism and constructivism argue that the effects of the international system depend on how actors perceive that system; and liberalism and Marxism argue that the effects of the international system are contingent on the domestic institutions of states.

Levels of Analysis
Comparing Traditions

Revisiting the Enduring Question and Looking Ahead

This chapter has surveyed five competing theoretical traditions in the field of international relations. These traditions each provide assumptions and arguments about the way the world works. Do we need to pick between these five theoretical traditions? Is one of them right and the others wrong? The answer is no. The world is an amazingly large and diverse place. Over the centuries, it has exhibited an extraordinary array of human endeavor. No one theoretical tradition can explain everything that puzzles us about international relations. They are all potentially useful as tools of explanation. As we explore the enduring problems of international relations, we want to have a lot of tools in our toolbox to explain what is going on. The arguments of one tradition or another may be more convincing in specific circumstances or historical episodes, but we want to keep all of them ready to be used.

It is useful to think of these theoretical traditions as *lenses* through which we observe international relations. The traditions tell us where to look, even if they cannot always confidently predict what we will find in any given situation. Each theoretical tradition offers a different lens, and each lens highlights different actors and activities in the international system. When we put on the realist lens, we see states and the struggle for power. We see the problems of anarchy everywhere – security dilemmas, power balancing, and nationalism. When we put on the liberal lens, we see individuals and groups engaged in complex activities of cooperation and institution building. We see states organizing open systems of trade and the emergence of communities of democracies. When we put on the Marxist lens, we see class conflict and economic struggle between the rich and poor across the globe. We see an ever-changing system of world capitalism shaping and reshaping conflict and cooperation around the world. When we put on the constructivist lens, we see great movements of ideas and norms. We see elites communicating and learning through international networks, and state identities shaping the way countries make foreign policy and organize the global system. When we put on the feminist lens, we see both the importance of gender differences and the role of gender in the perpetuation of political, social, and economic inequalities within and across states.

Each of these lenses allows us to see different things and raises specific actors and dynamics to the foreground and moves other actors and dynamics to the background. As we explore the history and evolving character of international relations, we want to keep all of these lenses at the ready. In looking at international history, as well as foreign policy of states in the present period, we also want to have the analytical tools that students of foreign policy have developed. It is to the examination of that toolbox for the analysis of foreign policy that we now direct our attention.

Visit www.palgrave.com/politics/Grieco to access extra resources for this chapter, including:

- Chapter summaries to help you review the material
- Multiple choice quizzes to test your understanding
- Flashcards to test your knowledge of the key terms in this chapter
- Outside resources, including links to contemporary articles and videos, that add to what you have learned in this chapter

Study Questions

1. Which theoretical tradition of international relations is most appealing to you? Which is the least appealing? Why?
2. Is it important that we have theories of international relations? Why or why not?
3. Realist theory has been the most central or prominent theory in the past. Do you think it will be as important in the future? Why or why not? Which theory seems to have a more promising future?
4. How do we know if one or another theory of international relations is more helpful to us as we try to understand international relations?
5. Which theoretical tradition of international relations do you wish national leaders in major countries like the United States and China, for example, paid closer attention to as they formulate their foreign policies?

Further Reading

Bull, Hedley (1977) *The Anarchical Society: A Study of Order in World Politics*, 3rd edn (Basingstoke, UK: Macmillan). A founding statement of the English School of international relations, emphasizing both the existence of anarchy among states and an international community.

Buzan, Barry (1983) *People, States, and Fear: The National Security Problem in International Relations* (Chapel Hill: University of North Carolina Press). A pioneering exploration of the concept of national security in international relations and its implications for the security dilemma.

Doyle, Michael (1997) *Ways of War and Peace: Realism, Liberalism, and Socialism* (New York: Norton). A magisterial survey of the leading theoretical traditions in the study of international relations. It includes portraits of the philosophical thinkers whose ideas have informed these traditions.

Jervis, Robert (1976) *Perception and Misperception in International Politics* (Princeton: Princeton University Press). Explores the way psychology and perceptions influence relations among states.

Keohane, Robert O. and Joseph S. Nye (1977) *Power and Interdependence: World Politics in Transition* (Boston: Little, Brown). Offers a liberal internationalist perspective on world politics, emphasizing the fragmented and decentralized character of power within a complex and evolving modern international system.

Waltz, Kenneth (1954) *Man, the State, and War: A Theoretical Analysis* (New York: Columbia University Press). A landmark study of the ideas of classical political theories on questions of war and peace. Waltz famously divides these theories into 'images' or levels of the international system and sources of war – the individual, state, and international structural levels.

Wendt, Alexander (1999) *Social Theory of International Politics* (Cambridge: Cambridge University Press). Wendt offers foundational thinking for the constructivist approach to international relations.

23

The Analysis of Foreign Policy

Enduring question: *What factors most influence the foreign policies of states* **?**

During the 1950s, China was allied with the Soviet Union and considered the United States its principle geopolitical adversary. China worked closely with the Soviet Union and fought opposite the United States during the Korean War of the 1950s and the Vietnam War of the 1960s. China did not even have diplomatic relations with the United States until the 1970s. Yet, by the end of the 1960s, Chinese foreign policy changed and China's leaders came to view the Soviet Union more as an adversary than as an ally. China and the Soviet Union fought a border war in 1969. By the 1980s, China not only established diplomatic relations, but moved closer to its former adversary, the United States, politically and economically.

Today, China enjoys cordial political relations, and limited economic relations, with Russia. It has close economic relations with the United States; in fact the two countries are highly dependent on each other commercially and financially. However, China's political relations with the United States are changing again, and have become significantly colder. Many believe the two countries are emerging as geopolitical competitors as they compete for influence in the South China Sea and in East Asia more generally.

These twists and turns in China's external relations point to the enduring question addressed in this chapter: which factors most influence the foreign policies of states? Also, which factors best account for significant changes in those foreign policies? We will address these questions by breaking them down into more manageable pieces in the sections to follow. First, we will consider the matter of what exactly is a foreign policy. Second, we will utilize the levels-of-analysis framework to investigate the sources of foreign policy or, more precisely, we will investigate the attributes of individuals, states, and the international system that influence the selection of foreign policies by governments.

Third, we will seek to identify the conditions under which states change their foreign policies.

The enduring question of what drives foreign policy is unresolved and consequential. Some analysts prefer 'inside-out' explanations; they focus on domestic sources of foreign policy, and debate the extent to which interest groups, public opinion, or the particular structure of government helps us to understand the behavior of states. 'Outside-in' analysts believe that international or external sources are the key determinants of foreign policy. External sources include how powerful or weak a country is relative to other countries, and the extent to which a country finds itself in a peaceful or threatening neighborhood. Scholarly debates over what accounts for foreign policy are unresolved in that no single factor is a clear analytical winner in explaining the foreign policies of different countries, across different issues, and across time. Understanding foreign policy is critical because the foreign policy choices that states make have profound implications for relations among states. Thus, it is important in an international relations text to devote sustained attention to the determinants of foreign policy.

© summersgraphicsinc–istockphoto.com.

Learning Objectives

By the end of this chapter, you will be able to:

→ Compare the study of international relations and the analysis of foreign policy, and appreciate how both are necessary to understand international affairs.

→ Identify the two core attributes, interests and strategies, of any country's foreign policy.

→ Analyze the range of policy instruments that a country may utilize in its foreign policy.

→ Apply the levels-of-analysis framework to explore the sources of a country's foreign policy.

→ Utilize the levels-of-analysis framework to identify the conditions under which a country may change its foreign policy.

Chapter Contents

- Foreign Policy Analysis: Connections to International Relations and Core Concepts
- The Sources of Foreign Policy
- How and Why States Change Their Foreign Policy
- Revisiting the Enduring Question and Looking Ahead
- Study Questions
- Further Reading

Foreign Policy Analysis: Connections to International Relations and Core Concepts

To explore the enduring question of which factors account for the foreign policies of states, we first examine how the analysis of foreign policy differs from and complements the study of international relations. We will then fine-tune language we introduced in Chapter 1 for the analysis of foreign policy, with particular attention paid to the two concepts of interest and strategy.

The Study of International Relations and the Analysis of Foreign Policy

In general, scholars of international relations are interested in interactions between two or more states, and particularly in why some of those interactions are cooperative while others are competitive and may even end in war. The theories we examined in Chapter 3 each fundamentally try to understand inter-state interactions, and especially the conditions that cause those interactions to be peaceful or in conflict. In contrast, foreign policy analysts want to understand why a *given country's government* has decided to take certain actions toward foreign governments or foreign non-state actors; why a government has decided that specific foreign policy interests are important to it; and why it has crafted a particular strategy to promote or defend those interests.

The negotiation of the Kyoto Protocol of 1997, which requires adherents (more than 191 states plus the European Union by the fall of 2012) to reduce greenhouse gases that contribute to global climate change, provides a good opportunity to see the differences between the relative emphases of scholars of international relations and scholars of foreign policy. A scholar of international relations would be interested in the international dynamics that brought the Kyoto Protocol into being. That scholar might ask whether the agreement on the Protocol was attained because more powerful countries bullied weaker countries into accepting it, because richer countries enticed poorer countries to do so, or because the global scientific community and globally active non-governmental organizations (NGOs) persuaded national leaders that global warming was a real threat and ought to be addressed through an international agreement.

A student of foreign policy might also be interested in how the Kyoto Protocol came about, but would focus on the decisions of specific countries on whether or not to adhere to it. So, for example, the student of foreign policy would want to understand why President Bill Clinton's administration helped negotiate the Kyoto Protocol in 1997 and signed the instrument in late 1998, but the Clinton team never submitted the Protocol to the US Senate for ratification, which the US Constitution requires in order for any treaty to come into force for the United States. Similarly, a foreign policy analyst might want to know why China and India, industrializing countries that produce significant amounts of greenhouse gases, were willing to sign and ratify an agreement that promised to constrain their future economic behavior. The study of foreign policy can focus on a particular country, such as the United States, India, or China, or can focus comparatively across the foreign policies of two or more countries.

Scholars of international relations and foreign policy specialists appreciate the importance of one another's work. Foreign policy analysts understand that a country's international context matters a great deal when its leaders identify interests and formulate strategies. In turn, students of international relations recognize that the international interactions of governments have firm roots in the foreign policies of the countries involved in those interactions. If you wish to understand international affairs and why countries sometimes work together, sometimes compete with each other, and sometimes even fight each other, then you must understand both sides of the coin in world affairs, international relations and foreign policy.

Foreign Policy Interests

We often say that a government is pursuing a particular foreign policy because it advances some interest (Jentleson 2010; George and Keohane 1980). An interest, as noted in Chapter 1, is a situation in the world that the leaders of a government want to exist, so much so that they are willing to pay costs to bring it about. National leaders often have to accept that there is a gap between their hopes to promote a given interest and their capacity to do so, and there are often trade-offs between interests; the pursuit of one requires giving up the pursuit of another.

For example, many US leaders believe that the extension of democracy and human rights to China is a US interest. However, those leaders often find it necessary to curtail their efforts to promote China's internal transformation due to the reality that they must gain the current Chinese government's cooperation in order to advance other US interests, including stabilization and growth of the international economy, finding a solution to global climate change, and management of numerous international security issues, including Iran's nuclear weapons program and North Korea's often provocative behavior toward South Korea. We explore in Making Connections Box 23.1 this clash between aspirations and realities involving the interest of US leaders in spreading human rights and democracy to present-day China while also working with its current government.

Foreign Policy Strategy

To advance or defend an interest, a government's leaders develop a foreign policy strategy. A foreign policy strategy, you will recall from Chapter 1, consists of the specification by leaders of objectives (the outcomes that help advance an interest), and policy instruments (the concrete measures the government takes to reach its objectives and thus advance its interest). For the purposes of discussion, we can distinguish between instruments that seek to reach policy objectives through the *persuasion* of a relevant foreign actor (that might be private or governmental in character), and those instruments that seek to reach policy objectives through the *coercion* of a foreign actor.

Instruments of Persuasion

Governments sometimes seek to achieve foreign policy objectives by trying to persuade foreign actors to act or desist from acting in one manner or another. One key instrument of such persuasion by governments is diplomacy. We will discuss diplomacy in more detail as a means toward peace in Chapter 6. However, diplomacy in general terms is the process by which representatives of two or more governments meet and discuss matters of common concern either bilaterally or in a multilateral forum. During these meetings, the representatives seek to persuade each other of the merits of their respective positions with a view toward finding a mutually agreeable solution to some problem or to develop a mechanism by which they can achieve individual gains through some form of joint action. These representatives may be ambassadors who are sent from their respective home countries to reside in the capital city of a host country, or they may be ministerial-rank officials, such as the British Foreign

Diplomacy: The process by which representatives of two or more governments meet and discuss matters of common concern.

US Foreign Policy toward China, 2009

US policy makers consistently argue that they place high value on the spread of democracy and human rights around the world. But, as this example shows, those concerns are often forced to take a back seat to other pressing issues such as climate change, the economic crisis then gripping the world, and security problems including the spread of nuclear weapons.

Aspiration: *Secretary of State Hillary Clinton on Human Rights and China, December 2009*

> The United States seeks positive relationships with China and Russia, and that means candid discussions of divergent views. In China, we call for protection of rights of minorities in Tibet and Xinxiang; for the rights to express oneself and worship freely; and for civil society and religious organizations to advocate their positions within a framework of the rule of law. And we believe strongly that those who advocate peacefully for reform within the constitution, such as Charter 2008 signatories, should not be prosecuted. With Russia, we deplore the murders of journalists and activists and support the courageous individuals who advocate at great peril for democracy. With China, Russia, and others, we are engaging on issues of mutual interest while also engaging societal actors in these same countries who are working to advance human rights and democracy. The assumption that we must either pursue human rights or our 'national interests' is wrong. The assumption that only coercion and isolation are effective tools for advancing democratic change is also wrong.

Source: Secretary of State Hillary Clinton, 'Remarks on the Human Rights Agenda for the 21st Century', address at Georgetown University, December 14, 2009.

Reality: *Secretary of State Hillary Clinton on Human Rights and China, February 2009*

In February 2009, Hillary Clinton was about to leave Seoul, South Korea, for Beijing, China, during an inaugural visit to Asia as Secretary of State. She told reporters that while she would raise with her Chinese hosts the controversial issues of human rights, as well as Chinese policy on Tibet and Taiwan, she thought it might be more productive to focus on issues on which real progress was possible, namely, climate change, the global economic crisis, and a range of security issues. According to the report in the *New York Times*, Clinton said 'There is a certain logic to that', and further, 'That doesn't mean that questions of Taiwan, Tibet, human rights, the whole range of challenges that we often engage on with the Chinese, are not part of the agenda', she said. 'But we pretty much know what they're going to say'. For that reason, according to Secretary Clinton, 'We have to continue to press them,' yet at the same time, she indicated 'But our pressing on those issues can't interfere with the global economic crisis, the global climate change crisis and the security crises. We have to have a dialogue that leads to an understanding and cooperation on each of those.'

Source: 'Clinton Softens Her Tone on China', *New York Times*, February 20, 2009.

Secretary or the Indian Minister of External Affairs, or they may be the heads of state or governments, such as the US President or the Canadian Prime Minister.

Diplomatic representatives from the five permanent members (P5) of the UN Security Council (China, France, Russia, the United Kingdom, and the United States) plus Germany have negotiated with representatives of the government of Iran in recent years on the latter's nuclear program. The P5 plus Germany have sought to persuade Iran that it should accept limitations on its nuclear activities since its past actions raise questions about its nuclear-weapons intentions. The Iranian representatives in turn have sought to persuade the P5 plus Germany that its nuclear activities are not directed toward the attainment of nuclear weapons, but instead are necessary for nuclear energy and medical research, and are in accord with Iran's rights and obligations as a signatory to the Nuclear Non-Proliferation Treaty (NPT). A diplomatic breakthrough occurred late in 2013, when Iran agreed to freeze temporarily much of its nuclear program and in exchange the P5 plus Germany agreed to grant Iran limited relief from international economic sanctions.

Diplomacy, then, is one instrument of persuasion in foreign policy. As the above example shows, economic incentives constitute another. Economic incentives are basically carrots: country A promises some economic gain to B, and delivers it if B does what A wants it to do. For example, West Germany extended very substantial economic aid to the Soviet Union to help facilitate Soviet acceptance in 1990 of the absorption of East Germany into West Germany (Newnham 2002). In the same vein, the European Union provided economic assistance to members such as Greece, Ireland, and Portugal to help those members meet their short-term funding requirements in the midst of the economic crisis that began in 2008, but on condition that they undertake internal reforms that will make them more competitive and self-supporting in the future.

Instruments of Coercion

Leaders sometimes find that diplomacy or incentives are not enough to cause another country to change its behavior. In those cases, leaders may turn to another class of foreign policy instruments, those that are designed to coerce a target government to act or stop from acting in some manner. One class of coercive policy instruments consists of economic sanctions (Hufbauer et al. 2007; Mastanduno 2011).

Economic sanctions are basically sticks: A threatens B with some form of economic loss if B does something A does not want it to do, or fails to do something A wants it to do. Such sanctions can include the imposition of tariffs or quotas on goods imported from a target country, the boycotting of purchases of particular goods from suppliers from the target country, or the seizure of financial assets owned by target-country residents that are held in the initiating country's banks or other financial institutions. In late 2011 and early 2012, the United States and member countries of the European Union began a boycott of purchases of oil from Iran, and a prohibition of financial transactions with Iran's central bank, in an effort to compel that country to negotiate an end to its efforts to build nuclear weapons. These actions were taken very seriously by the Iranian government: it raised the possibility that it might close the critically important Strait of Hormuz, through which passes approximately one-fifth of the world's oil exports (see Map 23.1). The United States responded that it would use military force to keep open the Strait of Hormuz – in other words, it would go to war with Iran. The deal the P5 plus Germany and Iran made in 2013 allowed the two

Economic incentive: An instrument of persuasion in foreign policy. Economic incentives are basically carrots: country A promises some economic gain to B, and delivers it if B does what A wants it to do.

Incentives: Rewards of some form offered by one state to another designed to influence the foreign policy of the recipient. Incentives are a form of persuasion.

Economic sanction: An instrument of coercion in foreign policy. Economic sanctions are basically sticks: A threatens B with some form of economic loss if B does something A does not want it to do, or fails to do something A wants it to do.

► **Map 23.1 Critical Waterway for Oil Exports: the Strait of Hormuz**

When in late 2011 and early 2012 the United States and its European allies sought to organize an oil embargo against Iran's oil exports, Iran threatened to retaliate by using naval forces to close the Strait of Hormuz, through which passes oil to world markets from such major producers as Kuwait and Saudi Arabia.

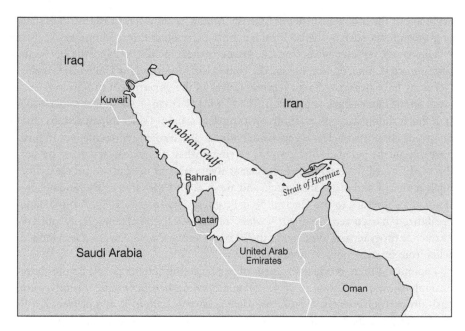

Covert operations: Activities that a government directs against the interests of another government or non-state actor in such a way that the foreign targets and others are kept from knowing that the initiating government is responsible for the activities.

Propaganda: The selective use of information, and at times misinformation, in order to advance a state's interests.

sides to scale back tensions. It also shows that yesterday's sticks (the initial imposition of economic sanctions) may be turned into today's carrots (the relaxation of those sanctions in exchange for some type of political concession).

Another class of coercive policy instruments involves covert operations and propaganda. Propaganda is the selective use of information, and at times misinformation, in order to advance a country's interests. Propaganda is frequently used as a tool to mobilize one's own population or to demoralize other populations in times of conflict or war. Nazi Germany, for example, relied on a Ministry of Public Enlightenment and Propaganda to produce documents and posters glorifying Germany's accomplishments and belittling its adversaries. During the Cold War, the United States used government-sponsored radio stations (Radio Liberty and Radio Free Europe) in an effort to influence the communist-controlled populations of the Soviet Union and Eastern Europe. Today, North Korea's autocratic government uses a steady stream of propaganda to keep its adversaries off balance, and to convince its deprived population that the more prosperous South Korea yearns to be 'purified' from capitalist influences and re-united with the communist North.

Covert operations are activities that a government directs against the interests of another government or non-state actor in such a way that the foreign targets and others are kept from knowing that the initiating government is responsible for the activities. In recent years Iran's government has provided covert support to anti-Israeli groups such as Hamas in Gaza and Hezbollah in southern Lebanon, and may have been providing logistical support to Shiite groups that had carried out lethal operations against US forces in Iraq. In May 2011, the United States killed Al Qaeda leader Osama bin Laden as the culmination of a covert operation in Pakistan, and did not inform the Pakistani government until after the actual raid against bin Laden's compound was completed, leading to a serious diplomatic rift between the two countries (Schmitt and Mazzetti 2011).

Similarly, the United States has used covert operations against Iran to try to cripple that country's nuclear program. In 2010 a highly destructive computer virus or 'worm'

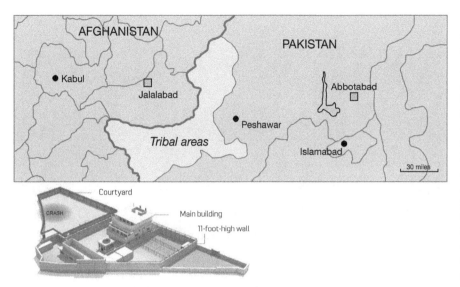

◀ Map 23.2 Covert Operation: the Killing of Osama bin Laden

As a result of US covert intelligence gathering, including covert on-site surveillance, Osama bin Laden was found to be living in a large compound in the Pakistani city of Abbottabad. The compound was attacked by a US Navy SEAL team early in the morning on May 2, 2011, and resulted in the killing of bin Laden.

Source: US Department of Defense image. (Use of military imagery does not imply or constitute endorsement of Palgrave Macmillan, its products, or services by the US Department of Defense.)

called Stuxnet was introduced into the computer systems that Iran was using to control important nuclear equipment, destroying much of it in the process. There are also signs that a country that does not want Iran to acquire nuclear weapons – it is probably Israel – has conducted covert operations in Iran that entail the assassination of Iranian nuclear scientists. Four Iranian scientists were killed in car bombings in the two years between January 2010 and January 2012, and Iran may have retaliated with covert bomb operations in February 2012 that sought to kill Israeli diplomats stationed in New Delhi, India, and Tbilisi, Georgia.

States may resort to coercive policy instruments involving differing degrees of military force. For example, a state sometimes may turn to coercive diplomacy – actions short of the immediate large-scale use of military force such as moving an aircraft carrier closer to the shores of another country to help convince it to rethink some behavior (Art and Cronin 2003). We noted in Chapter 1 that China and many of its neighbors have competing claims to the South China Sea and its potentially large undersea oil and gas reserves. On June 21, 2012 the parliament of Vietnam passed a bill that included an official reiteration of that country's claim of sovereignty over the two main island chains in that area, the Paracel Islands and the Spratly Islands. The Chinese escalated almost immediately to the non-violent use of military force. On June 28, China's government announced the undertaking of 'combat-ready patrols' in the areas claimed by Vietnam. On July 22, the Chinese government announced that Chinese military forces would establish a garrison at Yongxing Island (called Phu Lam Island by Vietnam), a 2.6-square-mile area of land where China maintains its main administrative outpost on the Paracel Islands (*The Economist* 2012). China used no actual military violence in response to the Vietnamese parliamentary action; however, it practiced coercive diplomacy by sending two non-violent military signals that it was preparing itself to use force to back its own territorial claims in the South China Sea.

Finally, the direct use of military force should also be considered a coercive foreign policy instrument. The German strategist Clausewitz famously stated that warfare is just the continuation of diplomacy by other means. After the 2001 terror attacks in New York and Washington, D C, the US government threatened the Taliban leaders in Afghanistan that they had to transfer Osama bin Laden and his aides to US custody, or

Coercive diplomacy: Aggressive actions short of the immediate large-scale use of military force (such as moving an aircraft carrier closer to the shores of another country) designed to convince a country to rethink some behavior.

▶ Photo 23.1 Chinese Administrative Facility, Paracel Islands, 2012

In July 2012 China reinforced its claim over the South China Sea by establishing a military garrison at its administrative post in Yongxing Island (known in Vietnam as Phu Lam Island). Notice in this photo that China has already constructed an air facility that takes up a good proportion of the island.

Source: © Zha Chunming/Xinhua Press/Corbis.

the US would go to war with the Taliban. The Taliban continued to harbor bin Laden and his Al Qaeda fighters. During 2001 and 2002, the United States used a combination of covert operations, air strikes, and ground forces to help local Afghan factions topple the Taliban authorities, forcing Al Qaeda to retreat to the west of Pakistan. Since 2002, the United States has provided most of the military forces operating in Afghanistan and is trying to keep the Taliban and its Al Qaeda allies from retaking power in that country.

In short, states have many interests, and they can select from a range of strategies to promote or protect them. Where do these interests come from, and why do governments choose particular strategies to pursue them?

Levels of Analysis

The Practice of Foreign Policy

Individual	🌐 International
National leaders choose which interests to promote in foreign policy, and select strategies (goals and instruments) to advance those interests.	Given that they usually need the active cooperation of other states to achieve their interests, most states find it necessary to make some trade-offs with other states in the pursuit of their interests.
Individuals are often the target of foreign policy: these individuals may be leaders of foreign governments; key diplomatic, military, or scientific personnel; or non-state actors like terrorist leaders.	

The Sources of Foreign Policy

What are the sources of foreign policy, or more precisely, the sources of foreign policy interests and strategies? The levels-of-analysis framework can be helpful in addressing this question. As we noted in Chapter 1, levels of analysis are used in different ways by scholars. A well-known approach to using levels to illuminate foreign policy was developed by Graham Allison in the early 1970s (Allison and Zelikow 1999).

Allison and Zelikow use three models to understand the origins, conduct, and ending of the Cuban Missile Crisis. These models focus respectively on a nation-state as a single, cohesive actor, on the operating procedures of particular government departments, and on political bargaining among top decision makers. The cohesive nation-state model is situated at the international level of analysis; the government department model is situated at the state level of analysis; and the political bargaining model, which largely centers on individuals and their interactions, is situated at the individual level of analysis. Although Allison's models have become a standard way to use the levels of analysis to study foreign policy, his framework does not take into account dynamics that reside within a country's society, such as interest groups and public opinion, that might also influence foreign policy, and they do not examine factors that operate at the level of the personal history or psychology of decision makers. Therefore, in this chapter we take a somewhat different and more comprehensive approach, yet one that still relies on levels of analysis.

Sources of Foreign Policy at the Individual Level of Analysis

National leaders play a disproportionately large role in defining a country's foreign policy (Bueno de Mesquita et al. 2003; Chiozza and Goemans 2011). It is useful and important to understand the beliefs of national leaders about foreign policy, for those beliefs are likely to shape how leaders assess threats and opportunities in the international arena (Jervis 2006; Saunders 2009).

Where do national leaders get their beliefs about foreign policy? One possibility is that leaders have well-established personalities before they assume office. These personalities arise from a host of sources, including genetic make-up, childhood socialization, and early adulthood experiences. These personalities in turn may powerfully influence what leaders think about international affairs and foreign policy. For example, some analysts have suggested that Barack Obama's racial identity and early childhood experience living in Indonesia make him America's first 'global' president with particular sensitivity to multi-ethnic and multi-racial concerns at home and abroad (Sharma 2011). Below we discuss how the personality and experiences of Saddam Hussein may have prompted him to take great risks in deciding to lead Iraq to war in the 1980s and 1990s.

Leaders may also subscribe to particular beliefs as a result of their having experienced, witnessed, or perhaps learned about some attitude-shaping event in the international domain. Such events might not only influence the ideas of leaders, but perhaps those of many individuals in a particular generation, and even in subsequent generations. In the first Iraq war in 1990–91, President George H.W. Bush behaved in ways that suggested two major past events were influencing his beliefs: Munich and Vietnam. On the one hand, in his arguments for using military force to eject Iraq from Kuwait, he compared Saddam Hussein's aggression against its weaker neighbor to that of Adolph Hitler against Czechoslovakia. Yet, Bush ended the war abruptly – right after Iraqi forces were expelled from Kuwait but with Saddam still in power in Baghdad – in part because he believed, on the basis of the US experience in Vietnam, that the American public would not support a long and costly war (Record 2002).

The field of political psychology offers rich insights about foreign policy decision-making at the individual level of analysis. Some psychologists argue, for example, that leaders are 'cognitive misers' who, instead of making comprehensive analyses of costs and benefits, rely on simple mental short-cuts when making decisions (Fiske and Taylor 1984). Decision makers become cognitive misers to save time and effort when confronted with large amounts of information or when dealing with a series of issues under conditions of uncertainty. In the above example, President Bush may have been acting as a cognitive miser; his mental short-cut was to assume that the Iraq crisis was similar to other salient international crises and therefore required a certain type of response. Along similar lines, Russell Leng has argued that because India and Pakistan have engaged over time in a series of confrontations and wars with each other, Indian and Pakistani leaders have adopted the mental short-cut of assuming the worst possible motives of the other in subsequent conflicts of interest (Leng 2005). To break the cycle of conflict requires new leaders with different experiences, or existing leaders to avoid this short-cut and make different cognitive assumptions, including the willingness to view new situations from the perspective of their rivals.

Sources of Foreign Policy at the State Level of Analysis

Every country's foreign policy is likely to be influenced to some degree by the domestic political, social, and economic institutions and dynamics of that country. For the purposes of discussion, we can place these institutions and dynamics into two general categories: those that are situated largely within the national government of the country under review, and those that are situated largely within its national society. We take up each category in turn, highlighting which dynamics in one or another of the categories spills over and influences dynamics in the other.

Institutions and Politics within National Governments

It is useful initially to distinguish democratic from non-democratic (that is, authoritarian or autocratic) types of national governments. In general, the foreign policy processes in democratic governments are less centralized and more accessible to society than those processes in non-democratic governments. As Box 23.2 shows, Iraq's decision to go to war against an international coalition in 1990–91 was driven largely by the preferences and calculations of that country's autocratic leader, Saddam Hussein. By comparison, before initiating that war, the democratically elected leaders in Great Britain and the United States (Margaret Thatcher and George H.W. Bush respectively) felt it necessary to mobilize the support of their respective legislatures and general publics. They also took the trouble to mobilize an international coalition, in part to convince their domestic populations that there existed a widespread global consensus for military action.

National leaders, both in democratic and autocratic regimes, do not make policy by themselves. Instead, they rely on officials in the executive branch of government (as opposed to the legislative or judicial branches), which consists of their immediate advisors, the heads of ministries or departments that are concerned with foreign affairs, and the professional staff of those ministries and departments. Leaders and their subordinates in a country's national government often engage in foreign policy debates, build coalitions, and generally seek to influence each other, and this bureaucratic politics can influence that country's interests and strategic choices.

This foreign policy process will look different across different countries. Compare, for example, the United States and China. In the United States, the parts of the executive branch that are chiefly concerned with foreign policy include the Departments of State and Defense, the Central Intelligence Agency, the Joint Chiefs of Staff on military matters and, on foreign economic matters, the Departments of Commerce and Treasury. To assist them in coordinating this large machinery of government, presidents since the late 1940s have had a National Security Advisor. At moments of major decision, the President, the National Security Advisor, and the heads of the departments most directly concerned meet as the National Security Council (NSC). The National Security Advisor and a staff of experts coordinate the activities of different

Bureaucratic politics: A possible influence on a country's strategy characterized by national leaders and their subordinates engaging in foreign policy debates, building coalitions, and generally seeking to influence each other.

In 1990 Iraq occupied its small, oil-rich neighbor Kuwait. An international coalition, led by the United States and Great Britain, formed to oust Iraq from Kuwait, first by imposing economic sanctions, and second by setting a deadline for Saddam Hussein to withdraw from Kuwait or face a devastating military attack. The coalition was far superior militarily and made strong efforts to convince Iraq that it would attack if Iraq did not retreat. Yet, Saddam Hussein refused to back down, ended up in a lopsided war and suffered a significant military defeat. How might we explain this puzzling Iraqi foreign policy choice? We cannot know for sure, but there are a number of plausible arguments from different analytical perspectives (Gause 2001).

Saddam's Personality

Leaders always matter in decisions to go to war, particularly so in non-democratic countries where political power is heavily concentrated in the hands of one or a few individuals. Saddam Hussein was ambitious and paranoid, had a proclivity towards violence, and was willing to take risks. Saddam ordered Iraq to invade a more powerful Iran in 1980, hoping to exploit Iran's revolutionary instability and gain advantage over its traditional adversary. That risky war ended as a bloody stalemate eight years later. Saddam also appeared to believe that international actors were continually conspiring against him. He perceived neighbors such as Saudi Arabia and Kuwait conspiring to squeeze Iraq economically, and others such as Israel and America conspiring to undermine his power at home.

Misperception and 'Groupthink'

Saddam may have believed that the coalition, and in particular the United States, would not carry through on their threat to attack. Saddam seemed influenced by the US experience in Lebanon in 1983. When a car bomb struck the US embassy and killed over 200 Marines, the Reagan administration pulled its peacekeeping force out of Lebanon. On the eve of the 1991 war, Saddam in effect told US Ambassador April Glaspie that the United States did not have the stomach for war because it was unwilling to suffer large numbers of casualties.

What about other Iraqi leaders, in particular the small group of Ba'ath Party officials that advised Saddam Hussein? Some appear to have worried that Iraq was about to suffer a big defeat given the forces arrayed against it. But, they were generally reluctant to disagree with Saddam or share with him views or information contrary to his preferred course of action. Saddam was intolerant of dissent; when he took power in 1979, he summarily executed two dozen Ba'ath Party leaders who had opposed his rise to power. He surrounded himself with like-minded individuals who, even if inclined to disagree, knew better than to do so.

National Economic Distress

The war with Iran exhausted Iraq financially. Iraq demanded 'contributions' from other Gulf states to finance its war effort. When the war ended and the money stopped flowing, Iraq was in severe economic distress. It needed oil prices to remain high to earn hard currency for economic recovery. Saddam believed Kuwait was overproducing oil and driving down the global price. But by taking over Kuwait he could control Kuwaiti oil supply and keep the global price higher. From this perspective, once Saddam had Kuwait he could not afford to give it up, and therefore he was willing to try to 'ride out' a coalition attack rather than back down.

Geopolitical Opportunism

Iraq under Saddam Hussein fashioned itself as a regional power and the leader of the Arab world. Saddam attacked Iran because its new fundamentalist Shiite regime (Iraq's Ba'ath Party leaders were Sunni Muslims) had aspired to dominate the region. He threatened the Arab world's common enemy, Israel. By taking Kuwait, he hoped to signal the Arab countries (especially Saudi Arabia) that Iraq was the regional leader and they should accommodate its wishes. By standing up to the United States and international coalition, even if he lost a war, Saddam may have believed that Iraq's prestige would be enhanced on the 'Arab street'.

Students should recognize the operation of the levels of analysis in the differing perspectives described above. Arguments for Iraq's seemingly puzzling decision to go to war range across individual, state, and international levels. Some explanations view Iraq as a rational actor making cost–benefit calculations, while others see non-rational personal characteristics and group dynamics driving the decision.

parts of the government on security and foreign policy matters.

At each point in this policy process, advisors and subordinates may or may not fully share the beliefs of the President about what the country should do abroad. If they do share those beliefs, they may differ about how best to act to advance US interests, or they may agree about goals but disagree about what their particular department or agency ought to be tasked with doing to contribute to the American effort on a given issue. These differences in

▲ Photo 23.2 A Difficult Partnership

Secretary Rumsfeld and National Security Advisor Condoleezza Rice often had sharp disagreements. Rice became Secretary of State in January 2005; Rumsfeld was fired by President Bush in November 2006.

Source: PA Images.

views occur in part because of the different life experiences officials may bring to their job, or because of differences in the interests of their respective organizations. An often-heard phrase in Washington is, 'Where you stand depends on where you sit.' In other words, if an official sits in the State Department he or she might give special emphasis to good diplomatic relations with other countries; if that same person were to sit in the Defense Department he or she might be more concerned about whether those countries can serve as a base for US forward military operations.

On looking forward to leaving office in 1952, President Harry Truman thought that General Dwight D. Eisenhower, if he were elected President, would incorrectly believe that executing the duties of that office was more or less the same as being a military commander. Truman said of Eisenhower, who had been a brilliant Supreme Commander of Allied Forces during World War II, that if he were to win the presidency, 'He'll sit here [the president's desk] and he'll say, "Do this! Do that!" And nothing will happen. Poor Ike – it won't be a bit like the Army. He'll find it very frustrating' (Neustadt, 1976).

The President is the key actor in the US foreign policy process. But the big executive bureaucracies play key roles as well and, as Photo 23.2 suggests, sometimes require the President to step in and resolve difficult inter-agency disputes. Unless the President is skilled in managing institutional and bureaucratic political maneuverings, he or she may inadvertently relinquish foreign policy leadership.

In China, political power over foreign policy is more concentrated. The key decision makers are found in the Politburo Standing Committee, China's top executive ruling body. Recently there have been important power transitions every decade or so, which happen behind closed doors and without voting or input from the mass public. China is a one-party state, but different factions within the Communist Party and especially within the elite Politburo compete for power generally and over China's foreign policy in particular. In recent decades 'reformers,' or top leaders who value

Name	Age	Confirmed and designated leadership post	Factional Background
Xi Jinping	59	Party Secretary General, Chairman of the Central Military Commission, PRC President	Princeling
Li Keqiang	57	Premier of the State Council	Tuanpai
Zhang Dejiang	66	Chairman of the National People's Congress (NPC)	Princeling
Yu Zhengsheng	67	Chairman of the Chinese People's Political Consultative Conference (CPPCC)	Princeling
Liu Yunshan	65	PRC Vice President, Executive Secretary of the Secretariat	Tuanpai (also close tie with Jiang)
Wang Qishan	64	Secretary of the Central Commission for Discipline Inspection (CCDI)	Princeling
Zhang Gaoli	66	Executive Vice Premier of the State Council	Jiang's protégé

◀ Table 23.1 China's New Top Leaders: The Politburo Standing Committee, 2012

Source: Cheng Li, Brookings Institution.

closer ties with Western countries and deeper Chinese integration into the world economy, have competed with 'conservatives' who place more emphasis on the state-run part of China's economy and who would prefer to see China act more assertively in East Asia and perhaps even globally. Some scholars make different factional distinctions, between 'generalists' who try to maintain initiative in the Chinese provinces and 'technocrats' seeking to maintain control in Beijing (Shih 2008).

An important political transition took place in China in 2012 (Li, 2012). The previous Communist Party Secretary General, Hu Jintao (in charge since 2002) handed power to a new leader, Xi Jinping. Xi is a 'princeling', or part of a faction of Chinese leaders who come from families of veteran revolutionaries (that is, the communist founding fathers) or other high-ranking officials, and are closely associated with a former Chinese leader Jiang Zemin. Another faction, known as *taunpai* includes leaders who build their careers by rising through the ranks of the Communist Party, usually starting from a young age. Professional China watchers note carefully the balance of power among these competing factions; in the 2012 transition princelings seemed to dominate, especially in the Politburo Standing Committee (see Table 23.1). Given the foreign policy preferences of princelings, this suggests, for example, that China will seek better relations with the United States and the West, and accelerate economic liberalization, all while seeking to avoid political liberalization and greater freedom for Chinese people domestically.

Dynamics between Executives and Legislatures

In democracies, executive-branch leaders must usually obtain cooperation, approval, or at least consent from the legislative branch for their foreign policies. This is true in parliamentary systems, such as that of Great Britain, in which the leader of the executive branch (the Prime Minister) and members of his or her cabinet are drawn directly from the elected legislative branch (the parliament). It is also true in presidential systems, in which the executive branch leader – for example, the Chancellor in Germany or the President in the United States – is elected independently of the legislature and appoints his or her own cabinet.

For example, the American political system presents important opportunities for the Congress to constrain the executive branch in foreign policy. The US Constitution stipulates that the President possesses the sole authority to negotiate any treaty with a foreign government, but the Constitution also mandates that any such treaty comes into force if and only if the US Senate ratifies the treaty by a two-thirds majority vote.

As we noted in Chapter 2, the significance of the Senate's treaty ratification power was evident in 1919–20 when the Senate refused to ratify the Versailles Treaty, frustrating President Woodrow Wilson's effort to engage the United States fully in the reconstruction of European security after World War I. President Jimmy Carter was thwarted in 1979 when the Senate refused to ratify the SALT II arms control treaty his administration negotiated with the Soviet Union, and in the late 1990s President Bill Clinton quietly gave up his efforts to get the Senate to ratify the Comprehensive Test Ban Treaty that his administration signed in 1996. As Box 23.3 shows, although different presidents approach Congress differently, it is impossible in the US system to ignore the role of Congress in foreign policy.

The need for executive leaders to engage politically and gain the support of the legislative branch is true, in varying degrees, across democracies. In 2013, British Prime Minister David Cameron preferred military action against Syria after there were claims that the Syrian regime used chemical weapons against rebel groups fighting for control of the Syrian capital, Damascus. However, the British parliament refused to go along and voted not to authorize Britain's use of force. British Members of Parliament, perhaps reflecting the unease of the British public, felt that the risks of getting involved in another Middle East war outweighed the sense of moral outrage directed at Syria's leader for using chemical weapons (*Guardian* 2013). Britain's response to Syria was being coordinated with that of the United States; after the British vote US President Barack Obama decided to step back and request formal approval from the US Congress before committing US military forces. Autocratic leaders, such as Syria's Bashar al-Assad, who was accused of using chemical weapons against the Syrian rebels, typically do not face similar types of domestic political constraints.

National Politics and Societal Actors

To this point, we have been focusing on political dynamics within governments as a source of foreign policy. Equally if not more important as a source of foreign policy are politics within a country as a whole (Snyder 1991). We explore below three particularly powerful classes of national political dynamics, and societal actors within countries, that influence foreign policy: public opinion and elections, the media, and interest groups.

Public Opinion and Elections

Public opinion and elections can play an important role in shaping foreign policy (Holsti 2004). The case of Syria, discussed above, is instructive. A survey conducted by the German Marshall Fund found that 72 percent of Europeans preferred that the European Union stay completely out of Syria's ongoing civil war. A majority of Americans – 62 percent – expressed a similar view of the role their government should play. In light of this clear public sentiment, it is not surprising that both European and American governments proved reluctant to intervene. That same survey revealed a more general difference between Europeans and Americans that both reinforces and

is reflected in the conduct of their respective approaches to foreign policy: 68 percent of Americans, but only 31 percent of Europeans, agreed with the statement that war is sometimes necessary to obtain justice (German Marshall Fund 2013: 6).

Scholars have demonstrated very clearly that US citizens vote on the basis not just of their views on domestic issues, but on foreign policy as well (Hurwitz and Peffley 1987). It is for this reason that presidential candidates spend significant time on foreign policy, and debate the subject. Moreover, there is good evidence that US presidents try to accom-modate American public opinion on foreign policy issues. For example, a recent study demonstrates that presidents from Lyndon Johnson to Bill Clinton were aware of public opinion on foreign policy matters, and that when it came to that issue area, presidents 'follow[ed] the polls for both governing and electoral purposes' (Sobel 2001: 238–9).

An important line of research on the matter of public opinion and foreign policy concerns the conditions under which public opinion is likely to turn against a war once hostilities have commenced. A long-standing thesis on this subject is that a dem-ocratic public will inexorably turn against a policy action that includes the use of force in direct proportion to the number of casualties (Mueller 1973). The Vietnam War, which the US public initially supported but gradually turned against, appears to support this thesis. A more recent alternative view is that the public does not neces-sarily turn against a war as casualties mount. Instead, according to this line of analysis, how the public assesses a war that entails growing casualties depends upon how that war is going: if the public believes that the country is winning, then it will support military operations notwithstanding battlefield casualties. World War II is a clear example of how the US public continued to support a war effort in spite of very high US battlefield casualties. It is the persistence of casualties and a loss in confidence that victory is likely, as occurred in Vietnam, which causes public opinion to turn against continuation of the war (Gelpi et al. 2009).

The relationship between national leaders and public opinion in the context of war is complex and multi-dimensional. War and, more generally, external conflicts often boost the popularity of a leader. This phenomenon is often termed the rally 'round the flag effect. Fidel Castro of Cuba became a more popular leader at home after the ill-fated Bay of Pigs invasion of 1961 because he was perceived as having stood up for Cuba against external aggression sponsored by the more powerful United States. Pres-ident George H. W. Bush enjoyed a spike in his approval ratings in 1991 after the United States and its allies expelled Saddam Hussein's forces from Kuwait, although

Rally 'round the flag effect:
A commonly observed
boost in the popularity of a
leader due to external conflicts or war.

that boost in approval did not carry over to the 1992 presidential election, when Bush was defeated by Bill Clinton in large part because of a lackluster US domestic economy. We noted above that a US covert operation killed Osama bin Laden in early May 2011: in the immediate aftermath President Barack Obama's overall job approval jumped 11 percentage points, from 46 to 57 percent (Dao and Sussman 2011). Not surprisingly, scholars and commentators sometimes suspect that political leaders fabricate or embellish external threats precisely to instigate a rally 'round the flag effect, and to deflect attention from other political problems.

The News Media and Foreign Policy

Foreign affairs media: Those individuals and organizations who report or comment on foreign developments in print, on television, over radio, and through the internet.

Framing: The process by which media participants select or present particular elements of a news story in such a way as to influence the opinions of recipients of the story.

The foreign affairs media are those individuals and organizations who report or comment on foreign developments in print, on television, over radio, and through the internet. For example, reporters play a key role in providing information about world events, often at great risk to themselves, and particularly when they operate in war zones (see Photo 23.4). However, the news media not only provides information; scholars have found that news media participants – reporters, commentators, and editors – can indirectly influence national leaders as they grapple with foreign policy problems. The mechanism by which this influence is exercised is termed framing. Framing is the process by which media participants select or present particular elements of a news story in such a way as to influence the opinions of recipients of the story (Entman 2004). The way the media frames a story can help shape public opinion on particular foreign policy matters; the choices media participants make about framing a particular issue can affect the degree of freedom political leaders have in positing interests and designing strategies.

A recent study systematically explored the degree to which media framing of a foreign policy matter can influence the recipients of such reporting (Berinsky and Kinder 2006). In an experiment carried out in two phases in the years 2000 and 2002, scholars recruited volunteers, divided them into three groups, and presented each group with slightly different sets of news stories about Serbian forces' brutal attacks in 1999 against civilian residents in the province of Kosovo, which ended with a NATO air strike campaign to stop the Serbian attacks. Volunteers in one group (the *control* group) were given news reports about the Serbia–Kosovo conflict that were, to the extent possible, devoid of a political slant. Individuals in the second group (what the research team termed the *humanitarian* group) were given reports that were largely the same as the straight news reports, but had been slightly adjusted to highlight the atrocities that the Serbs had been committing against the Kosovo residents. Members of the third group (what the team called the *risk to America* group) were given reports that highlighted the risks that American air force personnel could encounter in undertaking air attacks against Serbia. The research team found that, compared to the straight-news group and the risk-to-America group, those in the humanitarian group remembered more facts about the Kosovo case that related to Serbian atrocities and, looking back, they were more likely than individuals in the other two groups to say that the US decision to intervene against Serbia was the right thing to do. Even quite small differences across the groups in how the Serbia–Kosovo story was framed led to significant differences in what individuals in the different groups remembered about the issues at stake and how they assessed the wisdom of the air campaign against Serbia.

The media play a larger role in democratic countries than in autocratic countries, where the media typically face restrictions imposed by the central government, or are

expected to report and frame stories in a manner favorable to the central leaders. Technological changes, however, are making it more challenging even for autocratic governments to control the media. In China, for example, 'online public opinion' has become a new social force that is beginning to influence foreign policy. The Chinese Ministry of Foreign Affairs has become more sensitive to public sentiments because it recognizes how much and what types of international information ordinary Chinese people can obtain over the internet (Junhao 2005; Xin-An 2005). Although Chinese leaders still closely monitor and restrict internet coverage of foreign affairs, the government's monopoly of media control is gradually breaking down.

Interest Groups

An interest group consists of individuals or organizations that share a common set of political concerns. They band together in an association, which may be more or less institutionalized, and work through that association to persuade leaders and the public to pursue, support, or accept policies that are in accord with the preferences of the association. Interest groups can be found in virtually every country and type of political system. They tend to be most prominent in democracies in which freedom of expression and the right to organize are protected by law. In advanced democratic nations, business, ethnic-religious, humanitarian, and environmentalist groups have long been active in seeking to influence foreign policy (Mearsheimer and Walt 2007).

Interest groups usually organize according to issue; particular groups wish to influence, for instance, their government's trade policies, environmental policies, or overall policies toward a particular country. In France and Japan, politically connected farmers work effectively to influence their country's position in regional and global trade negotiations. In the United States, Jewish and Arab lobby groups try to influence US policy toward Israel and the Middle East. In many cases the preferences of interest groups are sensitive to geographic location. In China, corporations that operate in coastal areas, where factories assemble goods for export, are more supportive of China's integration in the world economy, while state-run enterprises that reside in China's interior and produce (inefficiently) goods for the local market are more skeptical of global integration. In Russia, the largest private energy companies (such as

Interest group: Individuals or organizations that share a common set of political concerns and band together in an association to persuade leaders and the public to pursue, support, or accept policies that are in accord with the preferences of the association.

Presidents Woodrow Wilson, Harry Truman, and Barack Obama on Working with Congress on Foreign Policy

Over time, American Presidents have gained more and more decision-making power, relative to Congress, in the conduct of foreign policy. However Presidents must still enlist the cooperation of Congress in order to carry out foreign policy effectively. This is as true today as it was one hundred years ago. Presidents who choose to ignore or disdain Congress sometimes pay a heavy price, as the experience of Woodrow Wilson demonstrates. Presidents who commit to cooperation with Congress will often reap foreign policy benefits, as the early presidential experience of Harry Truman demonstrated. When Presidents and Congress find themselves in confrontation, it is difficult to get very much done in domestic or foreign policy, as Barack Obama found.

Then: *President Woodrow Wilson, 1919*

In July 1919, President Wilson submitted to the US Senate the Treaty of Versailles and the Covenant for the League of Nations. Several senators who favored ratification wanted to add reservations that would limit US obligations under the Covenant to protect other League members in the event they were attacked.

Asked if he would accept such Senate-imposed reservations on the Covenant, President Wilson said, 'Anyone who opposes me in that, I'll crush.' The Senate ultimately refused to support Wilson's ambitious initiative, leaving him incapable of carrying out the US commitment to the League.

Source: Thomas G. Paterson, J. Garry Clifford, Shane J. Maddock, Deborah Kisatsky, and Kenneth J. Hagan (2006) *American Foreign Relations, Volume I: to 1920* (Boston: Houghton Mifflin).

Then: *President Harry Truman, 1946*

In a statement made before White House correspondents in November 1946, President Truman made it clear that he would continue his predecessor's efforts to work with the Congress, including members in the Republican Party, on matters relating to foreign policy.

Lukoil) are locked into West European energy markets; despite China's rise, and with the exception of arms exporters, no strong 'Asia lobby' is yet evident in Russian foreign economic policy (Rutland 2006). In light of China's ongoing demand for raw materials, it would not be surprising for such a lobby to emerge among powerful private actors in Russia's mineral-rich region of Siberia.

Since its independence in 1991, Ukraine's foreign policy has balanced between tilting toward Russia and edging closer to the European Union. Western and central Ukraine is home to Ukrainian-speaking Catholics who see their interests served by connecting with the West. In eastern and southern regions are a majority of Russian speakers and followers of the pro-Russian Orthodox Church, who more naturally lobby for their government to orient its foreign policy toward Moscow (Krushelnysky 2013). In 2013, Ukraine's President, Viktor Yanukovich, pivoted decisively towards Russia by accepting Russian leader Vladimir Putin's multi-billion dollar offer to bail out Ukraine's struggling economy. At the same time, Yanukovich turned away from Ukraine's planned economic partnership with the European Union. Pro-Western Ukrainians rose up in protest, taking to the streets, occupying local and regional gov-

Truman said at that time: 'I shall cooperate in every proper manner with members of the Congress, and my hope and prayer is that this spirit of cooperation will be reciprocated.' Truman faced a Congress generally reluctant to engage the United States deeply in European affairs after the war. Yet he managed to cultivate sufficient Congressional support for his signature foreign policy initiatives, the NATO alliance and the European Recovery Program (commonly known as the Marshall Plan).

Source: 'Statement by President Truman to White House Correspondents', November 11, 1946, in Henry Steele Commager (ed.) (1949) *Documents of American History*, fifth edition (New York: Appleton-Century-Crofts).

Now: *President Barack Obama, 2013*

Obama faced widespread Republican opposition to his legislative agenda during his first term (2009–12) and into his second. He and his Congressional adversaries proved unwilling or incapable of finding sufficient common ground to move policies forward. The result was a shutdown of the government due to the failure of the two sides to reach a budget compromise, and a lack of significant legislative achievement with the exception of Obama's controversial health care reform initiative which he managed to force through Congress only because his party held a majority in both houses during his first two years in office. In foreign policy, Congressional opponents sought to stymie Obama whenever possible, for example in his handling of an attack on the US consulate in Benghazi, Libya in 2012, and by opposing his 2013 diplomatic opening to Iran and lobbying for a tightening rather than a relaxation of economic sanctions against Iran.

On the morning that the US government reopened after having been shut down, Obama expressed his frustration directly to his Congressional opponents:

> You don't like a particular policy or a particular President? Then argue for your position. Go out and win an election. Don't break what our predecessors spent over two centuries building. That's not being faithful to what this country is about.'

Source: Leigh Ann Caldwell, 'Obama may have won now, but next three years could be tough', CNN, October 18, 2013.

ernment buildings, and declaring their loyalty to a People's Council set up by the political opponents of Yanukovich. Early in 2014, Yanukovich was chased from office, and Russian President Vladimir Putin intervened and eventually annexed Crimea, which is part of Ukraine, setting off an international crisis between Russia and the West.

Interest groups use a variety of means to try to influence national leaders and the public. In democratic states, interest groups publish or fund the publication of policy papers, purchase advertisements in major newspapers and other media, organize letter-writing campaigns to political representatives, and undertake lobbying, or personally meeting and speaking with members of legislatures and officials in executive departments. Interest groups also contribute to political candidates and political parties, or organize political fundraisers. As the Ukraine example above shows, some interest groups organize protests and demonstrations in major cities around their country in order to attract media attention to their concerns.

While we know that interest groups have sought to shape the foreign policies of most countries, foreign policy studies are only beginning to produce systematic research on how much influence such groups actually have on foreign policy-making.

Lobbying: Meeting and speaking with members of legislatures and officials in executive departments in an attempt to influence policy. Interest groups often engage in lobbying.

One challenge is that while we can observe instances in which interest groups have tried to influence leaders and officials responsible for foreign policy, it is difficult to know if they have been successful even if the government does what the groups have called for. For example, looking at some US policy decisions relating to trade with China or arms sales to Israel, we may know that one or more interest groups pressed for the United States to act in a particular manner on those issues, and we may also know that government leaders took the stance on these issues that matched the position the interest group or groups had been advocating. However, what we do not know is whether the leaders took the stance they did because of the interest groups, or if they would have taken the stance even if the groups had not been active. Scholars try to set up research strategies that allow them to isolate the preferences of interest groups and the impact of interest group activity on foreign policy. A nice example of this type of comparative foreign policy research is described in Box 23.4.

Sources of Foreign Policy at the International Level of Analysis

At least three factors that are situated at the international level of analysis may shape how a country's leaders define that country's interests and strategies: the country's geography, its relative economic development, and its overall relative capabilities, or power.

Geography

A country's geographic characteristics, combined with its demographics, are likely to influence how its leaders think about interests and strategy. During the nineteenth century Great Britain, separated from the great powers of Europe by the English Channel, developed its naval power and expanded its influence overseas while seeking to maintain a balance of power among the European states on the continent. Similarly, from the 1780s to the 1930s, many people in the United States believed that the country could remain free of European entanglements because it was separated from the Old World by the Atlantic Ocean. Mexican and Canadian leaders have also believed that geography matters. One of Mexico's longest-ruling autocratic leaders of the late nineteenth and early twentieth century, Porfirio Diaz, is reported to have said, 'Alas, poor Mexico! So far from God and so close to the United States!' In the same vein, Canada's Prime Minister Pierre Trudeau told an American audience at the National Press Club in Washington that 'Living next to you is in some ways like sleeping with an elephant. No matter how friendly and even-tempered is the beast, if I can call it that, one is affected by every twitch and grunt' (Canadian Broadcasting Company 1969).

A country's immediate neighborhood helps to shape its foreign policy. Israel's simultaneously defensive and aggressive foreign policy is influenced by the fact that Israel lives in close proximity to countries it has long seen as adversaries. India borders its traditional rivals, China and Pakistan; much of its foreign policy is pre-occupied with managing those relations. Germany's size and prominence in the center of Europe has long been a source of anxiety, and at times opportunity, for its smaller neighbors such as Poland. The United States is concerned by North Korea's behavior, but the stakes are arguably larger for China, which borders North Korea and worries that a collapse of that country would lead to large refugee flows into China.

Relative Level of Economic Development

A country's relative economic wealth, and the sources of that wealth, can influence how the country defines its interests and strategies. Historically, countries with the largest and most dynamic economies have had opportunities to translate their wealth

The Influence of Bankers on Foreign Policy across Countries

Theory

Marxists believe banks have significant influence over the decisions of governments to go to war. As we discussed in Chapter 1, Lenin's theory of imperialism, for example, expected big banks, or finance capital, in Western countries to press their governments to adopt aggressive foreign policies in order to obtain access to new markets. Lenin believed governments would comply in order to serve the interests of powerful economic actors.

Practice

Recent research suggests this theoretical approach may be off the mark. Jonathan Kirshner shows that bankers do have significant influence on foreign policy, though not always on the critical decision to go to war. More importantly, the preferences of bankers differ from what Marxists expect (Kirshner 2007). In a study of bankers in different countries across different time periods, Kirshner finds that bankers consistently prefer peace to war. Financial actors, whether in France in the 1920s, Japan in the 1930s, America in the 1890s, or Britain in the 1980s, are interested in economic stability above everything else. A stable economic environment is the best for profit-making, and war is disruptive to economic stability. Kirshner shows, for example, that British bankers failed to support their natural ally, Conservative Prime Minister Margaret Thatcher, during the Falklands crisis of 1981–82 in which Thatcher took Great Britain to war against Argentina. During the 1930s, Japanese financial interests opposed the aggressive turn in foreign policy which led Japan to occupy China in 1931 and again in 1937. Japanese bankers preferred a more cautious foreign policy, but were overwhelmed by the Japanese military which took control of the state and moved foreign policy in a more belligerent direction.

into military power and exert considerable influence in global affairs. This was true of Great Britain and eventually Germany in the nineteenth century, and the United States during the twentieth century. The rise of China in the early twenty-first century is a direct function of its rapid economic growth. A country's relative level of wealth and prosperity also affects how it views specific foreign policy issues. For example, many European countries, in possession of mature, developed economies, place a high priority on environmental protection. In sharp contrast, leaders in countries with industries that are only now reaching world-class competitiveness, such as India, Brazil, and especially China, do not believe that their countries are yet able to afford stronger environmental or worker standards, and these leaders have set as an interest the prevention of the imposition of stricter standards.

Relative National Capabilities

A country's relative capabilities are likely to condition both its interests and its selection of goals and policy instruments. A country's relative capabilities determine its international influence, its positive ability to cause others to act in ways it prefers, and its negative ability to resist the efforts of other countries to induce it to do things it would rather not do. A country's relative capabilities are a function of many factors: its demography (including population size but also the balance between young and old, working-age and retired); territorial expanse and such natural resources (if exploited wisely) as arable land, oil, and economically important minerals; literacy as well as scientific and technological sophistication; and the degree to which governing institutions are effective and enable leaders to convert national economic resources into military power and political influence (Mearsheimer 2001 and Waltz 1979).

Leaders of especially powerful countries often believe that, in the absence of an effective international government, they have a special responsibility to contribute to the existing international order (Gilpin 1975; Ikenberry 2001). In these circumstances foreign policy may be significantly influenced by a country's relative position in the international system. When war breaks out in central Africa, it is of great concern to Africans. When Serbs and Bosnians fight, it is of great concern to neighboring Europeans. But these situations are also of special interest to far away powerful states who believe, for better or worse, that they share responsibility for managing regional crises and assuring global order.

We have to this point explored what a foreign policy looks like and from what sources it emerges. We now may turn to the chapter's final question: why do states sometimes *change* their foreign policy?

Levels of Analysis *Sources of Foreign* *Policy*	👤 **Individual**	🏛 **State**	🌐 **International**
	A national leader's beliefs, which are likely to be shaped by his or her personality, formative political experiences, and motivated biases, play a large role in influencing that leader's approach to foreign policy.	Within a government, institutional and bureaucratic politics, as well as relations between different branches such as the executive and legislative in democratic systems, influence foreign policy.	Several international-level factors can influence both the foreign-policy interests and strategies of a country, including its geography, relative economic development, and relative overall power.
	Once a leader has made a foreign policy decision, cognitive dynamics may constrain his or her ability to change course in the face of new information.	Within a country, dynamics that largely take place within its society, including elections, public opinion, the news media, and interest groups, substantially shape its foreign policy.	

How and Why States Change Their Foreign Policy

We will organize our investigation of the sources of change in foreign policy with the aid of the levels-of-analysis framework, beginning with the individual, then focusing on domestic features of states, and ending with the international level of analysis.

Sources of Foreign Policy Change at the Individual Level of Analysis

At least two mechanisms that operate at the individual level of analysis have the capacity to bring about substantial changes in foreign policy. The first mechanism is that of learning by national leaders in such a way that they make significant shifts in foreign policy; the second is the sometimes dramatic impact of changes in leadership on foreign policy.

Leadership Learning and Changes in Foreign Policy

In accord with the expectations of constructivists that we discussed in Chapter 3, national leaders, as a result of their own foreign policy experiences or those of their predecessors, sometimes change their understanding of world politics or the particular circumstances of their country in the international system. Such learning can bring about significant changes in the way leaders define interests or what they consider to be the best strategies to promote them (Levy 1994).

For example, prior to the Great Depression, government leaders in the United States, Canada, Britain, Germany, and other industrialized countries mostly subscribed to *laissez-faire* economic ideas; governments should not interfere with market dynamics either at home or in the international sphere. As we saw in Chapter 2, at the outset of the Great Depression, those leaders had few international cooperative mechanisms available to them to deal with the collapse in national demand they were all experiencing, which in turn prompted them to turn to beggar-thy-neighbor prohibitive tariffs on imports or prohibitions on the inflow or outflow of capital. Since the Great Depression, government leaders in the United States, Canada, and Europe have largely believed that government should allow for the free operation of markets at home and overseas, *but* there is room for government intervention both through national monetary and fiscal policies and by way of international governmental coordination (as we will see in Chapter 8, through such entities as the International Monetary Fund and the Group of 20) to mitigate the kind of shocks that we have seen in the world economy during the crisis of 2008–13. The economic beliefs of leaders changed, and major changes in domestic and foreign economic policies were the result (Frieden 2006).

Similarly, an important line of recent research has shown that learning in the face of policy failure adds a key element to our understanding of why the United States switched from neutrality to internationalism at the close of World War II (Legro 2000). In particular, President Franklin Roosevelt reflected on President Wilson's failure to obtain America's entry into the League of Nations, and the United States' subsequent shift to a policy of political isolationism during the 1920s and 1930s, and learned that these failures enabled Nazi Germany, Fascist Italy, and Imperial Japan to pursue aggression. That aggression ultimately directly threatened America's security, Roosevelt thought, and that threat could have been averted or halted at lower cost had the United States been more active in world security matters and, in collaboration with other powerful states in a collective security organization, confronted the aggressors.

Roosevelt inferred that, to pursue its interest in security, the United States had to shift from a strategy of neutrality to one of internationalism, a strategy in which the US would be fully engaged with other states through institutionalized arrangements directed at maintaining world security and promoting global economic prosperity. The American strategy of neutrality during the 1930s clearly failed to keep the United States secure, and made Roosevelt's case for internationalism more credible in the US political system.

Over time, a given leader may change ideas about his or her country's interests or strategy. For example, Soviet leader Mikhail Gorbachev appears to have fundamentally changed his ideas about Soviet foreign policy from the time he took power in 1985 to the period during which he took steps that decisively ended the Cold War in 1988 (English 2005). At first, Gorbachev appears largely to have accepted the traditional Marxist ideas we discussed in Chapter 3: world politics is basically a continuation of domestic class struggles, the Soviet Union and the United States possessed fundamental conflicts of interest, and core Soviet interests in security could only be advanced by a strategy that included political dominance in Eastern Europe and, as

Isolationism: A strategy in which a state avoids or minimizes engaging with other states through any sort of international institutions or agreements and focuses solely on itself and its domestic politics.

Internationalism: A strategy in which a state is fully engaged with other states through institutionalized arrangements directed at maintaining world security and promoting global economic prosperity.

much as possible, military superiority over Western Europe. By 1988, however, Gorbachev radically shifted his foreign policy perspective to what was termed *new thinking* about Soviet foreign policy. Gone from Gorbachev's rhetoric and actions were global class struggle, permanent struggle with the United States, and the need for pro-Soviet regimes in Eastern Europe. He replaced these with an emphasis on shared interests with the West and acceptance of greater freedom of political choice in Eastern Europe.

Leaders' experiences with officials from other countries may change those leaders' beliefs about their own country's situation and strategic options. The experiences of leaders and policy officials in international institutions might also affect their perceptions and values. For example, Gorbachev moved to his *new thinking* stance on Soviet interests and the benefits of cooperation with Western countries as he interacted with decision makers from those countries, especially US Secretary of State George Shultz (Stein 1994). In the same vein, Chinese officials, as a result of participating in regular talks during the mid-1990s that included several East and Southeast countries, as well as the United States, appear to have moved from skepticism to support for the idea that regional dialogue is an effective mechanism by which China can reassure neighbors of its peaceful intentions (Johnston 2008).

The cases of Roosevelt, Gorbachev, and the recent leaders of China may leave us with the idea that policy makers typically learn what, from the viewpoint of a country's interests, are the *right* lessons from history, and then make the *right* policy adjustments. However, while learning may be a reasonably pervasive feature of foreign policy, the particular lessons leaders learn may not always yield successful outcomes. For example, while Belgian leaders inferred from World War I that neutrality had left them open to German invasion, the main diplomatic instrument they subsequently devised, a military alliance with France, did not prevent Germany from defeating and occupying Belgium in 1940. Many factors, not just correct learning, play a role in determining the success or failure of a country's national strategy.

Learning by leaders seems to occur in foreign policy-making, and such learning can materially influence how leaders view the interests of their countries and adjust their strategies to promote those interests. What is not guaranteed is that the lessons leaders learn necessarily increase or decrease their chances of success in foreign policy. An important scholarly task then is to identify and understand more fully the conditions under which leaders do or do not learn the right lessons in foreign affairs.

Leadership Turnover

Leaders play a key role in crafting foreign policy, so changes in leadership can bring about changes in foreign policy. Perhaps the most dramatic example of the impact of leadership change on foreign policy during the twentieth century occurred in the former Soviet Union in the 1980s. As we discussed in Chapter 2, Soviet leaders from Joseph Stalin to Leonid Brezhnev maintained iron-fisted control over Eastern Europe, using military force as necessary against Hungary in 1956 and Czechoslovakia in 1968. Mikhail Gorbachev between 1985 and 1988 reversed course on Soviet policy, most notably accepting the loss of Poland, Hungary, and other countries in what had been its empire in Eastern Europe, rather than relying on military force to keep them within the Soviet empire.

Postwar China offers a second example. From the 1950s until well into the 1970s, China was controlled by Mao Zedong, who was committed to making China communist, powerful, and independent through a strategy that combined a high level of state control over the national economy with an almost complete separation from global commerce. The coming to power of Deng Xiaoping in the late 1970s transformed China's economic and foreign policies from an emphasis on communist ideological purity toward to a more pragmatic strategy aimed at economic growth, a strategy that included economic engagement with capitalist countries.

Sources of Foreign Policy Change at the State Level of Analysis

Two mechanisms that originate and largely operate at the state level of analysis have the capacity to induce substantial change in a country's foreign policy: dramatic changes in a country's domestic political regime, and the political efforts of non-governmental organizations.

Domestic Regime Change and Shifts in Foreign Policy

Dramatic political changes within a country, such as a change in its political regime, may induce large changes in its foreign policy interests and strategies. A clear example of such an impact of regime change on foreign policy is Germany in the twentieth century.

At the outset of the 1900s, Germany had a political regime headed by the Kaiser and, as we saw in Chapter 2, his aggression, together with his unchecked control over Germany's foreign and military policies, led Germany to start but ultimately lose World War I. Germany's enemies in the war, Britain and France, with the acquiescence of the United States, imposed the very harsh Versailles peace treaty on Germany. By virtue of the Versailles Treaty, Germany lost much territory to its east, had Allied occupation forces in its western territories, was forbidden to have strong military forces, and was required to pay massive reparations to France, Britain, and other Allied countries.

In 1919, Germans succeeded temporarily in crafting a democratic constitution. This new Weimer Republic wanted to revise much of the Versailles Treaty. For example, Germany's new leaders wanted foreign forces out of Germany and a reduction in the reparations it owed to the countries it had fought during the war of 1914–18. However, Germany under the Weimar Republic pursued this goal in a cautious, non-confrontational manner, and sought revisions of the Versailles Treaty with the consent of the main European powers, particularly France and Britain, and in the framework of German integration into the League of Nations. In sharp contrast, when Adolph Hitler's Nazi regime came into power in 1933, it reversed Weimar's policies, overturned the Versailles settlement, and ultimately unleashed a war in Europe that almost perpetrated the destruction of all Jews in Europe. Then again, after World War II and the destruction of the Nazi regime, a new democratic Federal Republic in the western part of Germany turned to a policy of moderation and integration. West Germany aligned itself with the United States and Britain, became a loyal and important member of such Western institutions as NATO and the European Community (today's European Union), forged a durable peace with its eastern and western neighbors, especially France, and became a key supporter of the state of Israel.

The German case drives home a key point: what a state does abroad is likely to be influenced by how it is organized at home.

Why Did the United States and the European Community Impose Economic Sanctions against South Africa?

Background

South Africa long practiced a political system of institutionalized discrimination known as apartheid. A small minority of white South Africans ruled over a large majority of black South Africans. The apartheid regime controlled the economy and the political and legal system, and determined where black South Africans were allowed to work and live. Beginning in the early 1960s, a majority of members of the United Nations protested apartheid, imposed an arms embargo against South Africa, and sought to isolate the apartheid regime diplomatically. Several key countries, however, including Great Britain and the United States, maintained cordial political and close economic relations with South Africa until the 1980s. Then, in a significant policy shift, the United States and members of the European Community imposed economic sanctions against South Africa in 1986. What explains their initial reluctance to take action against apartheid, and their subsequent shift to opposing apartheid through the use of economic sanctions?

Realism: For realists, foreign policy is designed and executed to serve the core national interests of states. For the United States and its European allies, the central national security issue of the Cold War was the struggle against the Soviet Union and international communism. To Western leaders, South Africa's political regime was morally repugnant, but South Africa was an important ally in the global struggle against communism because it was an unambiguously anti-communist state in the key region of southern Africa. Western powers opted to maintain close ties with South Africa despite their distaste for apartheid. Security interests trumped democratic and human rights ideals.

The shift to sanctions in the 1980s is harder for the realist perspective to explain. One possibility is that once Mikhail Gorbachev came to power in the Soviet Union, the Cold War was moving towards its end, and thus support for the anti-communist regime in South Africa was less geopolitically vital. The problem with this explanation is that in 1986 it was difficult for Western leaders to foresee that the Cold War was actually ending and would do so within five years. A second and perhaps more persuasive realist argument is that the sanctions imposed were more symbolic than instrumental. They allowed Western leaders to take what had become a popular political stand against apartheid without doing significant damage to the South African economy. Realists might also point out that in the United States the sanctions were passed by Congress but opposed by President Ronald Reagan. Congress overrode the President's veto and the sanctions legislation became law. The US President, in other words, continued to pursue the national interest of close relations with South Africa; the foreign policy change was driven instead by the legislative branch, reflecting popular sentiment.

Constructivism: Constructivists focus on the importance of norms and ideas in international relations. For constructivists, the sanctions decision was the culmination of a gradual and global mass movement in favor of an anti-apartheid norm (Klotz 1995). The idea that apartheid was a politically and morally ➤

Non-Governmental Organizations and Changes in Foreign Policy

Constructivists, as we discussed in Chapter 3, argue that non-governmental organizations (NGOs) have had significant success in influencing the foreign policies of states, as well as the policies of international institutions those states control (Keck and Sikkink 1998). NGOs have sought to exercise this influence by working individually and in networks to persuade the leaders of national governments that they should broaden their definition of interests beyond traditional security or economic concerns, and to include in that definition issues such as human rights and the environment.

Some NGOs, such as Oxfam, Doctors Without Borders, and Catholic Charities, pursue projects in poorer countries relating to health or economic development, and unacceptable regime type for a state in the international community took hold and spread over time. This anti-apartheid normative movement was led as much by international organizations (such as the Organization for African Unity) and non-state actors as by the governments of nation-states.

By the 1980s, this anti-apartheid norm became too powerful even for major states to ignore; countries such as Great Britain and the United States that refused to isolate South Africa began to appear themselves as outliers in the international community. The pressure for foreign policy change in the United States and Western Europe came from below, from domestic political forces, and transnationally, from international and non-governmental organizations. Western leaders continued to place geopolitical value on the South African connection, but eventually were swept along by the movement and could no longer resist it. Global normative change trumped prior conceptions of national interest.

Constructivists might argue further that even if sanctions had limited economic impact on South Africa, their psychological impact on the South African government was significant. So long as Great Britain and the United States supported the regime, South Africa's minority government could continue to feel they were part of an anti-communist coalition rather than a pariah within the international community. The sanctions signaled that even their most loyal international supporters no longer considered apartheid tolerable.

Marxism: Marxists could explain the willingness of liberal Western governments to tolerate apartheid as a function of the economic interests of private economic actors. South Africa's economy was the largest and most profitable in southern Africa. Western banks, manufacturing firms, and raw material producers long considered South Africa a lucrative host for trade and investment. Government policy in Western countries followed and supported the interests of dominant economic classes.

How then to account for the shift to sanctions? Marxists argue that by the 1980s, South Africa was increasing less attractive as an economic partner. The well-publicized campaign, led by college students, to convince universities and other large resource holders to divest their portfolios from companies doing business in South Africa forced companies to calculate increasing 'social costs' of their South African activities. At the same time, domestic unrest and uprisings among the black majority population in South Africa (the Soweto uprisings of 1976 were a key turning point) created an atmosphere of economic uncertainty. The apartheid regime responded with repression including the declaration of a state of emergency in 1985. Shortly thereafter, Chase Manhattan Bank decided it would not renew its loans to South Africa, and other big banks followed suit. For Marxists, the key variable was that private economic actors reluctantly turned against South Africa for business reasons before Western governments signed on to economic sanctions against the regime. Government actors, in other words, followed rather than led a shift in private economic interests.

advocate for better foreign aid policies by wealthy donor countries like the United States and key international organizations like the World Bank and the International Monetary Fund. Other NGOs, such as Human Rights Watch and Amnesty International, publicize abuses of human and political rights in countries around the globe through newsletters, reports, and direct contacts with members of the news media. They also press national governments, as well as the European Union and United Nations Human Rights Council, for stronger international protections of such rights. Many environmental NGOs, such as the World Wildlife Fund, the Worldwatch Institute, and the International Union for the Conservation of Nature, use similar strategies to draw public and governmental attention to problems in the environmental realm. Others NGOs use more dramatic strategies: for example, Greenpeace has employed

► Photo 23.5
Greenpeace Protests

Greenpeace is an NGO that is especially adept at using public actions to draw attention to policies with which it disagrees. In this instance Samcheok villagers participate in a demonstration to oppose the planned construction of a nuclear power plant in their community, 192 km from Seoul.

Source: © Jean Chung/ Greenpeace.

small boats and a helicopter to interfere with what it considers to be illegal and immoral operations of large whaling ships.

There is evidence that internationally active NGOs have sometimes changed the ideas of policy makers and shaped, to some degree, their definition of foreign policy interests or strategies. For example, according to an important study by Margaret Keck and Kathryn Sikkink, networks linking international and domestic activist groups centered on Amnesty International and Americas Watch, helped move the US government to take more seriously human rights abuses in Latin America, particularly in Argentina and Mexico during the 1970s, 1980s, and early 1990s. The study reports similar dynamics involving NGOs influencing important governments in the issue areas of protection of women and the natural environment (Keck and Sikkink 1998).

Moreover, NGO advocacy groups have influenced the policy instruments that national governments employ to protect interests even in the sensitive area of national security. For example, during the 1990s, hundreds of NGOs, coordinated by the International Campaign to Ban Landmines and led by Jody Williams, who would receive a Nobel Peace Prize for her work with the campaign, publicized the manner in which innocent civilians were being killed by anti-personnel landmines. The work of the NGOs helped prompt 122 governments to ban that class of weapons by virtue of a treaty signed in Ottawa, Canada, in 1997 (Price 1998). As we will see, NGOs have sometimes been effective in influencing global policy regarding the natural environment. Finally, constructivists argue that NGOs played a decisive role in forcing leaders of Western countries to take a strong stand against South Africa's white minority government during the 1980s (Klotz 2005). As Box 23.5 shows, Marxists, constructivists, and realists rely on different types of explanations for that critical example of foreign policy change.

Sources of Foreign Policy Change at the International Level of Analysis

Finally, factors situated at the international level of analysis, in particular internationally-induced shocks and changes in the relative power of a country, can induce changes in its foreign policy.

External Shocks

National communities – leaders, officials, commentators, and politically attentive citizens – may sometimes be jarred out of their ideas about foreign policy by a major external shock. For example, the Japanese attack in December 1941 against the American naval fleet at Pearl Harbor discredited the isolationist position in American politics, and helped paved the way for the United States' more internationalist stance after World War II. In the same vein, the experience of Iran's revolutionary leaders after they attained power in 1979 – an invasion in 1980 by Saddam Hussein's Iraq, the receipt of no outside aid and, in fact, some American aid for Saddam Hussein – has probably scarred those leaders and made them deeply suspicious of the United States and committed to acquiring military power, including nuclear weapons.

Changes in Relative Power

You will recall from Chapter 2 that US leaders and much of the US political elite during and after World War II came to believe the United States had to do more to support a world order than had been true when the United States occupied a much less important place in the international system. In other words, as the US relative power position changed, so too did its conceptions of interest and appropriate strategy. These changes do not happen immediately; the United States was already very powerful by the 1930s but did not change its foreign policy significantly. Some analysts see China in a comparable position today – its relative power is rising, but it has not yet adjusted its foreign policy to do more to support international order. This 'lag effect' works in reverse as well. Great Britain and France maintained international responsibility typically associated with the strongest states in the system long after their power positions declined in relative terms.

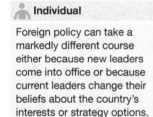

Individual	State	International
Foreign policy can take a markedly different course either because new leaders come into office or because current leaders change their beliefs about the country's interests or strategy options.	A change in country's political regime, or intensive lobbying by non-state actors within the country, can bring about large changes in a country's foreign policy.	External policy shocks as well as changes in a country's relative power may contribute to significant changes in foreign policy.

Levels of Analysis
Sources of Foreign Policy Change

Revisiting the Enduring Question and Looking Ahead

In this chapter, we have examined the enduring question of what accounts for the foreign policies of states. We reviewed the main elements of foreign policy, namely, interest and strategy, with the latter concept entailing two ideas of goals and policy instruments. We employed the levels-of-analysis framework both to understand why governments, by virtue of the influence of their national leaders, domestic institutions and societal actors, and international conditions, choose certain interests to advance and devise particular strategies to pursue them.

We used that same levels-of-analysis framework to investigate an important question derived from our central one: why do states' governments make substantial changes to their foreign policies? In accounting for both foreign policy and foreign policy change, the chapter has showcased the ongoing and unresolved debate among students of international relations and foreign policy. That debate cuts across the levels of analysis and also across the theoretical traditions introduced in Chapter 3. Students who grasp the different types of arguments made by scholars at different levels, and from different theoretical perspectives, will be well equipped to engage the literature on foreign policy analysis, to understand and explain current foreign policy decisions, and eventually to conduct their own research as well.

With this chapter and the previous chapter, we have explored the key language, ideas, and overall approaches that scholars, many media observers, and even some government leaders and officials employ when they think, write, and speak about international relations and foreign policy. As you reflect on these chapters, you will recall that we often talked about military disputes, including war. Although war is a rare event in world politics, it does occur and it can be awesome in its human lethality and political, social, and economic consequences. In the nuclear age, war can be a recipe for national self-destruction. Why do states sometimes turn to war? Fortified with knowledge of international history, aware of international relations theory, and in possession of analytical tools to explore foreign policy, we are now in a position to turn to and confront that fundamental problem in international relations.

Visit www.palgrave.com/politics/Grieco to access extra resources for this chapter, including:

- Chapter summaries to help you review the material
- Multiple choice quizzes to test your understanding
- Flashcards to test your knowledge of the key terms in this chapter
- An interactive simulation that invites you to go through the decision-making process of a world leader at a crucial political juncture
- Pivotal decisions in which you weigh up the pros and cons of complicated decisions with grave consequences
- Outside resources, including links to contemporary articles and videos, that add to what you have learned in this chapter

Study Questions

1. Is the formulation of a coherent strategy by a complex government like China, the United States, or Great Britain really possible? Aren't foreign policies the sum of bureaucratic and institutional in-fighting within governments, rather than the result of a rational, systematic assessment by national leaders of what's best for the country?
2. Can you think of how the geographic location of the United States, or Japan, or France has influenced its foreign policy? Has that influence continued or waned over time?
3. Do you think that a country's domestic political institutions influence its understanding of its interests in the foreign domain? Do those institutions play a role in influencing which instruments the country is likely to turn to in advancing its interests?
4. In general, do you think leaders are good 'learners' when it comes to foreign policy?
5. What makes it more or less likely that a leader will learn appropriate lessons from his or her experiences in foreign policy?
6. Do you think NGOs have too much, just about the right amount, or too little influence on the foreign policies of countries in the international system?

Further Reading

Allison, Graham and Philip Zelikow (1999) *Essence of Decision: Explaining the Cuban Missile Crisis*, 2nd edition (New York: Longman). This classic work, first published by Allison in 1971, shaped a generation of scholarship on foreign policy by showing that the same set of foreign policy decisions – the Soviet decision to place nuclear weapons in Cuba and the US response – could be understood several different ways. Allison challenged the then conventional rational-actor approach by looking 'inside' the state at the institutional and bureaucratic politics of governments.

Kang, David (2009) *China Rising: Peace, Power, and Order in East Asia* (New York: Columbia University Press). In this foreign policy analysis Kang argues that the states of East Asia are more likely to accommodate China than to balance against it. He draws on constructivist thinking to make the case that historical and cultural norms in East Asian countries lead states to embrace, rather than resist, a hierarchy of authority with China at the top.

Kapstein, Ethan B. and Michael Mastanduno (eds) (1999) *Unipolar Politics: Realism and State Strategies after the Cold War* (New York: Columbia University Press). A collection of essays that examine how the changing structure of the international system – the shift from a bipolar to a unipolar world – affects the foreign policy calculations of countries including China, Russia, France, Germany, Poland and the United States.

Legro, Jeffrey W. (2007) *Rethinking the World: Great Power Strategies and International Order* (Ithaca: Cornell University Press). Legro makes the case that ideas drive foreign policy change. He develops the argument in a broad comparative framework that includes analysis of major foreign policy transitions in Russia, China, Japan, and the United States.

Narizny, Kevin (2007) *The Political Economy of Grand Strategy* (Ithaca: Cornell University Press). Narizny argues that foreign policy strategies are driven by the particular pattern of interest group coalitions found within a country. He uses this framework to explain the overall foreign policies, or grand strategies, of Great Britain and the United States during the nineteenth and twentieth centuries.

CHAPTER 24

The State and Foreign Policy in a Global Age

'Traditional nation-states have become unnatural, even impossible units in a global economy.'

KENICHI OHMAE, *The End of the Nation State* (1996)

PREVIEW

The state has long been regarded as the most significant actor on the world stage, the basic 'unit' of global politics. Its predominance stems from its sovereign jurisdiction. As states exercise unchallengeable power within their borders, they operate, or should operate, as independent and autonomous entities in world affairs. However, the state is under threat, perhaps as never before. In particular, globalization, in its economic and political forms, has led to a process of state retreat, even fashioning what some have called the 'post-sovereign' state. Others, nevertheless, argue that conditions of flux and transformation underline the need for the order, stability and direction that (arguably) only the state can provide is greater than ever. Are states in decline, or are they in a process of revival? Globalizing trends have also had implications for the nature and processes of government. Once viewed as 'the brains' of the state, controlling the body politic from the centre, government has seemingly given way to 'governance', a looser and more amorphous set of processes that blur the distinction between the public and private realms, and often operate on supranational and subnational levels as well as the national level. Why and how has government been transformed into governance, and what have been the implications of this process? Finally, foreign policy is important as the mechanism through which, usually, national government manages the state's relations with other states and with international bodies, highlighting the role that choice and decision play in global politics. How are foreign policy decisions made, and what factors influence them?

KEY ISSUES

- Is sovereignty statehood compatible with a globalized world?
- Have nation-states been transformed into market or postmodern states?
- In what ways, and why, has the state become more important?
- To what extent has national government given way to multi-level governance?
- Is the concept of foreign policy any longer meaningful?
- What is the most persuasive theory of foreign policy decision-making?

STATES AND STATEHOOD IN FLUX

States and sovereignty

The state (see p. 118) is a historical institution: it emerged in fifteenth- and sixteenth-century Europe as a system of centralized rule that succeeded in subordinating all other institutions and groups, temporal and spiritual. The Peace of Westphalia (1648) is usually taken to have formalized the modern notion of statehood. By establishing states as sovereign entities, it made states the principal actors on the world stage. International politics was thus thought of as a 'state system'. The state system gradually expanded from Europe into North America, then, during the nineteenth century, into South America and Japan, becoming a truly global system in the twentieth century, largely thanks to the process of decolonization in Asia, Africa, the Caribbean and the Pacific. In the twenty-first century, statehood appears to be more popular and sought-after than ever before. In 2013, the United Nations recognized 193 states, compared with 50 in 1945, and there are a number of 'unrecognized' states waiting in the wings, including the Vatican (the Holy See), Taiwan, Kosovo and Northern Cyprus. The list of potential candidates for statehood is also impressive: Palestine, Kurdistan, Quebec, Chechnya, Western Sahara, Puerto Rico, Bermuda, Greenland and Scotland, to name but a few. However, what is a state, and what are the key features of statehood?

States have a dualistic structure, in that they have two faces, one looking outwards and the other looking inwards (Cerny 2010). The outward-looking face of the state deals with the state's relations with other states and its ability to provide protection against external attack. The classic definition of the state in international law is found in the Montevideo Convention on the Rights and Duties of the State (1933). According to Article 1 of the Montevideo Convention, the state has four features:

- A defined territory
- A permanent population
- An effective government
- The capacity to enter into relations with other states.

The Montevideo Connection advances a 'declaratory' theory of the state, in which states become states by virtue of meeting the minimal criteria for statehood, as opposed to a **'constitutive' theory of the state**. Even without recognition, the state has the right to defend its integrity and independence, to provide for its conservation and prosperity, and consequently to organize itself as it sees fit (Article 3).

The inward-looking face of the state deals with the state's relations with the individuals and groups that live within its borders and its ability to maintain domestic order. From this perspective, the state is usually viewed as an instrument of domination. The German sociologist Max Weber (1864–1920) thus defined the state in terms of its monopoly of the means of 'legitimate violence'. Joseph Schumpeter (1954) complemented this definition by pointing out that the state also has a monopoly of the right to tax citizens. In view of the state's dual structure, what can be called 'statehood' can be seen as the capacity both to protect against external attack and to maintain domestic order, and to do them simultaneously (Brenner 2004).

● **The constitutive theory of the state**: The theory that the political existence of a state is entirely dependent on its recognition by other states.

However, although not explicitly mentioned in the Montevideo Convention's list of state features, or in Weber's notion of a monopoly of the legitimate use of violence, the underlying character of the state is established by a single core characteristic: **sovereignty**. In the final analysis, states are states because they are capable of exercising sovereign jurisdiction within defined territorial borders, and so are autonomous and independent actors. In the billiard ball model of world politics, adopted by realist theorists, states are the billiard balls that collide with one another while sovereignty is the hard and impenetrable outer shell of the ball which enables it to withstand the impact of the collision. The first major theorist of sovereignty was the French political philosopher Jean Bodin (1530–96). He defined sovereignty as 'the absolute and perpetual power of a common wealth'. In his view, the only guarantee of political and social stability is the existence of a sovereign with final law-making power; in that sense, law reflects the 'will' of the sovereign. For Thomas Hobbes (see p. 14), the need for sovereignty arose from the self-seeking and power-interested nature of human beings, which meant that, in the absence of a sovereign ruler – that is, in a 'state of nature' – life would degenerate into a war of all against all, in which life would be 'solitary, poor, nasty, brutish and short'. He therefore defined sovereignty as a monopoly of coercive power and advocated that it be vested in the hands of a single ruler (whether this was a monarch, his preferred form of government, or an oligarchic group or even a democratic assembly). However, in line with the dual structure of the state, sovereignty can be understood in internal or external senses.

The concept of **internal sovereignty** refers to the location of power or authority *within* a state, and has been crucial to the development of state structures and systems of rule. Where, within a political system, should final and ultimate authority be located? Early thinkers, as already noted, were inclined to the belief that sovereignty should be vested in the hands of a single person, a monarch. Absolute monarchs described themselves as 'sovereigns', and could, as did Louis XIV of France in the seventeenth century, declare that they *were* the state. The most radical departure from this absolutist notion of sovereignty came in the eighteenth century with the Swiss political philosopher Jean-Jacques Rousseau's rejection of monarchical rule in favour of the notion of popular sovereignty. For Rousseau, ultimate authority was vested in the people themselves, expressed in the idea of the 'general will'. The doctrine of popular sovereignty has often been seen as the basis of the modern theory of democracy, inspiring, amongst other things, the liberal-democratic idea that the sole legitimate source of political authority is success in regular, fair and competitive elections. Nevertheless, some liberal thinkers warn that the concept of internal sovereignty is always tainted by its absolutist origins, arguing that the idea of an absolute and final source of authority is difficult to reconcile with the reality of diffused power and pluralist competition found within the modern democratic state. A state may, however, be considered sovereign over its people and territory despite the fact that there may be disputes or even confusion about the internal location of sovereign power. This is the notion of **external sovereignty**.

External sovereignty defines a state's relationship to other states and international actors. It establishes the state's capacity to act as an independent and autonomous entity in world affairs. As such, it is the form of sovereignty that is of crucial importance for global politics. External sovereignty, for example, provides the basis for international law (see p. 339). Not only does the United

● **Sovereignty**: The principle of absolute and unlimited power; the absence of a higher authority in either domestic or external affairs.

● **Internal sovereignty**: The notion of a supreme power/authority within the state, located in a body that makes decisions that are binding on all citizens, groups and institutions within the state's borders.

● **External sovereignty**: The absolute and unlimited authority of the state as an actor on the world stage, implying the absence of any higher authority in external affairs.

CONCEPT

The state

The state is a political association that establishes sovereign jurisdiction within defined territorial borders. In political theory, the state is usually defined in contrast to civil society: it encompasses institutions that are recognizably 'public' in that they are responsible for the collective organization of communal life, and are funded through taxation (the institutions of government, the courts, the military, nationalized industries, social security system, and so forth). In international politics, however, the state is usually defined from an external perspective, and so embraces civil society. In this view, a state is characterized by four features: a defined territory, a permanent population, an effective government and sovereignty. This means, in effect, that a state is equivalent to a country.

● Governance: Broadly, the various ways in which social life is coordinated, of which government is merely one.

Nations (UN) operate according to the principle of sovereign equality, allowing all states equal participation in international relations through membership of the General Assembly, but, most importantly, external sovereignty guarantees that the territorial integrity and political independence of each state is inviolable. Similarly, many of the deepest divisions in world politics involve disputed claims to external sovereignty. The Arab–Israeli conflict, for instance, turns on the question of external sovereignty. The Palestinians have long sought to establish a homeland and, ultimately, a sovereign state in territory claimed by Israel (see p. 119); in turn, Israel has traditionally seen such demands as a challenge to its own sovereignty.

Nevertheless, the notion of external sovereignty has been the subject of growing controversy, with questions being raised about both its moral implications and its practical significance. Moral concerns have been raised because external sovereignty appears to allow states to treat their citizens however they please, including, possibly, subjecting them to abuse, torture and perhaps even genocide (see p. 333). There is therefore tension between the principle of external sovereignty and the doctrine of human rights (see p. 311), and indeed any global or cosmopolitan standard of justice. This tension has been particularly evident in relation to the issue of humanitarian intervention (see p. 326), as discussed in Chapter 13. Concerns about the practical significance of external sovereignty have also become more acute. In a sense, the disparity in power between and amongst states has always raised questions about the meaningfulness of sovereignty, powerful states being able, sometimes routinely, to infringe on the independence and autonomy of weaker states. However, a range of modern developments have put states under pressure perhaps as never before, leading to predictions about the 'end of sovereignty' and even the 'twilight of the state'. The most important of these are linked to the advance of globalization.

The state and globalization

The rise of globalization has stimulated a major debate about the power and significance of the state in a globalized world. Three contrasting positions can be identified. In the first place, some theorists have boldly proclaimed the emergence of 'post-sovereign governance' (Scholte 2005), suggesting that the rise of globalization is inevitably marked by the decline of the state as a meaningful actor. In the most extreme version of this argument, advanced by so-called 'hyperglobalists', the state is seen to be so 'hollowed out' as to have become, in effect, redundant. Realists, on the other hand, tend to deny that globalization has altered the core feature of world politics, which is that, as in earlier eras, sovereign states are the primary determinants of what goes on within their borders, and remain the principal actors on the world stage. Between these two views, however, is a third position, which acknowledges that globalization has brought about qualitative changes in the role and significance of the state, and in the nature of sovereignty, but emphasizes that these have transformed the state, rather than simply reduced or increased its power.

It is very difficult to argue that the state and sovereignty have been unaffected by the forces of globalization. This particularly applies in the case of the territorial jurisdiction of the state. The traditional theory of sovereignty was based on the idea that states had supreme control over what took place within their

GLOBAL POLITICS IN ACTION . . .

The Palestinian quest for statehood

Events: In September 2011, Mahmoud Abbas, the chairman of the Palestine Liberation Organization (PLO), submitted a formal request for Palestine's admittance as a full-member state into the United Nations. The following month, the executive committee of UNESCO backed this bid in a 107–14 vote. In November 2012, the General Assembly of the UN voted overwhelmingly to recognize Palestine as a 'non-member observer state', giving Palestine access to other UN bodies, including the International Criminal Court. The emergence of a national consciousness amongst Palestinian Arabs can be traced back to a pre-WWI reaction against increasing Jewish immigration into Palestine (then loosely part of the Ottoman Empire), which was strengthened during WWI by British encouragement for Arab nationalism.

The establishment of the state of Israel in 1948 meant that the majority of Arab Palestinians became refugees, a problem exacerbated by the 1967 Six-Day War, after which Sinai, the Gaza Strip, the West Bank and the Golan Heights were occupied by Israel. The Oslo Accords of 1993, the first face-to-face meeting between the PLO and the government of Israel, prepared the way for the establishment in 1996 of the Palestinian National Authority, which assumed governmental authority, but not sovereignty, for the West Bank and the Gaza Strip.

Significance: The Palestinian quest for statehood has both legal and political dimensions. The legal status of Palestine is a matter of controversy and some confusion. The founding of the PLO in 1964, uniting a disparate collection of Palestinian Arab groups, did much to strengthen the notion of the Palestinians as a nation or people, separate from the larger Arab people and from existing states, such as Jordan, Egypt, Syria and Lebanon. However, it was not until the establishment of the Palestinian Authority that the Palestinians could be said to have a defined territory and an effective government, albeit one that lacked *de jure* and *de facto* sovereignty. The status of Palestine crucially underlines the role of the UN in establishing statehood through formal recognition. Palestine's transition from being a 'non-state entity' with an observer status in the UN General Assembly (granted in 1974) to being a 'non-member observer state' has not been endorsed by the UN Security Council and falls short of full membership of the UN, and thus full statehood.

Nevertheless, as of April 2013, 132 of the UN's 193 members had recognized the existence of the state of Palestine.

The political dimension of Palestinian statehood is substantially more important, however. The 'Palestinian problem' lies at the heart of the Arab–Israeli conflict and has poisoned the politics of the Middle East for decades. It is thus difficult to imagine meaningful progress in building mutual respect and understanding between the West and Islam, especially the Arab world, without improved relations between Israel and the Palestinians. Those who support Palestine's quest for statehood usually view the so-called 'two-state' solution as the only viable solution to the Israeli–Palestinian conflict. In this view, the continuing denial of the Palestinians' right to sovereign independence can only strengthen political extremism, hostility towards Israel and, probably, violence. However, the creation of a Palestinian state may be difficult to achieve in practical terms. Not only is the Palestinian Authority divided territorially and politically (Hamas, the Palestinian militant group, controls the Gaza Strip, while the Fatah wing of the PLO governs the West Bank), but if a Palestinian state were constructed in line with the 1967 borders, this would mean that some 500,000 Israelis would be defined as living in another country. Many in Israel, nevertheless, have deeper reservations about the 'two-state' solution. For them, implacable Palestinian hatred of the state of Israel would mean that a sovereign Palestinian state would pose an ongoing, and intolerable, threat to the security and survival of Israel itself.

borders, implying that they also controlled what crossed their borders. However, developments such as the rise of international migration and the spread of cultural globalization (see p. 151) have tended to make state borders increasingly 'permeable'. This can be seen in the growth of cross-border communications and information flows through, for instance, radio, satellite television, mobile telephones and the Internet, which occur both at a speed and in quantities that defy the capacity of any state to detect them, still less effectively control them. Most of the discussion about the changing nature and power of the state has, nevertheless, concerned the impact of economic globalization (see p. 98). One of the central features of economic globalization is the rise of 'supraterritoriality', reflected in the declining importance of territorial locations, geographical distance and state borders. An increasing range of economic activities take place within a 'borderless world' (Ohmae 1990). This is particularly clear in relation to financial markets that have become genuinely globalized, in that capital flows around the world seemingly instantaneously, meaning, for instance, that no state can be insulated from the impact of financial crises that take place in other parts of the world. It is also evident in the changing balance between the power of territorial states and 'de-territorialized' transnational corporations, which can switch investment and production to other parts of the world if state policy is not conducive to profit maximization and the pursuit of corporate interests. Globalization, furthermore, has been closely associated with a trend towards regionalization, reflected in the growing prominence of regional trading blocs such as the European Union (EU) and the North American Free Trade Agreement (NAFTA).

If borders have become permeable and old geographical certainties have been shaken, state sovereignty, at least in its traditional sense, cannot survive. This is the sense in which governance in the twenty-first century has assumed a genuinely post-sovereign character. It is difficult, in particular, to see how economic sovereignty can be reconciled with a globalized economy. Sovereign control over economic life was only possible in a world of discrete national economies; the tendency of national economies to be incorporated to a greater or lesser extent into a single globalized economy renders economic sovereignty meaningless. As Susan Strange (1996) put it, 'where states were once masters of markets, now it is the markets which, on many issues, are the masters over the governments of states'. However, the rhetoric of a 'borderless' global economy can be taken too far. For example, there is evidence that, while globalization may have changed the strategies that states adopt to ensure economic success, it has by no means rendered the state redundant as an economic actor. As discussed later in this section, states retain a vital role in bringing about economic modernization. At the very least, there is a growing recognition that market-based economies can only operate effectively within a context of legal and social order that only the state can provide. Moreover, although states, when acting separately, may have a diminished capacity to control transnational economic activity, they retain the facility to do so through macro frameworks of economic regulation, as provided by the G-20, the World Trade Organization (WTO), (see p.535) and the International Monetary Fund (IMF) (see p. 475).

The power and significance of the state has undoubtedly been affected by the process of political globalization (see p. 122). However, its impact has been complex and, in some ways, contradictory. On the one hand, international

● **Supraterritoriality**: A condition in which social life transcends territory through the growth of 'transborder' and 'transglobal' communications and interactions.

● **Economic sovereignty**: The absolute authority of the state over how economic life is conducted within its borders, involving independent control of fiscal and monetary policies, and trade and capital flows.

GROUP OF TWENTY

Type: International economic forum • **Established:** 1999 • **Membership:** 20 countries

The Group of Twenty (G-20) Finance Ministers and Central Bank Governors was established in 1999 in response both to the financial crises of the late 1990s and a growing recognition that key emerging states were not adequately included in the core of global economic discussion and governance. There are no formal criteria for G-20 membership and the composition of the group has remained unchanged since it was established (Argentina, Australia, Brazil, Canada, China, France, Germany, India, Indonesia, Italy, Japan, Mexico, Russia, Saudi Arabia, South Africa, South Korea, Turkey, the UK, the USA and the EU). The group includes most, but not all, the leading economies in the world, thereby comprising, collectively, around 90 per cent of world GNP, but factors such as geographical balance (members are drawn from all continents) and population representation (about two-thirds of the global population is represented) also played a major part. Like the G-7/8 (see p. 472), the G-20 operates as an informal forum to promote dialogue between finance ministers, central bankers and heads of government, with no permanent location and no permanent staff of its own. However, at its Pittsburgh Summit in September 2009, heads of government agreed to provide the G-20 with wider resources and a permanent staff. Within the G-20, each member has one voice, regardless of its economic strength or population size.

Significance: In its early years, the G-20 was a relatively peripheral body, certainly less significant than the G-8. This, however, changed with the outbreak of the global financial crisis in 2007–09. Developed states, recognizing that their economic fate depended largely on a globally-coordinated response to the crisis, were eager to join with developing states, and saw the G-20 as the forum for doing this. The G-8, by contrast, suddenly appeared to be hopelessly antiquated, particularly as it excluded the emerging economies of China, India, South Africa, Mexico and Brazil. The G-20's growing stature was underlined by the fact that the global response to the crisis largely emerged out of its Washington and London summits, in November 2008 and April 2009, respectively. At the heart of this response was the agreement by G-20 members to contribute $500 billion to a programme of global reflation. A start was also made on reforming the institutions of global economic governance by the agreement to expand the IMF's borrowing programme and by urging that voting shares on the IMF and the World Bank be rebalanced to boost the representation of the developing world. At the Pittsburgh summit, it was decided that the G-20 would replace the G-8 as the main forum for promoting international economic cooperation.

The rise of the G-20 has been heralded as marking a potentially historic shift. Its high degree of inclusion and representativeness may indicate the emergence of a new institutional world order that better reflects current economic realities and thereby enjoys greater global legitimacy. By comparison, the G-8, the IMF, the World Bank and the UN (through the Security Council) concentrate global decision-making in the hands of just a few states. The G-20 has, nevertheless, also attracted criticism. First, its prominence may be temporary and specifically linked to the peculiarities of a global financial crisis in which developed and developing states recognized that they were 'in the same boat'. Developing a globally-coordinated response over issues such as climate change and world trade, where the interests of the developed and developing worlds often diverge, may be much more difficult. Second, the G-20, even transformed into a permanent body, remains toothless. It castigates countries judged to be behaving irresponsibly, condemns weak financial regulation at national and global levels, and takes a stance on matters such as bankers' bonuses, but it lacks the capacity to impose its will, still less to punish transgressors. Third, although the G-20 clearly provides better representation than the G-8, its membership is selected arbitrarily and excludes some rich states and all the world's poorest states. The G-20's key players are also firmly wedded to a mainstream economic philosophy that favours the market and globalization, albeit a more regulated form of globalization.

● **Pooled sovereignty:** The combined sovereignty of two or more states; 'pooling' sovereignty implies gaining access to greater power and influence than state/national sovereignty.

● **Collectivized state:** A state that seeks to abolish private enterprise and sets up a centrally planned, or 'command', economy.

bodies such as the UN (see p. 456), the EU (see p. 509), NATO (see p. 259) and the WTO have undermined the capacity of states to operate as self-governing units. It is clear, for instance, that membership of the EU threatens state power, because a growing range of decisions (for example, on monetary policy, agricultural and fisheries policies, and the movement of goods and people within the EU) are made by European institutions rather than by member states. The range and importance of decisions that are made at an intergovernmental or supranational level has nevertheless undoubtedly increased, forcing states either to exert influence through regional or global bodies, or to operate within frameworks established by them. The WTO, for instance, operates as the judge and jury of global trade disputes and serves as a forum for negotiating trade deals between and among its members. Such tendencies reflect the fact that in an interconnected world, states have a diminishing capacity to act alone, because they are increasingly confronted by challenges and threats that have a transnational if not a global dimension.

On the other hand, political globalization opens up opportunities for the state as well as diminishing them. Working through international organizations and regimes (see p. 71) may expand the capacities of the state, allowing them to continue to extend their influence within a globalized and interconnected world. This occurs when states 'pool' their sovereignty. The notion of **pooled sovereignty** has been most explicitly developed in relation to the EU, but could just as well be applied to any other international organization. By 'pooling' sovereignty, member states transfer certain powers from national governments to EU institutions, thereby gaining access to a larger and more meaningful form of sovereignty. In this view, sovereignty is not a zero-sum game: the pooled sovereignty of the EU is, at least potentially, greater than the combined national sovereignties that compose it, because, in this case, a regional body is able to exert greater influence in a globalized world than the member states could if each acted individually.

State transformation

Globalizing tendencies have not only cast doubt over the continued relevance of the principle of state sovereignty, but also, arguably, reshaped the nature and role of the state itself. As a historical institution, the state has undergone a variety of transformations. The rise of nationalism from the early nineteenth century onwards led to the creation of the nation-state (see p. 168), which allied the state as a system of centralized rule to nationhood as a source of social cohesion and political legitimacy. Thereafter, the quest for national self-determination became the principal motor behind state construction (as discussed in Chapter 7). For much of the twentieth century, the state was characterized by its expanding social and economic role. The most extreme example of this was the development of **collectivized states**, which attempted to bring the entirety of economic life under state control. The best examples of such states were in orthodox communist countries such as the Soviet Union and throughout Eastern Europe. States in the capitalist world nevertheless also demonstrated a marked tendency towards economic and social intervention, albeit of a more modest kind. In their case, this involved the adoption of Keynesian strategies of economic management and a strengthening of social protection, leading to the development of the welfare state. The ability to deliver prosperity and to protect citizens from social deprivation thus became the principal source of legitimacy in most states.

Since the 1980s, however, many commentators have drawn attention to the progressive 'hollowing out' of the state, giving rise, allegedly, to a new state form. This has been variously described as the 'competition' state, the 'market' state (Bobbitt 2002) and the 'postmodern' state (Cooper 2004). The most common explanation for this has been the changed relationship between the state and the market that has been brought about by the pressures generated by economic globalization. This is reflected in the general trend towards neoliberalism (see p. 93), most dramatically demonstrated by the transition from collectivized to market-based economies in former communist countries during the 1990s, but it was also evident, to some degree, across the globe through the adoption of policies of privatization, deregulation and the 'rolling back' of welfare provision. Globalization can be seen to have promoted such developments in at least three ways. First, a greater exposure to global markets has encouraged many countries to adopt strategies designed to attract foreign capital and inward investment, namely policies of financial and economic deregulation. Second, intensified foreign competition forced countries to keep wage levels low and to promote labour flexibility, which meant scaling down welfare costs and other impediments to international competitiveness. Third, TNCs acquired growing influence at the expense of the state, by virtue of the ease with which they are able to relocate production and investment in a globalized economy if state policy is insufficiently responsive to corporate interests.

However, the changed relationship between markets and states may not simply mean a *reduced* role for the state but, rather, a *different* role for the state. The state may have been transformed, not eclipsed altogether (Sørensen 2004). Robert Cox (see p. 124) has argued that the growing global organization of production and finance had transformed conventional conceptions of government and society, leading to the 'internationalization of the state'. This is the process whereby national institutions, policies and practices become little more than an instrument for restructuring national economies in line with the dynamics of the global capitalist economy. Although this implies that states have lost substantial power over the economy, the process of economic globalization nevertheless requires a political framework that is provided by the state, notably in the form of the 'military-territorial power of an enforcer' (Cox 1994). In the modern global economy, this role has largely been assumed by the USA.

Bob Jessop (2002) described the advent of a more market-orientated state in terms of a move away from the 'Keynesian welfare national state', towards what he called the 'Schumpeterian competition state'. The competition state is a state that aims to secure economic growth within its borders by securing competitive advantages in the wider global economy. Competition states are distinguished by the recognition of the need to strengthen education and training as the principal way of guaranteeing economic success in the new technology-dependent economy, and this approach was adopted by the Asian 'tiger' economies from the 1970s onwards. Although they attempt to increase market responsiveness by promoting entrepreneurialism and labour flexibility, competition states are also aware of the need to combat social exclusion and bolster the moral foundations of society. To some extent, the advance of the competition state is evident in a

● Welfare state: A state that takes prime responsibility for the social welfare of its citizens, discharged through a range of social security, health, education and other services (albeit different in different counties).

● Competition state: A state that pursues strategies to ensure long-term competitiveness in the globalized economy.

Robert Cox (born 1926)

Canadian international political economist and leading exponent of critical theory. Cox worked in the International Labour Organization (ILO), before, in the early 1970s, taking up an academic career. Cox adopted a 'reflexive' approach to theory, in which theories are firmly linked to their context and subject. In his seminal work, *Production, Power, and World Order: Social Forces in the Making of History* (1987), he examined the relationship between material forces of production, ideas and institutions in three periods: the liberal international economy (1789–1873); the era of rival imperialisms (1873–1945); and the neoliberal world order (post-1945). His writing examines issues such as the implications of globalization and the nature of US global hegemony, in part to highlight the prospects for counter-hegemonic social forces. Cox's other major writings include (with H. Jacobson) *The Anatomy of Influence* (1972) and (with Timothy J. Sinclair) *Approaches to World Order* (1996).

wider shift from so-called 'demand-side' economics (which encourages consumers to consume, by, for instance, Keynesian reflation) to 'supply-side' economics (which encourages producers to produce, by, for example, improved education and training, labour flexibility and deregulation).

The notion of the 'postmodern state' has been associated in particular with the writings of Robert Cooper (2004). In Cooper's analysis, the post-Cold War world is divided into three parts, each characterized by a distinctive state structure – the 'pre-modern', 'modern' and 'postmodern' worlds. The postmodern world is a world in which force has been rejected as a means of resolving disputes, order being maintained instead through a respect for the rule of law and a willingness to operate through multilateral institutions. Security in such a world is based on transparency, mutual openness, interdependence and, above all, a recognition of mutual vulnerability. The states appropriate to such a world, 'postmodern' states, are more pluralist, more complex and less centralized than the bureaucratic 'modern' states they have replaced, and they also tend to be less nationalistic, allowing, even encouraging, multiple identities to thrive. Postmodern states are characterized by both the wider role played by private organizations in the processes of governance and the fact that government's role is increasingly orientated around the promotion of personal development and personal consumption. As Cooper (2004) put it, 'Individual consumption replaces collective glory as the dominant theme of national life'. In terms of their external orientation, postmodern states are distinguished by their unwarlike character, reflected in the application of moral consciousness to international relations and a rejection of the balance of power (see p. 262) as unworkable in the post-Cold War era. On this basis, the only clear examples of postmodern states are found in Europe, with the EU perhaps being an example of a postmodern proto-state.

However, the plight of the state is most serious in the case of the 'pre-modern' world. Cooper portrayed this as a world of post-imperial chaos, in which such state structures as exist are unable to establish (in Weber's words) a legitimate

THE STATE

Realist view

Realists tend to view states from the outside; that is, from the perspective of the international system. Above all, they take states to be unitary and coherent actors; indeed, they are commonly portrayed as the basic 'units' of the international system. Their unitary and cohesive character derives from the fact that, regardless of their domestic make-up, state leaders speak and act on behalf of their respective states and can deploy their populations and resources as they wish or choose. State behaviour is determined by a single, overriding motive – 'the wish to survive' (Waltz 2002) – although realists disagree about whether this implies merely a defensive desire to avoid invasion and attack or an aggressive wish to maximize power and achieve domination (see Offensive or defensive realism?). The social, constitutional, political and social composition of the state is therefore irrelevant to its external behaviour. In this sense, the state is a 'black box'. Neorealists in particular insist that states differ only in terms of their 'capabilities', or power resources (there are great powers, (see p. 6), minor powers and so on). All realists nevertheless agree that the state is the dominant global actor; hence they adopt a state-centric view of global politics. For example, from a realist perspective, globalization and the state are not separate or, still less, opposing forces: rather, globalization has been created by states and thus exists to serve their interests. Other actors thus only exert influence to the extent that the state allows.

Liberal view

Liberals believe that the state arises out of the needs of society and reflects the interests of individual citizens. 'Social contract theory' suggests that the state was established through an agreement amongst citizens to create a sovereign power in order to escape from the chaos and brutality of the 'state of nature' (a stateless, or pre-political, society). The core role of the state is thus to ensure order by arbitrating between the competing individuals and groups in society. The state thus acts as a referee or umpire. This implies that changes in the structure of society can and will alter the role and power of the state. Liberals, as a result,

have been less willing than realists to view the state as the dominant global actor, usually adopting instead a mixed-actor model of world politics. Indeed, liberals have generally accepted that globalization has been marked by the decline of the state (and perhaps the transition from nation-states to 'postmodern' or 'market' states), as power has shifted away from the state and towards, in particular, global markets and transnational corporations (TNCs) (see p. 94), but also to individuals. Furthermore, liberals insist that the constitutional and political make-up of the state has a crucial impact on its external behaviour. In particular, republican liberals argue that democratic states are inherently more peaceable than non-democratic states (Doyle 1986).

Critical views

Critical theorists reject both realist state-centrism and liberal assertions about the retreat of the state, but they do so in different ways. Neo-Marxists and post-Marxist theorists may have abandoned the orthodox Marxist belief that the (capitalist) state is merely a reflection of the class system, but they continue to argue that state structures and, for that matter, world orders are grounded in social relations. The mutual dependence between markets and states has in fact intensified as a result of globalization, leading to what Cox (1993) called the 'internationalization of the state'. Social constructivists deny that the state has a fixed and objective character; rather, the identity of the state is shaped by a variety of historical and sociological factors, and these, in turn, inform the interests of the state and its actions. Wendt (1999), for example, distinguished between the social identity of the state (shaped by the status, role or personality that international society ascribes to a state) and its corporate identity (shaped by internal material, ideological and cultural factors). Feminist theorists have been ambivalent about the state. While liberal feminists have believed that it is possible to reform the state from within, by increasing female representation at all levels, radical feminists have highlighted structural links between the state and the system of male power, believing that the state has an intrinsically patriarchal character.

CONCEPT

Failed state

A failed state is a state that is unable to perform its key role of ensuring domestic order by monopolizing the use of force within its territory. Examples of failed states in recent years include Cambodia, Haiti, Rwanda, Liberia and Somalia. Failed states are no longer able to operate as viable political units, in that they lack a credible system of law and order, often being gripped by civil war or warlordism. They are also no longer able to operate as viable economic units, in that they are incapable of providing for their citizens and have no functioning infrastructure. Although relatively few states collapse altogether, a much larger number barely function and are dangerously close to collapse.

monopoly of the use of force, thus leading to endemic **warlordism**, widespread criminality and social dislocation. Such conditions do not apply consistently to the developing world as a whole, however. In cases such as India, South Korea and Taiwan, developing world states have been highly successful in pursuing strategies of economic modernization and social development. Others, nevertheless, have been distinguished by their weakness, sometimes being portrayed as 'weak' states, 'quasi-states' or 'failed states'. Most of the weakest states in the world are concentrated in sub-Saharan Africa, classic examples being Somalia, Sierra Leone, Liberia and the Democratic Republic of the Congo. These states fail the most basic test of state power: they are unable to maintain domestic order and personal security, meaning that civil strife and even civil war become almost routine. Failed states are nevertheless not just a domestic problem. They often have a wider impact through, for instance, precipitating refugee crises, providing a refuge for drug dealers, arms smugglers and terrorist organizations, generating regional instability, and provoking external intervention to provide humanitarian relief and to keep the peace.

The failure of such states stems primarily from the experience of colonialism, which, when it ended (mainly in the post-1945 period) bequeathed formal political independence to societies that lacked an appropriate level of political, economic, social and educational development to function effectively as separate entities. As the borders of such states typically represented the extent of colonial ambition rather than the existence of a culturally cohesive population, postcolonial states also often encompassed deep ethnic, religious and tribal divisions. Failed states are thus failed, postcolonial states. Nevertheless, colonialism does not, on its own, explain the weakness or failure of the postcolonial state. Other sources of state failure include internal factors, such as the existence of social elites, backward institutions and parochial value systems which block the transition from pre-industrial, agrarian societies to modern industrial ones, and external factors, notably the impact of TNCs and neo-colonialism.

Return of the state

Discourse about the state in the early twenty-first century has been dominated by talk of retreat or decline. State sovereignty is routinely dismissed as an irrelevance and states are viewed as dinosaurs waiting to die. The reality is more complex, however. Realist and other state-centric commentators argue that the impact of globalization in its economic, cultural and political forms has always been exaggerated: states remain the decisive political actors. Nevertheless, a number of developments in recent years have helped to strengthen the state and to underline its essential importance. What explains the return of the state? In the first place, the state's unique capacity to maintain domestic order and protect its citizens from external attack has been strongly underlined by new security challenges that have emerged in the twenty-first century, notably those linked to transnational terrorism (see p. 294). This underlines what Bobbitt (2002) viewed as a basic truth: 'The State exists to master violence'; it is therefore essentially a 'warmaking institution'. The decline in military expenditure that occurred at the end of the Cold War, the so-called 'peace dividend', started to be reversed in the late 1990s, with global military expenditure rising steeply after the 9/11 terrorist attacks and the launch of the 'war on terror'. The USA with its massive military

● **Warlordism**: A condition in which locally-based militarized bands vie for power in the absence of a sovereign state.

Focus on ...
Problems of state-building

Why is the process of state-building often so difficult? What challenges does successful state-building have to overcome? At least three significant challenges stand out. The first is that new or reformed institutions and structures have to be constructed in a context of often deep political and ethnic tension and endemic poverty. For example, in Afghanistan, a country in which no internal or external power has ever long held sway, there are 50 ethnic or sub-tribal groups, 34 languages and 27 million people, together with widespread internecine feuds and counter-feuds. The task of developing a unifying national leadership in such a context is therefore highly problematical.

Second, indigenous leadership and new institutions need to enjoy a significant measure of legitimacy. This is why state-building is invariably linked to the promo-

tion of 'good governance', with the eradication of corruption being a key goal. However, the democratization that 'good governance' implies may make the task of state-building more difficult, not least by bringing ethnic and other tensions to the surface and by exposing the flaws and failings of emergent institutions. Finally, state-building may involve the imposition of an essentially western model of political organization unsuited to the needs of developing countries that are more accustomed to traditional tribal models of governance in which interdependent groups are united by a shared ethnic identity. If the western assumption that the state is a universal institution, the only viable alternative to chaos and brutality, is unfounded, then the task of state-building may be doomed.

budget has been the principal determinant of the current world trend, but military spending has also grown significantly in China, France, the UK, Russia and elsewhere. Moreover, many countries have taken steps to strengthen the inviolability of the state as a territorial unit by imposing tighter border controls. Counter-terrorism strategies have often meant that states have assumed wider powers of surveillance, control and sometimes detention, even becoming 'national security states'.

Second, although the days of command-and-control economic management may be over, the state has sometimes reasserted itself as an agent of modernization. The myth of neoliberalism is that prosperity and growth are purely a result of the dynamism of the market. In fact, market economies can only operate successfully in conditions of legal and social order that only states can guarantee. This applies particularly in the case of the rule of law and the enforcement of property rights, without which economic activity would end up being determined by threats, bribes and the use of violence. Beyond this, however, modernizing states develop and implement strategies to ensure long-term economic success. 'Competition states' do this by improving education and training in order to boost productivity and by providing support for key export industries. States such as China and Russia each modernized their economies by making significant concessions to the market, but an important element of state control has been retained or re-imposed (these developments are examined in more detail in Chapter 3 in relation to state capitalism). On a wider level, the state's vital role in economic affairs was underlined by the 2007–09 global financial crisis. Although the G-20 may have provided states with a forum to develop a

Debating . . .

Is state sovereignty now an outdated concept?

State sovereignty has traditionally been viewed as the core principle of the international system. However, while some argue that globalization and other developments have changed the international system fundamentally, others suggest that the basic contours of the international system remain essentially unchanged.

YES

Permeable borders. State borders, the traditional guarantee of territorial sovereignty, are permeable in that they have increasingly been penetrated by external forces. These include international tourism and the movement of knowledge and information via the Internet. Global financial markets and transnational capital flows mean that economic sovereignty has become redundant. If the conventional domestic/international divide is increasingly difficult to sustain, states are no longer meaningful territorial units.

Rise of non-state actors. States are no longer the only, or necessarily the dominant, actors on the world stage. Transnational corporations (TNCs) wield greater financial power than many states, and can effectively dictate state policy through their ability to relocate production and investment at ease in a globalized economy. Non-governmental organizations (NGOs) such as Greenpeace and Amnesty International exert global influence. And state security is as likely to be threatened by global terrorist organizations such as al-Qaeda as it is by other states.

Collective dilemmas. In modern circumstances, states are increasingly confronted by collective dilemmas, issues that are particularly taxing because they confound even the most powerful of states when acting alone. Quite simply, global problems require global solutions. An increasing range of issues have acquired a collective or even global character – climate change, terrorism, transnational crime, pandemic diseases, international migration and so on. Only international organizations, not supposedly sovereign states, can tackle these.

International human rights. Respect for state sovereignty has been eroded by the growing belief that there are standards of conduct to which all states should conform as far as the treatment of their domestic populations is concerned. Such a view is usually based on a belief in human rights (see p. 311), and the idea that the fundamental individual rights are morally superior to the state's right to independence and autonomy. This is evident in shifts in international law, Chapter 14), and in the wider acceptance of humanitarian intervention (see p. 326).

NO

Myth of the 'borderless world'. The image that world politics is dominated by transnational processes that elude state control is, at best, a gross exaggeration. For example, national economies have not simply been absorbed into a 'borderless' global economy, as much more economic activity takes place within state borders than it does across state borders. Furthermore, it is misleading to suggest that globalizing trends necessarily disempower states. Instead, states *choose* to engage in the global economy and do so for reasons of national self-interest.

States remain dominant. Although states are merely one actor amongst many on the world stage, they remain the most important actor. States exercise power in a way and to an extent that no other actor can. In particular, using the administrative processes of government and relying on unchallengeable coercive power, their control over what happens within their territories is rarely challenged. Only a tiny proportion of states, those classified as 'failed' or 'weak' states, have effectively lost control over what happens within their borders.

Pooled sovereignty. The advance of political globalization and the emergence of a framework of global governance have not brought about an erosion of sovereignty. Rather, they expand the opportunities available to states, particularly for achieving the benefits of cooperation. International organizations are bodies that are formed by states, for states; they are invariably used by states as tools to achieve their own ends. Indeed, by working together, states are able to pool their sovereignty, gaining greater capacity and influence than they would have possessed working alone.

Enduring attraction of the nation-state. There seems little likelihood that states will lose their dominance so long as they continue to enjoy the allegiance of the mass of their citizens. As most states are nation-states, this is ensured by the survival of nationalism as the world's most potent ideological force. Rival doctrines such as cosmopolitanism and allegiances based, for instance, on religion, culture or ethnicity are of minor significance compared with nationalism.

coordinated global response, the massive packages of fiscal and other interventions that were agreed were, and could only have been, implemented by states. Indeed, some have seen the crisis as marking the watershed between three decades of anti-statist neoliberal globalization and a new era of regulated globalization, in which states, through international organizations or sometimes acting alone, play a more active economic role.

Finally, there has been a growing recognition of the role of the state in promoting development. This is reflected in an increased emphasis on **state-building** as a key aspect of the larger process of peace-building (see p. 452). The provision of humanitarian relief and the task of conflict resolution become almost insuperably difficult in the absence of a functioning system of law and order. The wider acceptance of humanitarian intervention since the early 1990s has meant that ordered rule is often provided, initially at least, by external powers. However, this does not constitute a long-term solution. As examples such as Somalia, Iraq and Afghanistan demonstrate, externally-imposed order is only sustainable for a limited period of time, both because the economic and human cost to the intervening powers may be unsustainable in the long-run, and because, sooner or later, the presence of foreign troops and police provokes resentment and hostility. Foreign intervention has therefore come, over time, to focus increasingly on the construction of effective indigenous leadership and building legitimate national institutions, such as an army, a police force, a judiciary, a central bank, government departments, local administration, a tax collection agency and functioning education, transport, energy and healthcare systems. The process of state-building is nevertheless often profoundly difficult.

NATIONAL GOVERNMENT TO MULTI-LEVEL GOVERNANCE

From government to governance

● **State-building**: The construction of a functioning state through the establishment of legitimate institutions for the formulation and implementation of policy across key areas of government.

● **Good governance**: Standards for the process of decision-making in society, including (according to the UN) popular participation, respect for the rule of law, transparency, responsiveness and accountability.

● **Hierarchy**: An organization that is based on graded ranks and a clear and usually top-down authority structure.

Changes to the role and significance of the state have also had important implications for the nature and functioning of government. Government refers to the formal and institutional processes which operate at the national level to maintain order and facilitate collective action. Its central feature is the ability to make collective decisions and the capacity to enforce them. Since the 1980s, however, it has become increasingly fashionable for international theorists and political analysts to talk more in terms of 'governance' (see p. 130) rather than 'government', with terms such as 'global governance' (see p. 462), 'good governance' and 'corporate governance' becoming commonplace. The so-called 'governance turn' in the study of international and domestic politics has been a consequence of a variety of developments. At the heart of these is the growing redundancy of the traditional notion of government as a **hierarchy** or collection of hierarchies. For Max Weber (1948), hierarchy, in the form of what he termed bureaucracy, was the typical form of organization in modern industrialized societies. It was typified by the existence of fixed and official areas of jurisdiction, clear laws or rules, and a firmly ordered hierarchy based on an established chain of command. The virtue of such a command-and-control system was supposedly its rationality: bureaucratization, according to Weber, reflected the advance of a reliable,

CONCEPT

Governance

'Governance' is a broader term than 'government'. Although it still has no settled or agreed definition, it refers, in its wider sense, to the various ways through which social life is co-ordinated. Governance is therefore a process (or a complex of processes), its principal modes including markets, hierarchies and networks. Although government may be involved in governance, it is possible to have 'governance without government'. Governance is typified by a blurring of the state/society distinction (private bodies and institutions work closely with public ones) and the involvement of a number of levels or layers (potentially local, provincial, national, regional and global). The processes through which international affairs are coordinated are increasingly referred to as 'global governance'.

predictable and, above all, efficient means of social organization. Bureaucracies or hierarchies thus developed in the military and the police, in schools and universities, and throughout the modern state in the growth of government departments and executive agencies. Similarly, the emergence of capitalist economies generating pressure for greater economic efficiency made large-scale corporations the dominant form of business organization in the twentieth century.

The shift from government to governance is a political reflection of the advent of more fluid and differentiated societies (as discussed in Chapter 6). Top-down authority structures have, in this context, been exposed as ineffective, unresponsive and perhaps redundant. The advent of governance thus parallels economic trends which have seen a transition from 'Fordist' models of business organization, based on large-scale mass production, to 'post-Fordist' ones (see p. 141) that emphasize flexibility, innovation and decentralized decision-making. Pressure to adjust the way governments behave and how governing is carried out came from a variety of sources. These include the fiscal crisis of the state that was precipitated by the end of the 'long boom' and the down-turn of the global economy in the 1970s. Whereas sustained economic growth in the 1950s and 1960s had underwritten, in developed societies at least, an expansion in the welfare and social responsibilities of the state, helping to strengthen faith in the efficacy of government, reduced tax revenues created a mismatch between people's expectations of government and what government could actually deliver. Governments had either to reduce popular expectations of government or to find new and more imaginative ways of delivering government services more cheaply and efficiently. A further set of pressures were generated in the 1980s and 1990s by the ideological shift towards free-market or neoliberal priorities. Pursued most radically through Reaganism in the USA and Thatcherism in the UK but affecting almost all societies to some degree, this set out to dismantle 'big government' in the belief that the economy worked best when regulated by market forces and that the individual should be liberated from the tyranny of the 'nanny state'. Economic globalization has also played a major role in this process. The integration of national economies to a greater or lesser degree into a single global economy has exposed all countries to intensified competitive pressures, creating a 'race to the bottom' as governments seek to attract or retain private investment by cutting taxes, deregulating economic life and promoting more flexible labour markets.

How have governments adapted themselves in the light of these circumstances? The shift to a governance mode of governing has been evident in at least three, albeit related developments. First, the role of government has been redefined and in some senses narrowed. Instead of 'rowing' (that is, administering and delivering services), the tasks of government have increasingly been confined to 'steering' (that is, setting targets and strategic objectives). This, in part, acknowledges the inefficiency and unresponsiveness of traditional public administration by comparison in particular with private businesses or 'third sector' bodies such as charities, community groups and NGOs (see p. 10). In the USA, where such ideas were born and most enthusiastically embraced, the shift in responsibility for 'rowing' has been described as 'reinventing government' (Osborne and Gaebler 1992). Second, there has been a significant blurring of the distinction between government and markets and thus between the public and private realms. This has happened in a variety of ways: for example, through the 'contracting out' of public services or full-scale privatization, by the growth in public–private partnerships and the introduction of 'internal markets' in public service delivery, and by the introduction into the public sector of private sector management styles and structures through the so-called 'new public management'. Third, there has been a shift from hierarchies to networks within the processes of government, which has led Castells (1996) to proclaim the emergence of a 'network state' alongside the 'network society' and the 'network corporation'. For instance, the tasks of developing and sometimes implementing policy have increasingly been transferred from hierarchical departments to **policy networks**, as networks have proved to be particularly effective in facilitating the exchange of and coordinating social life in a context of increasing complexity.

Multi-level governance

The transition from government to governance is reflected not only in the more complex ways through which social life is now coordinated within modern societies – for example, through a wider role for markets and networks and the weakening of the public–private divide – but it is also evident in the 'stretching' of government across a number of levels. In other words, government can no longer be thought of as a specifically national activity which takes place within discrete societies. This has led to the phenomenon of '**multi-level governance**'. Policy-making responsibility has both been 'sucked up' and 'drawn down', creating a complex process of interactions (see Figure 24.1). The 'sucking up' of policy-making responsibility has occurred through the advent of political globalization and the growing importance of regional and global governance, as discussed earlier.

The 'drawing down' of policy-making responsibilities reflects a process of **decentralization**. For much of the twentieth century, most states exhibited a

● **Policy network**: A systematic set of relationships between political actors who share a common interest or general orientation in a particular area.

● **Multi-level governance**: A pattern of overlapping and interrelated public authority that stems from the growth, or growing importance, of supranational and subnational bodies.

● **Decentralization**: The expansion of local autonomy through the transfer of powers and responsibilities away from national bodies.

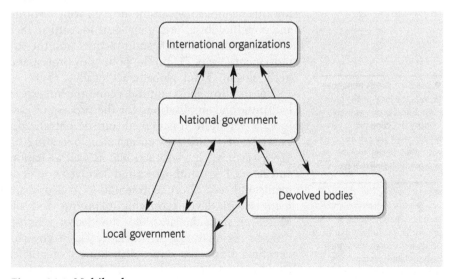

Figure 24.1 **Multilevel governance**

distinct trend towards centralization, largely as a consequence of their expanding economic and social roles. Central government has clear advantages over peripheral bodies in terms of its ability to manage the economy and deliver a widening range of public services, not least because of its significantly greater fiscal capacity. However, since about the 1960s this trend has often been reversed, giving way to a countervailing tendency towards **localization**. In many cases, this has been reflected in the growth or strengthening of peripheral or sub-national political bodies. For example, on achieving independence in 1947, India adopted a US-style federal system rather than a UK-style unitary one. As part of its transition to democratic government following the death of General Franco in 1975, Spain adopted a system of **devolution**, which led to the creation of 17 autonomous communities, each based on an elected assembly invested with broad control of domestic policy. In 1982, France developed its strategy of 'functional regionalism' into a fully-fledged system of regional government, based on 22 directly-elected regional councils. In the UK, the introduction of devolution in the late 1990s led to the creation of a Scottish Parliament, a Welsh Assembly and a Northern Ireland Assembly, and the emergence of a form of quasi-federalism.

Although localization may appear to be the antithesis of globalization, the two processes are closely, and perhaps intrinsically linked, as reflected in the notion of 'glocalization' (Robertson 1992). One of the key driving forces of localization has been the rise of cultural and ethnic politics, itself linked to the declining purchase of classical nationalism. In the late 1960s and early 1970s, secessionist groups and forms of ethnic nationalism sprang up in many parts of western Europe and North America. This was most evident in Quebec in Canada, Scotland and Wales in the UK, Catalonia and the Basque area in Spain, Corsica in France, and Flanders in Belgium. It created pressure for political decentralization, and sometimes, precipitated major constitutional upheavals. Similar manifestations of ethnic assertiveness were evident among the Native Americans in Canada and the USA, the Aboriginal peoples in Australia, and the Maoris in New Zealand. Other examples of localization include the tendency towards religious revivalism, through which Muslims, Christians, Hindus, Jews and even Buddhists have 'gone local' to reaffirm their faith through the adoption of fundamentalist beliefs and practices, and the stress within the anti-capitalist movement (see p. 74) on the politics of protest and political activism, reflected in the slogan: 'Think globally, act locally'.

Localization, in its cultural, economic but especially in its political form, has had profound implications for the process of governance, making the policy process yet more fragmented and decentralized. The EU provides the best example of multi-level governance, operating as it does through complex processes involving sub-national as well as national and supranational levels and actors. Local authorities and devolved bodies often bypass national governments and seek direct representation in Brussels, strengthening their involvement in EU-level economic planning and infrastructure development. Moreover, since the late 1980s the idea of a 'Europe of the Regions' has taken root, as regional and provincial levels of government have lobbied for, and benefited from, the direct distribution of aid from the European Regional Development Fund. Over time, regional aid has eclipsed agriculture as the largest single area of EU spending.

● **Localization**: A trend that favours the local as the basis for political action, cultural identity or economic organization, usually associated with the growing importance of sub-national governance.

● **Devolution**: The transfer of power from central government to subordinate regional or provincial institutions that have no share in sovereignty; their responsibilities and powers being derived entirely from the centre

CONCEPT

Federalism

Federalism (from the Latin *foedus*, meaning 'pact', or 'covenant') refers to legal and political structures that distribute power between two distinct levels of government, neither of which is subordinate to the other. Its central feature is therefore the principle of shared sovereignty. 'Classical' federations are few in number: the USA, Switzerland, Belgium, Canada and Australia. However, many more states have federal-type features. Most federal, or federal-type, states were formed by the coming together of a number of established political communities; they are often geographically large and may have culturally diverse populations. Federalism may nevertheless also have an international dimension, providing the basis, in particular, for regional integration, as in the case of 'European federalism'. (discussed in Chapter 20).

● Shared sovereignty: A constitutional arrangement in which sovereignty is divided between two levels of government, each exercising supreme and autonomous control over a specific range of issues.

● Foreign: (from the Latin *foris* meaning 'outside') Dealing or concerned with another country, area or people; implies strange or not familiar.

FOREIGN POLICY

End of foreign policy?

The making of foreign policy has traditionally been regarded as one of the key features of international politics. It reflects the importance of statecraft as an activity through which national governments manage their relations with other states and international bodies. Indeed, foreign policy-making has sometimes been thought of as a noble activity, seen as 'high' politics in that it deals with issues of sovereignty and security – in fact, the very survival of the state – as opposed to the 'low' politics of economics and other less important state activities. However, recent developments have called the concept of 'foreign policy' into question, certainly casting doubt on the conventional notion of foreign policy as a discrete activity, engaged in at a senior political level and involving formal diplomatic interactions between and amongst states. These pressures have came from various directions. In the first place, the emergence of neorealism in the late 1970s appeared to suggest that foreign policy, and indeed the wider process of decision-making in international politics, was simply no longer relevant. In the view of Kenneth Waltz (see p. 63) and others, state behaviour could essentially be explained through the power balances that shape the international system. As systemic factors were seen as decisively important, little or no role discretion was left to foreign policy actors, such as heads of government, foreign ministers, defence ministers, leading diplomats and so forth. The 'logic of anarchy' explained everything.

Further pressures have been generated by the advance of globalization and the growth of 'complex interdependence' (see p. 7). These developments dramatically widened and deepened the scope of the interactions between and amongst states. As the distinctions between home and abroad, inside and outside, and 'high' and 'low' politics became perhaps hopelessly blurred, the divide between 'foreign' politics and 'domestic' politics became increasingly difficult to sustain. If the notion of 'the foreign' is meaningless, can foreign policy any longer exist? The matter was made yet more problematical by the fact that globalizing trends have also been associated with the advent of post-sovereign governance and the burgeoning importance of non-state actors: TNCs, NGOs, terrorist groups, international organizations and so on. At the very least, this means that foreign policy can no longer be thought of simply as 'what states do to, or with, other states'.

Nevertheless, the study of foreign policy remains a worthwhile activity, for at least two reasons. First, although the foreign/domestic divide may have become blurred, it has not been rendered redundant. The simple fact is that the world is still more separated into distinctive communities than it is a single, homogenizing entity (Hill 2003). How these communities attempt to manage the relations between and among them therefore continues to be an interesting and important issue. Second, foreign policy highlights the crucial interplay between structure and agency, emphasizing that events can neither be explained entirely through 'top-down' systemic pressures nor entirely through 'bottom-up' individual decision-making (see Structure or agency? p. 76). In so doing, foreign policy underlines the crucial significance of a sphere of decision, choice and intentionality within global politics.

Foreign policy

Public policy lays out courses of action for government and its various agencies. Foreign policy refers, broadly, to attempts by governments to influence or manage events outside the state's borders, usually, but not exclusively, through their relations with foreign governments. Foreign policy-making involves the establishment of goals and the selection of means to achieve them. In view of the increased interpenetration of domestic and foreign affairs in modern global politics, the term 'external relations' is sometimes preferred to foreign policy, allowing for interactions that take place on multiple levels and which involve multiple actors. At the very least, the realm of foreign policy can no longer be confined simply to relations between foreign ministers/ ministries or between national diplomatic services.

How decisions are made

The making of decisions, and specifically of bundles of decisions, is clearly central to the policy process. Although policy-making also relates to the acts of initiation and implementation, the making of decisions and reaching of conclusions is usually seen as its key feature. However, it may be difficult to establish how and why decisions are made. In foreign policy-making a levels-of-analysis is commonly adopted, in line with the three levels at which Waltz (1959) analyzed the causes of war:

- The level of the *individual* decision-maker (involving personal priorities, psychological and cognitive dispositions and so on)
- The *nation-state* level (involving the nature of the state, type of government, bureaucratic structure and so on)
- The *systemic* level (involving power balances within the international system, the web of state interdependence, dynamics of global capitalism and so on).

Nevertheless, a number of general theories of political decision-making have been advanced. The most important of these are rational actor models, incremental models, bureaucratic organization models, and cognitive processes and belief-system models.

Rational actor models

Decision-making models that emphasize human rationality have generally been constructed on the basis of economic theories that have themselves been derived from utilitarianism. Developed by thinkers such as Anthony Downs (1957), these theories are usually based on the notion of 'economic man', a model of human nature that stresses the self-interested pursuit of material satisfaction, calculated in terms of utility (use-value; the balance of pleasure over pain). In this light, decisions can be seen to be reached using the following procedures:

- The nature of the problem is identified.
- An objective or goal is selected on the basis of an ordering of individual preferences.
- The available means of achieving this objective are evaluated in terms of their effectiveness, reliability, costs and so on.
- A decision is made through the selection of the means most likely to secure the desired end.

This type of process assumes both that clear-cut objectives exist, and that human beings are able to pursue them in a rational and consistent manner. The best example of such an approach to decision-making is found in the use of cost–benefit analysis in the making of business decisions. In line with the goal of profit maximization, business people make decisions that will ensure the least possible cost and the greatest possible benefit, both calculated in monetary terms. Realist theorists make similar assumptions about decision-making in

National interest

In broad terms, the national interest refers to foreign policy goals, objectives or policy preferences that benefit a society as a whole (the foreign policy equivalent of the 'public interest'). The concept is often vague and contested, however. It is most widely used by realist theorists, for whom it is defined by the structural implications of international anarchy and so is closely linked to national security, survival and the pursuit of power. For decision-making theorists, the national interest refers to the strategies and goals pursued by those responsible for the conduct of foreign policy, although this may mean that it degenerates into mere rhetoric. Alternatively, it may refer to foreign policy goals that have been endorsed through the democratic process.

● Incrementalism: The theory that decisions are made not in the light of clear-cut objectives, but through small adjustments dictated by changing circumstances.

international politics. In their view, foreign policy is guided by a single overriding goal: the pursuit of vital national interests, understood, at minimum, as ensuring state survival, and beyond that the pursuit of power to enable the state to achieve its national ambitions. This may be dictated by system-level pressures (as neorealists suggest) or by egoistical pressures that operate in and through the state itself (as classical realists argue); either way, it implies that the role of individual decision-makers is largely restricted to the selection of the best means of achieving a pre-determined end.

The rational actor model is attractive, in part, because it reflects how most people believe decisions *should* be made. Certainly, politicians and others are strongly inclined to portray their actions as both goal-orientated and the product of careful thought and deliberation. When examined more closely, however, rational calculation may not appear to be a particularly convincing model of decision-making. In the first place, in practice, decisions are often made on the basis of inadequate and sometimes inaccurate information. Such difficulties encouraged Herbert Simon (1983) to develop the notion of 'bounded rationality'. This acknowledges that, as it is impossible to analyze and select all possible courses of action, decision-making is essentially an act of compromising between differently valued and imprecisely calculated outcomes. Simon described this process as 'satisficing'. The second problem with rational actor models is that they ignore the role of perception; that is, the degree to which actions are shaped by beliefs and assumptions about reality, rather than by reality itself. Little or no importance is thus attached to individual and collective psychology or to the values and ideological leanings of decision-makers.

Incremental models

Incrementalism is often portrayed as the principal alternative to rational decision-making. David Braybrooke and Charles Lindblom (1963) termed this model 'disjointed incrementalism', neatly summed up by Lindblom (1959) as the 'science of muddling through'. This position holds that, in practice, decisions tend to be made on the basis of inadequate information and low levels of understanding, and this discourages decision-makers from pursuing bold and innovative courses of action. Policy-making is therefore a continuous, exploratory process: lacking overriding goals and clear-cut ends, policy-makers tend to operate within an existing pattern or framework, adjusting their position in the light of feedback in the form of information about the impact of earlier decisions. Indeed, incrementalism may suggest a strategy of avoidance or evasion, policy-makers being inclined to move away from problems, rather than trying to solve them.

Lindblom's case for incrementalism is normative as well as descriptive. In addition to providing a perhaps more accurate account of how decisions are made in the real world, he argued that this approach also has the merit of allowing for flexibility and the expression of divergent views. 'Muddling through' at least implies responsiveness and flexibility, consultation and compromise. However, the model is clearly best suited to situations in which policy-makers are more inclined towards inertia rather than innovation. It thus explains the foreign policy trends of pro-status quo states more easily than those that seek to revise or overturn the status quo. For example, incrementalism appears to explain the policy of appeasement, pursued by the UK and increasingly also France in the 1930s. This involved giving in to hostile demands from Hitler's Germany in the hope of avoiding war, but ended up emboldening Germany, if only by convincing Hitler that the western powers would never act to prevent Nazi expansionism. On the other hand, Nazi expansionism itself, the Japanese attack on Pearl Harbor in 1942, and, for that matter, more recent examples, such as the 2003 US invasion of Iraq, can hardly be described as incremental adjustments. Neorealists would further argue that the different foreign policy strategies of status-quo states and revisionist states can better be explained by the larger balance of power (see p. 262) than by an inclination amongst certain policy-makers to 'muddle through'. Finally, incrementalism places little or no emphasis on the role of beliefs and values, which may, for instance, have been a crucial factor driving foreign policy decision-making in Nazi Germany (see Hitler's war?, p. 35).

Bureaucratic organization models

Both rational actor and incremental models are essentially 'black box' theories of decision-making; neither pays attention to the impact that the structure of the policy-making process has on the resulting decisions. Operating on the nation-state level, bureaucratic or organizational models try, on the other hand, to get inside the black box by highlighting the degree to which process influences product. This approach was pioneered by Graham Allison (1971) in his examination of US and USSR decision-making during the Cuban Missile Crisis of 1962. Two contrasting, but related, models emerged from this study. The first, usually called the 'organizational process' model, highlights the impact on decisions of the values, assumptions and regular patterns of behaviour that are found in any large organization. Rather than corresponding to rational analysis and objective evaluation, decisions are seen to reflect the entrenched culture of the government department or agency that makes them. The second theory, the 'bureaucratic politics' model, emphasizes the impact on decisions of bargaining between personnel and agencies, each pursuing different perceived interests. This approach dismisses the idea of the state as a monolith united around a single view or a single interest, and suggests that decisions arise from an arena of contest in which the balance of advantage is constantly shifting.

Although these models undoubtedly draw attention to important aspects of decision-making, they also have their drawbacks. In the first place, the organizational process model allows little scope for political leadership to be imposed from above. It would be foolish, for example, to suggest that all decisions are shaped by organizational pressures and perceptions, for this would be to ignore the personal role played by, say, George W. Bush in initiating the 'war on terror', or Hitler's influence on Germany's decision to invade Poland. Second, it is simplistic to suggest, as the bureaucratic politics model does, that political actors simply hold views that are based on their own position and on the interests of the organizations in which they work. Although the aphorism 'where you stand depends on where you sit' may often be applicable, personal sympathies and individual goals cannot be altogether discounted. Finally, to explain decisions

Focus on . . .
Perception or misperception?

How are mistakes made in foreign policy? In particular, why do foreign policy-makers sometimes misinterpret or misunderstand the situations they are dealing with? Rational actor models of decision-making imply that policy blunders, when they occur, are primarily a consequence of inadequate or defective information. If decision-makers are able accurately to assess the costs and benefits of potential actions, they will usually select the one that best advances the national interest. Sadly, the history of international relations, and especially the frequency of war (which must damage the national interest of at least one side in the conflict), does not bear out this image of careful reasoning and dispassionate choice. A variety of factors that operate at the individual and small group levels of analysis may increase the likelihood of misperception. For example, time pressures often force policy-makers to 'rush to judgement', meaning that they may be disinclined to consider new or 'inconvenient' information and place unreasoned faith in information that supports a preferred course of action. Such pressures are exacerbated in a world of 24/7 news and current affairs, in which political leaders are expected to adopt a position on major events almost as soon as they happen. Crisis situations also compound such problems, meaning that policy is formulated in an atmosphere that is stressful and emotionally charged.

A further source of misperception stems from distorted images that actors have of themselves and of others. At one level, misperception is unavoidable because of the security dilemma (see p. 19), which systematically encourages policy-makers to overestimate the aggressive intent of potential enemies, interpreting defensive actions as hostile ones. An exaggerated or distorted image of an opposing leader, regime, people or ideology can significantly increase the scale of misperception, leading either to overreaction (for example, the escalation of the Cold War) or, at times, under-reaction (appeasement). Misperception is particularly common amongst small groups, where it may take on the characteristics of 'groupthink' (Janis 1982). This certainly occurs due to a tendency for leaders to select close advisers whose views correspond to their own, creating a tightly-knit 'in group'. Small groups, further, are prone to develop a sense of their own intellectual and moral superiority, sustained by stereotypes of their critics as weak, evil or stupid. Potential deviants within small groups often remain silent, rather than voicing their doubts or counter-arguments, as the strength of the group stems, in part, from an illusion of unanimity. Collective psychology thus inclines members to demonstrate their loyalty and commitment to a chosen path, rather than to 'rock the boat'.

entirely in terms of black box considerations is to fail to give any weight to the external pressures that emanate from the broader political, economic, cultural and ideological context.

Cognitive processes and belief-system models

Models of decision-making that place an emphasis on the role of cognitive processes and beliefs highlight the degree to which behaviour is structured by perception. What people see and understand is, to an extent, what their concepts and values allow them, or encourage them, to see and understand. This tendency is particularly entrenched because, in most cases, it is largely unconscious. Although decision-makers may believe that they are being

● **Ethnocentrism**: A mode of understanding in which the actions or intentions of other groups or peoples are understood through the application of values and theories drawn from the observer's own culture or experience.

● **Groupthink**: The phenomenon in which psychological and professional pressures conspire to encourage a group of decision-makers to adopt a unified and coherent position.

rational, rigorous and strictly impartial, their social and political values may act as a powerful filter, defining for them what is thinkable, what is possible, and what is desirable. Certain information and particular options are therefore not appreciated or even considered, while other pieces of information and other courses of action feature prominently in the calculus of decision-making. Indeed, Kenneth Boulding (1956) underlined the vital importance of this process by pointing out that, without a mechanism to filter information, decision-makers would simply be overwhelmed by the sheer volume of data confronting them.

However, there are different views about the origin and nature of this filtering process. Robert Jervis (1968, 1976), for instance, drew attention to evidence of consistent misperception (see p. 137) on the part of decision-makers in international affairs. In his view, this stemmed largely from **ethnocentrism**. The inclination of Anthony Eden and the UK government to view General Nasser as a 'second Hitler' during the 1956 Suez Crisis, and the tendency of the USA in 1959 to regard Fidel Castro as a Marxist revolutionary, may be examples of this phenomenon. Irving Janis (1982), on the other hand, suggested that many decisions in the field of international relations could be explained in terms of what he called '**groupthink**'. This helps to explain how and why contrary or inconvenient views may be squeezed out of consideration in the decision-making process.

Radical theorists, constructivists and feminists have each, in their different ways, highlighted the important role played by beliefs in the formulation of foreign policy. Radical theorists have tended to argue that senior policy-makers, both at a state level and within international organizations, are influenced by ideological biases that favour the interests of dominant economic and social groups. Capitalist economic structures are therefore seen as 'natural' and beneficial, meaning that free trade, market reforms and globalization are viewed in positive terms, with alternatives to them seldom being seriously considered. For Marxists, this is a reflection of ruling class ideology. Constructivists regard foreign policy-making as an intersubjective world, shaped more by ideas and identities than by supposedly objective facts. The interests that guide foreign policy do not therefore emerge out of the systemic pressures of the international system or from the nature of the state, but are fashioned by ideational processes at either a domestic or international level. In short, ideas and identities determine interests. Feminists, for their part, may argue that a preponderance of men amongst policy-makers ensures that the 'glue' of politics is provided by patriarchal ideas and values. This results in policy biases that help to sustain a system of male power.

SUMMARY

- The state has four key features: a defined territory, a permanent population, an effective government, and the capacity to enter into relations with other states. Its core feature, however, is sovereignty, the principle of absolute and unlimited power. There are, nevertheless, internal and external dimensions of sovereignty.

- Globalization has widely been seen to curtail state sovereignty, creating 'post-sovereign governance'. In particular, economic sovereignty has been compromised by transborder trading, capital and other flows. Some believe that such developments have transformed the nature of the state, giving rise to the 'competition' state, the 'market' state or the 'postmodern' state.

- Contrary to the 'declinist' literature, there is growing evidence of the return of state power. This has occurred as a response to new security threats, the increasing use of the state as an agent of economic modernization and through an emphasis on state-building as a means of promoting development.

- Changes in the environment in which the state operates have also, many claim, meant that government is being displaced by governance, implying a shift away from command-and-control and towards coordination. This trend has been associated with the 'stretching' of government across a number of levels, giving rise to multi-level governance.

- The making of foreign policy has traditionally been regarded as one of the key features of international politics, reflecting the importance of statecraft. However, some question whether foreign policy is any longer meaningful given factors such as the structural dynamics of the international system and the advance of globalization.

- A number of general theories of foreign policy decision-making have been advanced. The most important of these are rational actor models, incremental models, bureaucratic organization models and cognitive processes and belief-system models, although they are not necessarily incompatible.

Questions for discussion

- In what sense does the state have a dual structure?
- Why is sovereignty regarded as the core feature of the state?
- What are the major threats to external sovereignty?
- Is the notion of 'post-sovereign governance' meaningful?
- What are the implications for the state of the growth of international organizations?
- To what extent have globalizing tendencies reshaped the nature and role of the state?
- Is the 'return of the state' a myth or a reality?
- In what ways does governance differ from government?
- Is foreign policy-making best understood on an individual, national or systemic level?
- How has neorealism challenged the traditional conception of foreign policy?
- Why is it so difficult for foreign policy actors to make rational and balanced decisions?

Further reading

Bell, S. and A. Hindmoor, *Rethinking Governance: The Centrality of the State in Modern Society* (2009). A clear account of how modern states use a mixture of governance modes to address specific problems, which challenges the notion of the 'decentred' state.

Hay, C., M. Lister and D. Marsh (eds), *The State: Theories and Issues* (2006). An insightful collection that is international in scope and examines the nature of the state and the issue of state transformation.

Smith, S., A. Hadfield and T. Dunne (eds), *Foreign Policy: Theories, Actors, Cases* (2012). A collection of authoritative writings on the theory and practice of foreign policy, including useful case studies.

Sørensen, G., *The Transformation of the State: Beyond the Myth of Retreat* (2004). A systematic analysis that accepts the changing nature of statehood but stresses the state's continued importance in world affairs.

 ONLINE RESOURCES AVAILABLE

Links to relevant web resources can be found on the *Global Politics* website

Index